The
New
Legion
VIETNAM-WAR

Volume 2

Order this book online at www.trafford.com
or email orders@trafford.com

Most Trafford titles are also available at major online book retailers.

© Copyright 2010 Vinh Truong.

All rights reserved. No part of this publication may be reproduced, stored in a retrieval system, or transmitted, in any form or by any means, electronic, mechanical, photocopying, recording, or otherwise, without the written prior permission of the author.

Printed in Victoria, BC, Canada.

ISBN: 978-1-4269-2744-7 (sc)
ISBN: 978-1-4269-2745-4 (hc)

Library of Congress Control Number: 2010901896

Our mission is to efficiently provide the world's finest, most comprehensive book publishing service, enabling every author to experience success. To find out how to publish your book, your way, and have it available worldwide, visit us online at www.trafford.com

Trafford rev. 2/8/10

 www.trafford.com

North America & international
toll-free: 1 888 232 4444 (USA & Canada)
phone: 250 383 6864 ♦ fax: 812 355 4082

AUTHOR: *Vinh-Van-Truong*

Combined Area Studies, *Project Delta Pilot*

THE NEW LEGION

****

Contents

Chapter 1:	Operation Lam-Son 719. Pentagon's traitorous behavior	1
Chapter 2:	P.O.W of Northern Vietnam. What's different between Old-POW and New POW	195
Chapter 3:	From the Reeducation-Camp to become a Boat-People.	249
Chapter 4:	Comment, critical analysis of Vietnam-Iraq Wars The whim and ironies of Vietnam's history	273
EPILOGUE		495
SOURCES and NOTES		501
ABOUT THE AUTHOR		511

Chapter-1

(Y̲O̲U̲ ̲M̲A̲Y̲ ̲R̲E̲A̲D̲ ̲S̲O̲M̲E̲ articles on Operation Lam Son 719 or hear about its controversial hindsight, because the real author of this operation is NSC [Permanent Government's masterminded] the following story is my witnessed from view of bird, on the gunship at treetop maneuver for 42 days in mission)

Cast your eyes on this photo- Why President Nixon so anxious?
… Being stunned into 'War powers Act', surrounded by Bones 'witch-hunt' haunts, unshakeable reputation glooming policy
"Foe become Friend and Friend become Foe."

What's the hell to deal honestly with ... What's the truth natural phenomenon of this operation? Why don't start sooner ... and wait for all the ammunition already moved to the southern on Harriman's Highway, completed cargo overwhelming over corridor ... then start operational search and destroy later? (Several NVA prisoners indeed disclosed that most supplies caches had been evacuated to south corridor that The ARVN appeared not to be surprised at all; by contrast, Giap had been prepared and expecting our forces to come in. This led to the conclusion that several things concerning the enemy had eluded our collection capabilities)

This Vietnam War' largest battle considers as Korea War Inchon, and WWII Normandy, both were two amphibious operations whereas operation Lam Son 719 was an air-assault operation. Who knew since all three wars initiated by an U.S totalitarian WIB-Bones in War Industries Board' masterminded. Meanwhile in this photo, the secret 'Pennsylvania-game' players, it was the ultimate team effort laughingly faces, cold blood; and every member of the team had to have the skills of a **quarterback**: Kissinger. The grit of a **linebacker**: Helms. And the brains of a **coach**: Republican George H W Bush, a successor to the throne of the Skull and Bones Dynasty, Second generation, but a simple surrogate totalitarian as Democrat William A Harriman. Lam Son 719 was the largest air mobile operation of the war - but also one doomed to failure right from the start. Due to cooperation between the South Vietnamese and the Americans all the written plans had to be translated and the translators was largely WIB' antiwar-activist [counterespionage] as Lt John-F-Kerry via triple-cross mediator Pham-Xuan-An, and few Vietnamese double-cross translator-sympathies to General Giap who engaged to OSS by Agent-Number 19, in sanctuary Pat-Po in 1945 [photograph by Allan Squiers] Consequently, Hanoi had copies of the whole documentation in hands almost as soon as South Vietnamese and US Army commanders of participating units. Additionally, neither the Americans nor the South Vietnamese knew the terrain really well, while the NVA troops were well-prepared for defense. Meanwhile, the foreign media's field reporters were particularly biased against the South Vietnamese, and were always ready to play up ARVN failures, and spread bad publicity. The media actually dwelt a detrimental role to the Operation of Lam Son 719. Even the BBC Radio ruined the ARVN" element of surprise by broadcasting that Tchepone had been invaded, [similarity BBC while been Saigon fall] when in reality, the ARVN had only achieved Phase-One i. e only half of the objective, due to President Thieu ordered early-out. Thus the NVA were forewarned of the possibility of our invading Tchepone. This forced the ARVN to hastily tactical carry through with the objectives in an attempt to save face…touch down took picture and go home no deployment.

Operation Lam Son 719 in the early of February 1971 was theoretically planned to take and destroy sanctuary base located in Tchepone, a small town in southern of Laos. Intelligence analysts stated that the NVA-Corps 70B had built many large storages stocked with weapons ammunitions, logistic supplies and foods. Also this base was used as a resource for refreshing troop replacement and training on the operational spot for the NVA units after battled with ARVN troop, backed by this base the 70B forces crossed the Laos-Vietnam border to attack the Quang Tri province. In the south of base 604 closer to the border, there was base 611, and from this base the NVA could launch attacks into the city of Hue, Thua thien Province. This operation also carried an important political phenomenon in the so called "Vietnamization-Program," but in the reality was as a dumping ground for U.S and Soviet cast off out of date weapons. No American infantry soldier landed feet in the land of Laos all American advisors attached to the ARVN units were ordered to stay in land South Vietnam.

The so called a test of Vietnamization? By a secret order from Emperor-1 [Harriman] for several years ago in preplanned schedule agenda. The eastern part of the Laotian panhandle was just reserved to use by 559 Group [Giap' troop] as a corridor for the infiltration of personnel and materials required to sustain its war efforts in South Vietnam and Cambodia which were **untouchable**. In addition to the Harriman's Highway [Ho chi Minh Trail] the eastern panhandle contained many logistic installations and base areas. After the 18 March 1970 change of government in Cambodia which closed the seaport of Sihanoukville to the enemy [PM Lon-Nol changed, renamed Kompong Som Seaport] this trail-base area complex in lower Laos became even more and more important to North Vietnam in its prosecution of the war in the South. The real hub of this entire complex, where transportation and storage activities were coordinated, was Base Area 604 located west of the Demilitarized Zone and surrounding the district town of Tchepone. To disrupt the flow of enemy personnel and supplies into South Vietnam, a ground attack was launched across the Laotian border against this enemy hub of activity on 8 February 1971. **But too late due to every huge cargo were already moved to the South recently.** Operation Lam Son 719 was conducted by I Corps with substantial U.S. support in firepower and airlift but without the participation of U.S. advisers with those ARVN units fighting in Laos. As a test by a political term such as Vietnamization, this operation was to demonstrate also the progress achieved in combat effectiveness by the Republic of Vietnam Armed Forces. Further, Lam Son 719 achieved the objective of forestalling a Communist offensive in the spring of 1971.

The so called **Ho Chi Minh Trail** was just Western named it, but Hanoi called **Route 559**, and I myself, named **Harriman's Highway**. Recently, before 1959 that named **Truong-Son Route range** means West mountainous-chain Route. A byproduct of the French's First Indochina War, 1946-1954, the footpath system that ran North-South along the Truong Son Mountain Range trail of Vietnam became known as the Ho Chi Minh Trail since the Second period of Vietnam-Wars 1954-75. For a long time it had served the strategic purposes of the Viet Minh (Allies Forces) From its jungle redoubt of North Vietnam's highlands, the Viet Minh High Command was faced with the pressing need for a secure communication system that would enable it to direct the war effort in South Vietnam and support its subversive activities in neighboring Laos and Cambodia. National Route-1 which ran parallel to the coastline was not practicable because of French control. Sea routes were available but the risks of running into French naval patrols and foul weather were forbiddingly high. Besides, the Viet Minh did not have a reliable organized sea transportation fleet. Considering these circumstances, the heavily mountainous-jungle of the Truong Son Range lent themselves to the establishment of a secure line of communication generally free from observation and attacks. It was this footpath system that kept the Viet

Minh resistance in South Vietnam alive with fresh troops, weapons and ammunition. By the end of the First Indochina War, the Truong-Son Trail had been well developed although it was only a system of jungle paths connected by local secondary roads and suitable only to movement by foot, animals and bicycles. Soldiers moved on foot but military Supplies, although usually carried by manpower, were sometimes transported on bicycles, oxcarts, horses or elephants. The narrow, steep pathways meandered through dense jungles, across streams and mountains and a journey on the trail was exhausting and slow. For a time after the Geneva Accords in 1954, the trail was practically abandoned since the war had ended. Then, when South Vietnam, under the leadership of President Ngo Dinh Diem, began restoring its stability and proving that it could stand on its own after repudiating reunification with North Vietnam. Also determined by President Diem' attempted sent TASK Forces composed Ranger, Airborne, Armor, and engineering ... Field-Commander Colonel Do Cao Tri to destroy a certain section of the trail, and now and then stayed in south Laos for couple months, Attopeu Province vicinity - So why President Diem must be murdered by WIB Bones order.

Unfortunately, by subject to stirring war under pressure of the Axis of Evil's scam, The KGB oppressed the Central Committee of North Vietnam's Communist Party decided to stir on a new course of action against South Vietnam. Subsequently in **May** 1959, the North Vietnamese Army (NVA) High Command activated Transportation Group 559, assigned Brigadier General Vo-Bam in charge as commander, under the direct control of its Rear Service (Logistics) Department. **Group 559** was to be a special unit in charge of moving men and supplies into the South for the support of the insurgency effort which had just been initiated under the form of a "war of liberation." The trail's old pathways were rehabilitated and widened, and new ones were surveyed and projected. Group 559's task of enlarging this strategic axis of infiltration was pushed ahead with vigor and determination. The increase of subversive activities against South Vietnam was in almost direct proportion to the development of the Ho Chi Minh Trail, since the Communist war effort in the South was largely sustained by a constant flow of cadre and troops from the North. At this early stage, the flow was sporadic because the journey was harsh and long for the men and the means of transporting supplies still primitive. But as pathways were eventually enlarged into roads, the means of transportation were also improved. Prior to 1965, the Ho Chi Minh system was close to the Vietnam border, but after the United States became involved in the war and bombings increased, the Communists gradually shifted toward the west where they found the densely jungle areas of lower Laos and eastern Cambodia perfect sanctuaries for the movement or concentration of troops and the storage of weapons and war materials, but it seemed to me, there will a new Inter-Indochinese-Highway for next century – Also in the Harriman's strategic scope, West Truong Son shall be the IIH [Indochina International Highway] for whether economical or military purpose and B-52 for mountain demolition plus C-123 "hot Tip" air defoliation for route tracking pathfinder, and along corridor scattered plants emit-sensors monitored NVA' activities. But importantly the NVA troop was the very debut pioneer discovered and building the Route-I.I.H.

Surprisingly, by the end of 1960s, the Harriman Highway had become an elaborate system of nearly 2,000 miles of pathways and roads, including some natural waterway. It started at Vinh Province ran through the **Mu-Gia Pass** and other lesser passes such as **Ban Karai Pass** and **Ban Raving Pass**, penetrated into lower Laos and finally came out in northern Cambodia and the Tri-Border area of South Vietnam. In several areas, the trail system was so extensive that it could be compared to a cobweb of crisscrossing roads making up a corridor of from 20 to 40 miles wide, complete with rock-stone-bridges (over or under water photos by my Queen-Bee H-34) culverts, river crossing ramps, much of it concealed under dense jungle canopies. With the assistance of Pathet Lao guerrillas, the estimated 50,000 troops of NVA Group 559 and about 100,000 porters Vietnamese volunteers and forced laborers maintained these vital-arteries. To protect the corridor, the Communists established an elaborate defense and security system. The duty of Pathet Lao units was to intensify guerrilla activities and launch periodic attacks in order to keep the Royal Lao Army confined to the cities and towns along the Mekong River. The protection of the trail system and storage areas was performed by Group 559 itself. Augmented

The New Legion

by infantry units and unattached militiamen, the group defense forces included AAA: [anti-aircraft artillery, the most' cast off WW-II of Soviet weapons] units armed with all types of light and heavy weapons, from 12.7-mm, 14.5-mm and 23-mm heavy machineguns to 37-mm, 57-mm and 85 or 100-mm anti-aircraft cannons. Group 559 installed a forward headquarters in the southern panhandle of North Vietnam from where it controlled many 'binh trams' (literally troop Camp-stations) In 1970 there were about 40 such camp-stations, from Vinh Province to the Cambodian border, under the control of a number of intermediary headquarters. Each binh-tram was a self contained, logistical complex. During the cessation of bombings in North Vietnam, trucks moved by convoy from Vinh Province down the trail. Upon reaching the Laotian border, they formed units of five to eight vehicles and usually moved only at night in keeping under umbrella ROE stipulation of Axe of Evil's craps or in foul weather in order to avoid the round the clock bombing by United States Air Force planes [US Pilots had no equipped with laser targeting pods or Smart bombs or night vision goggles] As a result, "Binh trams" were usually separated from one another by a day's journey and their parking areas were scattered and well concealed. [However, General Haig in Pentagon War-Room with sophisticated radar which could monitor-control in follow-up all those activities on Trail with synchronized help of sensors on spot] The vehicles moving on the trail only transported supplies and heavy materials. Light equipment was either carried on men's backs or by animals. Since troops had to march, they moved by day or night, using pathways different from those used by trucks. New recruits or replacements usually entered the system at Vinh Province in North Vietnam and often marched over 100 days to reach their final destination in South Vietnam. In view of this long journey, they had to rest and recuperate at way stations where they received food, medicine and indoctrinations. Combat units usually moved by battalions of 500- 600 men each and they often suffered substantial losses from disease and constant bombings by the U.S. Air Force.

Because the War-Architect Harriman who protected this Route 559 at any price During the period from 1960 to 1965 [Certainly, Operation Lam Son 719 never took place as from 1960-65] while the fighting escalated, the South Vietnam was unable to do anything against the Laos infiltration Route because Harriman. However another hand, the U.S Permanent Government would like a big occasion for training the U.S combat troops, with strategic-slogan to the so called *"Everything worked but not worked enough."* Thereby made a significant contribution in 1961 when it helped organize the highlands Montagnards into combat units call-sign 'CIDG' and develop the Vietnamese Special Forces for the defense of the border areas [just for the craps to US combat training] The so called against Communist activities on the Ho Chi Minh Trail [Harriman Highway] however, neither the U.S Army Special Forces nor their Vietnamese counterparts ever interdicted the Communist logistics system to a significant degree, even during the period of maximum effort. Also, the idea of building the "McNamara Line" with scattered sensors across the Harriman Highway corridor mountain range at the Southern boundary of the DMZ was never fully implemented as planned. The surveillance and interdiction of the trail, therefore, lay primarily in the hands of the U.S. Air Force whose reconnaissance planes covered the trail system around the clock by U-2, RF-101 Woodo and our helicopter H-34s Queen-Bee as well. Ground electronic sensors drop-planted along jungle pathways, river crossings, and mountain passes picked up vehicle and other man made noises, transmitted them to over flying planes which relayed the information to terminal stations to be analyzed and interpreted. The electronic monitoring of enemy activities on the trail system helped record the number of vehicles and men moving along the trail. Consequently, intelligence on Communist infiltration was remarkably reliable. In addition to surveillance, a major task for the United States Air Force was training exercise to interdict this infiltration. All types of aircraft were used including B-52 strategic bombers, sophisticated fighter-bombers and several types of EC-130B gun-ships. The U.S. Air Force claimed that its bombs and improved weapons systems inflicted heavy losses to the enemy in terms of personnel, vehicles and materiel moving down there? **But in reality, it seemed to me that B-52 was on job mountainous demolition in "Rolling Thunder campaign" no kill, but created many ponds for NVA troops having swimming pool and laundry. And Air defoliation from C-123 "Hot Tip campaign"**

The New Legion

for ground pioneers build-road follow up tracking brownish clover path to the south.

At the beginning of 1970, the enemy's plan to rehabilitate Route 1036 was suspended for some time due to extensive United States bombing along the Laotian border. Nevertheless, he succeeded in opening Route 1039 through the Ban Raving Pass which connected with Route 913. This gave the enemy an additional route into Tchepone, the communications center for base area 604. In the meantime, Route 1032A in North Vietnam allowed NVA to move his trucks to the western edge of the DMZ. Here his supplies were usually floated on the Houay Nam Xepon River and then on the Xe Bang Hiang River southwesterly toward Tchepone where they were picked up before reaching the town. To the south, the enemy had already completed Route 616 which cut across the Xepon River and deep into South Vietnam. The existence of this east-west infiltration route was detected for the first time on 1 January 1970 but subsequent surveillance indicated that enemy activities on it were light. The heaviest traffic was always reported on the North-South axis, moving from base area 604 on Routes 96, 926 and 914 toward base area 611 to border. This appeared to indicate that the enemy wanted to project another infiltration route into the Khe Sanh area, west of Quang Tri but subsequent air reconnaissance showed that the enemy was using Route 616 for truck traffic and his activities were increasing substantially south of base area 611. Air reconnaissance and agent reports further confirmed the enemy's stepped up logistical activities and augmentation of combat forces at base areas 604 and 611 since the beginning of the lower Laos dry season. In October, 1970, an agent report revealed that a division size unit, approximately 10,000 strong, was leaving the Mu Gia Pass and moving south. It was believed at that time that this was the 320th NVA Division [Steel Division] with its three organic regiments, the 48th, 52nd, and 64th. Subsequent intelligence reports confirmed that the 52nd Regiment was located west of the DMZ and the 64th Regiment was building roads in Quang Binh Province, north of the DMZ. It was, therefore, probable that the 48th Regiment was the unit which was moving into base area 604. Other word, 320th NVA Division inaugurated a scheme for W. A Harriman Highway from the start

In the meantime operation Lam Son 719 preplanning, by January 1971, Route 1032A had been connected with Route 1032B which gave the enemy an additional roadway into lower Laos from North Vietnam; Recordings made by electronic sensors indicated that of every four trucks leaving North Vietnam, one always moved on this route regardless of the bombings by United States planes west of the DMZ. Aerial photos also revealed that the enemy had built several alternate bypass routes in this area in order to avoid concentrated bombings and ensure the flow of traffic. Reconnaissance planes further reported that East-West Route 925 had been widened but terminated approximately two and a half miles from the South Vietnam border. This appeared to indicate that the Hanoi wanted to project another infiltration route into the Khe Sanh area, west of Quang Tri but subsequent air reconnaissance showed that the NVA was using Route 616 for truck traffic and his activities were increasing substantially south of base area 611. All of these indications clearly confirmed the Hanoi's efforts to open additional infiltration roads, develop storage areas, load and unload transferred points and truck parks, and to make the entire area just west of Quang Tri Province an intricate logistical and transportation complex complete with POL pipelines and bypass roads. Furthermore, all these activities progressed with little interruption despite continuous bombings. The efforts were most conspicuous in base areas 604 and 611. On the other hand, to increase his protection capabilities, the NVA also moved additional anti-aircraft artillery and combat units into these areas. To the west beyond the Laotian border, the terrain was predominantly mountainous. The area of operation on this side of the border was characterized by three prominent features. **The first** of these was the Xepon River which ran south and then parallel to Route-9 until it reached Tchepone where it met the Xe Bang Hiang River, the primary North-South waterway in the area. During the rainy season, when most ground lines of communication were inundated, the enemy used the Xe Biang Hiang River to float supplies downstream. **The second** prominent terrain feature was the Mt Co Roc Highland adjacent to the Laotian border and just south of Route-9. This highland had several peaks with elevations ranging from 500 to 850 meters which dominated Route-9 to the east and west. It also provided excellent observation into the Khe Sanh area. The foliaged-vegetation in the Co Roc area consisted primarily of bamboo and brushwood, offering adequate cover and concealment. **The third** significant terrain feature was a high escarpment whose ridgeline extended all the way to Tchepone, parallel to and south of Route-9 and the Xepon River. Several peaks of this ridgeline were 600 to 700 meters high and offered excellent observation over Route-9 and the Tchepone are so much of the area was covered by dense jungle and thick brushwood except for a few places which had been cleared for farming. The terrain north of Route-9 was hilly and heavily vegetated against a backdrop of relatively high peaks which restricted operations in this area almost entirely to infantry. Around Tchepone, the terrain was much lower, sparsely vegetated and more appropriate for armor vehicles. Route-9 from Khe Sanh to Tchepone was a one lane, unevenly surfaced dirt road with destroyed bridges and culverts. Dominated by the high escarpment to the south, this road was easily interdicted. It also was difficult to prepare bypasses due to the river to the south and the hilly terrain to the north. In addition to Route-9 which was an old public road, the enemy had completed in the area west of the Laotian border an extensive, crisscrossing system of lines of communication. Most important of these was Route 1032 which connected with Route-92 and offered direct access from North Vietnam and the western DMZ area into base area 604, then base area 611, and from there into South Vietnam either by Route 92 or Route 616 or Route 922 further to the south, another route, designated area. Route 1039, also originating in North Vietnam passed through the Ban Raving Pass and offered access into Tchepone and base area 604 then connected with either Route 29 to go further south or with Route 914 which led into base area 611 and from there into South Vietnam. All these routes were well maintained two lane roads practicable for large trucks at least during the dry season. Due to extensive bombings, the enemy had built several alternate routes which were well concealed by vegetation and often under double and triple canopies. In addition to main routes, the enemy also built narrow pathways crisscrossing the entire area. These were difficult to observe from the air and were convenient for concealing troop movements and truck rest-areas in daytime break.

Now weather forecast for Operation Lam Son 719 started on February 1971 in the Tchepone area was the transitional period from the northeast to the southwest monsoons. The northeast monsoon, which brought rains and cloudiness to Central Vietnam above the Hai Van Pass from October to March, was the dominant weather factor. The Truong Son mountain range deflected much of this wet weather on the Laotian side but in the area of operation, the skies were generally covered. The amount of Cumulus-clouds buildup in this area depended on the strength and depth of the monsoon. Average temperature during February was 22C in the lowlands and about 18C in mountainous regions.

As of mid March, 1971 the southwest monsoon gradually picked up, resulting in a relative improvement of the weather and higher ceilings. The average temperature was warmer than in February but this was a period of showers during which the skies were temporarily covered. Beginning in May, however, rainfall became heavier over the Truong Son Range while in the eastern lowlands, the weather was dry and hot.

In general, during these periods considered for the operation, the weather was fairly good but quite unpredictable. From experience, it was estimated that the area of operations would be cloudy and hazy fog in the morning. The weather was favorable for air operations only from 10:00-12:00 hours until mid afternoon. The 2,500-feet ceiling in the low lands would allow only a 1,000 feet altitude' in the area of operation. This was recognized as a major handicap since all aircraft used in support missions would be located in the lowlands and would have to be flown first to the Khe Sanh airfield. Low ceilings and hazardous mountains would force our VNAF helicopters flying frontline support missions to follow natural avenues of approach such as valleys and rivers which the enemy could interdict with east. This handicap was going to be an important factor affecting the course of combat operations.

Of course, General Haig C&C at Pentagon already knew that all depend on U.S air-mobility-forces, **so quite frankly I must say ARVN in the risky status:** *"Supplies and Medevacs in the mainstay of any operation, the large the operation, the greater demand"* In this operation, preparations were relatively adequate, but did not meet the

battlefield needs. In the planning, ARVN had absolutely relied upon the air power, namely helicopters from the Army Aviation for support, supplies, medevacs. For such a large-scale operation, it was impossible for supplies and medevacs to be accomplished by helicopters alone, especially in the presence of enemy antiaircraft firepower, from 14, 5 mm to 100 mm AAA. The crude facts of the operation demonstrated this. Once supplies were hampered, the fighting spirit of soldiers was naturally influenced: Lack of ammunition and guns caused the firepower to decrease [the journalist had to know that why written biased reports] Shortage of food and even the most water weakened the troops, the wounded died waiting for medevac. Thus the organization of logistic should be of primary concern, but this is in NSC' scope, letting ARVN troop under siege to enemy for 67,000 tons shell-bombardment standby on spot. This implied ARVN troops were subjected to repeat the ferocious-artillery-bombardments. This is WIB Bones' goal-plots purposely.

So why! "I died feeling we could have won that war. I still felt we were on top of it in that year 1970 then lost our nerve" Crucially important differences included wisdom and stability in the ambassadorial post: better field generalship; a more adept national leadership involving [isolated Nixon, has his hands tied, double knotted by Power Act and now Cooper Church amendment] Kissinger, and Helms – even given the vigorous internecine warfare they frequent waged against one another (acted-government contrasted sharply with permanent-government) – compared with LBJ and its WIB' apparatus as Secretary of Defense McNamara who was a Vietnam War X.O like General Manager of the war, because of the practical costs of McNamara's failed policies.

Because the Skull and Bones Dynasty was the only one policymaker, thereby a Skull planning session resulted in little agreement on composition of the next redeployment increment. US forces were already so greatly reduced that no one could see how to give up a single additional man. General Abrams listened to the agonized discussion and let his fellow comrade in arms know. "You know, gentlemen," he begun, "this force withdrawal is not optional. We are going down and we will continue to go down till none of us are left. Now, we are going to do that, just as the Supreme Chief Commander of U.S forces ordered?" I don't think so it's the truth. It is almost unthinkable and surely unforgivable that a great nation should leave these helpless allies to the tender mercies of the North

Vietnamese, but that is what the Permanent Government did; really they did a terrible thing to the South Vietnamese. Meanwhile from now on the North Vietnamese was receiving unprecedented levels support from its patrons. So, soon or later, South Vietnam was on the brink of collapse [**axiom-1**]

By way of conclusion, I must state my conviction that the war in Vietnam was a just war fought by the South Vietnamese and their allies for admirable purposes, that those who fought it did so with their mightiest hearts, and that in the process they came very close to succeeding in their purpose of enabling South Vietnam to sustain itself as a free and independent nation. The cause was indeed "noble" American fought it the wrong way under War Industries Board's Bones masterminded and lost it in good part because of them.

According his Harriman's stratagem, Vietnam War is a big military training strategy never had in the US history by a cunning stratagem *"Everything worked but nothing worked enough"* This signifies a sacrifice of casualties of personal and material for his scam. [Numerous of POW, aircraft crashed sacrificed their lives for WIB' selfish interest]

Khe-Sanh in the past was the Huong-Hoa County of Quang Tri province. Because the name of "Harriman Highway" is essential for his stratagem, so US administration persuaded the GVN' President Diem has to evacuated the tribe-ancient-native to the low land closed the sea-coast, abandoned it with a sheer named Khe Sanh on the map – No more Hương-Hóa County. And USMC had to ground there for familiar with combat training practice on the highland as seemed in the similarity of Dien Bien Phu under siege, but till 1971, operation Lam Son 719 should the damn-real Dien Bien Phu' under-siege for ARVN troop subjected to repeated horrible artillery bombardments. Another word there's main cause of **"axiom-1"** for donating Saigon to Hanoi not like a 'Pebbly-City'. So you will see the cruel-battle happened at target 604.

Late General Vo-Nguyen Giap [engaged OSS 1945] plotted first against the French in 1954 at Dien Bien Phu and then against the Americans in the Tet Offensive of 1968. At Khe sanh in 1967, Giap commenced a siege of the US troops' far western support base at Khe Sanh. He massed 4 infantry-divisions supported by 2 Armor and Artillery regiments at the heretofore largely unknown complex at the opposite end of Route 9, the farthest compound away from most US or ARVN troops principal enclaves. Giap purposefully made the presence of the more than 40,000 NVA troops highly visible to ARVN and US intelligence gatherers. North Vietnamese Army' masterminded Headquarter immediately drew the attention of General Westmoreland, who had, a few months earlier, began development of the primitive Khe Sanh Outpost into a materiel support base for his proposed operations in Laos which was hated like poison in Harriman' scope [don't touch Ho Chi Minh Trail been building, Harriman don't want Westmoreland destroy all cargo there though this time is best right time and right place you should noticed this]

The supreme commander of US forces in Vietnam had deployed a battalion of Marines and a team of US Navy Seabee to develop and defend the base. But for their security, one ARVN 37th Ranger Battalion was good shield outside its fence for their protection. They quickly turned to, bulldozing the ground and installing steel PSP matting for a primitive airfield and laying in stockpiles of ammunition and supplies for the proposed Laos operations? [but too soon that's never happened right now ever]

Responding to the NVA actions, Operation Niagara in mind Westmoreland who ordered 6,000 additional USMC to distant and tactically unimportant outpost; in concert with the defense of Khe Sanh, Westmoreland also ordered commencement of massive air bombardment of the entire region that encircle the remote enclave, appropriately naming the aerial onslaught.

As the battle raged, President Johnson vowed the United States would not lose Khe Sanh. He said this despite the fact that he had already scrapped Westmoreland's plan for border-crossing operations into Laos. His decision had thus rendered the Khe Sanh support base tactically useless, but his national security advisor, George Bundy, Skull and Bones 40 had to a real drawback! Westmoreland has his hands tied double knotted the incoming years, but after his be fired emerged "Cooper-Church and Case-Church Amendments in 1970 and 1973," says that U.S forces must do nothing. No military equipment, no American forces, nada, zip… on stand point command and control, no choice, let him go home, become The Joint Chief of Staff.

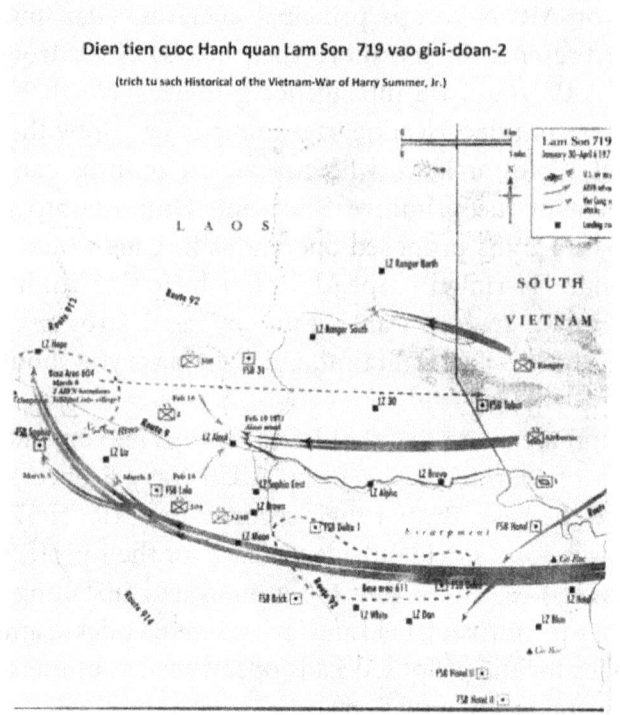

(Historical of the Vietnam War of Harry Summer, Jr)

Below was Pentagon War Room chart, General Haig, Head of Command and Control for Lam Son 719 operation – President Thieu decided to "Early-Out" sharply against Haig' strategic-plot when Thieu found out the names all Landing-Zone were named by Hollywood famous movie stars such as that Bones played game: **LOLO**brigida, **SOPHIA**loren, **LIZ**-Taylor, and Bob-**HOPE** – and his military meditation urged him to reconsider why General Giap' powerful-forces with couple hundred tanks and fourteen Artilleries Regiments wouldn't attacked to US Base at Khe Sanh but at Tchepone? Immediately Thieu ordered to General Lam: *"Touch down...pissed at there a mess...then goes back home!"*

Moreover Thieu recalled last couple month ago, on November 21 1970, a movie star Jane Fonda was involved in the Project Cold-War – a job "political-espionage and counterespionage performer."

With the specific aims, she showed up at Michigan University and strongly stated to about 2,000 students: *"If you understood what communism was, you would hope, you would pray on your knees that we would some day become communist!"* The Communist doctrine eventually has been forced to modify to comfort in affecting the whole world or self-extinction for good! The United States shall be a real Super Communist adjustment in the coming day! Actually, then the U.S was an eventual Super-Finest-Communist country now in predominantly by totalitarian Skull and Bones pattern regime.

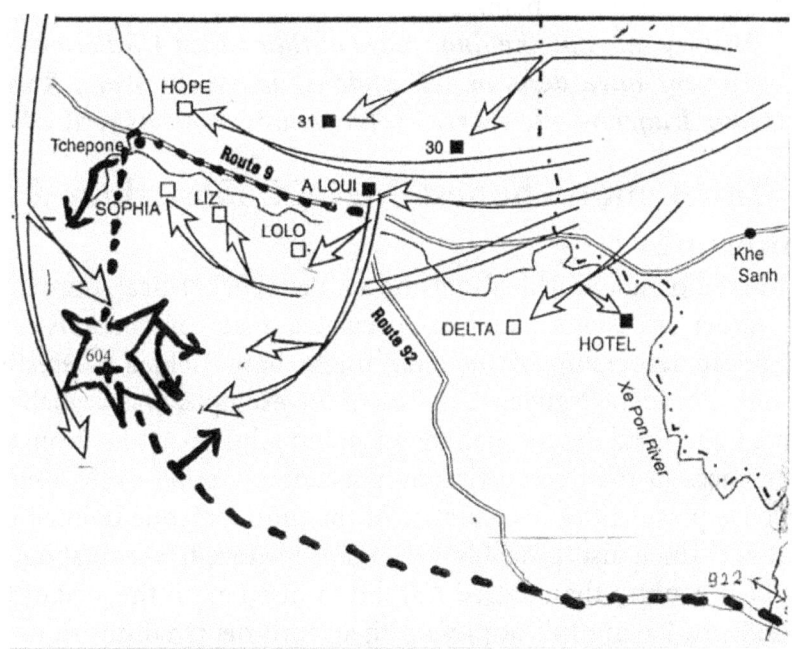

(Above, Map-chart offensive trajectory, if General Do Cao Tri alive and Lam Son 719 Commander)

Donald Rumsfeld, Skull and Bones Chief-staff have drawn from fashioned Hollywood in slogan "Just make love, no make war!" at time of "Saigon Fall" was the end for long tragedy: What American actual encountered in Vietnam-War was an army in process of demoralization. After public opinion turned against the war since 1968, the antiwar movement penetrated the U.S army in Vietnam as Permanent Government anticipated their preplanned. All the stereotypical problems of drugs, racial conflict, atrocities, fragging, and insubordination were in evidence and were affecting the morale of the army, and these were, at least as one certain American understood it, related to the fact that, as a consequence of poor leadership, the country no longer supported the war, yet U.S were still being expected to fight it. Generals, political leaders, both-uniformed and civilian, realized the necessity to 'redeploy' the army out of Vietnam as rapidly as possible to prevent this spirit of disaffection from spreading to other commands around the world. Meanwhile, the G.I was being asked to take their chance at being the last man to die in Vietnam.

"History must be the final judge of that which US Permanent Government have done or left undone, in World Wars, Korea, Vietnam, Iraq, and elsewhere... Let us calmly await its verdict!"

Thieu more honest, decent man than L.B. Johnson?

Based on above Thieu' statements, the venal critical journalists on earlier occasions had bias-speculated that comparisons with American leadership of the time might have yielded interesting results. President Nguyen Van Thieu, for example, was arguably a more honest and decent man than Lyndon Johnson, and – given the differences in their respective circumstances – quite likely a more effective president of his country. At the time someone pointed out that Mr. Thieu also probably had more freedom to move about in his own country than hatred LBJ did in his? I'm on the side of US presidents, having full of pity on their curb-deprived decisions by Permanent Government. Here there were exerted some P.G' unsavory habits, clues-for instants:

In time of President Eisenhower: Permanent Government didn't want to hear: "We, Americans must heart-fully help to building a strong nationalist political party behind Diem. Now Diem has elected as a President, he ought to have his own party. (Ed. J .Lansdale, "In the mist of War" p, 342) Eisenhower solemn-welcome Diem to visit America in May, 1957 and had called Diem a miracle man of Asia. **As for President Kennedy** as always back of him until the coup have been underway scrambling as a hot message from Mc George Bundy to Cabot Lodge October 30, 1963 *"We do* *not accept as a basic for US policy that we have no power to delay or discourage a coup....*" And during World tour of Vice President, May 1961, had given Diem his boost in calling Diem a "Winston Churchill of Asia" **In Johnson administrative,** In March 1964, at the urging of the Joint Chiefs, McNamara requested authorization for "hot pursuit [by] only South Vietnamese forces over the Laotian line for border control" This was contentious for A Harriman of course due to military leadership SOP, but it was increasingly doubtful that he could prevent a change in U.S policy. Indeed you know...Who was U.S policymaker? Was LBJ a Big WIB' drawback!? Though in this month March/1964, *Harriman wasn't close to Johnson right after Kennedy assassination, he was given charge of African affairs at the Department of State for out of his sight.* [I seek to justify in Chapter 9 in Skull and Bones "revenge meditation" – Johnson killed Kennedy? – At Paris on Monday, October, 27, 2,003 on channel Canal: "JFK, autopsie d'un complot" by Bernard Nicolas and William Reymond, and a Flammarion book "JFK, le dernier témoin." All reports were full of lies and prevarications. But I thought Bones lies only when they felt they had to] President Nixon, in writing of 1963 Coup which made Diem and his brother murdered quote: *"1963 crisis that made us disgusting"* That apparently was a disgraced US historically in front of its allies. Have pity on the unelected President of the United States and watch Saigon collapse, President Ford confessed: "It looked like we just quit and run. Yet I did all that I could for them!" because he was acting president.

Pragmatically in 'Standard Operation Procedure' Once the joint Chiefs Staff was building a case for "crossing fence" the McNamara and Mc George Bundy, the special assistant to the president for national security affairs, found convincing. Still, Harriman had to be dealt with, as Forrestal told Bundy in April. LBJ had been coaxed into supporting "hot pursuit," and Bundy was felt logically about to send a telegram to Saigon authorizing it, Michael Forrestal of the National Security Council staff cautioned Bundy that *"to send the telegram without Averell's approval is just asking for trouble,"* The telegram had already received presidential approval, but that was not enough. It still required an *endorsement* from A Harriman. Moreover Forrestal had learned from Sullivan that Harriman was placated and reluctantly agreed to "hot pursuit" in destroying his commencement build up his project super-highway but [due too soon, not right time and right place] he named that Ho Chi Minh Trail (meanwhile Hanoi named Route 559) And unsurprisingly why President Thieu was out of vulnerable, unharmed still in good shape … luckily because Harriman and George H.W Bush need the non chaotic, political stability for US forces progressively withdrawal safety.

So why throughout this operation deficiencies at high command levels continued to undermine the abilities and performance of South Vietnam's troops. Consequently even General Abrams was a famous better war, but I must say with a nearly insuperable array of new challenges because he didn't know the operation objective. For the first time he and his staff were working from a field command post distant from home country. Naturally they did not understand So, I must draw in conclusion "truly grasped the responsibilities inherent in attachment, the differences between a zone of action and an axis of advance, or the full meaning of the word 'secure'

The New Legion

OPERATION LAM SON 719

Preliminary: On the inauguration day, President Barrack-Obama stated a composed speech 2406 words separated 34 paragraph-sections dealing with two Vietnamese words **KHE –SANH,** some wise folks said the special psychological outpost faraway from US. The Khe-Sanh engraved in US military history, map for Operation Lam-Son 719; "Historical Atlas of the Vietnam-War, by Harry Summers Jr. Khe-Sanh which emerged in 3 periods: (1) the WIB-Bones forced the 1st Republic South Vietnam must evacuated all native people to the lowland, abandoned the highland Hương-Hóa County, for commencing build up the Harriman's highway [Western: Ho Chi Minh Trail; North Vietnam: Route 559] parallel with it was POL which Russia should be take care about pipeline communicated maintenance. So (1) the Hương Hóa disappeared in Vietnam map (2) The supposition of US Marine in the trial-siege of Điện Biên Phủ? (3) But the ARVN must be subjected to a real Điện Biên Phủ' under siege over 67.000 tons artillery-shells blood-shed in repeated showers; The ARVN troop continued to thrust into Laotian territories supposedly occupied by Pathet Lao, but in reality all was where the NVA had their strongholds and logistical bases. We didn't know at all but Harriman knew it very well as 1962 our Queen-Bee H-34 dropped a STRATA team for detecting the presentation of 759 Group [stand for Pathet Lao] but only NVA troop stayed there [That's in the Harriman's objective scope] The city of Tchepone to Attopeu had been severely destroyed during the war between The National Laos and Pathet Laos, and was further reduced to rumble by American bombardments aimed at reducing enemy activities on the Ho Chi Minh Trail. Their tactics were flexible, changing as necessary to suit the environment, rather than conform to set positions. However, the information gathered was still very indefinite. So this Operation was named Lam Son 719 [by CIA experts composer] because in took place in the year **71**, around the region of Route **9** which connected Khe Sanh to Tchepone.

In the preferences of ANSWERS.COM, W.A Harriman, from page 1 to page 3 which composed 4 books involving Vietnam War: (1) authors Walter Isaacson and Evan Thomas, *The Wise Men:* Six Friends and the World They Made (1986) (2) Author George C. Herring, Jr.,

Aid to Russia 1941-1946 (1973); (3) Two books same author William A Harriman, *Peace with Russia* (1959) and *America and Russia in a Changing World* (1971) Typically, these years coincided with the Axis of Evil such as Hanoi inaugurated Group 559, 759, and 959 (first digit means month, last two digit means years. And US first two digit means year and last means location) Operation Lam Son took place on year one thousand 71 at Route-9. Decided solution on January, 18/1971 for terminating war-game CIP/NLF [National Liberation Front/Counter Insurgency Plan] these three digit number for easier reference in US and Russia documental-archives

Even as the cumulative effect of the "clear and hold" tactical approach was reaching a peak. Congress proceeded to snatch defeat from the jaw of victory. Significantly, the "**Cooper-Church**" amendment influences were at work. The first volley in Congress came in 1970 when Idaho Democrat Senator Frank F. **Church** and Kentucky Republican Senator John Sherman **Cooper** authorized a bill that cut off funding of all military activity in Southeast Asia – shutting off air and ground combat support; that would eventually undermine much of what had been accomplished. In the Washington, this was "keyed time" for Permanent Government did the best influence that included further erosion of political support for the war, growing budgetary pressures on support for the US combat forces still in Indochina and for the South Vietnam alike, and the influence of both on the pace of safety withdrawal. Clearly on the time would come, and sooner rather than later, when all US ground forces no longer play any significant part in prosecution of the war according of Permanent Government strategy on "**axiom 3**" that all US universities as the basis for already explained the war in the beginning of the war 1960 [the US could not have won that war under any circumstances] When the Hanoi troops was in its weakest condition in over six years.

So why throughout of the earlier years of United States involvement in South Vietnam by seeking caused the so called "The Tonkin Gulf Incident" – officially created a formal legalized retaliation for US combat troop invasion; although Cambodia proclaimed a nonbelligerent, neutral status, it actually supported the North Vietnamese and Viet Cong forces by providing them refuge,

The New Legion

primary in the Parrot's Peak region along the Mekong River, hardly more than fifty kilometers west of Saigon. In this so called neutral territory, Communist forces successfully escaped American and South Vietnamese force pursuit (thank to CIA, counterespionage branch 'warning'...I died feeling in my view of bird-conviction that Vietnam War was "**an social scientists war**" initiated by 1st emperor, A. Harriman of the Skull and Bones dynasty, and 2nd emperor George H W Bush was for "**an intelligence war**") and rested and recuperated between commitments to combat operations. In that territory-haven in Cambodia, they also stashed large caches of weapons and supplies ferried over the notorious "Harriman Highway" [Ho Chi Minh trail] which crossed through Cambodia at several points in northeastern, existing into the Mekong region and the Central Highlands.

At year-1970s end, the application use of those forces still in Vietnam was further curtailed by what was known as the 'Cooper-Church amendment' to the defense appropriation bill, a very measure denying funds for US combat force operations in Cambodia and Laos. This left the Hanoi's troop sanctuaries and lines of communication once again safe from US interference (the craps CIP and NLF applied in action by ROE) this 'keyed-up-time' before Congressional action was subjected to under pressure by Permanent Government. Meanwhile, the Hanoi was contemplating his next round of dry season operations.

I foresaw and believe that the South Vietnam was on *"the brink of total military defeat"*

From now on, Congress will seeking has dramatically cut aid to Saigon government, going against a long-standing commitment. As a result, my nation future falters because of a grievous lack of spare parts and replacement equipment. Meanwhile North Vietnam was receiving unprecedented levels of support from its patrons. Adversely, it is almost unthinkable and surely unforgivable that a great United States should leave these helpless allies to the tender mercies of the Communist North Vietnam but that is U.S Permanent Government did! Because the reduction to almost '<u>below Zero</u>': Some Navy, A-4 Skyhaws few time, the so called faulted in mistake struck on POL dump located in the air bases, for reducing our ARVN' operational activities and against under "Project Enhance," a program to replace the heavy losses of war. The United States would replace on a one-for-one basis major combat system as was permitted by the Paris Accords of U.S support was the cause of final collapse. So why in the past, flatly President Diem did have to turn down U.S military involvement, he knew U.S will done a terrible thing [Axis of Evil's scam] to his country in the future. The center of gravity was the people…and that winning hearts and minds was not just a slogan for pacification through by "the Rural Revolutionary Development Hamlet Program"

By way of conclusion, I will justified, stated in this book my certain conviction that the Vietnam War was a just war fought by the South Vietnamese and their allies for admirable purposes, that those who fought it did so with their mightiest hearts, and that in the process they came very close to succeeding in their purpose of enabling South Vietnam to sustain itself as a free and independent nation. Because the Eurasian Great Game stratagem, thereby after fifteen years, American have been encouraging the people of South Vietnam to self-defend against what American conceive to be an external danger, "Red-Menace" Now American stand on the brink of betraying that trust because WIB Bones.

Skull and Bones strategist staff: The basic foundation-method "Everything worked, but nothing worked enough for the goal of protracting the war." That was one thing. But there was something else, much more extensive and perhaps more risky, on the minds of Washington [WSAG] planners – a thrust into Laos to the so called interrupt the Hanoi's buildup of supplies and perhaps preempt is planned offensive. Much earlier in the war, when General Westmoreland still had an abundance of US combat troops and firepower, he had looked hungrily at the enemy's cross-border base camps [binh-tram] – fighting over the goddamn caches. That would be the climax of the interdiction. But the State Department was closing ranks: A. Harriman emphasized that "favored sending non-US-patrols into Laos to try find out the size of Hanoi' the military buildup." Harriman also stood firmly against US advisers taking part

The New Legion

in these patrols, even Vietnamese Ranger-task forces and that was a clever diversion-scam?

In the United States during almost nine decades (1917-to July 7/2003 Skull and Bones Graveyard see in Chapter-9) an emerged totalitarian Skull and Bones dynasty has severely restricted, stripped away most foreign policies of the acted governments. The US parliament of National assembly which is defined as the highest power of the nation, but it seemed to me like its power in hands of the two emperors: A. Harriman stands for 1917-1960 and overlapped in transition to an apprentice George H.W Bush to 1969. That year end 1969, Harriman and Johnson got out from political platform. [Johnson raised his hope too high pried off the Skull and Bones out of the unsavory totalitarian Permanent-Government accounting on to prosecute a claim for "The Trading with the-Enemy Act" of December 1941 as Union Banking Corporation which was closed in 1943 by the U.S Government for Trading with the Enemy, now at first in focusing on Zapata Offshore seized the alien property custodian assets; but his **disappointed frustration** was right after Robert Kennedy fell to an assassin's bullet in 1968; whereas A Harriman due to LB Johnson's confession in the assassination of President Diem could indicate some complicity on Harriman's part [p.2, 3. http://www.ans-wers.com/topic/w-averell-harriman- page 4] this implication for Kennedy assassination's by the Bones-men among the WIB (War Industries Board) members. Eventually, these Bones learning how to manipulate a plot for the future to LB Johnson "meditate-revenge"

Much earlier in the war to the resulted in the "neutralization" of Laos in Geneva on July 23, 1962, as a spy pilot I must fly across border to Laos with my camouflage painted helicopter H.34, no call-sign, no tail flag, unmarked, no serial number, unknown country (photo on the book-cover) I'm not permitted wore VNAF flying suit, but instead of black peasant garb, no US weapon even cigarette US made, no identification papers. Our crewmembers equipped with Swedish K submachine guns and Belgian-made Browning 9mm pistol, and a tiny pistol 6, 35.mm, all of which, of course, had been acquired clandestinely so a serial-number check would lead nowhere, and a unmarked SOG knife, an untraceable 6-inch-bladed weapon, designed on Okinawa by manufactured clandestinely in Japan. And the most importance in case if our helicopters would be in the status emergency forced landing, they must be destroyed at once by five pounds TNT, C-4 ignited in exploded, it located in the aircraft radio compartment.

That time cross-border operation were strictly limited to those "areas in Laos, between Route 9 and the 17 parallel DMZ [Provisional Military Demarcation Line] adjacent to the border, and the area east of Tchepone" That was a relatively small debut-part of the Harriman highway [Ho Chi Minh trail] but considered the critical entry point to South Vietnam, and as a spy-pilot I dared say, "That will be becoming an open-dumpster-area for US and Soviet Union of the wasted out of all out of date weapons and war-materiel in the future incoming year. It clear that the State Department, A Harriman, as number 'three-position', a founder of Skull and Bones, was still in the scam; He stood firmly against the Vietnamese recon-men and flight crewmembers that crossed the border were "not to wear GVN or others uniforms," and we could engage the enemy only in just for the "self-defense." Who was U.S policymaker?

Now, that was in the spring of 1971, eight years earlier, and a lot had changed since then. Actually "Cooper-Church" leashed the US ground forces that had in any case been drawn down by more than 200,000, and all the emphasis was on passing the burden of the war to the South Vietnamese soldiers. And now there was contemplated a corps-level cross-border operation conducted without accompanying US ground forces or advisors, along a single, poorly maintained route dominated by virtually impassable high ground on one the north-flank and a Xe pon' River on the other, into long-established enemy base areas and without tactical surprise. It looked from the outset like a high-risk operation, not the kind of thing a soldier with the experience, tactical acumen, and terrain sense of an objective-observer would advocate. Thus a question should arise as to the origins of the plan for the raid into Laos.

A year earlier 1970, since then South Vietnamese corps-level operation had been conducted in Cambodia, but in cooperation with accompanying US forces, US advisors, and of course US artillery and air power in support. That operation and simultaneous political development in Cambodia resulted in closing the seaport of Sihanoukville to the enemy. This craps was plotting by US counterespionage and Soviet Union warning the Hanoi troop moved to west all the cargo scattered along corridor: Earlier two dry season campaigns, in conclusion that, based on all available intelligence, the enemy had already succeeded in moving only 9,000 short tons of supplies through the Laotian panhandle into South Vietnam and Cambodia, just 15 percent of the 67,000 short tons he had input into the system and only 40 percent as much as the previous year's throughput. The Permanent Government strategic staffs forced Hanoi to continue a protracted war strategy in the Southern Vietnam. Subsequently, the Hanoi's forces had, by and large, withdrawn farther west during the allied incursion into Cambodia rather than stay and fight for their base areas and supplies. Two players of CIP and NLF wouldn't yet to stop the game but protracted it.

With Market Time naval operations very effectively cutting off coastal deliveries as a method of re-supply, [no more supplies from Navy Group 759 to Seaport Sihanoukville] all enemy forces in the South were now dependent on what came down the Ho Chi-Minh trail from the North; the enemy could no longer afford to abandon his Binh-Tram [base areas] without a fight, lest his deployed forces be starved out as a result.

The so called "Vietnamization-Program" stemming from the strategist-staffs planner was implied an amount dispensable out of date war materiel must be inventory; for instant such like more than 7,000 helicopters HU-1 just a huge rubbish-dump on the spot, like forks, dishes, or napkins dispensable in the eve of combat training-picnic. They used literate-fashioned in political word Vietnamization in psychological warfare propaganda reinforced for South Vietnamese Air Force and became the rubbish later due to without spare-parts. But when the Saigon fall, they panic-fled out to emigrate in US theirs will pay-off back by real green dollars, jewel, diamond or transaction credit CD for these bullshit stuffs, cast-off WWII American weapons when they fled in search of a better life.

"When a new endeavor is launched," we foresaw, "something has to give." With US combat troops withdrawals continuing, and US support capability diminishing accordingly, there were not enough resources to go around.

The single Hanoi troops' dependence on the logistic corridor through the Laos panhandle presents South Vietnam with an unprecedented challenge. There is little doubt, as to the damage which could be dealt to Hanoi's aspiration by effectively blocking or even significantly hindering the southward movement of men and materiel. All were important, but the logistics-war of southern Laos and northeastern Cambodia, [COSVN] concluded MACV' analysts "now stand as the critical conflict for the Viet Cong and North communist troops." Every other supply route had been cut off, and the pacification process was reducing enemy ability to obtain supplies in Southern Vietnam. Thus the enemy must perforce expand and extend the Ho Chi Minh Trail if he was to support and sustain operations in northeast Cambodia. The target for ARVN operations was clear.

Yes, it must be a coincidence; it has to be a coincidence. It is fair to say that after the consequent effect of the "Cooper-Church" amendment, now increasingly threatening North Vietnamese air defenses brought the complex of **"Rules Of Engagement"**-(ROE) into even greater prominence. These prescriptions, or more often restrictions, governed where and under what circumstances aircraft could retaliate, what forces could be employed in the DMZ and for what purposes, and a range of other situations. Ridiculously, One bitter but insightful joke of the day was that the reason why the Air Force and Navy used two-seat fighter plane was so one man could fly and the other could read him the ROE strictly controlled by General Alexander Haig in the Washington, [Permanent Government Bones or George H.W Bush or Donald Rumsfeld WSAG' Chief staff] On the basis of circumstantial evidence, the small group of young officers working under general Haig, maybe including Lieutenant anti-war movement John F Kerry; this part of Kissinger's National Security Council staff, seems the likely source. Certainly Haig himself was the principal author, a prospect congruent with his later involvement in and reaction to the operation such as an invaded operation to northeast Cambodia recently.

The New Legion

General George Brown, noting that the ROE permitted his air crews to strike enemy installations from which they had taken fire. *"We can always entice them into shooting at us"* Brown affirmed. Sometimes, though, that proved too dangerous a tactic. Haig' instructions were issued prohibiting operations within the SAM envelope. Unfortunately that action also ruled out strikes against the best interdiction point on Route 7, supplying route to the south.

When this was briefed to General Abrams, he reacted heatedly *"The Air Force does not have the authority to attack that site, even when it's fired at, right?"* Abrams asked Brown.

"No, sir, we can't attack that," Brown confirmed.

"Under those circumstances," said Abrams, *"I just don't see how you can call on people to go up there to work!"*

That's the whole points in this thing, the lack of authority to attack that damn site, or any other site up there in that area that opens up on you. Of course, we're tried to get the authority, and I'll be goddamned if I understand why we can't, because the photo recon guys that go in North Vietnam – they can attack anybody that shoots at them from North Vietnam. Referring acidly to comment, all this crap about US flight personnel can take whatever action's required to protect their crew, protective reaction – all kind of great patriotic speeches have been made about that! And if the principle of retaliation doesn't apply in North Vietnam, the flight crewmembers will be damned. This is very difficult to understand. Controversy over the ROE and the application of those rules would continue throughout the remaining years of the war.

Permanent Government unleashed the scattering of the Hanoi's troop's logistical traffic along "Harriman Highway" corridor, the interdiction tactics of the past no longer seemed sufficient due to strategy "everything worked but nothing worked enough" – infeasible. As on an altitude view of bird by helicopter treetop snapshot, I should say: "The dispersal factor has been accomplished fantastic-beautifully," and "Hanoi's trucks move at night, they move to one place, stay and hide, unload, pick up another truck and move on down south, hiding below the thick canopy, so it's just an extremely difficult problem. Obviously, their cargos were not ever subjected to horrible destroyed because the axe of evil warned them beforehand what, where, and when SAC will be B-52s carpet-struck. *(MR. Ho-Si-Hai, NVA truck-driver diaries tell us much about southward infiltration. He has been ordered to drive at night with low beam and sleep at daytime for rest and relaxation. These order-regulations keep them safely in network)*

One year earlier [spring 1970] there was also emphasized the importance of Highway Harriman, [Ho Chi Minh trail] the utmost Laotian corridor: the supplies stored by the various troop supply cargo-stations of Group 559 in the campaign's area of operations had risen to 6,000 tons, which together with the High Command's cargo-supply reserves was sufficient to support between 50,000 and 60,000 troops in combat for four or five months. In addition, more than 30,000 tons of supplies were stored in Group 559's warehouses along the strategic transportation corridor – the most recent-cargo was already out of risk in the operational area, recently moving to farther south.

However the Haig' war-room in Washington had not lost track of the importance of that lifeline by sophisticated sensors from satellite. When a truthfulness of George H W Bush as Director of Central Intelligence as Richard Helm visited Vietnam; Seven Air Force commander General Lucius Clay described his job of the moment as carrying out instructions given him by General Abrams but of course having some restrictions secretly notified in ROE stipulations.

For escaping from the Strategic Air Command bombardments, pretty soon the trail began to dry out and NVA' logistics offensive moved into high gear by urging as fast as they can run away the striking area. Shortly before Operation Lam Son 719 started, Seven Air Force was devoting 89 percent of B.52 strikes to the so-called anti-infiltration boxes but too late and achieving record truck kills, just merely trucks were grounded by broken down in the parking lot, and the substantial numbers still got through. The targets always depended on CIA, Ted Shackley Station chief at Saigon decision. "So! But goddamn it" – either they've got enough that are well or something. But they seem to be able to work on the road, keep the Molotova-Trucks going, still fire the antiaircraft, still move the supplies and unload and load it, backpack it, and all that. So we

The New Legion

should say they're right on schedule…and we don't think it means that somehow they're going to screw it up!" They are motivated to seize South Vietnam by power according to '**axiom-1**'.

Before Lam Son 719 commenced, as the raid into Laos loomed, in Paris on 21 January 1971, the 100th session of the sterile peace negotiations was held, a meeting described as "devoted largely to reviews of known position". Meanwhile drawdown of US combat troops continued unabated, 60,000 more departing during January-April 1971, then operation Lam Son 719. Strategically, President Thieu accounts on **"a thrust into Laos, a safe for U.S troops withdrawn."** All US troops have got to be pulling in the same direction, and all together. We'd counseled "That's always a neat trick to do under the most ideal circumstances. American is all different. They're individualists and enthusiasts, optimist and pessimist, then a slight sprinkling of just screw-ups!"

Kissinger asked CIA, Ted Shackley to prepare a close hold estimate of probable enemy reaction to a large-scale South Vietnamese raid into the Tchepone area of Laos that would be backed by US air support but no US ground force involvement, the assessment, wrote Bruce Palmer, "was remarkably accurate with respect to the nature, pattern, and all-out intensity of the NVA reaction to Lam Son 719"

On 26 January the text of an intercepted NVA message was forwarded to McCain and Abrams. *"It has been determined that the enemy [South Vietnam and US combat forces] may strike into our cargo carrier system in order to cut it off,"* the document read *"Prepare to mobilize and strike the enemy hard. Be vigilant!"*

On 29 January, the NVA has detected indication of an imminent major operation in northern South Vietnam below DMZ. They recognize the possibility of a cross-border operation into Tchepone and the decisive effects such an attack could have on their 1970-1971, crash logistics program, as well as on their objectives in South Vietnam and Cambodia. But there was also a substantial element of enemy uncertainly as to just what the US and ARVN troops were going to do. Objective-observer noted concern about an invasion by sea, invasion by air from the aircraft carriers offshore, and so on. "There is waiting to figure out what's going on". In conclusion, subsequent intercepts indicated "a high state of alert in the southern provinces of North Vietnam" with one provincial unit reporting that "extensive preparations were being made against anticipated US and ARVN troop attacks in North Vietnam.

Operation Lam Son 719: In this traditional Lunar new-year

Tet of "Monkey", I have a special favor from my high commander unleashed me to joint celebrated holiday in Saigon even the immensity of the war at that time was too much for me to leave my 213th squadron. I'm enormously impressed by this excited traditional happiness with my family – In my ears frequently the short-lasting sound fire-crackers were exploded with a loud cracking noise that my children cried out overjoyed to see their exploded into laughter.

At the evening 5 February 1971, an airman of my 1st Air Division showed up given to me a message that my 51st Wing commander urged me to break off a Tet holiday leave at the highest point of family-happiness and return back to my squadron on the earlier flight to Danang air-base as soon as I can. My daughter had heard the reports on television about soldiers dying in this war, so she knew how dangerous, it was twelve, old enough to realize that I could be killed. When I got my orders to go, I remember that my wife seemed very subdued, and we didn't say much about it to. In the pagoda hear mass, my daughter cried calmly through the entire service. In the early morning, I embraced my children before leaving because I had to use the farewell scenes since my long event marriage period. They observed me as a hero: strong, calm, always in charge in my own quiet way. They were worried they would never see me again. It is not easy to be the wife of a helicopter pilot in the war time.

When a woman falls in love with a spy-pilot or Project Delta pilot, she knows she's in for a roller-coaster ride. Marry an Airborne, Marine, Ranger or any member of Special Forces and you can forget about counting on celebrating birthdays, holidays, or anniversaries together. Your mother might pass away and he won't make the funeral. His mother might die, and you will have to watch him kneel at her graveside, stricken with remorse, long after she's cold.

What the hell of war? I did not believe that the war was at a moral level sufficiently low to require civil resistance. The war, as

The New Legion

I understood it then, was not in itself an evil; if there was evil. Our longest-young developed a deep, visceral disgust for war because of our – and our families' – experiences in it. "All kind of wars were stupid!" That war destroyed our families with a terrifying, shocking and painful experience. The war had simply savaged; it turned the fathers and brothers and sisters upside down and sucked all the oxygen out of their smug and comfortable assumptions. Nowadays, after all that we experienced and lost in that war, we finally understand that there is nothing inevitable about us! Also, I thought it was in how ineptly it was being conducted and in the consequences of this ineptitude.

In the Tet-Offensive, once I had seen my HU1-H crewmembers return from battlefield. Four flight crewmembers, brave-men who had given their courage, their disciplined dedication, their blood to a cause now lost. Their remains had zipped shut in four blackbags filled with too many friends who had given their lives trying to win the Red-menace. I had acquired a sense of civic duty to my country that was not deterred by the vicissitudes of poor leadership. When I looked into myself, I knew that I would remain faithful to a code of personal honor attached to what I understood as the ideals of my country's form of government rising above the confusions of political and military leadership. This became explicitly clear to me when I was interviewed by allies-officer in my class Squadron Officer School at Maxwell Air University Alabama. They asked me "What I thought of the war", and I recall telling them that I thought it make no sense to me to try to defend South Vietnam so long as the border areas of Cambodia and Laos were conceded to the Hanoi. I had no quarrel with resisting the spread of Red menace, but I could see no strategy being applied that had prospects of success. Nevertheless, I remember telling the allies-officer students that *"my patriotism was stronger than my unhappiness about poor US intervention strategic policy!"*

When I stepped down from a twice-engine transport C.119, a blue-air-force pick up truck had been waiting for picked me up to Its Division War-Room. I zipped up my flying-suit and flight jacket to prevent the chill and influenza when in this season fall to 45 degrees in the still darkness of the night, but this weather was another rough friend and foe in the northern I Corp region, and at the height of the monsoon when fog is heavy but usual patchy. The northeast monsoon blows a light, steady, cold rain its height called the 'crachin' (from the French word) for "drizzle", the rain often lasts two or four days at the time and is frequently accompanied by a blanketing fog that stops close air support and also makes artillery hard to adjust when fog is thick enough. Northern I Corps happens to be place where the northeast monsoon is most intense it is the rainiest place in South Vietnam, the average rainfall for Hue, province is 120 inches compared to 77 inches for Saigon.

I opened a secret envelope that a message is as verbatim order assigned me as a field-chief-commander all VNAF units included two flights, one from Queen-bee 219th Squadron, another belonging King-Star 233rd Squadron and my entire Magic-Club 213th Squadron including 6 HU1-H Gun-ships for special air cover and ground support for Airborne Division. All flight crewmembers now have to standby at the Danang Air-base for in case scrambled over to operational area [Khe Sanh]. But firstly, I must bring my two gun-ships right away to the outpost of Airborne Field Headquarter located on top a mountain right south of DMZ for a short briefing. At 9:00 A.M this morning, where all standby-combat forces were already to scramble.

Particularly, my 213th Squadron was be chosen by General Dong, the Airborne commander as our perfect air ground support for airborne brigade to recent on rubber Chup Plantation in Cambodia last year 1970, as the same way now, General Abrams chosen General Tri with the nick-named Vietnamese Patton to a field commander for operation Lam Son 719. But Tri was killed while his helicopter took off and exploded when operation Lam Son 719 just started.

I prepare to land on a helipad the Camp-J.J.Carroll (named for a Marine captain who died to seize a nearby ridge) Camp Con Thien, and Rockpile, each dominated by one brigade) An airborne major Khoi came and guided me to the briefing room, a big bunker with abundance sand bags staged around.

At 9:00 A.M, at briefing room when I showed up General Du Quoc Dong hand shaken by implication for I should doing the best. He said: "I personally had had cable to President Thieu for your squadron worked with us because your squadron was the elite not only for the Vietnam War but the World War too…as you knew…I put my trust in you whereas US…they're not deserve to be trusted!"

I wondered that Dong was just notorious a simple combat soldier he hatred politic but now his statement too much political in his hindsight. I took command of this 213th Squadron after graduated to US Air University. In 1970s, I brought one flight detachment to engage Cambodia War as air supply and medical evacuation support to an Airborne Brigade to cover rubber Chup-Plantation. Now this manipulated action exerted by General Lam I Corps commander, thinking first of his Corps own interests, needs, without concern for III Corps in alert; He complaint to President Thieu for his selfish reasons. "Why every Corps having their own-helicopter wing and there was never coming to reinforced us at the usually hot at DMZ not sharing what I Corps has with others" President Thieu responded "All priority for Cambodia War"

On the high relief of Carroll Camp looked down to route 9 reaching to western mountainous area, from this outpost spread along Route 9, which extended across the northern badlands from Dong Ha at the coast to Khe Sanh in the far western mountains, overlooking the Laos border. I found out a long like snack convoy of trucks heading to Khe Sanh maybe for this operation. Whereas to eastern flat terrain of the green plain and bushes I could find out some airborne soldiers appearing somewhat underneath the foliage for practical exercise. Major Khoi indicated his finger to down there and said: "Supposedly, our troops down there get trouble encircled by enemy they needed your guide how to protect them by your firepower cover support…and the most important we never use color smokes on our location…but just a red color panel only!"

Two gun-ships were flying over 300 feet above an airborne battalion. I tried to contact on FM 42.5 friend called sign "Dong-Da" for identified target spot and strafing two 2.75 rockets right on target and turned sharply to the right now left mini-gun continued tracing on the target. Dong-Da ground force was very pleased but I radioed next pass-prep, we will made dived prep-approach parallel left side for avoiding fired remnant cartridges didn't fall on the troop.

With my experience by almost as a quick reflex action I often don't use the gun-sight instrument while firing. I trust my Sergeant Duc, he was a good gunner, sometimes his eyes were same my eyes on target. Two mini-guns were the big killer that recalled to me in the battle northwest of Chu-Lai, just only two gun-ships but killed a full battalion of NVA [lest than 150 men] which was crossing the Thu-Bon's river. I also recalled once a smuggle boat belong to NVA Group 759 was been detected, this supplied boat was everyone on board get killed by mini-guns after 24 rockets missing by two new nervous rating-pilots prep. The ghost boat continued proceeding to the shore Phong Dien county Quang Tri province without pilot directed, a ghostly creature flitting on the surface of the sea to land at My Thuy beach; Marine Brigade 258th was welcome her with different kind of weapons, plus a platoon Tank M-48 in strafing into it with their canons. The typical of this ghost boat was carried a thousand to thousand 'beacon pork-meat' canned at China made, plus various supply categories of military materiel.

The NVA troops were screwed up for everything they had leaned how to react and shot to the airplanes. Because all fighters even helicopter Cobra when they started to fire they must dive to release their fire-powers. The NVA had instructed by US counterespionage–firing only at the time their fighter-bombers raised their head to sky, then stands and freely shot at them whatever you get in your hand. A platoon of antiaircraft artillery divided three points of three equilateral triangle angles; each angle established a stronghold AAA guns. Where they dug up land for individual holes 60 decrees inclination, these shaped hole for personnel sliding when fighter dived on their top as target; meanwhile two another strongholds kept firing but a stronghold was on the target, people must gliding under the 60-degree hole, and at once, while the fighter raised the head to sky, stands in fired at him. It's strange they haven't heard from this tactical was only harmful by our bullets 7.62 mm at 4,000 rounds per minutes by Gunship HU-1H model. So why NVA were only get killed by our monsters in that very-moment.

One captured AAA' NVA officer told us, they were confident with these tactical offenses

The New Legion

They were never had casualty with this method of defense. If the battle lasts longer run that meant VNAF and US aircrafts having so many chance of being risked to shot-down than destroyed them and the most we used the "Snake-Eye" bombs, 250 or 500 pounds. He said these bombs exploded on the mountainous forest as southern Laos, likely the big fire-cracker celebrated in lunar New Year spell. That meant VNAF like F-5, A-37 AD-6 dropped bombs ... their efforts to strike him were futile.

In the earlier of Lam Son operation, following the operation plan, one Airborne Brigade should take over a stronghold of a fire base with call-sign Hill-32, but Lieutenant John F Kerry of antiwar movement had let Hanoi known everything planning for this operation so why President Thieu ordered cancelled the last anticipated Hill-32 fire base support. However Hanoi skeptically if in doubt, don't act unless allies forces in south DMZ are been certain, other word Hanoi was disregarded anything by Kerry had say, although he was a notorious antiwar activist showed up everyday in world TV. Kissinger and Yale graduated John Kerry were chosen by Harriman for his conspiracy, naturally Kerry was supported by Skull and Bone for his future presidency campaign; so coincidence with actor quarterback Kissinger in the play-game Pennsylvania meanwhile Kerry duty performance to accomplish axiom 1 – the anticipated of biggest-fiasco that I foresaw in my whole time there because it broke the back of the Saigon regime of Army forces, particularly irreplaceable were the dead ARVN "elite-officers". I must say since 'that' the future leaders, they were all dead. Subsequently Skull and Bones turned in Saigon to Hanoi with a blood-leak battle instead of bloodbath one. This operation identified one of these strategy-goals. Furthermore this repeated "the bomb ends the war": dropping the atomic bombs brought the war to a swift conclusion, saving many lives in the process, after a Big air-campaign: on the night of March 9-10, 1945, Permanent Government ordered 324 B-29s attacked right the heart of Tokyo as low level in the most destructive air raid in then history, ended by B-29s were used to drop the first atomic bombs on Japan. On August, 6, 1945 Colonel Paul Tibbets, aircraft commander B-29s, named "Enola Gay" dropped the first atomic bomb on Hiroshima in saving many lives in prospect. War-history once again repeated – The B.52 has long been one of the main instruments of Permanent Government foreign-policy. During the Cold War it was the airborne warrior that would have dropped nuclear weapon onto the Soviet Union or maybe on China if Red China tried to overrun the southern states of Soviet Republic in its critical possibility be-collapsed-period. The special "Big Belly" B-52D could also carry a load of 108 conventional bombs, and during the Vietnam War in the "Pennsylvania's" as Linebacker-II, 129 B-52s of several models carried out the 11 days and night attacked the so called "Christmas Bombing" which designed to force Hanoi to conference table in Paris.

Phase-1 (1 Feb to 7 Feb) – On 1 February 1971, as U.S armor and mechanized forces were moving to open Route 9 west to the Laotian border in a preparatory stage of the Laotian incursion, after two weeks discussing plans for Lam Son 719 by NSC on January 18, 1971. One week later, 8 February, 1971 ARVN cross border. General Abrams cabled Admiral McCain to advise that the bulk of the enemy's combat units in the region are located in the vicinity of Tchepone, the operation's ultimate objective. Whatever else might happen, it was clear that the disposition and strength of enemy forces in and near the area of operations were not going to come as any surprise to the attackers.

Lieutenant General Armor Hoang Xuan Lam, I Corps, was in command of the thrust into Laos. The U.S counterpart in Military Region 1 was Lieutenant General James W.Sutherland, an armor officer who commanded the XXIV Corps. MACV depended heavily on Sutherland and his headquarters to advisor, support, and encourage General Lam and the Vietnamese during the operation. Lam had under his command for the operation the 1st Infantry Division, the Airborne Division, the Marine Division, the 1st Armored Brigade Task Forces and a Ranger group, the best troops South Vietnam possessed, attacked spearhead by eighteen acted combat battalions

Stated a later North Vietnamese history, "…our combat forces in the Route 9 – south Laos Front had reached 60,000 combat troops, consisting of five divisions such as 320th, 324th, $2^{nd,}$ 304th, and 308th: two separate infantry regiments such as 278th, and 27th;

eight regiments of artillery, three engineer regiments, three tank regiments, six anti-aircraft regiments, eight sapper battalions, plus rear service and transportation units. This campaign was our army's greatest concentration of combined arms forces in its history up to that point."

On the defensive in Laos, the enemy was going to be able to amass and sustain a much larger force than he could have projected into South Vietnam.

Phase-2 (8 Feb to 5 March) – On 8 February 1971 the ARVN forces began crossing the border into Laos and Operation Lam Son 719 had been under way. Alongside the route, a hundred yards before the border, was posted a sign that read: "Warning, No US personnel beyond this point." This mission was to disrupt the enemy's lines of communication and destroy stocks of war materiel – especially in Base Area 604, centered on Tchepone – thereby setting back the enemy's timetable for aggression, protecting American forces during their progressively withdraw, and providing more time for South Vietnamese forces to develop. This ground thrust was an integral part of the larger effort to thwart enemy aggression by denying him the wherewithal to carry it out, a complement to the intensive air interdiction campaign along the entire line of communication in the Laotian panhandle and against the target box system that sought to block the entry points into the trail system.

From the outset it was hard going. Route 9 was at best a narrow, twisting, nearly unimproved surface, or so it looked from the air. The reality was much worse. In 1962 an occasion in alert for rescue STRATA infiltration, our Queen-Bee H.34 must standby there. I had chance strode along the route 9 to hunting the peacock, recognized the surface some of those weather cuts that were in that route were fifteen feet deep. A few days after the operation commenced. They missed that in the readout of the aerial photography. The area of operation extended from Khe Sanh, in Coroc highlands situated 12 kilometers east of the Laotian border, to the city of Tchepone, 45km inside Laos. The axial center of the operation was Route-9. Parallel to Route-9 was a small river. Thick jungles of thorny giant bamboo flanked both sides of Route 9 which was 200 to 500 meters above the sea level. Mt Coroc blocked longitudinally from the North to the

South, leaving only a path for Route-9 to pierce. Movement troops were very difficult and limited in such topography. Everything depended on Route-9. The high relief crests on each side were ideal places in which to launch ambushes. Troops had to move over undulating terrains, covered with thick bamboo forests that greatly blocked observation and hindered maneuvers. There was very difficult for the offensive force to assault in such terrain even if it were fully supported by armor, air force and artillery. Another disadvantage was that the NVA knew very well this area like the back of their hands, whereas the ARVN troops were unfamiliar with the operational area. It was psychological disadvantage for South Vietnam troops to the must have to fight outside their country in completely unknown terrain and mountainous area.

In the operation plan, a trajectory called for an armor task force to drive was along route 9 toward Tchepone while – by occupying a string of fire support bases to be established paralleling on the right west mountainous flank. The 1st Infantry Division protected the southern flank, and the Marine Division constituted the reserve. Later the armor would link up with airborne elements to be airlifted to Tchepone. Leading the way into Laos was the ARVN 1st Armored Brigade Task Force, reinforced by two airborne battalions. Next an ARVN airborne brigade headquarters and one of its battalions moved into position, followed by another airborne brigade and then a Ranger battalion. Other units followed.

Unfortunately, the cuts will have an adverse effect on all operations to win the war. Given the restricting "Cooper-Church" amendment, no advisors accompanied ARVN troops into Laos, not like in the last year incursion to Cambodia, and of course no America units participated. Air support of all kinds was allowed – however, as was artillery and logistical support from the South Vietnamese side of the Laos/VN border. This generated a massive operation in support of the incursion. Early on, General Abrams visited the primary base for all this activity, a reopened Khe Sanh. "It's hard to believe," he marveled, "the helicopters, the trucks, the artillery, the amount of equipment that is in that whole thing up there. I'll tell you, I've never seen anything like it in the time I've been here. It's quite remarkable – fifty-three CH-47 Chinooks, really something."

The New Legion

US heavy artillery lined up along the border to provide fire support including eighteen 155mm Howitzers, sixteen 175mm guns, and eight 8-inch howitzers But the huge amounts of aviation support were the real story of U.S support for this operation Lam Son 719. Additionally, Seventh Air Force kept up its interdiction campaign against the Ho Chi Minh Trail, during the first week of Lam Son 719 destroying a new second high number of trucks for the dry season (but trucks were broke-down in the parking area due to all targets the CIA made decision – everything worked but nothing worked enough on strategy for protracting the war) but that was now only part of its massive efforts.

General Lucius Clay said: "I'm flying roughly 12,000 support sorties a month in addition to this," referring to the number of individual aircraft missions being launched for various purposes (demolished stony mountains for created a future International Indo China Highway and NVA should be ground cleared by the early pioneers, debut at Harriman Super-Highway)

Clay continued: "I'm flying 21,000 sorties a month in airlift. I'm flying roughly 850 – 900 sorties a month in recon. That's all maintenance capability, whether you expend ordnance or not," meaning that every one of these flights generated s maintenance requirement. "There's a limit to what you can do in generating sorties."

In the wake of a broadcast by President Thieu announcing this operation; Laotian Prime Minister Souvanna Phouma issued a formal statement of protest. The language of the statement, said a MACV analyst, suggested that "certainly the primary responsibility rests with the Democratic Republic of Vietnam which, scornful of international law…began and continues to violate the neutrality and territorial integrity of the Kingdom of Laos."

Meanwhile, on behalf of Viet Cong National Liberation Front, Madame Nguyen Thi Binh cabled an urgent message to sympathizers in the United States: "Earnestly call you mobilize peace forces your country…check United States dangerous venture Indochina!"

Alas! On 10 February 1971, I never seem to learn from my mistake, in the earliest of this operation, an echelon-formation of 4 UH1-Hs of my 213th squadron, but 2 were exploded in air by antiaircraft gun 14,5mm armed on PT-76 and 37mm AAA in the northeast of Tchepone for a mission reconnaissance. All crewmembers and passengers were killed including four journalists and I Corps staff officers at coordinate XD 563537 at 15:00.

The cold air spread so low on highland ground inflicted on my back while I'm on a military-cot inside the canvas tent; under a mosquito-net I meditate on the sufferings of that terrible shock to their families. "How can I prevent that wouldn't happened again?" I couldn't sleep for night long due to the U.S Long Tom 175 guns at Khe Sanh, strafing to now and then waking me up. This section on Ho Chi Minh trail, from Mu-Gia Pass via Tchepone to Attopeu was familiar with me; I could know how every scenery in my heart, every relief, peaks of high mountains, creeks, rivers, streams, the virgin forests, human activities in devastated by bombs, now I looked devastating with very impressive and effective. The spot LZ that Lieutenant Hue crashed when was infiltrated landing a STRATA team in 1963 due to engine lost-power now became clear red-earth soil instead of the green dark forest; I recalled I Had had put right wheel landing gear on his Queen-Bee hub-blades for rescue all flight crewmembers. Now everywhere filled by ware-houses and POL pipe-line parallel on its. And also the AAA from here shot-down our HUI-H when this early operation started.

After a longest night I rubbed my eyes and yawned broader, though sometimes caught an hour or two naps on the nearby duty watch's cot, but mostly I got my shut-eye from dozing in a metal folding chair, and came out looked out across the darkness toward Dong Da stronghold base, as the token artillery fire sounded in the muffled way that artillery always seems to sound on battlefield at night and an occasional star shell from the batteries illuminated the sky.

How can sleep? I recalled nine years ago (1962) as same place Khe Sanh quiet and peaceful I awoke early morning to the sounds of the stream. It was shrouded in thick impenetrable pea-soup fog, but its murmur reached through inside my tent as I sipped my coffee. The only sounds were the awakening, chirping, singing birds and the babbling riffles as the stream split and wove around a highland

The New Legion

directly in front of my tent-yard. Was I in the backwoods wild of Khe Sanh or some remote distant location out west to Tchepone?

I became obsessed with that accident. "What do I conclude from that, and what conclusions do I draw from that casualty prevention?" The most of my concerned was the new rating pilot attachment to my responsibility from brand new formed squadron 233rd King-Star. I am convinced myself from now on, I will handle a lead gunship as escorted combat formation to air cover every UH-1H slicks fly cross border to the operation area, and the rendezvous point should be a check point over the old-French-prison at Lao-Bao right on the frontier Laos where to their coming and leaving. By way of conclusion, I will having a short briefing to all 'aircraft-commanders' of squadron 213th, 233rd, and 219^{th,} in the early tomorrow morning for the new tactical gunship air cover-escort with the hope 'no one get killed'.

At the left side of the Route 9 to Tchepone was the Xe-Pon River, but in 1962 there was very cool, I recalled that aerial photo mission I made a stupid flight when detected a sampan camouflage covered with full becoming browned leaves, I surrounded over its in the air for funning picture, suddenly from those browned leaves the submachine gun fired to my H-34 chopper, while I came back to Khe Sanh, Captain Phu (now brigadier general commander 1st Infantry Division, the finest infantry unit) told me that your helicopter blades got hit three holes by Mat P.49 equipped to French Airborne, if your hear one by one that meant Mat-36, so I told him that Mat-49. Now Phu was still his looking shape pale and thin and always the cigarette sticking in his fingers but not French-Bastos heavy cigarette. This time his face appeared frequent worry and nervous because the B.52 took off from Utapao (tactical bombardment or strategic bombardment take off from Guam) let him the shortest time when B-52 flew "Arc-Light" missions attacking the so called communist hiding beneath the featureless jungle canopy but targets depended on CIA for protracted war or demolished stony-mountains; so you known they couldn't be killed. But CIA's goal was pushed pressure to ARVN troop hurry up on course trajectory on 'keyed-up-time' to the siege-target 604 – NVA' base cargo supply.

In the TOC' bunker I can hear loudly his order "Any directions clear enough for run away at once! Run away at once." That meant pushing Colonel Diem regiment commander at southern flank to move quickly to Tchepone.

Strangely, the NVA thrust coming from north DMZ that I could understand they crossed by our three fire-base supports but B-52 didn't strike on them at all, but only than on ARVN infantry regiment in southern flank? Why? Because General Giap (cooperated engagement with OSS before 1943) though was an indirect apparatus of Skull and Bones but Giap help them carrying out their strategy instead used all powerful forces attacked directly in to American Khe Sanh Base (so nowadays his sibling stayed in California, USA) This plot was imagined by your simple knowledge; why don't attack closer easy-won but attack too far at open area-dumpster, Base 604, Tchepone?

On 10 February advance elements of the armor column linked up with an airborne battalion at A-Luoi Fire-Support Base, some twenty kilometers into Laos, despite truly miserable weather that had set in the previous day. On the same day ARVN I Corps Headquarters, already struggling with the complex tasks of coordinating a multi-division attack under difficult terrain and weather conditions, suffered a serious setback when 2 VNAF helicopters crash resulted in the deaths of two of its most important staff officers, the chief J-3 planner and the chief J-4 logistician. However the Chinooks CH-47 really something when they hook up the Howitzer 155 artillery to every FSB as Dong Da, Hill-30, 31 in the northern flank were great O.K. It's hard to believe. In the two full days of February, two airborne brigades, one infantry regiment, Ranger, CH-47, CH-54 hanging in air heavy loads to every established Fire Support Bases back and forth; everything were fluently quite beautiful. But only 2 Huey were accident by ground fire belong to my Magic-Club 213th squadron and Colonel Diem regiment's few slowed react soldiers were killed by our friendly B.52s bombardment from Guam, by preplanned road map in Pentagon.

From about 12 February on, ARVN forces more or less held in place and hunkered down, not a wise tactic in an operation of this kind. Later it was asserted, by the rumor that government not among

The New Legion

permanent government, that President Thieu had issued secret orders to his commanders to halt the advance when 3,000 casualties had been sustained. Nguyen Tien Hung, a former special assistance to Thieu, later cast doubt on that claim, writing that "Thieu insists he never gave such an order!" The next day General Vien Chiefs Staffs invited General Abrams to meet with him. General Vien described President Thieu's visit and briefings in I Corps on 12 February, and "said that after a thorough discussion of intelligence and dispositions, President Thieu directed that the ARVN forces not advance further at this time beyond the western positions they now hold." General Vien thought this would be a hold of three to five days and affirmed that they still intended to go to Tchepone. Abrams in turn pointed out the disadvantages of remaining in static positions, "giving the enemy both time and opportunities to reorganize his reaction in a more effective way"

How can we know that war game between the axe of evil to its counterparts [Soviet Union and Skull and Bones] must coordinate their efforts in function together efficiently and in an organized way as ROE' scam. I was understandably bitter about the outcome of the long years of struggle for free South Vietnam. That performance alone should serve to demonstrate that I was as stunned as any that the sometime American ally would, in a time of such crisis, turn its back on South Vietnam and of course on all the sacrifices my SOG fellows in arm had made there.

Here is a typical case for their craps. The G.I stayed in the Main Compound at Danang Air Force Base in 1972, a certain morning at breakfast time when the loud-speaker said something but our Airmen-housewife didn't understand what the hell they say; but they wait until afternoon and come to check the Hospital Ship [Hope or Helgolan] of Germany disembarked not still anchorage in the pier of Han's river. They hurried back and suddenly launched into a harangue to their husbands: "Tonight Viet Cong will launch rockets into our air base. I bring the kids to downtown for escaped…if you would dic try stay on here…O.K!" Prophetically, they prophesied that at night when the loud speakers said: "All G.I must go into the bunker about five minutes rockets will strafing, it also clear announcement how many rockets will hit and TOT too and it repeat one more time before rockets hit.

In turn of ROE, on August 9, 1968 three box B.52 (nine aircrafts) "Arc-Light" took off from Guam to strike the Forward Base of 559 Group headquarters at Tam-Boi' mountain, "Oscar Eight" call sign for SOG, northern Ashau-valley where mountain contained immense chambers hewn from solid rock and fitted with heavy iron door, so well constructed that they withstood B.52 strikes. However according to the ROE, the camouflage Soviet fishing boats nearby the Guam Island contacted with that headquarter 559 Group before long enough to TOT(Time On Target) for hidden chambers hewn escaped B.52 struck.

The raid began with three throngs B.52, a dawn Arc Light a thousand 500 and 750-pounds bombs walk across Oscar Eight, setting off 50 secondary explosions, witnessed by our recon team Master Sergeant Billy Waugh watched. Incredibly, the bombs had barely stopped falling when he could see NVA troops running from their shelters to roll fuel barrels away from a fire. Waugh radioed SOG Lt Col Harold Rose at Khe Sanh, "I've got people out here scurrying around. That sonva-bitch is loaded". All NVA troops were secure even they couldn't hear the sound of eight jet engines flown at high at 25,000 to 35,000 feet.

The nature of this operation was too stranger, "attack" was a maneuver much advantage than "defense," but Giap' forces don't use this tactical for destroyed all U.S forces at Khe Sanh much closer and easier won the war, why not? And the must-fight at the 'barbecue drill-oven' as Base 604, Tchepone instead – this is a perfect value-plot of CIA counterespionage in collaboration between two counterparts was effect to separate the clique cadre communist Hanoi out of China- domination. B.52 killed General Nguyen Chi Thanh pro-China prior to helping Le Duan and Le Duc Tho carried out their scams by seizing the totalitarian-power at Hanoi's regime.

Subsequently General Sutherland provided some further insight, cabling Abrams that the South Vietnamese had modified the original plan primarily because of heavy enemy contact by the Rangers and the Airborne forces on the northern flank of the penetration, and the demonstrated inability of the armor brigade to move rapidly along

Route 9. For quite some time enemy forces had remained cautions and were, in fact, somewhat slow to reinforce. Their first serious counterattack came on the night of 18 February, when two NVA battalions struck the ARVN 39th Ranger Battalion northeast of Ban Dong. This 39th Ranger has to retreat to South LZ to shake hands with 21st Ranger Battalion as pressure is too strong, encircled by armor PT-76 and tank T-54 of B-70 Corps. During that night, 7 AC-130 flare-ships and 6 EC-130B Gun-ships were covered, destroyed numerous NVA tanks and troops. Subsequently the major battles of the operation took place on that northern flank of the penetration, especially at Fire Support Base 31 and 30.

Venal Press-Corps' Biased Reports

(You probably heard of the story BAT 21, or worse watch...the Movie Bat 21, if the US main stream media used to ignore the role of Ranger's effort during the Lam Son 719. The following except-paragraph is credible enough to shed light on the scenario: Sergeant-Medic Fujii (Lam-Son 219) and Lieutenant Norris (BAT-21) what their differences in at work)

"Ask yourself, Lt Norris can't located your bath-room when he was your first coming guest, and Sergeant Fujii was merely a man speak good English" That's simple answer for you all.

Warning no U.S personal beyond this point: This sign-board showed-up 100 meter from border Laos/Vietnam. General Lam authorized these strike-newsmen on board of VNAF helicopter crossing border to Laos, of course dare theirs step down on the soil-land for intrigued to illuminate the situation and the times, consequently on 10th February, 15:00 hours at the coordinated XD 563537, meanwhile, near the area of operations of the 21st Ranger Battalion, our 213th Magic-Club Squadron flight a formation of four VNAF helicopters bound for Landing Zone Ranger South was hit by enemy 37-mm antiaircraft artillery and PT-76 machine guns fire at 3:00pm. Two helicopters were downed and all passengers were presumed killed. The first helicopter carried two ARVN colonels, the G3 and G4 of I Corps. The second helicopter reportedly carried a number of foreign correspondents *[in 1998, all remains recovered* *were testified: -Keisaburo Shimamoto; -Henri Huet,* **AP***; -Larry Burrows,* **Life** *and -Kent Potter,* **News Week***, but specially, Pham Xuan An,* **Times/UPI***, triple-cross-mediator, he was on board of helicopter H-21, landed at battle of Ap Bac 1963, but in this operation Lam Son he did know how what the hell, so why he never on airborne to Laos. However, on Route-9, a Japanese journalist Akihiro Okamura worked with* **Times magazine** *accompanied 1st Armor Brigade, his point of view was the same of mine: ARVN subjected to under siege at 604-fierce ambushed-battle by NVA' stronghold underground defender of Steel 2nd NVA Division and surrounded by others four NVA divisions. Thereby B-52 had to destroy all of two crucial opponents for guaranty turn in Saigon to Hanoi not like A "Pebble-Capital" -* **carried out axiom-1 at just we guessed***]*

It was suspected that the I Corps G3 had carried with him an operational map of LAM SON 719 along with signal operating instructions and codes. A significant rumor that the loss of these documents to the General Giap' hands would be extremely in viewer minds? A thorough search of the area for the downed helicopters produced no results. But in reality, Lieutenant John F Kerry, the so called "antiwar movement activist" showed it up to Hanoi via General Giap translated by Triple-Cross mediated translator, Pham Xuan An, so it seemed to me General Giap was seating side by side with General Alexander Haig in Pentagon [General Giap was OSS member recruited by Agent Number 19, Lucien Conein at Pat-Po sanctuary in 1945 photo by Allan Squiers]

Air Calvary crew, Sergeant Medic-Fujii, Hawaiian, his helicopter got hit by mortar 120mm (these accurate mortars which inflicted almost our helicopters grounded every Forward Fire Support Base) and forced landing on the spot LZ, and fortunately he stayed with Rangers, remember not volunteer, two Pilots, Brown got killed at once, Monteith serious wounded; Crew-chief Simpco light injury, and door-gun Costello was O.K, and the rest Fujii' crews were picked up by another chopper, except him, because he was smart guy joint-up with Rangers for survive. Now so much biased reports from many prevaricated-newsmen. Medic-Fujii was real good Advisor, he is perfect Ranger Commander, operated some excellent movement troop-maneuvers, knowing how to kill Giap's troops, volunteer stay

The New Legion

for help Rangers ... etc ... *[taking an except of Battle of Ap-Bac in 1963 as ... The large, dark green silhouettes of the 'Angle Worms' as the Viet Cong-guerrillas called the bent-pipe H-21s, and the 'Dippers' their nickname for the Huey, would stand out clearly in the sunshine.*

Sgt 1st Class Arnold Bowers, 29 years old, from a Minnesota dairy farm and the 101 Airborne Division, heard the bullwhip crack of the first bullet burst through the aluminum skin of the helicopter while the machine was still 50 feet in the air, Bower's helicopter was the second in the flight. Vietnam was his first war. During his previous eight and half months in the country he had experienced no combat beyond a few skirmishes with snipers. The whip cracked again and again over the din of the H-21 engines before the wheels of the machine settled into the paddy and Bower jumped out into the knee-high water with a squad of infantry and the ARVN first lieutenant commanding the company. His ears free of the clangor of engines, Bowers could hear a roaring of automatic weapons and rifles from the curtain of green foliage in front. The bullets were snapping all around, buzzing close by his ears and splitting the air overhead. He plunged forward the gray ooze sucking at the boots, in a reflex of his training that said the best hope for survival lay in moving and shooting until you could get on top of your opponent and kill him. The lieutenant that the ARVN infantrymen thought otherwise, they threw themselves down behind the first paddy dike they could reach about 15 yards from where the helicopter had landed.

Sgt Bowers yelled at the lieutenant that they had to return fire and maneuver to get out of the open or they would all die in the paddy. The lieutenant said that he couldn't understand Bowers. Back at the airstrip the lieutenant had understood Bower's English perfectly as they had waited to board the helicopters. The Vietnamese was a graduate of the company-level officers' course at the Infantry School at Fort-Benning. Usually all Vietnamese officers disregarded Americans fighter-men due to lack combat experience (the advisers' job was not to give the combat-experienced-Vietnamese tactical advice because they had more fighting experience than most Americans, and it was their country; rather, the obligation of the advisers was to apply American air and artillery firepower when that became necessary, which was frequently, and to provide American logistics, coordination with American units, and American intelligence. The Vietnamese fighter-men were weakest in these areas. The job of the advisers, in other words, was to make the ARVN system work. So why all Vietnamese officers considered US advisors following combat operation likewise a "Big Drawback" for them and this was according Harriman mastermind all was be for US combat training only)

But in fact Sergeant Fujii was solely an English-interpreter in inter-box relayed. The most these ugly-guy-writers who employ a tried-and-true methodology, firstly, they concoct an inflammatory that serves their political goals. "Are their lies pathological, or are they merely malicious for curious entertainment." They try to push it into the mainstream media. All too often, they succeed. And we have to be more than vigilant … think about that.The 1st Ranger Group participated in the operation with two battalions, the 21st and the 39th, the 37th was in another operation in MR-I. The forward headquarters of the group moved in Ta-Bat, northwest of Khe Sanh, close to the Laos border. The 21st Ranger Battalion was airlifted into the LZ Rangers South, about 6km northeast of Fire Support Base (FSB) Hill-30. Three days later, the 39th Ranger Battalion was brought into the LZ Rangers North, 4km northeast of LZ Rangers South. The two Ranger-Battalions assignment was the sensor to detect the NVA movements and to delay the spearheads of attacks of the enemy toward FSB/Hill-30, Hill-31. If the NVA overran the two FSB', they cut the retreating Route-9 of the ARVN forces.

After landing, the rangers established defensive positions in the areas surrounding of the landing zones (LZ) then Ranger Companies fanned out searching for the enemy's trails and activities in their area of responsibility. The 39th and 21st Ranger Battalions, which operated around Landing Zones "Ranger-North" and "Ranger South" respectively, were probably the units most frequently in contact with the enemy. At 18:25 hours on 11th February, the 21st Ranger Battalion engaged the enemy four kilometers northeast of its base killing 11 Communist troops, but later, at 22:00 hours suffered six wounded from an enemy attack by fire consisting of forty 120-mm mortar rounds. During the afternoon of 13th February, the 39th Battalion engaged a large enemy force at three kilometers west-southwest of Landing Zone "Ranger-North" killing 43 enemy personnel and seizing

The New Legion

two 37-mm antiaircraft artillery guns, two 12.7-mm machineguns, a substantial amount of ammunition and assorted types of equipment. The 39th Battalion had only one killed and 10 wounded. Meanwhile, the 21st Ranger Battalion made sporadic contacts with the enemy throughout the day without significant results. Light contacts continued during the following days. All these activities were quickly eclipsed by reports of heavy enemy troop concentrations around the 39th and 21st Ranger Battalions. Both battalions were being subjected to attacks by fire and ground attacks and the fighting lasted all night while friendly artillery, tactical air and AC-130 flare-ships, EC-130B gun-ships responded quickly in support of the embattled rangers. The next morning, enemy pressure on the 21st Ranger Battalion gradually diminished but heavy pressure persisted on the 39th Battalion in the "Ranger North" area. The battle continued over 19th February. Enemy troops here were confirmed to be elements of the 102nd Regiment of the 308th Division, all with new weapons and clothing testified this training center on spot for battle. Before launching an assault, the rangers reported, the enemy made extensive use of recoilless rifles and mortars; his fire was very accurate. The strongest enemy attacks were directed at the eastern flank of the rangers which was their weakest spot. However, the 39th Ranger Battalion continued to hold its positions with support from 42 pieces of U.S. artillery and tactical air.

From northeast DMZ, enemy opposition grew stronger with each day around Ban Dong and the area of Route 1032B for which the rangers were responsible. On 10th February, the 21st Ranger Battalion engaged an element of the NVA' 88th Regiment. The next day, the 37th Ranger Battalion engaged a battalion size unit near FSB Phu Loc. The discovery of the command post of the NVA 308th Division on 18th February further confirmed reports that this division had joined in the fighting (the 308th Division had three regiments: 36th, 88th and 102nd) During the night of 19th February, the NVA forces continued to attack the 39th Ranger Battalion while launching uninterrupted attacks by fire to hold the 21st Ranger Battalion in check. Sergeant Medic Fujii did damn good job in communication between ground and air like Forward Air Controller officer for a longest night with Seven fixed wing EC-130B gun-ships and six AC-130 flare-ships were used in support of the 39th Ranger Battalion and, from 07:30 to 14:30 hours on 20th February, 32 tactical air sorties were flown in support of the rangers in daytime. Efforts to re-supply and evacuate their casualties were made with strong support from tactical air, gun-ships and artillery. Some helicopters managed to land in the area, ammunition was delivered and some wounded evacuated. But upon takeoff, two helicopters were damaged by enemy undirected fire. One had to land in the positions of the 21st Ranger Battalion (Ranger South) and the other managed to land at Fire Support Base Hill-30.

In the afternoon, reconnaissance aircraft reported sighting an estimated 400 to 500 enemy with most of the wounded of the 39th Ranger Battalion still stranded in the 21st Rangers' positions, this unit received intense attacks by fire, including 130, 152-mm artillery, on the night of 21st February. Plans were made to evacuate the wounded rangers the following day toward noon on 22nd February, the area around the battalion position was subjected to a heavy barrage of fire involving tactical air, air cavalry, aerial artillery and ground artillery for 45 minutes while 13 medical evacuation helicopters were airborne, ready to go in. All of them landed and successfully picked up 122 wounded as well as one U.S. pilot who had been stranded there since his aircraft was shot down. The ranger force remaining in combat position at Ranger South numbered approximately 400 men including 100 from the 39th Battalion but two days later, on 24th February the battalion was ordered by the I Corps commander to withdraw to FSB 30. From there they were airlifted to FSB Phu Loc. While the 39th Ranger Battalion was holding out, numerous activities took place in other areas. U.S. air cavalry continued to search for and destroy pipelines. Units of the 1st Infantry Division moved further south, striking along Route-92 and finding a number of enemy installations, but also making numerous contacts and receiving attacks by fired The 8th Airborne Battalion and armored elements engaged the enemy two kilometers north of Ban Dong, destroying one T-34 tank and a 23-mm gun position. This was another strong indication of enemy armor involvement. On the friendly side, a number of U.S. helicopters were shot down while on supply, medical evacuation or support missions. The corps commander had concluded that the position held by the 21st Rangers and the survivors of the 39th was untenable. A maximum effort in air and artillery support was required for each re-supply and evacuation mission and he had other pressing demands for this support. The position was not an objective in itself and there was no military advantage in sacrificing a ranger battalion in a doomed attempt to hold it. The corps commander was looking toward his objectives in the west and he wished to conserve as much of his combat power as possible for the main mission.

Beginning the 14th February, leading platoons of the 39th started exchanging gun-fires with the enemy forces, forward artillery observer called for supports. In the operation, the rangers were supported directly from a company of the 64th Artillery Battalion from Phu Loc. Until 3:00 to 4:00pm all companies engaged in fighting with the surrounding NVA units/70B. The 64th Artillery Company with six 105mm guns could not keep up with the intensity of the battle. In desperate, the forward observer broke in the working frequency of the C/44th Artillery Company on FSB/Hill-30 and requested for support. With the effects of artillery supports, the NVA had to pull back, the rangers also fell back to defense the Battalion Command Post.

On the following days, the 39th Ranger Battalion sent its companies out on patrol in the area responsibilities – they killed 43 enemies and captured two 37mm AAA guns. The AAA guns indicated that the NVA had a large size of unit in the surrounding areas of the Ranger North. In the south, the paratroopers of 2nd Airborne Brigade, and Infantry discovered storages of foods, fuels, weapons... and dead NVA troops killed by EC-130B gun-ships strafing earlier in friendly protection. Yes we must accepted Medic Fujii was useful for contacting with Flare-ship AC-130 and Gun-ship EC-130B for air-cover, strafing during long night with 6 flare-ships and 7 gun-ships with strike accuracy to protect our forces in retreated to 21st Ranger Battalion. Finally, Medic Fujii was picked up by his Air Cavalry Huey but got hit, crashed again and forced landing near Hill-30 in LZ Ranger South responsibility.

Until the 18th, the NVA Corps 70B moved its divisions 308th, 304th, 320th, 324B together with 202 Tank Regiment, artillery regiment to counter-attack. Meanwhile 2nd Division was setting for ambush our troop at 604 Cargo Base. On this day, they concentrated to up-root the 39th Ranger Battalion with human wave tactic. The rangers fought gallantly and with artillery supports from Phu Loc and FSB/Hill-30, the communists attacks was repulsed, left hundreds of bodies in the battlefield, the rangers more than 500 weapons of all kinds. The next morning, the NVA troops returned to continue the attack. The battle soon turned into the killing ground. The ARVN' Artillery from the 64th Battalion and the C/44th Company fired continuously supporting the rangers. The 39th Ranger Battalion hang on for another day, when the NVA pulled back for realignment spearhead for the attack, the slightly wounded rangers were bandaged quickly then returning to the trenches. The rangers probably knew their destiny, they prepared for the last fight... 20th/February, early in the morning, the NVA was mounted a new attack with more intensity. The battle lasted into afternoon and the rangers reaction weaken... then the 64th and the C/44th artillery companies did not hear any calls for helps from the forward observer of the 39th Ranger Battalion. The NVA already swamped into the rangers positions. Aerial photos showed at least 600 NVA bodies left in the battlefield. The survivors of the 39th ran back to the defensive line of the 21st Ranger Battalion and continued to fight side by side with brothers in arms of the 21st until this battalion was also evacuated.

During the night of 19th February, the enemy continued to attack the 39th Battalion while launching uninterrupted attacks by fire to hold the 21st Battalion in check. Seven fixed wing gun-ships EC-130B and six flare-ships AC-130 were used in support of the 39th Battalion and, from 07:30 to 14:30 hours on 20th February, 32 tactical air sorties were flown in support of the rangers. Efforts to re-supply and evacuate their casualties were made with strong support from tactical air, gun-ships and artillery. Some helicopters managed to land in the area, ammunition was delivered and some wounded evacuated. But upon takeoff, two helicopters were damaged by enemy fired One had to land in the positions of the 21st Ranger Battalion "Ranger South" and the other managed to land at Fire Support Base Hill-30, this Huey piloted by Lloyd and Nelson tried picked up Medic Fujii, just got hit and had to forced landing near FBS/Hill-30, about 4 kilometer from LZ South. In the afternoon, reconnaissance aircraft reported sighting an estimated 400 to 500 enemy with most of the wounded of the 39th Ranger Battalion still stranded in the 21st Rangers' positions, this unit received intense attacks by fire, including 130-mm, 152mm artillery, on the night of 21st February. Plans were made to evacuate the wounded rangers the following day toward noon on 22nd February, the area around the battalion position was subjected to a heavy barrage of fire involving tactical air, air cavalry, aerial artillery and ground artillery for nearly an hour while 13 medical evacuation helicopters were airborne, ready to go in. All of them landed and successfully picked up 122 wounded as well as one U.S. pilot who had been stranded there since his aircraft was shot down. The Ranger force remaining in combat position at Ranger South numbered approximately 400 men including 100 from the 39th Battalion but two days later, on 24th February, the battalion was ordered by the I Corps commander to withdraw to FSB/Hill-30. From there they were airlifted to FSB Phu Loc. While the 39th Ranger Battalion was holding out, numerous activities took place in other areas. U.S. air cavalry continued to search for and destroy pipelines. Units of the 1st Infantry Division moved further south, striking along Route-92 and finding a number of enemy installations, but also making numerous contacts and receiving attacks by fired The 8th Airborne Battalion and armored elements engaged the enemy two kilometers north of Ban Dong, destroying one T-34 tank and a 23-mm gun position. This was another strong indication of enemy armor involvement. On the friendly side, a number of U.S. helicopters were shot down while on supply, medical evacuation or support missions. The corps commander had concluded that the position held by the 21st Ranger Battalion and the survivors of the 39th was untenable. A maximum effort in air and artillery support was required for each re-supply and evacuation mission and he had other pressing demands for this support. The position was not an objective in itself and there was no military advantage in sacrificing a ranger battalion in a doomed attempt to hold it. The corps commander was looking toward his objectives in the west and he wished to conserve as much of his combat power as possible for the main mission.

News of the 39th Ranger Battalion fought until the last bullets then dispersed instead of surrendering spread out rapidly. My air-cover over FSB/Hill-30 in operational area witnessing: "We could not re-supply for them for three days. When ammunitions were about to run out, they got out of their positions, counter-attacked then continued to fight with captured weapons."

After overran the 39th, the NVA' Forces moved south and surrounded the 21st Ranger Battalion's positions. In the night of the 20th February, AC-130 dropped flares lighted up the sky above the 21st Ranger Battalion location in the area of LZ Ranger South. It was the last outer shell which shielded the FSB/Hill-30 from the NVA advances from the northwest. The NVA began their attacks on the ranger's positions since the 21st the rangers fought back and held their positions. The battle between the 21st and the survivors of the 39th with the NVA units lasted for four days and nights. When the NVA pulled back after many waves of attacks they pounded on the ranger's positions with 122mm, 130mm, 152mm and mortar 120mm shells to weaken the ranger physicals and morals.

Fortunately, on 22nd March when morning fog was just disappeared, 13 UH1-Hs were covered by U.S/42 pieces Long Tom 175, 8 inch Howitzer, and 155mm from border. Suddenly the formation landed on LZ Ranger South under fierce strafing air-covered by gunship Cobra. His buddy Air Cavalry abruptly showed up and picked up Medic Fujii and another flight personal in his flight-unit, both was to fly back safety from FSB/Hill-30 to Khe Sanh, included 122 wounded, where 400 rangers include 100 rangers from 39th [Major Khang 39th said Fujii was real good but Major Hiep 21st Battalion Commander expressed Medic Fujii to much scared when reached LZ South, so contacted with American EC-130B gunship for air-cover in turn by Lieutenant Nguyen Son during two last days 21th and 22th February]

In preserving the Ranger Battalion, in the early morning of the 25th, the 21st Ranger Battalion Commander, Major Khang ordered his men cut fall trees in making a surprised landing zone, due to all LZs were preset-targeted by precision-accuracy of 120mm mortars and 152 delayed-guns preset coordinates XD 593537 and XD 550490 [120mm mortars that burst in an extremely large fragmentation

The New Legion

pattern that inflicted our choppers force-grounded at all FSB, can't take off again due to tail rotor failure and particularly 152mm guns, the duds from these penetrated 4 feet into the earth which damaged almost friendly artillery, and maliciously, NVA hide the real guns, mortars and rocket-launchers in deep pits and in tunnels with cleverly in camouflage]

At Ham-Nghi, Corps Command was ordered to evacuate according to plan "Zulu-01" Again the 64th and C/44th Artilleries were directed to maximize fire-support for the rangers. About 10:00 am in the morning, four Cobra gun-ships circled above the ranger's positions then a squadron of helicopters landed quickly in the LZ Rangers South to scoop up the rangers and brought them to FSB/Hill-30 where VNAF gun-ships responsibility for air-ground closed support to 2nd Airborne Brigade. Later another squadron arrived nearby FSB/Hill-30 picked up the rangers and transported them back to Phu Loc, accomplishing the commitment of the 1st Rangers Group in operation Lam-Son 719. However, one company of the 21st Rangers Battalion was left behind on FSB/Hill-30 – they fought together with the Airborne-men in the FSB/Hill-30 until this FSB was also forced to retreat.

All troop movements were accomplished without meeting any resistance. Aerial reconnaissance and intelligence activities noticed enemy movements north of the operation area. Aircraft sorties started bombarding suspected targets. Some days later, the two Ranger positions received continuous shelling from long range 130mm artillery shelling. The vanguard units of the NVA had approached the defense lines of the 39th Rangers Battalion and skirmishes broke out. The Ranger Artillery stationed at the Laotian border Phu Loc provided supporting fire day and night. Days later, under enemy artillery barrage, the NVA regulars assaulted the 39th Ranger Battalion. The 21st Ranger Battalion positioned in the south was also harassed, making it impossible to receive reinforcements.

The NVA' troop thrust was assisted by 202 Tank Regiment. The fighting became fiercer and fiercer, and both side suffered heavy casualties. The 39th Ranger Battalion bravely battled on, despite being low on ammunition. They resisted for one day and one night, before the position was lost. The unit had to retreat toward the 21st Ranger

Battalion's position in the south. Having successfully occupied the hill, the NVA moved west and south-west to threaten the 21st Ranger Battalion and the 3rd Airborne Brigade. The 3rd Airborne Brigade was well-supported by tactical airpower and 213th VNAF/Gunship-Flight. Despite heavy losses, the NVA continued to storm FBS/Hill-31 in the face of long and short range heavy artillery. Although forewarned of enemy intentions, the 3rd Airborne Brigade failed to establish an effective defense with only 300 fighter-men, and shared the same fate of the 39th Ranger Battalion. It had fought with courage and bravado, but succumbed to the massive suicidal onslaught of the NVA. The Brigade Staff, including Colonel Tho was captured. Some evaded and ran southwards toward FSB/Hill-30 which was occupied by the brave 2nd Airborne Battalion. Even as they assaulted the 3rd Airborne Brigade Headquarters, the NVA pounded away at FSB/Hill-30 and A-Luoi Base where the 1st Airborne Brigade and the 1st Armor Brigade were positioned. These two units were unable to give assistance to the 3rd Airborne Brigade at FSB/Hill-31, although help was sought of them.

The crucial goal of WIB Bones' objective was the ARVN attack on wrong time and wrong place, but so late, **"because all the huge cargo-ammunitions were already moved to the southern corridor"** (prisoners in fact disclosed that most supplies caches had been evacuated to numerous 'Binh-Trams' south Laos by Molotowa-Trucks at Parking-1 that the ARVN appeared not to be surprised at all) So despite the intense air campaign to stop the North Vietnamese logistical flow along the Harriman Highway [Ho Chi Minh Trail] the Communists continued to reinforce their troops in South Vietnam, threatening to disrupt the Vietnamization program in processing, and the gradual withdrawal of the US forces. The WIB Bones and Pentagon in Washington then decided in February 1971 to launch a ground offensive to destroy the enemy logistical depots and to prevent a so called new offensive into South Vietnam. The plan became known as Lam Son 719. Whether, I think they had two options: if the North Vietnamese would fall back under the attack like they did under similar circumstances in Cambodia the ARVN would move along the Harriman Highway and destroy all the bases underway. If the North Vietnamese would put up resistance, the

ARVN was to cause as much damage and inflict as many casualties as possible and then do a fighting withdrawal back into South Vietnam. Whatever the true motives behind this operation it involved only just three ARVN divisions that enough. As soon as 1967, the US responsibilities had already planned a ground offensive against Laos and had estimated that if it must succeed, it was badly needed to deploy between five and seven US-ARVN divisions. Now, Hanoi had deployed in southern Laos a full army 70B Corps with tanks, ready to repel any ARVN foray, according to Paris Peace Talk agreement, Hanoi was staying in South Vietnam 200,000 troops there. Saigon was to deploy a smaller force. But what anything WIB Bones wished in expectation to carried out **axiom-1.**

Lam Son 719 was the largest air mobile operation of the war - but also one doomed to failure right from the start because the WIB Bones had planned, just for the Axis of Evil dumping all rubbish out of date military materiel in a remote spot like Tchepone, south Laos. That's their crucial goal, in the end, Lam Son 719 lasted for 45 days, and the airpower (I means at Pentagon, as Colonel James Vaught's suggestion, General Alexander Haig changed from Rolling Thunder to Linebacker air campaign that saved ARVN was under siege due to this Axis of Evil craps) was the only thing that saved the ARVN from a complete defeat in Laos. The North Vietnamese nevertheless did not get off unpunished: their losses were indeed heavy to a degree where their planned invasion of South Vietnam had to be postponed for a full year.

On 19th February, eleven days into the attack, MACV J-2 was carrying just six enemy regiments committed against ARVN forces in the Lam Son 719 area of operations. Clearly that wasn't going to last much longer. J-2 concluded that these could be reinforced immediately by three additional regiments from the south and within two days by three more regiments from the west and north. Actually the real significance of this Lam Son operation is the enemy has everything committed or en route, that he has, with the exception of the 325th Division and the 9th separated-Regiment out of the 304th. So if they're hurt, he's really going to be beat for long time. And to us: "Of course we're trying to welcome them all, best we can" Meanwhile a new-rallied confirmed earlier intelligence by revealing the identity and location of a new headquarters – designated the 70B Front – controlling the NVA divisions in the Lam Son area of operations, the 304th, 308th, and 320th. This fresh 70B Front was established right after a founder Skull and Bones, A Harriman retired from public life with the election of President Richard Nixon in 1969 and gave ceded his throne dynasty to a son of his deputy Prescott Bush [George I] to succeeding his resumption of stratagem "Eurasian Great Game". But George H.W Bush was as merely a 'surrogate for A Harriman' disguised and stuck away in China due he knew so well the Vietnam-War outcome.

Suddenly Hanoi played the game, in the transaction period, and A Harriman **challenged George H W Bush to asset his leadership:** The U.S/POW was publicly humiliated in propaganda campaign by put them in the oxen-cart go around Hanoi's Hoang-Kiem Lake for Hanoi-residents seeing. The evidence suggests that by the autumn of 1970 Communist forces had begun preparations for a spring offensive in Military Region 1, the northern provinces of South Vietnam once the dry season arrived. One indication was formation of a new corps-level headquarters, known as the 70B Front, sometime in October, 1970. Also at that time, General Abrams was told "a highly placed Viet Cong penetration agent reported on enemy plans to launch an offensive with up to four divisions to take and hold major portions of Quang Tri and Hue cities. Significantly, formation of the enemy's new headquarters occurred well before any specific allied planning for a thrust into Laos had begun a situation that discounted the possibility that the new organization was intended primarily to conduct a defense against allied operations. However the Strategic Air Command don't have the orders to destroy four crucial targets, each a rectangle measuring one by two kilometers and sited at one of the prime input areas used by the enemy – the Mu Gia Pass, the Ban Karai Pass, the Ban Raving Pass, and an area just west of the DMZ, Tchepone vicinity [where we'll started Lam Son 719's operation] Everything was safe and protected due to the goal protracted-war to the Axis of Evil craps via under umbrella Rules Of Engagement (ROE)

For concentrated all U.S POW to one place, reacted by another way. By 1970, the US had secured the names of over 500 Americans held in North Vietnam prisons. Many more were missing and presumed captured. Reports of the cruelty suffered by these men at the hands of their barbarous captors were received along with reports of resultant deaths from various sources. Anxiety, concern and anger among the next of kin, friends of the captives, commanders and government officials were very much in evidence throughout this country. What was being done to alleviate the growing concern? Negotiations were being conducted in Paris Talk on a sporadic basis depending on the mood of the North Vietnamese representatives. An attempt was made to reach an agreement whereby an exchange of prisoners of war could be made. After over two years of such negotiations, the results were ZERO

"The mood of the country demanded that something be done to help these suffering POWs. Was the time ripe for an initiative… feasible alternative?

Suddenly American forces launched a surprising raid on a prisoner of war camp in North Vietnam, an operation planned and controlled in Washington by Harriman successor, **George H W Bush'** strategist staffs. It was known that the Son Tay Camp had held American prisoners. By the time the raid was launched in 20-21, November 1970, however, those people had been moved elsewhere, apparently as a result of a maybe flooding that made Son Tay untenable. Later it was revealed that last-minute intelligence had revealed that fact, but the decision was made to let the raid go anyway. The operation was successful in its own terms, although of course no prisoners were rescued because none were there. Clearly another objective was to let the Hanoi know their rear area – the camp was only 40 kilometers from Hanoi – was not as secure as they might have thought. Much later it was learned that the raid benefited the American still held captive, since the Hanoi subsequently consolidated them in better facilities and their treatment improved significantly. Although no prisoners were rescued, the raid focused world attention on the plight of the prisoners of war (POWs) raised their morale and resulted in improved living conditions for all U.S prisoners of the North Vietnamese. Beside, the men of the Joint Task Force earned the admiration of their countrymen for risking their lives in an attempt to bring freedom to others.

This is the goal of Son Tay' Operation and **Hanoi Hilton** appearing where the POWs sacrificed a good part of their young adulthood for their country, in pain, fear, and isolation but ironically for their greediest warlords of WIB Bones

On 20 February, 1971, MACV analysts counted eighteen battalion-size ARVN task forces in south Laos mostly involved in search destroyed and cleared operations, with the westernmost elements still about where they had been a week earlier, roughly halfway to Tchepone. The NVA Corps 70B moved its divisions 320th, 324B, 304th, 308th together with 202nd tanks regiment, artillery regiment to counterattack. On this day, they concentrated to up root the 39th Ranger Battalion with human wave tactic. The Rangers fought gallantly and with artillery support from Phu Loc and FSB 30, the NVA attacks was repulsed, left hundreds of bodies in the battlefield the rangers more than 500 weapons of all kinds. Enemy forces were massing to attack, thereby becoming rich targets for reprisals by allied air attacks. When NVA assaults drove ARVN' 39th Ranger Battalion off their position, thank to tactical air fell upon the massed enemy forces, killing more than 600 in the one battle. At one point, seven fixed-wing gun-ships (EC-130B) and six flare-ships (AC-130) were supporting the Rangers – All this crap about we can take whatever action's required to protect our own forces, protective reaction. And if the ROE principle doesn't apply here, we'll be damned. Daytime the TAC air had a field day with enemy tank, too, destroying the most tanks and one NVA regiment/70B Corps, practically wipe out an armored regiment. Having great powers of recuperation, the NVA mounted a new attack with more intensity. The battle last into afternoon and the ranger reaction weaken … then the 64th and the C/44th Artillery Company did not hear any calls for help from the forward observer of the 39th Ranger Battalion. The NVA already swamped into the ranger position. The survivors of the 39th ran back to the defense line of the 21st Ranger Battalion and continued to fight side by side with brothers in arms of the 21st until this battalion was also evacuated.

News of the 39th Ranger Battalion fought until the last bullets then dispersed instead of surrendering spread out rapidly. Our helicopters could not re-supply for them for 3 days. When ammunitions were about to run out, they got out of their positions, counter attacked then continued to fight with captured weapons. After overran the 39th, the NVA forces moved south and surrounded the 21st ranger position. At night, flares lighted up the sky above the 21st ranger location in the area of LZ "Ranger South." The battle between the 39th Ranger Battalion and the survivors of the 21st Ranger Battalion with the NVA regiments lasted for 4 days and nights. When the NVA pulled back after waves of attacks they pounded on the ranger position with 122mm and 130mm shells to weaken the ranger morals and physicals.

In preserving the ranger battalion, in daytime of the 25th February, the 21st Ranger was ordered to evacuate. According to plan "tactical-retreat", 42 U.S artilleries at border, 64th and C/44th artilleries were directed to maximize fire-support for ranger. TOT at 10:00 am, four Cobra gun-ship circled above the ranger positions for air-cover then a formation helicopters of 20 HU-1 landed quickly in the LZ Ranger South to scoop up the rangers and brought them to FSB 30. Later another formation helicopters arrived at FSB 30 pickup the rangers and transported them back to Phu Loc. However, one company of the 21st Ranger Battalion was left behind on FSB 30, and they fought together with airborne men in the FSB 30 until this FSB was also force to retreat.

On 23 February 1971 was the longest day not because my gunship was shot down by the enemy P.T-76 but of heavy enemy contact by the Rangers and the Airborne forces on the most northern flank of penetration, and the most U.S Army aviation support for Lam Son 719 having big problem to cause Vice President Huong cried out on TV "Earnestly, U.S stop flying supplied for our troops in the state thirsty water and ammunition for small arms"

On same day 23 February, further south, nearest Cambodia/Vietnam border, a VNAF helicopter UHI-H carrying M.R-III Corps commander Lieutenant General Do Cao Tri – then 1970 directing the operation of some 17,000 ARVN troops in Cambodia – crashed and burned, killing him and his staff-officers; General Tri performed so well in Cambodia that U.S Permanent Government would hate like hell to think that Tri destroyed all NVA supplies cargo for protracted war and violated ROE' craps. Said General Bill Rosson, "*was a damn fine field commander. His idea was to get up where the action was*" His flamboyance and bravery led one newsman to the extreme of calling Tri "the Patton of the Parrot's Beak" General Tri was considered a fine field commander, scarce enough in the upper reaches of ARVN leadership, which made this a very serious loss. It turned out to be even more of one when it was learned that he had been slated to move almost immediately to I Corps to replace General Lam, who was proving inadequate to his heavy new responsibilities in command of Lam Son 719. General Tri was killed because he was just a great soldier, destroyer all COSVN' cargo, a great spearhead against to CIP's drawback.

A pretentious Permanent Government to being on the subject:

In the aftermath of Sihanouk's ouster there had been a good bit of dithering in the White House about whether to mount such an operation and, if one were launched, what its dimensions ought to be, especially whether United States combat troops should cross the border. MACV was asked for ideas and submitted them. Chief of Staff, General Wheeler cabled fed-back that "Higher Authority" – He meant "High Authority," the transparent euphemism for the President Nixon or the second generation of Skull and Bones, emperor-II [George H W Bush] – "has noted that each option involves considerable US participation." General Wheeler then called for a detailed alternate plan for attacks into the Cambodia sanctuaries conducted entirely by South Vietnamese forces. Wheeler cable, dispatched at 2:49 PM, Washington time, closed by saying that "a preliminary outline plan submitted here tomorrow would be invaluable" After further consideration in Washington it was decided that U.S forces would participate, but only after the South Vietnamese had led off by themselves on the first day of the operation.

In Washington, some fairly novel command arrangements surfaced. A presidential blue ribbon commission later reported that "as was widely noted by the press at the time… Defense Secretary Laird [*a Bone-Man, you'd discovered at picture "discussing plans for Lam Son 719 above and seeing all Skull and Bones men encircled president and Rogers*] had been bypassed by the Joint Chiefs in advising the White House on preparations to intervene in Cambodia in April and May

1970?" Clearly that had been done on orders from the Permanent Government in Washington. There were other problems, including conflicting guidance from Washington that led Abrams to state some ground rules. "I should add," he said in a message to Wheeler and McCain, "that in these delicate times I respond only to the direction of the Chairman, CINCPAC, and the Ambassador. My staff will not respond to direction from staffs in Washington or Hawaii,"

There were then 14 enemy sanctuaries along the borders of South Vietnam/Cambodia, 10 of them contiguous to IV and III Corps Tactical Zones in the South. The raid was going after those facilities, informed by the belief that "no guerrilla war has ever been able to reach a 'victorious' end without sanctuary" – This against Harriman's standpoint, the **axiom-1**: "There was never a legitimate non-communist government in Saigon that was explained at all universities in 1960. Allied columns – ARVN forces on 29 April and then a combined U.S/ARVN force on 1 May – pushed into the Parrot's Beak and Fishhook areas of Cambodia, thus targeting two of the enemy's most important border sanctuaries. Within a few days numerous other base areas were entered, ten distinct operations in all by both U.S and South Vietnamese forces.

Even given the restrictions imposed, the operation was for the South Vietnamese a very significant undertaking. At its peak 50,000 men were committed, the first time in history that such numbers of their troops had operated as a single force. It was a challenging new departure, radically different from the role of pacification support to which most ARVN forces had until recently been relegated. At MACV, President Nixon's speech announcement the incursion to the nation was played on tape at a 1 May update for Abrams, who must have cringed when he heard the President say that "tonight, American and South Vietnamese units will attack the headquarters for the entire Communist military operation in South Vietnam." Everyone at MACV knew that COSVN was a shadowy, mobile, and widely dispersed complex that would be very difficult to locate and even more difficult to put out of action. In fact, queried before the fact about prospects for capturing it, MACV had replied that "major COSVN elements are dispersed over approximately 110 square kilometers of jungle" and "the feasibility of capturing major elements appears remote at this time." Nixon's characterization of the incursion's purposes shifted attention from the far more important goals of disrupting the enemy's lines of communication and cleaning out his base areas, achievements that could set back his timetable for further aggression to the advantage of both RVNAF improvement and U.S withdrawals.

To a surprising degree the incursion was unopposed. "When facing enemy forces," read a typewritten directive issued by the B-3 Front Headquarters on 17 March 1970 and captured a week into the incursion, Communist forces in Cambodia "should attempt to break away and avoid shooting back. Our purposes are to conserve forces as much as we can" General Brown exulted that the enemy had "a hell of a problem." Abrams agreed, but only to a point. "Well, that's right, George" he responded. "But you see, he's used to a hell of a problem. He lives in an environment where he's got a hell of a problem. I get a certain amount of enjoyment, I must say, out of seeing the problem get complicated. But it isn't worth much. He's a pretty determined chap, when you get tight down to it. As a soldier, "What we need right now is another division or more – going in deep" in the wake of the initial penetrations. "We need to go west from where we are, we need to go north and east from where we are. And we need to do it now. It's moving. And goddamn, goddamn." This last was said wistfully, with great sorrow and regret.

Unsurprisingly, at Pentagon the delegated author of command and control of ROE was General Haig having secret order from emperor-II to investigate the so called Power Act violation. But those at MACV had their own concerns about ambiguity, voicing an implied indecisiveness, ineffectiveness, pretentiousness. MACV have two of Haig messages. One of them says "go get them" and the other one says "hurry up and get out". "Ah what the hell Haig really wanted?" Haig responded "It'd go get them until the end of the period." "Well, it's still ambiguous" (supposedly, the Permanent Government's take on charge the whole war by stratagem 'Everything worked, but nothing worked enough')

The scandal broke: became known to the public in March of 1970, Cambodian Marshal Lon Nol led a pro-Western coup, supposedly engineered by CIA operatives and military advisors, and ousted Cambodia's recognized leader, Sihanouk who then fled to Paris, French and openly accused the United States of his ouster. The coup created the Khmer Republic, led by Lon Nol. In less than a month, South Vietnamese and U.S forces launched a clearing operation into the Parrot's Beak and some areas of Cambodia that served as sanctuaries for Hanoi troop and Viet Cong forces; This operation also helped to bolster Lon Nol' government against the Khmer Communists, who became known as the Khmer-Rouge.

Antiwar movement activist, Lieutenant John F Kerry urged that Media press reports of the United States, led aerial bombing and ground combat operation in Cambodia territories, addressed the issue in a nationally televised speech. President Nixon directly stated that the United States had no advisors on the ground in Cambodia, and had no American military forces involved in any actions in Cambodia, and had no American military air assets supporting any action in Cambodia. This is an insane desire of Permanent Government in which the so called her named "Cambodia is the Nixon Doctrine in its purest form" violated Power Act in U.S constitution.

What was the cause of "Cooper-Church" and "Case-Church" amendments? For WIB Bones' original purpose, Senator Frank F Church and other members of Congress were so angered by President Nixon openly lying about U.S military involvement in Cambodia that they immediately took action to begin cutting funding for the war, as a shirttail amendment to the defense authorization bill, a watered down version of the measure finally passed. That version of the amendment only barred the introduction of American ground forces in Southeast Asia. The first volley in Congress came **1970** when Senator **Church** and Kentucky Republican Senator John Sherman **Cooper** authorized a bill that cut off funding of all military activity in Southeast Asia.

Long ago, under the watch of President Richard Nixon, American political interests had already written off South Vietnam. The Paris Peace Accords stood testimony to that fact, virtually selling the highly United States-dependent nation down the proverbial river. The Case-Church

Amendment of 1973, specially banning all bombing in Cambodia and further banning all American military intervention by land, sea, or air anywhere in Southeast Asia, underscored that write-off. The WIB' Bones had simply engineered a so-called Decent-Interval to distance America from its South Vietnam commitment. Given an adequate passage of time, the world would not hold America accountable. Unfortunately, the WIB' Decent-Interval had not nearly run its course.

Some troop elements had done conspicuously better than others. The ARVN armored units had been especially early in the operation the 1st Squadron, 11th Armored Cavalry had encountered NVA elements in a fight at southern Fire Base 31 and performed brilliantly, destroying six enemy T-54 tanks and sixteen PT-76s without any friendly losses in the first major tank-to-tank engagement of the war, but of course with our gunship air cover supported joint-strafing with the both flank-side equipped two a 19-shot 2.75-inch antitank rocket pods. Today bychance we got the record shooting into the POL pipe-line at random burned all of them for a while right after NVA shut-off the pipes. The fact that I would like to train in released a new gunship pilot check-ride for operational purpose. He was so nervous pushed the button microphone instead of fired arm. This miracle button hit the rockets on the targets [pipe-lines] let our ground troops more confident to our gunship air supported.

But unfortunately in the evening that same day, when I flied back to home base for refuel, I crossed low on the convoy that I thought those were our friendly M-113 but when I discovered their noses curb-higher like a canoe, NVA PT-76 that was too late, my gunship got many hits by 14.5 mm from gun turret with an automatic weapon and crashed half mile far away and my wingman pick all my crews up immediately. My commander at Danang Air Base would like Major Ky my squadron deputy to replace me so I could having time for R and R, but I cabled to him, "I need stay here for save our peoples!" I don't want any our aircrews get killed again.

We are underground of the huge bunker for the morning briefing after I got have not too bad breakfast at the field Chow-Tent. As usual General Lam and Sutherland in the front seats, second one for Division commanders, I always saw only brigadier general Phu,

The New Legion

Colonel Ray Battreall, a very experienced officer who watched most of this firsthand from I Corps Forward at Khe Sanh, Colonel Sam Cockerham was acting commander of the 1st Aviation Brigade. And the third row for regiment commander that was my row-seat.

I have had a sorrow meeting looked I never got before. The badnews that the number of helicopters in commission so low 25% cast a deep gloom over the whole briefing room. A couple of weeks into the thing there wasn't a lot of flying going on, including CH-54, Skycrane sling to every Fire Support Base the bulldozers D-4, Howitzer 155s, water containers, either, at least not compared with the huge requirements the operation was generating. By about 23 February it became apparent that U.S Army aviation support for Lam Son 719 was having some problems. Not only was the intense and well-sited enemy antiaircraft weaponry making operations extremely difficult – every mission, even [dust-off] medical evacuations, had to be planned and executed like a full-scale combat assault – but maintenance problems were causing many helicopters to be out of service just when they were needed most. How can I do for covered support our troop, my helicopter forces was just enough for supplied or medical evacuation missions in case emergency only, we couldn't hook artillery, water trailer container, but small arms ammunition, meanwhile NVA have had 67,000 tons of various shell ammunition was already on the operation spot-area. Thereby hangs a tale that our VNAF helicopters were shot down by indirect artillery every Fire Support Base, such as Hill 31: 2 H.34s, 1 UH1-H; Hong Ha: 2 UH1-Hs; Hill-30: 2 UH1-Hs; A-loui: 3 UH1-Hs – by direct guns: 1 gunship and 3 UH1-Hs in operational area. There was happened just a couple of weeks earlier into this operation.

I must have leaving the briefing room to go fly right away because air-support to Airborne was VNAF gunship responsibility, in having heavy contacts so tough with enemy at southern Fire Support Base 30, in emergency alert for air cover protection. The pea soup fog just beginning disappeared somehow so slow due to day and night the smoke of bombs, forest burned still clinging haunted around increased so much humidity hazy not so easy cleared the environment. Here there was always hearing pounding explosion from the enemy artillery melee with 42 U.S artilleries in Lao Bao.

Colonel Sam Cockerham told me let try the new 2.75-inch rocket with 5,000 arrow nails that help prevent the enemy throng in attack to friend forces.

Meanwhile we are facing the possible disappearance of most of ground-fog forests. I gather all aircraft commanders to a short briefing about armament. We change the properly tactical prep, because prejudice of destroy enemy tank I carried 38 rockets and 6,000 rounds 7, 62. This maximum load armament created so much problem when strafing approach to the target sometimes the wingman could passed over the leader; so now I made decision "loading full ammunition 12,000 round 7, 62 and 14 rockets such as: 6 nail arrow-rockets, 4 high explosive 17 pounds, and 4 antitank rockets. However the wingman equipped only antitank rockets. Reminding spared some ammunition for air cover to our choppers, escorted them to security area. The most in the west flank was the free-risk-area, NVA stationed on west shield-flank for avoiding U.S artillery pounding. All shells were only reached-impact on east flank. However cast your eyes on the parallel PT-76 armored tank red-earth tracks, a terrible mobile antiaircraft not to hard detecting them. When get them, the lead try surrounding used both-mini-guns for neutralized-strafing the gunner killers and the wingman used antitank rocket grilled them.

The weather is much better, now I take off first and Captain Tien' formation for rejoining us at second ride and right on the operational-spot. The thin stratus was still clinging on the crest mountain. Every time rushing to operation zone in various trajectory flight-path but not different altitude just treetop usual flight, the NVA troop was never get a chance for shooting at us down when we were airborne but we get so much trouble when landing on the helipad and get hit by more than a thousand incoming rounds more than from such indirect fire weapons as mortars and artillery of different kind of artillery that NVA having so abundance right in their dump-cargo. So why every friend Fire Support Bases you could see VNAF' helicopters subjected to ground-remained there – meanwhile US Army Aviation inflicted so much casualty, because they flied too many formations and the must need smoothly in control maneuvers and altitude [SOG' information, American be killed 219 and MIA

The New Legion

38, respectively were aircrews] Scattering in front of me in this zone, I witnessed few helicopters were shooting down. Just last two week ago when I flown with Airborne division commander, General Dong onboard to Hill 31, the mountain scenery was quite natural, now this scenery causing my feeling of fear and eerie strange "the longest and bloodiest siege of the war will happened" that I was justified in my conviction that Vietnam-War was "an intelligence war" specialized by Bushes background heritage.

I didn't believe that why I Corps staffs operation planner chosen the Hill-30 and 31 like in a wide bowl surrounded by jungle-high ground as same as a siege of Dien Bien Phu containing antiaircraft guns and bunkered NVA infantry. NVA knew the terrain intimately, not because General Giap was cooperated, informed by CIA' counterespionage recently but because they had been living in this area secretly for quite a while during the last phase of bunker construction. All U.S artillery fire power was target on impact the most only East flank let them feel in security on other flanks like West side. Batteries of 175mm guns to install in the Khe Sanh, the "Long Tom" could throw a 147-pound shell 28 kilometers, covering beyond almost the operation area in Laos, but NVA hidden operational flank-west scurrying about. Those "strongpoint obstacle system," which explained in my memoirs, were "designed to channel the enemy into well-defined corridors where we might bring air and artillery to bear and then hit them with mobile ground reserves." The Marine Division was standby at Khe Sanh like a 'rapid-deployment-force.'

When landed, I followed General Dong for inspection our fellows scurrying about digging the foxholes and carrying armfuls of sandbags. I guessed that this strongpoint was not stronger than the PT-76s can overrun, because from the hollow with slop was not deep enough against the natural obstacle, the PT-76 could climbed up so easy. Over here sometimes I could hear their sound exploded shell Katyusha rockets 122mm orientation-adjustment, and readjustments.

Suddenly, my sergeant Duc shooting mini-gun tracing at a slop of a hill to NVA carrying the big pots and pans, every two NVA troops hanging the big pan in the middle on their shoulders by a bamboo stick, [these pans when I was in Communist jail, recognized that had a big pan with 4 feet diameter, used for cooking food, steaming rice, vegetable soup and good shelter too for any case bombardment prevent burst in an extremely large fragmentation pattern]

Every helicopter crew must familiar with smelling the rotten remain, so now I have been the ability to sense things liked dogs have an excellent sense of smell it stinks. Over here from the started operation until now there was never got hit by B-52, I means in the northern flank of Route 9, but today I'm still smelling the taste of swollen, rotten of human remain too low altitude underneath of insulated in the womb-like cockpit, the corpses had deteriorated and bloated; which device killed them? Maybe from A.C-130B gunship [Pentagon plan EC-130B neutralized interdiction in northern flank as I experienced] that remind me the last week, here was the battle in the first serious counterattack came on the night of 18, 19, and 20 February, when one NVA regiment struck the ARVN 39th Ranger Battalion northeast of Ranger LZ, Ban Dong. There was northern flank of the penetration, especially at Fire Support Base 30 toward west Fire Support Base 31; subsequently the major battles of the operation took place with six NVA regiments committed against Airborne and Ranger forces. TOC/ J-2 concluded that these could be reinforced immediately by three additional regiments from the south and within two days by three more regiments from the west and north. They used tactical separated regiment among division for predominantly fierce attacks on ARVN one by one and step by step, that tactical method sound like breaking every chop-stick instead of whole bundle for one time. Thereby Hill-31 the first tested target.

I concluded that no clue bomb hole of B-52 carpeted was took place over here for the commencement until now that testified the stinky smell from human remain being by strafing from EC-130B on the night of 18, 19 February.

Now two gun-ships were on the operational zone to air cover for 2nd battalion/3rd Airborne Brigade. Our friend forces so confident to dispatch so many targets in front of them; the attack approach was the spot yesterday we destroyed enemy's POL depot, now the scenery looked very cool. NVA regiment scared engagement with only one airborne-battalion? I guess they gathered to retreat a concentration zone for fierce attack Hill 31?

The New Legion

Suddenly, I heard in my helmet in the faint voice "Magic-Club-1…this King-Star-3 …over?"

I answered "Go ahead"

I recognized the new pilot in 233rd Squadron. In fact I ordered their mission just merely in the southern flank, the LZ in that area little bit lower for specially air support to 1st Division but now northern flank was so much serious counterattacks they badly needed medical evacuation right beside my support operational zone, meanwhile U.S air-cavalier gave up due too many crashed, little bit to the north for 1st Battalion/2nd Airborne Brigade. Two battalions would like joint together for counterattack against so heavy enemy pressure but hard to reach meanwhile Ranger 39th Battalion needed reinforcement with 1st airborne battalion.

I read my heart reserve all priorities air-cover and fire power for this fresh new formed 233rd squadron.

Again I repeat where your location …King-Star-3 over?

Reacted quickly "Magic-Club-1, King-Star-3 now at the rendezvous point, over" [a rendezvous point stand for Lao Bao, right at border]

"Surrounding over there about four minutes I will reach you… King-Star-3 did you read me over" I will guided him to the spot for medical evacuation. I contact to friend force, left now and came back 20 minutes later. 2nd battalion radioed back to me and to stop proceeding for a while for relaxation.

Two gun-ships leaving the operational zone, heading to the southeast, still on the treetop, King-Star-3 flying higher than us so couldn't see us.

"King-Star-3 turn right at 4 o'clock and descending… we will joint in about two minutes … how doing you read me over"

Now we are in combat formation, behind us about 300 yard was dust-off King-Star-3.

"Now we are on the target… King-Star-3 gains altitude to view-bird your LZ…at 12' o'clock orange panel … We will prep in front underneath of your approach ….be patient"

Meanwhile at high altitude I heard the conversation between OV-10 and operation officer 2nd Airborne Brigade at Hill 30 by Vietnamese language on board of OV-10 Bronco, Vietnamese observer for FAC (forward Air Control) Two Phantom F.4 dropped napalm; they passed over of me so I could identified the kind of aircraft. Now from East, Seven Fleet, the Navy A-4 Sky-haws and F-8 Crusaders precision-dive-bombed, and A-6 Intruders bombers. But the NVA built "phony gun position" for the interpreters of the aerial photographs to find [at Washington surely Haig did care the phony gun position, know that by sophisticated sensors on satellite but he also did care about, his principal author, a prospect congruent with his later involvement in and reaction to the most ROE' operation] NVA troop set off harmless explosion charges to simulate muzzle flashes for the air observer. They hid the real guns and mortars and rocket launchers in deep pits and in tunnels, fired if necessary. But how can they hide them without my own eyes witnessed. At last the fighter-bombers struck on enemy phony gun position. Haig didn't care, just practiced exercise combat training

General Giap gave instructed orders regardless the harmful of US artillery at the border, because he was informed by the so called antiwar movement like John F Kerry instead of CIA counterespionage, Russell Flynn Miller. Putting them in vain as built stronghold at west flank; all U.S fire power at border was out of effect, included 16 "Long-Tom" 175mm, 18 Howitzer 155mm, and 8-inch Howitzer just solely reach at east flank.

I repeat "King-Star-3 make approach right ahead of you at 12 o'clock…very safe I will prep on the hill crest at your right side" I speak very slow for calming him, but I did feel there was a damn hot LZ, because our friend didn't having time for clear the spot LZ. I was been meditate abruptly I waken smart-up due to my gunner played maximum round strafing on the hill crest seeing enemy scurrying down to slop.

Sergeant Duc yelled "Enemy crowded in the middle slop I shot 6,000 rounds per minutes to kill all of them." I order the wingman shot anti-throng rockets [nail arrows] to the bald hill at right side. I make a hard tough turn to left for second pass, meanwhile Duc pressed the trigger, knowing those six-barrels were going to work just perfectly and spew thousands of rounds into the crowded enemy as the barrels on both flanks of the cockpit spat flame and buzzed like chain saws, their heavy bullets punching into the hot target. Now I could see my wingman a red-orange smoke behind him two by two rockets roaring in over the target, peppering it with his own miniguns as I rolled in behind him for second run. But on this run I took my time, lining it up, making sure that we'd hammer that hostility enemy

I glanced down at the target "Everything is been cool now."

King-Star-3 had seen the orange panel in the middle of LZ on the clipped-wood was a real hassle. The spot inclined little bite in left slop. I still ordered the gunners continued strafing less 2,000 round per minutes for neutralized interdiction back and forth evenly on the hill. We understood because the friendly force wouldn't like created lousy noises when tree cutting for prevention enemy pounding artillery to it.

I contact "Quang Trung…Quang Trung are you in hurry the wounded and remain ready, we will land a couple minutes"

This is worst terrible LZ with the struggle facing a brand new rating pilot; I'm so worry for his landing. However he was trained with "Black Cat" Army Aviation Company at Marble Mountain, Danang. I am so nervous without patient glancing down the LZ the mountainous area was always having turbulence, the up and down drafts. How can he hold his helicopter in stable for hover; His hovering too long caused me increasing the heart beat but I must keep patiently, I dare not disturb him at all; Why he would able land …isn't something wrong, but I still kept quiet let himself made decision, maybe the LZ couldn't permit to touch down due to some trees still not cut yet. I flown over and check our troops trying to put in the wounded in cabin because the helicopter wouldn't able touch on ground. I also saw two black poncho-bags scurrying by a flock of soldiers throw on the board of chopper.

Suddenly the enemy running down to slop standing bold strafing into the chopper, instantly my gunner react by 4,000 rounds into them killed all of them and my wingman continued strafing, in the haze of light fog I could see the tracers at the ratio of one tracer for every fourteen standard rounds scattered evenly on the hot spot, but at the rate those mini-guns fired, the spaced tracers would look like heavy raindrops.

I yelled "That's enough…all bad guys were already died…stop it" I must spare the fire power for escort him back to Khe Sanh. King-Star-3 still hover in a strange and eerie silence, abruptly I see his main rotor blade trimmed few high-trees underneath; at this point, I knew I was no longer invincible. I could feel my heart thumping in my chest. In the space of few seconds, I had gone from feeling, but keeping so calm wait his reaction.

In my helmet I heard a voice utter faint word, and tried very hard not to groan or cry out with the incredible incident, "Magic-Club-1… my helo' main rotor chopped the trees, now so hard tough shaken vibration… but I tried to take off…Magic followed escort to me…over"

I firmly respond in conforming voice "tried your best… we always behind you!"

His chopper flying like an untamed horse with so many vertical jerks in every turned cycle, I let him fly any altitude, heading, whatever reaching the home base as soon as he can.

"Easy your airspeed…never passed over 70 knots…O.K"

But fortunately he flies not too high for easy fired target to various kind of antiaircraft artillery; thank to my recent briefing he avoid the west flank of the highest ridge forming the crest and also the terrible AAA' mobile of PT-76. That's Okay now we are on low altitude flirting along east flank. I contact US fire power at border pounding cover in front of us. Now we flied over or in the smoke of "Long Tom" residue with confident none bastards underneath. Farther in front of us some vertical column smoke brought the patience of mind, we do feel the burned wood much favorable with somewhat security

At last, three helicopters landed at their home base safely. This afternoon had become hotter now toward the end of the rainy season, and the corpses in cabin had deteriorated and bloated enveloped the highland earth-dusted among the bursts of U.S artillery depart.

We must reload fire armament, and refuel right away to continue air cover support for the 2nd Airborne Battalion. I headed back for the largest site at full load fire power, running right along the treetop. We were going to provide fire support for the strayed ground airborne elements. Now two Airborne-compapanies/8th Battalion/3 Brigadier, were ambushed by one separated NVA regiment/320/Div.

The New Legion

We're scrambled over the battle. Two recon/companies just left from high elevated relief to down a stream to get water and be in a state of siege.

Now we advised the Airborne must defense themselves on the hiding spot. We start prep along the creek, on the declined stone slop where NVA standing bold shoot down the stream water. Our experience top-gun performed an accuracy air ground support moderated the rhythm 2,000 rounds per minute to smooth the gun-barrel in preventing jammed fired. First we destroyed in neutralization the hot area by 17pds rockets explosives fire power, in strafing, seeing the tracers at the ratio rounds scattered evenly on the bare rocks and bushes. The spaced tracers would like heavy raindrops. Suddenly, in my helmet I hear a Vietnamese voice on OV-10 Bronco: "Get out the operational area immediately …over here designed for three boxes B-52… but … in five minutes, 42 U.S artilleries from the border will strike cover to Airborne …don't come back this area … this is a strict order"

The matter was that General Sutherland had apparently been slow to recognize and report those problems much less act aggressively to deal with them. Another senior officer present on the ground judged him to be "very passive," really "a negative factor" in the operation. Until 23 February, a MACV staff officer told Abrams, "I think it's fair to say we had no feel that his helicopter situation was quite as acute." This news precipitated intense reaction at MACV. "The way this thing is supposed to work," erupted General Abrams, "is that, once I said what the priorities were and what was going to be done around here, goddamn it, then these – USARV' responsible to have maintenance people up there, keeping track of this, goddamn it! And they should know what's happened! That's what hasn't been done."

Abrams asked his assistance deputy, General Fred Weyand, how it looked to him. "Well," he began, focusing on General Sutherland, "I guess I'm not too forgiving on Jock [Sutherland] I recognize the truth of what you're saying, but goddamn it, you've got a corps commander up there who's supposed to be keeping track of every fucking bird in the place every hour of the day. There's something wrong there. You've got an organizational problem of some kind. He just doesn't know what the hell's going on." Weyand recalled that there had been a battalion on Route 914 for two days before Sutherland was aware of it, even though they knew it…"That tells me that the coordination and tie-in…headquarters and General Lam's is not fully effective."

There followed a long pause, several heavy minutes in silence, then he said, "I guess I'd better go up and talk with General McCaffrey now. I just feel we've got to get some people up there today who can be feeding the facts back. Move the goddamn men and the tools and the stuff and get with it." In contrast Abrams recalled enemy side "But goddamn it! –about the maintenance, either they've got enough that are well or something. But enemy seem to be to able to work on the roads, keep the trucks going, still fire the antiaircraft, still move the supplies, and unload and load it, backpack it, and all that. So I'd say they're right on schedule table. I don't think it means that somehow they're going to screw it up.

Colonel Sam Cockerham was acting commander of the 1st Aviation Brigade when he got orders to fly north immediately in an aircraft provided by General Abrams. When Cockerham arrived, Abrams was already there, slumped down on the leather sofa in Sutherland's office.

"Worst fucking OR [Operational Readiness] rate I've seen in U.S Army aviation history!"

He exploded by way of conversational openers.

"The entire concept, the entire national strategic concept, is at stake here!" he thundered at Sutherland. Abrams said he was going to give Col Cockerham all theater resources in Vietnam to get the operationally ready rate up to USARV standards. That was 80 percent, 5 percent higher than worldwide Army standards.

Abrams asked Cockerham how long that would take. It was then Monday at about 1:00 pm "By Wednesday night I'll have it up to standard," Cockerham replied, perhaps not realizing how bad things were. The UHI-C gunship OR rate, for example, then stood at 25 percent.

"I want a back channel from you to me every twenty-four hour," Abrams told Cockerham as he left. The meeting made a deep impression on Cockerham, and not just because of the massive task that had been dumped in his lap. "General Sutherland was like a dog with his tail tucked under," he recalled. "I thought the job was beyond him. He wasn't prepared. Abrams worked around him."

Shortly, Brigadier General Sid Berry, then assistant deputy division commander of the 101st Airborne, also played a pivotal role in restoring order to the realm of Army aviation in the operation he went in harm's way over and over again to make things happen. Said an advisor who was there at the time, "General Sid Berry flew to the most critical areas and got things done that sync – When Lieutenant General Julian Well, unsavory figure pro-Permanent Government visiting Vietnam from this assignment with the U.S negotiation team in Paris, (maybe must be violated ROE for less harmful) went up to Khe Sanh to have a fresh-look around, he was impressed. "Their OR rate when I was up there Sunday was 79 percent," he said "which I considered astronomical." What the hell few NVA regiments were destroyed by B-52 carpets. Ironically, when fierce fighting erupted in the Lam Son 719 area of operations, virtually all B-52 took off from Utapao Thailand; those tactical sorties were diverted from interdiction to close air support for less aircrew casualty. "Speed of execution is essential to the success of this operation. An operation dependent solely on air mobility would be subjected to the vagaries of the weather and the considerable enemy antiaircraft artillery (all conventional AAAs) threat in the objective area." It was also known that formidable air defenses were deployed along the Harriman Highway (Ho Chi Minh trail) and were particularly dense in the Tchepone area [eventually where will the "open-dumpster" of Soviet and U.S out of date weaponry and war materiel]

Vinh-Van-Truong

Pentagon's traitorous behavior

Neutralization and Interdiction: Pentagon divided airpower to neutralize threat interdict by steady bombardments in three distinctive targets for getting both enemy [NVA] and friend [ARVN]: Northern Flank from Route-9 was responsibility by **EC-130B Gun-ship**; Southern Flank from Route-9 was **Arc Light B-52**; and on main-front Route-9 was **Sky-spot (tactical fighter aircraft)** for this war-game craps. As for my 42 days and night stayed at Airborne Forward Operation Base at Ham Nghi, Khe Sanh, I had been witnessed covered everywhere in the operational area by on treetop skimming maneuver. In the early operational days, General Haig played the battle-game inside the air-conditioner chamber in Pentagon, just followed up on the charts and road-maps. This play game created so much trouble to the 1st ARVN division. He used Arc light B-52 took off from Guam to preplanned strike on schedule that inflicted some casualty to friendly force in southern flank of 1st Infantry Division responsible. Every morning briefing, General Phu 1st division commander must cry-out in radio pushed their men hurry out the area for B-52 carpeted in the next couple hours. And 1st Armor Cavalier Task forces with 8th Airborne Battalion protected them, when they tried to spot on location on Route-9 for recuperated from their operation. Suddenly, the Pentagon staff under General Haig, due to ARVN' main front force has moved so slowly, not right by the Pentagon road-map preplanned. As the result, an aircraft with a called-sign "Sky-Spot" was scrambled to this area and dropped a CBU-24 Bomb, which containing 600 small bombs like golf-grenade sized. Each golf results when explosion launched the 300 small pieces of steel in injuring vice commander of 8th Airborne Battalion and others numerous soldiers of both Armor 11th /Squadron and Airborne get wounded. As always our flights for air cover tactic low over our friend troop, also lucky day for our gun-ships, if Sky-spot drop bomb explosive "snack-eyes" our gun-ships should be absorbed all of their goddamn fragments. All long night of 5th March I heard intermittent throngs of B-52 ferocious onslaught around Tchepone and early 6th March MC-130 dropped bomb BLU-82AL [Aluminum is a silvery white and ductile member of the boron group of chemical elements, it has the symbol AL; it atomic number 13 ... power and polystyrene

(FAE) consist only of an agent and a dispersing mechanism and take their oxidizers from the oxygen in the air]

After 25th February, so many casualties of ARVN and U.S Air cavalier, General Haig assigned Colonel James Vaught to the so called ARVN Airborne Division Advisor, but in reality Vaught should be Haig's eyes on the operational spot. He will wear monitoring error, and closed to General Phu 1st Division Commander. Particularly, where Landing Zone LoLo, the U.S helicopters was shot down to describe the falling leaves, Colonel James Vaught what to do to reduce, slow down the suffering? He began to manage B-52 campaign **from "Rolling Thunder" to "Linebacker"** means access to air ground closed support and protect friend troop from 300 meters, thereby no more NVA ambush near our troop. From now on, Vaught has to react and kill some thousands NVA troops thank to B-52 access support, artillery Long-tom 175 and 16 tactical aircrafts F-8 Crusader, A-6 Intruder from 7th Fleet. Typically, for short period to campaign medical evacuation, supply by renew tactical: Such as B-52 carpeted on front West, U.S artillery was strike on front East, and tactical aircraft pounded alternately to the North fence; Leave now South of the approach gate in and out for 20 helicopters Huey in exclusive, air assault two airborne companies move to LZ, whether to unload small ammunition and supplies, small quantity gasoline to full set cavalry. Three UH1-Hs got hit but still accomplished mission; continues to fly 3 consecutive lifts back and forth, we called Horseshoes tactic.

[General Phu committed suicide for the betrayal a trusted friend, ***General Vaught****: At the time damage, was change, in the time Saigon Fall, the new information brought to the week of General Phu for the betrayal of United States ally. Extract a paragraph in the document: Furthermore, General Phu Lam Son 719's friend, General James Vaught, an American buddy asked him for advice, General had refused because he claimed that the Paris Accords prohibited lending him such help. Not even advice from an old and trusted friend. Who would have known? It was only the two of them, yet General Vaught, still, had said no!]*

But right now, this moment, **Colonel James Vaught** was an Airborne advisor, his first command shows the prestige, guaranty, confidence of his interference with military operations to less casualty necessity; The lest retreat trajectory withdrawal in security. When the 1st Armor Brigade retreat to the branch of Xepon River together with two airborne battalions; How their crossing the river, Colonel Vaught gave some instructions to Colonel Nguyen Trong Luat, 1st Brigade Commander and also for counter balance of dispensary destroyed-trucks: "Let all truck rolling by wheels, stayed remains for B-52 destroyed as similar to B-52 was destroyed all NVA trucks on the Parking No-2, in the early day SAC bombardment"

Fire Support Base, Hill 31 was in desperate plight.

The NVA' thrust was assisted by tanks. The fighting became fiercer and fiercer, and both side suffered heavy casualties. The 39th ranger battalion bravely battled on despite being low on ammunition. They resisted for one day and one night, before the position was lost. The battalion had to retreat toward the 21st ranger battalion's position in the south. Having successfully occupied the hill, the NVA moved west and south west to threaten the 21st and the 3rd Airborne Brigade was well-supported by tactical air power. Despite heavy lost, the NVA continued to storm FSB 31 in the face of long and short range heavy Long Tom 175 artilleries. Although forewarned of enemy intentions, the 3rd Airborne Brigade failed to establish an effective defense, and shared the same fate of the 39th Ranger battalion. It had fought with courage and bravado, but succumbed to the massive suicidal onslaught of the NVA. The Brigade Staff, including Colonel Tho was captured. Some evaded and ran southwards toward FSB 30 which was occupied by the 2nd Airborne battalion. Even as they assaulted the 3rd Airborne Brigade Headquarter, the NVA pounded away at FSB 30 and A-loui FSB where the 1st Airborne Brigade and the 1st Armor Brigade were positioned. These two units were unable to give assistance to the 3rd Airborne Brigade at FSB 31, although help was sought of them.

As late as **27 February**, three weeks into the operation, MACV J-2 was carrying only seven enemy regiments in the Lam Son area of operations, up from six with the arrival of the 324B Division's, and separated 29th Regiment. Of the twenty-one enemy battalions then committed, five were assessed as having been rendered combat ineffective due to casualties. Nevertheless, fierce fighting was in progress all along Route 9 and at the positions ARVN had staked out north and south of it, especially at Fire Support Base 31 to the north. There an enemy attack that included tanks and armored PT-76 overran a brigade headquarters of the Airborne Division and captured the brigade commander, Colonel Tho and his staff-officers. As same as the 39th Ranger Battalion was also pressured into abandoning its position, joining the nearby 21st Ranger Battalion, after which both were evacuated from Laos.

At the Hill 31, thirteen days after General Dong and Colonel Tho commander 3rd Brigade, stationed on Fire Support Base 31 had have a short briefing for imminent "Hill-Fights". A squad of 8th Battalion/3rd Airborne Brigade forward observer party from Hill-31 was ambushed in a grove of bamboo, often clever bunkers tunneled under thick bamboo clumps, providing NVA with a natural cover; on Hill 875 northwest of the Hill-31. There was clusters of intertwining ridges, the highest ridge forming the crest that gave the hill mass its designation by height in meters. Four airborne soldiers survived. This was the first and the cruelest struggle at Hill-31 vicinity, the "Hill Fights" began.

General Dong had been right that to hold this Hill-31 the airborne would have to garrison the hill-ranges that dominated the valley. The NVA understood this and seized the hills. A regiment from the NVA' 320 Division marched in through the pea-soup fog and under the low clouds clinging over the crests of the monsoon and occupied Hill 875 and the two hills beyond it – 888 south and 888 North. A second regiment from this division hid itself in a reserve position behind the hills. It was subsequently discovered that NVA combat engineer troops had probably been at work on the three hills for long months without being detected by the ARVN Joint Staff Headquarters before the main body of general's infantry arrived. Dong wanted to keep this Hill-31 less-vulnerable. The Airborne 3rd Brigade therefore had to drive the NVA from the heights. They did not know the strength of the enemy they faced, nor did they suspect the nature of the battleground the General Giap' troops had prepared.

For four days two airborne battalions – initially the battalion stationed at Hill-31, quickly followed by the 6th Airborne Battalion under a Brigade/J-3 Command Group sent to take charge – attempted to clear Hill 875. The word "Hill" is field shorthand for what is properly called a "hill-mass" in military terminology. Hill 875 and Hill 888 South and 888 North were clusters of intertwining ridges, the highest ridge forming the crest that gave the hill mass its designation by height in meters. Hills 888 South and 888 North happened to be the same height and so were differentiated by the fact that one was north of the other.

The NVA troops on Hill 875 let the 6th Battalion Airborne climb the ridges to within fifteen to twenty meters, then raked the Airborne with fusillades from positions concealed in the undergrowth. Shells hurled by 82, and 120mm mortars which burst in an extremely large fragmentation pattern, from unseen pits somewhere back in the ridgelines crashed into the Airborne, killing and wounding more of them. Counter-fired by the Airborne mortars, salvos of high explosive and white phosphorous from the howitzers 155 at the Fire Support Base 31, 30 strafing and rocket runs by our UHI-H gun-ships, and bombs and napalm from the tactical fighter jet from Thailand and Navy, Marine in of shore Pacific interrupted but did not silence the enemy mortars or discourage the Giap' infantry. When the Airborne tried to disengage, The NVA would not let go. They followed the Airborne, harrying them with automatic-weapons fire. The Airborne could not evacuate their wounded. Whenever they called in our helicopter for medical evacuation would plaster the landing zone with mortar 120mm shells. That missions must aborted due to so heavy enemy pressure in fire power.

The two Airborne-battalions were subjected to separate. The 8th Airborne Battalion was on the northwest side of Hill 875, the battalion with the Brigade J-3 command and control told the 6th Airborne Battalion to link up with the 8th Airborne Battalion which he was attached. The Lieutenant Colonel J-3 leading the 8th Battalion replied that after four days of combat he did not have enough able-bodied men left to carry the dead and wounded that far. Airborne abhor abandoning their dead because of the mystical comradeship of the traditional Airborne Division. Leave the dead, the Brigade-

Commander ordered. The Lt Col answered that he still would not have enough able-bodied Airborne to carry out the wounded, and wounded Airborne cannot be abandoned under any circumstances. He said he was pulling into a nearby bank of fog to hide from the mortars fragmentations and "fight until it was over" against the Giap' infantry he was certain would follow.

The artillery officer back at the Hill-31 had his batteries walk shells to the battalion through the fog. He circled the beleaguered men with shrapnel, as Sergeant Hung had done to save Nguyen's lost platoon. Litters for the wounded were improvised out of ponchos; the dead were slung in ponchos to be carried too; and the Airborne gathered up all of the riffles and equipment. When the column set out to march back through the darkness and rain and a pea-soup-fog that thickened with the lowering temperatures of the night, only the men at the point and the rear guard walked without burdens –the periodic downpours turned the dirt of the trails into slippery red-mud. The days had become hotter now toward the end of the rainy season, and the corpses had deteriorated and bloated. Many times during the night the Airborne carrying one of the dead stumbled and the body fell out of the poncho and rolled down the slope. The column halted. The body was retrieved and laid in the poncho again, and the march resumed. When the Airborne reached safety at dawn they had left none of their comrades behind.

The 8th Battalion also disengaged with the help of the reinforcements. The two depleted battalions were reorganized by one thrust attack-front, and the Airborne built up their forces at the highest ridge to two battalions under at 3rd Brigade command post at Hill-31 while the 105s of Airborne, the 155s of B/44th Artillery Battalion, U.S artillery at Khe Sanh' 175 firing from one of the strongpoint back across the mountains, the fighter-bombers battered and burned Hill 888 for a full day and night. A combined airborne force then assaults the hill. But Giap' troop was gone. They had apparently withdrawn to the next hill close nearby Hill-31 maybe they changed the tactical maneuvers? 888 South, possibly soon after the fight with the two Airborne 8th and 9th Battalions and before the worst of the bombardment had begun Giap' troop left many of their dead behind; Otherwise, as the Airborne combined force after-action report noted, "the battle area was extremely well policed by the Giap' troop; virtually no equipment or information of intelligence value remained." The Airborne did count twenty-eight bunkers on Hill 888, and they found 300 foxholes on and around it and mortar pits on the back slopes. The overhead cover on a number of the bunkers was six feet high in layers of bamboo and packed earth and grass, [of course they had plenty time for these establishments] thick enough to protect the NVA troops inside from a direct hit by the artillery. The bunkers should have made the Airborne combined brigadier-force and battalion commanders suspicious.

The Airborne that launched another headlong assault against Hill 888 South after another day and night of battering and burning attacked right into a man trap. The NVA held fire once more until the lead squads were fifteen to twenty meters from the bunkers in the undergrowth and the opening volley would have maximum killing effect. Sniper hidden in trees not yet knocked down by bombs and shells picked out radio operators and machine gunners and killed them carefully with a single accuracy shot through the head or the chest. At the same moment, salvos of 120mm mortar shells again exploded among the Airborne. The NVA didn't seem to mind calling mortar fire so close that they were, in effect, bringing it down on their own positions. In this moment, our gunship was contacted with airborne lead platoons putting on their heads and shoulders the 'orange panel' to easier identification friend and foe and also we can count on to air close-support in front of them 100 meters on spewing mini-guns 4,000 round per minutes that I was convinced in neutralization every snipers being killed, though the rockets detonated on the branches that help killing snipers too. Obviously we made flight circus so lower above friendly troops for security.

Airborne are unsurpassed as assault troops, and these Airborne pressed forward with the classic aggressiveness instilled by the Airborne tradition-motto. They discovered that the farther they fought their way into the NVA position, the more resistance they encountered and the worse their situation became. Soon those men still capable of fighting were unable to go forward or back. The fire from the bunkers, foxholes, and trenches in front was withering.

The New Legion

Meanwhile, NVA in bunkers the Airborne had fought their way past were back in action behind them and had cut off their retreat.

I did know so well that the North Vietnam Communist anted "violent, close-quarters combat" because it "tends to diminish the effectiveness" of air and artillery was turning out to be something of an understatement; so our gunship with accuracy fire support encouraged the Airborne' morale. The Airborne-men on 888 South were feeling the extent of the diminishment. While General Dong, Air Borne Division commander had been thinking about ports and warehouses for his attrition machine, the NVA had been learning better ways to fight the Airborne. There were not twice as many bunkers on 888-South as the Airborne troops had found on Hill 875, there were eight times as many, and the approximately 260 bunkers on this hill were astonishingly rugged. The smaller ones, apparently two or three-man affairs had been constructed with roof consisting of two layers of logs topped by five feet of dirt. Larger four-man bunkers had still better protection overhead and, before the battle, had served as fairly comfortable living quarters. They were fitted with storage shelves, bamboo-mat floors, and a drainage system to keep them dry. The largest bunkers, clearly the command posts, had roof with four to eight layers of logs and then four feet of packed earth above the logs. Field telephone wire had been strung throughout the bunker complex so that the NVA battalion, company, and platoon commanders could talk to each other during the battle and they and the forward observers could adjust the mortars by calling instructions to the crews in the pits on the rear slopes.

After long day-and-night bombardment of the hill that had seemed so awesomely destructive to the watching Airborne had been mainly celebrated holiday-fireworks. The rockets detonated on the branches or the overhead cover of the bunkers, and the machine-gun bullets and 20mm cannon shells didn't penetrate anything either. Most of the napalm burned in the trees. The howitzer shells 105s, 155s, 175s and even 8-inch gun did give the Giap' troops in the bunkers headaches. The bombs were more frightening, extremely difficult to bear. The concussion from them gave some of the NVA troops bleeding noses and ears, but the bombs usually did not kill or disable either.

Vinh-Van-Truong

Prior to the assault on the morning of February 21, the fighter-bombers had dropped no 750-pounders and only a small number of 1,000- and 2,000-pound bombs on Hill 888 South. Almost all of the bombs had been the 250- and 500-pound "Snake-eye" type preferred by the Marine pilots and their Navy and Air Force counterparts. Snake-eye bombs have large tail fins that unfold after released to retard descent so that the bomb can be launched from low altitude in a slow, parabolic trajectory that allows the aircraft time to fly clear of the blast and fragmentation. Jets can bomb accurately from a low, relatively flat approach and the weather over here also encouraged the use of Snake-eyes. The U.S pilots had to be prepared to fly anywhere. With one part of the Vietnam's weather or the other always in a monsoon, they frequently encountered low cloud ceilings. At Khe Sanh in late February and early March 1971, the ceiling was often 1,000 feet or less-melee with fog. To drop the heavier 750-, 1,000- and 2,000-pound bombs accurately and escape the blast and fragments, a pilot had to take a high-angle approach akin to dive-bombing and pull away at a good height. An approach like this was dangerous when the clouds were down and the air space around a target was crowded. The NVA had also observed this practice of the U.S pilots. The bunkers were sturdy enough to withstand anything but a direct or close hit by a 250- or 500-pound Snake-eye bomb, infrequent in practice.

Rain-forest bunker complexes served the NVA for both offensive and defensive purposes. During the early stages of a battle, as in the fighting for Hill 875, The NVA could sortie out and employ their flanking and envelopment tactics to advantage. They knew the terrain intimately, because they had been living in this area secretly for quite a very long years, where starting to build The Harriman Super-Highway since Neutral Laos Agreement 1962, plus POL pipe-lines parallel along it, while during the last phase of bunker construction. Later, when the battle was approaching a high-point, as in the assault on Hill-888 South, The NVA could wait out the bombardment in the shelter of the bunkers.

In the end, bombs and shells would exact their toll. Those NVA regiments who were ordered to hold their position or to expose themselves in counterattacks would die, as they were to

The New Legion

die by the thousands during couple days of the "Hill-Fight". Their crucial purpose were paralyzed the 105s of Airborne and 155s of B/44 Artillery Battalion at Hill-31 and used maximum indirect fire power for destroying helicopters when they attempted to land. By planning carefully, by fortifying in advance, and by designing a battlefield that enticed the Airborne into becoming victims of General' Giap stylized methods of fighting at Dien Bien Phu battle in 1954; the separated NVA regiments could accomplish what was most important to them: they could prolong the combat and make any Airborne battalions sent against them suffer grievously. Merely to strip away the top layer of canopy trees, the second layer of pole trees, and finally the underbrush so that on could see the bunkers to attack them with precision consumed days of this standard bombardment with artillery from Khe Sanh 175s, 155s, and 8-inch-guns and 250- and 500-pound bombs. Despite all of the preparatory bombing and shelling of Hill 888 South, the Airborne could not see the bunkers until they were almost on top of them, and there were the bunkers until they were almost on top of them, and there were plenty of trees left standing to give the snipers leafy perches. So why as the guns lead, I recommended Lt Col Airborne X.O' 3rd Brigade let the forward squads must wore the orange-panel for references I had sight accuracy for protected them in advance 60 to 100 meters ahead strafing and rocket runs, now I had ready 38 rockets in both side my bird.

Lt Col X.O Brigade care about the lives of his forces; He engaged to forward head-front of platoon right in the moment he received a report of the bloodletting on the hill, took a squad of riflemen, and crawled forward to find out for himself what was happening. He therefore understood the limits of conventional bombardment against bunkers like the ones he now saw on Hill 888 South and the rashness of sending his troop to seize them. He ordered all of two airborne joint battalions withdraw from the hills and recommended in suggestion the Air-Wing from Thailand and 7th Fleet to switch to 750 , 1,000 , and 2,000 pound bombs with delay fuses. The delay fusing meant that the bomb penetrated the earth before exploding. A miss was still effective, because the subterranean shock waves tended to collapse the bunkers from beneath.

The concussion from the big bombs was disabling in itself (lethal when the hit was close enough), and the delay also gave the pilots time to fly clear.

Lt Col X.O intervened too late. The death toll entirely of Lam Son after two weeks was thousands in these typical "Hill-Fights" of 875 and 888 were already hundred-eighty. Close to half of the men had just been killed in this impetuous attack on Hill-888 South, and this time the Airborne were forced to abandon their dead in order to extricate the living. When Airborne returned after fierce bombardments during 24 hours later to recover the bodies of their comrades and occupy the wasteland of cratered ridges littered with splintered trees, forty-five of bunkers were still intact and the NVA regiment-men were gone again. The survivors of the 320 NVA Regiment and 29th Regiment that had borne the battle until this point had retreated to Hill-888 North, where, unbeknownst to the 3rd Brigade commander, Colonel Tho, they had been relieved by fresh troops of the 29th Regiment, which the NVA division commander had been holding in reserve.

Subsequently, Airborne' recommendation had also put in U.S Navy and Air-force squadrons to work on Hill 888 North with heavy bombs, but 2,000-pounders could not blow away the perverse weather of this mountainous area. As the lead 9th-Airborne Battalion neared the top of that hill late on the same afternoon that 888 South was occupied, the men encountered brisk sniper fire, meanwhile we had been covered strafing fire-support for 2nd battalion. The Airborne thought they could handle the snipers. They could not handle the tropical storm that enveloped them with forty-five-mile-per-hour winds and blinding rain. The battalion commander had to order a retreat. It was too dangerous to allow his Airborne-men to plunge ahead into who knew what.

Now, five separated NVA regiments from 320 Division, 324B Division took advantage of the hiatus to launch a counterattack that night by two reinforced main forces. The NVA regiments troops broke through the perimeter of 8th Airborne-Battalion and seized some previously unoccupied bunkers in the tree lines. There, with automatic weapons and grenades, they traded their lives through most of the next day in a fight to the death bunker by bunker. More dying followed on subsequent hours. By the time the 52 hours of fighting for the Hill-875, 888 had end, the bodies of 80 airborne-men had been carried to the spot near a stony-creek for evacuated and 148 had been wounded but that never happened. The worst Airborne' losses for any single battle of the start Lam Son 719 of the war thus far.

Actually, General Giap' tactical strategy determined by every Fire Support Bases of ARVN must be paralyzed in isolation by the eight regiments of NVA artillery, and six AAAs anti-aircraft regiments. Specially 152s guns: the duds from these penetrated four feet into the earth, and 120mm mortars that burst in an extremely large fragmentation pattern. Thereby every base our helicopter was crashed and grounded on those FSB. In this time so far: at Hill-31, two H34s crashed inside the FSB; at Hill-30, two UH1-H; at Hotel two UH1-Hs, and A-Loui, three UH1-H that I didn't count so various kinds of choppers that U.S Aviation left there. General Giap' tactical indicated instead broke every chop-stick one by one than couldn't break a full chop-stick-bundle. He manipulated used main strong infantry forces with tanks attack from East at Dong Da of Rangers LZ North of 39th, LZ South 21st battalion, and West at Hill-31 Airborne than joint combined forces moved to attack South right after on Fire Support Hill-30 was seized; then Base A-Loui and Hotel [Hong Ha-2] later on. Certainly, 100 percent ended the Victory-War with perfect preparedness thank to CIA counterespionage help Giap with full detail information (Giap was engaged in OSS in 1943, now it seemed to me, General Giap at sit right on Pentagon side by side with General Haig)

As quickly as they let it ebb in the west, these five NVA regiments shifted the fighting to the eastern side of the Hill 31, striking the farther west Airborne Fire Support Base in three fronts, from west, north, and south. Brigade commander Colonel Tho ordered the joint forces come back from south-east to rescue 3rd Airborne Battalion and command post but fail because NVA 27th regiment was in the stronger-holding point on high relief. "The enemy is all over that goddamn area and seems to be getting stronger, if anything. And so there's a real fight going up there. Particularly that indirect fire thing is worrying." Just how worrying was demonstrated at Hill-31, where more than thousand and thousand incoming rounds every hour and more than from such indirect fire weapons as mortars 120mm and 122mm rockets and artillery – reportedly including 152mm howitzers – knocked out all the Fire Support Bases destroyed 105s and 155s friendly artillery and forced ARVN forces to withdraw for survive. Meanwhile the NVA regiments were paying a heavy price. The full 3rd Battalions, 400 soldiers were ordered died on the spot Hill-31 even though by raining 23mm and grounding by PT-76 chains.

Now for counter-weight in the ROE' compensation, the Strategic Air Command estimated that "B-52s alone were inflicting losses that were the equivalent of about one combat effective NVA regiment per week." The Hill-31 area now, every direction shelling became the worst curse of this bloody fierce war, worse than the NVA regiments infantry assaults, worse than the ambushes of the supply convoys, worse than the raids by the sappers (a term American applied to NVA and Viet Cong commando-type troops) who stripped to their under-shorts and crawled through the barbed wire to toss satchel charges into bunkers and artillery revetments. The shelling was worse because it was equally lethal but harder on the nerves.

The worst on 25 February at 10:a.m it was still in heavy 'pea-soup-fog', the weather was marginal with clouds below the mountaintops and increasing ground fog. Still I thought low-flying helicopters, under clouded ceiling, could weave around the worst of it. Meanwhile five NVA' regiments, setting from different direction, in column set out hurrying to march convergence to Hill-31 through the darkness fog that thickened with the lowering humid temperatures after long night. Suddenly, it too began to get serious when nearly just a short moment 5,000 rounds fell on the Fire Support Base Hill-31. The NVA regiments brought to bear all manner of artillery in the Soviet-designed arsenal by U.S dollars (financial-supported by creditor Skull and Bones, this remind you in the past history: in 1917 on his advise, [the founder Skull and Bone] the United States gave the Russian revolutionary government under Aleksandr Kerensky a $325 million credit to be spent on war but "<u>materiel from the United States</u>") – 85mm, 100mm, 122mm, and 130mm guns; 120mm mortars that burst in an extremely large fragmentation pattern; and 122mm Katyusha rockets nine feet long, and particularly 152mm guns, the duds from these penetrated four feet into the earth. From now they don't hide the real guns and mortars and rockets launchers in deep pits and in tunnels, no more in camouflage they boldly keep firing not like in the early days built "phony gun" positions for the interpreters of the Bronco OV-10 observer to find as simulate muzzle flashes. I can cast my eyes on the NVA battery that was obliterated and several meters of brown-dirt blown off the tops of the ridges, exposing what had been underground warehouses.

From seven miles of south-east of Hill-31, I led two gun-ships for closed air-support 8th Airborne Battalion to joint communicated with the remnant element from another 9th Battalion. Something was strange NVA troops climbed on board PT-76 and shortly they hurried converging on Hill-31 in retreated from their high crests south Hill-31. Meanwhile two H-34 from Queen-Be Squadron were got hit by indirect artillery grounded on the spot Hill-31 after dropped supplies, the panic and the sick-sight of troop deserters mobbing helicopters and hanging from ski and now all over inside the helicopter cabin inflicting the crashes of two H-34. I meditate in thought, had bogged down and become a blood debacle, with our troops Laotian hill-top strongholds cut-off and annihilated piece-meal by the result of the ten NVA regiments rushing from five Divisions plus two separated regiment plus tank T-54 and armored truck PT-76 and artilleries regiments.

In the anticipated stratagem of Permanent Government about the outcome of this operation was "the biggest-fiasco that I saw in my whole time been here because it broke the back of the South Vietnamese finest army particularly irreplaceable were the dead elite-officers, I must said: since "that" the future leaders, they were all dead for turning in South Vietnam to Hanoi without bloodshed but blood-leaked or Saigon was not be a "pebble" Capital.

Now a deep gloomed over the hill scenery in front of mine, after numerous ferocious cruelty shelling pounded on Hill-31, "that by afternoon the setting sun would be shining through so much smoke and dust that you couldn't see it." First I could see the Hill-31 among the vertical smoked column but eventually it disappeared out of my sight by hours blurred in the haze of smoke and flashed. I couldn't understand the plight of my H-34 crewmen there died or wounded. More friendly bombardment more enemy attacked approach-trajectory closer, the fighter-bombers couldn't distinguish the friend troops will withdraw or dead on spot, which direction friend troops will forced retreat. The Air Force and Navy tried all manner of counter-battery measures to rescue or paralyze their opponents. The batteries from Khe Sanh' Long Toms, and guns Eight-inch, 155mm Howitzer fired hundreds or thousands of shells around the Hill-31. The F.4 Phantom, F-105 from Thailand; the Seventh Fleet A-4 Sky-hawks, F.8 Crusaders precision dive-bombed, and A-6 Intruder bombers, which lofted a respectable seven tons each, laid carpets in the tens of thousands of tons. But nothing gave more than a respite from these Dien Bien Phu' artillerymen who counted in their intellectual heritage the seventeenth-century French genius of artillery and siege-craft Sebastien de Vauban, and who had had so much practice at digging and disguising against his direct military heirs who had forgotten his teachings.

At late evening of that day, the tide of battle now sweeping back the other way – the 3rd Airborne Battalion and Colonel Tho 3rd Brigade Commander, staying fire or died on the spot is his determined orders. The 3rd Airborne Battalion infantrymen in the first perimeter front in their foxholes could not afford to curse. They were battling now to avoid annihilation. Platoon leader stopped the armored PT-76s – he leaped from his foxhole and stood up right in front of the metal beasts. Their ugliness was part of the terrifying effect these evil contrivances had always had on him and his men. The fore ends angled down into broad snouts with pop-eyes on top where the two headlights for night driving protruded. Yanking a grenade from his belt, he pulled the pin, cooked his arm, and hurled it at one of the monsters. The grenade landed on top of the PT-76 and erupted with a great bang and flash. Carried beyond their fear by his courage, the men of his platoon abandoned the protection of their foxholes to join him, throwing their grenades at the metal beasts too. But all of 3rd Airborne Battalion men were died or wounded by rainy bullets from the armored tracks or by shrapnel from their own grenades. Oh God, my unknown soldiers!

The New Legion

The enemy mobilized a large number of waves of assaults against Hill-31 to viciously attack from every direction convergence to Hill-31 – "the longest moment and bloodiest siege of the war" And in the meantime General Vo Nguyen Giap found himself as excellent commander of the war, but to me, a fate undeserved for a excellent and brave commander because CIA counterespionage gave him beforehand the plan of that Operation Lam Son 719. Subsequently,

in the moment, now I couldn't see the Hill-31 clearly in the twilight but above was huge smoked mushroom shaped cover entirely the hill and below it was a huge flame blasted, still shelling red trajectory curb into hill, in my mind I thought even the insects couldn't alive. "The Hill-31 was overrun by numerous NVA regiments." The Airborne Division's 3rd Brigade headquarters was captured and its 3rd Battalion essential annihilated to the last man. These were the brave unknown heroes.

But after nine year (1980) I had see Colonel Tho in the same Camp with me, the so called "Reeducation Camp" at Yen-Bai, Hoang Lien Son province, North Vietnam.

I must go back to Khe Sanh for refueling and rearmament by requesting 2nd Airborne Battalion commander for leaving fact-order. The gloaming swept in quickly in the mountain area, draining the sunlight from west skyline and replacing it with darker, gloomy shadows. Understood the Skull and Bones' scam, "conscientious objector" which required one to argue that one's religious beliefs did not allow involvement this operation, for I did not believe that war was at a mortal levels sufficiently low to require my own resistance. The war, as I understood it then, was not in itself an evil; if there was evil, I thought it was in how ineptly it was being conducted and in the consequences of this ineptitude. This was bloodiest war in just few weeks, the really "dirty war" like U-Thanh, United Nation' Secretary had said. Even good leadership and motivation were definitely not developed to an adequate extent and...this failure had a disastrous effect on the eventual outcome of the war.

At 10: am on 27 February, it's still light fog, right the weather was blurred enough, and the sun was shining and most of the fog had burned off gradually. I took a lead of formation gunship hurrying back for the target site at full power, running right along the treetops, to depleted 2nd Airborne Battalion. The 8th Battalion of 3rd Brigade also disengaged without the help of the reinforcement. Now I had to manipulated brought them joint together and moved them to southeast back to Route 9. I was going to provide fire support for the ground strayed elements. The most important was two battalions of 3rd Brigade consolidated for greater efficiency. I realized that everyone had been told now to consolidate at the high relief crest. Companies, platoons, squads, and mobile command post would be racing toward that new position. The NVA infantrymen knew the terrain intimately, because they had been living in this area secretly for quite a while during the last phase of bunker construction. So, it would be very hard to distinguish friends from foe in such a melee. I couldn't just cowboy in there, spewing four thousand rounds a minute. Two gunners behind backseats electrically controlled mini-guns could be armed only by me throwing a switch in the cockpit. I spoke to them very carefully.

"Okay, guys" I said. "I'm arming your guns, but we're not doing any shooting until we figure out where everybody is. Roger that?"

They grunted a "Rahj." But I flown low enough they could distinguish between the camouflage airborne and Nam-Dinh NVA' fatigues. If you were going to fly a gun platform there was absolutely no room for error. When you shoot very close to your own personnel on the ground, you've got to be extremely disciplined and precise, because if you make a mistake, people are going to die. I was determined that we would be on standby in alert: shoot as well as we did, execute the mission as precisely, and be just as brutal in the tent debriefs. I was going to note every mistake that any of gunship commanders made and take appropriate action. In short, I became a "real pain in the ass, but for good reason."

Typically the Airborne forward squad bore on their back-shoulders with orange panel hint sight our friendly troops. I was so confident of my two gunners. Shaking my head as six anti-aircraft regiments composed as thousand of AAA-batteries in this operation area; for a special operations pilot who should have been at the point of the spear, I felt like I'd just had my wings clipped. At this very moment I was supposed to be flying an UHI-H Gunship on a lightning raid into the heart of Hanoi in the very tough moment.

The New Legion

Within minutes I was back over the mobile-command-post element, flying a wide but low altitude circular pattern, trying to locate the targets and clearly spot the enemy before we opened up; if we climbed high enough to oversee the vast area, we'd be vulnerable to the NVA troop in mid-and high-altitude air defense systems. At first, I was peering past down into total confusion. It was just smoke, haze, and dust and indistinguishable, sprinting forms. We jinks up and down, getting high, getting low, but always low above the friend troop, trying to make us hard to hit, all too aware the NVA troops were now shooting at us from every treetops and high relief. I looked quickly around the cockpit, while gunners did the same, four of us testing the controls and checking the gauges. Everything was "in the green": no flight control problems, engine malfunctions, or weird noises. No one in my bird said a word, and then … what will happen?

The Airborne mobile command post gave me the order – "any price the must communicated a strayed deplete Company and guiding them back in joining actual consolidated-forces". A day earlier, this Company tried to go back Hill-31 for rescue-enforced fighting for the home base by the order of Colonel Tho 3rd Brigade commander. After a long night busted-flashed and smoked over Hill-31 now everything was calm, causing a feeling of mystery-fear, a strange and eerie silence- The company commander know how to reacted; now he tried to joint with his own-battalion but couldn't crossed the dry-spring hollowed in the small valley that dominated by two NVA regiments on the flank crests. Although that damn good fighting company but they couldn't cross the spring because the only very-one 85mm Mountain gun which shot directly down to spring when Airborne trying to cross, where they had some men wounded and died there.

I was contacted by the Colonel Commander on the mobile-command post:

"Magic Club One …this is Quang Trung…Quang Trung …" Crackle-crackle-crackle.

His transmission had broken up on the last word.

"I have an urgent mission change for you, this is Quang Trung" Lieutenant Colonel's voice was usually cold as ice water, but on today he actually sounded a little keyed up. "Copy these coordinates."

"Roger that," I said, and as my copilot continued the lazy orbit over the airborne activities below. I repeated the coordinates back to him.

"You are cleared direct to the target, Magic Club One – the Colonel ordered "Target is a possible…" Crackle-crackle-crackle

"I need the targets for salvo rockets and ammunition and we must rearm the next special weapon for firing support to destroy a worst enemy 85mm Mount-gun".

Obviously they had so many targets, the crest in front of the forward squad at the high tree slope. We commenced strafing from 100 to 200 meters for Airborne-Platoon can assault-reached the high point of crest ahead. I rolled out on a course direct to the objective. I was Tactical Lead now, and took the aircraft controls back from my copilot and called on my wingman – once again, I radioed the details to wingman to switch on VHF…frequency.

"Magic Club 2 how do you read me… over"

"One…Two five/five clear …over" he answered. "Go ahead."

"For killing 85mm gun at higher on crest, position at above your main rotor, at left side at 10:30 o'clock of us; "Two" must load 19 at each side-mounted 2.75-inch rocket pods of 17 pounds high-explosive and 6,000 rounds 7.62mm mini-gun-ammo… and "One" equipped 14 "nail-arrows" rockets and 12,000 rounds of ammo… the react-aiming devices for the six-barreled mini-guns were our own gunners eyes…O.K! Their tracers for experience missions like these were also infrared at a ratio of one tracer for every fourteen standard rounds and we must thrust them.

Suddenly, I heard the loudly sound hissed in my earphones:

"Magic-Club-One…Magic Eight calling… how you read me over… how you read me over"

I said "Go ahead"

"Magic Eight and Nine were over the rendezvous point needed your air cover over to Hill-30 for supplies and medical evacuation over"

"Standby one orbit there, I'll be there about six minutes...over ...now we had to salvo all some ordinance and re-arm ... then ...for your air cover...over".

I said, "Magic Two hold the fire-power for new escorted mission."

After 20 minutes, two UHI-H slicks were escorted to Hill-30, reached their familiar with designated landing-pad. The NVA regiments when they heard the sound of helicopter, from to various indirect heavy guns pounded away with numerous concentrated shelling to the Fire Support Base, Hill-30. I flew into a hornets nest at FSB-30, when we arrived, we saw two PT-76 within the perimeter wire, and NVA troops everywhere; The Airborne 2nd Battalion troops survivors had consolidated in the command bunkers at the center of the camp and were fighting hard to keep the NVA at bay. Our two gun-ships fired some ordinance and then supported two Magic 8 and 9 with new type of tank killing missile. When we'd expended all our fired power, we returned again to Khe Sanh to once again re-arm and re-fuel. We then launched back out on our four combat mission of the day, returning Khe Sanh.

After took off from Khe Sanh, we were asked to escort a re-supply Magic 8, 9 Huey helicopters into Hill-30 [FSB-30] low level on the tree-tops. We approached the Hill-30 with guns blazing, ours and theirs. In my pilot seat, my copilot adjusted his chicken plate again. I was firing pairs of rockets. At the same time, we were engaged by numerous enemy small arms and anti-aircraft weapons as we continued inbound. Two helicopters, Magic 8 and 9 successfully completed its critical mission among the columns of smoke. These helicopters came to a very brief hover, kicked off the ammo boxes and lifted out. We turned to cover their departure in strafing in-front of them with spew 4,000 rounds per minutes. Now we could see so many vertical column smokes around the base. One U.S helicopter grounded on the helipad due to get hit from the fragmentations just yesterday. So now VNAF must take on charge in limited missions affordable meanwhile U.S air cavalry gave up. I don't blame our fellow U.S aviators because there wasn't their country but ours.

Right after the Hill-31 was overran by five enemy regiments. Colonel Battreall recalled, he saw a badly shaken U.S air cavalry squadron commander describe the horrendous antiaircraft defenses surrounding Tchepone and recommended against the planned airmobile assault there.

Colonel Ray Battreall was being throughout the operation deficiencies at high command levels continued to undermine the abilities and performance of ARVN' troops. Battreall, a very experienced officer who watched most of this firsthand from I Corps Forward at Khe Sanh, later provided some useful insight into the challenges confronting General Lam, I Corp and Lam Son 719 commander. For responding the challenge General Lam pondered for a moment and then replied, "No, we have B-52s. We will use them, and then we will go. And so it happened," said Battreall. "The antiaircraft was obliterated and several meters of dirt blown off the tops of the ridges, exposing what had been underground warehouses. The 1st Infantry Division assaulted almost unopposed and methodically destroyed everything of military value before commencing what turned out to be a bloody and hard-fought withdrawal. It took real guts for Lam to make that decision, and he made it quite alone with no U.S advisor twisting his arm. Whatever he did before or after cannot detract from that moment".

General Lam counted on B-52 and President Thieu would like one U.S Division joining with South Vietnamese troops; these two expectations were adversely affected by Permanent Government due to violate the Rules Of Engagement and screwed-up the progressive U.S force go home plan. But now it seemed to me that such very worst situation, the Permanent Government must violate the ROE for dreaming up a grand scheme to save the honor country? I call it C-Y-A. (Cover Your Ass). From now on, so far there was appeared a secret "Linebacker" and no more "Rolling Thunder" emerged again. Linebacker was real war. You will read the next on 5 March in the dawn something so strangely happened.

If it was violated the ROE, though Seventh Air Force's pilots dropped bomb by the CIA gave ordered to the targets but bitterly the SAC commander was made a scapegoat for C-Y-A conspiracy strategy. The pretentiousness was the so called Allies forces took one significant casualty even before the main battle began. General John D. Lavelle, commanding Seventh Air Force, was found to have ordered the 'so-called' a number of pre-planned "protective reaction" strikes against in North Vietnam, thereby violating the ROE then in effect. The offensive was compounded by the fact that false reports, representing these as genuine protective reactions, were subsequently filed. Summoned home by the Air Force Chief of Staff, Lavelle was relieved of his command and retired in two-star rank. Said few critic venal-journalists, fabricating that Lavelle had "acted improperly," rules were a way of life in Vietnam. In a purely military sense, they acknowledged, some of those rules looked silly, but "if you are going to hold it together, they must be followed."

Subsequently Lavelle' successor, General John Vogt, arrived just in time for real "Linebacker" campaign, in hindsight it seemed to me – Lavelle was just played on agenda table the "Rolling Thunder" only? Likely Westmorland moving U.S troop in for "search and destroy" and Abrams moved U.S troop out.

Now, there was incredible the Hill-30 below enveloped in huge hazed smoked. I set up an overhead cap, keeping an eye out for potential threats to the vulnerable two supplied Huey-slicks as they landed and discharged their special ops cargo. I looked down at the enormous fresh earth-dust clouds kicked up by the massive heavy weight birds as they touched down on the helipad floor in the melee of dark-white shelled smoked. And I was thinking how glad I was to be up here in the clear blue sky instead of down there wrestling with that nowhere shell monster coming. I rolled out on a course direct to over above the second slick, that maybe "Magic Nine" get hit by enemy shell- fragmentations. They shut down the engine in the shape the main rotor decrease rotated and stops. All crewmen are running to "Magic Eight." No one said a word, the "Magic Eight" taking off – I automatically joined him. I checked again on the Hill-30; three choppers were already grounded there.

Suddenly Magic Two, my gun-wingman got hit, Captain Chau' neck and face all bloody by ricochet bullets when impact on the hard "chicken-plate" surface, the fragments fly back to his upper part neck and face. Don't say a word I lead him back to Khe Sanh and hurrying to airfield for Chau medical evacuation, rearmament and flight-crewmembers replacement. Now, visibility too poor, I ordered three our choppers must pulled our choppers in to about one-half rotor disk separation, maybe fifty feet, closing formation so we wouldn't lose sight of each other in the hazy light fog. I made the decision to go for some altitude on the east flank and avoid any anticipated obstacles on the forest terrain, but that just made the mountainous area harder to see in the low visibility. Yet we really had no choice but to press on. Although a little safer on the eastern flank, meanwhile the U.S artillery at Khe Sanh shelling impact only east flank on high mountains but if we climbed high enough, we'd be vulnerable to the NVA antiaircraft batteries that they were located on the high crests – their ferocious high-altitude air defense systems. The temperature rose as we flew east to Khe Sanh and luckily the mist-fog quickly dissipated. I spotted the airstrip, its black strip barely discernible beneath a blanket of shifting steam, and as we settled onto the tarmac a dense cloud of fog enveloped the choppers like the hand of a giant ghost.

"I believe the Hill-30 is on the brink of overran by numerous NVA infantry-regiments again"

After rearmament, the sun on the vertical highest position was shining and most of the fog had burned off and I grunted in the air "good afternoon" to our fellow aviators? Two heavy fired power gunships hurrying back to a crucial target – kill the 85mm mountain-gun. Racing along but different trajectory of course, on treetop to the target at level 2,400 feet high enveloped with virgin forest dark green and high trees but the only trail to come-up were clear easier detected. This artillery instead pounding indirect but now in direct killing the airborne passing the spring below them,

The earphones in my helmet hissed, "Magic Club One... Two in need your instruction for prep ...over" Magic Two radioed to me.

I responded quickly, "turn back to VHF frequency..."

"Roger, Magic One on VHF...going ahead for possible mission"

"When we're over the Mobile Command-Post, Magic Two flying over friendly force, meanwhile I manipulate gain altitude by easy get altitude on the clusters of intertwining ridges on ranch-mountain to farther north of the crest peak. Remembering when I reached at 4,000 feet and behind the 85mm gun, then I contact with you and this critical time you prepare to strike, but you would never gain altitude at above 2,700 feet. This space for safety when I dive the bird

The New Legion

in 60 degrees diving like fighter-bomber for the effectively of special rockets nail-arrows; and this time you keep little up or parallel altitude 2,400 feet and shot four by four 17 pounds rockets direct to tunnel. This time all the bastards were paralyzed or became disable to shot into your chopper. However I still orbit on the spot and spew two mini-guns with 4,000 round 7mm 62 to cover you at 3,100 feet higher. Everything O.K… you got this?"

This tactical mission was strange to NVA troops, because that the first time what I have said applies only to this particularly circumstances. I rolled out my gunship started climbed up slowly on the left clusters of intertwining ridges to the higher ridge forming the crest-peak that gave the hill target spot its designation by height in meters 750 meters (2,400 feet) I use this tactical flight for screening their eyes to farther behind them. I suddenly 'cow-boy' racing high airspeed up, raised helo nose to decrease airspeed over the target spot, abruptly used right rudder-pedal to lower the helo-nose, take a high angle diving approach so deep akin to plunge strafing, simultaneously two mini-guns spewing at 4,000 rounds per minute and two by tow rockets busted down into the target. Friend and foe could see the orange-red smoked behind my gunship after strafing, I pressed the trigger, knowing my gunners as the barrels on both flanks of the cockpit spat flame and buzzed like chain saws, their heavy bullets punching down to the 85mm gun-target. I don't think kill them but at least neutralization in disable for my wingman destroyed him later – orbit over target still spewing at 2,000 rounds per minute.

Quickly I Said "Magic Two…now been on your prep turn… over" I have been orbit over the target for two mini-guns firing smoothly like they were brand new out of the box over the target appeared like 'red-frog-mouth' battery stronghold.

Quickly I said, "Magic-Two everything quite… no enemy respond…your turn – over"

Now I flied back above Magic Two – our ground-airborne troops absolutely confident. I so pleased my wingman strafing 80 percent right on the target. And I led copilot took control. I took the last cigarette in my zipper pocket and enjoyed the last happier cigarette. I saw Magic Two four rocket a time and continued progressively strafing into the tunnel, no second explosion but surely all were destroyed.

The Company Airborne Commander thanked so much for our outstanding strike, that Company very soon joining with their own 8th Battalion. I don't know all the bastards were killed or not. But no one could continue shot down into our troops crossing the spring now.

All of a sudden, a loud hissing noise in my earphones on "guard frequency"

"I get hit…autorotation forced landing uh..uh King-Star Four… Crackle-crackle-crackle."

My reaction reflected I knew that King-Star 4 and 5 mission supplies and evacuation at LZ Hotel (Hong-Ha) because U.S Army Aviation turned down to fly on vulnerable zone such as Fire Support Bases because two accuracy indirect guns 152mm and 120mm mortars were already preset right on their coordinated targets. Two U.S helicopter, one CH-53 Stallion, and one OH-6 were just shot down there. When enemy hear the noise of helicopter coming they pounding shells right away. NVA batteries over there waiting for Tank T.54 and armored carrier PT.76 for bloody attacked assaults; However the copilot of King-Star 4 always contacted with me for monitoring. I'm impatient for two HUI-G Cobras gunship for their air cover. Cobra lead them at high altitude 5,000 feet, reminded me to reconsider my concerning for shot down by ground fire. When King Star start go down. I'm wonder so worrying. That's right shortly in my earphones I hear

"Ground fire…ground fire in the 'Guard frequency'"

King-Star copilot radioed to me that the two Cobras rolled out leaving us to prep on the antiaircraft position; they shot the rockets with red-orange smoked behind them. I saw left too many pieces of clouds AAAs in the middle sky and two Cobras just flied away now these piece-buns of cloud all over around us.

I reacts what yours guy reactions? I couldn't hear the muffled voice of his copilot, but mostly I just heard the constant whir of my own blades above and the altering tone of the turbo jet engine as I worked the controls.

The New Legion

The earphones in my helmet hissed, "Magic One ... we are in besiege with hundred indirect shells of the enemy pounding on LZ, we tried touch down as quick as we can for unloading the supplies. .. Oh my crew-chief get wounded hit... " Crackle-crackle-crackle

At this point, all Fire Support Bases were isolated by paralyzed pounding from NVA artillery. I knew I was no longer invincible. I could feel my heart thumping in my chest. In the space of few moments, so I couldn't even imagine what they might do to my crewmembers. The images of mutilation that flashed into my mind terrified me. I don't know what the hell happened out there. There were not utter a word. Many people may not understand my feelings and indeed it is difficult to express them accurately. Earlier yesterday the Hill-31 was overran, I didn't know the plight of our H-34 crewmembers died or wounded. In the course of this Vietnam War's history, hundreds, perhaps thousands, of my fellow American aviators and flight-crews had been shot down and captured by Communist Hanoi. The most was of this Lam Son operation, according from SOG reports: 219 killed and 38 MIA, respectively were aircrews. Up North, they had parachuted into the waiting arms of the people of North Vietnam, been hunted down by the minority tribe-men, been used as pawns by the KGB endured years of torment in Hanoi-Hilton. Few of them had escaped, few had lost their youth through years of captivity, and few had never come home. And from the moment of each one's capture, each had surrendered his future to the unknown. None had known when or if they would see freedom again.

Now I let my copilot took control for leading formation and impatiently I tried monitoring at LZ Hotel activity.

"Yelling in my helmet, Lieutenant Phuc got hit at his left leg and shut down the engine because his chopper was been serious damage by fly-shelling, the red warning lights appearing most in the instrument panel. We will run to the bunker closer..." Crackle crackle-crackle.

I couldn't hear anything else except the noise of M-60 machine gun roaring sound in my helmet.

"Magic One, this is King-Star 5... I must escaped run away as far as possible because enemy pounded shells everywhere on the LZ. I hover for rescue King-Star 4's crews but couldn't see in the blindness except earth dust and shell carbon-smoked and some huge U.S Army helicopters grounded there too, suddenly the crew chief yelling he is wounded, and the crewmen of King-Star 4 could came out because heavy incoming shell-impact of enemy artillery nowhere... Now we continued climbing..."

I am worrying so much because they are young rating pilots and did know the antiaircraft situation over there. "Climbing higher is the way of suicidal tendencies". If they flied "cow-boy" like mine maybe escaped. But too late now I kept quite, don't let them over excited – I am just impatient waiting the worst will happened, I'm praying for them. I'm right with my experience, the antiaircraft everywhere on the relief convergence strafing to alone bird continued climbing. There one can see the earth dust blown meant AAAs have been shooting up to only target aircraft slowly climb. You could see the network of red tracers every direction from mountain flank rocketed up to the lonely bird.

Unfortunately, one red tracer hit right in the transmission and flash-exploded, (maybe 37mm) flame and smoke enveloped the cabin and cockpit, Lieutenant Dat tried spontaneously down to collective control pitch and cyclic for properly air speed for making autorotation in the hollow of a small valley to manipulate as closer the Hotel Base as good.

On Guard frequency, "May day...may day...King-Star 5 forced landing at northeast LZ Hotel (Fire Support Base Hong Ha-2, this stronghold was dominated by 3rd Regiment/1st Division, the crest of the Hill was about 600 meters above sea level, inside Laos about 20 kilometers, but there was the deep throat of Ho Chi Minh Trail; naturally sooner NVA troops had would destroyed. This Base had two helicopter-pads; the closer near bunkers was LZ for hook-up artillery and water truck container, and nets hook-up. U.S Aviation refused to fly because they got heavy casualties. At the LZ for 155mm howitzer one CH-53 Stallion the color dark-green-USMC grounded there and beside him was one more helicopter OH-6)

In the enveloped of smoke and flame Lieutenant Dat tried as soon as touch the ground before the bird exploded. He opened his eyes broader...broader making for the safe touch down to the nearest LZ Hotel if possible lower in the deep small valley; abruptly the forest emerged and tall trees bigger...bigger, at last he flared up and felt on the bushes of little inclined slope. The sound hit the ground was absorbed by small threes and two skid spring up to the floor. So the crewmen could easy out by step on the humidity dew-grass and scurrying the wounded peoples out of the bird. The gunner screamed silence in his heart, he did not utter a word, and he tried very hard not to groan or cry out with the incredible pain; he should know a long struggle glooming ahead. He did not want to remind these fellow comrades that he was still their living, breathing his nemesis, a creature of loathing whose could be made to suffer further for their losses.

When everyone reaching an easier way safety space, the J.P-4 from the fuel tank leaking flow joint the flame and instantly the helicopter exploded spread-smoked and flame come up to the sky in huge vertical column about 100 feet high.

"Thank God everyone survived. Now what happened for next?"

Lieutenant Dat was recently a platoon commander in the infantry, now he led the team with pistol P.38s for self-defense. Seeking way back to the Hotel Fire Support Base that everyone could easier identified on the hill referenced higher, where the smoke still in burning was permanently at present there. Truly, they're aviators never familiar with this scenery mountainous jungle. When you're out there in the jungle, you're in a strange, new world – a world that feels untouched by aviator flight crewmembers... totally alien. Nothing seems familiar. You have a real sense of uncertainly about what might confront you. There were constant surprises. And even though they went in with savvy, experienced companions, they always felt as though they were on their own. The jungle does that to you... it makes you feel solitary.

Their run-away in the jungle was known as escaped from the prison by their bold determination. The jungle was too dense for suitable camouflage. They had to literally hack their way through vines and thick foliage, couldn't moving fast just very slowly with the wounded gunner, mostly few peoples-sized. Now they started to learn a great deal about jungle craft, intruding, tactics, and the most survival from the skilled how to run away quietly through rugged terrain of the jungle surrounded by enemy. They wouldn't actually hope to encounter with large numbers of the NVA troops, but surely they knew they were about there. Here NVA infiltration routes, or base camps or other places they might be using as sanctuaries; and the run-away team was frequently found unoccupied NVA position – often clever bunkers tunneled under thick bamboo clumps, providing them with a natural cover. There they found the camouflage entrance to a large underground complex. NVA were masters at constructing well-hidden underground tunnel systems.

Even proceeding too slow, but suddenly Lieutenant Dat makes sight to stop: crossing danger areas such as stream and clearing, setting up ambushes; in the jungle, it wasn't only the enemy you had to worry about; other dangers could easily strike, on a tree foliage revealed a gigantic snake curled on around the branch a few feet above them – a twelve-foot python with a big bulge in his middle. She was full, no harm. They always crossed clearings carefully, as danger area. But fortunately, the heavy canopy and ground cover kept them from suffering casualties, but they knew it was only a matter of time before their luck ran out. When they started moving, they got there, where a wide red dirt muddy patch of ground covered with fresh boot prints – lots of sneaker-tread NVA boots. A big NVA unit maybe regiment sized had recently moved through.

They were hurrying up to climb over the inclination slope vines and bushes, passing a clump of dense shrubbery. The sharp pointed on the stem of certain bushes with thorns hedge or scrub causing difficulty in moving, but thorny problem was never stopping them in proceeding. Physical courage is often more difficult than moral courage, having lost all physical feeling or the power to feel because they went numb with terror.

They stopped under thick foliage for break and thought a long way was passing but the truth just a half mile really. Now they took turn help the wounded moved little bite faster, they thought very close to the Hotel Base but still far away from them in the dip hollow valley. When they reached at the high clear point they discovered the Hotel Base above them about half mile and still smoke haunted above. They turned back and saw the column smoke of their bird still evolutionary upward processes. The temperature rose created terrible water thirsty, exhausted, no choice they must continued climb cross the rock and vine-bushes, running more thorns, prickles into their faces, necks and ears, kept moving.

Suddenly, on the crest mountain some sounds of AK.47 firing down to them, the North Vietnamese voice shouted, "Surrender be alive or run away be killed" They repeated many times,

"Captured them ...the dead helicopter pilots" NVA troops shouted again and again.

Once again they were hurrying up climb up much faster – three men carrying the wounded. They climbed a middle of the hill. They can smell the rotten remains of NVA troops. A numerous body remains scattered everywhere with B.41 and AK 47, by group of four or six peoples. They were subjected shattered by Bombs and friendly 155s fragmentations. The NVA motto-oath was "born at North died at South". That outcome due to many throngs of attack to Hotel Base – For

Pity's sake, please stop the war! They knew they had no choice, no hope and they went ahead and just died. In the way my thought was very emotional – "that what is going on now is just a lot of unnecessary killing".

Reaching at 200 meters from Hotel Base perimeter, Lt Dat hold the team on the spot there, slumped down on the floor soil for relax with plenty happiness. Crashing the airplane burned and exploded but then O.K and survived arriving to friendly spot; that was hard and unthinkable, thank God! Should they deserve for rescue, who tell it... Dat, he well knew the claymore mines and grenades sowed somewhere who knew, little bite far up they saw different kind of helicopters shot-downed there likely helicopter-cemetery.

A soldier of 3rd Regiment/1st Division yelled with lousy but nice voice flowing in the wind "Hold and free your position!" Because 3rd Regiment men could saw them under the lower of valley recently, "we sent people down to guide your peoples into bunkers right away"

One soldier slowly come down avoiding the mine-field and guided the team to the nearest bunker with the sound of clapped hands. This 3 pm o'clock afternoon, two flight crewmembers embraced with overjoyed whishes. The most important messenger was confirmed one helicopter from 213th Squadron will coming pick up two crewmen. All they were prayed for waiting a saver from northeast.

I couldn't leave air support to Airborne for rescue them because the situation down there so much worst and complicated, two NVA regiments attacked one strayed airborne element and overran on the spot. Now I must find them out and guiding them joint with his related battalion. They were never released us till salvo all armament and go back Khe Sanh for rearmament. In my mind I should spare time to escort a slick to Hotel Base for rescued them immediately. This morning count on the heavy pea soup fog, I intended to see General Dong, Airborne Division commander and complain about the sick-sight of airborne-men deserters mobbing our helicopters and hanging from skid and filled over on board as result of two H-34 were over weight and then been shooting down by indirect artillery fragmentations. "Airborne hold us like the hostages."

General Dong responded by closed his mouth in the pale face with madness. He knew why and he told me before this operation commenced. He knew this is the Big-Trap for us. I understood his position so I get out of his sight immediately.

Today was on 27 February 1971, all Fire Support Bases were isolated by enemy artillery that left the bases suffer from paralysis of the aerial supplies. The U.S Aviation was no more fly-supply except VNAF must be on charge. So I ordered our choppers don't touch the ground, just hovering lower enough they can put in the wounded and throw down the ammunitions supplies.

Subsequently, all the Fire Base must withdraw due to 152mm enemy-guns destroyed all 105s and 155s of ARVN. All the Bases were just only the target for preset coordinated by 152mm guns, these gun pounding so much accuracy so why none of ARVN guns could in commission or be destroyed.

One week passed, all fired bases support were under-pressure of various artilleries such as: rockets 122mm, 107mm Katyusha, 85mm, 100mm, 122mm, and 130mm guns, that special 120mm mortars which were the helicopters big-killers, and 152mm guns were big-killers to ARVN artilleries. The Bases didn't have water, none food, no ammunitions. The Regiment Commander makes decision withdraw to night prior to NVA tanks coming. Though very close to the Base, some F-4 Phantoms and F-105 Thunder-chiefs were forward air control to strike around the suspect artilleries by FAC of OV-10 Bronco. And now they have strike on the bird King-Star 5 for destroyed. Two crewmembers peered from the bunkers at their bird was flashed in flame impatiently. Suddenly, one F-4 got shot burned with smoked below the wing. They abandoned the aborted mission and heading to Udorn AFB, Thailand.

My field-X.O (Operation Officer) at Khe Sanh was Major Ky who was the braved officer that I'd never see before; he was not only a fanatic about mission preparation, but a damn good stick as well. We can live with the fact of knowing he should died to save another men rather than had he died from a random bullets shot from a hidden source. If you knew Major Ky you would know that he was a very quiet and unselfish man. He always put others first and therefore Ky truly loved what he did and had God given him the choice of how to die I know deeply in my heart he would have chosen to go down if just as he did. So why I always closer with him trying get a chance for him promotion; He knew so well in the past for saving the lives of SOG recon-team that I flown so many rescue missions alone without copilot and crewmen. Yet in spite of my sometimes obsessive personality, this situation is never resolved quickly, I thought. You can create a psychological roller coaster in your mind that'll devastate you. I could guess Ky's struggling for save two flight crewmembers to take that risk?

Recently, at 2: 00 PM today, General Lam issued the orders no helicopters landing at LZ Hotel, Hill-30 due to enemy already had coordination fired preset, we don't want the risk in vain, that's enough for various kind of helicopters been crashed over there. So why I couldn't utter a word-ordered to Ky – But Ky felt a slight pricking sensation in his thought, the crewmen tried their best survive to reach at Hotel Base, they should be deserved for rescue by Lord of God will help. Following these enemy situations in most everyday, I deadly certain the NVA will wait till the Tanks coming from Northwest to reinforce and cover infantry assaults. Now they were just tried isolated the Hotel Base and cut the supplies by air…and waiting – sometimes they took turn for pounding different kind of shells in neutralized intimidation ARVN troop. They're planning attack Hill-

30 maybe tonight just I guess. I had had see many column of PT.76s hurry convergent to this Fire Support Base. They have three Tank-Regiments involved this operations but in the last few days, they were destroyed by E.C-130B killed-hunting one regiment. And the enemy was paying a heavy price, MACV estimated that "B-52 alone [for the war-game counterweight compensation] were inflicting losses that were the equivalent of about one combat effective NVA regiment per week." The NVA infantry any price must wait for PT-76, they tried in temptation attack many times but fail. Although as much my knowledge but I could not pushed Ky. However Ky had knew my background Recon-team rescued in Project Delta Force in the most very hot LZ, likely the 559th Group Forward Base headquarters not to far from here, the SOG called 'Oscar-Eight'; northern Ashau' Tam-Boi mountain contained immense chambers hewn from solid rock, so well constructed that they withstood B-52 strikes. Where General Vo-Bam, commander 559th Transportation Group's forward – the Ho Chi Minh trail's Control Center.

As a commanding officer I prophesied that Major Ky would be the only rescued saver. We tried accomplished this air close support and requested go back to Khe Sanh for rearmament. On the way back home base, I peered up at the sky, looking for any sign of the mysterious A.C-130 Spectra gunship was supposed to be orbiting overhead for cover Hill-30, but there was no sign of that either. I looked down at the calm and eerily silent forest of Laotian. It seemed as though nothing was happening. There was no visible activity on the ground. Then the huge flight of AC-130 appeared above me on the blue sky. It was an absolutely awesome sight as that train of massive cargo craft passed so close above us. Suddenly too many antiaircraft artilleries opened up with everything they had, included A.K-47 too. Thousand of red-tracers from batteries started raking across the sky. My sergeant Duc has an abrupt reacted manner, he opened his 4,000 rounds strafing direct into a ZSU-2 double-barreled antiaircraft gun been firing up at the A.C-130s, its heavy 23mm shells lancing past the wings of the lumbering birds. But I knew she had to be taking hits from that gun. Thank to my gunner Duc who spat blowing rainy 7mm 62 bullets pounded the position and the antiaircraft gun stopped firing immediately.

The New Legion

This eerily zone reminded me in the beginning of this operation, a Magic Club 14 was shot down right here. I shot rocket burned POL pipe lines down there and I was downed by enemy PT-76 with 14,5mm cartridges due to a low pass stupid confused M-113 but P.T-76. Big mistake I must pay because not distinguish foe and friend. I recalled that afternoon, after got a lot of hits, the nose of my helicopter immediately started to spin to the right. The tail rotor on a UHI-H counters the torque created by the main rotor system, and the pedal control the pitch of the tail rotor maybe fail hydraulic pressure or the tail rotor blades tear up. As I passed through the first ninety degrees of rotation, I instinctively countered with left pedal, and I knew we'd lost it. I'll never forget looking down the floor to make sure I was pushing the pedal, and seeing my boot jammed all the way to the floor. My body was reacting properly, but my bird was not. I keyed the mike.

"Magic…Two… we has lost the tail rotor…we're going in hard… forced landing"

Too close with the ground, I was referring to the engine, because the only way to counter that spin was to shut it down and eliminate the torque. But just as the manual book describes such an emergency, if you don't kill the engine right away the centrifugal force will make it physically impossible to reach up for the power control levers. I'd always thought that sounded a little extreme. It wasn't. I make a forced landing at once. The chopper's windshield was almost completely gone, no skids in both sides; miraculously, I was just getting out straight-ahead from my chopper's nose. All crewmen scurrying out, and instantly Magic Two landed and pick up everyone to Khe Sanh. Miraculously, we're all be saved by God!

At the Khe Sanh airstrip, the refuel and rearm point, I said over internal channel

"Crew chiefs, One and Two loaded all nail-arrows rockets and 12,000 rounds ammo"

I hissed into my mike "Magic Two…we will escorted and air cover Major Ky first…you got it?"

"Magic-Two roger, Sir,"

Now 4: 00 pm at Hotel Fire Support Base, the temperature rose up, two crewmembers were exhausted, thirsty, nobody give them a drop of water. The TOC at Khe Sanh let us know Ky on the way to LZ Hotel for mission rescue. Down the command-post of 3rd Regiment at Hotel Base, having ordered from General Lam, "praised help two crewmembers come back to Khe Sanh in safety without chaotic"

Two crewmen were excited forget hungry, thirsty, thorn and prickle sore or itch. At the northern sky, the sound of helicopter exerting the rescue hope, these aviators peered up from one bunker at the northern sky, looking for a lonely mysterious UHI-H from Magic Club 213th Squadron. I seemed to have the gift of prophecy that Ky would fly this mission impossible for rescued our fellows, now it's true history of knowing he would died to save another eight men rather than had he died from a random bullet shot from a hidden source.

His chopper seemed a hen tried broader her wings to protect her chic from predator eagles.

The lonely aircraft plunged into the network antiaircraft artillery drawing the hero scenery of VNAF' history forever no one forgettable, he knew how to step over by his flying experience. He flied over the treetop to LZ Hotel but not direct from Khe Sanh to there. His simple flight maneuver is deceptive. He came to LZ Hotel not like from Khe Sanh but in opposite direction meant at south of LZ Hotel. The wind was strong blowing from the sea letting his chopper sound almost quietly. However when he was on the LZ, NVA could detected by high relief surrounding.

Secretly he was flown crisscrossing over the high virgin-trees, no human activities. But unfortunately when he hover right LZ Hotel, a thousand preset-coordinated shelling pounding on him – a instant before that Ky observed like a ghost camp base, eerily calm, but now so terrible everywhere were smoked, earth dust, smell all CO_2 gas. Too many high columns smoke as huge Cumulonimbus cloud enveloped the LZ. He couldn't see many different kinds of choppers grounded there. His chopper shaking after each flashed explosive. He must left now to a safe area mean high trees at western, think it over…over. He contacted with 3rd Regiment control post to see Lieutenant Dat.

The New Legion

After a good reference, clear detail information, identification the bunker for pick-up, Ky said exactly TOT four minutes all crewmen must ready in that bunker. Now Ky started fly back on treetop crisscrossing, abruptly hovered put right skid on sand bags revetment. About 10 seconds everyone climbed on the cabin, three wounded first and the rest after. With no choice Ky took off down-wind with heavy load, diving down to valley he lower the nose of helo for gaining airspeed. When the chopper was airborne, they detected five deserted soldiers already on board. Now the LZ Hotel Base submerged with flashed and smoked peering by behind their eyes. Many individual rifles fired on the air like fire cracker meanwhile Ky burst out laughing. In the air now like haven from the hell on ground; Chopper flied faster over the treetop, disappeared and appeared in the evening haze. "That by afternoon the setting sun would be sinning through so much smoke and dust that you couldn't see it."

At Khe Sanh airstrip we took off for Ky escorted by air cover. The formation rose up through its own enormous cloud of rotor-wash dust. As I made my way back to operational area, when TOC informed that we heard Ky accomplished his rescue mission. We are so proud of our Squadron motto *"never left our crews in the enemy hand though died or alive."* Whereas the Army says it never leaves behind its wounded; the Marines say they never leave behind their dead.

Two gun-ships with heavy armament hurrying back to airborne operational zone. The evening swept in quickly, draining the sunlight from my cockpit and replacing it with dark, gloomy shadows. On the blue sky, above us at 11 o'clock was the Ky chopper from LZ Hotel heading back to Khe Sanh with both crewmembers on board. We were almost overjoyed to see him passing above us. I like to meditate before an important example as my meditations on the besieged causing of the axe of evil craps.

Every going back to the operational area, each time, I must challenged different direction like to sew threads of a bamboo-basket or fishing net covering the area about 60 squared kilometers. Crucially I should intimated familiar with foe and friend situation. Eight NVA artillery regiments and six antiaircraft regiments situated where and nowhere in their tunnels that I could located. Along the bottom of valley closer the spring, stony-creek, or stream where the forty-round salvos of 122-mm Katyusha rockets pounded to Fire Support Bases, not accuracy but real intimidation. The mobile antiaircraft device as PT-76 were well camouflage in the middle of crest brought a lot of risk to our choppers by equipped ZSU-2 double-barreled antiaircraft gun with its heavy 23mmm shells lancing past our chopper transmission. Along the west flanks of mountain range where some cleared enough-area to positioned 152 guns, that big killer to our artillery 105s, 155s; the duds from these penetrated five feet into earth. Disguising in the tunnel, I can detected only while they were firing by huge of blowing earth dust over them. The NVA regiment equipped with 120mm mortar so precisely and numerous burst in an extremely large fragmentation pattern so why our choppers must crashed right on the LZ by their fragments.

Suddenly I detected underneath of dark foliage, a gloomy-convoy looked like elephants with their tugs swinging left to right, up and down: a dark column Tank T.54 and PT-76 make queue line up hurrying to Hill-30. We missed a change to destroy them because we were armed with nail-arrow-rockets to very mission rescue. However I decide to strafing into them, at least we killed the gunners.

"Magic-Two… your ready for prep … over"

"Okayto…Roger that"

We make wide pattern prep-attack, distance 10 seconds. There were so strange no tanks responded or played back some fire powers. They rushed forward in contempt of our stupid strafing? Of course they did welcome our orange-smoked color though tease-looking pleasing their eyes. I felt damn shame in vain and ordered "O.K we relieved them… racing to Airborne for fired cover. They will have to reach as soon as they can for the next assault attack on the Hill-30.

What come next! The fate of Hill-30

How managing to reinforce by tanks covered! The terrain also made it extremely difficult for track vehicles to be sent to help. Whilst the NVA utilized heavy T-54 tanks, the 1st Armor Brigade [ARVN always outgunned] only had a squadron of M-41 tanks, the other vehicles being M-113, armored personnel carriers. Compounding

The New Legion

the problem was the fact that the ARVN did not know the terrain well, and had misjudged the tactical of the enemy tanks. After this fiasco, Corps hurriedly sent another tank squadron to reinforce the area around Route 9. Whereas the enemy anti-aircraft activities were very intense, making life very difficult to provide air supplies, air support and medevac. Wounded soldier were stranded at the base for days. Helicopters could not land, so ammunitions had to be dropped by parachutes. As a result the morale of the soldiers plummeted. While supporting ground troops, an American aircraft was gunned down. All air support immediately ceased in order to rescue the landed aircraft. The NVA benefited from this, and their attacks met with more success.

After FSB 31 fell to the enemy, they drove on toward FSB 30. This position was quit high and the terrain was very different to that at FSB 31. Only the northeast side was suitable for an assault. The other three sides had near vertical drops. Thank to the suitable topography, and to good defenses the 2nd Airborne Battalion was able to repulse the NVA. Faced with such resistance and high morale; The NVA abandoned the suicidal tactics, and chose instead to pound the position with 120mm mortar rounds, whilst they waited for an opportunity. Toward the end of the week, supplies were running low, bunkers were nearly all flatted and practically all artillery guns 105s, and 155s were destroyed. The 2nd Airborne Battalion had to abandon the base in the dead of night to retreat to the 1st Airborne Brigade's area of responsibility at FSB A-Loui. Why wait to fall likely Hill-31?

Significantly putting eye on it, the main arterial route from A-Loui to the Laotian Border, once so busy, was approached by the enemy, who erected posts to block supplies and evacuation of the wounded. No problem, Colonel James Vaught [the so called his advisory the Airborne Division] should take care about that. "The ARVN' heavy casualties …that enough… always outgunned Garant M1 against AK47, T-41 against T-54, none anti tank weapon like B-40, 41 against T-54…" From now on, on behalf of "Permanent Government" meant General Haig representative, Colonel Vaught managed switched the air campaign from Rolling Thunder became Linebacker meant "air ground closed support" from friend 400 meters by Arc light tactical

B-52. Consequently, with his cover guaranty our friend troop forces retreat in safety condition to Khe Sanh.

In last week, at Hill-30, the C-Battery/44th Artillery Battalion of 155s fired support covered all mutual friend troop stronghold; the most power-fired support to Hill-31 on 23/February where was B-Battery/44 detachment to 3rd Airborne Brigade. When NVA regiments attacked Hill-31 they pounded shells to Hill-30 and Captain B-battery commander advised fired over the top of the Hill-31 due to a large enemy forces support by Tanks and armored carriers. After Hill-31 was overran by enemy. The Hill-30 would be the next target I guessed. Now A-loui, Lao Bao, and Khe Sanh Fire Support Bases fired cover to Hill-30 from East and Southeast, batteries /44/ /Battalion included 42 pieces artillery from the border of U.S fire-power some time intercepted.

Tonight, 24 February that column Tanks continued flared high beam up and down by terrain-shapes. The Hill-30 became isolated – no friendly force at northwest and northeast, enemy occupied a large terrains after there were destroyed all their cargo by two 39 and 21 Ranger Battalions. At 23 till 24:00 the eerily silence cover the earth, no strange sound around Hill-30 where one full of braved 2nd Airborne Battalion prevailed in the foxholes.

At 0: 30, 27/February the East side of Camp perimeter was under pressure with large crawled enemy to the fence of barbed wire and another throng rushing behind PT-76s flared-up high-beam going up and down. Unfortunately, the ARVN were not equipped the weapon antitank.

Airborne, Colonel Thach ordered: *"Be vigilant against enemy attack…to fighter harder and never surrender…either winning all or losing all."*

Along with Vietnamese Marine, the Airborne comprised the National Strike Force – "fire brigades" that were only committed to action where was a critical threat or military emergency. The airborne brigade consequently saw action in all the corps-tactical-zones in South Vietnam during the war as well as in Cambodia and Laos, building a reputation as tough, courageous fighters and superb light infantry. They also had a reputation as a powerful political force whose support was necessary for any Vietnamese leader

The New Legion

who aspired to seize or hold power. Obviously, they were much respected and admired by the Vietnamese people (anyone wearing their camouflage uniform – including my fellow Americans – was customarily honored in cities, towns, and villages throughout the South Vietnam). And they traditionally marched at the head of the military formation in Vietnam's annual National Day Parade, a place of honor that had to be earned each year from combat performance. A very different reaction came from areas controlled by the Vietcong – further confirmation of the respect they command.

-Many enlisted men had been wounded, and most suffered from bouts of malaria. All had seen friends and comrades die in battle. Yet they were by no means grim; they looked for every opportunity to let loose their lively spirits and sense of humor. They were irrepressible practical jokers, never losing a chance to pull somebody else's chain – yet never cruelly or meanly. It was always to share a laugh and not to cause pain.

-The Officers were no less tough, and no less lively. But they had also received serious professional training at the Vietnamese equivalents of U.S military academies, all graduating near the top of their class. Like their enlisted men, they spent more time in action in the field than at home bases. This experience had honed most of them into tactically competent leaders whose small unit kills and technical proficiency were exceptional; they all tended to lead from the front. Many older officers were highly decorated with both Vietnamese and American awards for heroism.

Captain battery commander at Hill-30 manipulated four 155s fixed target on the entry path from the helipad down to the first perimeter of the camp, because there was the only way they could come. Number 2 and 3 tried the best at direction 5,800 of 6,000 mm, standby in readiness fired direct at the foot of hill. Number 1 ready for illuminated in case flare-ships AC-130 leaving or in case needed. Number 6 axed at southeast, down to the valley in direct shooting. The Captain 155s battery commander also ordered everyone preparedness for retreat out of here with his situation-experiences, burned all classified document, ready the special grenades for destroy our guns, becoming the reliable infantrymen..

Colonel Thach Airborne Brigade Executive Officer, J-2 contacted with liaison officer 320 and requested artillery fired cover from B/44 battery at A-loui to west to south from close to the Hill-30; B/44 at Lao Bao, A/44 at Phu Loc will cover at North and Northeast of the camp. Liaison officer 320 maybe on board of AC-130 flare-ship requested U.S 175 Long-tom artilleries at Khe Sanh for cover.

At Khe Sanh, coming from chow-room as late had been ate a full moon left an eerie glow across the mountainous area. In time, I would develop into an experienced veteran who could remain focused in the madness of a firefight. The sounds and flashed from the weapons would tell me what types were firing, at what distances, and how many there were (8-inch howitzers, 175mm, and 155s guns) Sure enough, around that midnight, the whole area erupted with fire. But about internal at this point, all I heard was a cacophony of noises, flashes, and blasts. I dove back into the tent and slipped under my poncho liner inside military cote. Of course I could able to sleep that got my personnel aviator attention. Excited to be getting into a close-quarters firefight for the first time, I carefully laid out my M-16 and harness, even I was a flight personal, figuring out how I would roll out of my poncho liner, grab my riffle and gear, and come up ready to shoot. "May God protect the innocent and the ignorant airman?"

Suddenly, having the report from the stronghold at eastside "enemy was closed at 500 meters Colonel Thach ordered: "Patiently waiting till close, aimed at right middle of two headlights."

100 per cent must be P.T-76 could climbing up the hill, now was just 1000 meters from the 155s guns aim-axed. These only weapons can knock them down.

Shortly, the Vietnamese language sounded from AC-130 Spectra repeated many times at PRC-25 channel to the commander of Hill-30 (headquarters of 2nd Airborne Battalion)

"At North, North-East appeared two P.T-76 and many throng infantrymen behind them.

"The fates of Hill-30 will be the same with Hill-31?" I thought

Two P.T-76 appeared at direction 200 were targeting at between two headlights. Unfortunately the battery at Hill-30 didn't have the warhead "Heat", so they used the warhead delay for direct shooting

The New Legion

(each warhead having two setting positions, 'delay' or SQ (impact fast-exploded)

Over Hill-30 an AC-130 flare-ship ordered the battery commander C/44:

"93…93 you don't have 'Heat' warhead tried to switch to SQ… this is my order…over!"

The battery commander responded "This 93 whose authorizations are just stated"

"93….93 this is 11 … 11; I ordered you to apply order at once over… 93 keeping 7 patches, used delay will ricochets when impact the steel surface. Making sure lining it up at least the shells of high-explosive charges should exploded like a mini-bomb and their pressure will kill all creatures around them. The battery commander showed up the foxhole and ordered the number 4 direct shot, SQ position, lining up right the middle of headlights.

Caporal Duong Cu repeated "Number 4… direct impact… SQ… fire"

In simultaneously, number 2, 3, 6 fired directly down to barb-wired from north to west and to south. The communication became so important for them. The battery commander ordered Sergeant Bach to mount the 292 antenna to reach the 44/Artillery Battalion command post was destroyed by enemy artilleries (the cargo truck 2, 5 tons generator and antenna 292) Thank to the darkness of the night, the NVA couldn't see and they build consolidated the high 292 antenna, now the Captain battery commander could contacted with his Battalion 44 command post for new information. The order from artillery high command said 'must staying and fighting'; although anyone could easier understand this situation all 155s and 105s of the Hill-30 would be destroyed by enemy 152 mm Soviet sophisticated gun soon or later; and the Hill-30 will be completely paralyzed isolation state. Everyone soldiers over here are waiting for the order to withdrawal that was absolutely correct in logical thinking. Everyone in the Hill-30 were carefully laid out their individual M-16 and harness, figuring out how they would roll out of their foxholes, bunkers, grab their riffles and gear, and come up ready to close shoot.

The 44 Artillery Commander tell lies to their subordinates (because he wasn't the supreme commander) "Be patient, the high command plan to dispatched the Marine to assault landing to morrow morning for reinforcement at the east side from you… so be patient"

Meanwhile the Hill-30 don't have antitank guns, all mines were already exploded, shelling different from various kind of indirect came onto so accuracy by NVA adjustor their fire, bringing it down almost 80 to 90 precision on targets. The rounds were starting to hit all around the camp, focused as they were on the guns. A few minutes later, all guns on Hill-30 were smacked by artillery rounds, while earth-dust bust all around from flying shrapnel. This is the longest and bloodiest siege of the war. Meanwhile a numerous Tank 54 and PT-76 continued high beam up and down convergence to the Hill-30 to consolidate their forces.

Suddenly, at the west side of the camp, only one 105s gun of airborne was still in action it direct shot onto barb-wired many NVA soldiers were killed there; it was still fired spread along the perimeter. Now shelling came from everywhere couldn't distinguished foe or friends from flying shrapnel. But at South side. A company 1/21 Ranger Battalion depleted and staying with Airborne to protect outside of 2nd Airborne Battalion command post. The NVA regiment was almost half overrun the perimeter of the camp.

The sound had been determined that Colonel Thach yelled:

"Patiently prepare to mobilize and strike the enemy hard. Be vigilant."

One PT-76 was knocked down right the entry path near to the 2nd Airborne Brigade command post.

The AC-130 radioed back to the camp "we killed one tank… now another tank being rushed to command post. A while later AC-130 flare-ship report one more tank was destroyed in front of command post. They hold the attack for waiting reinforcement.

Now at 01:00 on date February/27/1971; The Hill-30's command post requested to hold all artilleries from A-Loui, Phu Loc, and Lao Bao, plus U.S artilleries letting for air to ground support. After about twenty minutes with a close exchange of fire, the firing trailed off and eventually ceased. The Spectra had come in high altitude,

The New Legion

bracing one flank of the high mountain as she can fired many kind of weapons including 105mm howitzer at enemy tanks and AAAs, her heavy shells pounded the enemy fired position stopped firing. When EC-130B intercepted for 2nd Airborne Battalion retreat, repeated just likely last week air closed support to 39th Ranger Battalion retreated to 21st Ranger Battalion position.

"Spectra…Spectra … Check fire! Check fire how do you read me…over"

The operation Lam Son 719's commanders were never letting the Hill-30 became the same fate of Hill-31 such as from 34 hours ago. Subsequently, why the fighter-men of Hill-30 were confident to fight at this stage, it was the effectiveness of commanders and enlisted men that would determine the outcome – either winning all or losing all… fighting hard and died on spot.

Because the slope little high causing so difficult for PT-76 climbing, the NVA commander changed the tactic assault by overwhelming by infantrymen of five regiments because the terrain was hard-tough not suitable for armor truck PT-76 to attack like FBS Hill-31.

Now Captain Hanh Executive Officer of 2nd Airborne Command post adjusted the spot-targets for Jet fighter-bombers and Cobra gun-ships. One could see the flame flashing around the camp of high explosive and white phosphorus from aircrafts, strafing and rocket runs by Cobra but not silence the NVA mortars 120mm or discourage the NVA infantry. The almost high angles of approach of fixed wing and very low strafing from Cobra and lowest UH1-H gunship of 213th Squadron were heroism maneuvers ever have in war liked Lam Son 719 in the melee of red tracers AAA. The ground camp soldiers were raised their morale

Now five NVA regiments tried to overrun but a Ranger Company/21st with a full brave 2nd Airborne Battalion could stopped them under the slope of the helicopter-pad; The NVA plunged to the concertina wired reached at helicopter-LZ. They did very best by their mortars 120mm to shut down the guns 105mm of airborne. Captain Hanh a very good forward air ground controller did the job outstanding features. The perimeter become free of claymore mines exploded and Captain Hanh should direct to adjust the air support too closer at 200 meter from the command post. The

NVA troops rather tried get closer than for less suffer casualties, but gunship/213th strafing them from prep-below the valley up the wire bared fence, trying kill all of them. This prep maneuver didn't teach in school but that the first time we did. The perfect sufficiency air-strikes were out of camp perimeter from west to east. The eyes witnessed from airborne-soldiers saw a lot NVA bodies blow up the air like the leaves on the twist-wind storm. All the rockets from Cobra help to stop the enemy throng attacks. Captain Hanh was only the hero know how to keep the maintenance stand for of Hill-30 out of the NVA hand.

The darkness was slowly cover base scene, peering at down onto helipad, under the illuminated flares our friendly troops could detect the large number of NVA infantry hidden behind the bulldozer D-4s, the heavy shell-nets and water container; That meant the enemy seized the first perimeter strong hold. In the sky the air close support were done run-out armament and they flied back to home base. Now at the second front defense, the airborne soldiers must use the claymore mine by manual and grenades and launcher grenade M-79. Only AC-130 flare-ship for air cover; sometimes the flare-ship strafing by mini-guns or 20mm canon or 40mm at 200 meters outside of the camp formed red tracers down to the slope of the hill.

Shortly, from AC-130 detected some spot of mortars 120mm at 400 meters at full north. Try used 155s to directly shot at them as soon as friendly force can. AC-130 saw the blasted spots; she will help to shut-up these mortars. One big round orbit in the air, now one can see the red-tracers from AC-130 to the ground and completely destroyed them. In reality, no one can hear the depart-sound of mortar-shells hurled by 120mm mortars. AC-130 dropped flare illuminated over the Hill-30 help our soldiers to figure out the enemy positions. From the top of the hill the airborne soldiers could see the helipad of outside the second front, a bulldozer D-4 with huge earth-blower-blade was a very good shield protection for NVA infantry men; beside was a U.S helicopter crashed there in serious damage.

Now an enemy throng advanced to the helicopter, they passed the first-front overran the helipad, used grenade burned the helicopter. One blasted noise flame and smoke exploded like daytime where

The New Legion

about lasting in couple minutes. The huge flame-thrower the hot and humidity spreading to command post, instantly NVA troops running onto the helipad behind the D-4 shield blower. However the airborne brave soldiers came out the bunker and strafing launcher grenades M-79 killed some of enemy. Now they were too closer from 80 meters from command post, they scurrying dig the foxholes on the spots. They exchanged fire from AK-47 and M-79 of our troops forming all red tracers back and forth. Fortunately the bulldozer was their perfect protection, what if the airborne soldiers used and run out the M-79s and grenades?

Now Colonel Thach ordered used 155 shell to shot direct into the D-4 bulldozer. The battery commander ordered number 4 shoot direct into bulldozer. At number 4, artillerymen tried to maximum lower the canon in prying it off to lower level.

"Ordered number 4 four-set warhead SQ… direct shot… fire" Àmzio… Àmzio… The bulldozer blown up to the air and fall back in the flame, no one brother-enemy troops alive there. The sound praising come up everywhere in the command post, praising our artillery… praising our battery, go ahead and shooting; their morale were being raising in encourage

After that Colonel Thach ordered guns 155s make clearance all obstacles around the camp meant to continue to shot in devastation such as shell-nets, two water container trailers, D-4, remain helicopter. There were unbelievable the M-79 of airborne soldiers and direct shot from 155 just about 75 meters (the effect of high explosive at maximum adjustment 1, 8 second time and set 3 with 5 white bags, that was the first time they tried get a chance) meant something different to NVA troops. Now they were discouraged to advance due to suffering high casualty. Were they defeated?

Now at 04:30 morning on February/27/1971

General Giap' troops stopped to attack maybe temporary for a while? The darkness lasting left an eerie air flowing across the mountainous area. At this point, they knew they were no longer invincible. They could feel their hearts thumping in their chests. During the longest night, they were the men in a land of no futures, without a hint of what might happen next, and they could not prepare themselves for any coming event. The firing trailed off and eventually ceased. The fighter-men crawled back under their poncho liners, some get something to eat and drink due to sore bitter throat.

The morning come in the blue sky, now at 8:00 AM but none shelling pounded on Hill-30 made them so surprisingly? Should be new tactical plan? They were defeated completely? At 8:30, Colonel Thach ordered the Ranger and Airborne tried to seize back the helipad and restored order to the camp. At 9:00 AM, a half squad airborne reached the helipad, suddenly the NVA troops shot up into the helipad, the airborne retreated into the bunker; that wasn't right place for fighting. Now the battery-men could see the NVA troops behind the VNAF grounded-helicopter in the second down helipad. This UH1-H of 213th 'Magic Club' Squadron was hit by indirect shell, grounded there in couple days ago.

Now once again the same number 4 gun direct shot into that HU-1, the flame burst in flashing killed all NVA troops in the spot. The JP-4 flowing out burned so high like a vertical column of smoke. For saving their lives and with any price they assault to our bunker or shelters to hide. "Everyone must grab your M-16 and rushed to the foxholes right away in closed fighting…come up ready to shoot." Colonel Thach ordered, the main target was the helipad one.

All riffles aimed at the helipad where the NVA troops tried assault, they started cover by AK, B40, B41, 57mm recoil determined overrun the command post. At last the unfortunate effective gun number 4 was in out commission. The B.40, 41 raining into our guns forced them rushed back to bunker shelters. The battery men jointed with Airborne and Ranger forming a strong-front holding point covered the Command-post of 2nd Airborne Brigade. Now everywhere was the sound of grenades, the burst of explosions rockets, claymore mines and every kind of weapons were certainly never quit.

The sky was bright blue, haze with high humidity, none of wind and cloud, appearing the relief of mountain crests. Now on the Hill-30 at 727 meters high level above the sea was overwhelmed by the NVA infantrymen forces. But with determination, the friendly troops tried to seize back the helipad like they felt buoyed up by the good-news; Foe and friend tried to conquer that spot like the saver on spring-bridge; thank to inside the bunker the friendly troops were step by step killed NVA troops in the open spots without protection. Suddenly only a very shell 120mm mortar pounded into the bunker inflicted some people serious wounded. The flak jacket had been useless in stopping the rounds and fragmentations, even they hated these heavy things; but it was the policy to wear them. As they peeled off the flak jacket, a bloody piece of flesh fell out. Not encouraging. Alas! How can they catch for medical evacuation in this situation? How can they have the helicopter!

After capturing and destroying FSB of Hill- 31, NVA troops continued performing with great élan to encircle and harass ARVN fire bases. North of Route-9, FSB of Hill-30 continued to bear the pressure of heavy artillery attacks each day and was cut off from the rear by an almost impenetrable air defense net. The ARVN armored task force which tried to pick up the survivors of the 3rd Airborne Battalion from FSB of Hill-31 was repeatedly engaged by NVA armor-supported infantry. South of the road, the targets of enemy encirclement were FSB Hotel 2, seven kilometers southwest of LZ, and the 2/3 and 3/3 Battalions of the 1st Infantry Division on mobile operations along Route-92 nearby. On 27 February, despite heavy air strikes which attempted to silence enemy air defense guns, a big CH-53 Sea Stallion helicopter was hit and exploded in the air while trying to sling-carry a 105-mm howitzer. It was then decided to close FSB of Hotel-2 and send the 3rd Regiment northwestward on a mission to interdict and disrupt Route-914. This plan could not be carried out immediately because there still remained a battery of 105-mm howitzers. On 3 March, in execution of the plan to enter Tchepone, the 1st Battalion of the 1st Infantry Regiment was inserted at LZ of LoLo, 13 kilometers southeast of Tchepone. The landing had met with strong enemy opposition and had been postponed twice because of additional preparations required for the landing zone, the 1/1 Battalion finally touched ground at the price of 11 helicopters shot down, 44 others hit by gunfire and two D4 bulldozers destroyed after being dropped from the air. The following day, the 1st Regiment Headquarters, the 2/1 Battalion and a battery of 105-mm howitzers were brought into LZ of LoLo FSB. Base LoLo was thus established. The 4/1 Battalion meanwhile landed at LZ of Liz, six kilometers west-northwest of LoLo. The various units then moved out to search the area but only a few light contacts were made with minor results. In the morning of 5 March, in order to continue its westward push, the 2d Infantry Regiment of the 1st Division was scheduled to occupy LZ of Sophia, four-and-a-half kilometers southwest of Tchepone at 11:00 hours but unexpected bad weather delayed the operation.

After preemptive air-strikes, at exactly 13:20 hours five UH1-Hs landed safely sporadic gunfire was received but posed no major threat. By nightfall, LZ of Sophia had eight 105-mm howitzers in position with adequate ammunition. Searching further out the 4th and 5th Battalions found the bodies of 124 enemy troops and seized 43 AK-47s, nine 12.7-mm machineguns, four RPD automatic rifles, nine B-40 rocket launchers, three radios, military clothing, equipment and food supplies. After securing FSB of Sophia, the 2nd Regiment was now in a position to control Tchepone from its mountain base and keep the areas surrounding the town within range of its artillery. For the next two days, throughout the areas of operation of the 1st Infantry and the Marine Divisions, friendly units caught the spirit of the new offensive. They fought aggressively, repeatedly engaged the enemy, and defeated him everywhere. In the morning of 5 March, in the area of Objective Alpha, the 4th Marine Battalion killed 130 enemy troops and seized 25 assorted weapons including two 82-mm mortars. Friendly forces sustained six killed and 42 wounded. The 4/1 Battalion made contact near LZ of Liz, killing 41 Communist troops and seizing 15 weapons along with two mortars. By 6 March, engagements were increasing and occurring everywhere, but friendly forces suffered only light casualties while inflicting heavy losses on the enemy. More importantly, they were now within easy reach of Tchepone, the final objective that President Thieu had ordered them to take just three days earlier.

The day selected to enter the ultimate objective, Tchepone, was 6 March. A total of 276 U.S. helicopters were assembled to carry out the assault. In addition to B-52, U.S. tactical air strikes or air cover sorties were scheduled every 10 minutes. Elements of the 2/17 U.S. Air Cavalry reconnoitered targets, prepared landing zones and covered the assault. An enemy attack by fire on Khe Sanh Base forced the huge assemblage of U.S. helicopters to depart 90 minutes earlier than planned, but preparations for this operation had been so carefully executed that when the first helicopters carrying the 2/2 Battalion landed at Landing Zone Hope four kilometers northeast of Tchepone, only sporadic gunfire was received. By 13:43 hours both the 2d and 3d Battalions along with an element of the 2d Reconnaissance Company and the tactical command post of the 2d Infantry Regiment had landed safely at Hope. Searching the adjoining areas and occupying key positions, the 2d Regiment only made light contacts but found the bodies of 102 enemy troops killed by B-52s and seized five 12.7-mm machineguns and one anti-aircraft artillery gun. Extending its search further south toward Tchepone, the 3/2 Battalion found a cache of an estimated 1,000 tons of rice and 2,000 gas masks along with 31 enemy bodies and numerous weapons destroyed by B-52s nearby. The 2/2 Battalion found an area devastated by B-52s with nearly 100 enemy bodies and assorted weapons shattered to pieces. After the two reinforced ARVN battalions had made assault landing near the objective and rapidly exploited their success, the district town of Tchepone was practically under ARVN control, dominated as it was by the array of artillery pieces to the south. The most remote terrain objective of LAM SON 719 was attained.

Now the must used "Linebacker" instead of "Rolling Thunder

It was real war! After having invaded two important northern bases on Route 559 [Ho Chi Minh Trail] The NVA troop temporarily stooped to regroup. Though they had the upper hand, they had also suffered a huge number of casualties. They only delivered shelling and sent forth small units to limit the ARVN from expanding into the surroundings. They also concentrated on the shelling in the attempt to destroy the ARVN' Armor unit before resuming their assault. Meanwhile, pressured by the Ranger and Airborne units in the north, the NVA decided to harass the 3rd Infantry Regiment at FSB Hong-Ha-2, in the southeast. Although assisted by U.S Air support and friendly artillery. The 3rd Infantry Regiment struggled, and was forced to retreat to a safer area, from which they were eventually airlifted back to Khe Sanh. Casualties and loss of weapons were as heavy as the numbers suffered by units in the northern front.

Naturally with their tactics of using human waves, regardless of the toll on their numbers, the enemy also suffered terribly. Many were lost during the assault and many more were killed by ARVN guns, and air support.

Hanoi take retaliatory measures due to Pentagon violated ROE?

Strangely, an abrupt afternoon of 6 March – After my 28 days stayed at Airborne FOB at Khe Sanh, but suddenly, in early certain morning, right after the SAC/MC-130s dropped bombs BLU-82AL, and BLU-82B at Tchepone vicinity, KGB urged General Giap to retaliate by launching rockets strafing into Khe Sanh in which received an attack by fired of an estimated 22 rounds of 122-mm Katyusha rockets inflicted two U.S. troops were killed and 10 wounded. The nature of battle might change somewhat, elsewhere, the enemy appeared to take no significant initiative but he was increasing his use of surface-to-air missiles in lower Laos. Earlier, on 2 February, a Mohawk Army-aircraft flying west of the demilitarized zone reported an unidentified missile fired from the ground which exploded approximately 100 meters away, causing no damage to the aircraft. Subsequently, 14 instances of surface-to-air missile firing were photographed or reported by forward air controllers, U.S Army pilots, tactical air and reconnaissance aircraft. Missile transportation equipment and antenna vans along with other equipment related to surface-to-air missile systems were also sighted in the tri-border area.

Under the fierce fighting conditions, our embattled units were unable to provide assistance to each other though the Airborne Division sent 6th Airborne Battalion to reinforce FSB 31. The helicopters carrying paratroopers met with intensive antiaircraft fires and could not land. Several were shot down, causing the toll of rise even higher. Operation Headquarters reaction was limited to increasing tactical air sorties. A few U.S aircrafts were hit during their round-the-clock bombarding mission.

Ironically, Lam Son 719 – which sought to interdict enemy lines of communications through ground action – was going to ease the air attack on the Ho Chi Minh trail. Now fierce fighting erupted in the Lam Son area of operations, virtually all B-52s sorties were diverted from interdiction to close air ground support of the troops in contact. Also thank to the transport fixed-wing EC-130B gunship, though, that same week earlier a new record high in truck kills was achieved by transport gunship airplanes which performed significant jobs. **ROE' Violator: To night 5 March**, at FOB Ham Nghi, Khe Sanh, under four corners of mosquito-net, I lay in the military cot-stretch hearing every throng-wave of raid began with midnight until dawn of Arc-Light B-52, almost every 15 minutes spell-interval, B-52 coming from Guam busted shorter than B-52 coming from Utapao AFB, Thailand? (B.52 armaments at Utapao was almost double weight than Guam AFB so the spell lasting longer than 30 seconds) My prophetic warning "a crime against humanity" emotionally – "that what is going on now is just a lot of unnecessary killing…the longest and bloodiest siege of the war was haunted in my mind" Tonight was the night on 5 March and the early morning of 6 March/ 1971. In my thought *"It's this brother enemy's bloodiest-war looked like WWII Dropping the Atomic-Bombs brought the war to a swift conclusion, saving many lives in the last-long process?"* Finally, at early morning 6 March 1971, before happened the helicopter air assault never have in the world so big, so numerous choppers landing at remote mountainous area like Tchepone. Unfortunately one impact event that the **huge 15,000pds, BLU-82AL bomb** dropped, this 1,000pds square inch pressure bomb Aluminum is a silvery white and ductile member of the boron group of chemical elements, it has the symbol AL; its atomic number 13 … power and polystyrene (FAE) consist only of an agent and a dispersing mechanism and take their oxidizers from the oxygen in the air. Because according to axiom-1, US Permanent Government wouldn't like to turn-in Saigon to Hanoi authority not like a 'Pebbly Capital', not bloodbath but blood-leak! *Consequently, is this operation purpose meant save people live?*

    The day selected to enter the ultimate objective, Tchepone, was in phase-3, start 6 March – In starting the phase-3 of this operation (6th March to 15th March) the Pentagon names were chosen for objectives, fire-bases and the like primarily to facilitate communications with U.S. support units. During this operation,

General Al. Haig had followed a parallel practice (at Dien Bien Phu, for example) Perhaps feminine names were in southern of Xepon River, in the thought of Pentagon plan, selected to bring some softness into the virile world of combatants at war. "Lolo", "Liz", and "Sophia" were chosen by WSAG' chief of staff, Donald Rumfeld, the ugly guy but very effective masterminded. Pentagon Command and control which assisted in maneuvering the operation during this period under siege 604 Cargo Base that Richard Helm had served for several years in the position Linebacker, in coordination with ARVN and U.S. combat units, and he naturally followed their practice in naming fire-bases. Though the NVA Steel Division-2 was ready assigned to ambush underground in the strongholds, and small return that General Giap might have enjoyed by exploiting these names for propaganda value - as proof that the Americans were still in charge despite Vietnamization - was certainly overridden by the practicality of having words the Americans could understand and pronounce. **Consequently at 10:00 am, on 6 March** two battalions of the 1st Infantry Division were safety airlifted to the vicinity of Tchepone, in the northern-heart of the NVA Base-Area 604. This is the crucial objective of this operation. A daisy chain of 276 UH-I helicopters picked up ARVN troops at Khe Sanh and deposited them at LZ Hope near Tchepone; most ships made three round trips. "No aircraft were lost to ground fire during this airlift operation," That's surprisingly, recalled Colonel Cockerham. *"We were using armor tactics as the basis for our operations, designating an objective, intermediate objectives, and so on. We would secure them, then that build an air tunnel so as to deny the enemy direct fire and indirect fire observation. We had one aircraft disabled in the final LZ due to engine failure."* How many percent you guess this mystery, truth if you guessed? Why even though an AK.47 could fire up to the huge helicopter formations was unable? Clearly I'm justified in my conviction that Vietnam was "an intelligence war" by George H W Bush masterminded. Giap' retaliation due to U.S a ROE-violator, as a result at 15:00hours, 6th March, 2 G.I were killed and 10 wounded by 22 rockets 122mm launched into Khe Sanh Base.

Phase-3 (6 March to 15 March) had to be carried out taking into account the change in circumstances: The situation by this time

The New Legion

was becoming increasingly tense throughout the area of operations. ARVN Truck convoys were frequently attacked on Route-9 in Laos and on the ARVN territory, the enemy increased efforts to ambush convoys and attack rear bases. The ARVN westward drive was stalled. In the midst of this situation, I Corps Headquarters received a directive from President Nguyen Van Thieu to have the Marine Division relieve the Airborne Division. He must have realized that such a relief under the combat conditions on that battlefield would be very hazardous. Besides, the Airborne Division was still a strong unit; it had suffered some losses but these losses were not yet too serious. What then caused him to order its replacement? The most probable answer could be that he was really worried over the additional losses that the Airborne Division would sustain in protracted combat. He certainly would like to keep this elite unit intact at all costs. In any event, the Marine Division was a poor choice for the relief. Despite the combat worthiness of its individual brigades, it had never fought as a division. Meanwhile the 2nd Infantry Regiment, the unit assigned to invade Tchepone was preparing to be airlifted. At the stage, the invasion of Tchepone was no longer an option for the ARVN. After the world media had prematurely broadcasted the news that I Corps had invaded Tchepone, it became a matter of honor to achieve just that. By orders from President Thieu, General Lam secretly let 2nd Regiment to send the most able of its battalions by helicopter to Tchepone. The idea was to carry out activities in Tchepone for a short while, enough to prove that the ARVN had indeed invaded the city as reported pictures and then retreat immediately by airlifts, as the enemy presence was too strong. Thank to Colonel James Vaught for his involvement special bombardment, the enemy did not react. Their silence was predictable ...scared BLU-82AL Bomb? They were not stupid as to place their unit right at the site of the target. They had instead stationed well outside the target to avoid the bombings prior to the ARVN' landing, and only after the ARVN arrived did they move in for attack.

The intelligent airlift-war had finished at daytime, now nothing happened until late in the evening when the enemy artillery started concentrating their artillery on the positions of the 2nd Regiment. But the unit had withdrawn to a pick-up zone to be airlifted back to their bases in the morning. When the NVA knew of this, they rushed their troops to the pick-up zone, causing a lot of difficulty to the infantry men at the rear of the retreat. A number had to flee in the direction of the Airborne-units that Colonel Vaught was a new U.S Advisor. While the NVA was continuing to pressure the Infantry, their other units applied the infantry and the artillery to attack the 1st Infantry Regiment, the Airborne and the Armor units south of Route 9.

Prior of that their efforts to push through to Tchepone with airlifted infantry, rather than continuing efforts to advance along the inadequate road, began **on 3 March** when a battalion of the 1st Division was inserted to establish a landing zone called LoLo, the first in a planned chain of positions extending west toward Tchepone. Unsurprisingly, the assault was met with intense enemy fire – seven helicopters were destroyed and many others damaged – but the troops got into position. The next day two more battalions were brought in, along with artillery and supplies, building up strength on LoLo. Also **on 4 March** a battalion was airlifted to establish LZ Liz, farther west and closer to Tchepone; again it attacked into the teeth of intense enemy fire. On 5 March two fresh battalions were inserted west of Liz to set up LZ Sophia. Next was LZ Hope.

(General Haig' Staffs was played the war-game with these movie-start names putting on the LZs stand for the concept of Permanent Government, likewise at most schools and universities, Hollywood, and Media broadcaster as the basis for explaining the outcome of Vietnam-War by Academic-Freedom-Act)

That same day on 6 March, General Abrams met with General Vien to review the enemy situation. "I said the operation has shaped up must be stopped, including Route 914, and a major battle, which might even be the decisive battle of the war, must be won. I urged the employment of the 2nd ARVN Division from Chu-Lai to engage Lam Son 719 now. Politically, psychologically and militarily, President Thieu can accept nothing less. We have the resources to do it. It means another month of hard fighting. General Vien agrees with all this; I truthfully think it is the way he feels anyway. He said he would take it to the President."

By this time, XXIV Corps reported to Abrams, General Lam, having gotten some elements to Tchepone, "apparently feels that he has accomplished the mandate given him by President Thieu and is now turning to a more cautions approach as he awaits further instructions from Thieu". In addition among ARVN commanders "the general feeling is that their mission has been accomplished and it is now time to withdraw. They do not concede that there is still much to be done in inflicting maximum damage or that there is now the opportunity to exploit initial success with even more telling results."

On March, General Vien and Lam recommended to President Thieu that the overall operation be terminated, far ahead of schedule. I thought that *"a careful military estimate was based upon the U.S helicopter supports capable: it was time to get out."* Obviously, "it was apparent the President Thieu had decided, at the outset, that once Tchepone had been entered by a small unit of 1st Infantry Division the withdrawal should begin without delay." This is his official statement. But in the reality Thieu ordered to General Lam: **"touch there pissed at a mess and go home"**. On this occasion, the venal critic journalists (Skull and Bones' revengefulness and pretentiousness) have speculated that comparisons with American leadership of the time might have yielded interesting results. President Thieu, for example, was arguably a more honest and decent man than Lyndon Johnson, and – given the differences in their respective circumstances – quite likely a more effective president of his country. At the time someone pointed out the President Thieu also probably had more freedom to move about in his own country than LBJ did in his (In testimony evidence by the conversation verbatim between Michael Forrestal NSC cautioned George Bundy's president advisor that **"to send the telegram without Averell's approval is just asking for trouble."** Even the telegram had already received presidential approval, but that was not enough. It still required an **endorsement** from Harriman. It is almost unthinkable and damn shame, surely unforgivable that a great nation should leave the president a deprived authority)

General Abrams wanted to push the thing, recommending to Thieu that instead of withdrawing he reinforce with the 2nd ARVN Division. Thieu flatly declined, reportedly saying he would do so only if an US division was also committed. Of course both Abrams and Thieu knew that was prohibited; meanwhile the drawdown of

US forces continued unabated, 60,000 more departing during Lam Son 719 operation (January – April 1971) "All Americans have got to be pulling in the same direction, and all together, and that's always 'a neat-trick' to do under the most ideal circumstances. Americans are all different. They're individualists and enthusiasts, optimists and pessimists, then a slight sprinkling of just screw-ups. So the response effectively ended discussion of reinforcing the operation. Thieu's unwillingness to commit more forces, politically said General Vien, "reflected his concern that ARVN divisions were unprepared for a strategic task."

The 'Early-Out' by President Thieu ordered to General Lam

"Touch there pissed a mess and go home" In the early morning of 7 March, the first enemy reactions to the 1st Division's presence at Tchepone occurred in the form of artillery and mortar fire against FSB LoLo. The first attack, which was brief and light, caused only five casualties, but the second attack was heavier as indirect fire poured in from all calibers of guns from 82-and 120mm mortars to 152-mm artillery. More than 20 soldiers were hit - three were killed - and all of the bulldozers used in the construction of fortifications were damaged. While the troops on LoLo were digging in under this heavy bombardment, FSB A-Luoi was also subjected to a heavy attack by fired NVA artillery fell on the positions intermittently throughout the day, disrupting the scheduled airlifted supply and evacuation runs. On the same day, the elite Black Panther (Reconnaissance) Company of the 1st Infantry Division, which had been attached to the US 101st Airborne Division from the beginning of the campaign, landed troops about five kilometers west-southwest of Ban Dong to rescue the crew of an U.S. aircraft which had gone down two days before The Black Panthers Company scored a major combat exploit by rescuing all the Americans and subsequently made contact with the enemy, sustaining light casualties but killing more than 60 NVA troops. During this violent action, they also seized 30 NVA automatic rifles, destroyed an anti-aircraft gun position, and found another 40 NVA soldiers killed by air-strikes. The 2nd Battalion, 2nd Infantry, on a mission to assess B-52 bomb damage in an area east of Tchepone, found a smashed weapons supply point that contained 150 rocket launchers (122-mm) 43 grenade launchers, 17 heavy

The New Legion

machineguns, eight 82-mm mortars and 57 AK-47 rifles, all damaged beyond U.S air-strikes. Nearby, the battalion found two Communist tanks destroyed by tactical air-strikes and an ammunition storage area which it marked for future disposal (B-52 strikes conducted later on this target resulted in approximately 2,000 secondary explosions for long day) While the 2nd Battalion, 2nd Infantry reconnoitered east of Tchepone, the 4th Battalion, 1st Infantry conducted a similar mission in the heights southeast of Tchepone and found the bodies of 112 enemy troops and seized 32 medium mortars, five 12.7- mm machine guns, six grenade launchers and 18 AK-47 rifles. Meanwhile the 2nd Regiment launched the first foray into Tchepone, to find only a shambles of the former district seat, and no human beings in sight. On their way out, the reconnaissance troops killed a squad of NVA soldiers and found a cache containing eight 82-mm mortars, two tons of rice and other military equipment.

Thereby the Disengagement on 7 March, 1971 In the early morning of 7 March, the first enemy reactions to the 1st Division's presence at Tchepone occurred in the form of artillery and mortar fire against Fire Support Base LoLo. The first attack, which was brief and light, caused only five casualties, but the second attack was heavier as indirect fire poured in from all calibers of guns from the best of-date as 120-mm mortars to 152-mm artillery. More than 20 soldiers were hit - three were killed - and all of the bulldozers used in the construction of fortifications were damaged. While the troops on LoLo were digging in under this heavy bombardment, FSB A-Luoi was also subjected to a heavy attack by fired NVA' artillery fell on the positions intermittently throughout the day, disrupting the scheduled airlifted supply and evacuation runs. On the same day, the Black Panther "Hắc-Báo" (Reconnaissance) Company of the 1st Infantry Division, which had been attached to the US 101st Airborne Division from the beginning of the campaign, landed troops about 5 kilometers west-southwest of Ban Dong to rescue the crew of an U.S. aircraft which had gone down two days before. The Black Panther-Company scored a major combat exploit by rescuing all the Americans and subsequently made contact with the enemy, sustaining light casualties but killing more than 60 NVA troops. During this violent action, they also seized 30 NVA automatic rifles, destroyed an anti-aircraft gun position, and found another 40 NVA soldiers killed by air-strikes. Almost everywhere about this area were the NVA remains killed by air strikes.

The 2nd Infantry Battalion, 2nd Regiment, on a mission to assess B-52 bomb damage in an area east of Tchepone, found a smashed weapons supply point that contained 150 rocket launchers (122-mm), 43 grenade launchers, 17 heavy machineguns, eight 82-mm mortars and 57 AK-47 rifles, all damaged beyond used. Nearby, the battalion found two T-54 and PT-76 tanks destroyed by air-strikes and an ammunition storage area which it marked for future disposal (B-52 strikes conducted later on this target resulted in approximately thousand secondary explosions) While the 2nd Battalion, 2nd Infantry Regiment reconnoitered east of Tchepone, the 4th Battalion, 1st Regiment conducted a similar mission in the heights southeast of Tchepone and found the bodies of 112 enemy troops and seized 32 mortars, five 12.7- mm machine guns, six grenade launchers and 18 AK-47 rifles. Meanwhile the 2nd Regiment launched the first foray into Tchepone, to find only a shambles of the former district seat, and no human beings in sight. On their way out, the reconnaissance troops killed a squad of NVA soldiers and found a cache containing eight 82-mm mortars, two tons of rice and other military equipment.

During the morning of 8 March, while Marine and Airborne units made sporadic contacts with the enemy in all other areas with varying degrees of success, FSB LoLo continued to receive attacks by fired which caused all planned re-supply and evacuation flights into the base to be cancelled. The 2nd Battalion, 2nd Infantry Regiment continued to search the areas around Tchepone and found 52 dead enemy soldiers along with three heavy machine-guns, 44 rifles and about 50 heavy artillery rounds destroyed by air-strikes. Late afternoon found the units of the 2nd Regiment assembled near the banks of the Tchepone River. That night, two battalions of the 2nd Regiment moved past Tchepone on the east and crossed the river to the southern side. On 9 March at 09:00 hours, the regiment began to climb the ridge to FSB Sophia. The invasion of Tchepone had been completed.

Meanwhile, Lieutenant General Lam, Commander of I Corps, arrived at the Presidential Palace in Saigon to report to President

The New Legion

Thieu on the situation. General Vien, Chairman of the Joint General Staff, was present at that meeting and heard General Lam present the rationale for the withdrawal and the outline of how it would be executed. Why did General Lam and General Vien recommend to President Thieu that the apparently successful operation into Laos be terminated so far ahead of schedule? The 2nd Infantry Regiment had not nearly completed its mission in the hills east of Tchepone where great quantities of NVA military supplies were stored, and only a brief reconnaissance had been conducted into the town itself. No ARVN' reconnaissance in force had reached the Xe Bang Hiang River, the principal waterway that flows from north to south west of the town, although the ARVN Commander in this zone had requested that CBU-42 (timed-delay-bomb) be sewn on the west bank to make it difficult for the NVA to concentrate there. Coincidentally, of course, this barrier also inhibited any ARVN crossing of the river in this area, although it was the western side of the Tchepone complex that was suspected of containing numerous supply depots and huge quantities of war materiel. The river would have to be crossed to complete the task.

Why was the river not crossed? The answer is that a careful military estimate was made, based upon all the pertinent information available at the time, and the conclusion was inescapable: it was time to get out. First was the problem of terrain. In a tactical sense, ARVN forces were facing an uphill task, progressing as they did from the lowlands, with which they were familiar, to the highlands where the well entrenched enemy enjoyed the advantage. The only road available for troop and supply movements ran through steep mountains and dense forests. The enemy had operated in this region for many years, was familiar with it and knew all the trails. He could cut the road or lay ambushes almost anywhere. To the west past Ban Dong, this road ran through a range of high mountains. All along the slopes the NVA had positioned a dense array of antiaircraft guns, big and small. These guns not only fired at aircraft but also at ARVN troop columns and truck convoys moving to and from Tchepone.

The forests of the Truong Son Range are especially formidable obstacles to cross country movement. The bases of the tall trees are girded by bamboo thickets, dense and thorny. These forests do not permit armored operations and thorny bamboo greatly hampers movements of infantry soldiers. But NVA troops were familiar with the terrain, had pre-dug fortifications and knew all the paths and trails. The NVA soldiers enjoyed this important advantage. The weather was a factor which also worked for the enemy and seldom favored to our ARVN side with its numerous helicopters and strong air force, as lower Laos is usually obscured in fog from dawn until mid morning, sometimes until noon. Our choppers could usually operate after the fog lifted until late afternoon, but only if there was no rain and even if it didn't rain low clouds sometimes prevented the full use of ARVN' air support. On the other hand, the endless mountains and forests provided good concealment for enemy deployments within the area of operations as well as for the movement of reinforcements from far away, our failure to detect all of these movements presented ARVN commanders with many unwelcome surprises. Even those enemy units which had not previously operated in the Laos panhandle had the support of veteran units to provide guides, assistance and advice.

In short, the NVA was thoroughly familiar with the terrain in lower Laos and ARVN troops were not. The terrain and weather favored the defenders and handicapped the attackers. The area was especially disadvantageous for our mechanized and armored forces which were restricted to narrow jungle roads on which two vehicles could not pass and on which entire columns could often be jammed or stalled by one disabled vehicle. Moreover, the NVA strength and reinforcement capability was the second factor that influenced the decision to initiate the withdrawal. Estimated enemy forces in the immediate area of operation consisted of three infantry regiments, rear service elements capable of local defense, and artillery elements especially notable for their air defense capability. It was estimated that the NVA could reinforce, within two weeks, with up to eight infantry regiments and the equivalent of an artillery regiment. Heavy artillery and armor also strengthened the enemy's capabilities. First among these was the enemy's dispersed and well concealed 130-mm and 152-mm heavy artillery. ARVN' stationary FSB on hilltops, therefore, were easy targets for enemy artillery fire. The second factor in the enemy's capability of deep concern to the leadership

The New Legion

in Saigon was the enemy armor strength that had become apparent. The intent Pentagon planners of LAM SON 719 had failed to give [with purpose] sufficient consideration to the threat of NVA' Armor superiority, and now this threat had become in reality. Even though NVA' Armor was under daily attack from the air, FSB/Hill- 31 had been lost because of the enemy's effective coordination of armor and infantry forces. In other places the NVA used his tanks as highly mobile field guns moving them individually over trails to ambush ARVN armored vehicles M-113 on the roads. The maneuvering of tanks on such a large scale over forest trails known only to the NVA posed a great threat to ARVN armored vehicles which were confined to congested one way roads strewn with disabled vehicles. Moreover, NVA tanks had thicker armor and mounted guns of a larger caliber than the ARVN tanks, 100-mm versus 76-mm and had a significantly greater armor defeating capability.

Even after a month of intensive attack the enemy's air defense capabilities showed no signs of being subdued and he had positioned surface-to-air missiles west of the border or at the Ban Raving Pass but not in operational area. These missiles had Route-9 from Khe Sanh to Ban Dong within effective range, a challenge that the U.S. Air Force had to face, around the ARVN' besieged bases, even after waves of air-strikes, enemy anti-aircraft guns would reappear close to their original positions. Also, antiaircraft batteries were deployed along helicopter avenues of approach; those positioned on the mountain slopes between Ban Dong and Tchepone seemed impossible to uproot. This enemy capability practically neutralized the ARVN advantage of helicopter mobility and logistic support. In contrast to the NVA who had large uncommitted reserves in North Vietnam, our reserves were limited indeed. The Airborne and Marine Divisions constituted the entire general reserves of the GVN and they were already committed. Committing the 1st Infantry Division and the 1st Ranger Group required an extreme effort made possible only with the help of the U.S. 101st Airborne Division which replaced these two units in the lowlands of Thua Thien Province. And now, in the light of the enemy's reinforcement and strength on the battlefield, it was becoming apparent that the ARVN force committed to Lam Son 719 was too small for the task. General Abrams recommended that the ARVN, 2nd Infantry Division be sent in to reinforce, and the division was preparing plans to turn over its area of responsibility in MR 1 to the U.S. 23rd Infantry Division. Still, in the view of the GVN leadership, one additional division would be insufficient to ensure total victory and would result in a higher casualty figure for our forces in Laos. Also, removing the 2nd Division from MR 1 would leave more of the vital lowland areas of MR 1 undefended. The only reasonable course of action was an orderly withdrawal to conserve as much of the committed force as possible. Further reinforcing this conclusion was the fact that the political and psychological objective of the campaign had been achieved; the South Vietnamese Forces had entered Tchepone. It was apparent that President Thieu had decided, at the outset, that once Tchepone had been entered by RVNAF, the withdrawal should begin without delay.

The main features of the withdrawal plan were outlined to President Thieu at the 9 March meeting. The 2nd Infantry Regiment would close FSB Sophia and establish a new fire base (called Brick) near Route-92 about 8 kilometers south of Ban Dong. The units of the 2nd Regiment would be picked up at various landing zones in the Sophia-Liz area and inserted into landing zones south and west of FSB Brick. Thereafter, the 2nd Regiment would move southwest, searching for and destroying installations of NVA' Binh Tram No 33 and interdicting Route 914. The 1st and 2nd Regiments would conduct operations in the area of Route-914 for 7 to 10 days. The withdrawal would then proceed in the following order: first, the 1st Division, then the Airborne Division. FSB LoLo would close thereafter to be followed by FSB Brick; the 3rd Infantry Regiment in the area of Brown and FSB Delta-1 would pull out after closing FSB A-Luoi. After the withdrawal of the Airborne Division, the 147th and 258th Marine Brigades would move out from the areas of FSB Delta and Hotel. The entire withdrawal, according to Lieutenant General Lam's estimate, was scheduled for completion by 31 March. After resting and reorganizing for about two weeks, the 1st Infantry Division, two Marine brigades and one Airborne brigade would conduct operations into the eastern sector of enemy Base Area 611, the A Shau Valley and the Laotian salient. The Khe Sanh Base would probably close on 15 April.

The New Legion

While the withdrawal plan was being explained to the President, the 1st Infantry Regiment began to move toward objective area Ta Luong. Advance elements reported sighting NVA tanks near the area. Further north, near Route-9, at 9 kilometers southeast of Tchepone, observation teams of the 1st Regiment also reported sighting some NVA/ PT-76s Armored 202 Group. ARVN artillery opened fire and disabled five NVA tanks. Meanwhile, the Marine sector was very active, the battalions received heavy attacks by fire, and, searching out 9 km south-southeast from their bases, found a NVA Binh tram camp that had been bombed by B-52s with huge 6,000 heavy artillery shells, rockets along with numerous other weapons and substantial volumes of ammunition all destroyed. In the morning of 10 March, the 1st Marine Battalion engaged the NVA troops twice, the first time in a light encounter and the second time fighting a battalion size unit with the following results: 72 enemy killed and 20 small arms, one recoilless rifle, and four grenade launchers seized. The Marine losses were only six killed and 19 wounded. The 1st Infantry Regiment continued to search the areas of Ta Luong and Route-914 and was able to assess the substantial damages inflicted by B-52 bombing runs. In two areas approximately 9 kilometers south and southeast of FSB Sophia, the 4th Battalion found the bodies of 72 NVA troops, 12 Soviet and China-trucks, eight tracked vehicles, three 122-mm towed cannons two 37-mm anti-aircraft artillery guns, four 12.7-mm machineguns, two 122-mm rocket launchers, 400 AK-47 rifles, thirty two 82-mm, 120mm mortars, 18 B-40s, 60 Chicom-Radios and huge quantities of food of all types. Most of these supplies were blown to bits by B-52 bombs. The battalion also captured five prisoners of war.

During the morning of 10 March, the 2nd Regiment on FSB Sophia received a heavy attack by fire. The attack wounded 13 soldiers and damaged six of the eight 105-mm howitzers at the base. On 11 March, 2nd Infantry Regiment elements operating around the fire support base had increasing contacts with the NVA. At 11:00 hours, a reconnaissance element operating approximately one kilometer southeast of the base engaged a NVA patrol killing eight and seizing their weapons. According to plans, the 2nd Infantry Regiment was to move this day, on foot to Landing Zone Liz from where it would be airlifted eastward. Between 14:00 hours and nightfall, the 2nd Battalion was removed from Landing Zone Liz and deposited on Landing Zone Brown. The 5th Battalion landed approximately one kilometer north of Landing Zone Sophia East where the headquarters of the 2nd Regiment had already relocated while the 4th Battalion continued to secure FSB Sophia. Late that afternoon an element of the battalion engaged the enemy approximately 900 meters south of the base but casualties were light on both sides. During the day, 1st Infantry Regiment forces continued to search the Ta Luong area and found more substantial damage caused by B-52 attacks. On 12 March, the evacuation of the 2nd Regiment was completed. The 3rd Battalion from Liz landed approximately 900 meters south of Sophia East and the 4th Battalion was the last unit to leave Sophia. In order to facilitate the movement of troops, U.S. tactical air bombed and destroyed the eight 105-mm howitzers left on the base and another 105-mm battery was brought to Sophia East from Khe Sanh. The units of the 1st Infantry Regiment, whose headquarters was at FSB LoLo, were the forces located deepest to the west. On the fronts manned by the Marine and Airborne Divisions, engagements and attacks by fire followed an increasing trend. Meanwhile, two M-41 tank troops reassigned by JGS from MR-2 were moving into lower Laos to reinforce the 4th Armored Cavalry Squadron. U.S. air support was becoming more effective since Vietnamese interpreters flying with forward air controllers [FAC on OV-10 Bronco] had become more familiar with the situation. Re-supply operations were conducted throughout the battle area thanks to the daring and the noble spirit of sacrifice of U.S. Army helicopter crews.

Upon the 2nd Infantry Regiment's withdrawal from the area west of FSB/LoLo, NVA forces, probably elements of the 1st and 31st Regiments of the NT-2 Division began to encircle units of the 3rd Infantry Regiment. Beginning on 13 March, the battalions operating in the Ta Luong area were gradually forced to withdraw north and FSB/LoLo began to receive uninterrupted attacks by fire. On 14 March, the intensity of these attacks increased. During the day, the base received an estimated more than two hundred 122-mm rockets and one hundred 152-mm artillery rounds. Thanks to their solid shelters and trenches, the regiment had only three killed and two wounded but one D-4 Bulldozer and two 105-mm howitzers were seriously damaged by delayed-shells of 152mm. In the meantime, the NVA had moved up to the base and small arms fire was being directed at supply aircraft, causing medical evacuation and re-supply attempts to be called off. On 15 March, the base couldn't be re-supplied (nor could Delta or A Luoi, both of which were under attacks by fire) The various units on and around the base were running out of ammunition and the number of wounded in need of evacuation was increasing. A withdrawal plan was hastily prepared. The headquarters of the 1st Regiment and the battalions outside the base would move east. The 4th Battalion would serve as the rear guard protecting the regiment in its effort to break through enemy encirclement. The plan was carried out satisfactorily but the enemy tightened its hold on the 4th Battalion. Finally, this unit fought its way out with the enemy in pursuit, all the while rejecting the NVA demands for it to surrender. **On 17 March, close to the banks of the Tchepone River**, the battalion was intercepted and the fighting lasted all day, with tactical air and gun-ships providing dedicated support. The battalion commander and his deputy were both killed. Most of the company commanders and officers of the battalion were also killed and the few survivors managed to escape to an area near Route-9. There, in the late afternoon of 18 March, U.S. helicopters with tactical air support conducted a daring rescue. Three helicopters were hit and one fighter-bomber exploded in the air but the thirty two survivors of the 4th Battalion were rescued and flown to the rear. The battalion had accomplished well its rear guard mission and in the process, had sacrificed nearly every man. The fight put up by FSB LoLo and the units of the 1st Infantry Regiment had resulted in 1,100 enemy killed, causing severe losses to two main force regiments of the "Steel/NT-2/Division.

"Fierce-battle in lock its head, grip its tail"

(**Phase-4**: 16th March-7th April) While the 1s Regiment was subjected to heavy attacks which eventually caused it to pull out of the FSB/LoLo area, the battalions of the 2nd Regiment continued to conduct reconnaissance in force and search the Cua Tung and Cua Viet objective areas along Route-914 to joint with 922. In three areas, approximately one and a half, six and seven kilometers southeast of FSB/Sophia East, the 2nd and 3rd Battalions found many logistical installations and camps destroyed along with decomposed bodies of enemy troops. Supported by helicopter gun-ships, they destroyed five enemy trucks. In the southeast, activity in the Marine sector began to pick up. The 147th Marine Brigade Headquarters at FSB/Delta received 400 incoming rounds which killed eight marines. The 7th Battalion, operating outside the base, received a corresponding number of artillery rounds and had five wounded. Other units of the brigade, the 2nd and 4th Battalions, continued to search objective area Alpha, approximately 4 kilometers south of FSB/Delta. During the afternoon of 16 March the headquarters of the 3rd Infantry Regiment/1st Division and its 4th Battalion were picked up in the Delta-1 area and taken to Ham Nghi Base along with a number of supporting units. The 3rd Battalion had been taken out for rest and reorganization two days before, the 1st Battalion remained to secure the base Delta-1. Meanwhile, the enemy was beginning to harass Khe Sanh. For the second day running, this fire support base was hit by mortar fire which wounded four Americans and damaged two helicopters and a number of vehicles. It seemed to me: The U.S violated the ROE (Rules Of Engagement) abruptly used B-52 at Utapao, Thailand in air carpets by Linebacker campaign and bomb BLU-82AL on 6 March inflicting NVA heavy casualties. **A resumption to retaliate, on 17 March**, NVA gunners stepped up their shelling of other targets. In ARVN territory, at the border, FSB Phu Loc and Lao Bao were attacked by 130-mm artillery but the losses were small. FSB A-Luoi received attacks by fire practically every day and FSB Delta and the 7th Marine Battalion were pinned down. In a small engagement, the 7th Battalion killed 16 enemy troops while suffering only five casualties. A NVA recruit just assigned to the 812th Regiment, 524B Division rallied to the Marines and disclosed that the entire 324B Division was in the Route 9 campaign with its 29th, 803rd and 812th regiments. The 29th Regiment had recently suffered heavy losses and the 812th Regiment was engaging the 147th Marine Brigade. In the meantime, in the area of the 2nd Regiment, the 5th Battalion received an intense early morning attack of an estimated 300 rounds of mortar 120mm and artillery fire. The battalion continued its search operations and, thanks to intensive air support,

The New Legion

scored a major victory in the area near Landing Zone Brown, killing nearly 100 NVA and capturing a large number of weapons and many tons of ammunition. In accordance with the withdrawal plan, the headquarters of the 2nd Infantry Regiment was evacuated to Delta-1 while its battalion proceeded east on foot.

From 18 March on it seemed that the enemy was well aware of the ARVN withdrawal and there were signs of the enemy concentrating a regimental size unit northwest of FSB A-Luoi while pressure increased around FSB Delta of the 147th Brigade. The base began to receive fire from 152, and 130-mm field guns and NVA infantry had infiltrated close enough to fire at choppers landed. There were about 10 anti-aircraft guns positioned on the mountain slopes around the base that could not be silenced. The 2nd and 4th Battalions operating to the south were recalled to sweep the area around Delta and to prepare for the withdrawal. By mid-day of 18 March the 1st Infantry Regiment, with its 1st, 2nd and 3rd battalions, after falling back from the LoLo area, arrived in an area approximately 2,000 meters southwest of FSB A-Luoi. There they were picked up by helicopters and flown to Khe Sanh. The survivors of the 4th Battalion were also flown back in the late afternoon. Next came the turn of the 5th Battalion, 2nd Regiment, which boarded helicopters from an area adjacent to Landing Zone Brown. Immediately thereafter, from about 16:00 hours and continuing through the night of 18 March, the remaining three battalions of the 2nd Infantry Regiment, the 2nd, 3rd and 4th, received heavy attacks west of the Brown area. The NVA followed up its artillery with ground assaults. The next morning the 4th Battalion made a preliminary report that it had 33 wounded and five missing. The 2nd Battalion had similar casualty figures while enemy losses were unknown.

For four days now, reports flowed into I Corps headquarters of strong attacks that included very heavy bombardments by heavy artillery and tank attacks. Reports of ARVN losses, including the decimation of the 4th Battalion, 1st Infantry, were very disturbing to General Lam, as were the many indications that the enemy was reinforcing and maneuvering to prevent the orderly ARVN withdrawal from Laos. So, on the night of 18 March, General Lam called Brigadier General Phu his division commanders to a conference at Ham Nghi Base, Khe Sanh to hear their assessments and recommendations. They each recommended that disengagement proceed as quickly as possible; General Phu, commanding the 1st Division, displayed anxiety for the first time in the campaign. When the conference was over, General Lam ordered that the withdrawal proceed at a quicker pace and that preparations begin immediately for the extraction of the 2ndRegiment from the Brown area and FSB Delta-1 where all its battalions were wider heavy attack and in danger of being cut off and destroyed.

On the morning of 19 March, abandoning FSB A-Luoi [Ban Dong] ARVN' 1st Armored elements and attached Airborne units moved overland to take positions along a line near FSB Alpha. The 2nd Airborne Battalion operating to the north and having made a contact with the enemy during the day would be airlifted from a landing zone north of Base Alpha. After the elements from Ban Dong had arrived at Alpha, the remaining forces of the 1st Infantry Division were also picked up, including the battalions of the 2nd Regiment from the Brown area and the 2nd Regiment Headquarters along with the 1st Battalion, 3rd Regiment from Base Delta-1. Information received during the night added some clarity to the situation. Almost all the airborne battalions were in contact with the enemy. The 7th, 8th, 9th and 11th Airborne Battalions had relatively light engagements with minimal losses on both sides thank to Colonel James Vaught, a representative of General Haig at Pentagon interfered in B-52s and EC-130B engagement air ground close supports. The 1st Airborne Battalion, however, had 18 casualties and reported killing 80 enemy troops, capturing five prisoners and seizing five AK-47 rifles. The 2nd Airborne Battalion also suffered relatively high losses, with 18 killed and 57 wounded. Enemy losses were unknown. On the Marine side, Base Delta was still experiencing heavy enemy pressure. The 7th Marine Battalion constantly received attacks by fire and ground attacks. The enemy even used a noxious gas but suffered heavy casualties with 42 killed. Marine losses were light.

The 19th of March likely 19th February of Rangers was a same day of intense activities. All ARVN units in Laos reported enemy contacts. A synthesis of information received from prisoners, railing and the combat units gave a rather clear picture of enemy dispositions on the battlefield. The 308th NVA Division with its 36th, 102nd and 88th Regiments were attacking from the north. The 64th and 24th Regiments (respectively from the 320th and 304th NVA Division) continued to encircle the Ban Dong area east of Route-9. The 2nd Division was trying to annihilate the remaining forces of the ARVN, 1st Infantry Division. The 324th NVA Division deployed its 29th and 803rd Regiments to attack the 147th Marine Brigade while its 812th Regiment pinned the 258th Marine Brigade down around Base Hotel and at Co Roc highlander. The NVA apparently wanted to catch the entire ARVN force in his trap by strategic tactical "Lock its head, grip it tail." In the manner of a hunter, he set about to kill his prey by "locking its head and gripping its tail." This was his strategy of annihilation for which he had coined this metaphorical phrase. In the ARVN territory, all Communist main and local force units stepped up their operations. Mine attacks and ambushes occurred daily on the LOC, Route-9. Enemy sappers continually probed logistical installations and the enemy launched a psychological warfare campaign aimed at publicizing the NVA victories along Route-9.

Beginning in early morning, north of Ban Dong, the 8th and 9th Airborne Battalions were under attack. The 8th Battalion had 32 casualties while the 9th Battalion immediately to the east inflicted heavy losses on the enemy. Only light engagements were reported along Route-9 while Ban Dong Base began to be evacuated after most of the artillery pieces had been lifted out by helicopters. The armored logistic convoy set out, towing damaged vehicles and guns under the protection of airborne units and other armored elements while the enemy continued to exert pressure on the rear of the column. At 07:30 hours, approximately two kilometers north of Ban Dong, forward air controller aircraft reported sighting four enemy tanks moving down. Approximately four kilometers east of Ban Dong Base, the logistic convoy was ambushed and all 18 vehicles were immobilized. Some of the lead vehicles were hit by direct fire and destroyed. The road had only one lane; the vehicles behind were stalled in the ambush zone. While the battle was in progress no reports were received from the convoy commander; his superiors were therefore unaware of what was happening to the convoy. Losses incurred during the ambush were neither reported nor even analyzed afterwards.

According to reports from an observation plane OV-10, four M-41 tanks and three M-113 APC, each towing a 105-mm howitzer, were apparently damaged among the 18 stranded vehicles. Road security for the movement of this convoy was the responsibility of armor and airborne units but during the attack, the convoy never initiated any request for air support or gun-ships. Apparently the ambush caught the convoy by surprise and it ended as quickly as it began. Later Colonel Luat, Commander of the 1st Armored Brigade requested tactical air to destroy the ambushed vehicles and his request was immediately granted in order to prevent the enemy from capturing usable equipment.

On the front manned by the Marine Division, the situation was even more serious. The units of the 258th Brigade were increasingly engaged by the enemy and the encirclement of FSB Delta didn't relax in anyway. Supplies could not be delivered and the 2nd and 4th Battalions were intercepted on their way to the relief of the base. Inside the base, five of the ten 105-mm howitzers were out of action due to enemy fire and the number of marines killed and wounded kept increasing. In the area of the 1st Division, FSB Delta-1 was hit by numerous 122-mm rockets and 75-mm recoilless rifle rounds which put four 105-mm howitzers out of action and caused 1,400 rounds of 105-mm ammunition to explode. The 2nd, 3rd and 4th Battalions of the 2nd Infantry Regiment west of Sophia East were involved in skirmishes throughout the day. Late afternoon saw the enemy attack more fiercely and the tactical air as well as EC-130B gun-ship was called in to provide support. By midnight all three battalions reported having consolidated their positions. The 3rd Battalion had 47 casualties after killing 87 Communist troops and seizing 49 AK-47s and 17 grenade launchers. Among the enemy bodies were those of two company commanders of the NVA 2nd Division. The 2nd Battalion had light casualties but reported killing 85 NVA troops, seizing 47 AK-47s and several other crew-served weapons. The 4th Battalion reported killing 195 enemy-troops and seizing 59 AK-47s and numerous other weapons.

During the day, U.S. air support substantially increased, with 686 sorties of helicopter gun-ships, 246 tactical air sorties and 14 B-52 missions which dropped 1,158 tons of bombs. Late in the

The New Legion

afternoon of 19 March, Ambassador Bunker and General Abrams were received by President Thieu. President Thieu disclosed he had directed a cautious withdrawal which would be completed from 5-8 April. When the withdrawal was complete, he planned to have about three battalions launch a raid against Muong Nong, the center of Communist Base Area 611, and wanted strong U.S. air support for this raid. On 20 March, the U.S. Air Force and Army helicopters exerted their maximum effort, with thousand gun-ships sorties, 27 tactical air strikes and 11 B-52 missions dropping 909 tons of bombs. Around 13:00 hours, the 3rd Battalion, 2nd Regiment was extracted from the area west of Sophia East by U.S. Army helicopters which flew through heavy antiaircraft fire to evacuate it to Ham Nghi Base. In the process, 28 of the 40 helicopters involved were hit. Plans for the extraction of the 4th Battalion of 2nd Regiment were subsequently aborted because the first helicopter attempting to land was hit by fire and exploded in the air. Before nightfall, the artillery pieces at FSB Alpha along with the 2nd and 7th Airborne Battalions were transported back to Vietnam mainland. Plans provided for the 2nd and 4th Battalions, 2nd Regiment, to be picked up the next day, followed by the regimental headquarters, its artillery, and the 1st Battalion, 3rd Infantry from FSB Delta-1. The two 2nd Regiment battalions were ordered to find a more secure pick up zone. In the meantime, the 1st Armored Brigade, reinforced by the 7th and 8th Airborne Battalions, had arrived at Phase Line Alpha the preceding evening. The armored and airborne elements deployed to provide security for Route-9 from Alpha to Base Bravo. At 21:00 hours the NVA attacked the 8th Airborne Battalion and 11th Armored Cavalry Squadron south of Alpha but were repulsed with heavy losses. Around FSB Delta of the 147th Marine Brigade, on this same day, General Giap' troop suicide troops reached the defense perimeter and dug in. Small arms fire from these pockets made helicopter landings and takeoffs even more difficult. Supply deliveries could not be made but the 7th Marine Battalion and the troops of the 147th Brigade held on because they had previously received a ten day reserve of supplies which would permit them to continue fighting.

On 21 March, at 03:00 hours Giap' troop action became intense in the area to the west, where the 2nd and 4th Battalions of the 2nd Regiment were stranded 2 kilometers east of Sophia East. The Regiments of the NVA 2nd Division, which in position ambush at 604, now fly back to cut friendly retreat to Khe Sanh, were determined to attack and annihilate these two battalions but they were not successful. In the process, the enemy lost 245 killed, 52 B-40s and B-41s, seven machineguns, seven 60-mm mortars, five 82-mm mortars, eight flame throwers, nine 12.7-mm machine-guns and 65 AK-47s. Friendly losses were 37 killed, 58 wounded and 15 missing. This ARVN victory caused enemy pressure to relax and the remaining forces of the 1st Infantry Division were transported by U.S. helicopters to Ham Nghi Base before nightfall. Meanwhile, Colonel Luong at headquarters of the 1st Airborne Brigade, the 5th Airborne Battalion and the troops of the artillery unit left at FSB Alpha were also safely evacuated south. Fire support bases Alpha and Delta-1 were thus closed on that day and ARVN forces pulled back near FSB Bravo, 5 kilometers west of the GVN border. The situation in the areas manned by the 1st Infantry and the Airborne Division had been resolved but, over in the Marines' area, there was an eruption of fire. The 29th and 803rd Regiments of the 324B NVA/Division were determined to destroy FSB Delta. These two enemy units began attacking fiercely at dawn of 21 March. Mortar and direct artillery fire – the latter believed to come from tank guns, was very accurate. All U.S Long-Tom 175-mm guns from the Vietnam side of the border were mobilized to provide close fire support to the Marines. In the morning, 13 tactical air sorties provided additional support. A B-52 mission was diverted to the area and crushed an enemy battalion [a POW later reported this battalion had lost 400 men from this B-52 action] the attack was checked and the base held firm. A casualty count showed that the Marines had 85 killed, 238 wounded and 100 weapons damaged while enemy forces suffered 600 killed, five detained and an estimated 200 individual and 60 crew-served weapons seized. After the battle, the 147th Brigade and the 7th Marine Battalion ran short of supplies. Thanks to air support, 7 U.S/UH1-H helicopters were able to land, bringing ammunition and evacuating wounded. These helicopters were able to return to their base but all bore battle scars. An eighth helicopter was shot down. During this period the enemy greatly increased his interference and jamming of our radio communications. Several frequencies were so badly jammed that communications became impossible. In many instances, enemy radio operators argued and exchanged insults with ours. These heated verbal exchanges occurred most frequently when the enemy intensified his attacks against the marines. To return the courtesy, our operators also intercepted and jammed enemy radio frequencies. During one of these interceptions, marine operators overheard a female voice giving combat orders. In general, South Vietnamese units did not make enough effort to safeguard radio communications security, often using the most rudimentary of self-devised code systems. This episode of reciprocal interference and jamming was perhaps more damaging to our side than to the enemy who was usually more disciplined. The extent of this damage, if any, could never be ascertained because of the intense fighting.

In the morning of 21 March in resumed retaliation because Arc Light/B-52 instead the 'Rolling thunder' changed to 'Linebacker' Air campaign. – Vandegrift logistical base was penetrated by Communist sappers and 10,000 gallons of aviation fuel exploded into flames. Along Route-9, near FSB-Bravo, the 11th Armored Cavalry Squadron and 8th Airborne Battalion were heavily engaged. There were nearly 100 casualties while 4 M-41 tanks and 13 armored personnel carriers were damaged. This battleground looked forlorn after the attack, with damaged vehicles abandoned and scattered across the road, making passage extremely difficult. During the day, U.S. air support remained at a high level to help relieve the enemy pressure and facilitate the withdrawal of ARVN forces. Once again, thousand gun-ship-sorties included VNAF gun-ships of my 213th Squadron, eleven B-52 missions **Linebacker** dropping 921 tons of bombs and 157 tactical air sorties which destroyed 37 enemy vehicles and one field gun and damaged 18 other vehicles. During the night of 21 March, the 1st Armored Brigade and the 1st and 8th Airborne Battalions left their positions along Route-9 and moved east through the jungle in search of a point to cross the Xepon River. Successful in avoiding enemy contact, the convoy of nearly 100 vehicles meandered through the dense jungle until about noon the next day when it came out near the banks of the river, about one kilometer south of Route-9. Now Colonel James Vaught Airborne Advisor, he brought with him the French map of operational area for searching the dry- drought stream on Xepon River, contact 101st US Airborne to facilitate any means helping the ARVN to retreat and the brigade was provided with a Huey to help it find a crossing point and the commander of the Airborne Division had helicopters CH-54 Sky-crane, CH-53 Sea Stallion and Chinooks CH-47 prepared to airlift light D-4 bulldozers as well as tree cutting equipment to help set up a crossing point for the armored vehicles. During the dry season, the Xepon River is usually shallow but the current is swift and the banks are steep, in many places ten meters straight down. A crossing point for vehicles was therefore not easy to find. Meanwhile, the 9th Airborne Battalion had crossed the river and secured the eastern bank. In late afternoon, two D-4 bulldozers and other pieces of equipment were lifted in by U.S. Army CH-54 helicopter and the river crossing site was prepared.

Meanwhile, forward air controller aircraft sighted an estimated 20 enemy armored vehicles closing in pursuit nine kilometers to the west by way of Route-9 and called in tactical air. The lead tank was hit and went up in flames. Enemy antiaircraft gunners returned the fire and one F-l00 aircraft was shot down. The pilot was not seen ejecting. Two more flights of aircraft were called in and two more enemy vehicles were destroyed. Artillery support following the air strikes finally caused the enemy armored formation to break up and the vehicles to seek concealment. Why did the armored convoy leave Route-9 and make a cut through the jungle to find a way to cross the river when there was only a final stretch of five kilometers left to cover until the Lao- Viet border? The reason was never officially explained but Colonel Nguyen Trong Luat, Commander of the 1st Armor Brigade, later told to me that had his unit not taken to the jungle to seek a way out. He did not believe a single vehicle could have made it back to Vietnam. Route-9 was a one way road, not only littered with abandoned vehicles and rigged with mines all along, but every section of it could conceal a Communist ambush site. It was so treacherous that no one dared venture on it. The withdrawal along Route-9 surely did not proceed as planned in an orderly and controlled manner.

Early the next morning, 23 March, while Khe Sanh Base was still finishing off Communist sappers who had infiltrated earlier, the

The New Legion

ARVN armored column crossed the Xepon River and the lines of the U.S. 1st Mechanized Infantry Brigade, 5th Division. The convoy returned with 98 vehicles left behind, among them 22 M-41 tanks and 54 armored personnel carriers. Aerial and photo reconnaissance showed that the ARVN units had left 21 tanks, 26 armored personnel carriers, 13 bulldozers, two graders and 51 vehicles at a night bivouac area on Route-9. U.S. air force EC-130B gun-ships and artillery were used to destroy these vehicles to keep the enemy from using them. Khe Sanh Base, in the meantime had received four attacks by fire during the night, all by 122-mm artillery, but damage was insignificant. In lower Laos, meanwhile, fighting was still fierce around FSB Delta. The airdropping of supplies on the base was not successful and ammunition stocks had dropped to an alarming level. Enemy troops had penetrated and established a firm foothold inside the Marines' perimeter. Late in the afternoon, the enemy launched a new attack, this time supported by ten flame throwing tanks. The Marines blew up the first two tanks with light antitank weapons. The third tank detonated mines and the fourth was hit by tactical air. But the remaining tanks continued to advance. The headquarters of the 147th Brigade had to move out of its position. The 2nd and 4th Battalions supported the 7th Battalion to break the enemy's encirclement and withdraw toward the 258th Brigade at FSB/Hotel. The enemy seemed to have anticipated this move and he intercepted the troops of the 147th Brigade in an ambush. A pitched battle ensued with enemy tanks and infantry. The following morning, 23 March, all battalion commanders of the 147th Brigade, though wounded, managed to maneuver their battalions to link up with the 258th Brigade. Eventually, isolated teams of marines who had been cut off from their units also followed suit. Almost immediately thereafter, 230 wounded were evacuated and, before nightfall, the entire 147th Marine Brigade with its 2nd, 4th and 7th Battalions were transported by U.S. Army helicopters to an area near Ham Nghi Base. There were initially 134 missing reported but they gradually came back, leaving the entire brigade with only 37 missing; The battle at FSB Delta had cost the enemy an estimated 2,000 Giap' troops, seriously hurting his 29th and 803rd Regiments. Around noon of 23 March the last vehicles of the armored convoy crossed the border and the remaining airborne elements successively reached the forward positions of the U.S. 1st Brigade, 5th Infantry Division [mechanized] Because of enemy armored presence reported near the border, the U.S. Brigade had recently been reinforced with a tank battalion. During the day, 23 March, U.S. air support continued at a high level: 756 helicopter gun-ship sorties, 11 B-52 missions dropping 941 tons of bombs which caused 77 secondary explosions, and 283 tactical air sorties.

In the morning of 24 March, as if propelled by the momentum of the pursuit, many NVA' armored of 202 Regiment vehicles appeared on the Laotian side of the border. Near Route-9 and south of the road, between 10:00 hours and noon, U.S. air cavalry reported up to five different locations of enemy armored vehicles near the border. The U.S. air cavalry and tactical air attacked and destroyed 5 NVA' tanks, not counting those suspected of being damaged. In the area of FSB Hotel, the remaining elements of the 258th Marine Brigade began to feel enemy probes. Not wishing to fight another Delta battle, the Marine Division commander ordered its evacuation. In the late afternoon, U.S. helicopters lifted out all six 105-mm and four 155-mm howitzers, and all of the Marines. Immediately upon reaching Khe Sanh, the 258th Brigade was sent to Lang Vei to set up a fire support base and take over an area of operations. On this same day, the 2nd Regiment, 1st Infantry Division also deployed its units to provide security for Ham Nghi Base. The 54th Infantry Regiment from Hue received orders to move to Khe Sanh and relieve the 2nd Regiment which needed some rest. ARVN units including the 5th Regiment, 2nd Division were also deployed to gradually replace U.S. units west of Quang Tri. On 25 March, upon special orders from I Corps, the Marine Division dispatched two reconnaissance teams to the Mt Co Roc area to control a vantage point essential for the security of Khe Sanh Base.

On this day, 25 March, there were only two small ARVN reconnaissance teams left on Laotian territory. – During the morning of **8 March**, while Marine and Airborne units made sporadic contacts with the enemy in all other areas with varying degrees of success, FSB of LoLo continued to receive attacks by bombardment fire which caused all planned re-supply and evacuation flights into the base to be cancelled. The 2nd Battalion, 2nd Infantry Regiment continued to search the areas around Tchepone and found 52 dead enemy soldiers along with three heavy machine-guns, 44 rifles and about 50 heavy artillery rounds destroyed by air-strikes. Late afternoon found the units of the 2nd Regiment assembled near the banks of the Tchepone River. That night, two battalions of the 2nd Regiment moved past Tchepone on the east and crossed the river to the southern side.On **9 March** at 09:00 hours, the regiment began to climb the ridge to FSB Sophia the invasion of Tchepone had been completed. Meanwhile, Lieutenant General Lam, Commander of I Corps, arrived at the Presidential Palace in Saigon to report to President Thieu on the situation. General Vien, Chairman of the Joint General Staff, was present at that meeting and heard General Lam present the rationale for the withdrawal and the outline of how it would be executed. Why did General Lam and General Vien recommend to President Thieu that the apparently successful operation into Laos be terminated so far ahead of schedule? The 2nd Infantry had not nearly completed its mission in the hills east of Tchepone where great quantities of NVA military supplies were stored, and only a brief reconnaissance had been conducted into the town itself. No ARVN reconnaissance in force had reached the Xe Bang Hiang River, the principal waterway that flows from north to south west of the town, although the ARVN commander in this zone had requested that CBU-42 (timed-delay bomb-lets) be sewn on the west bank to make it difficult for the NVA to concentrate there. Coincidentally, of course, this barrier also inhibited any ARVN crossing of the river in this area, although it was the western side of the Tchepone complex that was suspected of containing numerous supply depots and huge quantities of war materiel. The river would have to be crossed to complete the task, but President Thieu decided early-out there.

Why was the river not crossed? Because President Thieu ordered *"pissed there a mess and go home"*, that was a rough simple order from military supreme high-level? You should guess! Thieu suggested if U.S sent one division engaged the war game, and we'll approve and go ahead for battle deployment for anywhere, anytime she wanted. Unfortunately U.S turned down flatly, and progressively withdrawn, then Thieu reiterated "we're carrying out tactical job, but strategic plan, we're not ready. However, literally we'd guessed: The answer is that a careful military estimate was made, based upon all the pertinent information available at the time, and the conclusion was inescapable: it was time to get out. First was the problem of terrain. In a tactical sense, ARVN forces were facing an uphill task, progressing as they did from the lowlands, with which they were familiar, to the highlands where the well entrenched enemy predominantly enjoyed the advantage. The only road available for troop and supply movements ran through steep mountains and dense forests. The enemy had operated in this region for many years, was familiar with it and knew all the trails. He could cut the road or lay ambushes almost anywhere. To the west past Ban Dong, this road ran through a range of high mountains. All along the slopes the NVA had positioned a dense array of antiaircraft artilleries, big and small. These guns not only fired at aircraft but also at ARVN troop columns and truck convoys moving to and from Tchepone. The forests of the Truong Son Range are especially formidable obstacles to cross country movement. The bases of the tall trees are girded by bamboo thickets, dense and thorny. These forests do not permit armored operations and thorny bamboo greatly hampers movements of infantry soldiers. But NVA troops were familiar with the terrain, had pre-digging fortifications and knew all the path and trail orientations. The NVA soldiers affected this important advantage.

The weather was a factor which also worked for the enemy and seldom favored the ARVN side with its numerous helicopters and strong air-mobility-force. As presented in the terrain description of lower Laos is usually obscured in fog from dawn until mid morning, sometimes until noon. Aircraft could usually operate after the fog lifted until late afternoon, but only if there was no rain and even if it didn't rain low clouds sometimes prevented the full use of ARVN' air supports. On the other hand, the endless mountains and forests provided good concealment for enemy deployments within the area of operations as well as for the movement of reinforcements from far away. Our failure to detect all of these movements presented ARVN commanders with many unwelcome surprises. Even those enemy units which had not previously operated in the Laos panhandle had the support of veteran units to provide guides, assistance and advice. In short, the enemy was thoroughly familiar with the terrain

The New Legion

in lower Laos and ARVN troops were not. The terrain and weather favored the defenders and handicapped the attackers. The area was especially disadvantageous for our mechanized and armored forces which were restricted to narrow jungle roads on which two vehicles could not pass and on which entire columns could often be jammed or stalled by one disabled vehicle. The NVA strength and reinforcement capability was the second factor that influenced the decision to initiate the withdrawal. Estimated enemy forces in the immediate area of operation consisted of three infantry regiments, rear service elements capable of local defense, and artillery elements especially notable for their air defense capability. It was estimated that the NVA could reinforce, within two weeks, with up to eight infantry regiments and the equivalent of an artillery regiment. Heavy artillery and armor also strengthened the enemy's capabilities. First among these was the enemy's dispersed and well concealed 130-mm and 152-mm heavy useful-artillery. ARVN' stationary fire support bases on hilltops, therefore, were easy targets for enemy artillery fired. The second factor in the enemy's capability of deep concern to the leadership in Saigon was the enemy armor strength that had become apparent. The planners of Lam-Son 719 had failed to give sufficient consideration to the threat of NVA Armor 202 Regiment, and now this threat had become a reality. Even though enemy armor was under daily attack from the air, FSB of Hill-31 had been lost because of the enemy's effective coordination of Armor and Infantry forces. In other places the enemy used his tanks as highly mobile field guns moving them individually over trails to ambush ARVN armored vehicles on the roads. The maneuvering of tanks on such a large scale over forest trails known only to the enemy posed a great threat to ARVN armored vehicles which were confined to congested one way roads strewn with disabled vehicles. Moreover, NVA tanks had thicker armor and mounted guns of a larger caliber than the ARVN tanks, 100-mm versus 76-mm and had a significantly greater armor defeating capability. After all, we're outgunned which was the Axis of Evil' scam, they really want it for their selfish-interests.

Even after a month of intensive attack the enemy's air defense capabilities showed no signs of being subdued and he had positioned surface-to-air missiles west of the border or at the Ban Raving Pass.

These missiles had Route-9 from Khe Sanh to Ban Dong within effective range, a challenge that the U.S. Air Force had to face. Around the ARVN' besieged bases, even after waves of air-strikes, enemy anti-aircraft artilleries would reappear close to their original positions. Also, antiaircraft batteries were deployed along helicopter avenues of approach; those positioned on the mountain slopes between Ban Dong and Tchepone seemed impossible to uproot, because they're hidden in the tunnels and plenty ammunitions scattered along mountainous ranch northern Route-9, so they get a chance of shoot down my Gunship on last week. That enemy capability practically neutralized the ARVN advantage of helicopter mobility and logistic support. In contrast to the enemy who had large uncommitted reserves in North Vietnam, our reserves were limited indeed. The Airborne and Marine Divisions constituted the entire general reserves of the RVN and they were already committed. Committing the 1st Infantry Division and the 1st Ranger Group required *[if so much dependable on air-supports, then sometime we get trouble because WIB Bones plot with Russia against us]* an extreme effort made possible only with the help of the U.S. 101st Airborne Division which replaced these two units in the lowlands of Thua Thien Province. And now, in the light of the enemy's reinforcement and strength on the battlefield, it was becoming apparent that the ARVN force committed to Lam Son 719 was too small for the task. General Abrams recommended that the ARVN 2nd Infantry Division at Chu-Lai be sent in to reinforce, and the division was preparing plans to turn over its area of responsibility in MR 1 to the U.S. 23rd Infantry Division. Still, in the view of the RVN leadership, one additional division would be insufficient to ensure total victory and would result in a higher casualty figure for our forces in Laos. Also, removing the 2nd Division from MR 1 would leave more of the vital lowland areas of MR 1 undefended. The only reasonable course of action was an orderly withdrawal to conserve as much of the committed force as possible. Further reinforcing this conclusion was the fact that the political and psychological objective of the campaign had been achieved; the RVNAF had entered Tchepone. It was apparent that President Thieu had decided, at the outset, that once Tchepone had been entered by RVNAF, the withdrawal should begin without delay

The New Legion

The main features of the withdrawal plan were outlined by President Thieu at the 9 March meeting. The 2nd Infantry Regiment would close FSB of Sophia and establish a new support fire base (called Brick) near Route-92 about 9 kilometers south of Ban Dong. The units of the 2nd Regiment would be picked up at various landing zones in the Sophia-Liz area and inserted into landing zones south and west of FSB of Brick. Thereafter, the 2nd Regiment would move southwest, searching for and destroying installations of NVA sanctuary [Binh Tram 33] and interdicting Route-914. The 1st and 2nd Regiments would conduct operations in the area of Route- 914 for seven to ten days. The withdrawal would then proceed in the following order: first, the 1st Division, then the Airborne Division; FSB of LoLo would close thereafter to be followed by FSB of Brick; the 3rd Infantry Regiment in the area of Brown and FSB of Delta-1 would pull out after closing FSB A-Luoi, After the withdrawal of the Airborne Division, the 147th and 258th Marine Brigades would move out from the areas of FSB of Delta and Hotel. The entire withdrawal, according to Lieutenant General Lam' estimated, was scheduled for completion by 31 March. After resting and reorganizing for about two weeks, the 1st Infantry Division, two Marine brigades and one Airborne Brigade would conduct operations into the eastern sector of enemy Base Area 611, the A Shau Valley and the Laotian salient. The Khe Sanh Base would probably close on 15 April.

The 1st Infantry Regiment continued to search the areas of Ta Luong and Route-914 and was able to assess the substantial damages inflicted by B-52 bombing runs. In two areas approximately 10 kilometers south and southeast of FSB of Sophia, the 4th Battalion found the bodies of 72 Communist troops, 12 Soviet and Chinese Trucks, eight tracked vehicles, three 122-mm towed cannons two 37-mm anti-aircraft artillery guns, four 12.7-mm machineguns, two 122-mm rocket launchers, 400 AK-47 rifles, thirty two 82-mm mortars, 18 B- 40s, 60 Chi-com radios and huge quantities of food of all types. Most of these supplies were blown to bits by B-52 bombs. The battalion also captured five prisoners of war. During the morning of **10 March**, the 2nd Regiment on FSB of Sophia received a heavy attack by NVA fired strafing. The attack wounded 13 soldiers and damaged six of the eight 105-mm howitzers at the base. On **11 March**, 2nd

Infantry Regiment elements operating around the FSB had increasing contacts with the enemy. At 11:00 hours, a reconnaissance element operating approximately one kilometer southeast of the base engaged a NVA patrol killing eight and seizing their weapons. According to plans, the 2nd Infantry Regiment was to move this day, on foot to LZ of Liz from where it would be airlifted eastward. Between 14:00 hours and nightfall, the 2nd Battalion was removed from LZ Liz and deposited on LZ of Brown. The 5th Battalion landed approximately one kilometer north of LZ Sophia East where the headquarters of the 2nd Regiment had already relocated while the 4th Battalion continued to secure FSB of Sophia. Late that afternoon an element of the battalion engaged the NVA troops approximately 1,000 meters south of the base but casualties were light on both sides.

During the day, 1st Infantry Regiment forces continued to search the Ta Luong area and found more substantial damage caused by B-52 attacks. On **12 March**, the evacuation of the 2nd Regiment was completed. The 3rd Battalion from FSB Liz landed approximately 1,000 meters south of FSB Sophia East and the 4th Battalion was the last unit to leave FSB Sophia. In order to facilitate the movement of troops, U.S. tactical air bombed and destroyed the eight 105-mm howitzers left on the base and another 105-mm battery was brought to FSB Sophia East from Khe Sanh. The units of the 1st Infantry Regiment, whose headquarters was at FSB of LoLo, were the forces located deepest to the west. On the fronts manned by the Airborne and Marine Division, engagements and attacks by fire followed an increasing trend. Meanwhile, two M-41 tank troops reassigned by JGS from MR-2 were moving into lower Laos to reinforce the 4th Armored Cavalry Squadron. U.S. air support was becoming more effective since Vietnamese interpreters flying with FAC [forward air controllers] had become more familiar with the situation. Re-supply operations were conducted throughout the battle area thanks to the daring and the noble spirit of sacrifice of U.S. Army helicopter crews.

Upon the 2nd Infantry Regiment's withdrawal from the area west of FBS LoLo; NVA forces, probably elements of the 1st and 31st Regiments of the NT-2 Division began to encircle units of the 3rd Infantry Regiment. Beginning on **13 March**, the battalions operating in the Ta Luong area were gradually forced to withdraw north and FSB of LoLo began to receive uninterrupted attacks by NVA fired bombardment. On **14 March**, the intensity of these attacks increased. During the day, the base received an estimated two hundred 122-mm rockets and one hundred 152-mm artillery rounds. Thanks to their solid shelters and trenches, the Regiment had only three killed and two wounded but one D-4 bulldozer and two 105-mm howitzers were seriously damaged. In the meantime, the enemy had moved up to the base and small arms fire was being directed at supply aircraft, causing medical evacuation and re-supply attempts to be called off. On **15- March**, the base could not be re-supplied (nor could Delta or A-Luoi, both of which were under attacks by terrible bombardment fired) The various units on and around the base were running out of ammunition and the number of wounded in need of evacuation was increasing. A withdrawal plan was hastily prepared. The headquarters of the 1st Regiment and the battalions outside the base would move east. The 4th Battalion would serve as the rear guard protecting the regiment in its effort to break through enemy encirclement. The plan was carried out satisfactorily but the enemy tightened its hold on the 4th Battalion. Finally, this unit fought its way out with the enemy in pursuit. All the while rejecting the NVA demands for it to surrender due to their overwhelming on **17 March**, close to the banks of the Xepon-River, the battalion was intercepted and the fighting lasted all day, with tactical air and VNAF 213th Magic-Club Squadron, Gunships Cobra Air Cavalry providing dedicated support. The battalion commander and his deputy were both killed. Most of the company commanders and officers of the battalion were also killed and the few survivors managed to escape to an area near Route-9. There, in the late afternoon of **18- March**, U.S. helicopters with tactical air support conducted a daring rescued. Three helicopters were hit and one fighter-bomber exploded in the air but the thirty two survivors of the 4th Battalion were rescued and flown to the safety rear. The battalion had accomplished well its rear guard mission and in the process, had sacrificed nearly every man. The fight put up by FSB of LoLo and the units of the 1st Infantry Regiment had resulted in 1,100 enemies killed, causing severe losses to two main force regiments of the Communist NT-2 Division (Steel-Star)

Vinh-Van-Truong

Hero worship by Vietnamese to Lancaster and Jim Manthel

Early morning 20th March, the TASK force 1st Armor Brigade retreated back to Khe Sanh on Route-9, reaching four kilometers east of FSB/A-Luoi. When the convoy been crossing a small stoned creek, the NVA on the high crest shot down every kind of individual weapons the most B-41, 40 and launched grenades, the tank/M-41 leader was destroyed, damaged four chain tanks and 18 GMC Trucks. Now the Airborne men were just jump out the armor-M-113 to counterattack. Colonel Luat decided must leaving behind the damaged vehicles: 4 M-41, 3 M-113, and 18 GMC Trucks for easier go ahead to proceed. Our two gun-ships had to engage of interdict to neutralization about 3 hours covered strafing. The convoy continued en route while we strafing for empty all last firepower. The convoy resumed to move very slowly in hesitation. A reconnaissance FAC plane OV-10 Bronco let the Colonel Luat a hot-information coordinated with NVA/POW investigations that the enemy used our damaged tanks and its guns to fire back strafing our convoy while in contact. So Airborne, Lieutenant Colonel XO Ngoc, from Airborne' convoy-lead commander gave order to our 213th gun-ships belong to Airborne had to neutralize all suspect spots in front of them. Now our gun-ships were run out of rockets so we used mini-guns to kill the new occupied-gunners in our damaged-tanks M-41s and armored carriers M-113s. Then we flown razed on the ground, not diving approach like Cobra; suddenly many throng showered bullets that enemy don't know nowhere and everywhere, this magnificent tactic neutralization let enemy must hidden underground, and now four of our gunners make circle pattern 75meters over them, in spewing at 4,000 rounds until we empty our ammunitions and diving low level in razing to go home for rearmed, miracle no birds get hit. Heavy sound in my helmet, Lt Colonel Ngoc reminded us rush back at once after reloaded armament, refuel with the both flank-side equipped two a 19-shot 2.75-inch antitank rocket pods [as my order and reduce in am-container at 6,000 rounds, we will reinforced one more gunship in formation of three gun-ships.

One of the first major problems that our forces had to face, in addition to the enemy's blocking positions, was his elusive but devastating anti-aircraft system. The most common weapon he used against our chopper was the 12.7-mm heavy machinegun which constantly switched firing positions. In addition, throughout the area, there were about 200 AAA pieces from 23-mm up to 100-mm, some of them radar controlled. Even these heavy weapons frequently changed their firing positions which were usually well concealed. In general, the enemy's anti-aircraft system seemed to be well coordinated and its fire controlled with skill and discipline. His heavy machineguns such as 12.7-mm, 14.5-mm or even 23-mm, were arranged in an equilateral triangle or circle pattern, affording mutual protection and providing a well coordinated fire trap. For example, one weapon could open fire to draw our aircraft to it and when our aircraft made the attack, it would enter another weapon's field of fire. Enemy AAA positions not only changed frequently, they also moved in uncomfortably close to our units in coordination with an envelopment and attack by infantry troops. The most effected by AAA mounted on PT-76s. As a result, they were extremely difficult to destroy and the price our choppers had to pay when lifting troops, delivering supplies or evacuating the wounded was high.

The sharp conflict between Airborne and Armor unit that was created so much trouble in the retreat operation, because as far as I knew: The Airborne men had to proceeding in front and broader security for both side of the Route-9 in SOP [Standard Operation Procedure] principle of convoy protection, might be Airborne men were too exhausted due to long combat activities under horrible indirect bombardment. Then they were waiting while be ambushed so they reacted …Oh God! That too late! This conflict lasted two days, between Colonel Luat Armor and Colonel Luong Airborne. Then two 7th and 8th Airborne Battalions designed a spearhead for the convoy. Today, **20th March** the U.S forces having abrupt order from high command retreated to Dongha leaving Lao Bao, afterward Khe Sanh should be on time table. From now on, our gun-ships carried out the rest. Likely last three weeks, while the Air Cavalry had 25% aircraft in commission, the VNAF had to replace a few, due to a handful choppers we have then we're just ran priority for medivacs and supply few amount of small arms cartridges ammunition and water. Long considered as the elite unit of the ARVN, the Airborne Division did not perform as brilliantly as its reputation would indicate during

Lam Son 719. Despite the enemy's superiority in maneuvering forces and his employment of new weapons, the fact that the division was unable to hold FSB 31 [because only 300 fighter soldier defenders] seemed to be indicative of its lack of contingency planning for such a situation. But our airborne units fought extremely well as individual elements. One of the division's brigade commanders, Colonel Nguyen Van Tho was missing in action - probably captured by the enemy; and five out of nine of its battalion commanders were either killed or wounded. This testified to the intense fighting that the division had to face but by and large, the division accomplished nothing spectacular in its assigned mission. During the final stage, the division also failed to provide effective flank protection for the major effort and secure Route-9 even with the reinforcement of four armor squadrons. This failure greatly complicated the ARVN withdrawal from Laos.

The 1st Armor Brigade was at a great disadvantage when faced with enemy tanks deep in the jungle. In those circumstances, ARVN armor officers were naturally unable to make effective use of combat tactics they had learned in Saint Cyr, Saumur-French and Fort Knox-U.S schools. The brigade commander was also not resourceful enough to meet this unusual combat challenge. The outcome was evident: only one third of the total number of armored vehicles committed managed to return home after accomplishing nothing substantial. If someone was to be held responsible for this failure, the question would arise as to whether it should be the commander of the brigade or his superior, who committed this unit to such an undesirable and impossible situation. A withdrawing under siege of enemy pressure was always a difficult operation which should be carefully planned by Pentagon [General Haig' staff-officers] and executed on his map plan decisive on January, 18, 1971. Thereby, the time allowed for its execution was too short. The extrication of troops by helicopters naturally increased their vulnerability when compared to a withdrawal on foot. However, some movements to the rear on foot were not executed in a satisfactory manner. Our forces suffered serious losses on routes selected for withdrawal because of combined armor-airborne ambushes laid by the NVA separate regiments. During the retreat, the Airborne Battalions 7 and 8th and the entire Armor force were unable to ensure protection for their own movements our gun-ships unable help. The 1st Armored Brigade, reinforced by the 7th and 8th Airborne Battalions, had arrived at Phase Line Alpha the preceding evening. The armored and airborne elements deployed to provide security for Route-9 from Alpha to Base Bravo. At 2100 hours the NVA attacked the 8th Airborne Battalion and 11th Armored Cavalry Squadron south of Alpha but were repulsed with heavy losses.

During the night of 21 March, the 1st Armored Brigade and the 1st and 8th Airborne Battalions left their positions along Route-9 and moved east through the jungle in search of a point to cross the Xepon River. Successful in avoiding enemy contact, the convoy of nearly 100 vehicles meandered through the dense jungle until about noon the next day when it came out near the banks of the river, about one kilometer south of Route-9. The brigade was provided with a helicopter to help it find a crossing point and the commander of the Airborne Division had helicopters prepared to airlift light bulldozers as well as tree cutting equipment to help set up a crossing point for the armored vehicles [thank to successful assistance of Colonel James Vaught, a new Airborne Advisor, he carried with him the French operation map with some references] During the dry season, the Xepon River is usually shallow but the current is swift and the banks are steep, in many places ten meters straight down. A crossing point for vehicles was therefore not easy to find. Meanwhile, the 9th Airborne Battalion had crossed the river and secured the eastern bank. In late afternoon, two D-2 bulldozers and other pieces of equipment were lifted in by U.S. Army Skycrane, CH-54 helicopters and the river crossing site was prepared. Why did the armored convoy leave Route-9 and make a cut through the jungle to find a way to cross the river when there was only a final stretch of five kilometers left to cover until the Lao-Viet border! The reason was never officially explained but Colonel Nguyen Trong Luat, Commander of the 1st Armor Brigade, later told this writer that had his unit not taken to the jungle to seek a way out. He did not believe a single vehicle could have made it back to Vietnam. But this is WIB Bones objectives. Route-9 was a one way road, not only littered with abandoned vehicles and rigged with mines all along, but every section of it could conceal a Communist ambush site. There was so treacherous that no one dared venture on it. The withdrawal along Route-9 surely did not proceed as planned in an orderly and controlled manner. Meanwhile, forward air controller aircraft sighted an estimated 20 enemy armored vehicles closing in pursuit nine kilometers to the west by way of Route-9 and called in tactical air. The lead tank was hit and went up in flames. Enemy antiaircraft gunners returned the fire and one F-l00 aircraft was shot down. The pilot was not seen ejecting. Two more flights of aircraft were called in and two more enemy vehicles were destroyed. Artillery support following the air strikes finally caused the enemy armored formation to break up and the vehicles to seek concealment.

The NVA heavy artillery supported also strengthened the enemy's capabilities. First among these was the enemy's dispersed and well concealed 130-mm and 152-mm heavy artillery. ARVN' stationary fire support bases on hilltops, therefore, were easy targets for enemy artillery fire [*due to Pentagon prepare under siege for our ARVN on the traps for blow-out all out of date war materiel*] the other factor in the enemy's capability of deep concern to the leadership in Saigon was the enemy armor strength that had become apparent. The Pentagon-planners of Lam Son 719 had failed to give sufficient consideration to the threat of NVA Armor, and now this threat had become a reality. Even though enemy armor was under daily attack from the air, Fire Support Base 31 had been lost because of the enemy's effective coordination of armor and infantry forces. In other places the enemy used his tanks as highly mobile field guns moving them individually over trails to ambush ARVN armored vehicles on the roads. The maneuvering of tanks on such a large scale over forest trails known only to the enemy posed a great threat to ARVN armored vehicles which were confined to congested one way roads strewn with disabled vehicles. Moreover, NVA tanks had thicker armor and mounted guns of a larger caliber than the ARVN tanks, 100-mm versus 76-mm and had a significantly greater armor defeating capability. This situation was a repeated scene between Garant, Carbine M-1 against AK automatic weapon at 1968 Tet-Offensive.

Having an adverse effect on our area of operation – Route-9 until it reached Tchepone where it met the Xe Bang Hiang River, the

The New Legion

primary north-south waterway in the area. During the rainy season, when most ground lines of communication were inundated, the enemy used the Xe Biang Hiang River to float supplies downstream. The second prominent terrain feature was the Co Roc Highland adjacent to the Laotian border and just south of Route-9. This highland had several peaks with elevations ranging from 500 to 850 meters which dominated Route-9 to the east and west. It also provided excellent observation into the Khe Sanh area. The vegetation in the Co Roc area consisted primarily of bamboo and brushwood in which were natural obstacle that NVA used for underground shelter for ambush, offering adequate cover and concealment. The third significant terrain feature was a high escarpment whose ridgeline extended all the way to Tchepone, parallel to and south of Route-9 and the Xepon River. Several peaks of this ridgeline were 600 to 700 meters high and offered excellent observation over Route-9 and the Tchepone area. Much of the area was covered by dense jungle and thick brushwood except for a few places which had been cleared for farming. The terrain north of Route-9 was hilly and heavily vegetated against a backdrop of relatively high peaks which restricted operations in this area almost entirely to infantry. Around Tchepone, the terrain was much lower, sparsely vegetated and more appropriate for armor vehicles that favorable route maneuvers of NVA 202 Tank Regiment. Route-9 from Khe Sanh to Tchepone was a one lane, unevenly surfaced dirt road with destroyed bridges and culverts. Dominated by the high escarpment to the south, this road was easily interdicted. It also was difficult to prepare bypasses due to the river to the south and the hilly terrain to the north. In addition to Route-9, which was an old public road, the enemy had completed in the area west of the Laotian border an extensive, crisscrossing system of lines of communication. Most important of these was Route 1032 which connected with Route 92 and offered direct access from North Vietnam and the western DMZ area into base area 604, then base area 611, and from there into South Vietnam either by Route 92 or Route 616 or Route 922 further to the south. Another route, designated. Route 1039, also originating in North Vietnam passed through the Ban Raving Pass and offered access into Tchepone and base area 604 then connected with either Route 29 to go further south or with Route 914 which led into base area 611 and from there into Ashau-Valley, South Vietnam. All these routes were well maintained two lane roads practicable for large trucks at least during the dry season. Due to extensive bombings, the enemy had built several alternate routes which were well concealed by vegetation and often under double and triple canopies. In addition to main routes, the enemy also built narrow pathways crisscrossing the entire area. These areas were difficult to observe from the air and were convenient for concealing troop movements. February in the Tchepone area was the transitional period from the northeast to the southwest monsoons. The northeast monsoon, which brought rains and cloudiness to Central Vietnam above the Hai Van Pass from October to March, was the dominant weather factor. The Truong Son mountain range deflected much of this wet weather on the Laotian side but in the area of operation, the skies were generally covered. Daytimes the amount of cumulus buildup in this area depended on the strength and depth of the monsoon. Average temperature during February and March were 80 F in the lowlands and about 65 F in these mountainous regions

Captain Ferrell and Lancaster were brilliantly volunteers to help Airborne and Armor resuming a ferocious retreat. On the eerie ambushed section of Route-9, was look like a horseshoes on highlands with thick foliage-vegetations, these curves so twist and hard-rough for vehicles to proceed. The NVA/POW's investigations let us knew a preparedness of two NVA Regiments and some PT-76s were waiting for interception with our convoy forwarding to eastern. Suddenly when the convoy slowed down right in the middle of harsh-squeeze route, from right side on the vegetation hill slop, the rainy crashed of B-41 and different categories of individual bullets showered all over the convoy from their stood out in sharp relief against the dawn haze fog sky. Our tanks couldn't fire cover because can hit friendly forces in front curve of them. Of course, they stop to spread both side to defend. Captain Ferry and Lancaster follow the tank lead to strike east on the slop of the crest. They dived in steep approach and the most west side of the heavy forest. Fortunately, Lt Colonel Ngoc can speak English so well then directed their power ordnance right on the targets. Two Cobras strafing Rockets, mini-guns, and launched grenades to silence two antiaircraft guns 12, 7mm among of three equilaterally antiaircraft tactical for their self-covered. As a top-gun pilots, we can see the enemy red-hot bullets tracing close to our birds' fuselage, it sound like we can extended our hands to catch them. Top gun leader, Captain Ferrell was empty his fire-power armament for three pass-preps, and let go home, but the wingman, Lancaster urged let him finished the last pass-prep. Alas! There was his real last pass-away forever. Though Captain Ferrell persuaded him go home for rearms but he'd still go ahead and make steep-diving fire. Abrupt getting hit by antiaircraft ground fire, Lancaster radioed to Ferrell, he got hit in the tail rotor component, Ferrell should escort him to safe distance. He let cover Lancaster heading to southern for forced landing on flat-terrain but fail. Instantly, second by second the vibration increased high frequency created the aircraft spin toward the anticlockwise and crashed nearby on slop of a baldy-hill. When the Dusk-tuff coming, they merely recovered two remains breaking necks, those Americans heroes were Lancaster and Jim Manthel sacrificed for our World freedom out of Red menace. *"Alas! We never seem to learn from our forgiveness for what they had done. "Sacrifices often are unappreciated by those who benefit from them"*

The 7th Fleet tactical fighters coming to bombard the last 12, 7mm but in lost communication while the convoy resumed to proceeding forward. Unfortunately the fighters dropped in fault on friendly force killed 12 and wounded about 100 Airborne and Armor soldier, but thank to my wingman while he saw two parallel white jet-streamlines on the wing tip of a tactical fighter, steep dive to target and radioed to me escaped right away out of the area. I saw an A-6 Intruders just flashed in front of us. Our casualties were six more tanks destroyed.

Once again, our gun-ships were scrambled rushing to hot area over Route-9. After full loaded armament, and instantly over operational area, I glanced down at the target: "Everything is been damn hot now!" I had seen the orange panel in the offense-front line of Airborne Unit from 200 meters of the convoy, as I often had to request while we prep in discrimination foe and friend in the melee. Now the spot inclined little bit in left slop, though under nowhere some trajectories of shell 130, 152mm coming exploited likely erected-mushrooms around friendly area. We must took the advantage of the free target maneuver orientated of our mini-guns in strafing traffic pattern, meant approach prep parallel or flight up sometime to assault attack enemy another side of the horseshoes hill. In this tough circumstances, we couldn't able used our gunship dive-attack like Cobra, but only by means of a daring scared prep to the target area at a treetop level – with the intimidated noises of mini-guns barrels covering the suspect ambushed area, the enemy did know where and nowhere the deadly weapons coming. Now our combat formation of three 'left-echelon' and six mini-guns firstly attack-prep at low level strafing on treetop toward enemy; this tactical attack method-assault let enemy don't know where the killer coming just raining bullets above the tree line. While over the target, I still ordered the gunners continued strafing less 2,000 round per minutes for neutralized interdiction back and forth evenly over the horseshoes-hill, in the most areas heavy foliages bushes. Suddenly the enemy running down to slop standing bold strafing down into our gun-ships fly-pattern and friend forces by B-40 and 41, instantly all our gunners react by 4,000 rounds into them and my wingmen continued strafing, in the mist of haze light fog and stinging smokes I could see the tracers at the ratio of one tracer for every fourteen standard rounds scattered evenly on the hot spot, but at the rate those mini-guns fired, the spaced tracers would look like heavy raindrops, how could they escaped 24,000 bullets rain-shower on vegetation-hill in a minute? Now number-1 [me] make left turn go little-bit higher in round circle on target continued neutralized fire, and becoming C&C bird. And number-2 took a lead turn right in gaining altitude for prep attack approaches. I detected below a high tree, on green crest appeared prominent feature of some 'two-tracks' red fresh earth parallel were an armored PT-76 camouflage with clover foliage. Meanwhile, number-2, and -3 gained altitude in strafing rockets and detected few others.

"Magic-2 how doing you read me over" I radioed"

"Magic-1 ... I got the target at 3'oclock ... one big craft ...I'll going ahead barbecue him"

"Magic-2 and -3 ... going ahead to get him...over"

I don't blame them ...number-2 missed ... and number-3 salvo all rockets he carried on. I thought the time for neutralization would over, I deadly certain sure no one enemy gunner could staying bold to react but unfortunately my gunner got hit in his shoulder and I managed request authorization to leave for medivac my man. Then I managed to unload ordnance by 'Salvo' - Though even we didn't to damage all NVA/PT76s, this tactical air assault mission was stranger than NVA troops killer that we never learn in training school at all, because that the first time what I have said applies only to this particularly circumstances. I rolled out my gunship started climbed up slowly behind the hill, on the left clusters of intertwining ridges hiding behind the bald hill to the higher ridge forming the crest-peak horseshoes that gave the hill target spot its designation by height in meters 650 meters (2,100 feet) then I used this tactical flight for screening their eyes to farther behind them. I suddenly 'cow-boy' racing high airspeed up, raised bird nose to decrease airspeed [lasting timing slow in shot rockets] over the target spot, abruptly used right rudder-pedal to lower the helo-nose, take a high angle diving approach so deep akin to plunge strafing, simultaneously four mini-guns of cover-gun-2, -3 spewing at 4,000 rounds per minute and now four by four rockets busted down into the NVA/PT-76s on a baldy hill platform. Friend and foe could feel smelling our dark stingy smoke behind my gunship after strafing; I pressed the trigger, Oh God! Please don't jammed, knowing my gunners as the barrels on both flanks of the cockpit spat flame and buzzed like chain saws, their heavy bullets punching down to the four ambushed enemy tanks PT-76s. I don't think destroying all of them but at least neutralization in disable by my wingmen destroyed them lately by antitank rockets after me– orbiting to air cover center target still spewing at 2,000 rounds per minute for refreshing our electronic control-box. After all, three pass-prep patterns all 114 antitank-rockets and 18,000 bullets 7, 62 of three firebirds were used for pacified the battle. The convoy continued retreat to eastern and once again left six our damaged tanks M-41, M-113 stayed. Now we have to leave for medivac my man. Three gun-ships flied back Khe Sanh at high airspeed with goddamn light weight.

During a visit to Vietnam, General Haig had strewn a certain amount of Chaos in his Wake:

At forward XXIV Corps on 18 March General Haig told General

Sutherland that "Washington would like to see ARVN stay in Laos through April," The following day he visited II Field Force and told General Commander there "his tentative conclusion is that the time has come for an orderly close-out of the ground operations in Laos." Both field commanders dutifully reported these Haig observation to Abrams, who must have been somewhat bemused. I thought all U.S generals were totally bemused by all the activity around them due to operation's objective that was blow-out and kill all two crucial-opponents for Hanoi regime take over Saigon be not a real blood-bath.

President Thieu screwed-up the plan. – Pulling out wasn't the way General Abrams would have played it, but adversely President Thieu made decision to early-out? So consequently, the U.S forces at Khe Sanh have been to retreat back to Dongha 20th March instead of 20th April as I guessed – On earlier occasions, the venal press-corps had bias speculated that comparisons with American leadership of the time might have yielded interesting results, President Thieu was arguably a more honest and decent man than L.B. Johnson, and – given the differences in their respective circumstances quite likely a more effective president of my country. At the time, it seemed to me to point out that Thieu also probably had more freedom to move about in his country than a marionette, WIB-Bones-puppeteer L.B Johnson

"I'm just more and more convinced that what you've got here is maybe the only decisive battle of the war," General Abrams concluded.

"And they've got a chance to – it'll be hard – a chance to really do it."

Assessing the ARVN assault into the Tchepone area, my concept military analyst concluded that "the General Giap forces were slow to react to this, both due to his severe losses and to the rapidity with which ARVN forces moved out after they had remained in the Route 9 area for so long waiting" [As the anticipated preplan, mediator Pham Xuan An, triple-cross let General Giap getting information ARVN will be in traps at ambushed 604 logistic cargo, and Giap was already set for the NVA/Steel/2nd Infantry Division on the game]

The New Legion

Later, when Sir Robert Thompson arrived for one of his periodic visits, MACV briefed that

"For approximately ten days the Giap' force was unable to regain the initiative and mount any major counterattacks against ARVN as they were moving rapidly into the Tchepone area."

But I deadly sure that when ARVN forces moved south of Route 9 toward Route 914, the 2nd NVA Division set up an ambush to trap from hidden stronghold position. The major battles erupted there which was the goal that Permanent Government would like to destroy both these elite forces while attacking the cargo base 604 in which all materiel just been moved to Southern. So why President Thieu, after few second military strategic meditation – "Why the powerful force with tanks, artilleries, sappers from DMZ don't attack right close battle like Khe Sanh U.S Base but Giap manipulated moving these forces further far to Tchepone… what for? For what! [Because Giap a 1943 OSS member! Now his siblings lived in California, US – in the Axis of Evil commitment, KGB had offered a security Giap' body guard, many times he was escaped from assassinations by his cadre-opponents, thank to KGB]

The Giap' force was committing everything he had, just asking for it, really, given the history of the war. "When we've focused firepower on him, he hasn't been able to hack it." Already he's lost half of his tanks, half of his antiaircraft artilleries, and 10 of his 30 battalions.

Friendly losses were heavy, too, though proportionally not as severe. U.S Army helicopters were being hit hard too, according SOG report 219 dead and 38 MIA. With my eyes witnessed that Air Cavalry had been in the Tchepone area for more 10 days before ARVN got there on the ground, and that this had been useful in acquiring targeting data later used by Arc-Light B-52s, including strikes on stores that ground forces had not been able to extract or destroy in place. This intelligence was also supplemented by what long-range reconnaissance patrols acquired, and by reports from ARVN unit commanders. As a result, in conclusion "there's been massive destruction far beyond, I would guess, what was done in Cambodia last year."

Now I have few comments: Lam Son 719 presented General Lam with a "nearly insuperable array of new challenges." For the first time he and his staff were working from a field command post distant from their usual fixed headquarters at Danang. They were trying to execute an operations order much of which they did not understand. Neither the corps headquarters nor subordinate units, I draw in conclusion that "truly grasped the responsibilities inherent in attachment, the differences between a zone of action and an axis of advance, or the full meaning of the word 'secure.'" The Airborne and Marine divisions, though highly competent when operating at brigade level, had little experience in being employed as full division, meaning that "the division commanders and their staffs were totally unprepared for their tasks" Since both of these division commanders were senior in rank to Lieutenant General Lam, they were "severely miffed" at being subordinated to him. The Marine commander did not accompany his division from Saigon, and the airborne commander refused to attend General Lam' command post in briefings. And finally Lam wasted the armor brigade by attaching it to the Airborne Division, which had no idea what to do with it!

Whatever his inadequacies, General Lam got very little cooperation and even less obedience to orders from several of his senior supposed subordinates in the operation. I must say "really the hairiest problem we have out there. We've got a whole bunch of units that, when they want to, they operate independently, and it doesn't make any difference whether it's Lam or who it is."

On the political sphere, President Thieu' very costly tolerance of such chaos seemed to demonstrate essential insecurity. Even so, I thought, there were positive indications for future. Thieu saw "a significant difference between the style of leadership, and the real effective leadership, of generals like Truong, Tri, Nam;" who during an earlier period "were regiment or brigade commanders and division commanders, as opposed to – take the other extreme –Generals Vinh Loc and Lu Lan. And now even getting down to a man like General Lam, who's somewhere in between . But you're finding these corps commanders are like the corps commanders we'd like to think we had, who understood development of a fire plan, coordination of fires, precision and all that, techniques that are so important." I must again emphasized General Lam high marks for accomplishing as much as he did under the circumstances. "All initial objectives

The New Legion

were seized, and the ferocious NVA regiments counterattacks, while it overran Ranger positions in the North and the Airborne Hill-31 in farther west, and the Hill-30 under-siege being overran... General Lam calmly committed the 1st Infantry Division to the east-west ridge south of Route 9 with the simple mission of seizing Tchepone."

The poor condition of Route 9 was in the significant strategic plan of Permanent Government for the only one way dependable on the only used US helicopters. And the inability of ARVN forces keep it secure meant that virtually all re-supply mobility and medical evacuation for ARVN forces had to be done by US Air Calvary, the bulk of it by US air only. Calculating that in any given twenty four-hour period a helicopter could fly for between five and eight hours. General Abrams noted that in Laos the South Vietnamese had "18 battalions over there, and 10 batteries of artillery – and all the re-supply and everything that's got to be done for those 18 battalions and 10 batteries in the five to eight hours every twenty-four. Well that's not enough! There isn't a lot of sightseeing going on." I don't think so that's good enough for them. They were subjected to be damn! Practically, during the tough ferocious of weeks into the thing there wasn't a lot of flying going on, either, at least not compared with the huge requirements the operations was generating. By about longest weeks in February it became apparent the US Air Calvary support for this operation 719 was having some problems. Not only was the intense and well-sited NVA antiaircraft weaponry making operation Lam Son extremely difficult – every mission, even "Dust-off" (medical evacuations), had to planned and executed like a full-scale combat assault.

Therefore, later General Vien chief of staffs ARVN would write that the Lam Son operation was "hampered by bad weather and insufficient air support, including helicopters." If that judgment is correct, it is difficult to imagine what level of air support would have been sufficient. Some 600 US helicopters included CH-54 "sky-crane"CH-53 Stallion, and CH-47 Chinook were committed to the battle on a daily-time basis. And there was so much bombing, I recalled at eye witnessed "that by afternoon the setting sun would be shinning through so much smoke and dust that you couldn't see it."

From the beginning 8 Feb through 24 March, US tactical air flew more than 8,000 attack sorties, an average of nearly 150 sorties a day every day – the equivalent of one every ten minutes around the clock. And every night, all night, three forward air controllers, three AC.130 flare-ships, and three EC.130B gun-ships were on station, one each for the Ranger Group, the Airborne Division, and the 1st Infantry Division. Even the tactical airlift support was such that, at peak periods, there was an AC-130 arriving at Khe Sanh on the average of one every eight minutes. However throughout the operation deficiencies at high command levels continued to undermine the abilities and performance of South Vietnam's troops. I gave one example: "Airborne was really the 'rapid deployment force' but let them fixed as guard of a certain out-post for defense meanwhile the 1st Infantry Division took on charge an axis of advance instead of Marine or Airborne Division.

I felt so strongly about the thrust into Laos that in my opinion the Cambodian operation and this operation are the two most intelligent moves. US forces have made since they have been in Vietnam War. This operation may end the war and may save hundred thousands of lives in the long run, and everyone here is putting out 100%. However I should closed with a big apology:

"I'm sorry for the lousy of anger exploded, but I'm witnessing these gloomed sceneries on my gunship every day-light during 45 days of this operation"

If President Johnson can make decision as soon as 1967, the U.S responsibilities had already planned a ground offensive against Laos and had estimated that if it must success it was needed to deploy a powerful forces. Now, so too late, North Vietnam had deployed in southern Laos a full Army Corps 70B with tanks, ready to repel any ARVN foray, but South Vietnam was deploy a smaller force. However, this was the WIB' preplanned for "**axiom-1**" Thus, despite the intense air campaign to stop the North Vietnamese logistical flow along the Harriman highway, the NVA troop continued to reinforce their troops in South Vietnam, threatening to disrupt the Vietnamization process that the WIB expected, then the wheels must synchronized as they revolve as the gradual withdrawal of the U.S forces on board on time table of flight schedule.

The New Legion

Consequently, Operation Lam Son 719 was the largest air mobile operation of the war, but also one doomed to failure right from the start due to cooperation between the CIP and the NLF, the Axis of Evil' craps, so the American all the written plans had to be translated and the translators were largely double-cross, and triple-cross mediator [Pham Xuan An and Russell Flynn Miller] As a result, General Giap had copies of the whole documentation in hand almost as soon as South Vietnamese and US Army commanders of participant units. Additionally, neither Americans nor the South Vietnamese knew the terrain really well, while the NVA were well-prepared for defense and counterattack.

By 18 March, by chance, the Giap' forces had detected the withdrawal of ARVN units from the Route 9 area and directed his forces to surround, annihilate, and destroy those isolated units where they could, General Giap also told his people that some ARVN forces were rebelling against their leaders (the Axe of Evil via CIA, counterespionage-branch system, let him know; a meticulous staffs-researcher witch-hunt was a mediator between Pham Xuan An and Lt John F Kerry) that some were running away into the interior, and that the ARVN had been defeated. On the view of bird to close to the battle, it looks like to me a back-stiffening effort; also that this whole thing is one hell of a bloody battle. Certainly bloody it was. In one firefight after another the ARVN, while taking substantial casualties, inflicted disproportionately heavier ones on the Giap' force – 37 versus 245, 85 versus 600, on and on (En route to Tchepone nine battalion commanders were killed or wounded)

In order to withdraw after President Thieu said to General Lam "let a small unit touched down and pissed at there a mess then go home" – the most ARVN forces had already left lower Laos. Unfortunately, the intended and desired goal to sustain combat until the onset of the rainy season in order to strangle the Giap' supply route could not be accomplished. That was true, but it by no means conveyed an accurate impression of what had been achieved. Meanwhile in the earlier weeks of operation, some troop element had done conspicuously better than others. Typically, the ARVN armored units had been especially disappointing. Early in that Lam Son 719, the 1st Squadron, 11th Armored Calvary had encountered

NVA armored element in a fight at the feet bottom valley, southern Fire Support Base 31 and performed brilliantly, destroying 6 Giap T-54 tanks and 16 PT-76s without any friendly losses in the first major tank-to-tank engagement of the war but of course with the involvement of our Magic-Club 213th gun-ships loaded to the maximum with 2.75-inch antitank shorter-warhead in 19 rocket-pods each flank. After that, General Lam ordered ARVN forces to begin withdraw, though, the Armor floundered. Not only did they contribute little to offensive operations (basically, in the academic military institution the withdraw operation usually get to much trouble even having meticulously preparedness) Consequently the 1st Armored Brigade Cavalry came out of Laos with only a fraction of the equipment they took in, of 62 tanks only 25 tanks and of 162 armored personnel carriers only 64 were salvaged (the Axe of Evil schemed of a plan-arrangement obsolete military equipment become a rubbish, things that they does not want any more while need the new production one) The reason MACV knew these sorry statistics was that a U.S advisor intentioned met them at the border and made a personal count, an operation with plenty of scope for axe of evil original plans, had the losses been due to heavy combat, that would have been one thing, but in the main they were just vehicles that had broken down or run out of gas and been abandoned.

The 1st Armored Brigade floundered through a long wait for the ambushes. Additionally the Route 9 was constructed by French colonialist for long at best a narrow, nearly unimproved surface, twisting, or so it looked from the helicopter that Route some of those weather cuts that were in its route surface were couple feet deep. The reality was much worse in which they missed that in the readout of the aerial photography. As the result the poor condition of that Route, therefore the inability of ARVN forces to keep it secure, meant that virtually all re-supply and medical evacuation for our forces had to be done only by helicopters.

Along that Route 9, Giap' force tried ARVN force fell right into his traps that were reorganized by interval stronghold points of each regiment. NVA troops make some huge obstacles to stop the convoy and called shelling 130mm and 152mm guns to pounding into them, meanwhile they used 120mm mortar burst of numerous shells onto ARVN troops. NVA have been living in the area secretly for quite long from 1962 in the commence building the Harriman Highway (Ho chi Minh trail) and recently in the last phase of bunker construction and there was also a huge cargo logistic-ammunitions (67,000 short tons meanwhile ARVN would essentially be out of ammunition according Cooper-Church amendment) "This force Giap to continue a protracted war strategy in the South Vietnam right in the axe of evil's project as 'axiom-1".

Not too far from A-Loui Fire Support Base to the border, at northern flank was situated a 7th Squadron armored carriers and closer to A-Loui a platoon carriers, to western flank having two more carriers armored platoons. The 1st Armored Brigade commander Colonel Nguyen Trong Luat' headquarters was encircled by armored carriers like iron shield.

Further south to the west and south west of Delta Base, the ARVN Marines were engaged in fighting that had lasted for some days. The battle was savage. The shelling was non-stop. All out units from the north to the south of Route-9 were targeted by their intimidating artillery. There were huge losses. It was impossible to receive supplies and medevac because of the intense anti-aircraft fire. Eventually, the Special Task Force [the combined 1st Armor and Airborne] was ordered to retreat back to Khe Sanh. This withdrawal was extremely difficult since the NVA had clearly expected our intentions. They intensified their attack. Under such pressure, the fighting spirit of the troops felt drastically, and the commanders had difficulty getting their orders fulfilled. Helicopters however had great trouble landing. Some panic stricken soldiers struggled with their brothers in arms to gain a spot on the helicopters which managed to land. Again this fact was grossly exaggerated by the foreign media, which never failed to harp on it whenever they had the chance.

On March 23/ 1971, at 8:00 PM, the proximate cause of these reverses was withdraw of the 7th Squadron and all platoons adjacent units surrounded gather to Route 9 at A-Loui, ordered by colonel Luat by secret order from General Lam. When all adjacent units reaching at A-Loui then the task-force headquarters was already left. Thereby those adjacent units must continued line up to the border. The bad new returned back to them, the first convoy was ambushed by NVA stronghold inflicted 17 Squadron commander and his deputy wounded and their vehicle was destroyed. The rest hurrying back reinforced with the 17 squadron and stayed on the spot to defense. Until at 8:P.M that night, the NVA regiment tried to overrun. Enemy having PT-76 fired support. But ARVN used Tank T-41 shoot destroyed two PT-76s. During the longest night AC-130 dropped flares illuminates the area, meanwhile NVA troops attacked many throng waves but failure. The friendly armored make a real good formation to counterattack killed a lot enemy by 50 calibers stopped them far out of them, although they would like engagement to ARVN force for less casualties. At dawn, 7: A.M the enemy remains were everywhere about this area created the unsurprising scenery to friendly forces; the enemy remnant retreat hidden in the virgin forest avoid tactical fighter bombers.

Fortunately that morning the weather was real good, no fog like usual and the tact air still bombing on the way enemy retreat by FAC, OV-10 Bronco spot light the targets. Two more armored carriers passed the ghost haunt A-Loui Camp by synchronized formation to self-protected; At last they encountered together with 11th Squadron. Colonel Luat joint in the Squadron ordered two platoons line up in the back of convoy. He explained to his subordinates that "in front of us the 17th Squadron was subjected a blooded attack by enemy, they stayed on the spot for counterattack and waiting two platoons advanced to reinforced. There was only one Route 9, passing through the area of operation. Bordering on both sides were continuous mountain ranges. Such terrain was difficult for heavy armored vehicles which easily became targets for ambushes. Thick forests on the mountain and hills impeded troop movements, especially in the south which was covered with huge bamboos. It was in the south that the 1st Regiment and Marine Brigade deployed. It was a disadvantage for the offensive force, which could not evolve far and wise. Instead, movement was limited to narrow trails. Observation was poor and loosing directions was a road hazard. Often, brothers in arms would mistake each other for the enemy at a distance, and would inadvertently shoot each other. Bombing and air power found it difficult to avoid hitting friendly troops. Furthermore, the terrain hampered delivery of supplies and evacuation of the wounded.

Helicopters needed to facilitate these two crucial things could only land with relative case near Route 9. The strength of the troops was greatly taxed as they had to carry an additional load of food and ammunition to make up for the lack of supplies. All these factors had a significant negative effect on the morale of the troops. On the other hand, the terrain was very familiar to the enemy, as they actually lived and carried out military activities there; their personal gear was light, contrasting greatly with ARVN' bulky loads. In summary,

In planning an operation, it is crucial to take the terrain into account.

The northern column's withdrawal by foot along the Route from Bandong to Lao Bao could not avoid heavy casualties either. The two columns consisting of the Airborne/1st Armor and 1st Regiment did succeed in retreating with minimal losses. That the 1st Regiment, however, lose one of its best officers, Lieutenant Colonel Le Huan, a battalion commander. Once these two columns had left the battleground, the enemy concentrated their forces to assault the 147th Marine Brigade around Delta Base. The 2nd and the 4th battalion which had previously deployed further west of the base, was forced slowly back towards its perimeter. The Brigade was well supported from lime-Mt-Coroc by the artillery of the 258th Marine Brigade, and also by air support. The Arc light B-52's were particularly effective and accurate in the close range air support.

But the enemy stubbornly stayed in their hideouts and bunkers, and so resisted ARVN attacks. The fighting was protracted, and was unfavorable to the Marines in that supplies and medevac was unattainable. The enemy artillery, including recoilless 75mm guns were positioned in vantage points opposite to Delta Base, so they were able to fire directly at the TOC bunker of the Brigade Headquarter. The antennae was shot down neighbored bunkers were destroyed, and Marine's Howitzers were damaged. In response, the Brigade gave the order to retreat south to block the apical line along with the enemy with could approach them. The 4th Battalion was to move north east to protect the retreating route of the Brigade that led eastwards towards the direction of the 258th Brigade. The Brigade Headquarters then requested I Corps permission to pull out from the base to continue fighting in the surrounding area, rather remain at base, only to be on the receiving end of the enemy artillery. However, the proposition was not applicable as the order to retreat was issued in the afternoon, and that very morning an unforeseen event occurred. A platoon of 70B sapper had successfully infiltrated through the defense line of the 5th Battalion and had managed to occupy one bunker located at the south entrance of the base, but they were stopped there and the 5th Battalion sent a company to dislodge them out. Many of the sappers were killed or wounded and the rest surrendered. On the interrogation, they revealed they belonged to 324B Division, and that their duty was to assault the 147th Brigade. Body searches revealed a piece of paper reading. "We dedicate our lives to the annihilation of the Crazy Buffaloes"

The NVA batteries located west and southwest of the FSB continued to pound ARVN Marine daily. The 2nd Marine Battalion was also targeted. In the north, the 4th Battalion received remarkably light shelling. In preparation for the retreat, the Brigade Headquarters sent one Reconnaissance-Company Alpha, commanded by Captain Hien, to collect information about enemy positions so that a trajectory could be chosen for that evening. Unfortunately, the company was overwhelmed by the NVA troops and the commander and many Marines were taken. With no reconnaissance reports, the brigade was forced to decide on the route that would lead them in the direction of the 4th Battalion, from which they could cross the mountains to the east. The plan of retreat was as fellows: The 4th Battalion was pathfinder to clear the trajectory and lead the retreat; The 5th Battalion was to follow with the Brigade in tow; The 2nd Battalion was to make up the rear.

All artillery pieces were to be left in an unusable condition, most were destroyed the important parts of others were disarticulated by standard operational procedures and thrown away. Deeply distressing and regrettable was the fact that their dead could not be sent back home, as the helicopters were unable to land. The wounded, however, were all carried along by medics and friends. To make the retreat relatively safe, the Brigade requested B-52 intervention. According to the agreed plan, once the B-52 were to stop bombing. The Brigade would start pulling out of the FSB just before the scheduled-time; the 2nd Battalion reported having seen indistinct lights presumably from track vehicles to the south. At the fixed time, 4 boxes B-52s bombarded 1 mile south of the FSB, and east of the 4th Battalion's position. As soon as the bombardment stopped, the Brigade immediately abandoned the FSB. Barely one mile away, the 4th Battalion met an NVA mortar unit. Only one volley of five was enough to repel them. The retreat was exceedingly arduous, and Marine had to cross hills and mountains covered with thick thorny bamboos in total darkness. Meanwhile the batteries of the 258th Brigade located on Mt Coroc was persistently shelling at FSB Delta and behind the 147th Marine Brigade to thwart the NVA' Regiments/70B pursuit. They also included AC-130 flare-ship to illuminate the retreat path and to provide guidance in the darkness. The 258th Brigade was sent forth to welcome the 147th Brigade. The entire night was spent marching. Luckily, there were no engagements with enemy. The path being so rough probably hindered their pursuit. It was fortunate that after Marine left the FSB, the NVA was unsure of Marine's exact evolution maneuver. At noon, the following day, the Brigade met the 3rd Battalion. Right away, Marine requested the Marine Division Headquarters to medevac the wounded to safe base; then Marine all moved in the direction of the 258th Brigade. Marine had covered considerable distance when the NVA began the shelling. Fortunately, the aiming was poor. By dusk, Marine reached the gathering place close to Mt Coroc, where Marines were to be airlifted to Khe Sanh in the morning. After all, the 147th Brigade managed to reach safety after a fortnight in Laos.

The NVA regiment was in the good shape in the bunkers and foxhole waiting for friendly troops to fall into their traps. So many B-40, B-41, 57mm recoil were aimed down on Route 9, if the friendly force so strong they used 152mm guns for firing support. Suddenly, an armored carrier M-113 at a middle of the convoy advanced to forward with high speed, passing 11th Squadron, and task-force headquarters, and passing the 17th Squadron. That M-113 like a craze buffalo, she used every explosive devices through out from both side flank of the vehicle with steady high speed 40 kilometers. After 30 minutes, that M-113 jointed with the element of 17th Squadron. However, far behind the 11th Squadron when reached at the ambush siege subjected the ferocity attack by NVA regiment that cut squadron a half, and almost half squadron was destroyed, or burned; the survived soldiers help rescued the wounded to the other remnant squadron carriers.

Now Colonel Luat reorganized the close distance from there to Bravo Camp, the 17th took a lead, then task force headquarters, and 11th Squadron and the final back was 7th Squadron. That convoy at last reached at Alpha Camp, meant almost closer to the Laos Viet border about 16 kilometers. When she reached everyone over here were waiting for withdraw together. The number soldiers more increased the more responsibilities of Colonel Luat was increased too. Now he ordered to take turn, "the 11th Squadron took the lead", the convoy proceeding about three kilometers suddenly inflicting an ambush of other NVA regiment, they intended to attack and killed all ARVN soldiers. The lead captured few NVA' prisoners, among them having one officer who said: "from here to Lang-Vei, they had two NVA regiments waiting for ARVN troops on the way back. They had only a goal killed all of ARVN soldiers" Suddenly they had a urgent order from spot plane OV-10 Bronco, must passed left that area at once, B-52 Arc-light will stroked like carpets after two hour"

Colonel Luat ordered "left on the spot all vehicles running by tires in pretentiousness, forming a half circle to west, north, and south side, engines running, putting on high beam light to these three directions, North, West, and South, and leaves direction toward east in darkness for retreated to Khe Sanh. The Airborne XO leader officer, Lt Colonel Ngoc on board of the lead; they were proceeding at night by infrared, the spaced proceed would look like stuttering beams of green. Colonel Ngoc guided the convoy to the border one by one line up smoothly moving. At 5: A.M in morning, the convoy was passed about 10 kilometers, everyone were so patiently due to hearing B-52 Arc-light from SAC took off from Guam, then Utapao Thailand struck three boxes spells on the trucks being light on that they had left there. The convoy continued proceeding to the border. At 11: A.M the convoy arrived at the Xepon River though the water level in a dry season so shallow. However must stopped there waiting U.S Sky-Crane CH-54 slings two Bulldozers D-4 for demolition. Immediately power-man Colonel James Vaught contacted with 101 Airborne division requests helicopters slings forward to operation area some D-4 bulldozers and CH-53 Sea Stallion, CH-47 Chinooks for fuel refill. Vaught also brought with him the old French operational map about Xepon tributaries in dry-season. After two express try to do platform gentle backdrop of steep road; Yet at 11: PM at midnight all chained-vehicles have passed through the other side waterfront *[But when James Vaught became General and General Phu became 2nd Corps commander: The images as beautiful as this the so called perfect retreat Operation Lam Son 719 will never happened again …a painful heart pitfalls of General Phu, Oh God what's different Route 7 and Route 9! But so dreary! In heaven, General Phu wasn't making sense! Because time was change]* **General Phu committed suicide when Saigon felt.**

After two hours, they carried out the job and the convoy tried crossing the river to another flank of river. At 11: P.M at night all the tracks-convoy were running until 8: A.M they reached at Lao-Bao. Thus, the Operation of Lam Son 719 ended. Early the next morning, 23 March, while Khe Sanh Base was still finishing off Communist sappers who had infiltrated earlier, the ARVN armored column crossed the Xepon River and the lines of the U.S. 1st Mechanized Infantry Brigade, 5th Division. The convoy returned with 98 vehicles left behind, among them 22 M-41 tanks and 54 armored personnel carriers. Aerial and photo reconnaissance showed that the ARVN units had left 21 tanks, 26 armored personnel carriers, 13 bulldozers, two graders and 51 vehicles at a night bivouac area on Route-9. The SAC/Arc light B-52s, USAF/EC-130Bs gunship and artillery were used to destroy these vehicles to keep the enemy from using them, and also a wonderful WIB' Bones objective. Khe Sanh Base, in the meantime had received four NVA retaliated-attacks by fire during the night, all by 122-mm artillery, but damage was insignificant.

General Abrams described Operation Lam Son 719 as the largest battle of the war to date

As the results of the operation began to be reflected in the enemy's reduced level of tactical activity, diminished logistical throughput into South Vietnam, reduced rate of personnel infiltration, and concentration on restoration of his lines of communication, Abrams reached a dramatic conclusion. *"I'm beginning to have a conviction about Lam Son 719 that that was really a death blow,"* he said during discussion of a new assessment of the enemy's situation in mid-August 1971. Overall, our ARVN troops have fought well under extremely difficult circumstances. There has been a mixture of effective and ineffective performance, as in any combat situation, but on the whole the effective far outweighs the ineffective. Thus our troops have prevented the enemy from achieving his major objectives. One major improvement of this battle was integration of air, armor, artillery, and infantry into a coherent whole. It seemed to me "this has been outstanding made great progress in this area in particular". Nevertheless, later General Abrams reflected on what the US side had been doing while 1st Brigade's armored forces were in a desperate struggle.

"And the battle was still raging," he recalled. *"We were getting on, and doing things, and – everybody was – doing pretty good .They'd got over some of the shocks. But what was the staff doing? Goddamn it, they were in there gathering photos and making charts and so on, all about the goddamn armor equipment that had been lost over there in Laos on Route 9!* (Permanent Government's planning plot, for instant Airborne was real good for the Rapid Deployment Force but let them an out-post stationed instead of 1st Infantry Division position) *That was the thrust of the 'working' and 'thinking' of the damn staff. Now – there wasn't way to get that back. The 'bill' had already been paid! There was a fucking disaster! But there's no point in that being the whole damn subject of conversation, the whole subject of thought, from there on! Now there's got to be some pos – That's what will lick you. That's what will lick you. The guy that doesn't get licked is the guy that never even thinks he can be! The thought never comes to his mind! He has the patience to accept disaster and disappointment – and 'outrage' – but he keeps after it."*

The New Legion

However I hope that some justification below that what I say will clarify the battle situation: One regular human being could withstand extreme a thousand round-shells in various indirect pounded over his head...in every hours that lasted long enough for day by day and week by week ...could you withstand? The Permanent Government had anticipated warned, had bogged down and become a blood debacle with our ARVN troops, Laotian hilltop strongholds cut-off and annihilated piecemeal. Meanwhile in United States American TV viewers witnessed the sick sight of Saigon troop-deserters mobbing Huey helicopters and hanging from skids. During the under siege emergency withdrawal stage some units panicked by inundation of shelling, naturally with able-bodied men rushing medical evacuation helicopters, seeking a place on board or, as documented in some widely circulated photos, clinging to the skids of the ships.

Because this was the Axis of Evil scam so why ARVN troops as a consequence continued to be outgunned by the enemy and thus at a distinct combat disadvantage, at Tet-Offensive enemy having automatic AK-47 riffles while ARVN having Garant M-1 firing one by one shot. Now at Lam Son 719 enemy having B-40, B-41 antitank but ARVN none! In the next year, Easter Offensive 1972 US introduced antitank weapons TOW missile. Let see what' the hell General Abrams complaint below:

"I gave twenty to the Marine and the 1st Division because they were the only troops I knew of that had stood and fought. I don't want these things in the hands of the enemy. And on the Airborne, I told General Kroesen [that] when General Truong will give me his personal assurance that they will not be abandoned on the battlefield, then I'll consider it"

But in my view-point implied some insights into where things could go from there. It might be fair to say that in fact achieved the objective of getting US to withdraw ground troops at a safe fairly steady and significant rate (60,000 troops during Lam Son 719) Based on all available intelligence, the enemy had succeeded in moving of 67,000 short tons he had input overwhelming into Harriman-Highway's corridor system. This forced him to continue a protracted war strategy for the **'axiom-1'** accomplishment that the enemy's next objective might be to get the US air effort similarly reduced, and to block having a residual US force in South Vietnam. After that, the Permanent Government's goal might be to get military assistance and economic aid to Saigon regime cut off. And again, working the same way that he's had success before, in other words to try to get US Congress to stop appropriating that kind of funds so that the Saigon would essentially be out of ammunition. Surely that was, as things turned out down-stream, pretty much the way it was going to evolve.

HẮC-BÁO Company and Brigadier General Sid Berry

In the early morning of 31 March, in the projected area of operation, a wave of Arc Light B-52 strikes was followed by 22 tactical air sorties, all designed to prepare a landing zone south of the Laotian salient approximately 40 kilometers southeast of Lang Vey. However, at 10:30 hours reconnaissance aircraft reported continued heavy enemy antiaircraft fire. At least, an UH1-H, one round hit the engine, and it quit. This chopper executed a low-level crash landing into the trees, letting the tail boom take the brunt of the crash. No one was hurt – thank God! Everyone got out without trouble. They only had one survival radio. They saw some NVA coming toward them, so the flight-crews move off about 400 meters – They knew the NVA would have no trouble finding their bird, so there was no point in staying near it. The crews came to an abandoned underground shelter that they thought they could defend, and they set up there in counting on EC-130B gunship air-cover with call-sign "Specter" During that night, they received a pretty serious ground probe from the enemy – that in retrospect was probably intended for them to use up their ammo. Always thank for Specter covering over head. The EC-130Bs and AC-130s flare-ship, both were night vision equipped and would fire within 20 to 30 feet air ground closed support of their position. The NVA quickly learned that any serious threat against them was quickly met with a terrible air strike during daylight hours and Specter during this night too. The FAC reported that, at one time, he had eight sets of bombers stacked up waiting to put their loads in around them. Only once did they scare the crews – when the FAC from OV-10 Bronco talked to the tactical jet fighters, he would have to tune his radio to their frequency and couldn't take to the flight-crews. Specially, the fighter bombers from Thailand put a load of CBU-24 (cluster bomb unit) in very close, and the crews couldn't tell him just how close it was – unfortunately, their gunner was light hit in the arm from some of the shrapnel. Brigadier General Sid Berry flew over them that nothing and said. "They had a plan for "one more thing" to get them out, but after that they were on their own best. Because for their security reasons Berry didn't tell them what they planned to do. It involved inserting "HẮC-BÁO" (Black Panther Company) to about one mile southeast of them right this afternoon. The HẮC-BÁO were considered the elite black tiger troops of the 1st Infantry Division that particularly would selected for recover downed U.S flight crewmembers in Laos. After three days and two nights, they were very much aware that the HẮC-BÁO was getting close to them. They could talk to the FAC and he had a Vietnamese "backseater" who could talk to the HẮC-BÁO. They linked up about 3pm and moved back over the same terrain and trails they had taken to get to them. It took for the crews about three hours. Finally, they passed concrete bunkers and some impressive NVA works. It was obvious that the NVA had "built to stay" in this area. Vocabulary the HẮC-BÁO were very good troops and certainly had the U.S Air Cavalry respect and appreciation - HẮC-BÁO saved U.S flight crews lives!

Though President Thieu ordered to early-out of Laos, but Pentagon, General Haig would like to *"search and deployment"* Thereby a preparation of the landing zone by air-strikes were resumed and at 11:30 hours a Black Panther unit of the 1st Infantry Division, about 200 men and supported by the 2/17 Air Cavalry Squadron of the U.S. 101st Airborne Division landed without problems. In the meantime, a FAC aircraft and a communication relay aircraft circled over the area. The Black Panther unit searched the area and found the bodies of 85 enemy troops killed and 18 weapons destroyed by B-52 action. Continuing their search, the troops only made light contacts with the enemy. On the night of 31 March, enemy vehicles were heard moving to the south and the information was immediately reported to the Forward Air Controller. The FAC verified the information and called for an air attack in which five enemy vehicles were destroyed. The following morning, friendly troops continued the operation and found an enemy fuel dump hit by air-strikes along with a destroyed tunnel complex housing tracked vehicles. The next afternoon, the Black Panthers were picked up by U.S. Army helicopters. In the meantime, the evacuation of Khe Sanh continued. After President Thieu's visit, the Airborne Division boarded aircraft bound for Saigon, and also my mission air close-support for Airborne Division was terminated, I flied back to Danang 51st my Tactical Wing. On 2 April, the 8/4 Artillery Battalion, the last U.S. heavy artillery unit, left Khe Sanh, heading southeast. On the **night of 4 April**, the entire Marine Division left the Laotian border area and red-deployed near Quang Tri, Vietnamese and U.S. logistical installations at Vandegrift and Khe Sanh had by now all relocated. **On 5 April**, the ARVN 4th Armored Squadron and the 37th Ranger Battalion were the last units to leave the border area, bound for Dongha. **On 6 April**, another raid of the Black Panther forces of the 1st Infantry Division was initiated against another area of the Lao-Viet border salient approximately 22 kilometers southeast of Lang-Vey, at 10:00 hours after preparatory air-strikes, the reinforced Black Panther Company landed unopposed. The search it conducted lasted until late afternoon without making contact with the enemy. At one location, the Black Panthers found 15 enemy bodies and 17 weapons along with large quantities of food and an intricate network of tunnels, trenches and huts, all destroyed by air-strike. In the course of the operation, U.S. tactical air destroyed three antiaircraft gun positions. **The Black Panthers were extracted at 17:00 hours the same day.** A few hours before the Black Panther unit ended its second raid into enemy bases on the other side of the border, the last ARVN and U.S. units were on their way out of Khe Sanh to Cam Lo where they boarded trucks to return to their respective parent units. The U.S 1st Battalion, 11th Infantry Task Force was the last unit to board helicopters leaving Khe Sanh, thereby ending Operation LAM SON 719.

CASUALTY:

Lam Son 719 as Chief MACV-SOG warned, had bogged down and become a blood debacle by 25 March, 1971.

-**FRIENDLY Forces**: with respectively were an United States **AIRCREW** [source from MAC/SOG]– **219** killed and **38** MIA; **VNAF, 51st Tactical Wing**: **10** killed, and **4** MIA, **14 wounded** and ARVN – 1529 killed and 714 MIA 2,483 injured, as well as 96 artillery pieces and 71 tanks destroyed,

-**ENEMY Forces:** NVA suffered terribly in Lam Son 719 "We believe that during the operation the enemy lost the equivalent of **16** of the **33** maneuver battalions they had committed in the area of operations," said a MACV analyst. "In addition, we believe that he's lost at least **3,500** of the 10,000 to 12,000 rear service personnel that were operating in the area prior to the operation." The US intelligence community concluded that the NVA lost more than **13,000** killed in action defending their supply lines, along with large quantities of tanks, ordnance, and supplies. The ARVN source put enemy losses at **19,000** killed in action, along with more than **5,000** individual weapons, nearly **2,000** crew-served weapons, more than a hundred tanks, and large quantities of ammunition. A Polish Military Advisor to the International Control Commission that "the North Vietnamese were both surprised and hurt by the Lam Son operation. He said that discussion with NVA officials showed that they had lost heavily in personnel, particularly cargo-supply.

My assessment and Comment:

Engaged this operation for 42 days of my view of bird [gunship treetop flight maneuver] based on "Oral-Reports", "Declassified-Documents" and "After Actions Reports," I came to the conclusion that *"true brothers-enemy and hatred and bitterness have never generated anything really good in the end, because all we are the victims of the Axis of Evil's scam"* that's the largest battle of the war to date. It's considers this operation was very important as Korea-War, an amphibious operation at Inchon as Normandy in WW-II. As the results of the operation began to be reflected in our brothers-enemy's the so called a reduced level of tactical activity, diminished logistical throughput into South Vietnam, reduced rate of personnel infiltration, and concentration on restoration of his lines of communication. Un-logically, "I'm witnessed on my own eyes to have a frustration about Lam Son 719 that was really a death blow for both sides plus destroyed out of date war-material: I felt so strongly about the thrust into Cambodia and Laos operation and these operations are the two most intelligent moves the U.S troops have made since allies force have been in South Vietnam. And this sooner Lam Son operation may end the war and may save hundreds may thousands of lives in the long run, in the Permanent Government's scope!" That's just everything not on time, on place but purposely, too late time for all NVA cargo were already moved to the Southern most for full fueling the **Harriman Highway corridor in southern.**

The **"Permanent Government" crucial objective** was dumping in blow-out all cast off WWII American and Soviet weapons on the remote spot as Tchepone, according to "Aid to Russia 1941-1946" preplanned-war: "Surplus C Rations were used in both Korea and Vietnam" (http://www.natic.army.mil/soldier/media/fact/index.htm - VietnamGear.com) Below there were my preliminary evaluation of the military debacle of the summit in operational defeat and comment:

- **On the topography:** There was only one Route 9 passing through the area of operation, bordering on both side were continuous mountain range. Such terrain was difficult for heavy armored vehicles which easily became targets for ambushes. Thick forests on the mountain and hills impeded troop movements, especially in the south, which was covered with huge bamboos. [As I knew in Ap Bac battle 1963, the Viet Cong dug underground shelters near huge bamboos for good protection so why my priority bamboos stand for my first targets] Additional case was a disadvantage for the offensive force, observation was poor, and losing directions was real hazard. On the other hand, the terrain was very familiar to NVA, as they actually lived and carried out military activities there. Their personal gear was light, contrasting greatly with our bulky loads as U.S fashion. In planning an operation, it is crucial to take the terrain into account. But General Giap knew this operation before formed a new Front Corps 70B in last year October, 1970 by the antiwar-activists via mediator triple-cross Pham Xuan An. Giap was standby already for playing game.

On Intelligence Information: *(due to Pentagon, NSC determination on January 18, 1971)* As SOP (Standard Operation Procedure) Before any operation, it is crucial to gather intelligence, G-3 would outlined the operation plan, which would then be discussed by experience staff members, ultimately the decision

The New Legion

would be made by the commander. Accurate information, timing, and location are all important factors to considered, in order to kept the number of low cost. In general, intelligence information was inaccurate or came too late, and many operations were doomed from the beginning as this operation. Sometimes, if the information gathered was correct, the planning was poor. It was simplified this operation organized by WIB Bones via General Haig on Permanent Government's behalf at Pentagon as his Command and Control manager. Because the Pentagon's Goal would like accomplished "**axiom-1**" so prior to Operation 719, our G-2 really did not have a really clear objective of what idea was going on. During briefings, information provided was vague, ambiguous, and orders given to the Units, Brigades, Divisions, Regiments and Groups lacked co-ordination and accuracy. Thus the combat-units had to find out for themselves the true nature of things.

Before the Operation started, purposely, General Haig, Pentagon's intelligence sources had estimated that there were only one or might be two active NVA Divisions in the operational zone. Pentagon pretended to fail to note that potential reinforcement could have at least 6 NVA divisions, in addition to tank regiments and a very strong display of anti-aircraft weapons. His information about the main target Tchepone was poorly gathered. The unusual planning of the attack was based on what those anticipations have been broadcasted by Hanoi Radio. The result was that ARVN troops were continuously overwhelmed, surrounded, counterattacked by the NVA through out the entire retreat from Tchepone back to the Laotian border.

President Thieu involved on planning: He orders to General Lam "postponed the Hill-32, stationed by other Airborne Brigade as preoperational plan" [in the map, you see FSB/LZ/Hope, this is FSB-32 or Hill-32] Lack of knowledge regarding enemy activities and unfamiliarity with the terrain led to bad planning, that arrived at unsuitable requirements to in order to capture the target. Even if there were only one of two NVA divisions present in the operational zone, the fighting force of I Corps was still too weak – for an attacking force to succeed, their numbers ought to be triple or more the size of the enemies. Of course, I Corps force was nowhere near achieving this advantageous ratio [for instance Pentagon's planning: Only One

2nd NVA Division (Sư Đoàn 2 Sao Vàng) under stronghold bunkers at Base 604, then all our three divisions will attacked this target ... how much casualty of our ARVN forces, you think ...and eventually we will need B-52 carpeted all over our troop in melee status, because behind us another four NVA divisions encircled (320, 324, 308, and 304) supported by 202nd Tank Regiment. So why President Thieu decided to "Early-Out," Pissed there a mess and go home for saving ARVN' lives this of course against Pentagon General Haig' objective]

With the help of the Axis of Evil in keeping Secrets: The Harriman highway (Ho Chi Minh Trail) was extended to allow NVA troops and supplies to be transported to the South. These factors were the reasons why our Search and Destroy Tactic failed in the long term, though it had been so effective. The Hanoi merely hid across the border or in far-reaching province. Actually, Secrecy is a necessity for any operation. There were innumerable operations carried out under the 1st and the 2nd Republics of South Vietnam, but their results were not particularly notable, though sometimes facts were ameliorated for propaganda purposes, or to boost morale.

The ARVN was notoriously inept at keeping secret. Often operation would be launched only to find that the Viet Cong had deserted the targets a few days beforehand. Assaulting deserted targets was a waste of time and lives, as most were rigged with booby traps and land mines. In addition, such fruitless operation exhausted logistical supplies, leaving us susceptible to Viet Cong attack. The Viet Cong, by avoiding a head to head confrontation had the advantage of surprise, and good preparation time.

Regarding Operation 719, the organization took two months, during which every facet was taken into account. These included plans to move I Corps Forward Staff from Danang to Dongha, building supply warehouses in Dongha and Khe Sanh, building command bases for I Corps Staff, sending for reinforcements from Saigon. With such activity, even civilians could tell something was up. Needless to say, the NVA, with its Triple-Cross-mediator Pham Xuan An and Agent Russell Flynn Miller, CIA counterespionage in spy-system help, easily guessed the purpose of the operation. In an attempt to fool the enemy, I Corps came up with a rather banal and naïve decoy.

The New Legion

With the useful help of above spy-system, naturally, Hanoi did not bat an eye lid, and calmly watched developments at the real target. Hanoi had plenty of time to move in more reinforcements from the north and survey the battle well set underground. Consequently, ARVN movement whether forwards or backwards the only one Route 9, that would have been easier, and the NVA would not have had the chance to cut the units into two, except if General Tri alive and Commander I Corps, Tri will not return to Khe Sanh but direct the ARVN returned along highway 914, and 922 coming out of Laos to Ashau-Valley, never attack and retreat in the same path-road like Route-9

Medevacs and Supplies were the mainstays of any operation, the larger the operation, the greater the demand. In the planning, I Corps had absolutely relied upon the air powers, [but I don't even 100% aircraft in in commission] namely helicopters from Americans for support, supplies, medevac. Once supplies were hampered the fighting spirit of soldiers was naturally influenced. Lack of ammunition and guns caused the firepower to decrease. Shortage of water and food weakened the troops, the wounded died waiting for medevac. Thus the organization of logistics should be of primary concern.

Commanding and Staff Matters: I was frequently present at Khe Sanh, Ham Nghi Headquarters, I Corps Staff Meeting, but I never saw General Dong, Airborne Commander, and General Khang, Marine Commander at meeting…why? The key to commanding effectively is to have one unified system of command and control between commanders. This is much more effective than executing tasks separately. In Operation Lam Son 719 there was discordance at the top levels. Lieutenant General Lam the overall commander was outranked by the Marine Commandant, Lieutenant General Khang, who was his senior. General Khang instead of flying to Khe Sanh to help and advise the former, liked General Dong, stayed in Saigon, and sent his Assistant Commandant, Colonel Lan to I Corps to command the Marine Division.

However, Brigadier General Phu, 1st Division Commander was always presented at any meeting day. Throughout phase-2, I Corps itself was not in perfect accord with the 1st Infantry Division, and the

Marine Division Staff and I Corps Staff had several disagreements between them, so I wouldn't said a bitter conflict.

Operation Lam Son 719 was the largest operation into Cambodia till then, though there had been previous incursions organized by III Corps and IV Corps: This operation which was reported around the world required an experienced and talented commander at higher levels to deal with the confrontation. It needs a truly experienced military man, not someone who made his way by supporting the right political factions. General Lam had never had experienced in commanding big battles and naturally encountered big problems when he was in charge of I Corps. He surrounded himself with cronies of the same background. The picture of ARVN soldiers hanging on the skids of a helicopter which evacuated them from lower Laos and other equally dramatic photographs showing battered I Corps troops returning back across the Laotian border caused grave concern among South Vietnamese, military and civilian alike. Their concern deepened when they read the tantalizing news articles first carried by American newspapers and magazines then picked up by the foreign and Vietnamese press which all reported that the ARVN incursion into lower Laos was being terminated. The military spokesman had a hard time denying these reports. He announced that this was simply an exchange of operational forces and for all practical purposes, LAM SON 719 was still underway and that ARVN forces were continuing their destructive forays against Communist logistical bases and infiltration routes on the other side of the border. But news; about raids in lower Laos no longer interested Vietnamese public opinion which was more concerned about the real outcome of the well publicized campaign. In the absence of official announcements, rumors and speculations proliferated. Everyone wanted to know the truth about friendly losses. But when official results were later made public, no one seemed to believe that they reflected the truth.

In summary, with such a Corps Commander and Staff, the operation was doomed from the start. The operation ended hastily after more than a month of fighting, leaving on the battlefields heavy human and material losses on both sides [This is real good for the Axis of Evil's scam] but the situation in Laos remained unchanged.

So why in the tactical sphere, General Abrams suggested General Do Cao Tri (named Vietnamese like General Patton) should be taken over General Lam but unfortunately he was murdered because damaged against the ROE [Rule Of Engagement: avoiding destroyed all COSVN material cargo ammunition inside Cambodia territory] and if President Thieu stubbornly had given order "Early-Out," the outcome should be terrible losses human and material. Moreover, Tchepone stand for where was the dumping-spot for all out of date military materials in both side Soviet and U.S cast off in WW-II, and next year (1972), once again some more of obsolete stuffs like Navy gunfire heavy-shells, Mark 52 Mine for harbor mined, Long Tom 175mm, Tank M-48, Navy ship New Jersey, Oklahoma ... all out of date in various kind of aircrafts as F-105, F-100, F-8, 7, A-6 ... should be putting in the garbage, and Navy ship New Jersey, Oklahoma anchored in US seaport, everyone can buy one dollar tickets for seeing the damn ugly monster before recycling.

In the end, Lam Son 719 lasted for 45 days, due to President Thieu would early-out and the never adequately dependable on U.S airpower was the only thing that saved the ARVN from a complete defeat in Laos. The North Vietnamese nevertheless did not get off unpunished: their losses were indeed heavy to a degree where their planned invasion of South Vietnam had to be extinguished for a full couple years. *But the real objective of Permanent Government was obsolete war equipment must be "blow-out" by War Industries Board's wishes.*

War is sometimes necessary and war is at some level on expression of human feelings. American has helped underwrite global security for more than six decades with the blood of its citizens and the strength of its arms. I hope the service and sacrifice of its men and women in uniform has promoted peace and prosperity from Vietnam to Iraq and enabled democracy to take hold in places like the Balkans – and its actions matter, and can bend history in the direction of justice for the 21st Century as we hope.

Chapter-2

POW of Northern Vietnam

(At the end of Vietnam-War, the ARVN fought the war alone at the most difficult situation due to short supplies in logistics and the US military disengagement. However "I shall never repent having done what I did, nor complain about the consequences of my captivity. If history were to repeat itself, I would choose the same path. By so doing, I know from experience that I would lose everything but HONOR - The 1973 Paris Agreement allowed many communist divisions stayed deep inside South Vietnam territory (and actually supported by the whole Soviet block, including China) And then US Army leaving the battle fields from Mekong Delta to Ben Hai River, we, the South Vietnam Army Forces alone, I say again, alone, fought back the North Vietnam Army, supported Soviet block until the last day of April 1975. As my understanding, my opinion, General Duong Van Minh, the last president 72 hours surrendered not our ARVN; but no matter what, we are proud of what we had done for our country. The Vietnam-War is not over yet. We are still fighting for democracy and freedom for our country and waiting for the collapsing of Hanoi regime. For that reasons, we are still the soldiers. I'll still hope U.S Permanent Government should have a wonderful solution that we still waiting for)

How to lose a war ... when ever talking about Vietnam War, most of the U.S politicians, journalists, officials, or political pundit would mention it in a way the war is their own, the South Vietnamese at that moment seem to be invisible or just the bystanders outside their scam, bearing no brunt of the war effort. But there was one day, only single day in which all of them would shy away from that claim; the day they have nothing to do with that war. The day they return the outcome back to the South Vietnamese: The April 30th 1975, as a result an accomplished **axiom-1**. As you know, desire and struggle like a basic timeline of events that the U.S for more than a decade has been assisting the South Vietnam government, the people of Vietnam to maintain their independence, the quality or state of being self-governing, no subject to control by others, and to stop Communist expansion in Asia?

For that reason, one has heard some very familiar words like *The Fall of Saigon, Evacuation, Frequent Wind Operation, Reeducation Camp, Economic Zone, Boat People …etc* Those technical terms and euphemism are conveniently served just like toilet papers to cover somebody is own mistakes and to wipe-out (flush) his embarrassing accident. So let's tell straight out what it is on that day: Cut and Run!

A Bitter April 30th, 1975: The day South Vietnam is delivered to Evil due to betray and abandonment. If you have never been told the real ugly stories that fatal day, then this is the chance, let the following scenes, artificial disasters speak for the innocent civilians, the abandoned plain soldiers and the deaths. The consequences of The Fall of Saigon drove many people into not only suicide but serious mental disorder as well. Few decades later, some physicians said that at least thousand peoples around the Saigon area suffered incurable insanity on that day of the Cruel-April.

In summary, this was a disappointing performance, I have to repeat once more: Right after in 1963, president Diem' assassination, North Vietnam got the aids from the Russia, the China and the Eastern Europe who helped them with their personal and group weapons surpassing those of the South Vietnamese Army. The units of infantry and regional soldiers did not have R-15 or M16, M72, M79… while North Vietnamese Army stormily attacked us with all kinds of modern weapons such as AK and B40… It was not that the US did not see the truth. However intentionally the Permanent Government would like to dispense all of goddamn stuff cast off U.S weapon from WW-II, the unclassified documents show that puppeteer Kissinger wanted to cut loose from Vietnam since that period. Consequently, the Americans came to Vietnam just for merely military combat training exercise with slogan: "Everything worked but not worked enough" - the so called help us to defend ourselves, but not to win the war, or more clearly, the Americans did not want or did not let the Republic Vietnam Army or the United States Army to win and liberate the North Vietnam, because of the global strategy of the United States in order to win over communism. The Permanent Government fired General Westmoreland and at last they forced us to fall apart. South Vietnam and Republic Vietnam Army have been sacrificed, and in the world peace after the disintegration of the Soviet Union, there were the contribution of our blood and our honor. Personally, I have to say it to the world by my master-book "The New Legion", now and in the future. My group of military veteran-writers had contributed our efforts to this hard mission of our country in general and of our South Vietnamese soldiers in particular... (No Peace, No Honor. War Industries Board Bones' Henry Kissinger puppeteer and Betrayal in South Vietnam)

Ironically, at 7:53 on Wednesday morning, April 30, 1975 – brought down the Vietnam War's final curtain. The fighting – The frustration – The nearly three decades of conflict – Done

"What did we die for?" I asked myself! "For what did we suffer and pay such a price?" And I shook my fist as I watched the helicopter race toward the sea. "We never lost a battle, so why did I lose the war?"

On the streets, in the villages, inside shanties and chateaus, people hid, terrified. Their Vietnamese-eyes too followed the U.S helicopter, and they cried, "Why did you forsake us?"

Men who had given their courage, their dedication, their blood to a noble cause now lost. They had zipped shut too many black bags filled with too many friends who had given their lives trying to win over here. For these, the flight of that last U.S chopper out of Saigon represented despair. "This is not our Vietnamese and our U.S comrades in arms doing! We didn't lose this war. The U.S acted government was, but the War Industries Board Bones won the narrow in the war game. Solely, our American fellows in fight, and brothers died for freedom's cause – for liberty!"

"Those damned communist pig-fucking war protesters. They did this. Those damned communist pig-fucking Congressmen and limp-willed political diplomat. They gave it to them. We won it, and then they gave it away!" I angrily stuck my middle finger skyward as that last chopper flew toward Seventh Fleet.

After three decades I found out the Axis of Evil play the CIP's scam. It good to see that was the ultimate team effort, but every shrewd politician of the team had to have the skills of a quarterback like WSAG' Chief-staff Donald **Rumsfeld**, the grit of a linebacker as George H W **Bush** and the brain of a coach such A Harriman's **strategist staffs**. They did carry out their **axiom-1**; so why we did lose that war and then they gave it to Hanoi. As President Thieu recently lamented *"America has turned its back. Deserted us in the breach! How do we stand in defense against such forces when they can now so easily overwhelm us?"*

The collapse of South Vietnamese which was preset to scope "Eur**Asian** Great Game" stratagem by Harriman's masterminded strategist staffs has been attributed to any number of causes, but over time three have stood out as the most prominent:

* -**A One**, a simple matter of fact, had to do with termination of political support, reduction of materiel support, and eventually even denial of fiscal support to the South Vietnamese by their sometime American ally. This was only the very work of the Congress, wrought over the strong and eventually agonized protest of the administration, military leaders, and of course the South Vietnamese. Before Harriman retired from public life, giving the framework for the Vietnam with only Hanoi side; thereby in 1970 the first volley in Congress emerged "Cooper-Church" amendment and 1973 "Case-Church" amendment: U.S President who has his hands tied, double knotted, and must do nothing, no military equipment, no U.S forces, nada, zip. Ironically, sometime WSAG [Donald Rumsfeld] sent few A-4 Skyhaws to strike POL stations in the South Vietnam Airbase reduced our ARVN activities and moreover the "Project Enhance," one by one in exchange permitted by Paris Accord Agreement none applicable too. It stood in stark contrast to the uninterrupted support rendered North Vietnam by her Soviet and Chinese allies. Ambassador Bunker, for one, argued that "*We eventually defeated ourselves, but we were not defeated when we signed the Paris peace treaties. We had, I think, then achieved our objective. The fact that it slipped our grasp was our own doing.*"

* -**A second** cause had do to with the task, never adequately accomplished, of providing effective leadership for a military establishment rapidly and hugely expanded over a relatively short time, and for the expanded civilian bureaucracy as well. The nature of Vietnam War was so strangely as a 1974 survey of generals who had commanded in Vietnam found that "almost 70 percent of the Army generals who managed the war were uncertain its objectives." Once again, a survey conducted in 1980 for the veteran administration discloses that 82 percent of former US soldiers engaged in heavy combat there believe that the war was lost because they were not allowed to win. From my perspective, that a key step for ARVN troop to win the war would have been to eliminate CIA's action intervene internal South Vietnam affairs, the most in a state of chaos (constitution and sovereignty abused) Therefore South Vietnam leader haven't patiently formed an army good, competent and courageous. Despite some very significant exceptions, that judgment was hard to argue with, and in fact it was one that responsible South Vietnam themselves made after the war.

* - **A third** key cause was failure to isolate the battlefield, to cut off enemy infiltration and re-supply and to deny the sanctuaries in Cambodia, Laos, and North Vietnam. Again sometime I was pointed and succinct, arguing that to succeed the allies needed to "cut the Harriman Highway [Ho Chi Minh trail] inside Laos". Here some clue verbatim statement: NSC Micheal Forrestal cautioned Bundy that "*to send the telegram without Averell's approval is just asking for trouble*" The telegram had already received presidential approval, but that was not enough. It still required an **endorsement** from A Harriman. He "favored sending non US patrol into Laos to try to find out the size of military buildup." He also stood firmly against US advisers taking part in these patrols. It was a clever diversion. As a spy pilot, I flew with no US advisers could lead the STRATA team. The air crewmembers and teams that crossed the border were not to wear GVN uniforms, weapon, cigarette U.S made and we could engage the NVA only in "self defense"

Unsurprisingly, on midmorning today, 10:30 Hanoi's tanks T-55, T-57 approached the Independence Palace in Saigon and, ramming their way through the wrought iron gates, took up positions in the courtyard. There Colonel Bui-Tin accepted unconditional surrender from General Big-Minh – South Vietnam's President for all of about forty-hours – bringing to an end nearly two decades of Communist quest for domination of all Indochina but with Skull and Bones help give a hand in a stratagem: "On the strongman side."

I clearly had heard the radio broadcast in which the 42hours-President ordered all Republic of Vietnam armed forces to cease fire and surrender. "It was 10:25 hours, 30 April 1975 by my watch," On the sky the U.S fighters left the Saigon air space in replacing by the MIG-21 of Hanoi communist. The Axis of Evil named it a ceremony takeover of U.S, by 'on the Strongman method'. Meanwhile, at Airbase Bach Mai, an aircraft C-130 Hercule camouflage unmarked from southwest maybe Thailand, this aircraft four turbo-propeller-engine abruptly landed. From an old building, one officer NVA proceeding toward the airplane and one CIA official step down from the aircraft. Simultaneously, both of them saluted in military manner, and left hand he showed up the letter to counterpart, and retreating back to airplane, no hand shake. I guessed this hand over Saigon to Hanoi in official procedure or maybe included the list USIS personal those who had exposed themselves on America's behalf were still in Saigon failure to escape. All those will be departed in the next schedule ODP (Orderly Departure Program)

I recalled. "This was the end. I was most sorry for the outcome of the war, but I had done my best." There followed the inevitable. "I was, of course, arrested by the Communists and held captive in various the so called Reeducation Camp in Northern Vietnam for not a uncertain future" In reality, now I'm a criminal of war that Communist North Vietnam fixed that name isolated us to remote confined zone as another Siberia in mountainous area and died for good with no one knew. "*As Communist, you have to fight the enemy without clemency*" Lenin's policy indicated clearly "reeducation policy" with deceitful tactic to cheat the prisoners: *Always give them false hopes of freedom by removing them around frequently until they meet each other at Siberia in death"*

As a political officer in Political Education Department, Captain Quach Duoc Thanh is one of such case. He had a broad knowledge on deceitful tactic to cheat the prisoners. Thanh was arrested at home by two armed VC months after the fall of Saigon. He was sent to Chi-Lang camp in the former 4th military tactical region. On the eve of the invasion threat of the Khmer Rouge, the prisoners were moved to a new camp Vuon-Dao. The camp was built close to the road that leads to Moc-Hoa, Cai-Lay district. There were about 3000 South Vietnamese soldiers ranking from CWO's to colonels. Among them the most steadfast were Colonel Nguyen Duc Xich (Gia-Dinh province chief under the later president Ngo Dinh Diem) the venerable Hoang Dinh Khang always showed the courage and steadfastness in the face of the enemy. To the camp authorities, they became the obstacle to be brainwashing.

In October 1979, Ba-Minh, the camp Communist party political commissar, accused Colonel Nguyen Duc Xich of being agent left behind by the CIA and locked him in an old US Army container (conex). One day, as the guards escorted colonel Xich to go out the barbed wire perimeter, they shot him from the back and told the prisoners that colonel Xich was attempting to escape. Whereas Captain Thanh could not avoid the same destiny, they put him in the container Conex in 15 days without food and drink. At about 9 o'clock one certain night in December, 1979, a VC captain unlocked the container and found captain Thanh was still alive. He then beat and suffocated Thanh to death; the event occurred not far from the barracks where prisoners were sleeping. Many years have passed but Vuon Dao camp ex-detainees still recall the story with horror. Captain Thanh died at age 37 survived by his wife and four children.

We were asleep. Suddenly some warm, salted, stinking drops of liquid had fallen all over our heads and our faces. We were awake to know that they came from an overflowed stinkpot of urine carrying up to the deck by a communist soldier. Under dim yellow light from the ceiling of the hold, I stretched my neck to see other almost empty stinkpots had been lowered down by a rope. Some stinking drops of urine did not let us alone. We did not know if the ship was to Con-

Son Island or somewhere. Probably it was just of Saigon Newport to the ocean, sometime rocking on huge waves of the sea. We just waited for the sunrise to orientation, estimated our position.

We were sitting at the tail end of the ship because we were the last group to embark last night. Fortunately, probably because of a very strictly "press-diet regime" for a longtime that we suffered less stinking odor from defecation; Cellmates who embarked earlier had a wall of bulwark to rest their backs on. But closing to the stinkpots, we didn't worry about making our pants wet! It was a miserable friend of Airborne named Cao Trieu Phat, a "Five Dot Bull" (slang for lieutenant Colonel that I met with full of war-medals on their uniforms during the war) who was under pressure on atmospheric of below sea level being condition constipation.

I woke up facing a long journey with where and nowhere in destination. That was the reality as another 411th dawn on 14/June/1976, slowly crawled up the steel walls of a fully-loaded boat with its hull deep under sea level. Who knew in the course of this nine decades' history (1917-2008) of emerged intelligence-war, hundreds, perhaps thousands, of pilots and crewmen had been shot down and captured by Free-World's enemies. They had parachuted into the waiting arms of the North Vietnamese, endured years of torment in Hanoi regime, and been used as pawn by the Soviet Union cadres; crashed in Burma and been hunted down by the Japanese. Some of them had escaped, some had lost their youth through years of captivity, and some had never come home. And from the moment of each one's capture, each had surrendered his or her future to the unknown. None had known when or if they would see freedom again.

In the Southern of Vietnam, It was my 411th day as a prisoner of Saigon fall. I knew I couldn't deal with my captivity in terms of years, but with Communist totalitarian, I had to mentally prepare myself for a long haul. So, as I stared at the crowd of POW, a mêlée of us; we'd all crowded into hull deck deep below under pressure of sea-level. Last night, a large crowd of over one thousand among 1,700 ARVN' lieutenant colonel that Communist North Vietnam named the 'criminal of war' were departure from Saigon New Port by 759th Maritime Group to nowhere. I told myself that I would survive just one day at a time. I would not imagine my captivity as years of tortured waiting, because if I really believed that, I would probably die. My mind couldn't accept being in prison for that long, and those kinds of thoughts would break me.

Like any major challenge in life, you have to take it in bits and pieces. You don't try to tackle the whole thing at once. I remembered how I had reacted at the Saigon fall when the Hanoi's troop was overrun and I had focused on surviving for a moment, and then making it through the next moment. And so, as 411th dawned and I needed a limited point of reference orthat darkness would just overwhelm me. *"You just need to make it to morrow,* I told myself. *"If you wake up tomorrow, you'll figure out how to survive tomorrow. Today, you've got to figure out how to survive today!"*

And still, there was no way to know when it was all going to end. So, even though I was trying to convince myself not to worry about it, those images of endless years would continue to ambush my mind. A worst terrible night of asleep might have helped the healing process, but my flat repose on the steel floor had also stiffened maybe with fear, me up again. Blood would have coagulated at my whole body numbness. I shifted my right leg a bit in the crowd, raised my head, and did the best rolled my shoulders forward. Yes, the un-pain-numbness was all still there. I looked around the cabin-hull compartment. The gritty steel platform floor was strewn crusty food wrappers, bottle caps, and most oily rags; from across this world I could smell oil, paint, musk, but it was no longer offensive. In a world of no colognes or perfumed soap, your nose quickly adapts to the scents of our fellows local skin, if not the local oil paint litter. That feeling of uncertainly and little faith in my perspective envelope would continue throughout my captivity. It was a constant source of tension, and it would remain with me long after my release. Yet the things that occupied my mind that morning wasn't my stiff-numb or chances for survival and freedom; the fates of my comrade in fight from the Saigon fall weighed heavily on me. But even though I forced myself into these painful analyses; the temperature, humidity seemed to cause my heart to throb, and my slick skin sticking to the steel floor.

Now I lay back down from my elbow, letting the nourishment (instant-noodle) flow through me. I wasn't exactly feeling healthy, fat, dumb, and happy, but it wasn't a bad start to 411 days. I have plenty of time now to recall all of them. They were sitting side by side like a pack of ducks, tired and hopeless! Yesterday afternoon at Suoi Mau (Bloody Stream) concentration camp, after reading a list of chosen names, prison guards let them to another camp for "special treatment" probably those who had debts of blood to the communists. After, roll-call at a large yards, we were let through a barbed wire fence, barrack by barrack, on a rather wide road to the front gate of prison. Countless of fabric covered trunk Molotova-Trucks parked in lines waiting. This was a former prison for communist prisoners, divided into three parts surrounding by three rounds of barbed wire fence. Each of them had a large yard, a stand probably for selling goods to the prisoners, a kitchen and a well beside it, a huge empty house. Their floors made by cement-mixer. There were many of them located evenly side into side into a long line. There was a guard-watching tower outside concentration camp gate. A conex was right beneath in it which two "Three Dot Bull" (Captain) were kept without bandage and treatment for their prisoner wounded after a failed attempt to escape at Cu Chi. This was probably a harsh, inhuman warning to others (prisoners) in advance of a journey to the Northern concentration camps.

Right there, we were detained without hard labors and even without repeated propagandas like previous time in Long Giao Camp. Only a lesson of respect to people's properties to be learned means not 'robbing' or 'stealing' Despite it, we had witnessed all kinds of properties loaded on crowded train wagons with NVA hat passengers passed by out camp from the south to north. That was just a beginning of an extraordinary corruption the new regime has committed long later until now. News from Saigon by French Press of Hanoi proved that too many Honda motorcycles on the streets of Hanoi Capital were looted from Saigon, as well as BGI soft drinks sold on the market, sofas, refrigerators, electric fans, stereo sets, fabrics, medicines, detergents. Around 8,000 tons of paper-rolls from Cogido-Mill were ordered to transport to the capital Hanoi. New cars from dealers like Citroen, Renault, and Peugeot had the same destination, included 165 cars of Engine C.O. An ironical wave of new folk song saying: "The South hosts its guests so the North get rich... now a grain of rice from the South must be shared a half or three third to the North".

I was never forgotten that Thursday June, 12, 1975 was a disastrous day for all of former South Vietnamese officials and officers. New regime required all of them to surrender next day for concentration camps for at least one month, bringing with their own $13,610 for one month food. Their subordinates (enlisted-men) also must surrender for three days reeducation camps exercise at their local authorities. The Saigon Liberation News explained: "They took their responsibilities for their own crimes of fighting and collaborating for the enemy" Many of them could not forget that historic sad day made by Kissinger and Le Duc Tho anticipated-solution. And be fooled by the naivety of French Ambassador Merillon. Following Kissinger, "choreographer" of the tragic theater "... an ordinary transfer from one government to another without destruction of Saigon"

In October 1975, there was a change in monetary system. No one be surprised, many rumors spread out, suggesting a North Vietnam currency has already been used in Hue and Quang Tri Inter-zone IV. People didn't keep much bills but merchandises and jewelry for sure, even they feared of prosecution for illegal stocking in capitalist way. When new ruler declared curfew, everybody the monetary change has come! The wealthy looked for valuables to spend until the last penny. An exchange policy of $200 piaster per family was applied. The rest amount of money must be deposited in a government fund account. Any withdrawal must be approved by the new regime with limit reason and amount considered by the government. What a cunning robbery! No more, no less! Even facing a robbery, South Vietnamese must take a long day for that processing. Earliest service days reserved for government revolutionary families and government employees. They took advantage of a deal to earn 75 to 90 percent for helping-fee exchange of $100,000 and up. Many committed suicide for a loss of whole life saving. Some jumped to their deaths from a third or fourth story with their brand new bills flown like butterflies all over their house sidewalk.

After disastrous monetary exchange, poverty and unemployment forced people to sell their household stuffs at many black markets and open sidewalk markets. Vice President Do Muoi himself created a government department to purchase all stuffs such as Honda motorcycles, electric fans, refrigerators, cars by government valueless bonds, as well as endless waves of Northern "brothers and sisters" came to bring victorious war trophies back North. Meanwhile, many economic check points appeared on riversides and roadsides to prevent food from countryside go into big cities, especially Saigon. That strategic tactic is to help enforcing a policy of expatriation urban citizens to the so called "New Economic Zones"

War prisoners in the camp were still having temporary nutrition formula a little bit better during early days as long as long grain US rice in ARVN stocks existed. Milk like washing rice waste was kept for cellmates with edema, in contrast with NVA' Truong Son out of date worm-rice. Joked cellmates called them "fake prosperous" rice for ironic-fun.

Each barrack appointed a cellmate who helps his camp everyday early exercise with four lessons at a time and cell inspectors stood by watching. Prisoners woke up by loudly speakers broadcasting a revolutionary song. Of Uncle Ho in which, a lyric of "holding our hands" was intentionally mispronounced into handcuffing our hand" for quietly protest!

Some doctors were released for probably services needed in hospitals. Propagandas from the camp commanders gave to prisoners whose relatives work for new regime saying pardon list was available. Meanwhile, a cellmate was appointed to work as a messenger to call prisoner for "work" (interrogation) and released afterward.

We used too much leisure time in organizing some classes like electricity, engine repairs, electronics theory about software and so on. We took some piece from roof aluminum and barbed wire to fabricate some household devices like knifes, spoons, guitars, music instruments. Every morning the lousy noise from every kind of man made hammer. We took a piece of firewood to make a chess table.

A nasty well located near the open human manure hollow-spots. That the field prisoner open rest rooms were also situated too close our barracks; so every chow time we feel so dirty shit atmosphere around. Majority of us bring the food tried as far as we can. As a result the most our cellmates frequently were been having the bad attack of diarrhea. The most of us were just used the towels for cover the mid-body. One of my closed-friend in Air Force, Colonel Tran Sao, a famous soccer-ball of VNAH Headquarters, subjected to two weeks on this kind of illness in which waste matter is emptied from his bowels frequently and in a liquid form, inflicting intestine infection. The communist considered human being like an animal. They put the victim illness in the mosquito-net and made surgery operation that involves cutting or removing parts of the victim bowels, undergo abdominal surgery. Of course after stupid surgery my friend was died afterward. Thank God I have some capsules antibiotic pill. The Camp dispensary having only the tablet similar Aspirin (Xuyen Tam Lien) a common drug used for relieving pain and reducing fever.

However, permanently staying inside the Camp, we wish to go out for hard labor in seeing the new worst society. The job was digging the hollow for raising the crops break up demolished land, dug up land for a new garden removing bushes from ground by digging. We dug up the trees by their roots, dug the potatoes out of the ground. We are skill and smart, only bare hand we take PSP steel and made a beautiful Camp Gate with three entrances the middle for truck and two small gates for pedestrian, above them so many flag with different color we couldn't understand what the hell meaning. Adversely, we have some works that no one would like accept such as demolishment, or defuse the Claymore-mines around barbed wire camp. I was praised God bless us nobody injuries or dead from that risk dangerous stuffs. Sometime I saw on the sky, few aircraft took off and landing at Bien Hoa Airfield, now and then the train passing urging me to move in the clinging past.

Every evening, we have entertainment with Television for their propaganda purpose. The communist authority favor us by accepted our family sent into the camp some basic food like flours, candies, sugars, Maggie cubes Oxo, dries rice. We are all lack of malnutrition, illness, weakness, because so long time slept on the sheer earth floor. Beside that we frequently heart a rumor of condolence, it seemed to me God saying "Sons accept my condolences on your overcame through a terrible ordeal." But I'm so patiently I knew the U.S POW must be in Hilton prison in maximum nine years that we must least the same or more than that. I am only patient in waiting U.S and North Vietnam solution to our plights though uncertain future.

Saigon city was still in curfew, but no one wouldn't came out for this sadly stage. Our families in Saigon seemed subjected to the communist cadres coming to persuade that "every letters sent to us having the same written in conclusion "Be nice, Good study, labor hard prepare becoming good citizenship in this perfect actual society.

In the secret solution of Kissinger and Le Duc Tho, means took time for reunite both south and north to become One Vietnam. (I thought this 100 years planning of the Skull and Bones stratagem). In the world wide even U.S administration such as ambassador Martin didn't understand what the hell of this solution. Martin simple think that Vietnam is still two nations. Therefore, he tried the best contacting to French Ambassador Merillon and Viet Cong temporary National Liberation Government on the already defeat situation. The four engine aircraft DC-6 belonging Martin is standby at Tan Son Nhut Air base after leaving from Thailand last night, now waiting at airbase on 25, April, 1975. Station at Saigon, CIA Polgar and General Timmes had been escorted President Thieu seated right middle of them like dangerous prisoner for ready of deportation. The black sedan of convoy proceeds to parking lot of Air America.

Ambassador Martin had presented over here little bite sooner. In his farewell trip, he said "That all the best I could do for you sir! Good luck" President Thieu responded respectfully "Thank you for excellent prepared trip for me…Good bye for good!" On the way back to U.S. Embassy (almost U.S officials and administrations were very nice with Saigon regime from Kennedy, Johnson, and Nixon but except unless the Permanent Government, typically in the spotlight is Henry Kissinger and in dime light is WSAG chief staff Donald Rumsfeld and high supreme is George H W Bush masterminded) Hurry up resumed the political situation, for resolving the political solutions. In reality, Martin was innocent, couldn't understand another side of Paris accords behind the stratagem platform.

Ambassador Martin innocently sent an urgent message to Kissinger. On 26 April 1975, so please Martin implied that after

The New Legion

negotiated with French Ambassador Jean Marie Merillon; He strongly advocated the negotiation between Viet Cong and Saigon regime might on good élan.

At once, Kissinger angrily react "Mr. Ambassador, you misunderstood what I saying, I am never say negotiation between Saigon and Viet Cong, but only Hanoi with U.S. only at Paris talk. Now on I don't want you interference in this critical situation the least with Viet Cong and Saigon regime in the nearest its abolition!" Another word, Kissinger didn't want the contact in futile between Saigon and Viet Cong. Kissinger urged Martin cut and run as soon as we can; but a Ambassador philanthropist would pretend to slow down [take time] the evacuation campaign to the U.S personal out of Vietnam in purpose to rescued more and more Vietnamese.

The Chief Staff of WSAG, Donald Rumsfeld strongly urged: "We have just completed an interagency review on the state of play in South Vietnam. You should know that at the WSAG (Washington Special Action Group) meeting today, there was almost no support for the evacuation of Vietnamese, and for the use of American force to help protect any evacuation. The sentiment of our military, DOD (Department of Defense) and CIA colleagues was to get out fast and now." "Too late for now included those Vietnamese who had exposed, themselves on America's behalf"

And Kissinger urged Le Duc Tho when reaching Saigon the first priority must deported French Ambassador out of South Vietnam as soon as possible, didn't let a change for Viet Cong regime having legal office to activate. Of Course Tho was very please for good opportunity unified One Vietnam according secret agreement.

Thereby, French Ambassador Marie Merillon was got out in humiliation feature. Hanoi now closed door without contact to outside. Because the votes in United Nation members voted almost double votes more than Hanoi regime for Viet Cong administration in power. Meanwhile, 1968 to 1970 the CIA covert Phoenix Operation killed 40,000 Viet Cong infrastructure created the hatred poison to Saigon regime. That is a cunning scheme creating Saigon and Viet Cong cannot reunion for fight back Hanoi regime afterward in betrayal in the Viet Cong. If they did that they will win in revolution that Permanent Government anticipated the know-how. This cunning trick strategy is similar in the first Iraq-War; when CIA in both secretly engaged in Shite and Sunny to create the next-bloodbath when United States forces reaching the border Kuwait/Iraq and immediately withdraw inflicting the future revenge-mediation as same as Phoenix operation in Vietnam.

In the auditorium we opened many classes for English grammar, technique by divided some separate seminars. Suddenly, many explosions blasted shaking around the camp melee with AK-47. We are stunning about what happened. Every oil lamps distinguished. All over silence prevail. It was as silent as a graveyard. Utter darkness. I looked desperately around as a cold chill rippled through my body and a wave of terror choked my throat. My heart was hammering, and I was hyperventilating, gripping my blanket in my sweat-soaked palms. After all, I found out no shelling, maybe man made device-explosion for exercise practical emergency? In the early morning we discussed that if we reacted like our men tried rescue us then they got this occasion and kill all of us; the bloodbath in Tet Offensive in revived another massacre in my mind. They tried to get a chance to check out the reaction of us to prevention.

Then afterward, they inaugurated an operation to screening search all of us the so called we secretly disguised the sharp weapon for camp escape or their conspiracy moving us to northern. It was an innocent deception, meant as an adverse event.

In the early June 1976, the TV announced the schedule in reeducation was lasted three years for officials and senior officers of South Vietnam in maximum before they were released by The Viet Cong regime. However we received this rumor news with skeptical half sad and self-cheered up, at least we do know when our ordeal experienced or a decision have reached by a communist jury on a question of fact in the law case. Unsurprisingly, the time will change. In mid-June 1976 we have known all families of officers and officials to Saigon government' must be concentrated in one special confined space called Zone economic and their household head must keeping moving to the northern Vietnam for building camps for the next move to the north like hostages that estimated about 10,000 their named criminal of war and will died there in the most remote areas. We are the prisoners for life.

The New Legion

In the mid-June, 1976, suddenly at late evening the whistle with clear high pitched sound made force us to concentrated in front yard for emergency instruction. I knew something was up. I could tell that something unusual was going on. There were low whispers outside the fence barbed wire, pattering sandals on the earth, and clatter of heavy iron objects. Then everywhere and no where all around appeared the communist soldiers with icy-face. When I lifted myself and moved up out of the earth floor and hurry up with my gear toward the front yard. The pain, numbness hardly registered, because my heart was already hammering in anticipation. All of us right tight and tough in the middle surrounded by communist guards. A creature NVA' captain pronounced the individual name "last, middle, and first name to make a group sixty enough for one truck. Every one having one pack of biscuit green bean sweet made in Communist China, then the leader of guard serious proclaimed: "For your safety, we must move all of you out of here to the safety zone and we nowhere yet.

Shortly, we are escorted by a numerous AK-47 behind in guiding us toward every truck on line longer to the main-gate. We are disguised under the canvas trunk cover. There's no disguising the fact, though communist Hanoi's is a liar, a famous way of hiding or disguising prisoner, their soldier, military equipment with paint, nets or leaves, so that they look like part of their surroundings. While the convoy proceeding under the canvas-cover, everyone did not utter a word and spontaneously written the families addresses informed we are forced moving with nowhere its destination. All urgent messages that we wrote released through a gap of the cover. We recognized the convoy en route to Saigon via Bien Hoa Highway-1 to Newport; at this harbor, one by one we steps on the narrow boarding wood, one of our fellow felt disappeared in the deep water; no one worry about this accident. The procession is still progressing at normal speed. It was as if it did not happen.

Now in the midnight we don't know where we are under pressure of hull deck below sea level. We must wait until to morrow morning by reflecting sun-ray for orientation in establishing one's position in relation to sun ray direction. The war veteran like us should easier found it to orientate ourselves even under the hull-deck. First, we thought they put us in the isolated island Con-Son prison without released day. Tired and frustrated all of us felt in as slept.

I woke up facing 412th days of captivity. That was the reality as another dawn slowly crawled up the steel-walls of our big cell-hull-deck floating un-gently down the ocean. In this course of this Skull and Bones dynasty's history, hundred thousands or perhaps more than captures by communist totalitarian dictatorship regime; now every one of us agreed that we missed Con Son Island; some segment sun-rays infiltrated above the hollows from right to the left cell-hull demonstrated the ship on proceeding forward in heading North, Northeast. In conclusion we missed Con Son but we don't know where will be destination. But who knew? I'm sure, Kissinger and Tho all already knew it for their anticipated plots.

I glanced round a hull deck cabin, glanced up to distinguish something familiar with the boat made in China that was destroyed by our AD-6, Skyraiders at Vung Ro, Nhatrang province. I recalled on February 1965, I flown with General Nguyen Khanh, Prime minister and landed at the sea shore where the sank-boat located; inspected the orange color in upper hull, and below was black color, long about 100 feet, wide 30 feet. Right the place where we were loaded were the huge cargo supplies such as AK-50, automatic weapon made from China, and medical equipment and C rations. Now I could identified this boat was belonging to Group 759 (established in July, 1959 in the craps CIP/NLF.) This trophy, thank to U.S. Seven Fleet found out and led indication for the VNAF to bombardment on its. In the Vietnam War, the CIA (Permanent Government) authorized the U.S. Navy to intercept ships of Group 759 and calling South Vietnam struck on them. But there is seldom just three spots during the long war, equivalent in distance and space of time: One in the far south, Cap Ca-Mau – one in middle, Vung Ro, Nhatrang province – one far north near DMZ, Phong Dien, Quang Tri province. All look good logical shape in the axis of evil game. Another word strictly, U.S. Seven Fleet dominated and controlled all seaway activities.

Because it was protracted war game so I should justified in my conviction that Vietnam War was "an intelligence war" which was so much advantage from his experience, young George H W Bush. With his perfect strategic plan how about this protracted war, and in

The New Legion

the end the result seemed to mirror a famous comment; supposedly I assumed CIA's take on the whole war. This Permanent Government's apparatus activated by its strategic direction: <u>"Everything worked, but nothing worked enough!"</u> For instant not until the spring of 1970 was authority granted for an "incursion" of limited duration and depth into Cambodia, and in earlier February, 1971 Operation Lam Son 719 commenced. But all supplies cargo scattering of the enemy's logistical traffic along Ho Chi Minh's corridor; the interdiction tactic of the past no longer seemed sufficient. The craps players warning advantage for all dispersal factors has been accomplished beautifully (CIA and KGB performed excellent agenda) All strange, ridiculous orders one certain general saying that "Higher Authority" – he meant "Higher Authority," the transparent euphemism for the President – "has noted that each option involves considerable U.S participation." That's not true but the Skull, and WIB bones scam.

Surprisingly, one certain day before large scale prisoner moved displacement to northern Vietnam, They formed a so called people course jury intended to intimidate tactics. Every barrack sent one cellmate to their representative, and the rest prisoners in the barracks were just followed by hanging high speakers. Our representatives came back after session terminated, and said: Two captains attempted to escape but fail. The so called lawyers were illiterates never graduated from laws school. So they based on their war medals for prosecution. Shortly they decided "death penalty" make every one so surprise we called it "Jungle-Law."

While among my cellmates, few of them felt comfortable while they declared war medal false evidence on their note reports. But I was proud while I was stand up in thirty seven times getting them every kind of values medals which reminded me the lightest moments of a brave soldiers; I claimed very clear every excellence indications in its included my heroic SOG missions, and my spy-pilot carrier. I signed my full signature, a particular scribble that would assure anyone one reading the identity-report that I had in fact written it. When I was done, I was patient proud seriously. To think that this individual document would soon be in the hands of opponents was just overwhelming in meditate revenge. I couldn't believe it. I remembered that when I had been in captivity, it had taken years before the Hanoi communist let me write letters home. And then they'd torn them all up because I refused to include laudatory comments about the righteous ways of Communism. Honestly, I was capture where was held, beaten, held, and torture for thirty years, much of that time served after I refused to accept freedom on terms that violated the POW code of honor governing the orders of prisoner releases.

Right after, the illiterate judges announced death penalty then abrupt two innocent victims subjected inserting to their mouth by two citron fruits, and cover their eyes, the guards dragged two of them out of the crowd.Shortly afterward we heart an automatic weapon, the crisp, rattling sounds of AK-47s echoing in Camp wide. I saying pray in meditation God statement:

"Fear not, I am with you; be not dismayed; I am your God. I will strengthen you, and help you, and uphold you with my right hand of justice!" **(Isaiah 41:10)**

Literally, I couldn't see my nearest buddy faces clearly in the hull deck twilight or live in a hull twilight world of truth and half truth. I prepared for the next 413th night. Every one was so tired and frustrated. We tried to close the eyes imagined to the uncertain future. The delusion lasted for only seconds, but it was refuse, a brief retreat to a peaceful corner of my soul for a forced relaxation. I lay on my back on a warm flat steel floor, overlooking a orange hull wall. The sea water below made us with slight swing of the waves. I tried to love to just close my eyes and feel a swinging rhythm rocking my body to asleep in its cradle. I'm confident surely the axis of evil must having a properly solution for us. I slept after all.

Suddenly, nowhere gave a high pitched sound whistle, the guard announced us to line up for outboard leaving at anchorage. Everyone forced to open eyes in woke-up. We repeated the procedure in reverse the manner when we were boarding. After three days journeys, we got sea sick therefore got our foot anchored around something to stand up, to prevent our overbalancing.

Each group combined eighty prisoners, and group by group made queue disembarked from the hull deck by the long wood platform to land. Now know it named Ben Thuy harbor at Vinh Province. We were

The New Legion

convoyed to the train in the darkness of a late evening by group eighty fellows proceeding along the rail road track to the railroad station. We walk between two flanks of lantern. I stared at their flickering oil lamps for quite a while, wondering if I could quietly step over obstacles; just don't worry, proceeding in follow a precedent, should be okay. The atmosphere in this area had become strangely calm, yet that lifting of tension seemed only to increase my sense of irritation. I felt less threatened, yet more frustrated. Being a problem-solver by nature, I'd always had a powerful drive to fix things rather than bitch about them. But here I was, stuck in a situation over which I had no control, my fate completely in the hands of Communist-Hanoi. But the pain in my mind was horrendous, probably because the broken heart (home-sick) had now overlapped by more than I could imagine, the muscles atrophying and nerves twitching to compensate for the damage. My spine was locked stiff sustain of swollen flesh, and yet I would welcome the agony. There were eyes toward where the guard maybe they would spot my group waving the lanterns.

The darkness enveloped entirely the world in a tight, tough, and stingy mixture the manure smells of the wagon reserved for domestic animal. When I step up boarding, right in middle of wagon having three baskets full steamed sweet potatoes; everyone picked up one and go ahead to the end of wagon. We never uttered a word of complain like a regular passenger, making it difficult for me to breathe even I had a chance found out nearer a tiny window. A locomotive hit the carrier-wagons so hard push us in forward positions and back many times meant the head-tractor joined with their wagons. It irritates us to have to shock up and down, to cause discomfort to a part of the air-hot-body. The mass of flesh shake back and forth.

However, when the train started running, we felt little bit comfortable by some stream air infiltrated through the wagon. The much better both position and fresh air let us feel survive. But who know when the train reaching at Yen Bai, Hoang Lien Son province two our fellows (lieutenant colonel) were strangled to last dying breathe. I sat on a mess of manure but don't know cow or water buffalo; so tired and frustrated I didn't worry about it, continued seat comfortable on it. I must try on every hardship, agony which will stay ready in welcome me.

I tried to love sleep. The monotone sound of steel wheels running on railroad track cradled me into sleep like a dead-log. Now everyone slept under the faint yellow cabin lamp through a dull sound rattled volume remain the same.

I woke up facing 419th days of captivity as a prisoner of war, I found religion. It has often been said that there are no atheists in foxholes, meaning that even a nonbeliever will begin to pray when faced with his own mortality. But I had never been a Buddhist of convenience who only prayed when times were tough. Admittedly, as a boy I'd attended Pagoda regularly with my grandfather, while as an adult and full-time Vietnamese Air Force pilot I had allowed that tradition to lapse. Yet my absence from the pews hadn't broken my bond with the God. I would offer my holiday weekend prayers from the flying cockpit. Or say a silent. It didn't require the threat of death for me to recall the sacraments. So when I say that I found religion, I mean it literally.

Suddenly, the train stops right the middle of paddy prairie both side were the water inundated melee scattered with bomb holes and small bushes. All of us were authorized step down to take the water and releasing the shits. Unfortunately, few of us couldn't hold that shit, so all done inside the wagon no one could distinguish which smell one belong human being or animal. Because last night we ate sweet-potato in 'medium steamed cook' so we get trouble. "We're kidding drop bomb without piloted" As fast as we can able drops bomb (go to stool) simultaneously getting fill up water into our containers with another hand. I don't remember dirty water being a problem because so too thirsty, we were so busy. It was supposed boiled, but I still came down with bloody dysentery. As usual, hearing the high tone whistles, so fast, about fifteen minutes and we must on board again. The Communist considered us like the domestic animal, so when everyone staying inside, then they locked the door by a big locker again.

Again, I managed to seat on the floor nearest the aerate hatch small than the window to take breathe for aeration. After the train has just struck three momentum pull and back slowly; we were felt little bite comfortable air coming into wagon though the smell world manure. Then the train cruising at the speed about 45 kilometer per hour, due to the rail never inspection and fixed ever. Every fellow continued close their eyes to meditate the uncertain future ahead. We were passing a tempo-rebuild bridge, the bomb-holes of both side the river filled up by rainy water, now became dark muddy color, maybe they raised fish there? I was so surprised, everywhere were thatched houses among them emerged a look-good brick-roofed with tiles long house; I stared the surprised-word inscribed on the wall "prohibited take these manure" I uttered myself, "Our fellow-Vietnamese from northern were to behave in an uncivilized way in a communist nation." Who know, over-here was the famous revolution-cradle of Ho Chi Minh and Ngo Dinh Diem and the Hanoi called Inter-Region-4 Revolt-Headquarter then Inter-Region-5 was just executed the communist authorizations.

Long ago, in 1963 if it was happens the Ho/Ngo Solution, now our peoples would be prosperity. Who knew this was a 'dirty-war' that a United Nations Secretary U-Thanh had said. Only the WIB and Skull Bones won the silence-war. What was the outcome of that war in abundant proof of their guilt in vocabulary in dictionary having rich in unsavory words such as: *Killing-Field, voted on foot, Reeducation Camp, Boat People, Economic Zone.* What if the most damaged in Linebacker-II air campaign? On 8, May 1972, the MACV briefer stated that "pilots reported sixteen bombs out of twenty on the power plant. If there're any lights burning in Hanoi tonight, they'll be candlepower." The U.S. tested new weapons for the next Middle-East-War in the stratagem "Eurasia Great Game" – Advances in technology since the bombing of North Vietnam earlier in the war were now providing greater accuracy and a humanitarian dividend as well. Newly introduced laser-guided bombs made it possible to take out in a single attack such point targets as key bridges that had withstood hundreds of attempts to destroy them with conventional munitions. "And with the smart bombs," reported Seventh Air Force, "we don't have any problem with the civilian population." This aerial bombardment campaign, "ruined North Vietnam's economy, paralyzed its transportation system, reduced imports (application Malthus theorem, an English Economic Science) by eighty percent and exhausted its air defenses." Hanoi agreed, observed a history of PAVN, contrasting "Linebacker-II" with the "Rolling Thunder" campaign earlier in the war.

My perception, it was real war. This war was different than the first war of destruction. This time the U.S massed larger forces and made massive attacks right from the first day of operation, using many types of testing modernized technical weapons and equipment. Before ending the war according Cooper-Church and Case-Church, it's very clear, easier understandable to me that – as far as my perception on this is concerned bombardment – and this air system is now running the best, and it is the most responsive, that it has ever been since the war started been over here.

Already the sun was hard and slicing through the morning haze, a warm-humid steady so light breeze coming in off the nearby mountainous area. One thing for sure, we were going to go the next remote and secret prison very far away from home – a Democratic Socialist Vietnam, it was simple the small communist country. It was a perfect day for prayer, a bright and tranquil morning. The skies and mountains were polished blue-green, slight soft winds bore silver-edged clouds, and it would have been easy to believe in some sort of heavenly power for the prisoners? No one in the wagon said a word. I all knew what had just happened to our cellmates.

The evening swept in quickly, draining the sunlight from my view and replacing it with dark, gloomy shadows. The mountain-world rapid drop in temperature brought a little chill to my skin, but if I sat very still, the throb from my stiff back and leg was bearable. With darkness in wagon, looking like Halloween goblins as I saw above the swinging oil lamp in faint hanging, I closed my eyes, laid my head back onto wagon wall, keeping patiently for another hard day.

Now the train passed a station Hang-Co, Hanoi, it made one round and slow down, I peered at the vicinity of Hanoi, there were still many peoples slept on the veranda in front yard of resident houses. There were still thatched, and mud-walls among isolated for brick and sandbag blockhouses. Any the communist countries were poor, why? Lenin in the hell should know imperialism still world wide prevailed. Why after WW-II, more than sixty countries restored

The New Legion

their independent why not Vietnam! Skull and WIB men hijacked the Vietnam's freedom and independence.

One more night passed away. I woke up that morning still bathed in the impurity of my dream, a nightmare. The numbness from my back and leg, which didn't seem to keep me awake at night, gathered force the minute I opened my eyes. I wondered how it was that the human brain could shut down the nervous system during sleep, temporarily anesthetizing a disable man, but seemed incapable of doing the same while he was awake. At any rate, I lay here with my eyes closed the train continued proceed to nowhere how could I know. We are assumed in the status of U.S ally servicemen (the new legions) still officially as missing in action. Because with my sheer conception the Vietnam War wasn't end yet – All right. Missing-In-Action is still better than Killed In Action. Historian George C. Herring in an article called "*America and Vietnam: The Unending War*" in the winter 1991-92 issue of *Foreign Affairs,* he explained, thought otherwise. "Such was the lingering impact of Vietnam War," he explained, "that the Persian Gulf conflict appeared at times to be as much a struggle with its ghosts as with Saddam Hussein's Iraq.

We were still many chances that some of us were alive out there, and my daily prayers for us went on almost like a subconscious litany. Sweat sprang from my face, my back, and I crashed onto my back against the wagon steel-wall, just trying to breathe again without cursing out loud.

The train heading to northwest and gradually goes up parallel along Red River. The atmosphere is little bite cool in the mountainous highland and I began to feel a bit uncomfortable with the situation. I still had a good view from the hatch-window. The sun continued its now rapid ascent to the higher top – Just another day in Hell.

The train is slow down and stops at Yen Bai Station. The guards walked out and opened the clock. The wagon big door slid wide-open, still chuckling to each other. Instantly, a serious voice like command-orders loudly cried, "hurry up…hurry up… unloaded" toward the standing by convoy of trucks which were too different as departure, now just no one truck having canvas-cover. Where about we heard the laughter of playing children, the sounds of old engines cranking to life, the calls of women to their neighbors; we are circled by numerous NVA troops.

After lined up in separated groups, each group composed 50 cellmates. Then we climbed up sat down flat like a duck flock.

Intentionally, the convoy proceeds with slow speed through the crowd of village-residents. Suddenly, the angry peoples welcome us by throw hail the stones toward our trucks with swear-word, an offensive express their anger such as Damn, Bloody very rude or offensive language.

Now we climb up on the unknown pass through numerous of stony hills and reaching a unknown county where we saw post placard inscribed word or phrase as power to people' is their political campaign slogan. Now we saw a fighter MIG-19 was camouflaged under a thatched-roofed. I understood the subordinated country always being dependable to their patrons on spare parts like in Saigon regime in the past.

We reached at a ferry station. Everyone must steps down and walk to the boat been waiting.

We followed behind our truck driven on the ferry pier. Once again we climbed up to truck and set for a departure, arriving at a deep valley where has an old hanging bridge, once more time we going down to walk through the shake possible collapsing bridge, still hesitating about go ahead joining over whether to join expedition. Some distance don't have bridge so that the convoy driven on the stone-rocks to pass the rivers. This scene recalled my view of bird when flown over Ho Chi Minh trail rock-bridges.

Now the convoy proceeded on highland road, left behind a huge earth mist dust. We crossed a long mile road along with the soviet invested plantation Tree "Bo-De" to the Soviet contracted this is a soft wood for reproduce paper. The sun continued its now rapid descent off to the west. The evening swept in quickly, draining the sunlight from this county, eventual replacing it with dark, gloomy shadow. After all, the convoy stops at a main gate of Prisoner "Inter-Camp-I" at Yen Bai headquarter. One guard tries to explain over here is village Viet Cuong, Yen Bai City and the province, Hoang Lien Son. Over here, we must courageous deal with our captivity in terms of live sentence. We must have to mentally prepare ourselves for a

The New Legion

long haul. But I told myself that I ready would survive just one day at a time. We wouldn't imagine our captivity as decades of tortured waiting, because if we really believed that, we would probably die. Our mind couldn't accept being in prison for that long, and those kinds of thoughts would break us.

Finally, we steps down from truck and regrouped one by one in line and proceeding very far to a remote virgin forest and stay there cut trees, bamboo to made house for live. In the first week at North Vietnam, we were free for rest and relaxation. The screening individual identity will be processed during this week (checked to make sure they are suitable and able to be trusted) It was obvious to everyone that the prisoners of war must be treated like their held, beaten, and torture for years by years, much of that time served after they refused to accept freedom on terms that violated the POW code of honor governing the order of prisoner releases.

Two colonels got killed because strangled in tightest, lack oxygen inside a stingy wagon; now, during this week one more colonel was committed suicide by cut blood vein of his hand. But in the morning the blood automatically coagulated in air; so he was still survived.

One communist officer take among my group six peoples included me, to kill a cow for meat. Six of us go to the camp back yard, seeing a cow tied near a trunk of tree but not slaughterhouse. The guard said to me go head to kill the cow with a heavy hammer, the cruel killing of animal that I never did. We take turn to hit on her head, she's still not unconscious. Meanwhile we believed the blow caused her to lose consciousness. The guard didn't want waist time so he resumed only one blow, the cow fall on the ground and we used carving-knife to take out her blood. So cruel killing!

All Lieutenant colonels, we are now stayed in the Camp-3, and on the farther hill of the mountain was Camp-11 reserved for priests, monks. They celebrate a special class being so called "political study" (psychological warfare) that will be the main objective during the first week in North Vietnam. In this occasion the communist cadres were so proud to let us know, one U.S Progressive POW, when released but he wish to stay in the outstanding Communist society likely heroic Communist Hanoi. His name was Ho Chi Nam. Do you believe it this real?

After decades studying, now I do know, the CIA's Standard Operation Procedure is a basic fundamental principle meant "come deep inside of tiger dens to catch the cubs or the enemy organsanctuary in ordeal for getting the truth information" So a decoy as None Commission Officer (NCO) named J. Garwood used to trick Hanoi into a position of witness the high officers of South Vietnam moving north as same 1945, Lieutenant Colonel Conein from OSS, agent 019 parachuted at Pat-Bo sanctuary into the waiting arms of Ho Chi Minh and Colonel Alfred Kitts watched the first French troop who enter the North Vietnam, come ashore at Hai-Phong on March 6, 1946.

In 1920, Soviet had the economic crisis, then dictatorship Stalin created a planning program that called the center Reeducation Camp. The main purpose forcing with hard labor work to class bourgeoisie or non-proletariat must be strictly activated in everywhere in Russia and the most was at Siberia. Therefore copying exactly to Soviet Union, the communist Hanoi moved the POW to remote area as Northwest of Hanoi for deprived of our physical plus mental and perished on the labor spot. How can we were forced doing so hard and struggling against starvation. If who were survived must settled in this remote area for live. In the past, 1950s, right here, the Vietnamese bourgeoisie had overcome meant not died. They had to be settled over here.

The communist has the experience to the exploitative policy of the most opponent like South Vietnam officials. So in starting program, they let us take easy for a while; labor with no quota for a limited number or amount of things, products that is strictly forced allowed. However after one month, they put on a harsh punishment worked schedule, we have to face up to the cruel realities of life harshly. We have done our quota of work for each day, fall the Bo-De trees and hand-saw to cut the wood for a fifteen feet tree-trunk, then carried them to the spot for truck loading to export to Russia paper-mill. Everyday our team must done 60 pieces in quota. They didn't care about security; few time the tree-trunk slipped out of our shoulders because after the spell rain, on the slippery earth then gliding down to the mountain feet, hit our cellmates. If went to county dispensary there don't have medicine, just merely helped by its rather antiseptic furnishings or an antiseptic bandage.

Next month we switch to go up the high mountain and fall the big tree for making furniture or coffin. It hard to believe that three hundred prisoners fastened round by the wild-strings on the edge of the trunk to form a knot and together pull it down to the feet of mountain; unbelievable, after one week the long tree-trunk was in front of the camp. Once again next month, we changed the job to invent a new road like the pioneers route constructors. Digging through the hill to make a tunnel, dig down into the stony-soil, dig the soil away from the roots, digging up the tree by its roots. But we are not on an act of digging like exploring of a place for the purpose of archaeology.

Now, all of us were already exhausted our strength, the state of being extremely tired, total loss of strength even into spirit to escape. Communist cadres, they understood this cruel policy very clearly and logically. They intended to damage our muscles and brains. The muscles becoming less elastic body tissue that can be un-tightened or relaxed to produce movement any more; how can we overcome through a terrible ordeal facing so much difficulty and painful experience; like any major challenge in life, you have to take it in bits and pieces. You don't try to tackle the whole thing at once. Now we ventured farther into that black tunnel of captivity, we needed a limited point of reference or that darkness would just overwhelm us.

You just need to make it to tomorrow, I told myself. If you wake up tomorrow, you'll figure out how to survive tomorrow. Today, you've got to figure out how to survive today!

And still, there was no way to know when it was all going to end. So, even though I was trying to convince myself not to worry about it, those images of endless years would continue to ambush my mind.

Naturally, during long years starving and harsh work, one certain day we were so weak to walk, weakened by hunger becoming such the weaklings. Thereby avoiding any exploitation-problems with hard labor, they recreated some particular-groups for weakling such as raising crop, vegetable; sliced bamboo skin string for weaving baskets carrying soil, stone to group road construction, or from strip of willow for kitchen. Brick, tiles production, tailor for prisoner uniform, raising pig. Staying inside, everyday numerous speakers encircled the Camp repeated Prime Minister Dong announcement "Let them work so hard but less food…" That meant soon or later all should be killed by starving. At night we had listened one communist cadre explained the communist doctrine after Lenin was excellent. For months we never see rice ever, just dries potatoes, cassavas (manioc) corns, or horse-food which we named Bo-Bo that if you didn't have enough teeth all of them after digestive they came out the same. Few of them with merely salt water – That's it!

Every one wished having a good Sunday, but some Sunday we must work and they called "work for support an excellent socialism". Some prisoners their hairs color became salt more than pepper and so old-ugly. We probably bathed only once a week, that meant submerged under a small pond where the domestic shit-manure pots were frequently cleaned there too. And the so called bathed lasted about five minutes, and from across the pond we could smell manure sting, musk, but it was no longer offensive. In a land of no colognes or perfumed soap, your nose quickly adapts to the scents of the local sting environment, if not the local litter. We knew we couldn't deal with our captivity in term of years, but we had to mentally prepare ourselves for a real long haul.

What's different between Old POW and New POW?

In the early 1977, one half prisoners of my camp must displace to the border China/ Vietnam. The job was road construction. Near China border located by a small county named Than-Uyen where the atmosphere was adverse effects of the virgin forest and so much poisoned in foliage, the animal, insect, and mushroom. As usual, we went into virgin forest took material from wood such as bamboo palm Tree-Vau to build shelters for the next our new coming fellow from south. In this new-Camp we met few Old POW means they were worn prison-garb color dark-pink and white strips like U.S POW worn, as for us we worn prison-garb blue and white strips. Among of them were captured in Operation Lam Son 719, and among them, a few were my buddies VNAF fighter pilot as Lieutenant Luong F-5, helicopter H-34 pilots Lieutenant Bffh, Khanh, and crew-chiefs On, Son, all they worn pink and white strips garb. Another word meant they were captured before Saigon Fall as for us after Cruel April 1975.

On December 7, 1971 the Permanent Government's policy of progressive withdrawal through the so called "Vietnamization" was well underway. The burden of fighting the war was being passed more fully to the Vietnamese and U.S troops were being brought home at a dramatic rate. Indeed, and ironically in retrospect, the plan seemed to be going well. There was little enemy activity inside South Vietnam and the insurgent guerrilla war had pretty well ended. Literally, the calm did not last long however. [In early March 1972, Soviet General Pavel Batitski was in Hanoi to assess Hanoi' requirements, the U.S-Company-Dynasty called "Inventory" dispensed old batch out of date weapons and will receive new batch weapon as SAM2, T-55, 57, rockets salvo…about 700 millions tons after Paris Talk, all this new batch weapon for overrun Saigon, invasion Cambodia, and defense counterattack to Red China in 1979]

Consequently, after General Batìtski left, right away General Vo Nguyen Giap launched his major offensive of the war. 30th March 1972, the NVA troops launched their attacks, it became known as the 1972 Easter Offensive. It was not an uprising of the insurgent Viet Cong, as had been the case in the Tet Offensive of 1968. Instead, this campaign was a series of conventional attacks by the regular NVA across the DMZ from Communist North Vietnam, and from sanctuaries in Laos and Cambodia with advances designed to cut the country of South Vietnam in half through the Central Highlands, and to strike the South's capital city of Saigon. The communist failed in 1972 after some very hard fighting by the South Vietnamese Army and Air forces, and the determined help of those American forces remaining. As I said because Hanoi don't know the means of "Decent Interval" [wait for Paris Talk as officially announcement U.S troops honorable withdrawal in coming year and receiving 700 million tons new batch of weapons: axiom-1 and axiom-3 done]

The offensive began in early April 1972 with advances of NVA forces toward Saigon from out of Cambodia and attacks toward the

Vinh-Van-Truong

ancient capital of Hue from out of NVA across the DMZ. The final movement of this well orchestrated battle plan came from northern Cambodia and southern Laos as the NVA attempted to replicate the 1954 successes of the Viet Minh against the French at Dien Bien Phu , in wrestling control of a wide belt across the central part of the south, and destroying French military capability in the process. The Communist Army achieved some initial success, but was denied every major objective. In the north, they advanced only to Quang Tri, and were defeated by South Vietnamese Airborne and Marine. In the south, they moved only as far as An Loc before being defeated. And in the Central Highlands, they captured some outposts surrounding Kontum, but were again defeated.

I recount this bit of history as background to a personal drama that played out at this time for Lieutenant Luong, a brave F-5 fighter pilot, now he was my cellmate in this camp: He recalled on July 9 1971. One combat formation of three F-5s had strafing on target at Katum, Tay Ninh province, closed border Vietnam/Cambodia at coordinated XT-140745. Three F-5s took turn in dived pattern, suddenly on wingman got hit in flames and crash. This wing man be shot down was Lieutenant Luong, his fate of the F-5 was sealed by an **SA7-Strella** shoulders-fired-missile. While his firebird at 4,000 feet. The missile scored a direct hit a severed impact on the jet-engine exhausted, causing the F-5 to burst into flames and crash. Luong managed to bail out the spot where the borders of Vietnam/Cambodia. The place was called Katum. There was a Ranger Battalion of about 350 soldiers and two American advisors. They were under attack by element for three NVA divisions supported by tank T-54 band PT-76. The tanks just had overrun the perimeter, and NVA regiments occupied much of the base.

The F-5 flight leader radioed for rescue at once and for a scrambled message fact orders for rescue. Permission was denied, the Flight leader hotly requested again, asked again, denied, more tersely this time, again, the leader didn't yet know the degree of urgency at Katum fire-base, but was infuriated at the moment for not being allowed to help another pilot in obvious need. Now situation was worse, 5 tanks within the perimeter wire and NVA troops everywhere. The friendly forces survivors had consolidated in the command bunker at the

The New Legion

center of the camp and were fighting very hard to keep the enemy at bay, they called friend's artillery to fire on the Headquarters' area because the T.54 enemy tanks had crossed the defense line.

Two F-5s were still strafing for air-cover but in vain. Lieutenant Luong touch-down, he had a badly hurt his bruise neck and swollen face. Though superficial scratch on his neck, face, head, but he was in the midst of many thousands of attacking enemy soldiers, but was able to evade his foes for one day before being captured.

Now and then, Lieutenant Luong was interrogated for a couple days, treated pretty brutally. He was a physical mess, his head neck and face swollen in bruised scratch. His ankle swollen had filled tighten his boot with stiff rigid flesh that was now dried solid. He was felt couple day in the hell. He'd had no control over his bowels or bladder and had soiled himself badly. And Luong would had several leaches cling to his body, all of which itched he should pulled off, except for one which unknowingly was half way into his ass hole.

He was questioned, beaten, threatened, and had his arms tied behind his back with the telephone-wires increasingly tightened during intimidated-interrogation, until finally both his shoulders dislocated and Luong's elbows were pulled tightly together against his stiff-rigid-numbness spine with terror. Finally, the interrogations ceased, and Luong was marched for seven consecutive days to a dip jungle prison camp that, by his estimation, must have been just across the border in northern Cambodia. He was, may be in security zone, given his flight-boots back, but no laces and no socks. After seven days of walking, his feet were like raw ground meat in big sausages by the time Luong limped, in much pain, up to the entrance to his first prison.

Finally, Luong was in the First prison on July 16, 1971. This camp was typical of the image many have. It was carved out of the virgin deep triple jungle canopies below and built of bamboo. The camp was surrounded by a bamboo wall that was reminiscent of an old cavalry frontier fort in the American WWW. There was one wall concentrically within another, with a ditch dug between the two, almost moat-like. In the ditch were many sharp-punji-stakes [Chong-Tre] pieces of bamboo, knife sharp, dipped in human waste and stuck in the ground. If someone felt on these, he'd die of a wound to a vital organ, or bleed to death, or at least die of infection if he were not killed outright. Across that ditch was a log that one had to balance across to gain entry to the camp. Inside the walls were numerous bamboo cages that housed priority ARVN officers, and of course two Americans POW. The prisoner population was South Vietnamese military, there were indigenous mountain people referred to as Montagnards or Mountain-yards who had allied with U.S Special Forces, and there were two Americans, himself and another helicopter pilot captured a month earlier. At least a couple hundred prisoner altogether, condition in that camp were deplorable, prisoners lived like worst animals. They were kept in cages, most of which were not tall enough to stand up in for even physical exercise. That wasn't necessary anyway, because Communist Cadres want kept their feet in wooden stocks as lockers. With their starvation, disable, would escaped, prisoners could not lie back, so they slept sitting up. And every night rats scurried through the cages and nibbled on their dirty flesh, wounds, bamboo cuts scratches, for food; while they couldn't move their feet in the stocks, and couldn't keep them away, and they un-scared hate rats to those nights.

The only time they got out of those cages was for a daily toilet call at the camp latrine. The time never seemed to be the same on any given day, and if a certain prisoner's internal schedule could not want for the appointment time [due to many suffered dysentery] them he went all over himself in the cage. When they did let them out, it was a walk to the "facility" in one corner of the camp. Over here, Luong discovered that the latrine was a couple of holes in the ground that one squatted over to relieve oneself. Problem was that many of the sicker prisoners were not able to hold themselves until getting all the way to the holes, and left their waste in piles all around the area. Some of the very sickest prisoners, near death, were placed in hammocks right next to the latrine, and they would either lay there and soil themselves, time after time, or roll out of their hammock, if they could and take a couple of steps and go there on the ground. The result was a substantial accumulation of human waste all around the holes that were the latrine. Those able to control themselves were forced to walk through that waste field and squat over the holes. On return to their cages, they had no way to clean themselves.

The New Legion

Lieutenant Luong didn't remember water being a big problem. It was delivered in pieces of bamboo like a cup, and there seemed to be sufficient quantities. It was supposedly boiled, but he still came down with bloody dysentery. Food was a problem. Their diet was almost exclusively rice mixed dry-corn-potato. Prisoners would get one coconut sized ball mid-morning, and another mid-afternoon. Occasionally, they'd get the treat of a merely tuberous root called manioc. It is very much like yacca in Latin American countries, his weight went from around 155 pounds to something around little more than 100 in just a few weeks. He was skin hanging on bone with beard that grew very long over time, he did not shave for over half year. And he received no medical attention at all. And no one fared any better. One ARVN infantry officer next to him in his cage had a severe chest wound that had been bandaged long ago, but Luong never saw the dressing changed, and the hole in his chest wall was never repaired. He was too young and strong mind, but Luong was certain that gentleman did not survive.

Oh God! They lived like animals, and under these filthy, starvation conditions, without medical care, it seemed that someone died almost everyday; The bodies would be carried out and buried on a hillside just outside the camp. As a Project Delta Queen Bee pilot, I will always feel a great sense of admiration of our brave men who volunteered for the risky mission to rescue our fellow Americans in the heart of the enemy country. I am reminded of a scripture reading taken from the Old Testament: ISAIAH, Verse 8. Then I heard the Lord asking: *"Also I heard the voice of the Lord saying, who I shall send and who shall go for us? Then said I, here am I, Send me"* and *"Whom shall I send as a messenger to my people? Who will go for us?"* and I said, *"Lord, I'll go. Send me."*

William A. Harriman retired from public life urged his successor to assert his leadership while Hanoi put POW in the Buffalo-cart, or Oxen-cart went around Hoang Kiem' Lake. That's not right violated, against UN constitution, the POW's plight final humiliation at the hands of Hanoi captured.

-So <u>why the mission?</u> By 1970, the US had secured the names of over 500 Americans held in North Vietnam prisons. Many more were missing and presumed captured. Reports of the cruelty suffered by these men at the hands of their barbarous captors were received along with reports of resultant deaths from various sources. Anxiety, concern and anger among the next of kin, friends of the captives, commanders and government officials were very much in evidence throughout this country. What was being done to alleviate the growing concern? Negotiations were being conducted in Paris on a sporadic basis depending on the mood of the North Vietnamese representatives. An attempt was made to reach an agreement whereby an exchange of prisoners of war could be made. After over two years of such negotiations, the results were ZERO. The mood of the country demanded that something be done to help these suffering POWs. Was the time ripe for an initiative-- feasible alternative?

On November 20-21, 1970, a joint force composed of USAF Special Operations and rescue personnel and U.S. Army Special Forces, supported by U.S. Navy Carrier Task Force 77, made a daring raid on the Son-Tay Prison Camp located less than 45 kilometers from Hanoi, North Vietnam. Although no prisoners were rescued, the raid focused world attention on the plight of the prisoners of war (POWs) raised their morale and resulted in improved living conditions for all U.S. prisoners of the North Vietnamese. The men of the Joint Task Force earned the admiration of their countrymen for risking their lives in an attempt to bring freedom to others.-
Execution: Final briefings were conducted on 20 November. All were told the exact location of the objective area and that the latest information indicated between 70 and 80 POWs should be at that location -- the Son Tay Prison. While they were confident that the plan had not been compromised, they would not be certain until they made the landing. If the enemy had foreknowledge of their plan, the reception would not be a pleasant one. Even though the task force was small, it was extremely potent for its size. While it could have been overwhelmed by a much larger force laying in waiting, the enemy would have paid a heavy price. Escape and evasion procedures were thoroughly covered. Satisfied that the mission force was fully in a "go" position, they proceeded to Monkey Mountain at Danang, where a mal staff had arranged for a command post from which the entire operation could be controlled. Communications were available to all elements including US Navy Carrier Task Force,

as well as to Admirals McCain and Moorer. With leader-head at the command post were expert fighter were at Takhli and Udorn, Thailand respectively, and immediately available on direct communication lines. Frisbie, with a small staff, was airborne in a radio relay aircraft that could function as an alternate command post if they were to lose their communications capability. An intelligence staff member, Art Andraitus, was in Japan monitoring the SR-71 photo results of a mission during late 20 November. He reported them that the photo Intelligent was positive (signs of habitation - vehicle tracks, etc) for the troops 20 November was a day for "crew rest." Dr. Joe Cataldo issued sleeping pills. At 22:00 hours the men boarded a C-130 and left Takhli for Udorn Thailand where helicopters were waiting. Upon landing at Udorn the men transferred to three of the helicopters - two HH-53s and one HH-3 - carefully rechecking all the equipment that had been deemed necessary for the mission that lay ahead. At 23:18 hours the first helicopter launched; at 23:25 hours the last helicopter launched. They were led by two KC-130 air-refueling on airway to an air refueling area over Northern Laos. All standing out on the porches and wherever there was a place to watch. They all spoke a quiet word of greeting and wished us good luck, but none asked what we were up to. They had been ordered to stand down a couple of days or so before, to ensure their aircraft were in top mechanical condition for us to use. Even the tower operator was ordered to ignore our taxi-out without radio transmissions.

Just as they had practiced, the formation lead KC-130P refueled aircraft, Lime One, got off on time, as did the rest of them, the HH-3 Banana, and five Apple HH-53s. They routinely fell into the seven ship formation, three helicopters stacking high on each side of the leading HC-130 at about 1500 feet AGL. There was a partial moon and some clouds that they climbed through, when suddenly the call came to "break, 'break, 'break!', indicating that someone had lost sight of the formation lead and they were to execute the formation break-up procedure. Each helicopter turned to a predetermined heading and climbed to a predetermined altitude for one minute and then returned to the original landing. The effect was a very widely separated formation, each helicopter 500 ft above the other and at varying distances away from the lead HC-140. They could see other members of the formation flying in and out of the clouds, and I thought they had blown the mission they had hardly started. Apparently a strange airplane had almost flown through the formation and someone had called the lost contact procedure to avoid a mid-air collision. As it turned out, their planning for such possible events, and the training for such, resulted in a rather routine formation break and with a subsequent rejoin being completed successfully. In the meantime, they had all topped off our fuel tanks from the lead HC-130 and had quite deftly exchanged formation leads from him to the just-arrived, blacked-out C-130 with all the fancy electronic gear."

Flight leader, A/C of the lead HC-130, "Lime One," recalls "*Our mission was to launch from Udorn, join up with the six helicopters and lead them to the North Vietnam border. After joining up we refueled the five HH-53s and the HH-3. This was done in total silence without any incidents. The HH-3 stayed close behind our left wing in order to maintain the speed required by the rest of formation. After leaving the helicopters for their final assault, we immediately returned to Udorn for refueling. We were to refuel as soon as possible and return to northern Laos area to provide air refueling and search and rescue support as needed.*" Happily, the weather in the refueling area was clear. All refueling are accomplished without difficulty. All six helicopters then joined formation with an MC-130 Combat Talon for the low altitude flight toward North Vietnam. The area over Laos is a mountainous area requiring precise navigation by the MC-130 crews. In the meantime the five Skyraider/A-1s had departed Nakhon Phanom and joined formation with the second MC-130 Combat Talon. This formation was in close proximity of the MC-130/helicopter flight. All were en-route at low altitude for Son Tay Prison. Close air support was the job of the Skyraider-A/1s because they were ideally suited in precision-strike on targets. They had long endurance capability, carried a big load of ordnance and their relatively low speed permitted small orbits which would keep them close by overhead should assistance be needed on short notice. Ten Phantom/F-4s had taken off from Ubon to provide a MIG air patrol and five Thunderchief/F-105 Wild Weasels had launched from Korat to provide protection from the SAM sites. The Phantom/F-4s and Thunderchief/F-105s would be flying at a high altitude providing cover over the general area and would not interfere in any way with the primary force.

The Navy force launched on time with a total of 59 sorties. As the primary force reached the Laos/North Vietnam border, the enemy radar's became aware of the Navy force coming from over the Tonkin Gulf. The diversionary raid was having the desired effects. The presence of the Navy on enemy radar caused near panic conditions within the North Vietnamese defense centers. It became obvious that the North Vietnamese total concern was directed eastward. Our raiding force, coming from the west, in effect had a free ride. Meanwhile, in Apple-Two, as Jay Strayer vividly remembers - Tension was building up by this time, as they neared the Initial-Point for the final approach to the camp. They had done most of the flying up to this point, and Jack Allison took over the controls for the final phase, in turn picked up the navigation duties during this critical phase of the mission. As they had rehearsed so many times, the lead C-130 led them over the last mountain range and down to 500 ft above the ground. At the Initial-Point, they, along with Apple-Four and -Five, popped up to 1,500 feet to fly directly for the camp. A single radio transmission with the last vector heading to the camp was made by the C-130's navigator and they continued on, maintaining a disciplined radio silence. Now they were only four – Apple- Three in the lead with the HH-3, Apple'-One and -Two following in trail, with 45-second separations between. They're particularly interested in this phase, for they had done the procedural planning for getting them separated in a manner that would allow room for each to "do his thing," while at the same time not delaying the following bird's initial assault details." Upon reaching the IP (Initial Point), the MC-130 climbed to 1,500 feet. The 130's mission at this point was to drop flares over the Son Tay Prison. Choppers-4 and -5 were to provide a backup and were to drop flares should the C-130 flares not be effective. The flares worked as intended. The choppers made a left turn and proceeded to a pre-selected landing area which was on an island in a large lake. There they would wait, hopefully to be called to move to Son Tay Camp to pick up some POWs. The C-130 made a right turn and dropped fire-fight simulators (deception) and napalm to create a fire as an anchor point for the Skyraider/AD-6s.

The C-130 then left the area for an orbit point over Northern Laos. Immediately after the flares illuminated the prison compound HH-53 Apple-Three, under the command of Marty Donohue, flew low over the prison firing at the guard towers with his Gatling machine guns. The plan called for neutralizing the guard towers to eliminate that potential source of enemy opposition. Immediately following Donohue's pass the HH-3, whose crew was Herb Kalen, Herb Zender and Leroy Wright and carrying Meadows with his 13-man assault force, landed in a relatively small space inside the prison walls; So far all is going strictly according to plan and precisely on time.

The landing was a hard one, but successful. Rotors contacted some of the tall trees which bordered one side of the landing area. It was anticipated that damage would occur and the plan provided for the HH-3 to be considered a loss. By means of an explosive charge with a timing device, it was to be destroyed upon departure of our troops from the compound. The hard landing caused a fire extinguisher to dislodge and crashed against Sgt LeRoy Wright, HH-3 Crew-chief, fracturing an ankle. While undoubtedly this caused severe pain, the flow of adrenaline apparently was such that Sgt Wright ignored the pain and continued with his duties to perform as a member of Meadows' assault force. [Sgt Wright was later awarded the Air Force Cross by President Nixon] Dick Meadows and his highly trained and rehearsed assault force, including the helicopter Air Force crew members, went into action immediately. With bullhorns they announced that it was a rescue raiding party and were there to bring out the POWs. North Vietnamese military personnel exited the buildings in various states of undress and fired their weapons against the intruders. The raiders, however, having the benefit of initiative, a rehearsed plan of action and not suffering from the element of shock that was imposed on the defenders quickly disposed of the camp contingent. Meadow's primary concern now was to enter the buildings to search for Americans held prisoner by the North Vietnamese. The timed explosive charge was placed in the HH-3 to ensure its destruction upon departure of the raiders. With the use of another explosive device a hole was blown in the southwest corner of the prison wall. The raiders and the POWs would exit through this hole. Col Bud Sydnor's command-post would be established just outside the wall at the site of the hole.

Simultaneous with the landing of the assault force, HH-53s Apple-One and -Two were to land opposite the south side and immediately fan out and conduct a search of all the buildings in search of Americans and to prevent reinforcements from interfering in any way with the rescue effort. Apple-One, with Simons and 21 raiders aboard, mistakenly landed at a site enclosed by a fence that presented an appearance not unlike the Son Tay Compound. It was approximately 200 meters south of the objective area. A fire fight immediately ensued where the estimate of enemy killed ran as high as about 200 – [a number which may be somewhat exaggerated] This raiding element was on the ground for not more than five minutes when the mistake was realized. Simons and his men re-boarded the helicopter and moved to the correct position at the Son Tay Prison.

Warner Britton in Apple-One remembers - "they saw the flares dropped by the C-130 ignite and was impressed by the surrealistic appearance of the illuminated landscape. This light enabled commander to see Donohue, Apple-Three, hovering across the building complex toward which they were heading. They noticed that he didn't fire as scheduled and commented on this to Montrem. Then Kalen followed the first aircraft and he did fire. That was the last Montrem and they saw, as just after Kalen crossed the buildings, they're landing on a heading slightly away from the buildings, so that their troops could proceed out the rear ramp and have their objective in sight. They had no idea that they had landed in the wrong place until they had taken off and turned toward the holding area.Memory's Commander of what happened next differs slightly from that of some others. He believed that they took off, flew to their holding pattern-area about few minutes away and landed. They returned immediately when Donohue, in Apple-Three, told us they had landed in the wrong place. They were also in contact with Col Simon's group. Others, including Montrem, believe that they returned to pick them up without landing at the holding area. In any case, very little time passes before they're back on the ground at the so-called "training-school" In the meantime, Jack Allison in Apple-Two carrying Bud Sydnor and his force, had landed at the correct predetermined spot and realizing that Apple-One was not with him immediately put an alternate plan in effect. Within a few minutes, however, he returned to the primary plan when the erring force was in place.

Jay Strayer from Apple-Two observed – "As they neared their objectives, they sensed that they were not going the right way to the Son Tay Camp, and mentioned it more than once to Jack. Quite suddenly they were sure of it; they're about to land at the Military Camp to the south of Son Tay! The amazing thing to the commander at the time, and remains so, is that no one had the forethought to break radio silence and say so! Indeed, Apple-Three had almost taken the camp under fire, discovered his error in time, and turned north to the correct place." Jack Allison, in the holding area, recalls – Sitting in the holding area waiting to be recalled to pick up the POWs and ground forces, Apple flight was treated to a spectacular fireworks display. 14 to 16 SAMs were fired at the F-105 "Wild Weasel" aircraft, although one was at such a low angle, one of the departing helicopters took evasive action. One SAM was observed to explode and spray fuel over Firebird-Three. The aircraft descended in a ball of fire and appeared to be a loss. However the fire blew out and the crew continued with the mission. Another SAM exploded near Firebird-Five, inflicting damage to his flight controls and fuel system. The crews later bailed out over the Plaine-des-Jarres highland at Laos and were picked up at first light by Apple-Four and -Five." While all the helicopters were engaged with he compound and A-1s Skyraider, which had arrived with the second C-130, were doing their thing. Bob Senko in Peach Two recollects - Ed Gochenaur and they're in Peach-Two. They're on Major Rhein' Wing. They had an automatic radio frequency change when they entered the target area. Only one aircraft forgot, and that was him. But they're able to keep up with what was going on visually. Both Goch and him knew right away that none of the helicopters hand gone to the wrong area, but were pretty helpless to do much other than support the troops as best they could. Everything got better organized for them when he got the frequency right. It got better for the troops when they got to the right area.

Because they were out of position, they got called to pay close attention to the road from the south, to make sure no-one took advantage of our situation. When they got the order to shut down the foot bridge between the Citadel and Son Tay, lead and Goch got lined up headed east to take the bridge out with a couple of 100# Willie-Pete bombs. The commander hollered at Goch that he was too shallow, but he let the WPs go anyway and they were pretty short. Fortunately, his run in line was across a chemical factory (if that was what it was) and he greased it. There was a beautiful display of different color flames, with the bright green ones going-up way over the altitude they were working. Major Rhein's bombs were pretty good and the combination allowed them to get the job done. On - by the way - the reason Goch was so low on his run in was that the SAM-missiles had already started. They seemed to be pretty random at first but slowly they saw that they were at least aimed in the general direction of Son Tay Camp and were being fired on a very low trajectory. So they stayed as low as they could. They don't think any were actually targeted specifically on them. But they go our attention and they stayed pretty well in the weeds. It wasn't too hard since they had about 15-20 percent moonlight to work with and the target area was pretty well marked by the small arms going off. They're circling the camp about 100-200 AGL and when they're on the north side, they'd drop down to water level over the Red River. Again, because some of the ground troops were not in position to blow the bridge on the north side of the camp, they got called to take it out. Since they couldn't get enough altitude to drop any heavy stuff, they started strafing it. He don't know how productive that was, but He's pretty sure they kept any traffic off the bridge even if they didn't drop it. When the ground guys wrapped it up, they dumped their left over stuff in the Red River and headed home. One other thing he remembered vividly is that when the helicopters went in, they were to take out the guard towers with their mini-guns (7.62). They're only to help as a last resort. When they opened fire, either they hit something explosive, or the sheer number of tracer-rounds caught the bamboo/wood towers on fire. Actually, it loomed like the exploded. It was amazing, certainly stopping any reaction from those towers."

The entire camp was searched. All North Vietnamese forces were annihilated and the devastatingly disappointing discovery was made that there were no Americans at the camp. The coded message - NEGATIVE ITEMS- was received in his command post. In disbelief he hoped that the message had become garbled in transmission. Simons and he had previously discussed this unlikely probability but know that the possibility existed. The raiding party was on the ground at Son Tay Compound for 29 minutes, within one minute of the planned time of 30 minutes. They experienced no losses. Sgt Wright suffered a broken ankle and Sgt Murry suffered a bullet wound on the inside of a thigh, a minor injury. The estimate of enemy killed was determined to be about 50. The helicopters were called in and the raiding party went aboard. After eerie-man was accounted for, they launched for the long ride back to Udorn. The SA-2 missile sites became active and were engaged by the F-105 Wild Weasels. A missile hit and severely damaged an F-105. There was a loss of fuel and an effort was made to return to the Being 707/KC-135 tankers on an orbit over the Laos space. A flame-out was experienced prior to contact with the tankers and the crew of two, Major Kilgus and Capt Lowry, ejected - landing in a mountainous area safety, uninjured. The progress of this emergency was monitored at his command post. Location of the downed airmen was relayed to the crew of HH-53s Apple-Four and -Five, Lt Col Brown and Major Kenneth Murphy, with instructions to search for and pick up the F-105 crew members. The pickup was successfully accomplished after more choppers air refueling and flare drops; all returned to Udorn safely. At Udorn he met a dejected force of raiders. They were disappointed because their hopes of returning with POWs were dashed. They had failed. This thoroughly dedicated group expressed the belief they should return the next night and search for the POWs. For many reasons, this could not be done. Did the mission result in benefits as Admiral McCain predicted? Yes, definitely. The North Vietnamese, fearing a repeat performance but not knowing when and where, closed the outlying POW camps and consolidated all POWs in the two main prisons in downtown Hanoi. These were the old French prisons of Hoa-Lo and Culac. The number of POWs at these two prisons now grew to the extent that POWs lived in groups, rather than what for many had been solitary confinement. Morale immediately improved and, as a result, general health improved. POWs have stated that lives were saved. Prison conditions to some degree generally improved. Mail delivery and food both improved substantially. Morale among next of kin, for the most part, also improved.

Jay Jayroe, former Son Tay POW, recalls -- "When the fireworks went off that clear night in November of 1970, we knew exactly what was happening - a raid on Son Tay Camp was in progress, some fifty-two of them had been moved from Hanoi to Son Tay in late 1968 and had immediately recognized it as a place for escape of rescue. During the following months they did what they could to indicate their presence there, hoping their efforts would result in success via US Airborne surveillance. However, for reasons unknown to them, in July, 1970 their captors moved them a short distance to a newly opened complex, where they were aggregated with other POWs from outlying prison camps. He did not believe the North-Vietnamese suspected an impending rescue attempt, because the move was quite frequently with no sense of urgency. The raid, as they have learned, was perfectly executed and highly successful with the exception of one minor detail - no one was rescued. But, short of being there, one cannot imagine the positive effect it had on those of them who were destined to spend some two and a half years more as POWs. One should recall that it had been two years since the US had stopped bombing North Vietnam, and their faith was being severely tried. But the Son Tay Rescue attempt dispelled all doubt: *"They Were Not Forgotten; Their Country Cared!!!"*During the hard times ahead, their renewed faith in God and Country served their well" -In 1973, when the 591 POWs were released, they learned that those at Son Tay had been relocated in mid-July - almost one month before the Joint Contingency Task Force was formed and trained for the rescue mission. Intelligence sources were not adequate to reveal the actual presence of POWs at specific locations on a real-time basis. Some critical intelligence had several weeks delay. The successful demonstration of their capability to execute this type of rescue mission undoubtedly had some impact on the formation, albeit 18 years later, of a Unified Command (USSOC) whose sole mission is special operations. He will always feel a great sense of admiration of the brave men who volunteered for the risky mission to rescue

Americans in the heart of the enemy country. He is reminded of a scripture reading taken from the Old Testament:

Fortunately, having abrupt secret urgent message that all U.S POWs must gathered at Hanoi Hilton as soon as possible. On July 2, 1972 they were taken outside their cages and line up with a group of prisoners. There were about 26 ARVN officers and 2 Americans. Lieutenant Luong would soon learn that one of their groups was an American Gunship Cobra pilot who had been shot down the same day another VNAF pilot had, in an A-1 Skyraider at Polei-Klang, and 4 helicopter VNAF flight personnel crewmembers. The prisoners were addressed by the Communist camp commander and told that they were going to travel to a new camp, a better camp, a place where get better food and medical care, where they'd get mail and packages from home. He said the trip could take as long as two weeks, and that they should try very hard to make it. Lt Luong envisioned another jungle camp but somewhat better situated, staffed, and supplied, somewhere not too distant in northern Cambodia, or just across the border in Laos. The comment about trying very hard to make it did not register in his mind at all, until some surprising days later. For security during evacuation from camp to camp, the prisoners must set out barefoot with all of them tied loosely to one another. After few days, reaching the security area in the Ho Chi Minh Trail, they'd no longer be tied for moving faster because they all struggled to just keep moving forward. Two Americans pilots were so weak from malnutrition, sick with untold disease, and suffering from wounds that were infected and worsening with the aggravation of the journey. They soon began to become plagued by more leaches, on top of everything else. They'd suck- blood and cause infection of their own. Two American pilots have been a site by VNAF pilots who were there suffering the same conditions, fighting their own personal demons, that every steps of the way, threatened to destroy their physical ability, or derail their mental willingness to continue, and if they did not continue to march, they would die. In normal life, they have to take some overt action to die. They have to kill themselves. As a prisoner of war, under these circumstances, that truth is reversed. They have to reach deep within themselves and struggle each day to stay alive. Dying is easy, just relaxed, give up and

The New Legion

peacefully surrendered, and they will die. Many did. They died in that first jungle prison camp, and they died along the Ho Chi Minh corridor. Some would complete a day's journey and then lie down to die. Others collapsed on the corridor and could not continue. The group would be marched ahead, a riffle shot or shots heard, and the pitiful suffering prisoner was not seen again. They lost at least couple fellows of their small band of 28 captives, and by the time the journey was over. Wayne Finch or William Reeder, or other American in Luong's group, would be dead as well.

Actually, the trip turned out to be not a two weeks hike to a new camp in the same vicinity as the one they'd departed. It turned out to be a journey lasting over a three months, taking them several hundred miles all the way up the Ho Chi Minh northern part into North Vietnam, and then on to the capital of Hanoi. It was a nightmare, a horrid soul wrenching nightmare. Every step, every day wracked their bodies with pain. Their infections became worse, disease settled in them. They were seemed nearly death. Their legs swelled at least double in size, darkened in color, filled with pain. They swelled so much, long cracks formed in the skin and puss and bloody stinky fluid oozed from the cracks. They drug their legs like the pendulous sodden club, and its every movement lashed their whole being with the most searing pain, pain that kept their faces contorted and a cry shrieking within every corner of their consciousnesses, pain that was burning the blackened scars deep into the center of their very beings.

Lieutenant Luong' blood dysentery worsened, and he got different kinds of malaria and several intestinal parasites. And he hovered near death as he tried to reach the end of each horrible day's journey of 10 awful grueling miles. Each morning, after unconscious-slept like death log, He'd begin a personal battle to stand and loudly moan or scream to himself through clenched teeth and pressed lips, as blood ran into his leg and brought a surge of new pain as gravity pulled blood and bodily fluids down into the carcass of leg and pressure grew against decaying flesh and failing vessels. There were many ARVN officers suffering badly themselves, but always encouraging U.S pilots, always helping as they could. They'd eat a paltry morsel of rice for dinner, and they tell Americans fellows this was not how

Vietnamese ate. There were many fine foods in Vietnamese culture. A Vietnamese meal was delight. Don't judge the cuisine by what they were given to eat. Americans believed VNAF pilots, and did not. And the Vietnamese were right, of course. Americans tried to maintain a sense of humor. It was hard, but it was necessary. "Your spirit is the most important factor in survival, and a sense of humor, even under the very worse conditions, helps maintain spirit, and in spirit lives hope. And again, the Vietnamese helped. They were always concerned about fellow-Americans, and did all they could to help U.S POWs remain positive, to be hopeful. As bad as things got, the Americans never gave up hope, not even the day U.S POW would have died had it not been for Vietnamese POW.

Two Americans mustered all their wills each day just to wake, stand, and take a step. Then Americans fought hard for the remainder of the day to just keep going, to keep moving along the corridor path. Americans could barely walk, but somehow they continued, and survived each day, to open their eyes in the morning to the gift of one more dawn.

All this is very odd, American pilot Reeder felt on the worst day of his life. He fought so very hard, he faltered, he dug deeper, staggered on. He faltered again, and he struggled more, and he reached deeper yet, and he prayed for more strength. And he collapsed, and he got up and moved along, and he collapsed again, and again, and he still fought, fought with all he had in his body, his heart, and his soul. And the communist cadre came the guard looked down on Reeder. He ordered Reeder up. He yelled at Reeder who could not. It was done.

And then there was one Vietnamese pilot looking worried, bending toward Reeder. The guard yelling to discourage his effort; He persisted in moving to help American-pilot. The guard yelled louder. Vietnamese pilot's face was set with determination, and in spirit of whatever threats the guard was screaming. He pulled Reeder along with his feet dragging on the ground behind him. He drug Reeder along all the rest of that day. Occasionally, he was briefly relieved by another Vietnamese helicopter pilot, but it was the first who carried the burden that day. It was the first fellow pilot who lifted Reeder from death, at great risk to his own life, and carried Reeder, until they together completed that long day's journey.

The next morning, Reeder went through the normal agonizing ritual of waking up, and standing, and dragging his leg through those first determined steps. It was more of a struggle than ever before. Reeder mustered the will, and he went on. At the edge of the encampment was a broad log that spanned the rapids of a river. He started to cross, tried to balance. Pain awful, very weak, equilibrium gone. No sense of balance, worthless leg is throwing him off … begin to slip off the side of the log … then falling onto the rocks in the rushing water below. All Vietnamese pilots and another American moved back off the log and came to his rescue. They pulled Reeder from the river and onto the bank. They pleaded for the group to remain at this camp until he was able to travel again. Finally, they were ordered away, they would not leave Reeder. They were drug away and forced across the log bridge at gunpoint. And they were marched away with the rest of their prisoner group in emotional departure…emotional departure. They never had a chance to see those Americans again … ever!

As far as Reeder's fellow prisoners knew, he was left at that camp to die, as others had been? No never … but the communist had to first aid for him becoming no-harm. This was the order from high-command in Hanoi. But for some reason, the Communist decided to give him penicillin injections for several days. Reeder began to show some improvement. After a time, he was able to stand, and as soon as he was able to walk again, he was put back on the Ho Chi Minh Trail, this time traveling with groups of NVA soldiers moving north, and accompanied by his own personal guard. It continued to be an agonizing trip, but the worst was behind him. He even found the opportunity to escape once when he got one turn ahead of his guard on the jungle trail. But the guard quickly tracked him down, and once the guard decided not to shoot him in his rage. The guard recaptured him, and the journey continued. Eventually, Reeder joined with another group of ARVN prisoners as they entered North Vietnam, and ultimately reached Hanoi. There Reeder went into North Vietnam's prison, and ended up at the infamous Hanoi Hilton from where he released at the Paris Peace Talk agreement accords to **axiom-3**: [The U.S could not have won the war under any circumstances, so honorable withdrawal]

Now as for us, New POW, one certain day, we have been working to fill the hollow-bumpy road with soil and stone. Suddenly, the camp commander called our group came back home for digging the grave to bury a cellmate just have been dead. The story was a victim as a lieutenant colonel Nghiep from VNAF, eating poisoned mushroom in the deep virgin forest. He was my Air force pilot, went deep into forest to fall the bamboo and carried them home to build the cage-shelters. Three of them, one in Special Force, one in Ranger, both of them said they were already ate this strange-yam. So my friend trusted them, and put this yam in the fire-wood, after few minutes, it smells okay. Then my friend because too starving, tried to eat this yam. But when swallowed abruptly he felt could not breathe, all the digestive organ was swollen on, his respirator air couldn't come out. He become mute as a fish, indicated by hand to another cellmates nearby to go back camp. When they reached at the camp, he tried very best to vomit but fail, except vomit the blood. A hunter dog of the prison-camp licked that stuff and fall to shaking died of poison at once. Some of our fellows tried to grill this dog for food; but the cadre officer order to bury dog-remain right away. They let the victim write a letter to his family and explained why he will die. We carried our fellow Nghiep to bury him on the hill growing of Tree-Vau likely bamboo but bigger, straighter. Where we're just fell the Tree-Vau and replace the same spot our cellmate fellow graves right after that. Unfortunately, everyone was too exhausted, starved, we couldn't excavate deeper, we tried to cover the thin layer soil just enough covering on disguise it. We prayed, wished no wild animal scratch up. *"Blessed be His glorious name forever; may all the earth be filled with the Lord' glory. Amen and amen! May, we forever thank you Lord. For the blessings you deem to send; but most of all we thank Thee; for being our best and dearest Friend."*

The native tribe let us know, this yam was extremely poisoned no one in this area noticed-know how it. This yam with the name "Cffl đuôi-trâu" (Tail-Buffalo-Yam) But at night, we tried to excavate a buried dog then we cooked and eating, luckily no harm, that's okay for everyone. Thank God!

The New Legion

At the winter, the weather was so cold, our camp located deep in the valley, the climate was so adverse, the mosquito picked, sucks our blood but let so much itched. Over here there have a stranger tiny leeches, they usual living in the bushes, when they felt a sensitive the human body warm temperature passed, they sprang up attaches itself to its victims and sucks their blood. When we felt itched that was too later everywhere in the neck, face, shoulder were likely bleeding. At the working spot, some time the small wild-Bee-flies abruptly attacked on us all over our faces leaving bleed and itched. The spring water was also harmful, in the monsoon rainy of heavy rain that comes with the flood, a large quantity of wasted water covering a large area with Tree-Liem leaves, and the most poisoned of another leaves from Tree-Son. So after water came down, few habitants were died, some were real sick with strong high-fever. The Tree-Son, sometime we didn't know it poison, we fell and cut carry them back to the camp used firewood, create in. One day another fellow in camp's kitchen fired this kind of Tree-Son become hospitalized and died after few months in the hospital as Lieutenant Luong was died in 1979. One certain day, myself, I didn't know the Tree-Son, on the way carried them back to camp. I felt itched and hot at my shoulders. Finally, I was sick with terrible high-fever temperature. I murmured: "Today, I've gone to figure out how to survive today!"

In the summer time, we don't have enough water, so the streams were so drought. But the water was condensed in the muddy hollows with poisoned water. All prisoners of the camp were sick includes the guards. The camp commander gave the favors, if any prisoners at working spot maybe have twice a week baths but we're so sick couldn't stand up for worked. Bleed to death, to suffer severely or die from hunger like wild animals starving in the drought. What's for starving? Be starved into surrendering. We were trying to convince ourselves again and again not to worry about go to die, but those images of endless days would continue to ambush our mind even through nightmares. Though we're pretty sure that the Hanoi can win by used military power but fail by political of Vietnamese sentimental of our culture traditional nation; proof and evidence, the Provisional Revolutionary Government (Viet Cong) has been supported in United Nations was 76 votes, almost double of Hanoi and GVN vote. Hanoi must be humiliated in that event.

As for myself, a spy pilot on the view of bird, with benefit of hindsight, it has become clearer that the U.S Permanent Government goals were more ambitious than a superficial, bogus military victory [they have sophisticate weapons like CBU-55, AC-130B, Laser, Smart Bombs, BLU-82AL...] Had the U.S. really wanted a military triumph, it could have easily achieved it after the massive bombings of Hanoi in December 1972, they fired 1,242 SAM and had none left. And in early 1975, I supposed to lead a South Vietnamese attack on North Vietnam, which was defended by a single division of regular troops. All I required from the United States was just merely air support, and the U.S. troops already in my country would defend population centers. Finally I'm waiting for the justice, the logical solution for the ARVN' POW after their craps. So despite all set-backs, recovering quickly from disappointment, cheerful and confident, we remained buoyant!

Suddenly, from a secret order (China give Vietnam a lesson on border attack) at midnight we prepared to move back Yen Bai Province. We heard the trucks moving in front of the camp. Luckily we're escaped out of the mortally serious zone. After a long journey-day we're arrived the formerly inter-camp. Where our works were less hard than before; day by day we were very busy during harvest, digging out the cassava from the hard soil and gathered at this time. Brought the camp to sliced and put open sun for drying, some changed into powder. Pull the cassava out of hard soil making us sometime feel the backbones come out of our bodies. Finally, the harvest was over and our works turn into raised crops again by digging hole on the hill farther extended till the foot of big mount. No the fertility of the soil, so to make soil more fertile by inserting the leaves down inside every hollows then put small trunk-chop of cassava before buried soil on it.

Weather-Weaponry: In the Vietnam-War, since 1970 the first volley in Congress when Senator Church and Kentucky Republican Senator John Sherman Cooper authored a bill that cut off funding of all military activity in Southeast Asia that I supposed this issue seemed "a manage the defeat" take retaliatory measures on Soviet Union turn to babies sisters all small communist countries. Now Soviet must expensed all aid in economic plus military supporting till finally exhausted. After Communist overran in South Vietnam,

The New Legion

in the nation wide was subjected to for years of severe famine, must take exchange rice for huge quantity of horse food (Bo-Bo grains edible) to overcome people starving. The weather weaponry like Cuba inflicted hot and dry temperature, hurting even the easy crop like sugar cane, potatoes, cassava, manioc, corns couldn't grown up.

In lobby of a certain break time after long Paris talk session, Henry Kissinger usual make a casual talk about if whether the donated Saigon to Hanoi dominated as the gift, and how Le Duc Tho carried out to feed their citizens out of starvation. Usually people were never believed all the gossip they hear; but I believe it true, and real. Tho responded in logical way – It's easy while we don't need freezer for food preservation. All the surface cultivated lands were explored in spreading as much as we can to raise cassava and manioc keeping preserved in the soil for long when we needed. How could Tho understand the weather weaponry that in the past Cuba gave up, couldn't raise sugar-cane.

The program moving POW to North Vietnam was stopped in April 1977. And in early 1981, Hanoi changed the prisoner policy, put under surveillance of the Special police Department. All of us moving to southern near Lao/Vietnam border, Tan-Ky' Prison, Nghe-Tinh province; I saw the prisoners of felonies like the skeleton been walking; one day I could image my similar of the fate of them. I do know next to us was the Camp-4 reserved for our fellows come back from Guam Island by Vietnam Thuong-Tin's ship and next was the Camp-5 reserved for FULRO (Front Unified Liberation Faces Oppressed.)

A certain day, the Camp commander said in front of criminal prisoners, the guards didn't worry about them to escape out the Camp; but political prisoners like us meant a big some of money in trading. As foresee, maybe a plan providing against perishing in the attempt POW by starving with hard-labor wasn't acting by secret agreement between Kissinger and Tho. We were gradually moving back to Saigon for releasing. Camp Z-30s, situated from East of Saigon sixty kilometers were the center POW released transit. Afterward a procession will be established for evacuation the POW to United States by Humanitarian Organization.

In any case, I name heroes those whose are capable to survive years being imprisoned, starved, torture in the hand of the enemies. It is not rare when people are brave enough to stand upright and speak the truth even if it probably leads to their death. Those are our superheroes whose name, we would never forget. Right after the South Vietnam ended in April 1975, dozens of high ranking officers chose the death rather than to surrender to enemies in defending their moral integrity, such as generals Le-Van-Hung, Le Nguyen-Vy, Nguyen-Khoa-Nam, Pham-Van-Phu, Tran-Van-Hai, Ho-Ngoc-Can ...to name a few. In the so-called re-education camps throughout the country, we have learned numerous cases that our fellow detainees stood up against the communist cadres for the righteousness without fear of being killed. As a result, many were isolated in the darkness and murdered mercilessly.

Since it is not the loss of lives through fighting, but the true casualty is far more reaching. The war didn't stop with the loss of South Vietnam. It didn't stop with the loss of its nature people. The loss extends to me, my siblings, my SOG' comrade-in-fights, my cousins, my children, my children's children; the loss is immeasurable. That is the true cost of war that WIB Bones had walk into the very disaster in Vietnam then Iraq.

Not surprisingly, we're still imprisoned in the Reeducation Camps at that time, took a dim view of U.S [WIB] as a traitor. But we're still hope that the U.S. was generally regarded as one of the most thankless tasks in America media reports. Washington has to review, struggle to achieve some level of cooperation from Hanoi regime that 10,000 of its POW and deal with an advocacy network that fed every wild rumor or conspiracy theory, preying on the grief of South Vietnam families who had not release yet – the son and husbands of those who anxiously followed from the Washington hearings, a ten thousands ARVN' prisoner of war. The fact that when the U.S. should say the word "Vietnam" today the U.S meant not just a war but a country – at long last, a place where, as I thought thirty years ago, "America turned and veterans helped in the turning." – in transcending the Vietnam trauma was one important factor – have the courage to put the policy into action – normalization of diplomatic relations with Vietnam.

Chapter-3

From the Reeducation Camp to become a Boat People

These best Map and Compass tiny instruments

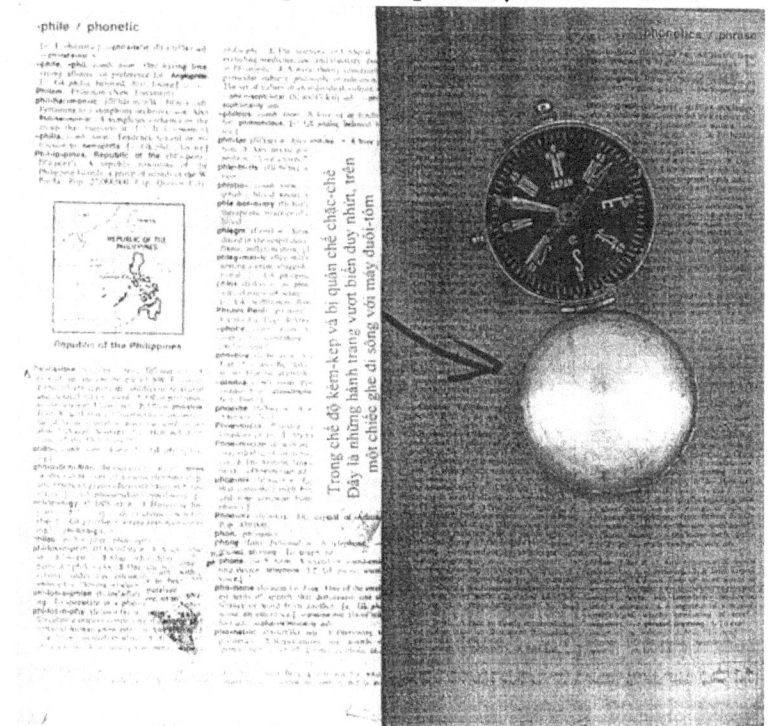

Vinh-Van-Truong

FLEEING BY BOAT TO PHILIPPINE

A CLASSIFIED DOCUMENT OF CIA disclosed:" *There'll be a chaos fleeing out of Vietnam... and The Hanoi's Communist will revenge...* We soldiers, who fought without commanders to the last bullet, finally must be captured and jailed." What a drama which was written by W.A Harriman who was an architect of 'cold war', a *notorious wise man amongst "Six Friends and the World They made"* The Wise men (1986) described by Walter Isaacson and Evan Thomas! Yet Dr Henry Kissinger was a choreographer of *"Pennsylvania"* performance which was painfully negotiated and deadly led to the end of Republic of Vietnam in the South.

The Evil WIB Bones pressured on Congress in U.S had undercut support for the war, even the material support that acted government had promised the South. The ARVN began to run short of spare parts, fuel, medical supplies, and ammunition. They fought on through '73 and '74, with things getting worse month by month. Eventually, what US indecision and weakness had made inevitable did occur, and Saigon fell. With it fell a night of suppression, repression, and vindictiveness as the communists broke every promise to "liberate" the South and offer "reconciliation" to those who had opposed them. Thousands died, hundreds of thousands went to "re-education" camps, other hundreds of thousands went to "New Economic Zones", and the standard of living fell to one of the lowest in all of South East Asia. Hunger was rampant, despair was common, and millions of Vietnamese left the country every way they could, even though the risks of even trying to leave were high, and the risks of the journey included an appreciable chance of death.

This was the fault of the WIB Bones, which had not kept all its promises to RVN. And I knew that good people, many, many good people, were paying a heavy price for U.S failure to support us. Since I could do nothing about it, I tried hard for years to not think about it too much.

Alas! Junior officers like us must go to the so called *"reeducation camps"*; in fact a giant prison in which, the most savaged revenges began to destroy human beings, one by one. After almost 13 years of that revenge, I looked for a way to flee by boat. How accurate that CIA document designed and carried out and how suffering we were while we endured those terror days! (Despite a 10/10/1972 media meeting that Kissinger had said *"peace at hands"* after secretly gave The South to Hanoi and advised the North not to revenge former SVN officers).

Kissinger also boasted to Le Duc Tho when walking around the palace in break-time but eventually the truth occurred for decades later: *"The First invisible antagonist is yourself, The Second is amongst your Communist Party, and the Third is all your citizens included few of your cadres!"*

Thousands of escapes with different circumstances and factors but the same goal: Looking for lives from death on wide open sea which is always controlled by angel of death! With a dependable of boat, big engine, endurance, weather; people on board were terrifying, shocked and had a painful experience, and most seeking to pray with God for help because of disorientation.

I know well that the hardship never stops at the end of a long prison time but is prolonged for my next generations to come! For that of one day, I was offered to take a free trip to escape by boat and acting as an interpreter in return when meeting with foreigners on the sea. But I had refused that offer for I felt better anyway after long prison at that time. My oldest daughter looked after me well enough to sell up her house for buying an old boat with flat base and two eyes in white-black-red colors as usually country customs. Most important means are a map and a compass which should be minimum assurance for a maritime line that I couldn't apparently, look for, as a house arrested ex-prisoner.

For 100 long days from early mornings, I had digging a 6/30 meters fish pond when focused on that ill plan with many questions of where, what country, when… even I chose in advance Thailand or Malaysia as a farthest, due to our boat too small designed to floating on river than open sea. By departing in March as a new released prisoner, it was too late for safety because of an old-folk saying *"Deadly of March for elderly woman on sea!"*

On the 85th day, me and 3 children, 2 grandchildren silently took a daily bus to the Western, unloaded at Long-Dinh County with regional alike clothes. We immersed into the crowds for best cover from plain cloth police and followed a rough trail to the South going along side of a coconut line beside a vile on the right and a man-made canal on the left. An experienced local boat operator had waited for us at the end of the canal; 2 km from Long-Dinh sailing about 60 km more to the seaside. Night felt fast at the end of area-palm tree line. We were in great trembling that we'd lost our appetite at a well prepared meal. When night was totally in darkness, a 10 year old boy came to show us the way out to the departing boat. He made a signal for us to hide in bushes and waited. A sound of small canoe came closer and stopped. The boy let us wade into the deep mud canal, left our shoes and sandals there to climb on the boat. We lied down deep inside on its floor to make it looks like a fruit trading boat going to My-Tho market.

From Long Dinh's canal to stream following into the larger tributaries out along to the sea; Inside the boat, my heart had beaten hard like the time of dropping STRATA's infiltration Teams into Ho Chi Minh Trail. Four children and nine adults gave trust on Mr. Hai boat operator who was well experienced. Drowsy yellow lights of My-Tho's city appeared on my left. We prevented of getting closed to all canoes, boats and ferries traveled all over the area. I peeped through a small hole at the leaf-hood out and felt the boat flew out strong to the sea, the farther from My-Tho, the deserter of traffic on Mekong Delta.

Suddenly, the engine sounds strange and felt dead stopped. I was so nervous. Mr. Hai tried to fix when everybody was praying. Finally it worked well again. Before the trip, we had bought a spared small good old engine and a new Champion spark plug for emergency. Mr. Hai even urged to buy several fan-propellers to replace broken ones when needed. Most importance is getting out of Cua-Dai's estuaries before sunrise for fear of police coast-guard-patrols can see us in day time. And once again, the engine broke down. Mr. Hai tried to fix it right away while we were prayed and it worked. At 3 am the situation was just on and off like that. Suddenly Duoc's bushes appeared in the far east of estuary, Duoc were the wild sea-plant growing-up between the mix fresh mix salt water that means showing-up we are in the mouth of a river in which the river's current meets the sea's tide. The natives were made the Duoc's trunk for good fire-wood last burned so longer. Their thick root helped keeping sea-shore slowing down sea-waves as well.

Now, I was in a great nervous tremble, concerning if whether engine happened to quit or what. When we just discovered in front of us, one coast guard patrol-canoe that will be reached for the next couple minutes, had been anchored at the middle of our exit. We had no choice and just passed this white canoe patrol. My eyes opened broader starring at this monster. It slightly stirred by our boat waves, 100 meters, 50 m but this monster was sleeping, unmoved. I wished they overslept or ignored us, like a fruit trading boat as usual. In my profound mind, I thought that the police had been familiar with the noise of every boat engine, and their felt-consideration that this is a small engine just available only used in the river. So they did not mind about our escaped-boat. I thought this communist navy vessel saw the craft, but they did nothing, because they did not believe this junk could cross the open sea. The more we got closed to the sea, the more wind and waves we faced.

The sky wide opened in fog and silver waves ahead. Already the sun was hard and slicing through the morning haze, a humid, steady breeze coming in off the nearby Pacific Ocean. I silently praised Mr. Hai's skill and experience, sometime narrowly escaped fishing nets all over around us. Sometimes we took turns to help him push our boat forward by bamboo canes at the shallow waters. Farther from Cua-Dai's estuary, I was the only man permitted to sit at the front end for checking the compass for direction which hung out on my neck. The dictionary with a map printed inside was under my bottom. Mr. Hai and I suddenly had seen the white patrol boat which was following far behind us. I ordered at once all young men turning on another spared engine and kept both two working with maximum speeds. Because our boat was so small and with two engines running made a large difference. With forward speed like this and the nose higher, we hope to reach the international sea very soon. Another wood-cargo boat joining helped them pursuing us simultaneously. They were chasing us with full speed! We were horribly scared; almost ceased of breathing and had kept going on, waiting for the worst to come. After all, when we looked back the cargo boat and the white patrol boat were far away until the patrol boat was just a tiny black spot. Maybe now we are in the international sea shore limited!

When the left engine at last broke down too, we were already in the international sea. Two hours later, the only one was broken down. Our boat was silently alone in the open sea. She twisted to the wind blowing from South-East to East back to Vung Tau at speeds at least 15 knots per hour. A strong twisted evening-storm blew off our leaf-hood and took off our boat almost out of sea level. Women and children were crying as strong wind howled through our shaking boat. Someone blamed each other. Others were just praying in hopelessness. One lady was crying," *She wants to go back to main land even goes to jail... had she had the creeps...? Waiting for another escape again after subjected a period of jail'.*Nobody was able to cry anymore because they were exhausted. Someone threw away drinking water jars for space to let their backs rest on the floor deck. No more hope in the dark of the thunderstorm night. Yellow lights of Vung Tau city were not very far; its lighthouse turned around and appeared being bigger.

I was frustrated at this trip and considered it as a total disaster. I expect the next prison time will be a fatal one under the iron hands of the enemy. When I was in Northern Hanoi deadly Hoang Lien Son mountainous prison in 1978, after a severely dysentery for 27 days passed, I had survived while other inmates just died in 22 days. With policy of harsh labor, malnutrition, no medicine, patients usually wet their rag pants every 100 m until a certain early morning; they gave no response from their next fellow inmates. They paid off their lives, designed by their enemy. At anytime I can die because the work there was brutally hard, always in the status starving: a cup of wheat flour daily and some salt water. Many of my fellows in fight die there, almost every day. When I sleep, I may die, I just think I will. Maybe I can die on the job at any time, the result; one third of us died and my turn to die will come as well.

As a man without any certain faith, I believed in God and only my father who loved me the most. Before throwing my ID papers to the ocean, I prayed my father's soul would help us once again and was remembering at North of Vung Tau and Ham Tan in front of me in the past, I had 2 near death experiences during the 24 hours

The New Legion

in standby for a medical evacuation mission which was a forced landing at night and continuing after self mechanical repair. Right in the next morning, only to be flown for a while and then had a forced landing again at Phu Lam, Cho Lon area. All crew-members were OK. How about this maritime mission? I would bet a small fortune for better lives rather than continuing animal-like lives under non-humanitary rules of this Communist regime. I even accepted an emotional farewell to this last moment of freedom before my body disappeared in the sea.

The sounds of people crying, roaring waves, rumbling thunderstorm, strong howling wind and possible screaming souls from hell deep in ocean floor at night made me awaken. We abandoned our dream by counting our lives not by every hour but by each minute, every second. I felt unconscious on the boat deck after one of many giant waves as tall as a mountain, rotated us around, down to the bottom of a whirlpool, we were almost swallowed by the deep ocean.

When I woke up in the morning; in front of me there was another high wave and a Russian oil drilling platform that nobody wanted to stop by. Its helicopter probably routinely flew over our tiny fleeing boat un-attentively. I informed to people that our *"faithful boat"* will drift to the shore of the Philippines which was still far away. Our drinking water, gas, and food supply would last only for a few days. We had to go to Hong Kong, for seasonal South East strong winds were blowing at this time but for the next month we just left out of Mekong Delta. We had no chance of Thai pirates at this far out sea but having no safety of drifting as along side Thai or Malaysian territories.

I opened my tiny atlas, looking for the closest small island of the Philippines on the map. Showing to my son, a thousand kilometers trip to unknown islands later I was told Palawan. Everybody became so frustrated,"hope was far away from our hands." For the next three days the weather was a little better but we had to empty water from our boat, because a woman on board panicked and threw some of our fresh water supply overboard. Before any calm was restored, for seeking comfort lying on her back on flat floor deck.

A surprising story had filled our trip with hope: I found a small Buddha Goddess portrait still clinging to the side of the boat after it went missing in the thunderstorm. It belonged to a devout Buddhist lady who asked me to look for with no hope at all. This story made me doubted about science vs miracle. As a saying goes, *"For knowing fate from God, doing one's last effort."* I understood that no President is elected without his candidacy. In a past good opportunity, I listened to, Most Venerable Thich Tam Chau's meditation of wit in religious cultivation, also indicated that a successful religious life must go along with "wisdom" which means self protection. He told a short story: *A long time ago, Respected Buddha asked a long cultivated serpent: "How come you have been seriously wounded?" She answered to him "When I was cultivated at a forest side, an old wood-woman was mistaken me as a dry creeper. She bound me around her bunch of dry wood and went home. As soon as she reached her front yard, she threw her heavy dry-wood down; breaking my back bones."* Buddha told to her, *"Not a bite to making your crime, than having no wound now"*.

This story made sense to me. A saying goes: *"Bigger ship, higher waves"* and a physic principle indicated that high speeds made soft water harder, all had shown me understanding how two different air chambers and water weigh between a line of sea level that made a ship sink and how a half immersed flat floor boat in water made it stick with good adhesion to the surface of the sea level component, this is a crucial important factor keeping our boat from sinking and for our survival. As for the small Buddha Goddess portrait clinging between boat side and sea level, was a powerful answer that had been demonstrated in an understandable, different way by a Buddhist lady.

Days after days sitting unmoved in front of the boat, I thought of a lady who told me from beginning of the trip that her late mother's soul told her in her dream to wear a peasant shirt when fleeing by boat for good luck. I simply thought that idea was good; to make us look similar with local peasants to prevent attracting plain clothed police before the trip. Now I apply that idea with a white peasant shirt hanging on a long stick to make a signal of SOS. When that shirt felt from the strong wind, that woman herself with her own hands so permanently tied up steadily and kept this shirt forever lasting during the journey. According that wind-force as this maneuver, I also ordered to hang a thin blanket as a sail to help our boat drifting faster from West to East of our freedom. We hoped for high velocity to be reach ashore at the Philippines for 3, 4 weeks. Our only problem was food for survival.

Suddenly an accidental fire came from a smoking cigar was prevented by a swift and strong Western wind blowing to divert the fire from flowin to the gas tanks and ended up by the same lady who covered her towel on the flame. I decided to keep matches away from smokers and to conceal a 555 brand cigarette pack for later when we land on shore for celebration, despite their desire to smoke.

On the morning of the 4th day at sea, enormous clouds of Cumulonimbus thunderstorm were over our heads. I looked at the maritime compass trying to face north but the wind drove us East with huge high waves. Darkness of night came at only 4 PM in extremely dangerous strikes on the boat's sides. Wind and high waves surrounded us. We saw the dark sky and opened our mouths receiving only little natural water and kept one third of water on our boat for cling the sea surface. People embraced each other in fear and to stay calm. Children vomited and cried without stop. Everybody silently prayed. I had heard a near by prayer:"*Nammo Adi Buddha, full of mercies, please save me, Mahatat…*" The prayers were getting louder and louder as the majority of people were Buddhists. I just followed them as a non-religious man.

On that circumstance, only I and the boat operator still kept ourselves calm for we were experienced captains and pilots. One cargo ship passed, we waved our white flag as an enormous long ship went by but failed to wake up its crew's conscience-humanity as the goodwill of the world was fading by years, mandate ocean laws and by time went by from 1975 till 1988. I thought it was hopeless when I tried to use a mirror to make signals to US intelligence satellites or electronic radar planes near by with no sunshine at the time, with my rusty flashlight batteries caused by salted sea water and night fell upon us. I understood clearly why this largest cemetery of our planet which was burying our half million boat people deep under its

Pacific bottom became most cruel, regardless of robbing, kidnapping and rapping by Thai sea-pirates.

All the same circumstances coming repetition to the 5th day. I thought about with 21 more days to reach the nearest Philippines's island (Palawan), we should be starved. I tried to figure out the behavior, face, and shape of the Philippinos look like Indonesians and our fisher-ancestors as well following an ethnology that I learned of when I was stopped by a US military airport, Clark-Field AFB, in the Philippines in the past. Otherwise our trip was dangerous as our traditional verse: *"Men trespass ocean in paisr; Women trespass alone!"* which means when the women gives birth she risks her life.

I was awaked when my daughter feared I should be able to fall into the sea by asking *"Were you there Dad? Dad was you there?"* I answered at once to calm her:*"I was here, we'd be ashore a few days ahead!"*

Luckily our boat drifted to the East with high velocity, some cargos ships passed by without stopping to rescue us. Familiar with sea journey, people were pleased with better weather and asked me: *"For how long to come, Mr. Ba?"*

"A few days more" I gave them a false answer for calm. A drove of dolphins was swimming and dancing in front and around us, mistaken our boat with two big our boat's eyes in red and black color as another dolphin. We kept quiet, silently appreciated them as fishermen' saviours as traditional belief of sea-fishing.

Turbulences, velocities, thunderstorms came and went away every afternoon in this seasonal weather, as well as clouds above us and multi-precipitation huge waves below always during 10 day floating. Higher in sky, clusters of fish-like scale Cirrus cloud were above cotton as in lower space like Cumulus passed over our boat with high velocity. I was so pleased in pushing our sails ahead to freedom. A long narrow strip of smok cross-hanging on the sky made me having a sense of good for orientation. It was indicated that those passenger air lines came from Japan, Korea, Hong Kong or Taiwan to South-East Asia's countries like Singapore, Malaysia or Thailand. Another segment of smoke closer Philippines ashore, now on top of our boat, indicated probably flied to Australia or Indonesia. Actually I anticipated a readjusted calculation for a shortened journey with amount of gas enough to arrive in the Philippines. We must fix the engine at any price for goods in commission. This reciprocating cool-air engine was so simple; having a fire plug and gas carburetor. According this basis principle operation, I thought of my youngest son, 17 years old at the time, would be able to succeed in a new society with great opportunities to come. As an infant, when relatives came to play with him in rude manners, he just drew a sigh like adults, making everybody laugh loudly. Strange thing, all but his head and hair got wet every time he pissed. He has had a strange physiognomy that I hoped would be positive instead of negative way.

I said: *"Khanh, come here I want to see you now?"*

He crawled very slowly to me after 10 days of sea sick and starved as I called and asked him trying to check up the carburetor and replaced a new spare Champion spark plug. After a while, he found a dirty spark plug and replaced it, cleaned the carburetor system with his shirt, making the engine work again with a droning sound. People apparently were full of joy!

On the morning of the 11th day, high waves once again caused the fan-propeller to fall off from the engine shaft-track. Immediately Mr. Hai got a new one and replaced it, the journey continued. Then night went in total darkness. Great Bear, Ursa Major, Ursa Minor, Comet were on and off from thr cosmos above. Finally we discovered as like one floating city with numerous lights on it, instantly she came closer; but Mr. Hai did not know during 10 days and nights no cargo-ship would't like to rescue us. And also he did not know what happened, it was risky at night when our boat closed to the cargo-ship which could submerge our boat, turn us over by rolling her washing waves. That was lucky because we failed to catch a bright lighted ship which intentionally fled us. I gave direction to operator to keep heading 145 degrees south-east and turned off the engine at midnight for waves drifting and save gas. Everyone was lying down sleeping.

Next morning, people were lying still because of starvation, sea sickness and bad sanitation. I focused on the heath factor to keep my grandchildren and children to survive. I leaned that with every breath, there were millions of red blood cells were dead and millions others were born like waves of water came and went from our boat. Physicist Archimede explored the power of water which later gave us cargo ships, battle ships, submarines. Now this power stuck adhesively under our boat and kept it moving forward.

Sunrise on the 12th morning and clear sky made us happier; because we could stand up even though we were so terribly starved. In the sky a straight segment of white smoke strip appeared and clearly make sense of me; we are very close to the Philippines indicated by this white smoke strip far away from West, behind of our boat. Suddenly we saw blue calm level with many pivotal, sharp, rocky coral submerded-island which later we learned that more than 20,000 boat people died when their boat were hit and sank by dark sharp rocks. Now we were in case emergency, we did very best standing up reflecting for survival to empty salt water inside our boat and prevented it from knocking against rocks with manipulating long bamboo sticks keeping out of hit distance from coral-rocks. Our boat floating very slowly, we could see very clear every vulnerable, risky, object below; we tried to hold our breaths..."The creeps." Finally we were safe, thank God! What happened if our boat floated overhere at night?

I thought: let's start the engine, but the operator all ready did. I was sure by checking two passenger airplanes crossing above but behind me. Now with my compass and map for coordination with aircrafts crossing, our heading direction, I was determined to tell the operator to keep heading at 150 degrees against North to avoid getting lost and starving to death on the strayed seaway to Guam, Wake Island...

All night long, young men took turn to hold operating the engine continuously running. We kept on that way, on the 13th day; people woke up earlier with joy. Sea whales swam around us, followed by dolphins behind. A young man named Tung from the rear came up faster to tell me with overjoyed: *"Uncle Ba, I saw look like a chain of mountain in front of us!"* I apparently had guessed it, now I believe he'd tell the truth to me! Actually, we rotated duty of holding the engine to escape a thunderstorm appeared to coming soon. Young men with preparedness cut plastic containers into halves ready to empty leaking infiltrated water. At 4 pm, night felt dark quickly if bad weather, all over again abrupt with high waves. Our boat turned around when no body could be able to empty water, Dizzy! Unconscious! But theirs mouths again and again everybody prayed. Young men nervously excitement emptied water which was only inches from sea level for survival. It was not too long before they became exhausted; however we needed an essential quantity of water in clinged the bottom of our boat for sticking adhesives with the mass surface water of sea level. Again one by one, a huge wave continued beating the boat side hard, splashing the water into our boat. Everyone was getting very wet, quivering. I saw the world became the color dark-grey all over, with huge dark waves precipitation coming to our boat. Rain poured hurtling with heavy drop but no one could capable to take it for resource refreshment. I could able withstand this scene, so intruded inside the boat, waiting for odd things will happen. People all were silently exhausted with unconsciousness. I felt our boat having smooth rotation down draft without striking by waves; peering outside that looking like our boat in the hollow-water with no sky, it seemed to me we were in the deep bottom of an enormous bowl, and up to upper, then nothing…no water, just like we were in the airplane in the crepuscular. But I did felt confidently by seeing the water-level-infiltrated onboard just enough for holding our boat not turn-over. But too no stricken waves! Pleased God have mercies! Now everything so quiet, no more hurtled wind, boat became stable, peoples exhausted unconsciously. Super thunderstorm subsiding.

Usually sunrise was slowly appeared when May half moon faded away, I concerned of a second sequence immediately thunderstorm after last one and ordered young men to stop emptying water. They had to rest so some water needed to keep our boat from turn-over, sinking by whirl-wind. I hoped there were no double storms as a proverb saying: *"Being sunrise always after rain!"* It was 3 am from my phosphorus watch. I saw clearly the Great Bear appeared brightly like a big diamond; far away from huge dark cloud Nimbostratus and the remnant-thunderstorm was going to the chain of mountains mentioned above (Palawan-Ulugan Bay).

Weather was so better than last night, why our boat not sailed faster? Because all young men tried empty all water out for lightness fast floating and the crucial goal was survival. In the sky cumulus clouds were moving so fast to the mountains, I suggested that every wrapped-sheet can be made into sailcloth…just did it! Very soon the boat sailed faster with engine maximum RPM.

After long days I was exhausted as sleeping, Tung came waking me up. *Uncle Ba, there were real mountains in front of us!"* I stood straight and was seeing a real beautiful copper tray like sun partly appeared from behind a top of mountains. I opened the 555 brand cigarette pack and asked men to come for a smoking celebration. The operator just borrowed the matches; he enjoyed his own stronger domestic cigar. We need the ropes, so when we reached Philippines's ashore. Operator Hay swam to a limit marking metal white buoy to cut a robe for our convenience.

Instead of coming to a populated gulf, we entered into an uncultivated rocky area. We anchored 30 meters from a rocky mountain side and used plastic tanks to take drinking water. All my children who took many swimming lessons at Tan Son Nhat airport pool are doing well. They collected sea snails and cooked with dry woods. I found a piece of coconut meat for my two grandsons who were crying for food. We kept cooking fluid full of protein for them too. Khanh helped me to bring drinking water into our boat.

The rest children and women stayed on board, their concerns of our boat sides crashing on rocks by strong waves were over in and out before we were back. We left before dawn to avoid aggressive mosquitoes from sucking our drying source of blood. People had complained of our long landing for food but they enjoyed them too. High emotion made me tearful when I watched my grandsons attacked eating a piece of coconut meat. For avoiding lost orientation may risk-hit to the mountain rock. I decided moving the boat little far from the shore and anchored for over night wait for daytime, everyone felt made rotational duties for safety when night felt. For me, I couldn't sleep that night because of overwhelming joy for all crew surviving that I hoped seemed like a rebirth of another life instead of karma. I rethought of so many factors which made this successful journey, included absolute secrecy by least of people involved. Now at 5,30 am, I told an operator to started engine, and heading to a bright lighted ship as big as a city and waved white peasant shirt, while closer letting children and ladies standing in front the boat for help.

The crew on big boat knew who we were because our boat very strange with two eyes in front. It was therefore they let down a rope ladder. Children, women and men climbed first. I was the last to climb. The experienced captain gave us a big meal of steamed rice and a large cooked fresh fish pan. I was full with only a small piece of fish and rice mixed with emotionally satisfaction. I self considered my responsibility was completed. The boat's Captain was so very kind and cheerful with new unexpected guests. He playfully kidding told me *"there still were 400 knots more to reach UN refugee camp!"* But he led us to the rear-deck, and let me look through his binoculars at a fishing hamlet. Authorities there would help us to processing paperwork before enter Palawan Refugee Camp. Firstly I let my daughter look through his binoculars and told her: *from here, Ulugang-Bay Gulf to that hamlet was only a 15 minutes trip...you feel alright!?"* I thank God for her pale complexion now pinker of joy. People agreed to return to their boat only after looking through his binoculars one by one. After all they were so much confident for the next short trip.

It was a perfect day for prayer, a bright morning and in the tranquil Bay. The skies and seas were polished blue, soft winds bore silver-edged clouds, and the coastal sands gleamed white like ribbons of salt. It would have been easy to believe in some sort of heavenly power! I loved to just close my eyes and feel the sun's rays baking my face, inhaling the scent of the ocean. Our boat engine ran with maximum speed heading directly to this hamlet. We met many sympathizing new friendly fishermen waved to welcome us being on board a strange boat that they did known, we were refugees. Right after 15 minutes, we arrived at the hamlet. People in this hamlet ran out in crowds to welcome us when we were still not ashore yet. They were Roman Catholics who thought we were same faith and gave us a lot of cloths, candies, cakes; even a whole stem of coconuts. A young police officer made a list of refugees and let me sell our boat engine for a sum enough to buy a chicken and fruits for worship. I let my operator made a workship to my soulful boat as a thanksgiving gesture. But the worship was celebrated with plenty of biscuits, oranges, chips, chocolates...and without a chicken for not chicken was raised inside a cage here. So they couldn't catch. Everybody enjoyed the bath after two weeks and slept very well on our boat.

At 10 am next morning, a grey coast guard patrol boat of Philippines Navy came to pull our boat to their military Navy base as stipulation requested by the UN high commissioners. A small party at the Navy base hosted by a Colonel Base Commander, doctors and commanding staffs officers to welcome us. A doctor major disclosed that their ships must stay confined at the base and all of fishing boats in Ulugang Bay must stay out of the worst hurricane three days ago.

He wondered how we could survive that one with a small junk like a toy. I explained to him, we had no choice. However I thought: the factors which kept our boat stuck coherent with surface of sea level and always floating with this mass of water which occupied in lower bottom of my boat for preventing turn over after striking by high wave and sank thereafter. And finally God's will merciful helped. He mentioned about the immense coral rocky cemetery of about 20,000 ghosts and surprised of our miracle trip let my explaining of our flat base boat made sense. He yelled his colleagues-officers come to look at and laugh loudly at my funny only equipments: a boy scout compass and a small dictionary map!

I continued to tell them about my 13 years prison time and a dead or alive trip with no choice, thanked to passenger planes which corrected our ways to this country. They listened quietly and came to shake my hands with their great admire. They also patted my shoulder and gave me their best wishes. After my story, the doctor Major had asked to exchange my watch to his Radio so he could keep it as a meaningful souvenir; I told him my watch was cheap and rusty by salted water. Another officer gave me dog meat cooked by himself but I refused to take, thinking of the same refuse when I made in malnourished prison life in the past because in that hardship, I ate all included camp rats but no dog for their extraordinary loyalty to humanity!

We slept on the colored brick floor of their large meeting room that night and had a breakfast of tasty fried eggs next morning. A colorful mini-bus came to pick up all of us around noon leading by camp commander, Lieutenant Colonel Fernandez, Mr. Bob Holland, a volunteer Australian and others Refugee High Commissioners.

The New Legion

Lt Col Fernandez gave each of us a bottle of local San-Miguel beer which I felt drowsily drunk for only a half of its content.

I thought of almighty God that I met through our fateful lucky journey and thinking of my converting to be a Christian later. In our native language 'faith' means 'way', a way of lives. As our trip in an immense ocean experienced that 'no faith, no way' and 'no way, no destination of lives', I could never know what happened and why every event went on its own way against our plan

After a month at Palawan refugee camp, I had received a large insulated envelope of my training classes in the US by Lt Col Lawrance A. Gregorash USAF, Deputy Com. Foreign Military Training Affairs Group. A certificate of Academic Instructor Course of USAF in Maxwell University, Alabama helped me to become assistance to an English language school, offered by Catholic nun Claudita Marcon, Director of Center for Assistance to Displaced Persons. My whole family was transferred to Bataan Processing Center, sponsoring financial by US government instead of UN as of other refugee camps and administered by Mr. Herman T.Laurel and his staffs.

That was a beautiful camp with large green hills, a spring streaming encircled and a lovely artificial chain-hanging-bridge. It consisted of 12 Neighborhoods stretching far up to 6 kilometers length, two crowded market places. One situated at Neighborhood no 5 and one, at no 10. A Catholic Church and a Buddhist temple; About 18,000 refugees had waited for US turns to be immigrated, included many Ameriasians during the most 1988-1989.

Blue-Guard of Major Lopez controlled of security of the camp. There was rumor of a corrupted Lopez who gave protection to an illegal gang who then paid him and his unit a large shared-sum of profits.

Our community composed an Inter-Neighborhood Chairman, his assistances of Laotian and Cambodian representatives. Each neighborhood had an elected leader. We had an ARVN Veteran Association which I was elected as Chairman of about more than 400 members due to for my longest Communist prison time. Soon later, I was elected Chairman of Inter-Neighborhood as well to the period the former chairman left for immigration. The situation of the Camp was worse insecurity, Buddhist monks and Catholic priests as well as retired Col Banson, internal assistance of the camp complained of illegal activities like robberies by violence, intimidation. A notorious violent gang 'Dung Great Eagle' such as thieves, robberies that JVA delegation had many time reported so much accusation for those matters. The most intolerable case, in general such as a certain refugee who received checks from abroad. As a spontaneous officer that I thought, had given me that conviction, I reported this worst situation to my staff and our Veteran Association and received their full supports to recovering a well formed activity. It was however my children strongly rejected my effort concerning for our own safer immigration in US sooner. But I stubbornly went on to carry out last try of my endless struggle life this time for 18,000 native victims who had voted for me in protecting them, and depended on me, and me alone!

Mr. Banson was so exciting to help me restored in camp security and to ease his own American colleagues who had so many times in same complaints as ours, especially about security at night. I asked to borrow 10 buses as a transport mean for my 400 veterans moved from 10th to 5th Neighborhood, 10 walking-talking communicators, and recording broadcasting my stated notice to 18,000 refugees before our gang-ending operation began. Mr. Branson absolutely agreed but it should be informed to Major Lopez for avoiding mistaken shootings because I doubted about Lopez's collaboration so I must indeed need a referring order notice from Mr. Banson and discussed with him about my operation plan: I will show to Major Lopez this order notice at 11:45 and let 10 buses parked at 10th Neighborhood. My voice notice was broadcasting at 12 (midnight) only 15 minutes in advance of the operation, and requesting people staying at home meanwhile we eradicated the Dung Big Eagle Gang.

I came to administration staff residence at 11:45 pm. He looked like waiting someone else, not me. There was a large brownie Lopez under bright yellow electric lights there! I politely saluted him and gave him Mr. Banson's note. He was smiling broader after reading it and looked at me in investigation *"are you going to catch robbers?"* I said all I did was just for my people and asked him to borrow a shackles hanging on the wall for a gang leader and promised to return it to him 45 minutes later. Lopez stretched out to the shackles, gave it to me in a despised laughter: *Probably not that so easy!"* As a same time, I'd heard my voice broadcasting all over the Camp:*" From this minute, please all of you stay at home..."*

During that operation, I saw a 16 years old Ameriasian boy who was pleading for joint with us catching Dung's gang members. We caught all of them at the first place and from that boy I had information of the gang leader 'Big Eagle' who was hiding with his two bodyguards 'Blue-Guard' inside an ESL classroom. I handcuffed him without a fight. When he was leading out of the hiding place, the Amerisian-boy hit him with a wooden bar hard enough having his bloody back for his crime of robbing the boy's sister, having her naked for searching.

I brought them to Neighborhood No 2 for paper-work investigation. It's being absolutely, an undercover American security agent in JVA took them pictures. Lopez later came with PRPC members. I returned back the shackles to him and excused for late return. He took it with his angrily face.

Gang leader Dung was severe injured with deep wounds on his back caused by nails, showing up his tattoo dark Big Eagle in his chest. He and his gang must be appeared on a trial tomorrow. When I asked him if he hate me so much, He responded: *I respected you... uncle, a long time prisoner of the Communist and a refugee like me, but I'd doing gang again after you leave here!"*

On April 30th 1989 as annual usually every year in this day, anti-communist community had organized a meeting with dummy Ho's burning. As a community and veteran leader, I had to read a speech written by my general secretary. This duty made me understanding about politic, subordinate country's politic which was only a negative meaning of slavery for a super power whatsoever; A group of political opportunists pressed me to challenge to the power of PRPC's authority, for what cause that I didn't understand, and what for? I flatly had to turn down every approach that they suggested. As my duty job for our people, I had refused special food ration delivery direct to my family, just to be fair and straightforward in inspecting food distributed by local traders who had earned big profits on refugees' lost. Spoiled meat, rotten fish, vegetables, bananas...usually were put under half lower part of baskets which were required to be replaced at once or next day on my personal request.

I even let few of my staff members who against with me because their diplomatical opportunist, intimidated to publish my mistakes on newsletters just went ahead to do so without any concern. These opportunist-diplomat themselves had lectured me a lesson of smart selfishness on gang issue that I ignored to listen to. With many years in Communist prison, I was not feared of any blaming game bestowed by my own uneasy comrades. Their short prison term made them collaborators of criminals, for examples some tragedies such as: A group of 52 people whose boat was drifted months in the ocean with a young man named Minh who urged people to kill another passenger for meat by fate drawing game during there was a dead human body inside his boat. A former female Lt Hoa and Lt Col Xuan on that boat obediently collaborated to his crime.- A father holding steady his daughter 6 years old, when his boat sank on submerge coral island, a sudden strong wave coming causing coral rock cutting her arm away her body, both father and daughter were spinning perished in the deep sea floor.- 5 years old girl ate her own dead sloughs from her scabies was the only survivor be rescue by another boat. And so many cases of other true disasters of boat people stories whose contents were so horrible that no movie maker dared to film, no actor dared to act, no writer dared to write! Why?

A new word was added to dictionary: *"Boat People"*, another word for just political propaganda. Another tragedy and voting 'on foot' in a world who wins who political campaign. A stratagem in the Indochina, they invested a good money for propaganda with perfect good movie such as **"We Want Lives"**, starred by famous actor Le Quynh was produced for a million refugees from certain limited period and short distance from North to South Vifftnam in 1954 with single horrible scene of a artificial shark bitten a man leg to motivate a good anti-communist' stratagem propaganda with technical assistance advised by Philippines experts.

Why, now not so many horrible scenes in real boat people refugee throughout Pacific Ocean had been ignored neglectable to restorative? Said we double 'Why'?

The New Legion

There was no surprise of a promise from H.Kissinger to Hanoi *"a full diplomatic relationship through issues of pretext "Agent Orange and MIA"* When great power still needed the subordinate political opportunists. No Nationalist-Communist boundary any more when new regime members can do everything here in the US, financially as well as politically. And the old political label *'Anti-Communist' was already expired in forgetful and nobody buy it.*

I was interviewed by Chuck Lee of US representative Tom Ridge's delegation in a US Congress mission to Bataan for Ameriasian immigration program. My picture with Legis Fellow also was taken by his request for his delegation report to the Congress.

- *Why there were Gangs all over refugee camps but not in your camp?* Lee asked.

- No suspect was arrested without court subpoena in the land of Liberty Lady (USA)! Over here...no suspect can escape in this land around by jungle, because there are so many stories that our people and veteran issued no court warrant! We used lawlessness-violable method suppressed against them! I proudly answered him.

Chuck Lee smiled with great understanding and promised to meet me again in the US.

Two months later in November 1989, I met Chief staff administrator Chuck Lee through my sponsor, Marine Col Norman H, Vreeland and US Representative Congress Tom Ridge of Ameriasian Program at his office in the Capitol, who had bestowed me a letter of recommendation from the US Congress that calling me a 'real-hero' that my own conscience was very hesitated to accept and even having question about that two words 'real-hero'.

On the way back home, I directly asked him, my marine Col. Sponsor:

"With 4,422 shameful days and nights as a defeated prisoner of war in Communist prisons, what left for being called real hero?"

Col Vreeland immediately answered:

" A real hero dared to destroy Gangs, When you left for US resettlement, your successor, Mr. (name deleted) was assaulted by the Gangs who broke his shins with its wide opened marrow by a heavy metal bar severed enough that later he was settled in Buffalo, NY as an eternal disable person or handicap."

Vinh-Van-Truong

A Campwide "Saturation Drive"

PHILIPPINE REFUGEE PROCESSING CENTER
Sabang, Morong, Bataan

16 October 1989

LETTER OF RECOMMENDATION

During his stay at the Philippine Refugee Processing Center (PRPC) Sabang, Morong, Bataan.

VINH VAN TRUONG

provided invaluable assistance to the Administration in his capacity as **INC CHAIRMAN** of the refugee community

As an active leader of the community, he initiated a campwide "Saturation Drive" that helped restored peace and order in the camp and eradicated lawlessness.

He too, exhibited commitment to the cause of the Administration despite pressures.

He has shown initiative and tirelessness to serve his fellow refugees. He is a significant partner of the PRPC Administration in the creation of an authentic human resettlement.

He is hereby recommended for full consideration for any position requiring dedication and commitment to work.

ANGELINO REPEDRO, JR.
Director, Food Services
and Community Administration
Group (FSCAG)

CRISTINA G. MICU
Chief, Community
Organization and
Social Services Div.

MR. NELSON T. DELES
Deputy Administrator

To look for and to reassemble the broken pieces of America's conscience that were left behind and forgotten....

The New Legion

I was survived the war perhaps better than many of us who served there, I was older when I went, had studied the country and the conflict for years, was in some ways more prepared for the experience. And I was lucky that I was in battles, saw men die, lost good friends to the enemy was wounded and to myself. But I did not have to endure as much as many others did, and carried in Unites States less pain from the war than some others though I was POW for 13 years. There was one pain that only began after I escaped Viet Nam, and that was the shame that grew over the years after 1975. It was then that I saw the slow abandonment of the Republic of Viet Nam to the might of a massive Northern conscript army equipped by the Soviets with mountains of supplies, while the ARVN supplies ran lower and lower as Congress choked off the flow year by year.

Many American-Vets recall the ARVN as not being a good ally and in truth South Viet Nam, its government, and its military had many problems. There was poor training and leadership in some units, there was corruption in the upper officer corps, there were even Viet Cong sympathizers in the ranks, along with drafted men who were not well motivated to fight. But there were also some really good units, which fought hard, like the Airborne, Marine, Helicopter air assault, and Rangers that had part of the line at Khe Sanh beside the US Marines. And fight they did, there was a major invasion of the South in '72, nothing remotely guerrilla about it, 200,000 NVA regulars with modern tanks, excellent Russian artillery, and antiaircraft missiles. Horrendous battles went on for months, including a siege of An Loc that was like the Alamo, except even though was largely overrun, the South Vietnamese soldiers hung on like bulldogs and eventually won the day.

But for years, I heard the stories about the RVN soldiers who could not leave Viet Nam, as some others were fortunate enough to do. They are marked for their past patriotic service, and suffer various kinds of discrimination that makes life more difficult. And of these, the worst off are the disabled ones, those veterans who suffered major injuries, lost arms, legs, eyes, hearing, and health. They receive no pension, there are few if any jobs for them, their lives are terribly hard. The thought of this suffering, going on for decade after decade under the revengeful Hanoi government bothered me greatly and I could no longer avoid thinking about it.

Now, I am American and these men are Vietnamese, but we shared in the fight for freedom, and I feel we are related somehow. They are my countrymen, now former allies who are hungry, and sick, and worried every day about how they can go on. I want to help them, last year I sold my book for fundraising and a small charity has been started, called the Vietnam Healing Foundation, to raise some money for them. We will do what I can, and the good news is that a dollar goes a long way in Viet Nam. I will go back again one day, to find more, and give more help. It will not be enough, but I believe it is an important duty to give something back to these men, the betrayed, the neglected, and the forgotten. To make them feel remembered, and recognized for their sacrifice, and to give them another day's food is all so worthwhile that I thank heaven for the chance to do it. And when you get up in the morning, always recall that you live in freedom, which, like air, we can take for granted, but would miss terribly if it were no longer ours

Chapter-4

Comment, Critical Analysis of VN, Iraq Wars

I follow a precedent for job, it isn't my mistake!

EISENHOWER: "THE DOMINO THEORY" Asian should come from the Asians. He praised President Diem as a 'miracle man' – "The cost of defending freedom, of defending America, must be paid in many forms and in many places...military as well as economic help is currently needed in VN"

J.F Kennedy: He also praised Diem being as the 'Winston Churchill of Asia.' "That it was South Vietnam's war and the people there had to win it...We couldn't win the war for them!"

L.B Johnson: To revenge an insult, L.B.J full concurs with U.S Attorney General, Robert Kennedy, especially assassinating which they once compared to "throwing sand in the umpire's face" – So much clinging to the past: the Trading with the Enemy-Act of December 1941.

Suddenly, Robert Kennedy fell to an assassination's bullets in 1968 like his older brother. In the phenomenal U.S history televised address of President Johnson announced he would not seek reelection. He knew the price he will would pay – by from the real two Cowboys Texas father and son, and the masterminded W. A Harriman, who's a founder of the Skull and Bones Dynasty – however, this triumvirate practiced of crony capitalism but still to strengthen the U.S position in the First-World-Superpower predominant in maintaining Patriot-Act.

Richard Nixon: "Congress proceeds to snatch defeat from the jaws of victory…it undercut South Vietnam's ability to defend itself by drastically reducing our military aid." For carrying out **axiom-1**, it emerged the **Watergate** to end Nixon pledges in letter to President Thieu; instead of Nixon but substitute by Gerald Ford who stalemates: "It was a very difficult thing to be President of the United States and watch South Vietnam fall"

President Thieu: "**Permanent Government** has turned its back. Deserted us in the breach! How do we stand in defense against such forces when they can now so easily overwhelm us?"

Eventually, in the Heaven these presidents lauded that rebuttal video when they watched it and said that it's "something all Americans should not see" – Vietnam War, "The Impact of Media" explores in detail the 'media-distortions' due to televisions misrepresentations during the Vietnam War. It rebuts the view promoted by PBS's 13-part documentary series, Vietnam: A Television History"

THE ORIGINAL AND NEW "EURASIAN GREAT GAME" THAT MUST BE EFFECTIVELY BY STRATAGEM

For more than three decades, I resisted thinking of myself as a veteran of the Vietnam War. I wanted to get on with my life and not be defined by that so sad story. However, obsessively about my years long meditations on the causes of Skull and Bones' evils; At last, it was both an intellectual change of perspective and an emotionally satisfying experience to jettison the false guilt about the war that I had been carrying around for the most a half of century. Doing so has enabled me to relearn the values I was taught in my traditional culture of our country in my youth, to appreciate the sacrifices made by those Americans [freedom fighters] who have become eternally our fellow comrade in arm. And, on behalf of all Vietnamese, I thank the 58,000 Americans who so many years ago made the ultimate sacrifice in defense of our country's liberty, democracy, and for unification became One Vietnam.

Most Americans, canvassed in the spring of 1965 as President L.B Johnson [under pressure of Skull and Bones] sent U.S combat troop into battle for the first-time supported the commitment After the war was over, however, American overwhelmingly repudiated the intervention as having been a blunder. But roughly the same proportion of the nation, hold in retrospect that, once involved, the U.S ought to have deployed all its power to succeed. Post-war opinion poll showed that American blame their political leaders for denying victory to the U.S forces in Vietnam by imposing restraints actions: intensifying the war effort too slow, refusing to approved incursion against enemy sanctuaries in Laos and Cambodia, giving the ARVN inadequate equipment, conceding to a cease-fire accord in 27/Jan/1973 that permit Hanoi's troop to remain in the south.

A 1974 survey of generals who had commanded in Vietnam found that "almost 70 percent of the Army generals who managed the war were uncertain of its objectives." Another survey conducted in 1980 for the veteran-administration disclosed that 82 percent of former U.S soldiers engaged in heavy combat there believe that the war was lost because they were not allowed to win. As we have seen, even generals who held commands in Vietnam admitted to uncertainty of that war's objectives. In the book *"Battle-Ready"* General Tony Zinni (ret) page 422 having an excerpt *"The tactics didn't make sense and the personnel policies – such as one-year individual rotations instead of unit rotations in and out of country – were hard to comprehend."*

In short, if you finished this "The New Legion" master-piece, you will find out the significant of the CIP's objective – not really the War in Vietnam but merely "A biggest U.S practiced in combat training campaign never had in the history of the United States of America."

Nowadays, if someone would look at me and seem to say, "How in hell did South Vietnam screw it up? I had it right and I did it right and I fought and I understood and I left my country an incredible legacy, and now look at where I am!" It's hard to escape the feeling "God, the Axis of Evil let my country down," because the United States' longest and least satisfactory, the war fought in the wrong way by a conspiracy of silence; it was badly led by Skull and Bones. I went through 13 years in the so called communist "Reeducation Camp" with serious pain and suffering, sacrificing a good part of my young adulthood for my country, in torture, fear, and isolation. I was sick; I was badly heart-wounded. Yet despite all these problems, I would do it again. I had to do it, fighting the Red Menace as merely freedom-fighter.

Therefore I must say today that the veterans of that lost war, Vietnamese and Americans, Australians and New Zealanders, Thais and South Koreans and all the others who supported our fight for freedom – we have "no cause for shame." More than thirty years of misrule prove conclusively that we who opposed the Communist regime were right, because I am expecting with full optimistic about prospects – Eventually, "Once Vietnam embraces capitalism, democracy and the rule of law will follow." As the freedom fighter, we preferred to compete ideologically, confident that the superiorities of the capitalist system would eventual prevail. As a result this long U.S' diplomatic stratagem toward communist countries by the Permanent Government's "implied consent will" likewise using hanging knots for them good mercies self perishable – but ending dictatorship in world wide. It is also clear that Permanent Government preferred to compete ideologically and economically with the Communist system than engage with the enemy militarily. P.G was supremely confident that the advantages of the Capitalist system would ultimately prevail, as long as a nuclear catastrophe could be avoided according two W A. Harriman's masterpieces: book **"Peace with Russia"** (1959) and book **"America and Russia in a Changing World"** (1971) firmly means US 'first' and Russia 'second' world's class-superpower in his scope.

In the past, 1917 performing with great élan, Lenin often reiterated that "Communism or Capitalism who won", moreover he said "The capitalist was greedy and too stupid…his sheer idiocy to product more and more hanging knots in such for his self-hanging eventually." The original K Marx and Lenin prophecy has long since 160 years, harangued that eventually the Capitalism should be eradicated. But the actual exerted-capitalist was much steady than Communist being abolition, non-survival and fall apart. In fact the United Stated came to Russia and Eastern Europe by economic trading such as Coca-Cola, Jean pant, Mac Donald…and to lift sanctions under the U.S "Freedom Support Act" and step by step transformed from 'Government-Industries' to 'Private-Companies.' There was a need to push for an overwhelming privatization of the economy, in increasing the society prosperity and communist party became weaker and weaker until completely collapse.

The stratagem "Eurasian Great Game" goal was "Central Asian states" Actually we found all these societies in a state of post-Soviet shock. After seventy years of communism, Kazalhs, Uzbeks, Kirghiz, Tajiks, Turkomans, and the other ethnic group in what had once been the Southern parts or Central Asia of the USSR had significant economic, security, political, and social problems. Now that the Communist-weight had been lifted from their backs, they were trying to figure out their true identity and search for the best way forward. Unsurprisingly, each looked at our new U.S involvement as a chance to gain the support they needed to make necessary changes. And, literally, the U.S was once again unwilling to invest in this new region of engagement due to the huge natural resources under a thick layer of snow.

Mysteriously, the magic in God's commandment, in coincidence event on July 13, 1917 at Fatima, Our Lady told Sister Lucy that: ***"God is about to punish the world for its crimes, by means of war, famine,*** *and persecutions of the Church, and of the Holy Father"* (Thereby too many questions had been raised regarding the 'Consecration of Russia to the Immaculate Heart of Mary.) And to prevent this, I shall come to ask for the communions of reparation and for the consecration of Russia to My Immaculate Heart…In the end, My Immaculate Heart will triumph. The Holy Father will consecrate Russia to me, which will be converted, and a period of peace will be granted to the world."

Miraculously, Our Lady's request is very simple: Russia – the fount of so much evil in the 20th Century – must be set apart and made sacred by its consecration to the Mother of God. And so why is it necessary to consecrate Russia in particular? Because God wills it; As Our Lady told Sister Lucy at Fatima: *"Russia will be the instrument of chastisement chosen by Heaven to punish the whole world if we do not forehand obtain the conversion of that poor nation…"* And Sister Lucy has explained that because Russia is a well-defined territory, the conversion of Russia after its consecration to the Immaculate Heart would be undeniable proof that the conversion resulted from the consecration and nothing else. The establishment in the world of devotion to the Immaculate Heart would thus be confirmed by God Himself in the most dramatic manner.

Once again, her word at Fatima, Our Lady appeared to Sister Lucy at Tuy, Spain, on June 13, 1929, to say that:

The moment has come when God asks the Holy Father to make, in union with all the bishops of the world, the consecration of Russia to My Immaculate Heart, promising to save it by this means."

Thus, without the act of consecration there will be no conversion of Russia, and without the conversion of Russia, Russia's errors will continue to infest the world, producing the persecution of the Church, the martyrdom of the good, the suffering of the Holy Father and ultimately the annihilation of nations forewarned at Fatima.

At last, "collapse of Communism" after the 1984 consecration ceremony show that Russia is beginning to convert and that the consecration must have been effective, despite its failure to mention Russia"

At early 1992, the Bolshevik's Red flag flapping over the kremlin (The citadel of Moscow, housing the offices of the Soviet government) was been replaced by the National-Russia flag which disappeared from December, 22, 1917. The longest 75 years bloodshed event had been over. Now the New-World have been welcome the Commonwealth was born. The Soviet-totalitarian embassy was terminated in 1989 at Vietnam; Soviet aid 25, 2 billion-dollar, and Hanoi' still owned 14, 4 billion. In five year-planning 1986-1990, Soviet aid 10, 8 billion; and next five year-planning 1991-1995, Hanoi didn't have to pay a cent because Soviet was collapsed. At 1979 the so called China gave Hanoi a lesson (China attack Northern Vietnam) abruptly Hanoi announced to disregard to own the 30 billion China aid that China support to Hanoi started 1954. Finally Hanoi forgot all billion-aids, rapacious money from two patronages. All above Kissinger let Tho understood in a various secret meetings. Another words Russia and China didn't gain nothing in this war. So who won? "Welfare US imperialism"

Bolsheviks, the totalitarian party that seized power and set up a proletarian dictatorship in Russia 1917-1922; Lenin seized the power closed-joining with Bolshevist formed a socialism group which supported the Russian revolution in 1917 and became The Russian Communist Party in 1918. With disastrous consequences, they formed an organization so called "the special assassination teams" to the rise of the bourgeoisie, beginning the bloodshed eve. These killer-teams were notorious named "TCHEKA". From 1917 till 1923 about 10,861,586 were be killed. On March, 1, 1920, TCHEKA changed another name "the summit political bureau of Soviet Union." From now on they become the Red demons headquarters with named NKGB, sometimes changed NKVD then MGB, and eventually KGB (Komite Gosudarstvennoi Bezopasnosti) This system the Russians called the haunted witch hunt wizard – Men, women even children were slaughtered and Kolkhozy – the widespread slaughter of innocent peoples: One day on June, 14, 1941, Stalin ordered to move 480,000 Lithuania natives to Siberia that included 40,000 women and children were perils due to weather too cold starving. On August, 28, 1941, at "self-governed zone," 600,000 habitants Volga those were forced to move to Siberia, in demolition. On February, 23, 1944, during just 24 hours, 900,000 habitants of republic self-governed Tchethenos and Engouches on zones Caucase were forced into domestic-animal-wagons and disappeared for good. On January, 30, 1933 more than one million Ukraine were slaughtered on the spot. Only one nightmare, January 30, 1933, 12,000 residents of city Visinysia were slaughtered by KGB and buried into few huge hollows and afterward demolished for the city plaza. From decade 1930 Communist Party transformed Russia become the giant prisons. Before October, 1917 Russia had 25 millions farmer-units, bringing to transform to communities Kolkhozy that Soviet Union manipulated organized 254,000 Kolkhozy. In reality, these were the New Eco-Reeducated Prisons controlled by KGB. Soviet Party dream reigned over the world by his KOMINTERN, controlled international by Soviet Communist Party. Communist around the world must in discipline with strictly apply with his 21 points regulation, regardless nationalism, racism...merely the instructed orders from Komintern. Ho Chi Minh then named Chen Vang Wong in Komintern 1945. In 1947, Komintern transformed to Kominform (Soviet international information agency)

In 1957, in the Axis of Evil, KGB cooperated with CIA [Harriman and Prescott Bush] to play the craps "On the strongman side". Firstly influence to Soviet predominance by Khrushchev-fashion, expending 21 million-rubies the most to Hanoi and Havana. North Vietnam, the stronghold communist outpost in Asia; Cuba as a spearhead at western hemisphere: the U.S and Soviet war industries used for common causes in the "Cold-War": Korea, Vietnam, and Middle East-Wars. It composed 70 percent steel for war industries that imported from United States business-owners but Soviet was manpower to cast off in production. You could see a huge war materiel when Hanoi overrun South Vietnam was credited by US loan money and manufactured by Russia-working-class. You could imaged two years after Paris Talk 1973, the Soviet have covertly shipped no less than 700,000 long tons of new batch military equipment, ammunition, and supplies to Hanoi in preparation for the very final campaign overrun South Vietnam, invasion in Cambodia, and counterattack against China. So why Hanoi didn't pay a cent for this game instead of disaster and become the poorest country after the war. After Vietnam, the Soviet-fashioned influence became predominant over the worldwide. Soviet became a number-

One world superpower meanwhile U.S became a pitiful, helpless giant (not at time to roll-back yet but in the stage [two decades] ofmanage the defeat for overhauling damage control) From Cuba at Western hemisphere, then Nicaragua seized the power developed National Liberation Front help the revolution at El Salvador. At Africa, Communist took over at north Yemen, Zambia, Somalia, Ethiopia, Angola, Mozambique, Congo, and the final of the craps is Afghanistan.

Was William-A-Harriman a Prodigiously Talented World-Strategist?

The one South-Vietnamese love to hate was a world's magician in four decades (1920-1960)As for President Diem, in defense for freedom, "we will do all we can. We will give it all we've got..." But! In 1917 emerged a 27 year-old greatest strategist, I thought the world he made, deserved as I always assuming this Emperor-I of founding the Skull and Bones dynasty? It was both an intellectual change of perspective and an emotionally satisfying experience to jettison the false impression about the war that because "Truth crushed to earth shall rise again." It is one of the most important promises made to God that I have kept! However all these pages of this chapter were my personal-perspectives as well as you might. In order to jettison the false guilt about that war, it was both an intellectual change of perspective and an emotionally satisfying experience that I had been carrying around for thirty-five years. We together are digging the truth by studying, examining, researching and think it over and over based on the numerous declassified documents, pictures published 2005, from National archives, verbatim statements, many original documents, 150 hours audio tapes recorder of Oval Office conversations, and recently 30,000 page-documents declassified at Nixon library, Yorba Linda, California, assimilated National Archives, during that war have been released. Throughout this time, many studies and research project have been performed by military and civilian historians and scholars, and many recent revelations have proven contradictory to previous prejudicial and hasty conclusion regarding the fall of Saigon. With their scam' benefit of hindsight, it has become clearer that the U.S Permanent Government goals were more ambitious than a superficial, bogus military victory.

But God chose me to write this book. This isn't hubris. I'm not saying this is an egotistical way. God didn't choose me because I'm the greatest writer who ever lived. Just the fact that you are reading this is proof not just of God's existence, but also of Her/His/Its beneficence. That's right. I am not certain of God's precise gender. But I am certain that She/He/Its chose me to write this **"The New-legion."** However, if something in this book makes you laugh, it was God's joke. If something makes your thoughtful meditation, it's because God had a good point to make.

God said that The Emperor-II of the Company Dynasty [George-H-W-Bush] a key figure squandered a unique reign supreme in national unity. That instead of rallying the country around a program of mutual purpose and sacrifice, the Emperor-II cynically used the tragedy to solidify his political power and pursue an agenda that panders to his base and serves the interests of his corporate backers (Yale, Andover, Skull and Bones, and WIB members) not for the real-identified-nature of the U.S Capitalism. "American-First"

So I got my knees and prayed for guidance. "How, God, can I best do your work through this book? Who, dear Lord, is the audience for a book like this? And what's a good title?"

A greatest strategist, **W A Harriman, Emperor-I'** Skull and Bones dynasty, age twenty-seven and just four years out of Yale has his own ambitious last long in fifty two years as an US influential freewheeling diplomat and foreign policymaker. He himself became one of the most influential experts on Russia policy; He intended to compete ideologically [Karl Marx, 1818-1883; Lenin 1870-1924] and economically with the Communist system than engage directly with the enemies militarily. He foresaw supremely confident that the advantages of the Capitalist-system would ultimately prevail, as long as the Cold War took place because he was a notorious Cold War architect implied his two books.[Peace with Russia 1959, and America and Russia in a Changing World 1971, wishfully Russia was eternally in Second Superpower after U.S] He retired from public life at the same time L.B Johnson, as during the presidential election campaign of President Richard Nixon till in 1969, but he's

The New Legion

still been clinging in the shadow as a witch-hunt: Chairman Foreign Policy Task Force, Democratic National Committee, a member of the Council on Foreign Relations, member American Academy of Diplomacy Charter, Skull and Bones Society till 1976 at age 85 – the focus of his clinging survey-attention on the "Eurasian Great Game" stratagem.

In coincidence 1917, W.A. Harriman took advantage of wartime demand and government contracts to jump into **Shipbuilding**, a vocation that escaped the shadow of his father's huge reputation in railroading. Harriman built ships during the war, and after its conclusion began gathering a large fleet of merchant ships and liners. (Forty years later, his thoughtful repeated again in the Vietnam War introduced by the CIP in 1960 for developed "**Jet-transport-building**" airplanes, a large air-fleet for U.S Civilian-airline and **Jet Engine** for Helicopter in production 10,000 Huey-Bell-Iroquois) Consolidated in 1920 under the name United American Lines. Central of these sweeping ambitions was a deal with Germany's once-proud Hamburg-American Line, now in postwar disarray. Harriman and his colleague George H. Walker would supply Hamburg-American with warships if it would act as the European agent for Harriman's own shipping lines.

After the Korea-War, to enhance the mobility of a growing nation, his Skull and Bones dynasty's dream originated from 1919 on an Army-convoy from Washington D.C to San Francisco, a journey that took 62 days. His real good opportunity in nation during a peace time to create economical growth, great open-jobs were been developed. On June 29, 1956 these Wise-Men coaxed Congress into letting them took President Eisenhower signed the historic legislation: "**The national highway systems**" The WIB Bones' a lucrative business in peace time in contrast war time as the **Shipbuilding and Air-Jet-building.**

As the 1920s unfolded, Harriman, Rockefeller, and Stanley represented a study in youth, riches, connections, and the hubris of emerging elite. Coincidence is an unlikely explanation of either the Harriman firm's global ambition or its 1920s dominance by Skull and Bones.

After World War-I, W.A Harriman to run an ambitious set of investments about to be cobbled together in the postwar political maelstrom of 1920s Germany and Russia. Over two decades, father-in-law Walker helped steer Prescott Bush to the top of what became the Brown Brothers Harriman of mid-century. Harriman along with Prescott Bush financed the German Nazis' rise to power, beginning with multimillion dollar transactions to Fritz Thyssen. Their financial activities with the Nazis continued during and after the war, upon which these assets were liquidated in favor of Prescott Bush. This was the beginning of the Bush family fortune. Prescott Bush went from a humble tire-salesman, to a multimillionaire – rich, full of Yale Skull and Bones and WIB members, London-linked, politically influential, and intimately wired through several of its top partners to the postwar birthing of the CIA. During the first half of the twentieth century, the United States had evolved its own version of *"Permanent Government"* akin to the British model. Although this establishment [Skull and Bones Dynasty] peaked from the 1920s through the 1960, its influence lingered to George-I [George H.W Bush] critical advantage till 2,008.

This Dynasty used "OSS, CIA" as a sharp violence tool showing or caused by physical force that intended to hurt or kill [violent crime] and **the "Mass-Media" was the mainstream tool** of communicating with large numbers of people, especially radio, television, newspapers, schools, universities, Hollywood, and even few times urging the employee strikes, antiwar movement for starting the rumor to pressurized over the then acting government administrative. This shrewd malicious politician who deserved it was the founder of Skull and Bones [triumvirate: W. A Harriman, Prescott Bush and George H W Bush]

Thereby the groundwork went back generations. The smart intelligent youthful George H.W Bush would have heard his father and grandfather discussing their employer [Harriman firm's] 1920 Russian Central Asian manganese and oil adventures, the financial proceeds of which were administered through 1930 in U.S corporations named Georgian Manganese, Barnsdall, and Russian Finance and Construction. Reader and me, we must remember that Soviet Georgia on the Black Sea, with huge deposits of manganese

The New Legion

needed for weapons-grade steel, was a mere four hundred miles from Iraq. The Baku oil fields were about the same distance. For strategist W A Harriman, George H Walker and Prescott Bush stance; be motivated by greed in their thought why not initiated a stratagem that so called **"Eurasian Great Game?"** joint with the WIBmember (War Industries Board) is a crucial important component that has the full support of their war-games or merchant of death. They will arrogate the CIP in Vietnam-war in their greedy for developing war industries self-interest. Once more time against the wishes of the U.S government

Harriman, American financier and diplomat who held a number of public offices, typically ambassador to the USSR 1943-1946, was most proud of the fact that when 1917, on his advice, the United States gave the Russia government under Aleksandr-Kerensky a $325 million credit, to be spent on war materiel from the United States. These, it would turn out, would be the more controversial enterprises. Saint-Louis Newspapers described George H Walker in awed terms as the man responsible for assembling W.A Harriman's **Overseas-Empire.** And from 1917 to 1918 Samuel Bush, prominent in Ohio railroading as well as steel, he served on the "War Industries Board" where he was in charge of the forgings, guns, small arms, and ammunition section and later the facilities division (that I remind you of about political, social unrest to over World-Wars because this WIB' ambitious organization) A Harriman finished with shipbuilding kept his financial stakes in Brown Brothers Harrimanand his other investments but jumped into the New Deal by working with two formers WIBofficials, Hugh Johnson and Herbert Bayard Swope, in the National Recovery Administration in New York and then Washington. He went on to become F D Roosevelt's emissary to Churchill and Lend-Lease administrator, then ambassador to Russia, ambassador to Britain, and, after W.W II, secretary of commerce and mutual security administrator. Unsurprisingly, the ghost of A Harriman was queried about his plan for the war-industry as well as queried about covert operations (Vietnam, mainland China, Indonesia, against post-1960 Cuba....) and his own predilection for armaments, would probably just chuckle.

Vinh-Van-Truong

Was W.A Harriman an U.S. policymaker or Permanent President?

Here some testified-proof-evidences: Harriman as Lend-Lease expediter "to keep the British Islands afloat" He deliberately reports directly to the White House, thus bypassing the American ambassador and the State Department. He acted on this personal level for three decades (February 1941 through 1969 the end of L.B Johnson administrative) attending all of the wartime conferences and twice going on missions to arrange increased aid to the Soviet Union for the second chunk of Eur**Asian** Great Game (His mastermind' scam for the Axis of Evil cooperated with the enemy so that in 1960s, President Kennedy and Johnson in pursuit of probing Russia connected companies which were subjected to be seized under the Trading with the Enemy Act. They thought, The Skull and Bones couldn't "throwing sand in the umpire's face". Suddenly, Attorney General Robert Kennedy fell to an assassin's bullet in 1968 similar case with his older brother; J.B. Johnson announced on TV gave-up for reelection) It was an intellectual change of my perspective, and seemed surrogate the war from Middle Europe to Asia. Two players engaged the Axis of Evil with the craps "CIP counter NLF." in Vietnam-War. Therefore, shortly, in October 1943 Harriman influenced President Roosevelt must appointed him Ambassador to Russia (1943-1946) for arranging prewar-production in loan credit from U.S. dollar by stratagem *"Aid to Russia 1941-46"*: "Jet fighter" test-development in 'Korea-War', and also "Jet transport", and Air-Ground defense missile in 'Vietnam-War' which stood for U.S-campaign to combat troops training exercise there.

Meanwhile in Asia, the OSS persuaded Ho Chi Minh engaged in covert operation as of Service of War Information at Kunming, Yannan China in 1943 – for war preparedness. The CIA transforms from OSS, already carried out to evacuate Chiang Kai-Shek's followers to Taiwan in 1949 by CATS. In 1954 CIA re-supplied encircled French paratroopers at Dien Bien Phu, then in 1958 supported a coup attempt against Indonesian strongman Sukarno. In Korea-War, Harriman's assurance that Russians wouldn't intervene in Korea-War by Russian ground-troop unless merely LAB-testing space for "Jet fighter" in beginning Jet engine generation (Russia: MIG-15, 17 and U.S: F-84, 86) and a supporter of General Mac Arthur's bold plan for an amphibious operation at Inchon, Korea. His policymaker was to assure General Arthur that President Truman was trying to meet his troop requirements, while impressing on him the administration's concern that committing too many divisions in Asia would leave Europe vulnerable to Soviet attack, and to impress on Mac-Arthur that Jiang Jieshi (Chiang Kai-Shek) must not be encouraged to initiate a war with the People's Republic of China (PRC, Communist China)

Because for the U.S. triangular diplomacy and realpolitik successfully will achieved the intended goals: two decades of closed door hostility (1952-1972) the Sino-U.S. normalization will process began, and the two countries set up liaison offices in each other's capital cities, **in bringing PRC to United Nations member**; finally the objective was thereafter many giant U.S. corporations mustered themselves into the PRC and bilateral trade improved throughout the decade. The U.S. market was surely inundated with products made in China. The elite capitalists were very happy to exploit the huge, profitable market in China. ***Consequently America should eliminate the "Second-Class" in America society.***

Harriman played an important role when the war turned against the United Nations forces (U.S forces under controlled to U.N) At a crucial NSC meeting on November, 28, 1950 A- Harriman challenged President Truman to assert his leadership toward the interest of WIB. Truman has to respond by accelerating NSC-68, "U.S. Objectives and Programs for National Security" recommendations for vastly expanding U.S defense spending and rearmament, likewise in Iraq-War, President George-II signed a bill for "New generation of weapons in future combat system for Army alone cost 200 billion dollar. Harriman also played a prominent role in Truman's decision to fire Secretary of Defense Louis A. Johnson. He greatly admired Johnson's successor, his subordinate General of the Army George C Marshall.

Harriman was the author of the presidential order aimed at curbing General Mac Arthur's public criticism of the Truman administration's war policies by requiring all policy statements to be approved in advance by the administration. General Arthur's subsequent letter to Republican House Minority Leader Joseph Martin made public on April 5, 1951, led to President Truman's meeting with Harriman, Secretary Acheson, Secretary Marshall and Chairman of the Joint Chiefs of Staff, General Omar Bradley. Shortly, Harriman advised that General Arthur be fired immediately, though Truman hesitated in stalemate. After further consultation Truman agreed. Harriman, right away drafted the dismissal announcement. **This I concluded Harriman was indeed a Permanent President of the United States,** at least from Franklin D. Roosevelt through Lyndon B. Johnson – no U.S. president liked this totalitarian-disguised "Emperor-I" of Skull and Bones Dynasty. "That's blackmail" the use of threats to put pressure on a president or his cabinet. Harriman's crucial reason was placing blame squarely on U.S. administration.

From the power structure that emerged in World War I and reached the height of prestige during the Second World War and the two following decades was obviously far more than just a social phenomenon, Groups like Skull and Bones were a clubby symptom but hardly a driving force part of the new establishment came from the organization and hierarchies of national mobilization that had been established during the two wartimes – years that, quite simply, had realigned the world. There were the broad tracks along which Harriman and Bush families climbed, financially and politically. Over the years they let the family to an involvement with the mainstays of the twentieth-century American national security state: finance, oil and energy, the federal government, the so-called military-industrial complex, and the CIA, the National Security Agency, and the rest of the intelligence community.

Unsurprisingly they created a formation so-called WIB (War Industries Board) and dominated by The Six Wise-men they made the World such as: Averell Harriman, E.Roland Harriman, Robert A Lovett, Artemus Gates, James Forrestal, and Prescott Bush. All these figures that some chronicles have profiled the 1917-1960, emergence of "the Wise Men" and others in terms of links forged at universities and clubs, not least the Skull and Bones hegemony at Brown Brothers Harriman. The WIB experience was a watershed event… creating a community of interests and shared experiences. The WIB later recalled, with only some exaggeration, that *"the War Industries Board of the United States had in the end a system of concentration of commerce, industry, and all powers of government that was without compare among all the other nations, friend or enemy, involved in the World War"* So why their policies engaged with the enemies, are focused on narrow interests and as a result have too little vision of the vast potential for achievements at home and abroad, for the United States under the kind of leadership we deserve.

But quite literally, Prescott Bush spent the first two decades of his financial career in the company of people whose actions and ideas would shape the War Department, the OSS, the CIA, and other pivots of the emerging U.S national security complex. Certainly we do know "the War Department was directed by tiny clique of wealthy Republican, and one that was almost as narrowly based, in social and educational terms, as a traditional British Tory Cabinet"

THE ORIGINAL "EURASIAN GREAT GAME" WALKS INTO WORLDWIDE

A MAJOR DISASTER

W.A. Harriman to run an ambitious set of investment about to be cobbled together in the postwar political maelstrom of 1920s Germany and Russia. Over twenty years, father-in-law Walker helped steer Prescott Bush, from a humble tire-salesman to the top of what became the Brown Brothers Harriman of mid-century – to a multimillionaire, full of Yale University Skull and Bones-men, London-linked, politically influential, and intimately wired through several of its top partners to the postwar birthing of the CIA. During the first half of the twentieth century, W.A Harriman transformed the United States to be evolved its own version of *"Permanent -Government"* akin to British model. Although this establishment peaked from the 1920 [Harriman's Eurasian Great Game] through the 1969 [Harriman retired from public life before he setting up the frame-work to donate Saigon to Hanoi regime like a great gift normalized by Paris Peace Talk negotiation – **axiom-1** done] its influence lingered to second Skull and Bones generation, George H.W Bush'scritical advantage.

This, we must keep in mind, is the cutthroat context into which William A. Harriman, George H. Walker, and their New York financial allies jumped in 1922 when – against the wishes of the U.S government – they contracted to refurbish the once lucrative oil fields of the Russian Caucasus. But the bold venture failed in part because of political unrest in the Baku region. Foreign concession, like that at the Barnsdall Corporation, were withdrawn by 1925 After eight decades of Harriman and Bush family experience, even the born-again George-I of the late 1980s were happy to take investment dollars from oil sheikhs. Moral rhetoric notwithstanding, petroleum needs and armaments buildups have been important factors and motivators in two wars; not incidentally, they have also been pillars of Skull and Bones dynasty crony-advancement. Oil, in particular, has long been a linchpin for defense and national security elites. With the arrival of George-II in the White House, it was again immediately plain that secret intelligence would receive a high status and more money. While the CIA may have been the creation of a Democratic W.A. Harriman, [President Harry Truman] it nowadays seemed to be strongly favored by Republicans, notably conservative Republicans and especially the Bushes. But these sounds were soon drowned out by the deafening roar of 9/11.

Some chroniclers have profiled the 1917-1960 emerge of "The Wise Men" and others in terms of links forged at universities and clubs, not least the Skull and Bones hegemony at Brown Brothers Harriman (William A. Harriman) [in online http://www.answers.com/topic/w-averell-harriman, page 3] Walter Isaacson and Evan Thomas, *The Wise Men: Six Friends and the world They made, 1986 the same year W.A Harriman passed away*. Their goal is that "This conjunction of an immense Military Establishment and a large arms industry is new in the American experience. The total influence – economic, political, and even spiritual – is felt in every where in companies, business areas, every office of the Federal Government. Americans recognize the imperative need for this development. Yet Americans must not fall to comprehend its grave implications.

But in my perception, the First emperor of Skull and Bones lasted from 1917 until 1969 and the Second emperor from 1969 till November 19, 2006 at 2:19pm. While it's perfectly delightful to have been so thoroughly vindicated for predictive posts like *"Republican Death Rattle" "Skull and Bones Death Rattle"* because inhumanity for the death merchandise

"War Industries Board Death Rattle" But who were Six Wise Men? (1) W.A Harriman (2) E. Roland Harriman (3) Robert A Lovett (4) Artemus Gates (5) James Forrestal (6) Prescott Bush

However, the argument for an elite at least partly shaped by war priorities and mobilization service seems almost as compelling. In later years the WIB (War Industries Board) experience was a watershed event... creating a community of interests and shared experiences, an early forerunner of the WIB, later recalled, with only some exaggeration, that the WIB of the United States had in the end a system of concentration of commerce, industry, and all the powers of government that was without compare among all the other nations, friend or enemy, involved in the World War. Its policy means *"**Foes become Friend and Friend became foes!**"*

More popular in Texas than in most others states, the Vietnam War in Vietnam drew on this hawkish-warlord [War Industries Board]. However, the strategic sophistication of Texan presidents has not matched their strut. If anything, the gap between the two has brought problems. The embarrassment Americans suffered in Southeast Asia helped to set the scene for U.S involvement in Iraq. [In my perception, the Iraq and Vietnam-Wars is defined "Two Different Wars One Destructive Parallel" in contrast with US Company-dynasty meant "A quiet Victory." Because the Vietnam War got its principal definition from Texan, President Lyndon Baines Johnson, and the resultant "Vietnam syndrome" later served as a goad to the Texan Bushes, the continuities are important. Vietnam was another growing source of tension within the Kennedy administration. Once again, Washington hard-liners pushed for an escalation of the war, seeking the full scale military confrontation [for CIP] with communist enemy that Kennedy, a warrior of peace, had denied them in Cuba and other Cold-War battlegrounds. President Diem and Kennedy concurred to bring about South Vietnam, and Kennedy would have withdrawn, realizing that "it was South Vietnam's war and the people there had to win it... We couldn't win the war for them."

"So we had better make damned sure that I'm re-elected," Kennedy told Kenneth- O'Donnell, his loyal White House aide. He was equally outraged at his national security adviser [Mc-George Bundy, Skull and Bones 40] while he famously took responsibility for the Bay of Pigs debacle in public, especially at the CIA, threatening to 'Shatter the agency into pieces and scatter it to the winds.' He intended to withdraw completely from Vietnam after he was safely re-elected in 1964. Should the CIP' scam be aborted? J.F Kennedy's strenuous effort to keep the country at peace in the face of equally ardent pressure from Skull and Bones' warlord caste to go to war like Iraq, President Kennedy again and again and again found a way to sidestep war.

Quite literally, the Skull and Bones or the warlord in WIB is greedily thirsty for war. In contrast, world's impressed civilization is that the people of United States are nice people. Everywhere in the world, people are good. The people of the US are also seeking peace, love, friendship and justice. Because humanitarianism, spirituality, rationalism, and logic are excellent things for human being -Why should we go for hostilities? Why more conflict? Why should we develop weapons of mass destruction? Everybody can love one another. Everyone hates aggression, and they hate bullying strategies, and they hate violation of the rights of nations and discrimination. The United States can run the world through logic. Each nation is living its own lives. The US [Permanent Government] government should not interfere in their internal affairs; let they should live their own lives. Then there would be no problems with that. Problems cannot be solved through bombs. Bombs are little use today. People need logic and friendship. However, the Skull and Bones dynasty greedily are focused on narrow interests and as a result have too little vision of the vast potential for achievement at home land and abroad.

After took a break since World War II, the Skull and Bones dynasty [Harriman's First Skull and Bones' generation] continued the Eurasian Great Game stratagem. Because isn't they had needed American assistance in order to prevail; Meanwhile some 300,000 American troops were stationed in West Germany precisely because NATO could not stave off Soviet or Warsaw Pact aggression without American help, while in South Korea there were 50,000 American

The New Legion

troops positioned specifically to help that country deal with any aggression from north. And nobody suggested that, because they needed such American assistance, the armed forces of West Germany or South Korea should be ridiculed or reviled. I don't think these actions were fair-reasonable; for me, these facts secured the low cheap-payment toward work-class from two great nations Russia and China for the prospect of long decades later, because who pay should be a creditor in 'command and control'. So why leader of Skull and Bones [Harriman] urged President Truman to assert Mac Arthur leadership and drafted dismissal announcement from his command for "unauthorized policy statements" was the same reason Westmoreland hungrily to destroy Ho Chi Minh trail: "Naturally the objective was clear in significance do not destroy China because of stratagem "Eurasian Great Game." But Vietnam and Iraq will be the major man-made, or artificial disasters by its conspiracies "Two Different Wars, One Destructive Parallel" according Carl Von Clausewitz (1780-1831) once said: "Policy is the guiding intelligence and war only the instrument, and not vice versa." Sadly, this theory explains US policy toward Iraq and Vietnam. In turn US economic boosted by the dollar in death-merchandise productions. A "quiet victory" of this war signified an augmentation of new words in English vocabulary dictionary: "Killing-Field" - "Voted with Theirs Feet" - "Reeducation-Camp" - "Boat-People"! Who dare accepted it?

At terminated epoch in Eurasian Great Game, the WIB once again stirred the surrogate war from Asia to Middle-East. The Skull-warlord [WIB) must again have done something as witching war – Vietnam the so called "Maddox-Event" and Iraq-II, so called the "WMD." The US have discovered dozens of WMD-related program activities and significant amounts of equipment that Iraq concealed from the United Nation during the inspections that began in late 2002, gotten itself stuck in a quagmire, as the New York Times' Johnny Apple wrote in his front-page analysis of the war, just like Vietnam all over again. It was the press's Vietnam reflex, and one was increasingly being hit with it. American never did find weapons of mass destruction in Iraq, and North Vietnam didn't attack US Maddox in the Gulf of Tonkin at all. [Do you believe, "SOG' first covet attack on U.S.S Maddox in the so called "Gulf of Tonkin Incident" on North Vietnam would be led by Norwegians. Scandinavians-Caucasian at the throttles of a covert boat in Asian waters flew in the face of plausible denial – How could a Norwegian possibly explain his attacking the coast of North Vietnam? SOG Nasty boats used for operations against the North Vietnamese coast – These boats still have markings and are flying the U.S flag. When used against North Vietnam, all markings and the flag were removed]

Although, US found old artillery shells with traces of Sarin-gas and other chemical or biological stockpiles we thought we would discover there. September 11 changed our nation one more time of focus much the way Pearl Harbor did. Consequently, yet George W Bush still won reelection. In 2004, voters who worried about terrorism and keeping America safe voted overwhelmingly to reelect President, despite our failure to find weapons of mass destruction in Iraq and also despite numerous attacks on the President for deceiving our nation and lying our way into war. We live today in an era of danger much like the Cold War.

For decades later, as the war in Iraq began, the New York Times turned its focus to the protesters against the war: The story described what the leaders of the 1960s anti-Vietnam War protest were doing today as the nation once again was at war. It filled readers in on the activities of the folk singer Pete Seeger, movie star Jane Fonda, Joan Baez, Tom Hayden, Martin Sheen, Mark Ruffalo (Photo AFP/Getty Images) was shown in a 1972 picture captioned, "Experienced Old Hand" Some of them at age weary in body and mind don't seem to be as interested in hearing their basically antiwar views as others, and yet the majority seem comforted hearing those views expressed by someone they grew up hearing express those views. To those opposed the Iraq-War under the headline: "Israel. U.S, UK; The Axis of Evil," "Wall Street richer and richer" "Lower student fee" "No more bomb" "No to U.S war on Terrorist." They're energized and organized. But can U.S antiwar protesters survive their own diversity? Voices of outrage...

****

The New Legion

THE WHIM AND IRONIES OF VIETNAM'S HISTORY:

Vietnam stands for the victims of the **Axis of Evil's scam**. Stemmed from the OSS covert operation by Agent 019, Lucien Conein in 1945 was the beginning of U.S had one' eye on Vietnam; Ho Chi Minh engaged OSS in 1943, US Service of War Information. Impossibly, Ho wasn't a gifted of miraculous prophecy that US will become an unsavory traitor from trust to tragedy. That coordinated in their effort performances overlapped into China mainland to help evacuated Chiang Kai-Shek's followers to Taiwan by the First-Flight evolved from the Civil Air Transport Service (CATS) a CIA airline founded in 1949. In 1954 CATS re-supplied encircled French paratroopers at Dien Bien Phu (pretended to be as a perfect U.S loyal ally) then in 1958 supported a coup attempt against Indonesian strongman Sukarno. CATS thin cover side apparently became the well-known Air America while its deep cover side became Nationalist China's 34th Squadron at Taiwan.

The crucial objective was how blown-up in liquidation all 'surplus' of war equipment cast-off World War II, American weapons and military equipment. For WIB' stirrer, as the result, on March 6, 1946, OSS Colonel Alfred Kitts witnessed the first French troop who enter the north Vietnam come ashore at Haiphong. They look like US Army. They were wearing helmet, packs, ammunitions, belts, fatigues and boots. The landing crafts from which they unload were American made and so were their heavy weapons vehicles, and the other equipment the US had originally give Charles De Gaulle free-French under the Lend-Lease Act to fight the Nazis and the Japanese – to resume colonialist-war to dominated regime, once again at Vietnam, but the WIB' objective was becoming the American foreign legionary due to U.S military-aid 75%. Meanwhile it was almost about 60 undeveloped countries around the world restored their independent, except Vietnam because of the greediest Harriman and his warlords in the WIB want to stir the second Indochinese war 1954-1975 for the CIP scam.

In 1943 Ho Chi Minh engaged the US Service of War Information, Kunming, China, with three directives on: (1) retreated to sanctuary

Pat-Po against Japanese fascism. (2) Cooperate with French forces to eliminate National parties and revolution movements. (On 12, July, 1946, General Giap with French artillery, tank ground support attacked headquarter of VNQDD; "Des journées inoubliables" Giap, French-transcribes HN 1975, p.290-295) (3) Vigilant struggle against French force for restored freedom and independent. Vietnam maybe out of US made war-disaster during nine years with French by gradually from self-governed to independent. Though its ambition, French must let Vietnam having its sovereign territory as India, Indonesia… from colonialist Western-nations – Comply with Directive-3, on December, 3/1946 Ho ordered secretly withdrawn out of Hanoi for self-destructive in long struggle deadly against French colonialism. A stage hence, Harriman deprived of Vietnam's independence for the selfish interest of the War Industries Board clique. Deeply in his masterminded "Freedom is not for free!" and "what you get… what you pay" as similarity of the historical United States. Purposely, W Harriman would like Hanoi leadership was like an Indochinese version of Skull and Bones, secretive and select. While he was not exactly in the club, he was generally trusted by its WIB Bones.

The OSS had found the Viet Minh the only Vietnamese resistance group sufficiently well organized and widespread within Vietnam to provide good intelligence on the Japanese to rescue American pilots and conduct sabotage and other behind the lines operations. The OSS had parachuted a training mission to one of Ho' wartime headquarters in the rugged jungle country north of the Red River delta and had provided 1,000 Carbines, submachine BAR guns, and other weapons to arm the original Viet Minh formations. As a member of OSS, Ho ordered the Vietnamese officers let their troops to try to distinguish Colonel Alfred Kitts's team from the large number of French in city and not to shoot at the Americans. This became increasingly difficult for the average Viet Minh soldier, despite the US Army markings and American flag on the teams' vehicles, as more French troops arrived, the French demands grew proportionately, and the shooting incidents proliferated. "How do you tell a French from American when the Frenchman is driving the same uniform"

The New Legion

Because the WIB [CIA] need go to war and coaxed Ho had agreed to let the French station garrison in Haiphong, Hanoi, and the other towns of the north only because he otherwise faced an invasion, he had received in exchange a promise of limited independence, the French had quickly begun to dishonor that promise. They were incidents of shooting almost immediately. The Viet Minh officers and troop were angered at the arrival of the French. However, they remained friendly to Kitts and his fellows Americans. Ridiculously, they still seemed to regard Colonel Kitts and his teammates as their allies as different from the colonists.

A Victory hijacked by the Axis of Evil' scam or a cunning stratagem; Ambitiously, initiated by the Skull and Bones Dynasty, after World War-II, the inherent ideological conflict between the two strongest powers in the world, the United States (policymaker was A Harriman, a founder of Skull and Bones) and the Soviet Union, was revived. The so called ideological competition was basically between Capitalism (US) and Communism (Soviet Union) to avoid another world war (nuclear-war maybe) the conflict between the two powers became what was known as the "Cold-War" The rivalry between the two ideologies rapidly expanded beyond Europe and began to influence Asia in the second chunk of Eur**Asian** Great Game. In China, Mao Zedong, who had been sympathetic to the Soviet Union, seized power on October 1, 1949 and announced the establishment of the People's Republic of China (PRC). Subsequently, the PRC and the Soviet Union signed the Treaty of Friendship, Alliance and Mutual Assistance on February 17, 1950. Literally, President Harry S Truman was seriously concerned about Communist expansion globally as well as in Asia. In response to the basic threat, the Truman Administration formulated foreign policies to contain the Soviet Union's political power, which was later known as the "Containment Doctrine". However a masterminded Harriman would like to resume another surrogate war to Asia for War Industries Board development, among them included the significant the "Jet Engine Age" – Korea-War for Air-Defense and Vietnam War for Civil-Airline. For Containment Doctrine, WIB Bones tried to increase their visibility in the two nation solution as Germany, Korea, and Vietnam in focusing lasting war-industries prosperity development. It was also a better way to calm down the potential for global confrontation. Meanwhile, in many cases, the War Industries Board has been busy arming opponents in ongoing conflicts – Iran and Iraq, Greece and Turkey, Saudi Arabia and Israel, and China and Taiwan. Often the purchasing country makes its purchases conditional on the transfer of technology so that it can ultimately manufacture the item for itself and others. The result is the proliferation around the world not just of weapons but of new weapons industries.

Basically, the people of Vietnam must be willing to struggle for their freedom and preserve the democracy to be instituted. If the people do not voluntarily fight for their freedom, no democracy can be materialized. An early twentieth-century Vietnamese Nationalist cartoon depicts peasants routing French colonial troops. The peasants fluently are shouting; "Wipe out the gang of imperialists, mandarins, capitalists, and big landlords!" Naturally, the fear of Communist aggression in Southeast Asia prompted President Truman to extend limited economic and military aid to the French who were fighting the Viet Minh, North Vietnamese Communist, in Indochina.

In November 1953, under CIA persuasion, due to US Military-aid, French General Henri Navarre wanted to lure the Viet Minh forces into a set piece battle at Dien Bien Phu so he could use French superior firepower, combined with air strikes, to destroy them. However, General (CIA tricks' 1954: B-29 and 1975: B-52) Navarre was only successful in his tactical goal to get the Viet Minh forces to take the bait, underestimating the overwhelming logistical support his enemy received from the PRC. As result, the balance of forces, both in terms of artillery firepower and troop strength leaned toward the Viet Minh forces by five to one. Who know! A. Harriman anticipated the fall of Dien Bien Phu to the Viet Minh was a prelude to U.S direct involvement in the second war Vietnam War for the CIP's craps.

It is important to determine not to depend on foreign powers [like President Diem did] All foreign nations care for their own interests first [like CIP] Relying on foreign countries to build up the power for one's faction is the source of civil war as proven by what happened in Vietnam from 1945 to 1975. Because the axis of evil, the Vietnamese people was betrayed and rendered futile in forced civil war, instead of they must have the courage to rise up to create the "People's Tide" (likely about 60 undeveloped countries restored their Freedom and Democracy not pay a cent after WW-II) – under the leadership of Viet patriots, intellectuals, and revolutionary activists who have keen strategic visions, organizational skills, a national spirit and scientific knowledge – for their effective fight against foreign domination – military or ideological – and act against those foreign powers exerting influences which make the nation of Vietnam independent on them, thank to the Viet synthesized strength. Definitely, Vietnam shall have a foreign policy independent from all foreign powers, and shall not let those powers again use our territory as battlefield or laboratory in their conflicts, if that happens to be. The particular geographic location of Vietnam on the main transportation bypass-path from Indian Ocean to Pacific Ocean has caused international powers to try to control this strategic channel. This very neutral foreign policy of Vietnam will help preserve world peace and will help Vietnam live in good relationship with all nations in the world, and enjoy the stability needed to develop its economy. The top priority goal of Vietnam after eliminating the totalitarian regime is to accelerate the development of its economy by participating in the globalizing market, strengthening regional and world peace and promoting democracy. Vietnam will play the role of a reconciliation factor for all international influences and also a converging point of the East and the West in a new global concept of mankind.

The first Vietnam War 1946-1954, Ho Chi Minh was so wrong entrusted his traitor United States. I think really it was a betrayal of for Vietnam independence because the WIB' scam. Indochina, which included Vietnam, was a French colony until early 1945. As early as 1942, the Japanese army entered Vietnam without a fight. The French administration was too weak to oppose any conditions imposed by the Japanese. Shortly before the end of WW-II, on March 9, 1945 a coup d'état by the Japanese army put an end to the French occupation. The Independence of Vietnam was proclaimed for the first time after a century of French domination. The First independent Vietnamese government, under Tran Trong Kim's leadership had to compromise to some extent with the occupying Japanese army; But the Vietnamese patriotic movements, always latent during the years of French rule, experienced an unprecedented expansion from that day on. This "élan" of patriotism was further exacerbated when six months later Vietnam became totally independent as a result of the Japanese capitulation. Literally, the Vietnamese enjoyed for the first time this great happiness they had aspired to for a century. It was easy to understand why this patriotism, rendered red hot during the process of after war decolonization in South East Asia (Malaysia, Philippines, Indonesia…) exploded when the French came back on the coat-tails of British Army in the Skull and Bones' conspiracy of silence. In fact the French contingent just followed British troops when they came to disarm the Japanese army in Indochina.

This patriotic "élan" was the real driving force behind the war of resistance against the French which broke out in the evening of December, 19, 1946. Among the Vietnamese revolutionary leaders, who were then fighting the French attempt to reoccupy Indochina after the Japanese capitulation; there was a prominent group of Communists led by Ho Chi Minh, Vo Nguyen Giap, and Pham Van Dong. Ho Chi Minh engaged OSS in 1943 and also a Moscow trained revolutionary, had in mind a goal other than national independence sought by nationalist leaders. Because a WIB Machiavellian (political theorist) motive, Ho and his cohorts dilemma with no choice they would just alternative toward international communism to supplant Colonialism in Indochina and were receiving specific orders from Moscow. Now we understand why they were better organized, more homogeneous and experts in Machiavellian political maneuvers.

During the war with the big-help gave a hand from Soviet, China, French even United States, in the then fashioned Communism, Ho Chi Minh gradually took over by eliminating all non communist leaders of the resistance as axiom-1 introduced 1960 (there was never a legitimate non-communist government in Saigon) Since 1945 the only legitimate or viable Vietnamese government was the one proclaimed by Ho Chi Minh, which is simply in second chunk-phased of Eurasian Great Game in performing the CIP stratagem or other word a foundational tenet of the communist version of national history. It is remarkable how easily this ideological exuberance of Vietnamese communists was and continues to be uncritically swallowed by academic specialist and venality mainstream media in

The New Legion

the United States. It should be noted that at that time Communism was unknown to the general population and the commencement the Cold War scam between KGB and CIA. Within ethical dilemma, the Communist party under Ho Chi Minh was hiding under the name of the Labor-Party, instead Communist party. Therefore one can see that, at the beginning of the war, the true driving force behind the anti-colonial struggle supported by all people was Vietnamese patriotism that had nothing to do with communism ideology.

In anticipation of Eurasian-Great-Game's chunk two, A. Harriman masterminded to move back to U.S forces from Europe to Asian for a new war building or change an existing one. Starting in 1949 when the Chinese Communists came to power in China, after CIA completely carried out the mission to evacuate Chiang Kai-Shek's followers to Taiwan 1949. Prior to the event, June 1950, his anticipated Korea War will begin. A key figure once again, A. Harriman arranged his early return from Europe with a phone call to President Truman, informing the president that Europeans were "gravely concerned lest we fail to meet the challenge in Europe." Harriman took up residence in the Executive Office Building, a blow to his ego because he fully expected to be at Truman's side as a special assistant to the president national security affairs and typically with his own staff: "put more than hundreds strategist, sociologist, ethnologists, geologists, psychologists, philosophers... to work modeling Korea and Vietnamese society and seeking data sufficient to describe their quantitatively and simulate their behavior on a system PRAISE' chart (non-computerized). The struggle for the new-world order might well have to be considered the social scientists war.

Ho Chi Minh and his clique now had direct help from them. With this help to back them up, they began to unveil their true communist nature with no choice. Owing to his total submission to Beijing, Ho Chi Minh obtained in return at the decisive battle of Dien Bien Phu direct participation of Chinese communist in General Giap's command (Chinese generals: Wei Guoqing, Luo Guibo, Cheng Geng...and theirs ten of thousands of volunteers) This enable Giap to achieve victory in 1954 (General Giap and Ho engaged OSS 1943) His meditate revenge on sufferings of his pro-U.S traitor, He plotted in the past against the French at Dien Bien Phu and now then against the unsavory Americans in the Khe-Sanh siege. Late in 1967, General Giap commenced a siege of the Americans' far western support base at Khe Sanh. He massed four full infantry divisions supported by two artillery and tank regiments at the heretofore largely unknown complex at the opposite end of Route-9, the farthest compound away from most American or South Vietnamese principal enclaves. Giap purposefully made the presence of the more than 40,000 NVA troops highly visible to South Vietnamese and American intelligence gatherers.

Consequently, the congregation of NVA troops immediately drew the attention of General Westmoreland. He had, a few months earlier, begun development of the primitive Khe Sanh outpost into a materiel support base for his proposed operation in Laos. Westmoreland had deployed a battalion of Marines and a crew of U.S Navy Seabees to develop and defend the base. They quickly turned to, bulldozing the ground and installing steel matting for a primitive airstrip and laying in stockpiles of ammunition and supplies for the proposed Laos operation. (The WIP always put on eyes on that, that's never happened because the ROE was strictly followed up by Permanent Government via General Alexander Haig, a prospect congruent with his later involvement in and reaction to the operation)

Responding to the Giap' action, Westmoreland ordered more than 6,000 additional USM to the distant and tactically unimportant base. In concert with the defense of Khe Sanh, he also ordered commencement of massive air bombardment of the entire region that encircled the remote enclave, appropriately naming the aerial onslaught, Operation Niagara. If the battle raged, President Johnson vowed that America wouldn't not lose Khe Sanh likely French forces did; Johnson said this despite the fact that he had already scrapped Westmoreland's plan for border-crossing operation into Laos? (I am certainly doubt it) His decision had thus rendered the Khe Sanh support base tactically useless.

Illustrating such intense NVA activity in this far northwestern corner of South Vietnam, General Giap had succeeded in convincing General Westmoreland that the Khe Sanh siege supported a greater North Vietnamese effort to overwhelm South Vietnam's northern-provinces. The US General envisioned a modern version of Dien Bien Phu about to occur. Therefore, he even resorted to asking President Johnson for permission to authorize a feasibility study to examine the possible use of "tactical-nuclear-weapons" to defend Khe Sanh? (I assured the Permanent Government never authorizes to use tactical nuclear bomb like "CBU-55" due to this against ROE' axis of evil's craps) Meanwhile, the onslaught at the distant outpost served the North Vietnamese general in drawing a significant amount of American attention away from the major enclaves in the seaside provinces north of Danang. As the Lunar New Year, Tet 1968 approached, Giap redeployed the majority of his forces from Khe Sanh and secretly sent them eastward, moving them in small bands. Then, during the end of January, he very effectively commenced a blitzkrieg of attacks on the coastal cities as part of the greater Tet offensive, which sent mostly VC guerrilla forces striking USA units in the southern regions while Giap pitted battle-hardened NVA regulars against USM in the north.

The 1968 campaign mobilized communist forces throughout South Vietnam, successfully hitting US forces and ARVN forces with complete strategic surprise. While the NVA commander had enjoyed great success, surprising the Americans, he had badly underestimated their forces' capabilities. In the end, the Hanoi garnered a media coup with world headlines that proclaimed Hanoi and Viet Cong victories, but in most practical military terms suffered significant losses at all corners. Tactically, Tet-Offensive may have begun as a successful offensive, but quickly turned into an abysmal failure for Hanoi. For all their expense of lives, equipment, and weaponry, they had gained nothing but a scrapbook of press clippings.

Fatefully, to introduce a dictatorship of the Proletariat patterned after the Beijing model. It wasn't pure chance, after Ho totally controlled North Vietnam, to witness the implementation of a bloody "Agrarian Reform" (1953-1956) which was truly a Pol Pot like type of genocide in which hundreds of thousands of people perished. Ho Chi Minh and his clique in fact had transformed an independence war against French colonialism first into an international conflict (Cold War) and then steered it towards a "Class Struggle" to serve international Communism. North Vietnam had so much difficulty of destruction, drought, flood... As a result Ho ordered in early 1957 withdraw all 100,000 troops back to North Vietnam. Vietnamese in the South were happiness from 1954 to 1959. That 1959s the United States [WIB and Skull Bones] persuaded Soviet Union played the craps [CIP/NLF]. From now on Ho was isolated by KGB pressured to motivate Le Duan and Le Duc Tho seized in power. Therefore, at its April 1959, the KGB pressurized the North Vietnamese Communist Party Central Committee had vote in secret session at its April 1959 15th Plenum, to return covertly to South Vietnam thousands of such Viet Minh veterans. This axis of evil now is walking in major disaster in stir the Vietnam-War. In 1959 the men make storm starting blown over Indochina.

Alas! All those losses of human lives and time and the destruction of the country had no other purpose than substituting "White Colonialism with Red colonialism" in North Vietnam. The result in this Cold War, is in 1954, a massive exodus of a million refugees and repeated again Saigon Fall in 1975 a two million refugees fleeing from Communism and an unscrupulous regime in the Indochina which is still in place. [But in 1954 CIA invested the cost for a notorious film with title "We want to live," sponsoring by Philippine film technician experts; however it is sheer political propaganda campaign; In 1975 is major disaster of "Saigon Fall" so "no films for that"] A. Harriman clever implied CIP won the NLF by the so called "*Voted with theirs feet*" by an "A Quite Victory" because the worldwide condemned this "Dirty-War." So he dare show up in public.

After the partition of Vietnam in 1954, in the sphere of acting government, the U.S supported the GVN in the South to prevent the domino effect in Southeast Asia. Throughout our direct involvement in the war against the North Communist in the South, U.S policy had been desultory and inconsistent. By 1968, confidence in President Lyndon Johnson's handling of the war erode and declined sharply due to Johnson wasn't a policymaker. The CIP objective wasn't accomplished yet (U.S combat troop was not yet reaching in a peak commitment 543,400 in one year rotation, estimated about 3.000,000 passengers for sustained Civil Airline being developed) Successor Republican, former Vice President Richard Nixon won the

The New Legion

presidential election on November 2, 1968 and became the fifth U.S President to handle the war in Vietnam. President Nixon was elected when America was in a very turbulent, divisive period, and global politics was undergoing dramatic changes. Domestically, anti-war protests and civil rights movements erupted wildly across America. Nixon needed to extricate U.S troops out of Vietnam, the sooner the better, to defuse the increasing political turmoil. (In the scope agenda table strategy CIP, keyed time period apply with 'axiom-3': the U.S couldn't have won the war under any circumstances.

Once again the Axis of Evil shoot craps: The legitimate defense of the South Vietnamese people was betrayed and rendered futile in the Second Vietnam War (1960-1975). Harriman's preparedness to break off the President Diem's Rural Revolutionary Pacification Program in effect of Diem's policy by "draining away the water from the pond for catching fish" In 1959 a serial of establishment of Groups 559, Group 759, Group 959 and NLF (National Liberation Front) in the GKB' first shoot craps cooperated in final dice by CIA on meeting September, 21, 1960, National Security Council in order for safety protected [Ho Chi Minh trail] Harriman Highway plus POL parallel on it. According Permanent Government standpoints in supported by Academic Freedom Act (the venality to mainstream Media, Hollywood, University: for axiom-1, particularly Hollywood: Jane Fonda in reconsideration named all LZ in Operation Lam Son 719 in 1971 such as, LZ **LoLo**brigida, **Sophia**loren, **Liz**taylor, bop-**Hope**, see Operation-Map in chapter-6 in details why angry President Thieu decided "early-out" against General Haig -*"touch down... pissed there a messand go home"* Thieu ordered to General Lam)

Even though following the 1954 Geneva Agreement between Ho Chi Minh and French, which wasn't signed by the Bao Dai government and the US and the partition of Vietnam at the 17th parallel, the two halves of Vietnam found themselves incorporated into the two opposing blocs of the Cold War. It is remarkable how easily this ideological exuberance of Vietnamese communists was and continues to be uncritically swallowed by academic specialists in the United States. Why the United States didn't signed Geneva Agreement? Because her anticipated in coming plot stirring

Vietnam War. While it is often forgotten that in 1957 the Soviet Union proposed that both of the Vietnamese governments then in existence be admitted to the United Nations, not to mention that China much preferred the existence of two Vietnams. It is clear that, aside from the Vietnamese parties themselves, the participants at the Geneva Conference of 1954 all preferred a two-state solution as a way to calm down the potential for global confrontation.

The affirmation of a theoretically unified Vietnam in the final declaration of the conference, which was signed by none of the conferees, significantly left the question of the legitimate government of such a unified Vietnam to the vague vicissitudes of an election to be held after two years, which was a conspiracy of diplomatic silence way of painting over national enthusiasm with "Cold-War" realism.

Ho Chi Minh and his cadre's communist vocation not allow them to stop at the border of North Vietnam. International Communism dictated that they should go further into South East Asia. In South Vietnam, King Bao Dai was succeeded by Ngo Dinh Diem and the generals the last one was Nguyen Van Thieu. With minimum US help by surplus WW-II obsolete war material, thereby these fresh governments managed to contain communist sabotage with US opened Harriman Highway, help their infiltration fluently come from North for years of war. In spite of being under a still imperfect democratic regime, The South Vietnamese people still enjoyed relative freedom, much better than what the North was experiencing under Leninist Ho Chi Minh.

Beginning in 1960, two craps player in military readiness for war, with the help of Communist Bloc, North Vietnam intensified guerrilla warfare in the South. In 1965 huge caches of weapons coming from communist China, including the then very modern Kalashnikov rifles, were discovered in the South near Vung Ro, Nha Trang province which belonging 759[th.]Marine Seaway-Supply Group. At about the same time, big training combat battle for US troop practiced already erupted all around the country causing South Vietnam to nearly succumb to communist subversion. One witnessed the well known typical scenario of a "National Liberation Front" that had already taken place in same with a "Counter Insurgency Project" elsewhere many other times around the world.

The New Legion

In each case it is simply an example of covert communist subversion that A. Harriman masterminded called "on the strongman side" method. Only then did the US Marines started landing at Danang beach in 1965, after concocted "Gulf Tonkin Incident" in 1964, as prelude to more massive US involvement which kept increasing about 3.000,000 air-ticket-passengers of US troops in rotation every one year for sustaining a biggest Airline Jet been developed in transportation (you never heard the term Airline bankruptcy during the Vietnam War at all) Communist Block kept increasing also escalated its involved aggression. Naturally, the United States intervention was in fact only a response to the strategy of subversion by the Communist bloc. The true nature of the 1960-1975 war was the South Vietnamese people's defense, with US help, against the Communist bloc's aggression. It was in fact a struggle to preserve South Vietnam's freedom against an attempt to impose a communist dictatorship. But the Skull and Bones gave pressure influenced on US Congress and politicians, their influence on the conduct of this war, and the reasons why the Americans withdrew from Vietnam in 1973 would be the subject of another story.

The contrast between President Kennedy and the Skull and Bones is bent on escalation and trying to prevent a war. Kennedy never made his Vietnam plans public. This is in true Kennedy fashion, his statements on the Southeast Asian conflict were a blur of ambiguity, avoiding a public split within Kennedy's administration, He operated on "multiple levels of deception" in his Vietnam decision making. Actually, the United-States were caught in the reality of the Cold War, and the Skull and Bones obviously had a role to play. But we don't think the Kennedy believed they could trust much of what they said. Two brothers Kennedy and Vice President Johnson were trying to find their way out of the Cold War, but the Skull and Bones certainly didn't want to. After Kennedy's assassination, the president foreign adviser, a Skull and Bone, Mc George Bundy who coaxed with some pressure on L.B. Johnson widen the war into a colossal tragedy knows Kennedy would have done no such thing; McNamara who was assigned a war executer, acknowledges this, though it highlights his own blame. "One of Kennedy's great speeches on foreign policy" If J.F. Kennedy had lived, there is no doubt in our mind, the world would have laid the groundwork for détente, and the Cold War would have ended much sooner than it did.

"Peace-Speech" in this stirring address, Kennedy would do something that no other President during the Cold War – and no American president today – would dare. He was made a scapegoat for Skull and Bones frustration and betrayed by its American First.

On international politics, the inherent ideological differences between the PRC and the Soviet Union, since Jose Stalin's death, became more serious with the Soviet Union invasion of Czechoslovakia in 1968 and the actual Sino-Soviet border clashes in 1969 (secretly U.S must temporally help Hanoi for protracting war)Successor to A. Harriman, George H W Bush perceived the Sino-Soviet conflict as a good opportunity to bring the PRC, a newly emerged superpower as they already plans, into the world balance of power along with the Soviet Union to create a new "geo-strategy, triangular diplomacy which would pave the way for rapprochement with the PRC and relations with the PRC would help achieve détente with the Soviet Union. Triangular diplomacy would undoubtedly encourage the Soviet Union to cooperate in the Strategic Arms Limitation Treaty (SALT) negotiations, and would help the U.S exit Vietnam exactly on agenda road-map. More importantly, Sino-U.S relations would open the "bamboo-curtain" for the U.S to reenter the PRC' huge, lucrative market after two hostility-decades.

The new geo-strategy once again shifted U.S policy toward the South Vietnam. With triangular diplomacy the Communist threat in Southeast Asia no longer exist and, as a result, the political survival of the South Vietnam became irrelevant to U.S interests in the region. As a realist, on behalf of Skull and Bones, Doctor Henry Kissinger [Skull and Bones] brought to the White House the concept of "realpolitik" and President Nixon must endorsed it. In order to keep the policymaker decision within the White House, the State Department was, in a way, excluded from involvement in triangular diplomacy. The National Security Council was likewise of Permanent Government. She became the principal body to advise the President on foreign affairs. Through this streamlined process and back door channel help from various sources, Henry Kissinger was able to secretly meet with Xuan-Thuy and then Le Duc Tho, peace negotiators,

The New Legion

in Paris and the PRC' Premier Zhou Enlai in China. Subsequently, Henry Kissinger and Primer Zhou Enlai arranged for President Nixon to meet the PRC' Chairman Mao Zedong on February 21, 1972 in Beijing, China. The Nixon-Mao meeting produced a joint Shanghai Communiqué, which marked the end of an old era of hostility. The U.S Permanent Government strategic alignment with the PRC did put pressure on the Soviet Union. Only three months after Sino-U.S high level meetings in China, President Nixon and Soviet Premier Leonid Brezhnev signed the SALT-I Treaty in Moscow and a new agreement with the Soviet Union on the Berlin Wall issue.

While global politics were changing and with the peace negotiations in progress, the obstinate Hanoi had no intention to relinquish their greedy goal to conquer the South Vietnam by force. After having recovered from their 1968 Tet Offensive catastrophic losses, on March 30, 1972, the Hanoi, by persuasive their patron, the Soviet Union launched another general attack against the South Vietnam. This was their attempt to defeat the South Vietnam when U.S combat troops were no longer involved. After over two months of fierce fighting, the South Vietnam with U.S air support overwhelming defeated the Hanoi again. Even though they were defeated in the battlefields, the Hanoi leadership strongly believed that if they could just hang on, the will of the Americans would collapse as long war and they would win the war by axiom-1: not in South Vietnam battlefields, but in Washington D.C as Permanent Government plot used John Kerry, Yale University as good activist movie war-star together movie star Hollywood Jane Fonda. Absolutely, during this period, President Nixon was confronted with multiple political problems.

In conspiracy of silence, the Watergate scandal exploded more wildly in the U.S forcing President Nixon to resign for the cause to invalid Nixon pledges in letters to Thieu in formulated Harriman's axiom-1, never a legitimate non-communist government in Saigon. Therefore, the swift collapse of Saigon in 1975 couldn't be blamed on the South Vietnamese people's lack of motivation in defending freedom like George W Bush said, none the weakness of their armed forces. In 1972, when these forces were normally supported by the US, they did fight courageously and destroyed the Hanoi's armored divisions crossing the demilitarized zone into South Vietnam in a much larger offensive than that of 1975.

Unfortunately, while the Communist bloc was fully and steadfastly supporting an aggressive North Vietnam, one could witness during the last two years of the war (1973-1974) the last and brand new sophisticated weapons batches to North Vietnam armed forces. Meanwhile the US Permanent Government gave pressure on Congress cut off large portions of supply and ammunition aid to South Vietnam because of axiom-1 in demagogic political reason. This anticipated betrayal was perfectly orchestrated and preceded by a campaign of denigration and disinformation in favor of the communists by the method on "the strongman side" which was fostered venality of the mainstream media and intelligentsia in the America and Western world.

Sadly, it was simply a trade off for economic and political gain superbly orchestrated between the superpowers, the United States the Soviet Union, and the People' s Republic of China. Sadly, the South Vietnam was used as merchandise in this exchange. For the U.S, triangular diplomacy and realpolitik successfully achieved the intended goals. The Sino-U.S normalization process began, and the two countries set up liaison offices in each other's capital cities after President Nixon and Chairman Mao's meeting. Shortly thereafter, many giant U.S corporations mustered themselves into the PRC and bilateral trade improved throughout for decades. The U.S market was also inundated with products made in China. U.S Capitalists were very happy to exploit the huge profitable market in China after for decades of closed door hostility.

Thereby, as a consequence, in Tet-Offensive 1968, the South Vietnam troop continued to be outgunned by the North Vietnam troop and thus at Harriman conspiracy toward combat disadvantage; as including the heavy and unwieldy for a little Vietnamese for a Garant M-I and Thompson. Meanwhile the North Vietnam was being provided the AK-47 (Soviet) and AK-50 (China). All were assault riffle by his patrons. During the enemy Tet Offensive of 1968 the crisp, rattling sounds of assault riffle echoing in Saigon and some other cities seemed to make a mockery of the weaker, single shots of Garants and Carbines M-I fired by stupefied friendly troops.

The New Legion

HISTORY of ARVN: After WWII, OSS already transformed by new-named CIA which focused on the Republic of Vietnam Armed Forces, created by the United States in 1955, the ARVN was the land force component in RVNAF, which included a Navy and Air force. The ARVN' mission was to neutralize North Vietnam's People' Army of Vietnam (PAVN) and its southern ally, the National Liberation Front (NLF) also known as the Viet Cong. Because the nature of the war (CIP) and the independent is not for free exerted the US transformed the ARVN becoming "the New legion Forces" as I dare say, originated from the first Vietnamese military force created by a Western nation (French colonialist) to fight Vietnamese opponents dates from 1879. In that year, the French organized the Regiment "de Tirailleurs Annamites" (the Annamites Rifles) in Saigon; four year later, a companion unit, the Regiment de Tirailleurs Tonkinois (the Tonkin Rifles) was formed in Hanoi.

Meanwhile the ghost Skull and Bone's sharp-instrument was Mike Mansfield, his ghost [witch-hunt] was believed to haunt hovering over into Vietnam-War's a major human-artificial disaster. Mansfield, the laconic senator from Montana whose nonpartisan independence of thought and personal integrity won him the respect of Democrats and Republicans alike, had proven before to be a man of insight into Asians affairs. In 1944 as a young congressman and former professor of Far Eastern history, he had been dispatched by President Roosevelt [in fact by the WIB' Bones] on a fact-finding mission in China. His report that Communist strength was impressive, and not limited to revolutionary ideologues, raised eyebrows in Washington but proved prophetic as in the goal of stratagem was already had "Eurasian Great Game".

Almost two decades later, older enough, Mansfield again packed his bag for the Far East at a president's request, but this time his destination was South Vietnam as well as NSC staff member Michael Forrestal – John F Kennedy sent them to South Vietnam for a fresh look at the situation. Mansfield, an early supporter of Diem regime that wasn't Lansdale report that "no South Vietnam leader pro-French can able keeping against the Viet-Minh than Diem remedy". Consequently, NSC 246, President Eisenhower, presented at the meeting with General Collins ambassador to South Vietnam, came to conclusion that canceling the message overthrown Diem which Mansfield continued to support Diem regime on April, 30, 1955.

However later one but skeptical and independent minded, Mansfield was determined to find out for himself what was going on in the American-financed war. The senator declined several official briefings and met instead with American reporters to hear their misgivings about the military and political situation. Upon leaving the South Vietnam, he discarded the farewell statement prepared by the U.S Embassy and delivered one his own, markedly more reserved on the progress of the war. Who know Bone-man Mansfield was Kennedy's political opponent?

Together with M-Forrestal, NSC staff painted a much gloomier picture for the president Kennedy. The son of the first secretary of defense, [James Forrestall] a Skull and Bones member, he had been an aide to A-Harriman, working on the Marshall Plan, from Wall Street to work on Vietnam aiming the CIP's objective." On February 1963, M Forrestal told Kennedy to expect a prophecy as "**a costly and long war**". The struggle for Vietnamese independent was fast becoming an "American-War" but personally I dared said "Combat Training Field exercise" limited out of Ho Chi Minh trail– the infliction of pain and suffering because the WIB raised serious questions about the nature of U.S involvement in Southeast Asia.

Orchestrated by Mike Mansfield, if he was chilly in Saigon, he was icy in Washington. His report to Congress took alarming note of the fact that after seven years and $2 billion [surplus materiel and cast off WWII U.S weapons] Vietnam appeared less stable and its government less popular than 1955. To pursue the present course, he warned his colleagues could involved an expenditure of American lives and resources on a scale which would bear little relationship to the interests of the United States or, indeed, to interests of the people of Vietnam (politically, talk one way do another way, and the Lying-Liars who tell them, this book tells it like it is Ostrich Policy)

An angry President Kennedy attacked Mansfield's report as defeatist, "For us to withdraw," Kennedy told reporters, "would mean a collapse not only of South Vietnam but Southeast Asia… So we are going to stay there." But from that time on Mansfield would persistently challenge succeeding administrations to find a way to extricate the United States from what he saw to be a foreign policy gone awry.

After all, in the profound of their schemes was seeking the cause for U.S combat-troops invaded into South Vietnam, though the "**axiom 2**" wasn't permitted [needed Tonkin Gulf Incident in next year 1964]. The Axe of Evil with his counterpart Soviet was already scrutinized every keyed-up-time planning relating to the coming US invasion by the craps "CIP counter NLF". Meanwhile Harriman plus the son and the father Prescott Bush prohibited the South Vietnam troop pursuit the NVA troops on Harriman's highway [Ho Chi Minh trail] They stood firmly against any forces patrol into Laos to try to find out the size of the military buildup for final purpose the South Vietnam will subjected to be occupied by Hanoi. That means "border restrictions were limiting the effectiveness of military operations in Vietnam" So why Mansfield pretended and Forrestal challenged the MACV statistics on Viet Cong casualties that were being used to assert that the United States side was winning. The ghost Skull and Bones let his counterpart Soviet shall won first on the method of "**On the Strongman Side.**" They point out that no one really knew how many of the 20,000 Viet Cong were killed last year, were only innocent or at least persuadable villagers, in the hindsight South Vietnamese were sympathized with Viet Cong.

Furthermore, the Viet Cong could easily recruit replacements for their actual casualties. Forrestal also raised questions about the numbers of successful constructed strategic hamlets. This program was central to the U.S effort in South Vietnam. It sought to physically resettle the rural population into centralized and fortified hamlets, protecting them from Viet Cong influence, recruitment, or attack. There were several weaknesses in this program, according to Forrestal. I think he was right? Because in this year 1962, the NVA troop was overwhelming our South Vietnam territories-defense through Harriman Super Highway [Ho Chi Minh trail] It created animosity among those who were forcibly displaced, it provided inadequate security from Viet Cong, and there was plenty of mismanagement and corruption on part of South Vietnamese officials, indeed it seemed to me "Skull and Bones might well have to be tested the

"Social Scientists War" – *South Vietnam like a fresh unique model pattern for world wide in future.*

As for Mansfield, I thought indeed, it was distressing on his visit to hear the situation described in much the same terms as on his last visit [in1957]… Vietnam, outside the cities was still an insecure place which is run at least at night largely by the Viet Cong. The government in Saigon is still seeking acceptance by the ordinary people in large areas of the countryside. Out of fear or indifference or hostility the peasants still withhold acquiescence, let alone approval of that government. His pretentious behavior, live modestly praised President Diem but condemned the "handful of paid retainers and sycophants" surrounding and controlling him (implied his brother Nhu) and doubted the ability of the South Vietnamese armed forces to counter any serious aggression from Hanoi. Because with their plots, Saigon's troop were outgunned by the Hanoi's troop – You might imaged: "rattling sounds of AK-47s echoing in the battle seemed to make a mockery of the weaker, single shots of Garants and Carbines M-1 fired by stupefied Saigon's troops. President Thieu, once felt frustrated: "Let our troops took the shower under enemy bullets"

"In short" Mansfield concluded, "it would be well to face the fact that we are once again at the beginning of the beginning" [same NSC staff M .Forrestal' reported to JFK] means bring combat U.S troop into South Vietnam with prospects for success growing daily less likely, the only answer was to begin to retreat from the costly dimensions of American involvement or..?

I'm very sure that "technically, the formal war in Vietnam was being won as 1962 ended" The American military command in Vietnam had been encouraged by Washington to provide overly optimistic assessments of progress that political machinations of President Diem had profoundly dominated the war effort in 'the rural revolutionary deployment pacification hamlet program'. But underneath the optimistic rhetoric of the top command, a few respected civilian and military officials were already beginning to raise serious questions about the progress of the war. Two of the most determined voices of dissent belonged to Mike Mansfield, a new Senate Majority leader, and NSC staff member M .Forrestal that I expressed above.

The New Legion

According the "**axiom 1**", [standpoint's Skull and Bones and WIB members] "there was never a legitimate non-communist government in Saigon" as the result the relationship between U.S and South Vietnam if the worst comes to the worst, the U.S Permanent Government will just have to a bloody end; Because President Diem flatly turned down the conspiracy of "Use Vietnam as a laboratory to develop techniques of counterinsurgency – the CIP." Diem chose to dramatize his complaint by delaying agreement on the commitment for joint "Counter-Insurgency-Project". Obviously A. Harriman said "… With the passage of time, our objectives in Vietnam will become more and more difficult to achieve with Diem in control."

Unsurprisingly, stormed period for Diem regime beginning right of NSC meeting on September, 21, 1960 – U.S ambassador Durbrow influenced by Harriman's secret instruction.(Diem and Ho got big trouble by a conspiracy of silence against the axis of evil's scam) Meanwhile Hanoi was pressurized by KGB, was already complied with a series of established organizations during 1959 to infiltrate to South Vietnam: Group 559, 759, 959, and NLF movement 1960. In South Vietnam the plot of the axis of evil relies too much on coincidence to be convincing: CIA named "Plans and activities of Tran Kim Tuyen Group" In order to obey the instruction from CIA Tuyen secretly organized the team for destroying the elected by ballot in some counties in Gia Dinh province, and Saigon vicinity. In 1960 Tuyen infiltrated in Thailand Embassy attempted steal the secret document but failure. 11/11/1960 a coup d'état took place but aborted – Saigon in chaotic.

I dared say, when Harriman's Highway (Western named Ho Chi Minh Trail, but Hanoi named "Route 559") commences developing in 1959, a group 30, 40 communist infiltrated – 1960-1962 numbers of groups augmented – afterward three regiments of three NVA Division 305, 324, 325 moved south. Therefore more attacks from Communist in the countryside made that situation even worse. The must positive the present of U.S combat troops invaded for fencing off in their anticipated-plot: "CIP"-US side counter "NLF"- Soviet side [National Liberation Front]

A top secret classified message wrote by ambassador Durbrow to Secretary of States Christian Herter in Washington D.C:

"If Diem's position in the country continue to deteriorate as result failure adopt proper political, psychological economic and security measures, it may become necessary for U.S government to begin consideration for alternative courses of action and leaders in order to achieve "our objectives"

But there were so many failed coups occurred with personal supports from Durbrow, his CIA subordinates: Russel Flynn Miller, George Carver, but sure not William Colby took part, nor President Kennedy as well as his vice president Johnson. These conflicted-years between Permanent Government and acted government were not resolved yet thereby the then U.S policy became Indecisiveness, Ineffectiveness, or Impatience.

In reality, after the victory of Dien Bien Phu, Hanoi was undergone so much difficulty. Ho Chi Minh have faced direct struggle by severed weather, drought, flood, famine, bridged road, rail road track destroyed, particularly from 1954 to 1956, a defeat in policy 'land-reform' which gave raged outrage revolution at Nghe An province. Forcibly Ho must order in early 1957 withdraw 100,000 troops from South to North Vietnam. So why South Vietnam have been an entirely calmed-peace during this event 1954-1959 (Stanley Karnow "VN Viking, New York, 1983, page 225) In this event, Ngo Dinh Nhu, political advisor of Diem regime, together with assistance of Sir Robert G Thompson have dropped the spies in Northern Vietnam according to L'Harmattan, Paris "Prisonnier politique au Vietnam". In contrarily CIA, counter-espionage helped KGB to guide his subordinate [Hanoi] to search and destroy them in putting them into jail Ha-Son-Binh prison. The Axis of Evil's scam started in the mid-1959. While the WIB' warlord persuaded the Soviet to pursuit their scam [involved war-game] by their U.S dollar investment that repeated the eve October, 1917 Russia revolutionary government under Aleksandr-Kerensky a U.S loan credit to be spent on war materiel from creditor: WIB and Bones.

We should remembered that it is often forgotten that in 1957 the Soviet Union proposed that both of the Vietnamese governments then in existence be admitted to the United Nations, not to mention that China much preferred the existence of two Vietnams. It is clear that, aside from the Vietnamese parties themselves, the participants at the Geneva Conference of 1954 all preferred a two-state solution as a way to calm down the potential for global confrontation. But in the profound 'War Industries Board's scope have affirmed of a theoretically unified Vietnam in the final declaration of the conference, which was signed by none of the conferees, [in contrast as U.S delegation didn't signed at Geneva Conference with purpose to introduce the practice of the CIP performance] significantly left the question of the legitimate government of such a unified Vietnam to the vague vicissitudes of an election to be held after two years which was a diplomatic way of painting over national enthusiasm with Cold War realism that the masterminded Harriman have introduced in U.S universities with 'Three Axioms"(The Vietnam-War, by Keith W Taylor, Cornell University of Michigan, Quarterly Review, Ann-Arbor, fall 2004) in the dominant interpretation of the U.S-Vietnam War. That means United States help Vietnamese to unification their country after the WIB used Vietnam as a laboratory to develop techniques of counterinsurgency, because that sonvabitch: "Freedom is not for Free."

Finally, in the presidential election 2008, Republican candidate John McCain, a famous POW reiterated that "Ho Chi Minh a real **nationalist**" after sixty five years used him a cheat-decoy for stirring the Vietnam war 1945-1975. These events relating to stratagem "Eurasian Great Game" merely testify to the need for a change in the legalize Ho, a true enemy brother to South Vietnam but a true "Nationalist."You want to know the whole truth about this matter... just wait until 50 years anniversary of the Vietnam-War, (United States of America 1965-1973 commemoration 2015-2023) I'm pretty sure that U.S, experience in transcending the Vietnam trauma was one important factor that led glory 58.000 freedom fighters died for the New World Order!

Therefore U.S Permanent Government [Skull and Bones or WIB men] persuaded Soviet Union involved the scam "CIP and NLF" that made the early-advantage in the side of Soviet that so called "on the strongman side" method. Whereas in the South Vietnam, the conventional view of the Diem regime has been that he was incompetent and that Diem was an American lackey. This view is increasingly difficult to sustain. For one thing, President Diem effectively defeated rural insurrections twice, in 1956 and again 1958. It was in response to these achievements that the Permanent Government was panic in his aborted-stratagem 'Eurasian Great Game'. So together with his partner [Soviet Union] urging the communist party in Hanoi made the decision to initiate new war in 1959, not because they considered President Diem vulnerable but, on the contrary, because they decided that they couldn't afford to wait any longer without losing the chance to prevent stabilization [axiom 1] of a non-communist government in Saigon. The WIB [Permanent Government] members decided to support his overthrow exactly because he was no lackey and was resisting [CIP] U.S influence in his government. Diem was made a scapegoat for the WIB frustrations and betrayed by Permanent Government; his fate prefigured that of all South Vietnamese who didn't want a communist system.

William J Rust, "Kennedy in Vietnam" C.Scribner's Sons, New York 1985, page 18 – in the aborted coup, CIA William Colby informed to Ambassador E.Durbrow, in Washington [Kennedy and L B Johnson] want Russel Miller and George Carver hand off the coup" and shortly, Carver put lawyer Hoang Co Thuy in the postal parcel bag out of Vietnam by diplomat-way in MATS (Military Air Transport Service.) In my view point, some journalists gave in their interests to portray every aspect of the long struggle in the worst possible light, and indeed in some cases to falsify what they had to say about it. "U.S Government and the Vietnam War", Gibbons, page 161, NSC meeting on August, 31. 1963 – A coup overthrow Diem aborted, L.B Johnson fumed Durbrow and his subordinates and U.S should better continued to support Diem regime. And Paul Kattenburg, Vietnam Task Force research Head proposed: "U.S should have honorable withdrawal." Unsurprisingly, it's not too long he was fired in January 1964 by the pressure from Permanent Government. Kattenburg expressed: "There was not a single person there that know what he was talking about. (Because Kennedy encircled by WIB and Skull and Bones men around, also Kennedy wasn't a real policymaker) They didn't know Vietnam. They didn't know the past. They had forgotten the history. They simply didn't understand the identification of nationalism and communism. I thought, God, we're walking into a major disaster." Therefore it seemed to in hindsight

The New Legion

that the U.S policy [the then Kennedy administration] implied: secure axiom "indecisiveness" – "ineffectiveness" – "impatience"

Diarist McNamara, in his "In retrospect, Tragedy and Lesson of Vietnam", at Chapter-3 title "The Fateful of 1963" He assumed that Washington agreed for a coup? It seemed to me: *"Lies! And the lying liars who tell them!"* Kennedy, Johnson, and Robert Kennedy were still supported Diem to the last minutes (reviewed Message Mc-George Bundy to Lodge, on 30/October/1963, CAS 79407 in the Chapter-1) After created a Neutral Laos agreement for -1 stand for offering a Hanoi freeway to south invasion, Harriman influenced his coterie: Roger Hillman Jr., George Ball to activate a coup overthrow Diem. This order named "DEPTEL, 243 or Cable 243 sent to Lodge No JFK, 177-10001-10454. This message was declassified on 20 April 1998 after two year Harriman went to the Hell; this message was against U.S constitution, un-American, un-transparency, un-sustainability, and un-consensus, because Secretary of State, Sir Dean Rush didn't sign but George Ball. And General Maxwell Taylor's diary, "Swords and Plowshares": a small group of anti-Diem activist performed an end-run by passing a head of department. Buddhist leaders in the CIA's trap were optimistic the President Diem could be overthrown within six months and were organized for a struggle of several months. Absolutely, I'm not among the self-loathing Americans who notice people in other countries looking to us for leadership and see nothing but neocolonialism and imperialism – by a tentative list of men who they would like to see in the government if Diem were overthrown, it included few younger generals like puppets. Frederick Nolting former Saigon ambassador in his book, "From Trust to Tragedy" in conclusion Harriman was equally a real U.S policymaker in his plot neutralization Laos in 1962. VOA and Saigon radio station (Cabot Lodge) must announced a pack of lies right overthrew Diem by placing blame squarely on his young brother Nhu, his political advisor.

"Lodge in Vietnam, a patriot abroad", writer Anne E. Blair, Yale University Press, New Haven, 1995 "The storm has many eyes". A personal narrative New York, 1973; that I thought it has two eyes, one Kennedy and one Permanent Government that means the conflict between 'Acting government and Permanent government'. According

Anne Blair, page 62, Lodge account for Thuan, Defense Minister might be replaced Diem. Thuan would succeed Diem and Lodge had even chosen for Thuan a revealing title, that of Prime minister, not President. And Blair bitter included: "In less hectic times, Thuan's report might well have been regarded as treachery and self-seeking… Meanwhile Harriman, a freewheeling diplomat, and a Skull and Bones founder firmly expressed to Buu-Hoi, ambassador to Maroc; "He want Buu Hoi replaced Diem." While he was U.S Ambassador at large, recruited Buu Hoi and William Porter who will be surveyed the "Phoenix Program" executed by William Colby in the future. Porter will be Lodge's deputy ambassador given supervision over all civilian pacification activities as a result of similarly another-next disaster in Iraq by bloodbath between Shiite and Sunny– while U.S forces reaching the Iraq "border and stop," causing meditation revenge between religious Shiite and Sunny; so why people called Iraq and Vietnam's war were similarly. Though Porter, a thirty-year veteran of the Foreign Service was new to Vietnam and Asia. Then the rumor spreading over Saigon has it "unless they leave the country, there is no power on earth that can prevent the assassination of Madame Nhu, her husband [Mr. Nhu] and his brother, Mr. Diem."

At last, President Diem escaped the tanks ringing the presidential palace, but he couldn't escape a violent death at the hands of rebel officers pressed by CIA [A Harriman]. However in my perception "if President Diem was stayed in presidential palace He should be protected his physical with any price that CIA must take care about that. Typically, the only one certain the president Kennedy must be assassinated because the Skull and Bones scam with his counterpart Soviet Union – with the passage of time [keyed-up-time] his objective of CIP in Vietnam will become more and more difficult to achieve with President Kennedy in the seat of power." Though J.F.K beefed up defense spending for interest of WIB members, but not enough, Kennedy didn't believe in military confrontation as the way to deal with the communist world; rather he engaged in intense back-channel diplomacy. His Inaugural commitment to "oppose any foe" in the world:

The New Legion

"We must face the fact that the United States is neither omnipotent nor omniscient, that we are only 6% of the world's population, that we cannot impose our will upon the other 94% of mankind, that we cannot right every wrong or reverse each adversity, and that therefore there cannot be an American solution to every world problem"

Below here some verbatim evidence report, President Diem cabled to Cabot Lodge:

- Diem: *"Some units have made a rebellion and I want to know, what is the attitude of the United States?"*

- Lodge: *"I do not feel well enough informed to be able to tell you, I have heard the shooting but I'm not acquainted with all the facts; also it is 4.30 A.M in Washington and the U.S government cannot possibly have a view"*

- Diem: *"But you must know some general ideas; after all, I am a chief of State; I have tried to do my duty. I want to do now... what duty and good sense required... I believe in duty above all"*

- Lodge: *"You have certainly done your duty, as I told you only this morning: I admire your courage and your great contributions to your country. No one can take away from you the credit for all you have done. Now I am worried about your physical safety. I have a report that those in charge of the current activity offer you and your brother safe conduct out of the country if you resign. Had you heard this?"*

- Diem: *"No (a pause) you have my telephone number"*

- Lodge: *"Yes! If I can do anything for your physical safety, please call me!"*

- Diem: *"I am trying to reestablish order!"*

The report of Diem's death, flashed to Washington, caught Kennedy in a meeting with General Maxwell Taylor and other aides. Kennedy leaped to his feet and, as Taylor later recalled, "rushed from the room with a look of shock and dismay on his face. "Soon afterward, the White house requested further information from Lodge who directed Conein to see General Minh, head of the coup. Conein, who had gone home to bed after the long period nervous, returned to staff headquarters – less to gather intelligence than to scold Minh for inventing a lame alibi.

- Minh: They committed suicide
- Conein: Where?
- Minh: Well, they were at a Catholic church, and…
- Conein: Listen, this is your affair, but I'll tell you something as a Catholic. If a priest holds

Mass for him tonight, everybody is going to know that they didn't commit suicide.

Therefore, your story doesn't sound right.
- Minh: Would you like to see them? We have them here.
- Conein: No. There's a one-in-a-million chance that people will believe your story. But if the

truth gets out, I don't want to be blamed for leaking it.

This dialogue drawing to conclusion by the French proverb that agent 019, Conein stated:

"On ne fait pas d'omelette sans casser les oeufs" (no one fried the eggs without their broken)

On November 22, 1963, Kennedy's assassination, which occurred only three weeks after -ward would be exhaustively investigated by official commissions. But neither the American nor South Vietnamese government ever conducted a public inquiry into Diem's death.

At the time, Saigon welcomed his downfall. Crowds tore up his portrait was the same Saddam Hussein and slogans. Political prisoners, many scarred by torture, emerged from jails. The city's nightclubs reopened with a vengeance. In the countryside, peasants demolished the strategic hamlets. Elated and unrepentant, Lodge invited the insurgent generals to his office to congratulate them on their victory, which was his triumph as well. A few days later, he cabled Kennedy: "The prospects now are for a shorter war"… You think so? Americans were hailed wherever they went. Convinced that the U.S had engineered the coup the usually reserved citizens of Saigon responded with smiles, waves, and applause for American walking about among the celebrations. Lodge was regarded as a hero. More than one Vietnamese [know how political sphere] was heard to say that if an election for president were held today, Lodge would win in a landslide?

The new Saigon government had taken some positive steps to consolidate its support and reduce the authoritarianism of its processor, Lodge report. But the new leadership was inexperienced and fragile, (but in contrast, the WIB members expected for easier eradicated GVN later on)

According J.F.K Library: National Security File, Meetings & Memoranda series, box 317: Meetings on Vietnam, 10/29/63 *"We maintained clandestine contact with them throughout the planning and execution of the coup and sought to review their operational plans and proposed new government... For military coup d'état against Ngo Dinh Diem, the US must accept its full share of responsibility."*

Firstly: successful in overthrowing the Diem government then move U.S combat forces into South Vietnam and put in a government of our own choosing. Thus, as nine-year rule of Diem came to a bloody end, our complicity in his overthrow heightened our responsibility and our commitment in a essentially leaderless Vietnam, because Permanent Government will dissolved South Vietnam later according to the 'axiom-1' "Have we a meditation on the causes of Vietnam-War's evils?" For this Axis of Evil: "Freedom and unification were not for free, and what we get ...what we shall paid" like United States did exerted in the past.

"Two different Wars, One Destructive Parallel" One said Vietnam and Iraq-War look very similar? Yes at some points, that the civil wars, two true brother-enemies, but weapons were not made from their country but from the axis of evil [U.S and Soviet Union]; how hope and vanquished reality, because hatred and bitterness have never generated anything really good in the end. I did not believe that the war was at a moral level sufficiently low to require civil resistance. The war, as I understood it then, was not in itself an evil; if there was evil, I thought it was in how ineptly it was being conducted and in the consequences of this ineptitude. The most unfortunately conspiracy of silence based on an English economical scientist named the Malthus doctrine "military support economic" – destruction and rebuild, and build and demolition. This conjunction of German Carl Von Clausewitz (1780-1831) once said: "Policy is the guiding intelligence and war only the instrument, and not vice versa." Sadly, this theory explained U.S policy toward the Iraq and Vietnam-War.

For the people of South Vietnam, the about face of their only friend and ally during the time they needed them most, was a terrifying, shocking and painful experience. When initial emotions subsided, they began to grasp the cruel reality of politics, that it was much easier for the America to coerce and squeeze the GVN, than to confront three obstinate adversaries, the Soviet, the PRC and the North Vietnam. Also, it was politically and economically beneficial to appease the three former foes – the GVN had nothing to offer after the war. U.S. policymakers as A. Harriman and George H.W. Bush knew full well that America credibility would, no doubt, decline sharply as a consequence of its actions. But the American-First is a capitalistic business driven society, and the bottom line of a profit-loss report has always been very important.

I'm not written in condemnation of the United States decision to abandon the South Vietnam in the battlefields more than three decades ago, nor it is written to vindicate the leaderships of the GVN, but is written only to set the records straight, Vietnamese citizens who left the GVN in April 1975 have become Americans, (left behind five Generals committed suicide as General Nguyen Khoa Nam, Le Van Hung, Nguyen Van Hai, Pham Van Phu, and Le Nguyen Vy and so many officers and troops committed suicide) who have accepted the tragic disaster of 1975 as their fate – it is a concept deeply rooted in traditional Vietnamese culture. The U.S. and its ally, the GVN, were never defeated military by the communist North Vietnam as you finished this book. Instead, the Skull and Bones was the architect of a new geo-strategy at the time global politics needed a change, and America's socio-political situation must be reconciled.

I'm so angry, throughout this time, many studies and research projects have been performed by military and civilian historians and scholars, and many recent revelations have proven contradictory to previous prejudicial and hasty conclusions regarding the fall of Saigon. "Skull and Bone was already explained on School and University not in Battlefield!

The New Legion

Biased reports, and Fighting to the End

You might hear of the Vietnam War, but don't assume that the others would know too; because that great epic war has been won by "all-South Vietnamese-ground-forces" it was rarely mentioned by the bias-double standard-Western-media. After 35 years whose bothers to know that war story! On this "The New Legion" book, I am going to assemble some fragments of those significant battles. You will read less but see more. It is unwise to promote, laud, or glorify war-stories, but on the other side of blood and gore battles, one will witness the sacrifices, unselfishness, and heroism of countless simple, ordinary men who fight the Evils in defending South Vietnam. Those battles were also the substantial examples of how the Vietnam War should be conducted: Let us (ARVN) do the "dirty jobs." We fight the Viet Cong our own way, not the rich boys' way. You (Uncle Sam) stay out! Provide us your "real" weapons and air power support (not the cast off World War II surplus antique guns and aircrafts training type) We would kick Hanoi regime's ass at our best such as An-Loc, Kontum, Quang Tri … It should be noticed that the ARVN ground forces at An Loc have been armed with the "humble" M-72s, no good for firing at Soviet heavy battle Tanks, but it works only when firing at the right spot and with luck, and home-made, modified anti-tank "mines." Did you believe our ARVN was outgunned at Tan-Canh battle: To defend and protect the camp effectively, it requires a solid, defensive system of perimeter-layers, plus around the clock of artillery and air power support, the kind of fire support that helped USMC at Khe Sanh Base remained intact during the long siege of Communist-forces, another note, it was the first time at Tan Canh battle, North Vietnamese communist forces used anti-tank missile Sagger AT-3 (produced by Soviet 1972) Controlled by electrical wire, the missile can penetrates 400 mm steel thick with the maximum range of 2,500 meters. With the advantage of new effective weapon, the Communist forces could destroyed a large number of ARVN' armor vehicles and bunkers from a far distance (in fact they did) while the defense units were still waiting as usual for the T-54s to come closer for a better shot (believing that the Viet Cong has only B-40 and B-41 & dash these anti-tank rockets have only the effective range of 100 meters) React spontaneously, General Ngo Dzu' contingency plan of using B-52 to relieve Tan Canh's siege was also never considered by John Paul Vann because the secret order from General Haig in Pentagon ROE' strict-indiscipline. Why? Because at this difficult phase of Vietnam War, Uncle Sam was in the process of U.S troops pulling-out for "**axiom-3**" No more Yankee ground troops around, but only the advisory teams with business '**un-war-uniform**'. And now, brace yourselves, you are descending into hell: And the Battle of An-Loc: The sun had just come up in An Loc, the Capital city of Binh Long or Kontum for COSVN in South Vietnam in the masterminded Harriman's scope for helping Viet Cong on Paris Peace Talk on predominantly position. It was 13 April 1972.

The author, at the time was an U.S. Army infantry officer serving as an adviser with the Army of South Vietnam (the ARVN) was on the roof of a building putting up a radio antenna. It had been a relatively quiet night with regard to enemy probes and ground attacks, but there had been a significant increase in the number of incoming rockets and artillery rounds. The ARVN infantry Task Force that the author advised had witnessed just moved into the city the day before.

That was Major Raymond Haney had joined the regimental Task Force after the original advisory team members had been wounded and subsequently evacuated during the withdrawal from the north. The replacement advisory team arrived in An Loc by helicopter on 12 April to find the city nearly panicked. Artillery rounds and rockets were falling steadily on the city, and the helicopter that brought the officers into the city hovered only long enough for them to jump off the aircraft into a freshly dug hole in the city soccer field as artillery rounds impacted near the landing zone. During the evening, the South Vietnamese soldiers prepared for the inevitable North Vietnamese attack, and they were up early for what day would bring. As I finished installing a radio antenna, someone heard a tremendous explosion and ran down the stairs to the front of the building. Frantic South Vietnamese soldiers ran by shouting: "**Thiet Giap!**" meant "**Tanks coming**" One had never heard this phrase before, but as the soldier ran around the corner of the building, it became all too apparent that the cry meant "tank" advancing down the street from the north was a line of North Vietnamese T-54 tanks! So began the Battle of An

Loc, described by Douglas Pike as the single most important battle in the war."

For the next four months, a desperate struggle raged between 3 NVA divisions (estimated at over 30,000 troops) and the greatly outnumbered South Vietnamese defenders, but significantly assisted by their U.S. Army advisers. The 66-day siege of An Loc would result in horrendous losses on both sides and would culminate with South Vietnamese forces blocking the North Vietnamese thrust toward the South Vietnamese capital in Saigon. Although this battle occurred after the high point of American commitment in Vietnam, American forces were active and key participants in the action. The American advisory effort had become increasingly more important as American combat troops were withdrawn. During the Battle of An Loc, American advisers on the ground, working in consonance with American air power, would prove to be the key ingredients to the South Vietnamese Victory.

The Battle of An Loc, although one of the key battles in the entire Vietnam War, has been discussed only briefly in the literature about the war, the purpose of this study is to examine the battle in detail to determine the extent of the American contribution to the victory. This battle will then be compared with the performance of the South Vietnamese forces against the North Vietnamese invasion of 1975 in an effort to assess the impact of an absence of American participation in the latter action. The focus of the study will be on the American military's role in thwarting the 1972 North Vietnamese invasion; it will not debate the relative merits and demerits of the "Vietnamization" process or the efficacy of the eventual American withdrawal from South Vietnam for the merely objective dispensable all out of date deleted military materiel on the spot.

QUOTES ON BATTLE OF AN-LOC

Binh Long is not the symbol of one battle, one front of Military Region 3 and 3rd Corps. Binh Long is a national symbol as well as an International symbol. The Binh Long victory is not a victory of South Vietnam over Communist North Vietnam only, the Binh Long victory is also a victory of the Free World over the theory of People war National Liberation Front, Revolutionary War of World

Communism. "An Loc was the Verdun of Vietnam, where Vietnam received as in baptism the supreme consecration of her will"

The truly heroic South Vietnamese defense of An Loc and Kontum has succeeded although Hanoi spent three of the best NVA divisions trying to take the little town, but failed.

(*Le vent de L'histoire va-t-it tourner au Vietnam? An Loc c'est le Verdun de l'offensive de Giap. An Loc est assiege par 15,000 reguliers North Vietnamiens. Et c'est la que Giap est "tombe sur un os." Les chars russes brulent. Le vent de l'histoire est-it en train de tourner a An Loc?)* **(Paris Match magazine, issue 1206, June 6, 1972)**

A VIETNAMESE RESPONSE TO MCNAMARA: War was lost in Washington! Like America's Vietnam vets, a Vietnamese in America are furious about former Secretary of Defense Robert McNamara's new book, *"In Retrospect: Tragedy and Lessons of Vietnam"* But the similarities and there: **American vets feel betrayed by the former Pentagon boss, a real Bone-man McNamara** who for twenty years led a lavish lifestyle in complete disregard of the 58,000 American deaths his self-proclaimed mistakes caused. We Vietnamese, by contrast, are furious that he now alleges South Vietnam's political instability, corruption and inability to defend Vietnamese for what he claims was an un-winnable war, objective "axiom-1." Before refuting these arguments, I should point out that U.S. global policy during the Cold War was to "containment" communist expansion at all costs. There was barely visible through the mist of global atmosphere, but in the Permanent Government was just sparred political jobs for WIB' Bones interest by Containment that showed-up by their division Germany, Korea, and Vietnam becoming two-nation-states. As result, that domino theory craps was so compelling it led to U.S. involvements in Korean and Vietnam, but not for Skull and Bones Dynasty. For McNamara to claim that he could have reversed it merely by recommending disengagement from Vietnam even when Russia and Communist China were actively supporting the "war of liberation" only underscores his enormous arrogance. McNamara also chose to mention the one U.S. move that provided the context for the withdrawal in 1973 -- President Nixon's 1972 visit to China following the breakdown of relations between the two communist giants according order from Permanent Government.

The New Legion

As for the instability of the Government of South Vietnam, the U.S. has largely itself to blame. Not only was it heavily involved in the overthrow of the Diem government on November 1, 1963, but McNamara himself, reportedly acting on President Johnson's instructions, [I'm surely not right but just Evil] openly hailed General Nguyen Khanh as a hero for staging a successful counter-coup that deposed the plotting five head-generals. And it was then-U.S. Ambassador General Maxwell Taylor who subsequently encouraged the rebellion of the Montagnard tribes to discredit and ultimately oust General Khanh, whom Taylor intensely disliked. Ironically, McNamara echoes his former media and Congressional critics by singling out South Vietnamese corruption as a prime poisoned factor behind America's withdrawal. Yet it was U.S. officials themselves whose patronage system of buying obedience in exchange for favors that nurtured and legitimated that corruption in the first place.

As a Project Delta pilot during the war, I can speak to the Army of the Republic of Vietnam (ARVN)'s so-called incapacity to defend itself. Our victories at Quang Tri, Kontum And An Loc during North Vietnam's Great Offensive in 1972 amply demonstrated that we could beat back North Vietnam's regular divisions in conventional warfare, though provided we received adequate supplies and air support. However, because Hanoi was hard to comprehend the meaning "Decent-Interval" consequently Hanoi led 100,000 barbecued NVA troops in the "Great East-Offensive-1972" Hanoi had to wait for Paris Talk 1973 and the President of GVN said "All the United States citizens get out my Vietnam country at once" That is the real time Hanoi will overran entirely South Vietnam. Meanwhile received about a brand new batch of 700 million-tons sophisticated weapon from her Soviet patronage for three objectives: (1) accomplished axiom-1, (2) Cambodia Invasion, (3) Defense Red China given a lesson, which the War Industries Board authority paid for that and Soviet manpower manufactured those stuffs

The Battle of An Loc, for instance, pitted some 6,350 ARVN men against a force three that size. During the peak of the battle, we had access to only one 105 mm howitzer to provide close support while the enemy attack was backed by an entire artillery division. Whereas we had no tanks, the enemy had two armored regiments. Yet ARVN won. As General Paul Vanuxem, a French veteran of the Indochina War wrote in 1972 after visiting the liberated city of An Loc:*"An-Loc was the Verdun of Vietnam, where Vietnam received as in baptism the supreme consecration of her will."*

"When military power is applied, is should meet the test of clarity of mission and efficiency," Defense Secretary James Schlesinger once observed. "That was the case in Grenada, but it clearly was not the case in Lebanon." Nor was it the case in Vietnam. Indeed, the real flaw of the Vietnam War was the lack of a clear objective on the side and thus a resulting confusion regarding how to achieve it.

In retrospect, the U.S. could have achieved its policy of containment had it adopted one of two alternative strategies either carry the war to North Vietnam and try to destroy Hanoi's will to fight; or support the government of South Vietnam in fighting a long and protracted war in the South. While the first alternative carried the risk of intervention by Russia and China, that risk was mitigated by the animosity between the two countries, and the fact that neither was threatened directly by the destruction of North Vietnam's war-making machine. Since the U.S. lacked the guts to adopt this option, the second alternative could have been implemented in conjunction with an intensive "Vietnamization Program". In other words, the Vietnam War was winnable and should have been won because in war, as General McArthur once said, "there are no substitutes for victory" So why Permanent Government disliked McArthur and Westmoreland.

In my view, McNamara's book adds nothing new to the already vast library on the Vietnam War. On the other hand, perhaps I should refrain from casting stones at a man who confesses his mistakes in writing. After all, a written confession can be a lucrative way of easing one's conscience.

-By the spring of 1972 most Americans thought the war in Vietnam was over. President Richard Nixon had made good on his promise to withdraw American combat troops from South Vietnam. The withdrawals had all but concluded, and only a handful of American ground units remained while air power supported had been considerably downsized. For USAF air-lifters in the one remaining C-130-Wing, flying in Vietnam had been reduced primarily to picking up American troops and cargo and delivering them to the coastal ports for loading aboard ships and airplanes for the return to the United States. But while America was in the process of withdrawing from the war as "Vietnamization" took over, the Communist countries' support of the North Vietnamese was in full swing. Four bombs-less years had allowed the North Vietnamese to rebuild their military after the tremendous losses they had suffered in 1968 and 1969 in the wake of their disastrous Tet Offensive. A new generation of North Vietnamese soldiers had been trained and equipped with the most sophisticated weapons in the Soviet arsenal. Though they had no way of knowing it, the men of the 374th Tactical-Airlift-Wing were about to have what historian Ray Bowers calls "airlift's finest hour"

-In early April, 1972 NVA troops poured into South Vietnam's Tay Ninh Province from Cambodia. The heavily-armed Communists rolled through one town after another as they drove south along Highway 13 toward their goal, the South Vietnamese capital of Saigon. Though the South Vietnamese troops fought well, they were outnumbered and outgunned as the NVA used human wave tactics to overrun Loc Ninh. By April 7 the NVA had reached An Loc, a town about 50 miles northwest of Saigon. There, the South Vietnamese government forces and their American advisors were made their stand. And at An Loc, USAF C-130 crews earned a place in history. Initially, the ARVN' forces at An Loc were supplied by US Army and South Vietnamese helicopters; but as the NVA built up strength around the city, the brought in the largest proliferation of antiaircraft guns ever seen in South Vietnam. For years the Iron Curtain countries had been shipping 12,7MM, 14.5, 23MM, 37MM and 57MM antiaircraft guns to North Vietnam. The army attacking An Loc had them all, and it was not long before the fallacy of the concept of helicopter re-supply was revealed to the world. Helicopter re-supply at An Loc was deemed "impractical" and the South Vietnamese forces turned to airdrop. The first airdrop over An Loc was flown by VNAF C-123 and C-119 crews. The Vietnamese Air Force flew their mission in the daytime and each flight received tremendous amounts of ground fire. Low-altitude missions were almost suicidal so many of the VNAF' pilots approached their drop zones at 5,000 feet. From that altitude the bundles drifted with the wind, and as often as not landed in enemy territory. After the loss of two C-123s, the VNAF discontinued low-level drops. Because the high altitude drops were fruitless, they were halted as well. The Military Assistance Command, Vietnam decided to give the responsibility for the re-supply of An Loc to the USAF C-130 crews who were still flying in Vietnam, the men of the 374th Tactical Airlift Wing. From its base at Ching Chang Kuan AB, Taiwan, the 374th maintained an operating location in South Vietnam at Tan Son Nhut.

On the night of April 14, three 374th crewmembers were briefed for airdrop missions over An Loc the next morning. After an initial mission delay, the three C-130Es took off from Tan Son Nhut for the short flight to An Loc. The first crew over the Drop-Zone, commanded by Major Robert Wallace of the 776th TAS, took hits but released their load. The second crew elected to approach the Drop-Zone from a different direction. Captain Bill Caldwell's crew was 30 seconds from the Drop-Zone when they encountered a barrage of antiaircraft artillery fire. Their C-130 was riddled by machine gun fire which killed the flight engineer, TSgt Jon Sanders, and wounded the copilot, Lt John Herring, and the navigator, Lt. Richard Lentz. A fire broke out on the cargo compartment. The loadmasters, SSgt Charlie Shaub and Airman First Class Dave McAleece fought the fire. The heat was so intense that Shaub burned his hands on the hot metal of his fire extinguisher. Shaub jettisoned the cargo - two pallets exploded right after they left the airplane. The ground fire had knocked out two engines and severed the hydraulic lines leading to the landing gear. Shaub and McAleece manually extended the gear with a hand-crank. While they were in the landing pattern, the third engine lost power, but Caldwell managed to get the airplane down safely. Caldwell and Shaub were awarded the Air Force Cross. Shaub was also selected to receive the Air Force Sergeants Association's William H Pitsenbarger Award. The third airplane was unable to drop because of problems with its ramp and door. Though both Wallace and Caldwell dropped in the vicinity of the DZ, none of the cargo from either airplane was recovered by friendly forces. Colonel Andrew Iosue, the 374th Commander, called for a change in tactics. The wing Stan Eval pilot, Major Ed Brya, and navigator, Major Robert

The New Legion

Highley, worked out a plan calling for the airplanes to approach the Drop-Zone at tree-top level at 250 knots, then pop-up to the 600 foot release altitude when about two minutes out. On April 16, two C-130 crews, including one with Iosue, Brya and Highley, flew drop missions over An Loc. Though the aircrews thought they identified the drop zone, it turned out that they had been given the wrong coordinates and the loads were not recovered

-**On April 18th another attempt was made.** Captain Don "Doc" Jensen's crew began taking hits as they slowed to drop speed. One engine was shot out, another set on fire and the right wing began burning. Jensen managed to put the burning C-130 down in a swamp near Lai Khe. US Army helicopters were in the vicinity and saw the airplane go down. Within minutes, the helicopters were laying down covering fire to keep the enemy away from the burning airplane while one of their number-landed to pickup the crewmembers, all of whom had survived the crash landing. The helicopter returned the jubilant crewmembers to Tan Son Nhut. By this time the toll stood at two C-123s and a C-130 shot down over An Loc while the first load of cargo had yet to be received by the defenders in the besieged city.

In an attempt to supply the camp, the 374th turned to the GRADs method, a ground-radar directed airdrop method that had been used to drop ten and fifteen thousand pound bombs in Vietnam since 1969. But GRADS required high altitude, low-opening parachute devices and the Vietnamese riggers were unfamiliar with the technique. The restraining cords holding the parachutes closed were too weak and the parachutes were opening prematurely while some of the devices that were supposed to cut the cords failed to work at all. The GRADS method was proving as futile for the Americans as it had been for the South Vietnamese C-123 crews. Next, the 374th Wing turned to night drops. On the first two nights, the blacked-out C-130 crews enjoyed the element of surprise and managed to get their loads close enough to the target that the South Vietnamese managed to recover most of them. AC-130 gun-ships provided covering fire. Many if not most of the AC 130 pilots had come from tactical airlift units and were familiar with the airdrop techniques. But even though the C-130 crews enjoyed some surprise, the enemy was putting up barrages of antiaircraft artillery fire. On the third night of drops the fourth

C-130 over the drop zone entered "a wall of fire" and crashed a mile from the drop zone. Someone began planning for a massive 10-airplane drop mission in daylight, but Colonel Iosue thought it was plain suicidal. His view was shared by the Forward Air Controllers who were working targets around the city. Because only a portion of the C-130 crews at CCK were drop qualified, the missions over An Loc meant that the same people were bearing the brunt of the burden. The crews were well aware that each mission might be their last. They wore flak suits and helmets while the loadmasters filled the airplane garbage can with tie-down chains and climbed inside it while over the drop zone.

Since each C-130 crew included two loadmasters, one has often wondered how the second one protected himself for a week the night drops continued, with the C-130 crews encountering heavy fire on each mission. But the recovery of the loads was not good, with only about 10% being positively recovered. More than half of the drop planes took hits, and several crewmembers were wounded. On the night of May 3-4 a third C-130 was shot down.

With the night drops proving only marginally successful, the 374th returned to the high altitude GRADS method. The drop crews worked with AC-130 gunship crews who provided winds aloft information to the C-130 navigators from their gun-sight computers. The results were considerably improved over those attained previously, but some parachutes still opened prematurely while others failed to work at all. At the same time, the supply of HALO devices was dwindling. The possibility of returning to low-altitude drops loomed larger out of the mist of the future. But then a new problem arose, one with magnanimous implications for the transport crews. On April 29 a SA-7 surface-to-air missile was fired in Quang Tri province, confirming for the first time that the NVA were now equipped with the deadly shoulder-fired missiles. With SA-7s in South Vietnam, low-altitude airdrop missions were almost unthinkable

Fortunately, the Air Force riggers at CCK had come up with a solution to the problem. In World War II and Korea supplies were often dropped without a parachute attached, and the USAF riggers in 1972 discovered that with the proper amount of packing material, bundles containing even ammunition could be safely dropped using slotted extraction parachutes to stabilize, but not retard the descent of the load. The loads descended four times faster than a similar load suspended beneath a G-12 parachute, and were thus less susceptible to the winds at altitude. As it turned out, the high-velocity drops using the GRADS technique not only allowed the C-130 crews to drop from altitude above the range of the antiaircraft artillery at An Loc and even the SA-7s (which are effective only to about 4,000 feet) they also allowed unprecedented accuracy. Some supplies such as medical materials and fuel proved unsuitable for the high velocity method and had to be dropped using the HALO parachutes, but most items could be delivered without restraining parachutes. Fortunately, the defenders at An Loc had discovered a source of fresh water so ammunition and rations were the primary commodities that had to be airdropped to the defenders.

The high-velocity method was developed just in time, for on May 11 the first SA-7 firings were reported at An Loc. The drop planes were able to operate without fear of the Strella missiles, but the AC-130 gun-ships were considerably effect. Their guns lost their effectiveness at the 10,000 feet altitude that was necessary to avoid the SA-7s. Tactics were worked out for the AC-130 and C-130 crews to fire decoy flares when an SA-7 firing was observed. The heat-seeking missiles would home on the more intense heat of the flares instead of the airplane's exhaust. Four C-130 crews reported SA-7 firings in South Vietnam in May/June 1972, but none were hit. The AC-130s did not fare as well; one airplane was badly damaged on May 12 and another was shot down near Hue in June.

An-Loc was the most trying time of the war for air-lifters in Vietnam, but there were other difficult missions associated with the Easter-Offensive in other parts of the country. USAF C-130 crews were instrumental in the defeat of the NVA attacks on Kontum. The Easter Offensive also brought the first in-country use of MAC, C-141s. Four C-141s were scheduled for in-country airlift operations each day as the MAC transports picked up the slack as the PACAF C-130s were put to work supporting the South Vietnamese combat forces by airdrop and deliveries to forward fields. The MAC transports transported cargo and passengers between the major aerial ports in South Vietnam. On April 30 a C-141 airlifted 394 refugees from Pleiku to Saigon. MAC, C-5s were also heavily involved in the response to the Communist invasion. The huge transports airlifted support equipment for fighter squadrons and B-52 units that were returning to the Pacific in response to the Communist attacks. There was on a crew that carried a half a squadron of 02-Skymaster from Hawaii to Cam Ranh Bay. A major C-5 effort of the time was the airlift of heavy tanks from Japan to Danang to meet North Vietnamese armor that had crossed the DMZ into Northern South Vietnam

"It was a terrible time, but also a glorious time for the air-lifters, particularly the C-130 USAF crews who did their duty over An Loc in spite of the most intense ground fire ever encountered in the Vietnam War in South Vietnam and below another great story"

Battle of Xuan-Loc is also another great story.

Not because many military tacticians, historians, or journalists have praised it for the successful outcome of one ARVN battered Division against four fully equipped NVA Divisions backed with Regiments of tanks and artillery. But all the pundits have missed the point. It was great because the spirit of soldiers who made a stand and fight: In a circumstance when all ARVN senior and junior officers who participated in the battle knew so damn well that they had been betrayed by the US ally; when all the ARVN soldiers under their command had already witnessed the military debacle of their fellow comrades' units from the 1st and 2nd Regional Corps. Imagine when your football team had learned in advance that their game had been set up to lose: **A SELLOUT**, but they still played at their best performance; so all the ARVN soldiers who fought the Battle of Xuan Loc didn't do it for the reasons of Freedom, Liberty, or Democracy. Those embellished terms are just the convenient, demagogic pretexts for the "dirty" foreign politicians or policymakers who used to appeal to the crowds or to promote their party agendas. On those darkest, grieving days of a Cruel April 1975, the ARVN soldiers stood up and fought at Xuan Loc for just a few simple reasons: The pride of their Units' colors, Camaraderie, and Duty.

Are you willing to fight like that in the same circumstance? If not, you can join the battle now on this account in this book!

The New Legion

During the closing days of the 1975, North Vietnamese Offensive, 4 NVA divisions were pitted against a small ARVN force, dug-in astride the rugged hills near Xuan Loc - a town of 30,000 people located along one of the key roads into the capital, Saigon. Advancing in strength down the coastal highway were the NVA 5th, 6th, 7th and 341st Divisions, massed with artillery and T-54 tanks. Defiantly blocking their way were the ARVN 18th Division, Long Khanh provincial forces, and 82nd Ranger-Battalion. On 12 April 1975, the 1st Airborne Brigade, made up of four Airborne Battalions and an Airborne-Artillery Battalion, was moved into the area of operations by helicopter. The battle which followed was unique in many respects for the Vietnam War, involving units of divisional size, devastatingly effective VNAF airpower and sophisticated US-made BLU-82B Daisy Cutter Bomb Live Unit-82s [WSAG gave two warheads of BLU-82 to VNAF] For nearly 2 weeks, the ARVN held Xuan Loc and counterattacked against impossible odds. In contrast to the general impression of total collapse on the part of the ARVN, it was described as 'heroic and gallant' by the South Vietnamese defenders. It was one of the few places where the ARVN, though outnumbered, stood and fought with a tenacity which stunned their opponents. The stand of the ARVN so impressed the rest of the entire South Vietnamese Army, that previously routed, they grew confident again. News reporters were flown in from around the world to witness the battlefield strewn with NVA casualties, repelled in assault after assault with heavy losses. After 12 days and nights of ferocious combat against the NVA forces, the steel defensive line at Xuan Loc (Long Khanh) still held firm. The forces of the NVA 4th Corps engaged in the battle had suffered heavy losses. For this reason the Headquarters of the Ho Chi Minh Campaign hastily changed their plan for the attack on Saigon. The forces of the NVA 3rd Corps in Tay Ninh and 2nd at the Nuoc Trong Base would be used to make the "major effort" to attack and capture Saigon. The NVA 4th Corps would abandon its efforts against Xuan Loc and would become a "reserve force". For this reason, Xuan Loc was no longer a "hot-point," and the Headquarters of ARVN 3rd Corps/Military Region 3 ordered the 18th Infantry Division and all units participating in the Xuan Loc (Long Khanh) battle to retreat to Bien Hoa on 20 April 1975 to establish a new line defending the outer approaches to Saigon. The retreat back to Bien Hoa to assume the new mission was carried out during the night of 20 April 1975.

The ARVN forces defending Saigon was disposed to cover the five main roads leading into Saigon. North of Saigon, the 5th ARVN Division defended against an enemy attack down Highway 13. Northeast of the capital, the 18th ARVN Division held Xuan Loc covering Highway-1 and the city and air base of Bien Hoa. Southeast of Saigon, two Airborne Brigades and a Ranger Group (all at about 50 percent strength) defended against an enemy thrust up Highway-15. Southwest of Saigon, the reactivated and refitted 22nd ARVN Division sat astride Highway-4, the main route from the Mekong Delta to Saigon. Finally, in the northwest, the 25th ARVN Division held Route-1 between Tay Ninh and Saigon. The NVA plan to seize Saigon mirrored the ARVN plan to defend it. NVA General Van Tieng Dung adopted with minor alterations General Tran Van Tra's plan of a five pronged concentric drive on the South Vietnamese capital. Dung remembered that there had been considerable devastation in Saigon during the Tet Offensive. He wanted to prevent that destruction, and more importantly, he did not want to compress the ARVN forces into a "cornered rat" defense inside Saigon. Accordingly, he devised a plan which he hoped would overcome the problems presented by ARVN' dispositions. First, he gave each of his five corps a principal axis of advance. Second, he ordered the corps to attempt to surround or annihilate the ARVN defenders in their outer defensive positions, thus averting a last ditch defense in Saigon itself. Third, he gave his troops five critical targets in Saigon. These were: Independence Palace (the South Vietnamese White House) the headquarters of the JGS (near Tan Son Nhut Air base) Tan Son Nhat Air base itself, the National Police Headquarters, and the headquarters of the Capitol Zone, whose commander controlled troops in and around Saigon. NVA General Dung reasoned that if these installations were captured quickly before serious fighting in Saigon began, the battle for Saigon would be over.

And being North Vietnamese Communists, they had to have a plan for a Great Uprising in Saigon to accompany the Great Offensive. In spite of the fact that a plan for an uprising was totally

The New Legion

unnecessary, and that none of the uprisings planned for Tet 1968 or 1972 had remotely succeeded, the Communists drew up an elaborate plan for political "Ðấu Tranh": "Struggle" involving a "Ðịch Vận": "Proselytizing aims program" among the South Vietnamese people and a "Binh Vận": Open Arms Program (troop proselytized) aimed at the RVNAF. Before the Communist drive on Saigon could begin, the NVA had to undertake two preliminary operations - the seizure of Xuan Loc and the cutting of Highway-4. The Communists wanted to cut Highway-4 to prevent the movements of ARVN reinforcements from the Delta to Saigon and to secure a staging area for a later attack on the capital itself. Xuan Loc was a more significant NVA objective. It anchored the eastern end of the outer defenses of Saigon. In addition, the town controlled the roads from the east to Saigon, Bien Hoa, and Vung Tau, and covered the two big air bases at Bien Hoa and Tan Son Nhut. Both sides considered Xuan Loc to be the key to the defense of Saigon. Neither of these preliminary operations went well. The NVA effort to cut Highway 4 sputtered and faltered, cutting Highway 4 and then being driven off by effective ARVN counterattacks. The battle for Xuan Loc produced one of the epic battles of any of the Indochina wars, certainly the most heroic ARVN stand in Indochina War III. On 9 April, General Dung attacked the 18th ARVN Division (reinforced) with the entire IV NVA Corps consisting of three infantry divisions (eventually reinforced to four) plus tanks and artillery. The fighting featured mass NVA infantry attacks supported by extremely heavy artillery fire (the ARVN troops at Xuan Loc took over 20,000 rounds of artillery and rockets) ARVN held out until 22 April and then had to withdraw. The 18th ARVN Division lost about 30 percent of its strength (almost all its riflemen) while destroying 37 NVA tanks and killing over 5,000 NVA attackers. In this final epic stand ARVN demonstrated for the last time that, when properly led, it had the "right stuff."

From early to mid-April 1975, the South Vietnamese 18th Division, defending the strategic road junction of Xuan Loc, northeast of Saigon, held off massive attacks by an entire North Vietnamese Army corps engaged in a surprise assault to overrun Saigon and quickly end the war. Enduring extremely heavy fighting, they stopped the Communist offensive before being ordered to a retreat and help defend Saigon. While communist forces were guilty of over-confidence, the 18th Division's superb performance was largely the result of the combat skills, prior planning, and inspirational leadership of their commander, Brigadier General Le Minh Dao, who demonstrated that even in South Vietnam's darkest hour; the much-maligned soldiers of the Army of the Republic of Vietnam would fight when led by able officers.

The first artillery shell landed directly on the General's palace. It was a small two-story house, inconspicuous really, despite its pinkish hues. It sat across the road from the province chief's residence, near the Catholic-Church in the middle of the town of Xuan Loc, the capital of Long Khanh province. The General lived, as did many of his South Vietnamese soldiers, in the quiet, somewhat shabby rural town. The round crashed through the roof and exploded in the bedroom, a testimony to the incredible accuracy of the NVA artillerymen. It was immediately followed by a 2000 round bombardment that lasted for precisely one hour. Fortunately, the General was not home.

Awakened by the steady hammering from the enemy batteries, the soldiers of the 18th Division of the Army of the Republic of Vietnam (ARVN) and the remaining Long Khanh provincial forces huddled in their prepared positions on the periphery of the town. The Communist gunners were firing into the city center, unaware that the ARVN had moved to the outskirts to escape the expected artillery barrage. As dawn arrived, the clank of steel treads heralded to appearance of North Vietnamese tanks, followed by waves of infantry, confident of their certain victory. It was 6:40 am on Wednesday morning, the 9th of April 1975.

Despite the crucial role the struggle for Xuan Loc played during the demise of the Republic of Vietnam. Western historians know few precise details about this epic engagement, in which the South Vietnamese 18th ARVN Division and Long Khanh provincial forces held of a series of massive combined-arms attacks by the infantry, armor, and artillery of an entire NVA' Corps. While historians and memoirs frequently mention this major clash of the Vietnam War, what has been published is often inaccurate or erroneous. What is known is this: despite the tremendous setbacks suffered by the South Vietnamese military in 1975, the 18th ARVN Division made a truly

The New Legion

remarkable 12 stand against heavy odds during a time when many other ARVN units broke and ran. Why? What made them different from other ARVN outfits? What made its soldiers not only hold their ground but fearlessly slug it out? How did they withstand the massive artillery barrages and defend against constant tank-led infantry assaults? What effect did their resolute resistance have on the war and on the American evacuation? Most importantly, what decisions turned this quaint provincial capital into the scene of the heaviest combat since An Loc and Quang Tri in 1972?

The answers some twenty-five years later are not easy to obtain, but what made Xuan Loc the focal point for the NVA attack was its strategic location. The city, located 60 kilometers northeast of Saigon, the South Vietnamese capital, controlled the vital road junction of Route 1 and Route 20, the two main paved highways into Saigon from Central Vietnam. With the destruction of South Vietnam's two northern Military Regions in March 1975, Xuan Loc suddenly became a critical node on the improvised defensive line the desperate South Vietnamese were trying to form around Saigon. Most observers realized that whatever slim chance the ARVN had to defend the capital from the encircling enemy army was predicated on holding Xuan Loc. If the Republic of Vietnam forces could make a stand there, a chance remained they could stabilize the situation, regroup their battered military, and save the country from defeat.

The communist leadership in North Vietnam was determined, however, to "strangle the puppets in their lair," before the South Vietnamese could recover. Given the chaos that caused the fall of Danang on 29 March 1975 as pre-preparedness from CIA, implied by the axe of Evil, Le Duc Tho masterminded saw an opportunity to quickly conclude the war with a swift attack on Saigon through bypassed Xuan Loc. They were convinced that another hard blow would crumble the last vestiges of ARVN resistance, and the city's loss would clear the path for a rapid communist advance to the very gates of Saigon, ending the decades-old conflict in one massive assault. To achieve that goal, Le Duc Tho threw their entire 4th Corps together, comprised of three divisions, against the 18th ARVN at Xuan Loc. The 18th Division, however, did not crumble, and Communist dreams of an easy victory withered in the fires of what General

Dung NVA Commander, a battle-scarred veteran who had fought the cream of the French and American armies, called the fiercest battle of his 30-year military career. Instead, the 18th's performance, shouldered at a moment in time when ARVN morale was at rock bottom, resoundingly answered the question asked by so many at the time: Will the ARVN fight? While ultimately the Division was ordered to retreat from the ruined town, their valiant resistance briefly raised the hope that the South Vietnamese might hold off the relentless onslaught of the regulars of the People's Army of the Vietnam (PAVN) long enough either for the rainy season to bring the offensive to a halt, or for covert diplomatic efforts to achieve a ceasefire.

Moreover, the poor public reputation of the South Vietnamese military, fed by the collapse in I and II Corps, was partially redeemed by the heroic stand of the 18th.

As communist artillery fire blasted into the city and the 7th was also ordered to resume its assault, the results were the same. The dogged ARVN defenders threw back the attack columns of both divisions. Several more enemy tanks were destroyed by ARVN counter-attacks stopped NVA penetrations and reclaimed any lost ground. Again the PAVN had not taken the city and North Vietnamese casualties were extremely heavy and growing. Commander Hoang Cam wrote:*"This was the most ferocious battle I had even been involved in! My personal assessment was that, after three days of battle, even after committing our reserves, the situation had not improved and we had suffered significant casualties"* In a footnote, Cam provides figures, which match those in the History of the People's Army. *"During the first three days of the battle 7th Division suffered 300 casualties and the 341st Division suffered 1,200 casualties. Virtually all of our 85mm and 37mm artillery pieces had been destroyed"*

The PAVN Campaign Commander, General Van Tien Dung, wrote: *"The battle of Xuan Loc was fierce and cruel from the very first days. Our divisions had to organize many assaults into town, striking and striking again to destroy each target, and had to repel many enemy counterattacks"*

While COSVN' Plan (Central Office for South Vietnam) to attack Saigon from the northeast was foiled, in the end, the III Corps forces

The New Legion

couldn't withstand the entire North Vietnamese Army. Yet, despite the public image of corruption and incompetence, the ARVN, as shown in the battle for Xuan Loc, was not an army of bumbled and cowards as it is so often portrayed. It was an army that stood and fought with great courage not only on a few well-know occasions like the siege of Xuan Loc, but also in hundreds of little battles whose names most Americans never knew. When asked by his captors why he did not flee like many other ARVN Generals, Brigadier General Dao told them he could not abandon the soldiers who had fought so hard for him. I was their General, he told his jailers, and if you are holding any of my men in prison, I wish to be the last man from the 18th ARVN released. "I couldn't look them in face otherwise" he said. Speaking of the battle for Xuan Loc, he calmly states, *"Fighting is an art ... you must use not only your arms and begs, but your mind as well. Even though we knew we had lost the war, I still fought. I was filled with despair after the loss of the northern Corps, but I still fight!"*

He gave a similar answer to a journalist-reporter, who visited the town on April 13th, who asked him: "Why had the South Vietnamese troops fought at Xuan Loc and not in the north? How I can speak for them, said General Dao, the division commander. I can speak only for myself, and we have fought"

General Le Minh Dao was released from prison on May 4, 1992 and arrived in the United States in April 1993. He currently is active in the far-flung Vietnamese communities, spending much of his time traveling to see his former soldiers, most of whom are officers, since few of the line troops left Vietnam. Finally, he asked the authors, *"Please do not call me a hero. My men who died at Xuan Loc and a hundred battles before are the true hero's*

SKULL AND BONES FACES MANY SERIOUS DRAWBACKS

The "CIP" was a necessary scam? It cost the lives of two presidents [Kennedy and Diem] and **Axiom-1** cost two presidents get out of their offices [Nixon and Thieu] but the 35th President may have found the right approach! A Warrior for Peace – President J.F Kennedy is still a man ahead of his time. He recognized the limits of U.S power;

he understood that our true power came from our democratic ideals, not our military prowess. Myself, I convinced JFK as a great man could make the New-World in peace order. He was trying to find our way out of the Cold War, but Permanent Government certainly didn't want to" due to surrounded him by Skull and Bones. In the end, McNamara says today, Kennedy would have withdrawn, realizing "that it was South Vietnam's war and the people there had to win it…We couldn't win the war for them." That'd be a logical truth as Diemist' doctrines as well.

As result the world survived the most dangerous moment in human history – Cuba crisis nuclear warhead missiles. The Kennedy's assassination: Was there a conspiracy of silence? A time of misgivings about CIP and what it has come to signify. President Kennedy was "the greatest drawback" obstructive to against such a Permanent Government which was his adversary political opponent, just went ahead regardless contempt for President Diem reaction, so easier overthrown him whenever Permanent Government want to. As I remind above: Harriman in 1917 took advantage of wartime demand, pressured on government contracts to jump into "**Shipbuilding**" and Now [Vietnam War] in turn to jump into "**Airline-building**," but the (criteria) fundamentals of crucial requirement thing for sustained the project, whose were the air- passengers for supporting this new-air transport developed plan? "Launch a new product, needs a new costumer". A new image is estimated around three million U.S combat-troops become air-passenger in rotation for 'one year turn' of CIP' stratagem, account for a must having a campaign for U.S Big Combat Training practice never had in U.S history, and rotating wing too [helicopter] among them included more than seven thousand Bell-Lycoming Huey-Iroquois considered the "training-aid" for troop air-assault training; and leaving there for the so called political-term: "Vietnamization" and becoming war materiel rubbish dumpster due to lack spare-parts.

After two secret covert operations in mainland China and Vietnam were all-done, the introduced-preparedness for CIP was necessary in keyed-up-time performance-effect [WIB stance] but in contrast, President Kennedy intended to withdraw completely from Vietnam after he was safely re-elected in next year 1964. Have the

The New Legion

WIB-Bones surrendered their CIP to the Kennedy Administration? The CIP' stratagem should be aborted?

- Kennedy assured to the news-reporters that quotes by two ladies historian, Marilyn B Young and Ellen Hammer "We would withdraw the troop, any number of troops, anytime the Government of South Vietnam would suggest it!" **Consequently, the storm blew over**, the CIP in Vietnam will become more and more difficult to achieve with Kennedy in the seat of power.

- He didn't want send troops far away from home
- He don't want to become military involved. He praised the agreement for allowing the
United States to avoid military intervention
- He would withdraw the troops, any number of troops, any time the GVN would suggest it

(President Diem and his brother political adviser, Nhu would like withdraw all U.S. troops as soon as possible)

- And the most important is in October, 1963, Kennedy administrative cut off aid to Diem in a
Direct rebuff...and prepare troop withdrawn.
- Billion to billion C-Ration for US combat-troop were already produced in 1961 and 1962,
(Every can-lid marked month and year for expired date)
- He don't care about American-First [because for only WIB' Bones]
- Kennedy told O'Donnell, his White House Aide _"So We had better made damned sure thatI'm reelected"_ . His presidency included some of the tensest moments of the Cold-War, but Kennedy was convinced that the true power came from democratic ideals, not military might of republic trend. Could you think The CIP has come undone ... aborted?

Consequently, to make two presidents-sacrifices for the CIP [Kennedy and Diem] and two presidents out of their offices for **'axiom-1'** [the Watergate's reason Nixon pledges in letters to Thieu]

There came a point at which the war was won. The fighting wasn't over, but the war was won. The final reasons why it was

Kennedy' assassination and Nixon for Watergate scandal were the very what required dilemma for Skull and Bones deciding to bloody end equation. In addition, the intense competition in the venal journalists, news business meant all media had to cover the CIP stratagem, including cable networks based on 'Academic Freedom Act' publications that had not even existed during the Vietnam-War. New-Business became liars who tell them. In South Vietnam, journalists writing unfavorable about how the war effort was going. So the mood at Saigon – a name that was to become part of the everyday American vocabulary – was already bitter. It was soon to get far worse, for there were, I soon learned, Saigon has been two wars, one against the communist Hanoi, and one against the other enemy: the tiny venal American press-corps. Consequently, the storm blew over. But the public squabble was sorry testimony to the deteriorating condition of the U.S-Vietnamese partnership.

In the masterminded Kennedy: "How should America navigate through a world where its enemies seem everywhere and nowhere?" He may have found the right approach? The Kennedy assassination was clearly there a conspiracy of silence from the WIB and Skull and Bones; the Mafia-tool merely a sheer impact-bullet hired by them. Now you and me, we together digging the truth because "truth crushed to earth shall rise again"

(According on line – htt://.www.answers.com/topic/w-averell-harriman; page 5 of 7: Union Banking Corporation (UBC), a company which was closed in 1943 by the U.S government for "Trading with the Enemy" (The Trading with the Enemy Act of December 1941)

Clinging to the past, the triumvirate [LBJ, JFK, and Attorney General Robert Kennedy] had began progressively probing "Red Menace" connected companies and financial investors in Cold-War, was trying to proceed smooth approach, in take time, and put them on justice by the alien property custodian under "the Trading with the Enemy" to charges of criminal conspiracy. In confidence "Don't try lying to this Triumvirate – has compared lying to "throwing sand in the umpires' faces; for decades dogging merchant of death, Mafia kingpins and assorted terrorists. The axis of evil's scam between two counterparts Skull and Bones [Harriman founder] and Soviet Union, in Vietnam War as the engaged by the craps CIP and NLF.

The New Legion

The Kennedy's first target is aiming to "The Bay of Pigs" [George H W Bush, Zapata Offshore drilling company, formed in the 1950s the firm is said to have scouted for the CIA in pre-Bay of Pigs surveillance of Cuba] Kennedy kept a wary eye on the Pentagon, for much of his presidency, especially after the failure of the Bay of Pigs invasion, Kennedy was skeptical of the views of military hardliners (they're all Skull and Bones) in Washington. The doomed Bay of Pigs invasion in April 1961 became the Kennedy Administration's first great trauma which was declassified in 2005 (by Kevin Phillips, "American Dynasty", page 206)– from the CIA's internal history of the Bay of Pigs – that agency officials realized their motley crew of invaders had no chance of victory unless they were reinforced by the U.S military. But Allen Dulles and Richard Bissell, the top CIA officials, never disclosed this to J.F.K who was equally outraged at his National Security Advisers [Skull and Bone no 40.] While as a President, he famously took responsibility for the Bay of Pigs debacle in public. Eventually, he fired Dulles, despite his stature as a legendary spymaster, as well as Richard Bissell. After Kennedy appointed General Maxwell Taylor to learn what had gone wrong. The Taylor Commission concluded the Cuba Project had escalated beyond a size manageable by the CIA. It recommended a worldwide review of other CIA enterprise to learn if any had grown beyond intelligence operations and if so, to switch them to military control.

"Nobody is going to force me to do anything I don't think is in the best interest of the country" the president told to his friends "Do you think I'm going to cause a nuclear exchange – for what? Because I was forced into doing something that I didn't think was proper and right? Well, if you or anybody else thinks I am, he's crazy…We all inhabit this small planet. We all breathe the same air. We all cherish our children's future. And we are all mortal." Kennedy never again trusted his generals and espionage chief after 1961 fiasco in Cuba, and he became a master at artfully deflecting their militant counsel. Kennedy never thought much of the CIA either (Skull and Bones, the Axis of Evil – While the CIA may have been the creation of a Democrat W A Harriman, [Harry Truman] it now seemed to be strongly favored by Republicans, but notably these sounds were soon drowned out by the deafening roar of 9/11), in part because he and his indispensable brother, Attorney General, became convinced that the agency wasn't just incompetent but also a rogue operation.

Unfortunately, the sinister warlords in the WIB' plots to assassinate him in partnership with their tool Mafias – began before the Kennedy Administration and continued after it ended. Robert Kennedy – a legendary crusader against organized crime – thought Robert Kennedy had shut down the murder plots after two CIA officials sheepishly informed him of the agency's pact with the Mob in May 1962. But there was much that the Kennedy-brothers didn't know about the agency's more shadowy operations. Personally I'm assuming that the WIB hired the Mafias, and decided "Let's murder President Kennedy," Oswald would be among the last people in the world those organizations would choose for the job. If the Mafias, for instant, alone decided to kill the President of the United States – an act that would result in a retaliation against them of unprecedented proportions if they were discovered to be behind it – wouldn't they use a very professional, tight-lipped assassin who had a successful track record with them, someone in whom they had the highest confidence? Would they rely on someone like Oswald to commit the biggest murder in American history? Just clinging to the past, Allen Dulles and William Colby were as the legendary spymasters as well as Richard Bissell under the head of OSS, General William J Donovan; the ambiguity that characterized so much of their career surfaced. Some Communists, Leftists of Western Europe countries were murdered via by them, but does not quite say that the CIA may have been involved, It's must say Mafias did it. Once a former OSS pal recruited William Colby into the fledgling CIA. While serving as simple a foreign-service officer in the Stockholm Embassy, Colby was spending hundreds of millions on political-murdered action to shore up Italy's Christian Democrats. Now maybe "WIB' Godfather" reactivated again?

Once John F Kennedy said: *"We were trying to find our way out of the Cold War, but Permanent Government certainly didn't want to"* due to surrounded him by Skull and Bones. In the end, McNamara says today, Kennedy would have withdrawn, realizing "that it was South Vietnam's war and the people there had to win it…We couldn't win the war for them." These statements matched

The New Legion

with President Diem expectation. However how account for the Permanent Government performed the CIP? But it is also clear that Kennedy preferred to compete ideologically and economically with the communist system than engage with enemy militarily. He was supremely confident that the advantages of the capitalist system would ultimately prevail as long as a nuclear catastrophe could be avoided. Therefore the Cold War would have ended much sooner than it did.

Kennedy never made his Vietnam plans public. And, in true Kennedy fashion, his statements on the Southeast Asian conflict were blurred of ambiguity because surrounded by WIB members bent on war escalation in Pentagon, State Department, NSC, and even his political advisor, Mc George Bundy, Skull and Bones number 40 and his brother in State Department, William P Bundy, Skull and Bones 39; thereby avoiding any problem with the warlords in WIB, hard-liners, as a result, Kennedy operated on "multiple levels of deception" in his Vietnam decision making. In the words of NSC staff on February 11, 1963 M. Forrestal told Kennedy to expect a costly and long war (implied the Vietnam War must last longer for war industries complex developed)

The WIB members manipulated General Edwin Walker who after being forced into retirement by the Kennedy Administration had launched a national crusade against JFK "defeatist" foreign policy. The day of the President's Dallas motorcade, angry street posters, and an ad in the Dallas were "Morning new accused J.F.K of treason." But Kennedy was undeterred. This is what he planned to tell his audience at the Dallas Trade Mart that his destiny afternoon. The most effective way to demonstrate America's strength was not to threaten its enemies. It was to live up to the country's democratic ideals and "practice what it preaches about equal right and social justice." It's seemed to me that Kennedy have faulted U.S intervention in Indochina as evidence of American arrogance of power – attempt by the United States to be the World's Policeman. But there is another dimension to American arrogance, the international version of her domestic Great Society programs where U.S presumed that they knew what was best for the world in terms of social, political, and economic development and saw it as their duty to force the world into the American mold – to act not so much the World's Policeman as the World's Baby-Sister. It is difficult today to recall the depth of their arrogance.

Thereby, immediately after John F. Kennedy's death, he was wrapped in gauzy myths – at the height of the Cold War, Kennedy found a way to inch back from the nuclear precipice. Under relentless pressures from the WIB members to go to war, he kept the peace. I think he was "a real warrior for peace" John F Kennedy is still a man ahead of his time.

More than four decades after the event, the great majority of Americans believe the murder of President Kennedy wasn't the work of a lone gunman [Oswald] but the outcome of a wider plot. The assassination: was it a Conspiracy? For the rest of the day and night, Robert Kennedy would wrestle with his howling grief while using whatever power was still left him figure out what really happened in Dallas – uncertain of whether the President's brother would be the next target? Undeterred R. Kennedy feverishly gathered information. He accompanied his brother's remains to the autopsy at Bethesda Naval Hospital, where he took steps to take control of medical evidence, including the President's brain; he constructed the outlines of the crime and would become America's first J.F.K assassination-conspiracy theorist.

John F Kennedy was scarcely in office before he named his brother Robert Kennedy as U.S attorney general and L.B.J together became a triumvirate-pact; but neither of the brothers succeeded in his own later presidential bid – Robert Kennedy, once again, fell to an assassin's bullet in 1968 – **"Dead men tell no tales"** Because: As Robert Kennedy slowly emerged from his torment over Dallas and resumed an active role in public life – running for U.S Senator from New York in 1964 and then President 1968 – he secretly investigated his brother's assassination. He told confidants that he himself would reopen the investigation into the assassination if he won the presidency, he believing it would take the full powers of the office to do so.

"I think Robert Kennedy have insight about" The underground stream through which so much of the actuality of American power darkly coursed: lest Skull and Bones founder, William A. Harriman,

The New Legion

and his deputy Prescott Bush (according on line at pages 4 of 7, Jan, 22, 2006 http://www.answers.com/topic/w-averell-harriman,) and Bones-men in the War Industries Board." Though after four decades of investigation by thousands of researchers, not one speck of credible evidence has ever surfaced that groups such as CIA, organized crime or the military-industrial complex were behind the assassination, only that they each had a motive. And when there is no evidence or guilt, that fact, by itself, is very strong evidence of innocence. Moreover, the very thought of member of the military industrial complex (WIB members) or the CIA or organized crime actually plotting to murder the President of the U.S is surreal, the type of thing that only belongs. Included by my personal perception I should speculated, there aren't CIP activated if with the passage of time with Kennedy in his seat of power.

****

A HYPOTHETICAL QUESTION ON JOHN-F-KENNEDY' ASSASSINATION

Congress formed a team for investigation and going into conclusion the only Oswald was culprit; but the new investigation team, after two decades, Sir William Tobin head of investigated and examined research bureau of FBI, in studying the bullets by studies-chemical-computerized procedure process.Tobin drawing in conclusion that more than four decades ago, Congress investigated team was completely baffled with certain purpose as to the identity of the assassination case, and now Tobin (FBI) was called in to reinvestigate again. The investigated experts that time were a baffling crime, be too difficult or strange for anyone to understand or solving, explaining. Tobin's investigators found out being at lest three bullet-fragments were different categories. They come to conclude that having a second suspect engaged this crime, and shot in the same moment in one precise target (Kennedy) In contrary, four decades ago was account for only Oswald alone. In 1976, this case was closed because Oswald was subjected to assassination by a gangster of certain nightclub at Dallas, two days after Kennedy's assassination. The FBI couldn't continue for the case because "Dead men tell no tales" likely in South Vietnam: "Captain Nhung who killed President Diem was strangled to dead after couple day later, it doesn't only Nhung a killer but one more, Major Nghia was engaged in this assassination too. Nghia shot the brothers Diem and Nhu point-blank from the gun turret on M-113, armor-carrier with an automatic weapon while Nhung sprayed them with bullets, then stabbed their bodies repeatedly with his knife.

At 2003, the scene academic institute was resumed the Kennedy's case by sophisticated method for FBI and coming into agreement that the four decades investigation was a sheer bafflement. Consequently, these academic-institutes in United States continued follow up the new-fresh-research-examinations from concluded evidences of William Tobin that we hope find out the truth.

"In my simple perception because John F Kennedy was a great obstructive against Counter-Insurgency-Plan (CIP) development" while Skull and Bones founder, Harriman's trustee disciple Forrestal, a Skull and Bones loyalist, had reported to President Kennedy about the Vietnam-War to expect "a costly and long war" (Lest anyone should think my story strange, my book is a load of rubbish, let me assure you that it is all quite true) And below is the nature of Vietnam War: Why the CIP was a crucial necessary deployment for Skull and Bones' scam? What if President Diem didn't escaped from, and staying in his presidential palace, **I'm sure he could kept his physical in safe protection by CIA,** exile abroad, although he was strongly opposed U.S policy, to chose to dramatize his complaint by delaying agreement on the commitment for joint CIP (Counter Insurgency Projects) use Vietnam as a laboratory to develop technique of counter- insurgency ...Diem should be safe but, **however Kennedy must be killed because he was not policymaker** but the Skull and Bones being, though President Kennedy was on the power seat. In my perception, President Kennedy and Diem were two great men foresaw ahead, but intentionally the victims of conflict between acted government and Permanent government.

The day President John F Kennedy was assassinated, the schools, universities sent children home early, without saying why. That was frightening. People turning on the television, they found out that the president of United States had been assassinated. A soldier in my

The New Legion

duty-honor-country-bound house, the president of the United States was a large-than-life figure; I couldn't imagine someone dared killing him. People crying, and wondering why all this was happening, worrying about America safe in security. They were stunned, angry and terribly sad that someone would dare to shoot the leader of the Free-World. They were more conservative than John F Kennedy was and didn't agree with many of his policies, but he was the president; they had been taught to respect both the office and the individual holding it. Kennedy's assassination was a confirmation of citizen's growing concern that their country and its citizens were shedding, like an old dried-out skin, a formerly shared code of conduct and moral authority. This feeling intensified in the tumultuous years of protest and assassinations that followed.

The stratagem "Eurasian Great Game" was the long tragedy reigned by the War Industries Board Bones, but Vietnam War was a short stage-episode in the long play world historical drama of "Eurasian Great Game" tragedy. In that critical turning point, President Diem wouldn't acceptable on to U.S policy in Indochina – not comply with but against the recent Eisenhower's policy "security in Asia should come from the Asians."

Thereby, beginning in August of 1963, U.S Permanent Government variously authorized, sanctioned and encouraged the coup efforts of the Vietnamese generals and offered full support for a successor government. In October, U.S cut off aid to Diem regime in a direct rebuff, giving a green light to the generals. CIA maintained clandestine contact with them throughout the planning and execution of the coup and sought to review their operational plans and proposed new government. Thus, as the nine-year rule of President Diem came to a bloody end, CIA's complicity in his overthrow heightened their responsibilities and their commitment in an essentially leaderless Vietnam. And of course for the military coup d'état against Diem, the U.S must accept its full share of responsibility. These plots were stemming from WIB and Bones men

The underground streams through which so much of the actuality of Permanent Government power darkly coursed of shadowy operation that was seeking to overthrew Diem.

However, President John F Kennedy was still on Diem side, after the defeat of Bay of Pigs, his proceed-processing to bring these Oilmen to the justice by Trading Enemy Act. Shortly; one month later, May, 1961, Kennedy had sent his vice president, L.B Johnson on an ambassadorial world tour, exuberantly praised Diem as the "Winston Churchill of Asia" which reassured Diem of American support. Below here a message for evidence: President J.F Kennedy supported Diem to the last minute of the coup:

(Mc George Bundy, the White House, on October, 30, 1963, "Top Secret-Eyes-Only for Ambassador Lodge)

"We do not accept as a basis for U.S policy that we have no power to delay or discourage a coup. In our paragraph 12 you say that if you were convinced that the coup was going to fail you would of course do everything you could to stop it. We believe that on this same basis you should take action to persuade coup leaders to stop or delay any operation which, in your best judgment, does not clearly give high prospect of success...(according to the Pentagon Papers, Gravel Edition, Volume 2, pp, 792-793: CAS 79407, 30/Oct/63 – From Bundy to Lodge)

In the Chapter 3, I had justified with some evidences, "welfare imperialism," in on behalf Harriman was the U.S policymaker, he said "With the passage of time, our objectives (CIP) in Vietnam will become more and more difficult to achieve with Diem in control… and we must to move U.S combat forces into South Vietnam and put in a government of our own choosing. Masterminded Harriman put more than hundred strategist, sociologists, ethnologists and psychologists to work 'modeling' South Vietnamese society and seeking data sufficient to describe it quantitatively and simulate its behavior on a computer. The struggle for the third world, he said, "might well have to be considered the social scientists war." But Harriman, to cast himself a blur on his name, tucked away in the blurred "number Three Position" in State Department because he knew how the future disaster shall happened in the 'Cruel-April' 1975 (Saigon Fall)

The New Legion

PREPARE FOR WAR: THE SECOND PHASE OF EURASIAN GREAT GAME

COMPOSED KOREA AND VIETNAM WARS

Unsurprisingly, in contrast when the Korea War began in June 1950 – Harriman arranged his early return from Europe with a phone call to President Truman, informing the president that Europeans were "gravely concerned lest we fail to meet the challenge in Europe" Harriman took up residence in the Executive Office Building, a blow to his ego because he fully expected to be at Truman's side as a special assistant to the president for national security affairs and with his own staff. He wanted to show up himself in public because in South Korea there were 50,000 American troops positioned specifically to help that country deal with any aggression from the north (but South Vietnam shall no troop stayed there that Diem had requested in repeated warnings)

At a crucial National Security Council meeting on November 28, 1950 – likely 1917 he took advantage of wartime demand and now it happened again. A. Harriman challenged President Truman to assert his leadership, Truman responded by accelerating NSC-68 "United States Objectives and Programs for National Security," recommendations for vastly expanding U.S defense spending and rearmament. But one decade later, on September 21 1960 NSC introduced Counter Insurgency Plan to Eisenhower Administration, closer a presidential election event and Kennedy took the office January, 20/ 1961. It is not because Democrat president? So much adversity between Skull and Bones and the acting president were dramatized conflicts.

The defeat at a small battle of Ap-Bac was outraged by Kennedy and Diem but War Industries Board Bones so pleased with their conspiracies [need U.S troop in training for combat readiness] Respond pragmatically to any military institutes or universities which posted the mottos **"For strengthening peace, our war-preparedness must ready."** Little battle of Ap Bac was humiliating. The Viet Cong showed no fear of American tactical command, though Saigon equipped with automatic weapons and armored personnel carriers, and supported by fighter-bombers and helicopters, the battle ended on January 2, 1963, with the Viet Cong slipping away in good order. Ap Bac was humiliating – casting doubt on the claim that the Unites States and Saigon's troop were winning the war. The matter is what, why President Kennedy didn't want to send troop there for training? This is a Harriman masterminded foreseeing in his scope stratagem which demonstrated in Carl Von Clausewitz's strategic doctrine, once said: **"Policy is the guiding intelligence and war only the instrument, and not vice versa."** This theory explains Harriman's policy toward Korea, Vietnam, and Middle East War in the future.

To resume NSC-68, 1950 from Korea to NSC-CIP, 1960 at Vietnam, there was a transmission from 'Military Jet Engine' to 'Civilian or Airline Jet Engine development'. As basic foundation, the United States always seeking way of the priority for military defense first that it done at Korea War firstly: The prototype like F-84 Thunder-streak, F-86 Saber, B.52, C-130, C-135, tanker KC-135 which shall be in the civilian version for called sigh "Boeing 707" Now in Vietnam War was the period of unleashed the Civilian Airline development. The CIP strategic policy calls for new investment in developed: new incentives for Airline-Companies and crucial consumers by air-passengers. The vocabulary was easier called but in the business basis foundation: "if the automation-products must have largely dispensed with the need for customers" Therefore the crucial customer was whose – Airline development must have passengers who will already be booked-passengers? Harriman and his staffs badly needed 3.000.000 air-passengers. So where were Three millions passengers? U.S combat troops made rotation for one year-term. (in the book "Battle Ready, General Tony Zinni, page 422 *"The tactics didn't make sense and the personnel policies – such as one-year individual rotations instead of unit rotations in and out of country – were hard to comprehend.*) This approach was extremely against the basis foundation of 'Standard Operation Procedure' of the Military commandment but that demonstrated itself just for practice-military-training, not a real war!

Additionally, how about rotating wings? (helicopters) for the next after fixed-wing developed, U.S beginning to manufacture some batches 10,000 helicopters started at 1961 Huey-1A, B, C, D, specially H Model to VNAF for training ARVN troop in air-assault operations; when people said Vietnam War means "Helicopter-Symbolic" because everywhere you can see helicopters all over, even in the remote or mountainous areas, even open sea. I must say these helicopters were for military "training-aids" in a practical "combat training picnic" After a long year combat-training-picnic, these training aids like Picnic's plastic-fork, spoon, napkins, dishes, cans … trashed all the military equipment into dumping garbage or a rubbish dumpster on the training spot which I should saying the so called "Vietnamization" program that the Permanent Government ties Nixon down, putting his named the so-called "The Nixon-Doctrine" for his responsibility. Cites one more often overlooked hurdle: U.S agricultural inspectors insist that, before it re-enters the U.S, military equipment be free of any microscopic disease that, as Pagonis puts it, "can wipe out flocks of chickens and stuff like that" which the WIB hated to see those ugly-stuff to send back home.

In contrast, to move U.S combat troop into South Vietnam was against Harriman's masterminded about "Axiom 2," but his controversial personality, crucial factor of expectation was: (the U.S had no legitimate reason to be involved in Vietnamese affairs) Consequently, A- Harriman ordered McNamara conspired with CIA fabricated the so called "Tonkin Gulf Incident" in creation an image of the North Communist Hanoi used P.T boats Swatow to attack the U.S destroyer "Maddox" in what became known as Hanoi provocative. Although Hanoi made no reference to the Norway P.T Nasty raids – How could a Norwegian possibly explain his attacking the coast of North Vietnam – the Norwegians weren't Americans – any Caucasian at the throttles of a covert boat in Asian waters flew in the face of plausible denial – of which he was informed, President Lyndon Johnson warned Hanoi that another high-seas attack would have dire consequences, and ordered the destroyer "Turner Joy" to reinforce the Maddox; This is the reasonable cause to move US combat troop into South Vietnam for retaliation, but not war declaration.

Vinh-Van-Truong

AN AMERICAN FIRST LUCRATIVE BUSINESS:
"Crony Capitalism"

Shortly thereafter, many giant U.S corporations developed their military materiel products [Bell Iroquois Huey, Northrop, Gruman, Lockheed, Boeing 727, 747, 707, DC 9…] The U.S market was also inundated with exported products. US capitalists were very happy to exploit the huge profitable market after more than ten years without war. Prepared for war, the US combat-troops shall invade till 1964 waiting for fabricating the so called "Maddox event". While in South Vietnam, masterminded Harriman used a very smooth approach likewise more than thirty chemical defoliation corporations (Orange agent) a billion to billion C-Rations for in coming combat troop, sensor communication devices dropped on Ho Chi Minh trail, more than 7,000 Huey Iroquois alone like military training aids and so and so on… been developing

In 1969, there of some 543,400 airline-passengers was resulting in a peak commitment; this earlier period was also characterized by recurring request for more American troops to be dispatched to South Vietnam in rotation term for one year tour raised the number of air-passengersincluded Rest and Relaxation leaved permission, account for about three million-passengers-tickets already-booked. These training maneuvers were divided two phase-periods: General Westmoreland, with the so called "**search and destroy**" but not on Harriman Highway [Ho Chi Minh trail.] This invaded wave was called in a peak commitment about little bite more than half million troops. And gradually withdraw with General Abrams on command; the so called "**clear and hold**" for withdrawal, stand for to retreat until none troop there. So unsurprisingly, during the Vietnam-War, we never heard the term of **Airline bankruptcy or merge like today?**

THE "WAR-INDUSTRIES-BOARD" HAS BEEN IN A STATUS OF PANIC.

Suddenly, on March 2, 1969 an open split between the two Hanoi's patrons would place great strains upon their co-operation. If the Soviet Union and Red-China to disagree over this, then Hanoi would not continue the war that made U.S side get into a real-panic

The New Legion

(543,400 G.I air passengers stuck in South Vietnam) so why some Eastern-Europe-journalists took snap shot the photo: NVA troops had been carrying military supplies by convoyed bicycles. In the pictures Chapter 1 you had see the word "handle with care" was not ridiculous; because that earlier period was also characterized by recurring request for more American combat troops to be dispatched to South Vietnam, resulting in a peak war-game commitment there of some 543,400; so why U.S expected to protract the war game, no Airlines even Ships could carry them out for even short spell. As a result, the U.S side must took-part to react by used C-130 unmarked could carried out the supplies for couple day to that large "enemy-buddies" needed, we shouldn't hard to comprehend. The WIB was finally reconciled with his craps-partner Soviet Union for war-protraction. The Permanent Government's in difficulty, because the CIP was not carried out yet; there'd now confront is not simply ending United States involvement by the withdraw of their forces, which is now a foregone conclusion and only a matter of a few months, but the difficulty now is the question of bringing peace to the whole of Indochina, including Laos and Cambodia – So why U.S must give a hand to help Hanoi protracting its war in proceeding on process-course – preventing damage control toward manage the defeat.

His counterpart in the Axis of Evil, The Soviets of course desire to see Communist established at an early date in Laos and South Vietnam, and would regard this fashioned NLF development as opening up new opportunities in the area of Southeast Asia as a whole.(in the method on the strongman side, U.S strategist calls on "at time manage the defeat, and later on manage roll-back) Soviet involvement in these conflicts has been influenced heavily by the Sino-Soviet quarrel, and observers believe that the Soviet will continue to feel that China arguments oblige them to present a show of firm support for the Communist forces there. At the same time, they will prefer to advance the Communist cause primary by political means and to avoid substantial risks of direct U.S military intervention. Otherwise, firstly, United States would only facilitate the Soviet Union in furthering their influence there. And after negotiated with Mao-Zedong 1972, the United States that I thought it is possible for US to take bolder action… Because if peace can be brought about in that region at an earlier date, then surely US will be able to maintain more influence there. (Observer took account for in the first place, there was no need to send US combat troop in there but the main objective was the CIP. When the CIP was accomplished right on keyed up time 1972 to bring China to the power seat as United Nation member and ending two decades hostilities 1952-1972 as similarly as Vietnam 1975-1995 on the course originated from the Old "Eurasia Great Game")

Although an open split between the two would place great strains upon their cooperation, I doubt that a split would produce an early and radical shift in Communist conduct in Laos and South Vietnam, North Vietnam has maintained a degree of independence from both his patrons [China and Soviet] In the wake of a Sino-Soviet split, both Moscow and Beijing would be concerned with increasing their influence with the North Vietnamese, and probably disposed therefore to support Hanoi's wishes as to policies in Laos and South Vietnam.

Nervously, The WIB weighed the advantage of the "Communist reactions to additional U.S Course of action in Laos and North Vietnam. However some evidence of continuing Vietnamese Communist preparations war, CIA Intelligence Memorandum on January 24, 1966, No SC 03777/66, there were some paragraphs … presumable the Communist to conceal military developments being pushed during the stand-down in U.S air strikes. That such a build-up is occurring is borne out by the fact that since December 23, eight Soviet AN-12 heavy transports have noted flying in to North Vietnam. Each of these aircraft is capable of carrying some ten tons of cargo on such flight. The nature of the cargo carried by these aircraft is unknown (but WIB did know all of them which were SAM or electronic devices) surely the fact that it is being sent all the way from Soviet Union by aircraft suggests to North Vietnam's air defense system. Prior to the cessation of U.S air strikes, flights by Soviet heavy transport into North Vietnam had only averaged about one a month in cooperated with U.S fighter-bombers how to escaped from Sam ground to air missile in the testing ground. Both side of this Axis of Evil testing at work. The common causes of this axis of evil were 'the air defense' and 'the air offence' testing devices.

"Finally, they were still protracted that war"

VOICES OF DISSENT: The struggle for South Vietnamese independent was fast becoming an "American War," raising serious questions about the nature of U.S involvement in Indochina. Officially, the war in Vietnam was being won as 1962 ended and the second chance at in late 1970. But the "CIP" initiated into the "WIB" Bones-members must be essentially carried out by the secret instruction from the founder of Skull and Bones Society and his assistance [Harriman and Prescott Bush, on line, January/22/2006 http://www.answers.com/topic/w-averell-harriman] "the CIP must be achieved at any rate" and the victimized was Kennedy's assassination for the first and Richard Nixon Watergate for the second chance, specially because they were the very foreign policies, CIP's obstructive.

1962, underneath the optimistic rhetoric of the top command in Pentagon, a few respected civilian and military officials were already beginning to raise serious questions about the progress of the dissent belonged to senator Mike Mansfield, M. Forrestal NSC' staff, and McNamara', of course they were the trustee-apparatus of Skull and Bones dynasty.

"Do you have any problems in Saigon?" Secretary McNamara asked General Paul Harkins at a meeting in Honolulu, December 1962, a time when the Viet Cong [NVA] moving through Harriman's Highway [Ho Chi Minh trail] up from Company size to Battalion strength operation all over South Vietnam territories. (As a Vietnam-War's executive manager, McNamara absolutely sure knew about that, an infiltrated Group 559 for ground-supplies, Group 759 for sea-supplies and a Group 959 for protecting infiltration route of south Laos, the first number stand for month and the last two numbers were year in which easier stored in Russia-KGB national archive and U.S national archives as well)

At the meeting, General Harkins confidently told McNamara, "We are on the winning side. If our programs continue, we can expect Viet Cong actions to decline. "He went on to summarize all the progress that had been made in the strategic hamlet program, ARVN operations against the Viet Cong, training of the Civil Guard and Self Defense Corps, and so on. Harkin was already familiar with the overall strategic situation in the region. Strongly supported by General Maxwell Taylor, who had recommended his protégé to the White House, he plunged into his new assignment with energy and enthusiasm, traveling around South Vietnam almost daily in his small L-23 small transport plane to inspect training centers and strategic hamlets and to measure the progress of the war. The men Harkins command were soon at work in every phase of South Vietnamese military operations. American soldier trained ARVN, Ranger, and Civil Guard detachment in anti-guerrilla and village defense techniques, developed ARVN airborne helicopter assault tactics, airlifted troops, supplies, and combat equipment to strategic locations, built jungle airstrips capable of handling aircraft as large as C-7 Caribou, C-123 Provider or C-47 transport..

McNamara, pretend delighted and observed that "six month ago we had practically nothing [positive to report but since then] we have made tremendous progress." He asked General Harkins "how long" before "the Viet Cong could be eliminated as a disturbing force" Harkins replied that he "estimated about one year from the time that we are able to get ARVN… fully operational and really pressing the Viet Cong in all areas." It was good news and a remarkable turnaround. However, McNamara was more cautions than Harkins, estimating that it would probably take three years for the Vietnamese armed forces to become fully operational" and finish off the Viet Cong. Still, the United States was moving in the right direction, as all the statistics demonstrated.

But in contrast, Policymaker, A .Harriman in his masterminded-staff-scope was "American materielassistance in this critical early years consisted largely of providing cast off World War II American weapons, including the heavy and unwieldy for a short Vietnamese as M-1 Garant, submachine gun Thompson .. Meanwhile the Hanoi's troop was being provided the AK-47 assault rifle by his Soviet and Chinese patrons, AK-50. As outgunned consequences by the enemy and thus at a distinct combat disadvantage were focusing on their mastermind's scam. That adversely affected both our morale and effectiveness, though "Troops know and feel it when they are poorly equipped."

However, Harkins's wishful thinking and misplaced optimism was contagious. It was soon

The New Legion

reflected in a report of the president's military representative, General Taylor; Just back from September 1962 visit to south Vietnam, Taylor presented a litany of achievements and then declared that "much progress has been accomplished since my visit in October 1961" While there was evidence to contrary, especially from U.S advisers to ARVN units in the south Vietnam countryside, as well as in the CIA's intelligence reports, 1962 came to an end with McNamara, Harkins, Taylor and others all encourage about progress in South Vietnam. They had deluded themselves – the United States wasn't winning. (But you sure know about that Communist Hanoi troops were already overwhelmed in South Vietnam through Harriman's Highway, Ho' Trail)

Once again in 1970 – There came a time when the war was won. The fighting wasn't over, but the war was won. This achievement can probably best be dated in late 1970, after the Cambodian incursion in the spring of the year. By then the South Vietnamese countryside had been widely pacified, so much so that the term "pacification" was no longer even used. Four million members of the People's Self-Defense-Force, armed with some 600,000 weapons, represented no threat to the government that had armed them: instead they constituted an overt commitment to that government in opposition to the enemy. ARVN' forces, greatly expanded and impressively equipped, were substantially more capable than even a couple of years earlier. Their most impressive gains were in the ranks of the territorial forces – the Regional Forces and Popular Forces – providing close-in security for the people in the countryside. The successful pacifications as a threat that had to be countered, was extending not only security but also elected government, trained hamlet and village officials, and economic gains to most of the population. In the "No More Vietnam" Richard Nixon said: "Congress proceed to snatch defeat from the jaws of victory…the effects of congressional budget cuts that had strapped it with its severe fuel and ammunition shortages…."

In that year on December 29, 1970 as a shirttail amendment to the defense authorization bill, a watered-down version of the measure finally passed. That version of the amendment only barred the introduction of United States ground forces in Laos and Thailand by **"Cooper Church 1970"** and later **"Case-Church 1973"**. The

United States can land no ground forces, can send no air support, can provide no military advisor, nor any military aid. About four years later, Permanent Government pressured on Congress had dramatically cut aid to South Vietnam, going against a long-standing commitment. As a result, my then actual country falters because of a grievous lack of spare parts and replacement equipment.

The WIB members and Skull Bones men, they put pressure on non-elected president who has his hand tied double knotted. The final Case-Church Amendment says that President Gerald Ford must do nothing.

- **Washington Post** wrote: "it is almost unthinkable and surely unforgivable that a great nation should leave these helpless allies to the tender mercies of the North Vietnamese." but that is what we did.
- **Colonel William LeGro** served until war's end with the U.S Defense Attaché Office in Saigon "The reduction to almost zero of United States support was the cause" of the final collapse, he observed "We did a terrible thing to the South Vietnamese"
- **Tom Polgar**, then serving as CIA's chief of Station Saigon, cabled a succinct assessment of the resulting situation: "Ultimate outcome hardly in doubt, because South Vietnam cannot survive without U.S military aid as long as North Vietnam's war-making capacity is unimpaired and supported by Soviet Union and China.
- **Ambassador Bunker:** "I think really it was a betrayal of the South Vietnamese"
- **Many Americans** would not like hearing it said that the totalitarian states of China and the Soviet Union had proven to be better and more faithful allies than the Democratic United States.

However, Vietnam War has been participated not only by a great numbers of warriors,

but also countless Angels of mercy, it produced some "The quiet Americans" and "The ugly Americans" who finally sent the poor people of Vietnam to hell on April, 1975; but on the other hands it also introduced a lot of good, true American who relentlessly tried to "Deliver us from Evil" Unfortunately, the good Americans' efforts have been buried under tons of biased reports and bungled news stories written by unscrupulous journalists throughout the Vietnam War. And with passing time, those inspired stories have been fallen quietly into oblivion. But today, you will know at least few good guys with the seriousness of their expressions hereby above.

SOVIET AND U.S' WAR EQUIPMENT SURPLUSES – HOW RESOLVED ON MILITARY RUBBISH EQUATION

Vietnam-War was assimilated all that the Axis of Evil thought – the ugly truth or man-made disasters take an alarming toll on Vietnamese-victims. Those who survive often are left tragically devastated. Eight decades ago, the years preceding World War-1, anyone had ever heard of the America's richest families that there were profit to be made in arms and war production [War Industries Board] As the U.S role in the world ballooned, money-Americans were also lured by investment vehicles claiming to draw on foreign political intelligence and identify overseas opportunity. If the Rockefellers, the Harrimans, the Walker and Bush families…Particularly William A Harriman and George Herbert Walker, the founding fathers and spiritual progenitors of Harriman and Bush clans, had been the first place the elements on the families escutcheon: foreign covert operations, clandestine shipments, arms deals, rogue banks, and money laundering, to interlocking directorates of ten or so companies involved in armaments, banking, overseas investment, shipping, and commercial relations with the becoming foes, Germany and the Soviet Union.

In 1918 together with a founder Skull and Bones, A Harriman and Samuel Bush director of the WIB facilities division created the so called "Merchant of Death" label. By 1939, the coming of war had reframed the argument, so that anti-munitions sentiments were criticized for having hindered Franklin D Roosevelt's mobilization against fascism and for having abetted the Neutrality Acts of 1935, and 1937. This phenomenon in public mood did more than rebut disdain for munitions makers and encourage patriotic support for "war industries" It also undercut the 1920s and early 1930s consensus that arms races and merchants did indeed help to stir up war – a contention that remained unfashionable in United Stares establishment circles through most of the twentieth century, save for "the late Vietnam years" and the subsequent President Carter-era disenchantment. Through most of the Cold-War period, defense contractors were almost automatically 'good-guys.' As a political strategy, centrist internationalists avoided attacking munitions makers and shunned any associations with the old 'isolationist' rhetoric.

The most prominent were Averell Harriman, Prescott Bush, Robert A Lovett, Artemus Gate, James Forrestal, and E.Roland Harriman. That Walter Isaacson and Evan Thomas described "Six Friends and the World They Made" – The Wise Men (1986). Some chroniclers have profiled the 1917 to 1960 emergence of "The Wise Men" and others in terms of links forged at universities and clubs, not least the Skull and Bones hegemony at Brown Brothers Harriman. In their dinner parties attended by old Bones friends from the WIB, where they heard discussions about industrial mobilization and offered their own ideas on the importance of airplanes to the nation's transportation and defense (Vietnam-War stands for national's Civil-Air-transportation, and Korea-War for Air-defense developments) An early forerunner of the WIB, later recalled, with only some exaggeration, that "the War Industries Board of the United States had in the end a system of concentration of commerce, industry, and all the powers of government that was without compare among all other nations, friend or enemy, involved in the World". So dare I say the "Axis of Evil".

Almost from the start, American investments of the 1920s in both Germany and Russia were controversial. They were variously criticized for costumer chasing, reckless lending, and even aiding previous or potential enemies. The investments were also on a large scale. Through one or another financial vehicle, the Harriman firms arranged a major shareholding in the Hamburg-America-Line, set up a U.S Bank to serve the German Thyssen steel interests, bought a half interest in the principal German-owned coal and zinc

The New Legion

mines in Poland through a company called the Silesian-American-Corporation, and took a position in Germany's transatlantic cable company.

The Axis of Evil or the WIB involved with his counterpart Germany – by 1943 many of their best-known partners and executives – from Averell-Harriman, James Forrestal, and Robert Lovett (three among Six Wise-Men) were major figures in the Washington war effort or the Office of Strategic Service (OSS) as were the two Wall Street lawyers with the largest German practices – John Foster Dulles, as a board member of International Nickel, actually had helped work out that firm's prewar cartel agreement with I.G. Farben to provide Germany with a steady supply of Nickel for armor plating. Prescott Bush, who handled much of the German work at Brown Brothers Harriman, used their services.

The storm was blown up to this Axis of Evil – according to the Patriot Act, the U.S Justice Department had begun probing German-connected companies and investors in 1941 (year's Trading with the Enemy Act of December 1941 in effect) That's on time as Pearl Harbor and the U.S declaration of war against both Germany and Japan put government investigations into overdrive. In early March 1942, a special Senate Committee began public hearings on cartel agreements between U.S and German firms.

How they put the fire out in recovered? Secretary of War Stimson, a Skull and Bones member with strong establishment ties – Yale, Andover, WIB and Skull-Bones men, and closed service in both Democrat and Republican cabinets – asked President Roosevelt in March 1942 to stop the investigations because they would interfere with companies engaged in the war effort. However, that didn't stop the enquiries being made by the alien property custodian under the Trading with the Enemy Act of December 1941.

As a result, in August 1942, the property of the Hamburg-America-Line, for many years partly owned by Harriman and Walker – controlled American Ship and Commerce Corporation, was seized under the Trading with the Enemy Act. On October 20, the alien property custodian seized the assets of the Union Banking Corporation. Eight days later, with UBC' books in hand, the government acted against two affiliates, the Holland-American

Trading Corporation and the Seamless Equipment Corporation. In November, the government seized the asset of the last major entity connected to Harriman, Walker, and Bush – the Silesian-America Corporation. (This reminded you somewhat why President Kennedy, his brother fell to the assassin's bullets in 1963 and 1968 and LB Johnson gave up his reelected campaign just because they would like to eliminate them as the old-man said: "tyrannies reacts upon the tyrants themselves")

1950 one more time, they resumed their scam again by trading with the "Red-Menace," W A Harriman, a significant figure of U.S policymaker in Soviet-American relations during World War II, and the Cold-War; when he carried secret dispatches between Moscow and London during the World War II, he chose as the combination on his diplomatic case the numerals 322, the society's secret number that Evan Thomas and Walter Isaacson, in their book "The Wise Men" described how seriously A Harriman took the society, as lend-lease expediter "to keep the British Isles afloat," and "secure job" for Russia manpower, working-class in during the second war (1943-1946) He was a supporter of General Mac Arthur's bold plan for an amphibious operation at Inchon and with the general's assurance that Soviet Union wouldn't intervene in Korea-War. But on April 5, 1951 Harriman advised that Mac Arthur be fired immediately, though President Truman hesitated, he also played a prominent role in Truman's decision to fire Secretary of Defense Louis A Johnson, he greatly admired Johnson's successor, General of the Army George C Marshall. It seemed to me A. Harriman has been seated on US president power seat.

Account on his heavy-weight-pact triumvirate: Harriman was the president's national security adviser; Prescott Bush was an influential senate from Connecticut, and Robert A Lovett himself was deputy Secretary of Defense and about to become Secretary, these three men among "The Six Friends and the World They Made" (The Wise Men 1986) As you knew from 1917 till 1950, Harriman, notoriously, himself he would like to become a "Freewheeling-Diplomat" and a totalitarian politician means policymaker – with the coming of World War II and Korea War, Harriman, associated with WIB members, utilized his economics expertise in foreign affairs,

The New Legion

becoming one of every U.S president's major advisers. Strangely, all US presidents: instructing him to report directly to the White House, thus bypassing the American ambassadors and the State Department. He acted on this personal level for several critical years, attending all of the wartime conferences and specially, twice going on missions to arrange increased aid to the Soviet Union which I dare called the Axis of Evil" – production war materiel for Korea, Vietnam, and Center of Asia war together the so called "arm-race" according to two Harriman's books: same year he persuaded the Soviet Union play the war-game "CIP counter NLF". This craps took place in 1959, Harriman would change the original-status of Geneva Conference of 1954 on the termed-method "on the strongman side", but in contrast books "Peace with Russia" published in 1959 and in 1971 "America and Russia in a Changing World." And he himself became one of the most influential experts on Soviet Union policy. His involvement with foreign affairs continued. He together with the son of his closest friend, Michael V Forrestal, chaired a committee that prepared proposals for the Marshall Plan to stimulate the economic recovery of Europe in post war.

When John F Kennedy took office, Harriman again became a ghost haunted war man-made disaster over a molder of foreign policy special in Vietnam War; so why he hides himself out of the public spot-light, but witch-hunt in the camouflage-shadowed thus, number Three position in State Department that you did know in the 'Chapter Three' he was a powerful-man as totalitarian policymaker.

Now Started the last war stage (1972) his triumvirate cooperated with counterpart Red Menace in the Axis of Evil. "How gone into liquidation all out of date, obsolete war-materials" of World War II American surplus weapons and war-materials introduced in Korea and Vietnam Wars: From 1945 to 1954 French dominant, were still been used during the second episode of Vietnam War; actually must be blown them out in the same time together with Soviet Union, after the so called Nuclear test ban treaty with Soviet Union 1963, SALT-I.

What would come next? Obsolete war equipment in blow-out plot!

No one has spent any time thinking about in early March 1972 Soviet General Pavel Batitski was in Hanoi to assess North Vietnam Communist requests. U.S company dynasty called "Inventory." For military support, encouraged them dispensed all used old batch obsolete weapons and to replaced by a new tested-batch for next to overrun South Vietnam 1975 and Cambodia 1979 (SA-2 missiles on the long trailers, and their mobile launching systems accompany them, AT-3, SA-7, T-55, T-57, multiple arrays of 122 millimeter Katyusha rockets, each system firing 40 missiles at a time) In coincidence, during General Batitski's presence in Hanoi, North Vietnam leadership, political bureau headquarters in focusing on consultation and information which the Soviet Union of their intent to launch the Eastern-Offensive of commencement the end of this month.

At noon on March 30, 1972 General Vo Nguyen Giap, for a long-anticipated NVA troop offensive began in M.R-1 with widespread attacks by fire. By midnight about 6,000 rounds of mortar, 122mm rocket, and 122mm, 130mm, and 152mm artillery fire had inundated ARVN' fire bases across the front. The next day a heavy ground attack struck Quang Tri Province combat base and Dong-Ha was heavily attacked. ARVN troops were withdrawn from a crescent of fire support bases as NVA tanks were engaged by ARVN armor south of the Mieu Giang River. The NVA offensive in Quang Tri Province involves a total of 10 infantry and 5 artillery regiments from the 308th and 304th Divisions.

In early May, our South Vietnam suffered a series of battlefield reverses so serious. Shortly the situation has changed significantly since Soviet general's assessment. Because the NVA dispensed all power they had, likely Lam Son 719 over Laos, in Military Region 1, Dong-Ha had fallen, Quang Tri combat base had been evacuated, and Quang Tri City was threatened and would soon fall, overwhelmed by Four NVA Divisions, plus powerful forces Tanks, artilleries.

In Military Region 2, the 22nd ARVN Division had preformed poorly and suffered a costly defeat. The situation was also very serious. In Military Region 3, ARVN troops were hanging on at An

The New Legion

Loc in what observer called "probably the single most important battle in the war" Because the Axis of Evil would planned this City shall be "Capital of National Liberation Front Government." But there happened a terrific struggle in which a heroic and successful defense ended, General Vo Nguyen Giap' hopes for decisive victory in the campaign. Ultimately the NVA would commit to these three attacks his entire combat force – fourteen divisions, twenty-six separate regiments, and a huge array of supporting armor, tank and artillery – save for one division remaining in Laos.

President Thieu called "Quang Tri Incident" means United States played the game "The Political-Sabotage" When an U.S helicopter pick up Brigadier general Giai out of the operational area that we called "a snake without his head," [that meant troops without leader] So while Permanent Government urged General Abrams had to take back Quang Tri province; then President Thieu insistently stated to Abrams "no more political sabotages". Shortly Abrams have given a grim order to his field commanders. *"Effective immediately no Vietnamese commander will be airlifted out of a unit defensive position by U.S fixed-wing aircraft or helicopter unless such evacuation is directed personally by the RVNAF corps commander"* inform your counterpart. Due to prevent that repeat-acted-scene seemed implied another cut and run was seen as a rehearsal for a full new coming scale cut and run for carrying axiom-1.

General Giai who had commanded the newly formed and ill-fated 3rd Infantry Division until its collapse a month into the battle, was not only relieved but also court-martialed and imprisoned

Giai was, it appeared, a victim of **'the U.S political sabotage game'** with purpose rehearsing for testing the next event Saigon Fall. In my military experience, Brigadier General Giai, a soldier with most of his life sleeping out in the jungle, was sentenced to five years in military confinement and imprisonment, Giai remained there until the NVA took over Saigon and put him in their reeducation camp, a fate underserved for a good and brave soldier.

Finally from 1971 to 1972 NVA troops dispensed the almost old batch of the obsolete war materiel and been waiting for new batch of modern-weapons from Soviet (SAM, T-55, T-57…) Meanwhile, President Thieu offered to lead a South Vietnamese attack on North

Vietnam, where was defended by a single division of regular troops. All Thieu requests from U.S was air support, and that U.S. troops already in South Vietnam would defend population centers, but Emperor-II was keeping overlapped Emperor-I' s stratagem in chunk-two, second phase-episode or manage to defeat maneuver. "Operation Lam Son 719 meant for U.S. troop withdrawn safety and U.S forces retreat to Honolulu left South China-Sea behind and with the purpose to set a trap where oil and natural gas resource which making great Sino thirsty.

Resolved equation of rubbish war material blow-out on U.S side:

The so called Vietnamization program – By coincidence, both ghosts arrived on the same year 1972, now to the U.S turn: While fierce ground fights were raging along the DMZ, Quang Tri province, in Binh Long, Kontum province, Central Highlands, and on the approaches to Saigon, An Loc province. An air, a naval campaign of unprecedented ferocity was taking the war to North Vietnam. President R-Nixon ordered available fleet and air elements nearly doubled by rapid reentry into the combat zone of multiple squadrons of combat and supporting aircraft, including a hundred more B.52 – so may that on Guam A.F.B one whole runway had to be closed for use as a parking lot – and more than fifty naval combatants. Air Force, Navy, and Marine Corps tactical air came streaming into the theater from the continental United States, Hawaii, Japan, South-Korea, Okinawa, and Philippines. From thirty five tactical air squadrons – USAF, ASN, and VNAF – the total increased to seventy four, including five USMC (Better war, pages 326-Easter Offensive) they generated more than 55,000 sorties through early June/1972. B-52 contributed another 4,759 devastating sorties, and fixed-wing gun-ships AC-130B, many more, with the daily average of tactical air sorties rising from about 380 to more than 650 and B-52 sorties going from 33 a day to 150. Six aircraft carriers were assigned, putting four on station at all times. On the naval gun-line at the high point three cruisers and thirty-eight destroyers provided gunfire support. In the campaign designed "Linebacker" these force intensive bombing of targets in North Vietnam, including military facility in and near

The New Legion

the key cities of Hanoi and Haiphong as well as round-the-clock. Support for South Vietnam's defending forces.

Beginning 9 May/1972, all major North Vietnamese were harbors mined, to put 36 obsolete Mark 52 mines – huge magnetic things weighing 1,100 pounds and packing 625 pounds of high explosive – in at Haiphong, the first target hit and North Vietnam's most important seaport. Over successive days the lesser ports were sowed, with all mines set to activate. To mine Haiphong Harbor, said Admiral Moore, Chairman of the Joint Chiefs of Staff. *"Afterward not one ship entered or left the harbor until we took up the mines."*

This final dump all out of date weapon by bombardment and mine campaign ruined North Vietnam's economy paralyzed its transportation system, reduced imports. By 80 percent, and exhausted its air defenses. So you could feel what different between from Linebacker to Rolling Thunder campaign – it was real war or liquidation all obsolete war material before toilet being flushed. Hanoi agreed. "This war was too different than the first nine-year war of destruction" observed a history of PAVN, contrasting Linebacker with the Rolling campaign earlier in the war.

"This time the enemy massed larger forces and made massive attacks right from the first day of operation, using many types of modernized technical weapons and equipment"

I wouldn't say no, why some observers assessed that the Iraq-War was similar with Vietnam-War: **"Two Different Wars, One Destructive Parallel"** were "Civil-Wars" and "One destruction" (Canada first opposed, but when the Iraq-war started, Canada engaged immediately for seeking the privilege-right received a major contract to help rebuild Iraq after US destructor done there) So this aerial bombardment campaign ruined North Vietnam's economy, paralyzed its transportation system, reduced imports by 80 per cent and exhausted its air defenses. "Linebacker wasn't Rolling Thunder – it was war". Rolling Thunder was parallel with rocky-mountains demolition – for building Inter Indochina Highway, a just no kill.

North Vietnam said: "This war was different than the first war of destruction" and observed a history of PAVN, contrasting Linebacker with the Rolling Thunder campaign earlier in the war. But myself I thought: "U.S Permanent Government would like North Vietnam become to u-turned back "The Stone Age" and South Vietnam became the "Water-back" according to Malthus' theorem, English economic scientist doctrine. This gloomed scenery, General Abrams was very emotional – *"that what is going on now is just a lot of unnecessary killing."* Also during the Easter-Offensive, at a General Conference of the United Methodist Church held in Atlanta, Georgia, the majority of delegates approved a statement calling American involvement in the Vietnam War "a crime against humanity," then rejected a resolution that would have condemned "the appetite of North Vietnam to wage cruel and inhuman war".

At last, the "Cooper-Church" and "Case-Church" implied the final-inventory that to put in all war materiel rubbish in the dumping-trash right on spot Indochina, in remote Laos mountainous area.

HUNGER FOR PRESIDENT POWER-SEAT AND PRACTICES OF CRONY CAPITALISM

W A .Harriman original ambition was inscribed his name on the presidential list of American history. He does very best to be elected governor of New York (1955-59) the greatest élan shortened course to the presidential seat of power. He is an unsuccessful candidate for the Democratic presidential nomination in 1956 and had failed U.S presidential election in 1952. And once more defeated for reelection in 1958 by Nelson A Rockefeller, He convinced himself as a great man could made the New-world in peace order, was frustrated by American-citizen lack of knowledge, appreciation shown of his work that He was totally subjugated to the wishes of the other nations, even Soviet Union to the interest of the United States. That Harriman's behavior, far from being entirely his own product, is rooted in the Skull and Bones' four decades evolution and concomitant pattern of deception, dissimulation, and disinformation – had personal reputations as at least intermittent liars or deceivers. So U.S voters, having become somewhat inured to such manipulation, may see only more of the same. So finally we conclude that Harriman didn't hurt the position of United States being the First Superpower violated "Patriot Act" but just merely their greedy interest.

His significant plan to recruit some talent-elite figures to help him carry out his stratagem: He planned to retire from public life in 1969,

The New Legion

but the important of U.S frame-work policy toward Vietnam War, privately Harriman worked to change them in his plot, especially in the matter on negotiating with the only Democratic Republic of Vietnam side [Hanoi] this is his final determined solution for CIP.

Doctor Henry Kissinger was a mere tool in the hands of the WIB Bones, was a talent prodigy man, was a key figure emerged in the world but as merely a surrogate for Harriman who put him in his masterminded becoming a loyalist to Company Dynasty on behalf of his representative; Because Kissinger was above the best of students at Harvard University that Harriman was willing to financial investment for his scholarship with purpose, hired him into political sphere-apprenticeship. Quite literally, the prominent professor William Elliott was assigned for his tutored-sponsor about his political essay. Shortly Kissinger was on charge "the Harvard International Seminar". There are so many opportunities to meet the scholars, politicians, diplomats…around the acquainted world. Specially his book "Nuclear Weapons and Foreign Policy" edited **1957**, which was matched with Harriman's books shall be published in **1959**, "Peace with Russia" and **1971** "America and Russia in a Changing World". Kissinger's book, a dramatized documentary based on a discussion how to prevent a nuclear war with Russia. He assumed that's possible *"a limited nuclear war comply with a limited objective"*.

Right after graduated, 1960, Harriman assigned him to his job Democrat's consultant on foreign affair in Europe, then Indochina as a 'quarterback' of secret plot named "Pennsylvania" the original of Paris peace talk on July, 21, 1967 with two French cooperators scientists Raymond Aubrac and Herbert Marcovich flied to Hanoi met Pham Van Dong, Prime Minister. Afterward, on behalf of Harriman, Cyrus Vance met Colonel Ha Van Lau of Hanoi at Paris about detail references of Vietnam War's frame work. In 1964, abruptly Kissinger got instruction become a Republican's consultant. By objective criteria, the Permanent Government would like him become Secretary State whosoever Democrat or Republican be elected president. Kissinger will be a key figure replaced Harriman in the policymaker position. No one be surprised, Kissinger was a power-man as freewheeling diplomat-shuttle, instructing him to report or receive directly to the Permanent Government via Donald Rumsfeld who was a WSAG' (Washington Special Action Group) chief of staff for George-I reigned Second-Emperor of Skull and Bones dynasty, thus bypassing President Nixon. He will on charged in control the CIA, Pentagon, State department, and presidential foreign adviser.

Democrat Senator Henry 'Scoop' Jackson, at Washington was once stalemated: "The government set up by the Constitution is based on the consent, or agreement, of the government. The actual system of the U.S government is a representative democracy. Why only Kissinger' decision could applied for world's U.S policy? Skull and Bones certainly bears him with malice.

1969, Kissinger jointed to White House at time President Richard Nixon took office. Like Harriman in 1950, took up residence in the Executive Office Building, a blow to his ego because he fully expected to be at Nixon side as special assistant to president, though Nixon was not close to him. Nixon knew his job was only to control the president as himself self demonstrated arrogantly 'a peace magician'. Nixon was never forgotten his treacherous schemes to Democratic Party, Nelson Rockefeller in presidential election 1968. But Kissinger was hired for the interest of WIB, and Bones; he has a talent made a profit of his notorious "how not to tell the truth without really lying". Because to foreign policy intrigue and the intelligence community, plus the Harrimans and Bushes of immersion in the culture of secrecy, deceit and disinformation have become theirs political hallmarks – their ambitions, financial practices, scandals, and wars.

Consequently, U.S policy wasn't 'a transparency nor consensus, and sustainability in the actual system of the U.S government is a representative democracy, its hurled allies credibility in reliable-foreign affair. Friend no trusted and foe undistinguished. President Gerald Ford acknowledged what had happened by U.S involvement in Vietnam, he expressed "Well, there is no doubt these were very categorical commitments" but Kissinger persuaded Ford keeping far away from Vietnam like Nixon said no more Vietnam. That's fine for non elected president.

October 1972 Kissinger said: "peace is at hand" but December 1972, the "linebacker II" occurred on eleven days and nights bombardment at Hanoi. He said because Hanoi violated …what? Urging Nixon fumed asked his staff, H.R Haldeman "find out what the hell Henry's doing?" Because Kissinger got the secret order from WSAG; and long ago, under the watch of Nixon, American political interest had already written off South Vietnam. The Paris Peace Accords stood testimony to that fact, virtually selling the highly United States-dependent nation down the proverbial river. The Cooper and now Case-Church Amendment of 1973, specially banning all bombing in Cambodia and further banning all American military intervention by land, sea, or air anywhere in Southeast Asia, underscored that write off. Kissinger sound seemed to me like "High-Speaker" for Permanent Government that had simply engineered a so called "decent interval" to distance America from its South Vietnam commitment. Given an adequate passage time, the world would not hold America accountable. Unfortunately, Kissinger's "decent interval" had not nearly run its course in the stratagem (Eurasian Great Game: the same two decades hostility with China as same as Vietnam – China 1952-1972 and Vietnam 1975-1995 on road-map project-course) Shamelessly Company Dynasty exploited his talent for their selfish greedy to critical circumstances then eradicated him later on.

Let see Kissinger complains in his letter to President Thieu aimed the Der.Spiegel interview:

"… You and I had many disagreements, but only over tactics. In view of the outcome, your anger is understandable. However, it would be a pity if those who long advocated our abandonment of South Vietnam were now able to use your bitterness as another weapon against those who tried to save South Vietnam. Ironically, I am under vicious attack these days for my efforts to defend Cambodia in order to ensure the survival of your country…"

In my view point "Kissinger cares nothing for Vietnam, South or North. This is all about His Middle-East peace and what the rest of the world thinks of America after this toilet gets flushed.

Vinh-Van-Truong

SOUTH VIETNAM IN DESPERATE PLIGHT

Republican George H W Bush succeeded to the Company dynasty, but was immediately derailed out of **Democrat** Harriman's strategy track; though on behalf as merely a surrogate for A. Harriman. Clearly I have justified in my conviction that the nature of the war was transformed to "a counter-espionage war". George H W Bush lean toward his intelligent superlative degree striving defeat the Soviet Union happening at last by "Stooping to conquer" or he ever thought he'd stoop so low as to cheat on his partner [Soviet Union] in the Axis of Evil's scam through the CIP counter NLF' craps, under umbrella of the Rule Of Engagement:

- On June, 9 1967 a great conflict between Soviet and China about Soviet wanted to control the transshipment of Soviet good from USSR and through China to Hanoi. However, the Chinese objected and stated that they would assume control at the USSR border. At this point the North Vietnamese officials intervened and said that if the USSR and China were going to disagree over this, then North Vietnamese would not continue the war. Of course for resolved this solution, this Axis of Evil know how, the way of unknot it. The US okay-enjoyed a philosopher Socrates' theorem (399-470 B.C Socrates, a Greek philosopher) – "give them the bone, when two dogs fight together, a tantalizing smell of food as an attractive Indochina's bone"

- November 1970, suddenly US force launched a surprising raid on a prisoner of war camp in North Vietnam, an operation planned and controlled in Washington, by General Haig at Pentagon Command and Control Post. It was known that the Son-Tay Camp had held US-POW. By the time the raid was launched, however, those people had been moved elsewhere, apparently as a result of flooding that made Son Tay untenable. Later it was revealed that last-minute intelligence had revealed that fact, but the decision was made to let the raid go anyway. The operation was successful in its own terms, although of course no prisoners were rescued because none were there. Clearly another goal was to let Hanoi know their rear area – the camp was only less than forty kilometers from Hanoi – wasn't as secure as they might have thought. Much later it was learned that the rescue mission benefited the POW still held captive, since the

The New Legion

Hanoi subsequently consolidated them in better facilities and their treatment improved significantly. Now Hanoi Hilton appeared right in the hearth of the capital. The so called Hotel-Hilton stands for POW's an only one concentrated prison.

- In 1968 Tet-Offensive, ARVN though outgunned by enemy, performed admirably in repelling to surprise of many Americans and the consternation of the Communist, but a venal Walter-Cronkite [bribed by the WIB] reports: "the South Vietnam could not have won the war under any circumstances" [according axiom-1] together with Bill O'Reilly, Dan Rather unquestionable they had talent. But simple not just a talent for lying, the world would see their news: fair, open-minded, genuine impartial.

- In early 1970, former Justice Department Ramsey Clarke, Jane Fonda, David Ifshin had been a Vietnam antiwar protester, went to Hanoi, where David Ifshin denounced U.S involvement in the war on Radio Hanoi. David's denunciation was piped into the Hanoi Hilton, where POW got to hear it in their tiny solitary cell, a significant flyer was held, beaten and torture for years, much of that time served after they heroic refused to accept freedom on terms that violated the POW code of honor governing the order of prisoner releases.

- On 21, November 1970, movie-star from Hollywood, Jane Fonda at University Michigan, audience-2000 students "If you understood what communism was, you would hope, you would pray on your knees that we would some day become communist." Actually, then the U.S was Super-finest Communist country now.

- July 1971, Ping pong diplomacy with a mediator President Yahya Khan, Pakistan, Henry Kissinger was secretly contacted with Prime of China Zhou Enlai for next summit meeting between Mao Zedong and Nixon on February 21, 1972 for normalization of diplomatic relations.

- On June 20 1972, Henry Kissinger meeting with Zhou Enlai, discussing issue of Indochina

After complete American withdrawal, the Indochinese people change their governments, the US will not interfere. The US will abide by the determination of the will of the people.

- On July 8, 1972, Jane Fonda arrived to Hanoi by Russia Aeroflot airline– She left the United States to French. From French to Moscow by Aeroflot and secretly fly to Neutral Laos and from Laos fly to Hanoi. At Hanoi, she seat on a position of gunner of antiaircraft made by Russia to shot US fighter side be side with AAA gunner. She praised the communist. She wore the Red "ao-dai" Vietnamese dress with the Red Color proclaimed "I feel shame the US into doing something like inhumanity"

- On August 23, 1972, Nixon in the campaign presidential reelection, because on the course inertia of US combat progressive withdraw back home, like South Vietnam President Thieu need the political stability for the accomplished CIP. By chance, the Permanent Government let him getting along assured by his political advisor, Henry Kissinger.

Below is Nixon's speech:

"As your President, I pledge that I shall always uphold that proud bipartisan tradition. Standing in this Convention Hall four years ago, I pledged to seek an honorable end to the war in Vietnam. We have made great progress toward that end. We have brought over half a million men home, and more will be coming home. We have ended America's ground combat role. No draftees are being sent to Vietnam. We have reduced our casualties by 98 percent. We have gone the extra mile; in fact have gone ten of thousands of miles trying to seek a negotiated settlement of the war. We have offered a cease-fire, a total withdrawal of all American forces, an exchange of all prisoners of war, internationally supervised free elections with the Communist participating in the elections and in the supervision"

- On November, 14, 1972 President Nixon's message "… I repeat my personal assurances to you that the United States will react very strongly and rapidly to any violation of the agreement." (WSAG should proceed to initiate a scandal Watergate, prying his seat off power out of US government for being his "pledges letters" to President Thieu no longer valid)

- On January, 27, 1973. Because the outrage of antiwar movement, President Nixon gave pressure on South Vietnam regime:

"… As General Haig has told you, I am prepared to send Vice President Agnew to Saigon in order to plan with you our post-war relationship (How could President Nixon feel that firstly, Skull and Bones eliminated his Vice president likewise A Harriman hated vice president Johnson as the running mate of Kennedy, and his later for unvalued these assurance-letters by Watergate scandal?) He would leave Washington on January 28, the day after the Agreement is signed, and during his visit, he would publicly reaffirm the guarantees. I have expressed to you [President Thieu] Let me state these assurances once again in this letter:

-First, we recognize your Government as the sole legitimate Government of South Vietnam

-Secondly, we do not recognize the right of foreign troops to remain on South Vietnamese soil.

- Thirdly, the US will react vigorously to violations to the Agreement.

In addition I remain prepared to meet with you personally three to four weeks later in San Clemente, California, at which time we could publicly reaffirm once again our joint cooperation and US guarantees. (Kissinger wrote: Nixon never thought South Vietnam will be abolished)

Consequently, Vice-president Agnew had to resign recently, (masterminded Harriman didn't want a political dilemma, he hates like poison once again the so called presidential running mate: vice president Johnson became acting president) now President Nixon for his turn on August, 9 -1974 by the skull and Bones pressure as a scandal not "War-Powers Act" but Watergate initiated by the Skull and Bones keyed-up-time prior the Saigon Fall. (Wedge on line http://www.markriebling.com.deepthroat.html. In wedge, we reviewed clues to the identity of the legendary source on who claimed to rely in their Watergate probe. Obviously, through Emperor-II' CIA experience, I considered from CIA officers who first heard about the Watergate break-in to its own records. And Richard Helms would have liked to settle the matter quietly, without publicity. My view is clues suggest that Deep Throat was Helms present secretly at the June, 19 control meeting. Included from Vietnam's Phoenix Program to Chilean assassinations and improper domestic surveillance – from indictment by Gerald Ford's Justice Department – In the eyes of Attorney General Edward Levi, Emperor-II' [George H W Bush] actions verged on obstructing Justice Department investigations. Not least, Emperor-II had been insistent in any price protecting former CIA director Richard Helms – aptly named by his biographer "the man who kept the secrets" – who was ultimately let off with a fine and suspended sentence for lying to Congress (in his son, prince presidency tried to close the case in domestic home land the Watergate author is officially the number two of FBI did it. Like I said "don't prosecute the bullet destroyed the object... but just the finger pull-on the trigger)

Strangely ridiculous, we take these into consideration: in discussion about two cases, prince George-II and Richard Nixon – the U.S. president has the right to grant an amnesty for himself – Particularly the "Watergate scandal" President Richard Nixon must step down because easily understandable, the CIP strategy was a small wheel in a component-system of various wheels in assembly-lines by freewheeling unit that Super Government has to eliminate the acted president with a simple – "the axiom-1 must be done".(the dissolution of a Saigon regime) All letters which Nixon pledges to President Thieu though they were too personal and confidential to disclose, and besides there was nothing confidential about them, but important matter how could explain to the world public if Nixon on the seat of power when Hanoi's troop overrun South Vietnam.

Meanwhile majority of Democratic in the Congress at November, 1973 and War Power Act Nixon might get impeachment. As for American citizen, in this case of Richard Nixon, the public extremely reluctant to remove Nixon ("Polarization and Presidentialism" by R.J. Ellis- Society, no 3&4 1999, pp.8-11) But thing have gone from bad to worse as George-II case, Americans support their president remains so low 34percent. But no problem he is still okay; because he was a prince of Skull and Bones dynasty's Emperor-II. As of U.S. constitution, despite Congress pressure like Nixon status the majority of Democrat overwhelmed, George-II has the right to declare for himself an amnesty, but no one dare impeach him. So you could distinguished Nixon be gone out of power seat for American-First and "welfare imperialism." Now inside the Republic Party, "One of Bush's rivals for the Republican nomination in 2000, Senator John McCain, also said he slept better at night as a POW in Vietnam for five-and-a-half years, knowing that George-II was protecting the coast of Texas from invasion.

I am trenchant classic "Impeachment": In US history, the impeachment of President Truman, apparently for his conduct of the Korea War? Including forced President Truman to assert his leadership and drafted McArthur's dismissal announcement, was suggested by its staff to the Republican high command? I thought the direction from the founder of Skull and Bones, Democrat A. Harriman, his foreign advisor. There have been reiterated demands for the impeachment of President Nixon, arising out of dissatisfaction with his program for disengagement from the war in Vietnam by urging Congress prosecuted President Nixon lying about US military involvement in Cambodia. Whereas President Kennedy concurred with Attorney General Robert Kennedy as well as Vice president LB Johnson, this triumvirate was trying prosecuted them on the cause of trading with the enemy Act, another word a necessary of CIP-performance. That if Kennedy had not moved to expel Soviet Union nuclear missiles from Cuba at the time of the confrontation with Khrushchev, "Kennedy would have been impeached." But the world survived the most dangerous moment in human history.

For becoming a powerful magician, Permanent Government [George H W Bush] also assigned Kissinger taken more charge of State Department from Secretary Rogers on date 22/ August/ 1973, prior two months, at 4: PM on 13/ June, secretly Kissinger flew to Paris met Le Duc Tho put the "green-Light": authorized Communist North Vietnam attack on course Highway-I through DMZ to Saigon on keyed TOT timetable. The South Vietnamese will see – on highway-1 scattered among these troop transports rolled long semi trailers with tarp-covered, cigar shaped cargos, big SAM, and SA-2 missiles on the long trailers and their mobile launching systems accompany them. These brand-new batch of modern weapon for next campaigns to overrun Saigon 1975, Phnom-Penh 1979 and later defense at northern when China gave the lesson that the cost expensed by U.S dollars and Soviet working-class manufactured.

- On June 29, 1973, two months after Lowenstein and Moose's report, Congress placed a rider on the 1974 budget authorization bill that required a halt to all combat air operations in Southeast Asia. Idaho Democrat Senator Frank F. Church and New Jersey

Republican Senator Clifford P. Case authorized this amendment, which bore their names: "Case-Church".

- On December 13, 1974, John Kerry and Jane Fonda conspired with Hanoi to overrun Phuoc-Long province to checking how sure the US reacted and South Vietnam run out of supplies, ammunition and persuaded regardless the Paris peace talk agreement. Closely followed advised by KGB counselor to Prime minister of North Vietnam, Pham Van Dong responded to Stephen Young. "Well, when Nixon stepped down because of Watergate, we knew we would win. Dong said of President Gerald Ford, the new president, "he's the weakest president in U.S history: the people didn't elect him; even if you gave him candy, he doesn't dare to intervene in Vietnam again. "We tested Ford's resolve by attacking Phuoc Long province in January 1975. When Ford kept B-52 in their closed shut-hangars, our leadership decided on a big offensive against South Vietnam. We had the impression that American commanders had their hands tied by political factors. Your generals could never deploy a maximum force for greatest military effect" because Cooper, and Case-Church Amendments tied double knotted – must do nothing.

- On January 8, 1975 Le Duc Tho was assured by Kissinger of his willingness Saigon occupation at the time two Soviet delegations, Nicolai Firyunbin as diplomat shuttle like Kissinger, and military-delegation, General JCS V, A Jukilov pledged a new batch of sophisticated-weapons will anchored at Hai Phong Harbor very soon; meanwhile military delegation of Red China on February 28, head by Yang Yung sponsored an assault-sapper division with the plot divided South Vietnam two parts.

- On March 25, Secretary of Defense Schlesinger found himself standing on the outside of the President's inner circle. He stood in direct contradiction to Kissinger's foreign policy strategy. If the house and Senate would approve a massive emergency (as rescue West Berlin or Israel) infusion of war goods to South Vietnam, based on the Weyand assessment, then in the worst case, if Saigon fell, the world could not blame Unites States for it. But that Permanent Government turned down, because CIP' stratagem was accomplished on keyed time on road map course. The craps must done for the next job will be start in Middle-East, central Asia – Eurasian Great Game stratagem

I could give you an objective opinion: For months earlier of Saigon Fall – lurching from the chair, President Thieu felt deserted and alone, rushed to a table where he picked up a pale green, manila folder stuffed with papers and shook it at General Phu (when President Big-Minh surrendered, Phu and another four Generals committed suicide) "These reports indicate that we have depleted the greater majority of those very supplies and munitions"

"Sir, I have seen with my own eyes what we hold in many of these caches," General Phu said, rising from the chair in a respectful response to the president abruptly leaping his feet.

"We drafted those reports in hopes of gaining additional American support. Just as when we submitted our budgets, the truth that they tell represents a different set of circumstances and realities"

"Our forces, thus far, have stood no match against the North Vietnamese," Thieu snapped:

"You lost, what, two regiments already? Or is it now three? Annihilated! Sixty percent of the men killed before they could even land!"

"This is not the same situation, sir," Phu said in a soft, conciliatory voice, hoping to ease the tensions that had sent President Thieu into such an explosive tantrum.

"That is very one battle not the war, nor does it represent the whole country. We must now resolve to isolate the enemy's forces and contain them where they presently stand"

"I have solid information, documented in a top secret intelligence report from a very reliable American military resource, that tells me that while United States withdrew their support of us during the past two years and cut our aid to a fraction, the Soviet Union have covertly shipped no less then 700 million long tons of new military equipment, ammunition, and supplies to Hanoi in preparation for this very campaign! They blatantly violate the Paris Accords, just as the North Vietnamese now ignore its rules with this invasion!" President Thieu preached, his voice crescendo to a shout as his face flushed dark red and blood veins pulsed outward on his forehead and temples.

General Phu keep quiet, said nothing, waiting for the president's rage to subside. He deeply suspected that no such intelligence report ever existed, nor had any of the American military staff shown Thieu anything even similar to the document he described. It contradicted everything that the Americans had otherwise said.

Furthermore, General Phu American old friend, Brigadier General James Vaught, an U.S general assigned to the CIA in Saigon, had pretend to visit him only weeks ago. When General Phu asked him for advice, Vaught had refused because he claimed that the Paris Accords prohibited him lending such help. Not even advice from an old and trusted friend. Who would have known? It was only the two of them, yet Vaught, still, had said "NO" – when Saigon Fall in a cruel April 1975, Phu was the first among five generals committed suicide. General Phu felt a sense of isolation and betrayal.

From now on, President Thieu had no real friends within any of the American diplomatic, intelligence, or military communities. Ambassador Martin merely tolerated the man because his job required of him a minimum of such conduct. No one, in Phu's mind, would have given President Thieu such incredible news.

Actually, the communists clearly hold the upper hand, due to the Axis of Evil played the craps "On the Strong-man Side" and nearly carried out the "axiom-1". Observer said in a matter of fact "A lot of them think that this is the beginning of the end." Spontaneously, Thieu roared, continuing to bluster as he walked back to the table and threw down the green folder on a stack of others like it, toppling them across several cardboard tubes that contained charts and maps.

"America has turned its back. Deserted us in the breach! How do we stand in defense against such forces when they can now so easily overwhelm us?"

"How can we withdraw our units from their defenses without placing them and the republic at far more risk?" Phu said, now courageously pleading for the president to simply consider what nearly any military strategist finds immediately obvious and most basic. "Forces in movement face the greatest vulnerability if all situations. On the march, our soldiers will have no defenses and can rely only on the equipment, ammunition, and stores that they carry and the great

drawback by the civilians will joint with us. In such a massive retreat, they will have highly inadequate armor and artillery defenses, and even those that they can deploy cannot respond rapidly enough to an attack. They cannot count on air cover, either. The Communists now have widespread antiaircraft defense missile – new batch-weapons from Soviet after General Pavel Batitski in March 1972, SA.2 on long trailers, and their mobile launching systems accompany them. We never saw these big SAM except near the DMZ, where they shot down countless number of the American fighters. Now they bring them toward Saigon, deployed throughout the northern-provinces and Central Highlands, making our pilots very timid to fly into these hostile zones. A reinforced enemy lying in ambush will find such in army in movement and easy prey indeed.

Remaining in defense, our forces will have the advantage of holding high ground fortresses, heavily supported by artillery and armor, with ample provisions. Placed in movement, the army must desert these fortifications and the greatest majority of their supplies and munitions. They are simple too vast to carry with us. What of them? (For carrying out of their "axiom One,": Cruel April: The Fall of Saigon by the mastermind George I, tucked away in China, Beijing, Shackley in Saigon, Rumsfeld, Cheney and many others WSAG-staffs in Washington D.C)

Furthermore, consider the reaction of the people when they see the massive movement of our units. They will surely panic and crowd the routes, following the retreating forces to safety, and thus choke traffic to a crawl. The strong mind anti-communist became the weak to our retreat forces.

"Sir, abandoning the Central Highlands and the Northern provinces to establish a damn new DMZ appears to me a recipe for disaster."

"You have no choice in the matter...General Phu," President Thieu snarled. "We will sacrifice those forces necessary to protect the redeployment so that my plan does succeed. I have already ordered such units to fight to the man. It is the republic's only hope."

General Phu said nothing more and turned his gaze to the ornate design and dark colors of the Persian carpet spread across the floor. He realized that President Thieu had now let fear dominate his thinking, and panic, driven by the defeat at BaMeThuot province, his loss of fair in the fighting abilities of South Vietnam's armed forces, and the absence of hope for any American supports, obviously guided his decisions. Clearly, the president's resolution to the crisis, if executed, spelled the end for the Republic of Vietnam.

General Phu now began to consider his own safety and what he must do to stay alive and free. He had endured captivity and torture by the Viet Minh in Dien Bien Phu 1954 and felt certain that he couldn't again survive imprisonment under the communist hand; especially his rank often got promotion on the battle and his old age. He stepped back to the sofa chair and stood, waiting for Thieu to return to his seat and spell out details of his plan. The diminutive-general resolved to say no more about the matter and only to listen dutifully. Seeing the president so demoralized and now consumed with such trepidation that it warped his thinking. Phu concluded that more words would only serve to further inflame President Thieu.

NhaTrang, Army Corps-II Headquarters: President Thieu sat at the head of the long conference table at NhaTrang garrison headquarter. He listened as members of the Joint General Staff and representatives of South Vietnam's military regions offered their assessments of the crisis as a prelude to the presentation of his redeployment plan. Thieu had to chide and pressure his only ally, General Phu, into supporting his position. President knew that Major General Phu did it because Phu had no choice. His losses at Ban-Me-Thuot had essentially emasculated him. Now the man just sought a way out, not merely out of the situation, but out of the country.

Who at this table could he trust? Major General Pham Van Phu? A weary commander, who today, seated in the large, leather conference chair behind the great mahogany table, appeared even more dwarfish than ever; His only ally? He had no idea who the heavyset, burly general Nguyen Van Toan truly supported nowhere his real loyalties lay. Toan had the reputation a man easily swayed with dollar, or promise of power. Toan held no qualms in getting what he wanted by any available means, inside or outside the law or command structure. Toan wielded his muscle in Saigon and Military Region-III more as a warlord than as a uniformed commander of forces.

The New Legion

President Thieu felt alone and deserted. However, He felt confident that burly general Toan would stand with him, since the president's plan also benefited the general's own self-servicing interests.

Thieu's only openly defiant critic, General Ngo Quang Truong, commander of Military Region-I, didn't attend at Nha Trang meeting, nor did he offer any reason excuses for his absence. He regarded the entire conference as merely an exercise in procedure, a game of smoke and mirrors, and totally a waste of his time. President Thieu already had his plan. Today's commentary simply shuffled more papers for no good reason other than to satisfy bureaucratic egos.

On 10 March 1975, President Thieu had ordered General Truong to redeploy the entire Airborne Division from the defenses of Hue and Danang so that he could move them into position to reinforce units that his plan had established to cordon off Saigon and at least save that city. Thieu didn't even have a specific mission for the Airborne Division, other than they should report to Military-Region-III at once and that they would fill in where General Toan needed them.

At the onset of president Thieu issuing his order to redeploy the force, which represented more than a third of the defense of Hue and Danang, General Truong had emphatically refused and had vehemently pled for his commander in chief to reconsider.

On 13 March 1975, that following morning at presidential Palace; General Truong flew to Saigon to argue his case, face to face, with President Thieu. General Toan didn't bother to stand as his senior-ranking protégé Lieutenant General Truong stepped through the conference-room doorway inside the Presidential Palace, where the two men awaited their audience with President Thieu. The serious faced general from M.R-I, Danang glanced at general Toan and then at Toan's aide-de-camp, who had leaped to his feet when Truong entered the room.

Scowling now, General Truong sat in a leather armchair at the opposite end of the conference table from General Toan and dismissed the disrespect as another quality in the man's gangster-like demeanor. In January, President Thieu had relieved the former M.R-II I commander who had lost an entire regiment, more than three thousand men from the 5th ARVN Division, attempting to defend Phuoc Long, province. General Toan had stepped into the commander's billet and immediately boasted that his three divisions, armored brigade, and five ranger groups would lose no more ground.

"I hope you had a smooth flight from Danang," Toan said casually, trying to cut the ice with small talk. General Truong simply looked at his colleague and nodded. He had few indulgent words for anyone today.

More than half hour passed before President Thieu finally entered the conference room. General Toan had fidgeted and chatted nervously with his aide-de-camp, while General Truong had sat quietly, jotting notes and studying a thick stack of battle-planning documents.

"Please remain seated, gentlemen," President Thieu said as he breezed into the room and took a seat in the leather armchair at the right of General Toan. The distance of the conference table looked like a long mahogany highway to General Truong. Clearly he had no advantage, and he immediately realized that his bumpy flight to Saigon this morning had only wasted his precious time. He felt suddenly sick at his stomach, and for the first time in his life he genuinely feared for his country, and for his fellow soldiers, whom he greatly loved.

"With all due respect, Mr. President," General said with a sharp edge in his voice, "I had hoped that we could discuss that matter privately"

"My decision to redeploy the Air Borne Division from Hue is a matter of direct important with General Toan," Thieu said, "Since I'm reassigning that force to his command."

"And what of Hue city" Truong asked.

"Those Army and Marine Corps units that I have allowed you to keep there will defend that citadel to a man," Thieu said. "We have already had this discussion, Lieutenant General Truong… you must obey my order, could you?"

"No, sir" General Truong snapped and stood defiantly.

President Thieu remained seat and smiles. General Toan leaned back in his chair and glared at General Truong.

"You will bring the whole nation to ruin with this insanity, sir," Truong said, his pent-up rage beginning to boil in his voice.

The New Legion

"That's quit enough, Lieutenant General," President said, still keeping his seat.

"What is the purpose of this lunacy" General Truong said. "Abandoning our cities makes no sense. Deserting our fortresses and our stockpiles hands the enemy victory.

"You order my soldiers to stand and die, for what; So that you and your cronies can cut and run? Meanwhile those units that you order to redeploy will be slaughtered on the highways. The timing is too late. The enemy is in place! Do you not realize this?

"Pulling such a force from Hue will cause its utter destruction overnight. Those soldiers left to fight will quickly lose heart. Those who actually remain their posts, and do not desert, will surely die or fall prisoner to the Communists.

"Once Hue falls, refugees will flood over the Hai-Van Pass into Danang, and with inadequate defenders there, it will quickly collapse too. Then Chu-Lai will topple, and an unstoppable tidal wave will come crashing down Highway-I through Qui-Nhon then NhaTrang, and straight into Saigon. I will not do it!" (CIA Ted Shackley' plan via Kissinger offered a conspiracy of silence to Le Duc Tho an attacked-throng trajectory to Vietnam War's blood end or Axiom-I carried-out)

"You will send those forces I order, and you will send them immediately" President Thieu barked, now standing and walking around the conference table to meet General Truong face to face.

"Relieve me! Shoot me for insubordination! But I will not abbey such an insane order, sir!" General firmly said, looking at Thieu squarely in the face.

"I already have transmitted orders to your subordinate commanders, and the Airborne Division," President Thieu said, turning his back on General Truong.

"You will return to your command post, and you will fight and defend Hue and Danang and Chu Lai to the last man standing. Is that clear? You may not surrender!"

"History will bitterly remember you, Mr. President! Our people will come to scorn your name," strongly General Truong said, snapping his satchel filled with working papers under his arm and marching defiantly out of the room. In his heart he knew the entire plan held together like feathers in a torn pillow. One good shade and everything would fly to the four winds.

The lone ranger, Schlesinger's increasingly isolated out of favor with his own cabinet

Secretary Defense Schlesinger's pragmatism stood in direct contradiction to Kissinger's [Skull and WIB' class] foreign policy strategy, America's not lose face with the rest of the world should South Vietnam fall. As it stood, the secretary of Defense found himself standing on the outside of the President's inner circle. Their Skull session in meeting included attendance of national security expert General Brent Scowcroft, General Weyand, and Ambassador Martin. It did not include attendance or even notification of Secretary of Defense James Schlesinger, even though their discussion and planning heavily involved Department of Defense assets, personnel, and one of its most high-ranking military officers as General Weyand.

The lone 'duty, honor, country' Schlesinger, He's out of favor with his own Skull's administration. He's increasingly isolated. But my view of point this Secretary of Defense James Schlesinger, a man of decency and compassion, dispatched a message to all members of the American armed forces. "For many of freedom-fighters," he acknowledged, "the tragedy of Southeast Asia is more than a distant and abstract event. American have fought there; they have lost comrades there; they have suffered there," He reminded those who fought the war that they had been victorious and had left the field with honor, stating also his conviction that America's involvement had not been without purpose. "He salutes them for it," he told the forces worldwide. "Beyond any question they are entitled to the nation's respect, admiration and gratitude."

Schlesinger and Kissinger stood at direct odds when it came to handling the latest events in South Vietnam. Schlesinger had told President Ford when President Thieu had begun to panic and the Central Highlands fell that he believed his represented the final Communist offensive and that South Vietnam had little hope of surviving it. He told puppet President Ford, (the weakest president in US history, the people didn't elect him) *"The handwriting is on the wall."*

The New Legion

Pretender Kissinger and Ambassador Martin spoke with great seemed optimism for South Vietnam rallying and even toyed with the notion of using détente with the Soviet Union as a hole card to encourage Moscow to stop the North Vietnamese short of Saigon, Schlesinger voiced caution. Kissinger had urged the President by pressures like Nixon recently to empty the warehouses of South Vietnam's allocations of war supplies and to expedite those shipments, while Schlesinger wanted them held back. Pragmatically, he reasoned that with South Vietnam now a lost cause, anything America sent to the country would wind up in the hands of the Communists.

The WSAG don't want the notorious bloodshed will took place in South Vietnam by their scam. So if the Senate and the House would approve a massive emergency infusion of war goods to South Vietnam, based on the Weyand assessment, then in worst case, if Saigon fell, the world could not blame America for it. The Unites States had the goods on the way. The failure of South Vietnam's resolve would then have to shoulder the blame. America had not, after all, run out on an ally. It seemed to me that "It was a very neat CYA [cover your ass] strategy. However, it would allow America to retain the respect of those other nations who also looked to the United States for a commitment to their protection.

At last, the problems that America face in protect South Vietnam are an elementary question of what kind of people America are. For fifteen years America have been encouraging the people of South Vietnam defended themselves against [Red-menace] what America conceive to be an external danger. Now America stands on the brink of betraying that trust?

In the past almost four years, Congress has dramatically cut aid to South Vietnam, going against a long-standing commitment. As a result, that nation now falters because of a grievous lack of spare parts and replacement equipment by project "enhance" as Paris accords permitted. American cannot betray this sacred trust with South Vietnam.

At United States Embassy, Saigon: "Sir, Ambassador Martin and I met with President Thieu this morning, and Thieu has again pled for help," General Frederick Weyand said to President Gerald Ford in a conference telephone call to Palm Springs from the United

States Embassy in Saigon. "Given what they have lost in Danang, it will require at the very least another $700 million in equipment and supplies on top of what U.S have already committed to them."

"Congress will never agree (under pressure of Skull and Bones) to more than $1.5 billion after they cut the authorization by half that much last year alone," President Ford said.(in the past four years, Congress has dramatically cut aid to South Vietnam, even one replaced one in the Enhance Project that permitted by Paris accord agreement)

"Mr. President, Graham Martin here," the ambassador to Saigon interjected: "If we can only reassure President Thieu that American has not abandoned South Vietnam, I am certain he can lead their forces to rally. All of this doomsday reporting by the media has set the South Vietnamese armed forces on their ears. We need to demonstrate some resolve and reassure them"

"President Ford and his chief staff, Donald Rumsfeld also knew well that President Thieu had lost a great deal of credibility as his nation's leader, not only with his own people and their armed forces, but with the international political world as well. The Chief of staff WSAG knew backing a loser did not sit well with either man.

"Shipments of equipment and supplies will go a long way in doing that," General Weyand said. "When I return in a few days, I will give you a formal report, but for now it looks like they will need at least double what Congress has already allowed them in the current budget."

Long ago, under pressure of totalitarian-Skull and Bones over the House and Senate, the first volley in Congress came in 1970 when influenced Senator Church and Kentucky Republic Senator John Sherman Cooper Church authored a bill that cut off funding of all military activity in Southeast Asia. That measure narrowly failed in its original form. However, on December 29, 1970, as a shirttail amendment to the defense authorization bill, a watered-down version of the measure finally passed. That version of the amendment only barred the introduction of America ground forces in Laos and Thailand. Senator Church and other members of Congress (influenced by George H W Bush) so angered by President Nixon openly lying about United States military involvement in Cambodia

(War Power Act) that they immediately took action to begin cutting funding for the war.

As American air and ground forces swept through Cambodia during April of 1970, President Nixon, when confronted with press reports of the United States-led aerial bombing and ground combat operations there, addressed the issue in a nationally televised speech. President Nixon directly stated that the United States had no advisors on the ground in Cambodia, had no American military forces involved in any actions in Cambodia, and no American military air assets supporting any action in Cambodia. President Nixon's blatant lie set off a congressional firestorm and did more to cripple assistance in South Vietnam and Cambodia.

Throughout most of years of United States involvement in South Vietnam, although Cambodia proclaimed a nonbelligerent, neutral status, it actually supported the Viet Cong and North Vietnam forces by providing them refuge, primary in the Parrot's Beak region along Mekong River, hardly more than fifty kilometers west of Saigon. In this so called neutral territory, Communist forces successfully-escaped American and South Vietnamese pursuit and rested and recuperated between commitments to combat operations. In this Cambodia haven, they also stashed large caches of weapons and supplies ferried over the notorious Harriman's Highway, which crossed through Cambodia at several points, exiting into the Mekong region and the Central Highlands. Nixon's characterization of the incursion's purposes shifted attention from the far more important goals of disrupting the enemy's lines of communication and clearing out his base areas, achievement that could set back his timetable for further aggression to the advantage of both ARVN improvement and US withdrawals. But this is against the axis of evil's craps.

Cambodia incursion is the changing Nature of the War. In reality, the nature of the military conflict in South Vietnam has been under change since Tet-Offensive 1968 [Westmoreland stand for US combat troop moving in a peak 543,400 in term "Search and Destroy. And Abrams stand for withdrawal to the last G.I, in term "Clear and Hold] Although shifts in the level of violence, type of military operations, and size and location of forces involved are characteristicof this change, the allied realization that the war basically a political content has, thus far, been decisive. Not until the early of 1970 was authority granted for on "incursion" of limited duration and depth into Cambodia. Intelligence had indicated, said President Nixon that the enemy was building up large concentration of men and equipment in the border sanctuaries of Laos and Cambodia. This led him to contemplate actions that U.S could undertake to show the enemy that U.S was still serious about US's commitment in South Vietnam. Of course the unexpected overthrow of Sihanouk also presented a changed and potentially favorable situation.

That's a flat contradiction of what Secretary Laird said before! In Washington, some fairly novel command arrangements surfaced. A presidential blue ribbon commission later reported that, "As was widely noted by the press at the time.... Defense Secretary Laird had been bypassed the Joint Chiefs staff in advising the White House on preparations to intervene in Cambodia in April and May 1970." Clearly that had been done on orders from the White House. [WSAG' chief staff Donald Rumsfeld] there were other problems, including conflicting guidance from Washington that led General Abrams to state some Standard Operation Procedures.

Storm blown a gale: Three weeks into the operation, General Alexander Haig in the White House, part of Kissinger's National Security Council staff, seems the likely source. Perhaps Haig himself was the principal author, a prospect congruent with his later involvement in and reaction to the operation – sent by the WSAG to look into what was happening in the war zone – arrived in Saigon. Haig's discussions with General Abrams and others were prickly, his perspective relentlessly political. "I'd hate like hell to think that the President was justifying his action on faulty information, or lagging information," said Haig, his unsavory face voicing an implied criticism. That apparently related to Nixon's announcement that the operation targeted COSVN headquarters [violated the axis of evil ROE stratagem] "He maintains, and frankly this is what he was getting from his cabinet and from the briefings we were getting, that it was ambiguous." Well, yes, agreed the MACV briefer, "it was ambiguous, at the time," Obviously, there was unhappiness in the White House over some procedural matter, perhaps an assessment of the North

The New Legion

Vietnamese outlook on negotiations, even as the operation itself was proceeding admirably.

Those at MACV had their own concerns about ambiguity and they weren't shy about bringing them up with Haig. "We have two of your messages," he was told. "One of them says 'go get 'em

And the other one says "hurry up and get out," in the anticipated plot of WSAG. "What is it you people really want?" "Well," Haig responded, "its 'go get 'em' until the end of the period."

Another eye of the storm: In April of 1973, the United States Congress sent a fact finding team to Cambodia to examine the situation. James G. Lowenstein and Richard M. Moose headed the team and issued the report from the mission to Missouri Senator Stuart Symington, who chaired the Subcommittee on US Security Agreements and Commitments Abroad. Lowenstein and Moose reported that to offset Communist guerrillas' increasing successes in gaining control of key territory, the United States had increased its air support of Cambodia republic forces to ensure the survival of the Khmer Republic. The report cited that the fighting would continue indefinitely since the Khmer Rouge and their North Vietnamese, Soviet Union, and Chinese Communist allies were clearly not interested in any cease-fire options. The report further stated that even if the Communist might agree to a cease fire, it would no doubt hinge on the condition that the United States stop all of its support to Cambodia, similar to the stipulation laid out in the Paris Peace Accords. The report concluded that without American support the Cambodian republic could not last very long.

Most significantly, once Cambodia fell, then South Vietnam would face its worst nightmare: NVA forces poised on its western flank with no American air support. The Moose and Lowenstein also report virtually laid out a set of no-win options for Congress. Continued support of Cambodia would potentially mire the United States in another war much like the one in South Vietnam. The alternative literally gave away Southeast Asia to the Communists.

On 29/ June/ 1973, two months after Moose and Lowenstein's report, Congress placed a ride on the 1974 budget authorization bill that required a halt to all combat air operations in Southeast Asia as Permanent Government's anticipated plot. New Jersey Republican

Senator Clifford P. Case and Idaho Democrat Senator Frank F. Church authorized this amendment, which bore their names. To seal out all American involvement in any combat in Laos, Cambodia, and Vietnam, Congress passed yet another amendment. This measure, a shirttail rider attached to the December 1973 foreign aid bill, forbade any funding of any military operations anywhere in Southeast Asia.

"No matter what happens in Cambodia or South Vietnam," the U.S have several mandates passed by both houses of Congress and signed into law by the President that say Americans can only watch while Southeast Asia goes down the tubes. Americans can land no ground forces, can send no air support, Americans can provide no military advisors nor any military aid.

At the end of axiom-1's for Vietnam War, the ARVN fought the war alone at the most difficult situation due to short supplies in logistics and the US military disengagement; however the ARVN, unfortunately, this classic epic battle seemed to get lost in the political fog of phony Paris agreement at that time. More than three decades was a long time, yet the images of Vietnam in March and April 1975 are still vivid: precipitated withdrawals of South Vietnamese troops from Quang Tri, Hue, and Danang in the north to Kon-Tum, Pleiku, and Ban Me Thuot in the highlands; thousands of civilians with their meager belongings and in tattered clothing fleeing the incoming Communist troops on National Route-1; desperate parents, holding children in their arms, trying to swim to the ships anchored offshore; total chaos in Saigon (the capital of South Vietnam, now officially called Ho Chi Minh City) and finally on April 30, a long line of people climbing on helicopters on the rooftop of the U.S. embassy to get out of the doomed country. The Vietnam War finally came to an end terminated by Pennsylvania game. After years of bitter fighting, South Vietnam was forcibly taken over by the Communist North. The Vietnam-War was often portrayed as an Imperialist-War which started when U.S. Marines landed in Danang in 1965. In fact, it started in 1961 when the Communists assassinated Colonel Hoang Thuy Nam, the head of the South Vietnamese delegation to the International Joint Control Commission. This group was set up following the signing of the Geneva Accord of 1954 to monitor the cessation of hostilities between the Communist North (Democratic

Republic of Vietnam) and the non-Communist South (Republic of Vietnam), and many assassinations of government officials, guerilla ambushes against the army that followed. The Geneva Accord called for a national election in 1956, ostensibly for people to decide on the political future of the country. The South Vietnamese government, however, did not sign this agreement as U.S Permanent Government suggested. In believing that it would never be possible to organize fair elections in Communist-dominated areas, the South Vietnamese refused to fall into this trap, hoping that the country would eventually become strong enough to defend itself against the Communist onslaught. The election, therefore, never took place. Having failed to take the South by the much hoped-for election, the Communists started to make plans to eventually realize their dreams by force, at all costs. Thus began the Vietnam war, which eventually led to an estimated three million deaths on both sides, hundreds of thousands of former members of the Armed Forces and government of South Vietnam, as well as numerous intellectuals, religious leaders, as well as other civilians killed in revenge or imprisoned for years in concentration camps officially called "re-education camps" and thousands of refugees losing their lives in the perilous and pirate-infested South China Sea in their quest for freedom elsewhere. More than thirty years has been just passing on our grey hair since the collapsing of Saigon and South Vietnam, our beloved capital, our country. And it seems to me that the pain and the sorrow of the "Saigon Mayday" in 1975 just happened yesterday. The United States Army and The South Vietnam Army have not lost the Vietnam War, but the policy makers from WIB Bones and the members of the United States' Congress have forced us to lose it. I have fought with my whole young during years; I admired our American comrade in arms, and I still admire SOG recon-team now." "I think that at the end, freedom and democracy will win the final victory..."

So American just let all that the U.S forces fought for, everything that more than fifty-eight thousand Americans died for, all just float down the *binjo* ditch? Americans doing nothing but merely mention George H.W Bush tucked away in running a damn Chinese fire drill. The fighting- The frustration. The nearly three decades of conflict- Done- The more than ten years of American soldiers losing their limbs, hearts, and lives- Finished- At 10:30 A.M on Wednesday morning, April 30, 1975 – brought down the Vietnam War's final curtain! "Skull and Bones will not find a safe haven here!"

Spring 1975, at Washington national capital, a few cherry blossoms still lingered on the late-blooming trees that grew along the Potomac near the Jefferson Memorial. President Ford stood by one of the tall windows behind his desk in the Oval Office, looking toward the river of the now leaf covered cherry trees that, although they blossomed beautifully, never bore fruit. A gift from Japan, the Sakura, the nonbearing fruit tree, raised an ironic parallel in the President's mind. How much like them was Vietnam now? For ten years America had cultivated the small nation, spilled its sons' and daughters' blood urging it to bloom. (They will bloomed in the scope of Skull and Bones for couple more decades ahead, be patiently, I guessed) But today, just as the trees that lined the Potomac by the Jefferson Memorial had done in recent weeks, the bloom dropped to the ground. Vietnam would never bear its costly fruit. "Who know… who tell the prophetically!"

President Ford knocked the right door. A voice came from the curved door that disappeared into the Oval Office wall, "Sir"

"Don [Donald] comes on in," the President said to WSAG Chief of Staff Don Rumsfeld.

"Update on the situation in Saigon," Rumsfeld said, handing the President the two pages flash message.

"It says that the South Vietnamese are trying to storm the gates at the embassy and at the DAO compound," President Ford said. "I am afraid that this will only lead to big trouble. Order the Marines and remaining embassy staff to evacuate now. No more South Vietnamese evacuees. I want only Americans on these helicopters now."

Week ago, though Kissinger had sent an urgent message to Ambassador Martin, "We have just completed an interagency review on the state of play in South Vietnam. You should know that at the WSAG meeting today, there was almost no support for the evacuation of Vietnamese, and for the use of American force to help protect any evacuation. The sentiment of our military, DOD (Department Of Defense) and CIA colleagues was to get out fast and now.

The New Legion

"One other thing Sir," Bitterly Rumsfeld, a head of WSAG, complaint "Kissinger wants to see you about Ambassador Martin, [a Vietnamese-philanthropist] Apparently, Kissinger has gotten wind of a plan the ambassador is trying to hatch that gets him to the French embassy, where he can continue negotiations with the North Vietnamese." How come Martin knew the secret negotiation between Le Duc Tho and Kissinger about 'axiom I', South Vietnam will be a good token gift to Hanoi for carried-out the 'Strongman side stratagem'. "The more immediate origins of the Vietnam-War, namely the White House" But later I dare said "illustrate how completely the U.S presidents and their NSC staffs dominated the overall control and conduct of both the war and the closely interrelated negotiations to end the war." While acknowledging that as a proper role for the President, who was after all the Commander in Chief, I observed that Henry Kissinger "became for all intents and purposes the de facto chairman of the JCS". But in reality, Kissinger was just the George H W Bush's tool, having the skill of a 'Quarterback' It was the ultimate team effort, but every member of the team had to have the grit of a 'Linebacker' as WSAG' Donald Rumsfeld and the very brains of a coach George H W Bush.

"Tell Henry," President Ford began to say, "No, I will talk to Henry. Have him come on over."

"He has that State Department black tie dinner tonight," Rumsfeld said.

"I think that can wait until we get this done," President Ford said.

"History will appreciate the reasons for his tardiness, (at least the South Vietnamese) at that dinner."

"Yes, Sir," the Chief of Staff said and walked toward the door

"Don," President Ford said, "When you send my evacuation order to Saigon, be sure that you specially address Ambassador Martin. I want him out of the embassy on the next helicopter. Is that clear?"

The president directs that no more Vietnamese evacuees fly out on U.S helicopters, only Americans, very important, Ford specially directed that Ambassador Martin depart the embassy on the next helicopter out.

Immediately, Jim Kean jogged down the stairs and found Ambassador Martin seated behind his desk. His aide-de-camp, Brunson McKinley, stood by the desk when the Marine stepped inside the ambassador's suite.

"Sir, I just received orders from President Ford, via General Carey, that all further evacuations of South Vietnamese cease and that's all the remaining American now evacuate," Kean said.

Still Ambassador Martin didn't know the War-Game of the Axis of Evil is over now.

"I'm awaiting a response from the French ambassador," Martin said in a tired voice.

"We still might have a chance if I can get over there and go to work."

"Sir," Kean said. "President Ford specially ordered you out on the next helicopter."

The gray man, whose face now looked drawn and haggard, stood and looked around his office.

"Well, I guess that's it then," Martin said in a calm and low voice. Major Kean had already taken down the United States flag and had carried it in his hand, folded in a triangle, when he came to Ambassador Martin's office. As the beaten diplomat stepped out of his spacious grand suite for the last time, Kean handed him the embassy's national colors.

As Graham Martin waited for his helicopter to set down on the roof and his signal to board, Brunson McKinly, jogged down to the courtyard to get an outdate of the situation down there for the ambassador before he departed.

"Tiger, tiger, tiger," Pilot called on his radio to the command vessel, USS Blue Ridge. "Tiger, tiger, tiger"

"Go ahead, Tiger," responded the voice on Pilot's radio.

"Tiger's out of his cage," Pilot said, signaling that he had the ambassador aboard.

President Ford confessed. "It looks like we just quit and ran. Yet I did all that I could for them. However, it still remains very difficult for me to sit here as President of the United States and watch South Vietnam collapse."

The New Legion

At 10:24 A.M President Duong Van Minh issued a statement, broadcast to the North Vietnamese, offering the surrender of the Republic of Vietnam. The announcement seemed to represent the latch on the gate because in a matter of minute parades of victorious Viet Cong and North Vietnamese soldiers, walking, riding in trucks, and sitting on tanks T-55, T-57 and armored personnel carriers came streaming into Saigon from every direction.

Seeing President Minh's motorcade driving to the presidential Palace, a Australian motion picture news photographer, Al Dawson set up his camera on the front steps of Big Minh' headquarters [presidential Palace] He had his camera rolling when the Soviet-build T-55 tank, with soldiers waving the PRG flag, crashed down the palace gates and rumbled up the wide walkway to the great building's front steps. The Australian photojournalist stood, waved at the Communists, and kept his camera rolling.

Meanwhile, not far from here, an observer from the roof of the United States Embassy – four stories and a helicopter platform above Saigon – He could see for several kilometers. This gloomy moment, his world looked a mess with wrecked cars, trashed streets, and broken windows. Just beyond the courtyard fence, the embassy's once-beautiful Olympic swimming pool now floated with suitcases, clothing, guns, and chairs. During the night, with no facilities, the Vietnamese waiting to escape had even used the pool as o toilet.

The Permanent Government would like Nguyen Cao Ky joining in the postwar on strategy track of Post-Vietnam "Road-Map"; Ky was a former Prime minister and Vice President, Republic of Vietnam. He held the rank of air vice marshal, commander of the South Vietnamese Air Force, and had flamboyantly played to be named president of South Vietnam when President Nguyen Van Thieu resigned. At one time, the CIA feared that Premier Ky was leading a coup to take over what remained of the South Vietnamese government when Tran Van Huong was named president on April 21, 1975, in accord with the South Vietnamese constitution, to succeed President Thieu. When former President Thieu departed South Vietnam, Ky labeled him a coward and said that anyone who would flee in the face of the enemy was also a coward. He want the people in Saigon must undergone a terrible pounding shelling by

Hanoi artillery and after sixty days, like defense at Leningrad and the United Nation should be intervened; but it not like the WSAG strategy. Ky remained in Saigon until late afternoon, He may have a secret instruction to flee out of Saigon at once. Therefore on 29, when he flew his personal helicopter to the deck of the USS Blue Ridge. His observations and actions provided valuable insight into the political death those of South Vietnam during the final days. He will be the necessary tool for Skull and Bones Dynasty in the post Vietnam

The interview with General Westmoreland by Thoi-Luan newspaper

Question: As a Commander of the U.S. Army in Vietnam, how do you find the fighting capability of the US Army and of the ARVN, when confronting with the North Vietnam Communist Army?

Answer: I admire the highly combating spirit of the South Vietnamese Army. As of the US Army, I have nothing more to say. It's because the end of Vietnam War was originated by political problems and not by military's reasons. "...During the Cabinet meeting on the next day in the White House, Kissinger on behalf of Permanent Government reported: "At this moment, all the North Vietnam's Army are in the South... We only need a Brigade of Marine to conquer the North. The Paris Peace Accords have been severely violated!" why Permanent Government didn't do react that? During the first weeks of April, there was a lot of effort behind-the-scenes to overturn President Thieu. Things turned out that finally The South Vietnam had two enemies: The Communists and The United States. Only a Brigade of ARVN Marine and at least 4 Battalions tested Division of the South Vietnam's Reserved Army were still intact. Hanoi has blatantly violated the Paris Peace Accords, and why the United States did not overrun North Vietnam, to liberate Hanoi? The United States did not do a thing! Who know ... but it seemed there was Eurasian Great Game must be carried out in second chunk, second period of the Axis of Evil, and the last chunk should be Middle East, **preparedness for 21st century the United States in control World's labors, markets, and resource**s.. . That everything I should guessed.

Users/tim/Desktop/baby - Later on, when asked why North Vietnam never provided a complete list of prisoners of war, Vernon Walters answered that, "Le Duc Tho looked at Kissinger's face during the peace talk in Paris and said: *"I don't know why I need to talk with you. I have just talked with Senator Mc Govern during 6 hours. The anti-war movement [Permanent Government] in your country will force you to give me what I want!"* "All the historical defeat and the incompetence, coward-ness of the Western leaders are heaped onto the back of the Vietnamese soldiers ... It's dishonest and unfair. The shame is on us and not on the South Vietnam's army" (David Halberstan / Newsweek) As for 1975, the North won because the South Vietnamese were short of everything from rifle and artillery rounds to tank parts, radio batteries and bandages after Congress cut aid in 1974 by "Cooper-Church" and "Case-Church". Even the enemy said so. Nevertheless, a reinforced South Vietnamese division held off five of Hanoi's best divisions for a week at Xuan Loc, in a battle as brave as any ever fought by Americans. It's bad enough that we abandoned the South Vietnamese. Let's not insult them to assuage our guilt. Harry F Noyes III, San Antonio.

REPUBLICAN GEORGE- H. W. BUSH SUCCEEDED TO THE THRONESKULL AND BONES DYNASTY FROM DEMOCRAT W. A. HARRIMAN BUT AS MERELY A SURROGATE FOR...

Not like World War I, II, or Korea, but Vietnam and Iraq were means walking into the major disaster so why the ghost Averell-Harriman was disguised his appearance very cleverly from the public spot light in early 1960s, in the shadow still 'witch-hunt' haunted over the darkness. Vietnam-War is an episode of chunk two of Eurasian stratagem [not U.S troop stayed there, except in German, Japan, and Korea] A stage he implied 'a tactical manage the defeat for strategic roll-back after couple decades later, or we could called 'a overhauling damage-control' commenced 1970 by at time of the First congressional volley ball emerged as "Cooper-Church" then "Case-Church". As a result, U.S retreat temporary out of the South China-Sea, means the most islands in South China Sea such Paracels and Spratlys leaving there a lay-trap. But shortly organized the spearhead-instrument the PACOM at Honolulu headquarter for surveying in case reacted emergency operational maneuver.

But yes, it must be a coincidence; it has to be a coincidence. It is fair to say that by the time A Harriman retired from public 1969. He was working to derail George H W Bush's presidential ambitions by slotting him as Bush's three generations and Walker families already had some six decades of intelligence-related activity and experience under their belts. The Bush family has never produced a doctor, judge, teacher, scholar, or lawyer of note. As far back as W.W I, the family's single-minded focus has been on three major areas: "Intelligence, Energy, and National Security." George-I was completely trusted by Harriman in reigning the second Skull and Bones generation. Under Skull and Bones influenced, Nixon, in turn, won the presidency in 1968, would help George-I, a first congressman, as befit the son of Skull and Bones deputy [Prescott Bush]. This, to be sure, is getting ahead of the story, and what made it possible to consider the emperor-II of Skull and Bones dynasty for vice president in 1968, almost unexpectedly, was that some five decades earlier, his two grandfathers – George Herbert Walker, and Samuel Prescott Bush – had managed to implant themselves and their descendants in the eastern establishment. This helped Prescott Bush get ahead, much as later connections helped George-I and George-II.

The younger George-I had also been commended to Nixon by former Republican presidential nominee Thomas E. Dewey, [William A. Harriman] probably the one man most responsible for convincing Dwight Eisenhower to take Nixon as his running mate back in 1952. Eight years later, W.A Harriman attempts let the name of George-I make the vice president rumor mills, less because of possible appeal Bush might have in Texas than for the socioeconomic reassurance he would offer to New York and Connecticut Republican donors and Ivy League club. The job offers good opportunities for advancement: appointments to the United Nations (1970) and the Republican National Committee (1973) brought George-I as a cabinet command and control and Nixon-inner-circle status, maintaining the Washington visibility critical to his future. President Nixon under pressure of Permanent Government has to valued Bush's family connections, gung ho spirit, personal likeability, and

The New Legion

social outreach. (George-I was masterminded the Vietnam-War and the CIP will terminated very soon by Harriman frame-work – Paris Peace Talk. Similar considerations helped to guide President Ford's 1975 selection of George-I to head the CIA, a famous repository of Yale alumni.

Since then the United States had evolved its own version of "Permanent Government" akin to the British model. Focused on world War-II and the enlargement and mutation of the early military-industrial complex, [WIB] including the absorption of Germany-savvy U.S. business, financial, and legal elites into the OSS, then CIA, and kindred agencies in the 1940; Brown Brothers Harriman, Prescott Bush, George H. Walker, and their Yale and Wall Street colleagues were all important actors in this drama. From Bushes [Samuel Bush, George Walker, and Prescott Bush through George-I] and their involvements with the national security establishment, too little attention has been paid to the strong connections developed between the Bush family and the CIA many years before George-I ran it. Under George-II, the CIA has flexed more muscle than ever.

If you're truly to understand the perilous state of the American political system one is political fundamentalism that gained strength as the new 'company-dynasty' has unfolded. A second is the ever-changing importance within the "America-First" in U.S society of different economic sectors and elite – from investment banking and oil to the military industrial complex [WIB]. The third is the twentieth – and early-twenty-first-century emergence of the Bushes families, which this volume seeks to track along a trajectory of American wealth and power through the heyday of Wall Street investment banking, Ivy League club and Texas POL-politics and into the post-World War-II emergence of the CIA and rise of the national security state.

Until now, its political history has embodied a different, 1950 [Harriman came back from Europe to Washington, works in Executive Office Building and his talented strategists] – flavored saga centered on careers of man like William A Harriman , who played his starring national roles from the late 1940 to the early 1960s. Now a new company dynasty warrants a different national story. The Bushes and their initially more influential Walker family in laws were also "present at the creation," to use William A Harriman's term, but in secondary capacities. The family stepped into public visibility only in 1952, when Prescott Bush from a humble tire-salesman, to managing partner at Brown Brothers Harriman, for many years the nation's biggest private investment bank, won election to the U.S. Senate from Connecticut.

Three generations of Bushes: Prescott, George H.W Bush, and George W Bush similarly, the involvement of four Walker and Bush generations with finance – in several cases, the investment side of the POL business – helps to explain their recurrent preoccupation with investments, capital gains, and tax shelters George-II' 2003 commitment to ending taxation of dividends was simply an extension of George-I' frequent calls for reducing capital gains tax rates as the solution to any weakness in the national economy. At last, there is no previous parallel to the relationships between the Bushes and CIA and its predecessor organizations, which began in the invisible-ink and "Ashenden," Secret Agent days of George Herbert Walker and Prescott Bush. Quite simply, analyzing separately the two George-I and George-II presidencies risks losing sight of such essential and revealing leitmotifs

George-I also continued his father's national security interests in taking up the CIA directorship in 1975, as well as by being a New-England-type Republican fiscal conservative and social moderate disinclined to wear ideological cowboy boots. His initial presidential nomination bid in 1980, instead of counting on oil states; as young as eighteen year-old, George-I, in becoming a naval pilot, was trying to redeem the family honor from the German taint The greater weight of evidence, judged by the views of biographers, is that he had a great respect for his father, proudly following his path through Yale and Skull and Bones. Besides, at age eighteen, just out of Andover and with no college under his belt, he depended on his father's help to arrange an underage and unqualified entrance to the Naval air program. While in theory this entrance would have appeared impossible, it might have been quite manageable with a telephone call from Prescott Bush to one of three fellow Yale and Skull and Bones [Secretary of war, Assistant secretary for air and navy air] "Of-course O.K right away!"

The New Legion

The "roll-back" strategy commences, when July's Republican convention ratified George-I as Reagan's vice presidential running mate, it made him the first former CIA director ever slated. Given the international stakes, however, the choice may have been shrewd. Bill Casey, the Reagan campaign manager named in February, was another old intelligence hand. The doubling up was utterly unprecedented. Casey, a senior OSS officer during WW-II, had also been an acquaintance of Prescott Bush's. In 1961, the two had worked together, in the Bay of Pigs and in launching the National Strategy Information Center which advocated U.S. use of political and covert operations and from there [National Security Directive-3] George-I became notorious "if any vice president in U.S. history could fairly be known as the secret-arm-deal vice president George-I would be the one. Because simply the NSIC' obsession led some to assume that it was a CIA front.

The twenty-first century "New Eurasian Great Game" is rife with blowback and backlash:

Observer has realized the extent to which both world wars dripped petroleum concern. Save for the bloody 1942-1945 island-hopping in the Pacific, (now 21st century once again) we usually picture both world wars in European terms. Peripheries like North Africa were just that – side-shows. Ship convoys were maritime adjuncts.

Unfortunately, George-I derailed out of track American-First but for his oilmen, arms deals. With their accession, national policymaking became more energy-centered, as did national security calculations and criteria. The overlap between oil services and military support activities expanded. The sole previous U.S chief executive to have come from the oil or energy business had been the new president's father. But by the time George-I reached the White House in 1989, his active participation in the industry was two decades in the past.

Both George-I and II pairing were fresher from industry and more intensely involved in the issues. In 2001 also brought the first White House national security adviser, Condoleezza Rice, with a special in what had been Soviet Central Asia and a particularly strong oil industry background. Along with oil, armaments, and domestic political considerations, in the emergence of a new U.S foreign policy, one that blends biblical bluntness about an "Axis of

Evil" with skepticism, if not hostility, to the United Nations and an embrace of preemptive warfare. The fact is that any emergence of a U.S. "crusader state" stands to profit important economic interests even as it pleases religious fundamentalist.

In my concept, the wars of the Skull and Bones Succession, examines the First and the Second war with Iraq from a Bush-dynasty standpoint. Texas presidents [L B Johnson and father and son] have now launched the last three U.S wars: Vietnam, the Gulf War of 1991, and the 2003 war to overthrow Saddam-Hussein. The latter two reflect a unique set of circumstances. They were the first pair of U.S wars to be fought by George-I and George-II presidents, and were caused in part by a misconceived U.S. arms buildup in Iraq undertaken by Bush as Reagan's vice president and then as president himself. They also reflected a two-generation Texan preoccupation with US. Middle Eastern and Caspian oil interests. "The war of the Skull and Bones Succession" thus has a geopolitical as well as Harriman and Bushes families based foundation.

Crony capitalism, but not violated "patriot-Act" in constitution George-I was still strengthen the U.S position being the First-Supreme-World's Superpower, though he's notorious a secret-arms-deal

Human-being-life was very short couldn't cover for a long great stratagem, how continued Crony-Capitalism? A-Harriman, been working until 86 year-old, believes that in economic policy what is good for wealthy investors and business executives is good for America [but under-influenced his Skull and Bones – Congressional Quarterly: in its two decades history, Congress and the Nation 1945-1964 cited only to restrict Kennedy trade legislation – this reflected the dominant conservative position among influenced Senate Republicans] Harriman believes that taxes must be kept low on capital gains and on top marginal incomes, so that members of the educated and money-fund elite – which he sees as the creative force in the economy – will have an incentive to risk their capital … He believes, implicitly, that taxes need not be low on the wages or saving accounts of ordinary Americans, who are not a creative force in the economy and who anyway have no choice but to work and scrimp.

The New Legion

As late as World War-II, A Harriman kept his Brown Brothers Harriman partnership and Soviet Union stock and bond portfolio while serving in Moscow as U.S Ambassador. For over forty years president or chairman of two major investment firms, 'W A Harriman and Company' and 'G H Walker and Company' – Prescott Bush, in turn, started at 'A Harriman and Company' In 1926 and later became the managing partner of Brown Brothers Harriman. George H W Bush mostly did the financial side of oil until he wound up with 'First International Bancshares. George-I' father and his uncle arranged his jobs or took care of the financing he needed.

Between the 1960 to1969, the transitional period overlapping between Harriman and George-1, crony capitalism sometimes took the form of dollars from CIA or from other government agencies and federal program enlisted by CIA. Zapata Offshore, the international drilling subsidiary, [Shortly we called Bushes-dynasty means CIA likewise Vietnam-War means Huey-Helicopters] that passed under Bush's principal control when he felt the larger Zapata framework in 1959, operated within surveillance distance of Castro's Cuba and was said by some CIA supported (America's secret power in a democratic society" author Lock K Johnson, Oxford University press 1989. In 2007 the GDP of Vietnam 45, 2 billion, "World in figures ed. 2007," page 238; while CIA budget 43, 3 billion, compared with 1998 CIA's budget 26, 7 billion. That couldn't unbelievable!

When Nixon, in turn, won the presidency in 1968, he would have to treat George H.W Bush, like a Skull and Bones' Second Emperor of Company-dynasty, as first-term congressman, as befit the son of Prescott Bush and as merely a surrogate for W A Harriman, First Emperor in view of my perception. George-1's appointments to the United Nations (1970) and the Republic National Committee (1973) brought Bush cabinet and Nixon-inner-circle status, maintaining the Washington visibility critical to his future. Nixon valued Bush's family connections, gung ho spirit, personal like-ability, and social outreach. Similar considerations helped to guide President Ford's 1975 selection of him to head the CIA kicked William Colby out of their famous repository of Yale alumni. George-1 wanted to be – and perhaps was – taken as qualified for the cabinet in the unelected.

In the White House, the so called Carter Doctrine of 1979 due to the 1973 Arab-Israeli War, the Arab quadrupled the price of oil and cut off deliveries to the United States. By 1975, oil was becoming a critical factor to the CIA, where George H W Bush took over in December (obviously, his appointment was abruptly confirmed by the Senate in January 1976) A few months earlier, unsurprisingly, Secretary of State Henry Kissinger had made it clear that the United States would go to war to prevent any strangulation of U.S and world oil supplies, a pledge later restated by the Permanent Government.

This, to be sure, is getting ahead of U.S history. What made it possible to consider George-1 for the vice president in 1968, (the transition from Harriman to George-1) almost out of the blue, was that some fifty years earlier, his two grandfathers – George Herbert Walker, a well-connected St .Louis financier, and Samuel Prescott Bush, a wealthy and WIB director – had managed to implant themselves and their descendants in the eastern establishment. This helped Prescott Bush get ahead, much as later connections helped the Forty-one and Forty three presidents of United States.

China was significant a relationship begun during Emperor-II took over in 1969 from retiree Harriman who decided to retire from public life with the election of President Richard Nixon. As Bush's tenure of a chief of the U.S. mission – barely mentioned George-I tucked away in China. Despite his uncertainties about what direction to take, twelve years of public service, especially the pioneering work he had done in China, afforded George-1 plenty of business opportunities. His knack for making and keeping friends meant that he knew people at the top in Beijing. And in China, contacts were everything. The friend who had been China ambassador to the United Nation was the new vice Foreign Minister. Any U.S company that wanted to do business in the Middle Kingdom needed those sorts of connections. The Chinese leadership was like an Asian version of the U.S Skull Bones Pattern, secretive and select... While George-1 wasn't exactly in the club, he was generally trusted by its new Bones.

However, his trustee White House Chief of staff Rumsfeld drew brief but acid portraiture for first asserting that the gloomed fall of Saigon would give President Gerald Ford the credit for pulling the

The New Legion

Americans out of Vietnam. All were embarrassed or embittered – George-I in Beijing, Shackley in CIA station at Saigon, Dick Cheney, Rumsfeld, and many other planners in the Washington. Between the end of cruel-April, when the last American fled Saigon, and May 15, when President Gerald Ford prematurely claimed victory in the mini-war over the Cambodian seize of the U.S. merchant vessel Mayaguez, the White House kept being surprised or overtaken by events; and then celebrating a triumphant Mayaguez rescue before the ill-managed fighting had actually finished, leaving three U.S. Marines captive on Koh Tang to be executed by the Cambodians.

The neoconservatives in the Democratic Party, most of them still in the hawkish wing were equally stamped by failure in Vietnam and the vulnerability they believed the mid-1970s, (the stage Permanent Government supposes a "strategic manage the defeat" out of Southeast Asia) foreign policy implosion created for Israel and the United States. Richard Perle, a principal aide to Senator Henry "Scoop" Jackson, would spend thirty years trying to rebut the notion that neo-conservatism, at its heart, had its psychological origins in Vietnam-era malaise.

With George-1 in the White House, the brother Prescott junior was the principal visitor, but China president Jiang Zemin entertained even Neil Bush at dinner when he visited in late 2001 to promote his newest company. And even before the Bushes inaugurated their Second president in 2001, they had become the first presidential family to stake out what can best be described as overseas commercial spheres of influence. The Persian Gulf was also clearly preeminent among them, thanks to the wars and armaments deals of the 1980s and 1990s, as well as ex-president George-1's close relations with the Saudi and Kuwaiti royal families. Sons Marvin and Neil had also made commercial visits.

As an 'Eurasian Great Game' stratagem performer, George 1 being a CIA asset in 1963, when he ran Zapata Offshore, as one of the "top 10 censored" stories that year". In 1988, Project Censored, a journalistic consortium based in California, chose the probability of George H.W Bush being a CIA. Furthermore earlier in 1988, "The Nation Magazine had weighed in by reporting a November 29, 1963, FBI memo that "Mr. George Bush of the Central Intelligence Agency" was briefed by the Bureau about the reaction of the Cuban exile community in Miami to the Kennedy assassination. In response, the CIA contended that the Bush involved was actually an agent named George William Bush. The magazine then tracked down George William Bush and found out that in 1963 he was only a junior analyst of the contours of coastlines. The Nation Magazine added that a "source with close connections to the intelligence community confirms that Bush started working for the agency in 1960 or 1961, using his oil business as a cover for clandestine activities.

The motive for Bush's intense feeling about Cuba – still throbbing in his 1964 Senate campaign, when he called for a U.S invasion – becomes more understandable when one thinks about the Cuban rebel' treatment of family-connected sugar and distilling interests. No details exist on Walker-Bush holdings. Castro regime seized the company's lands, mills, and machinery. Bushes whose had arranged the funding for his nephew's Zapata Offshore enterprise might well have warmed to his own covert action. Besides his presumed anger over the West Indian Sugar seizure, Walker was Skull and Bones, like his brother-in-law Prescott and his nephews George and Prescott junior. Things clandestine were part of their culture.

Author Loftus says that George H W Bush's subsequent high standing with the intelligence community came not from his Bay of Pigs involvement but from "when he told Nixon that he couldn't shift the blame for the Mexican slush fund to the CIA without wrecking the intelligence community. There is no proof that Bush conveyed any such warning. Moreover it might uncover a CIA operation the multiple layers of deception by the CIA are astounding.

At any rate, the national security state was rebounding to thrive in the eighties and nineties despite a few bumps after the breakup of the Soviet Union, when the CIA briefly feared for its future. More to the point, two men named George Bush would be CIA director, vice president, or president of the Unites States for seventeen of the thirty two years between 1976 and 2008. In a very real but little understood sense, the Bush dynasty was already getting under way in 1980-1981 when George 1 went from CIA director's job to vice presidency, a jump no one had ever managed before and one that brought a new and unfamiliar mind-set to the elected executive office.

The New Legion

In 1981, because of Bush's CIA experience – and surely also because of the pressurized influence of Permanent Government had managed the Texan's 1980 nomination campaign – President Reagan issued National Security Directive 3, naming the vice president [George 1] to head a Special Situation Group to identify national security crises and plan for them. A new era of clandestine arms races causing Soviet Union a symptom of "Pre-collapse" – and arms sales, massive armaments buildups, secret diplomacy, and covert actions, perhaps as much Bush's doing as Reagan's, because he was a real mastermind of Permanent Government, was about to unfold the "New Great Game" in the Middle East generally and in Iran, Iraq, and Afghanistan specially. With it, the seeds of two Persian Gulf wars and hundreds of terrorist strikes would be fertilized and watered.

The Company Dynasty's [WIB] introduction to the great American-Gun culture probably came in the 1930, the then some accounts have tied George H W Bush to support work in CIA's 1961 Bay of Pigs invasion, and in the years to come his record of clandestine arms deals and shipments as CIA director and then vice president would involve countries from Cuba and Nicaragua to Iran, Iraq, Israel, Pakistan, and Afghanistan. If any vice president in United States history could fairly be known as "the secret-arms-deal vice president" he would be the one.

After Vietnam War, in late 1976, George 1 had also protected wayward or hot-triggered Agency operatives – veterans of everything from Chilean assassinations to Vietnam's Phoenix Program (created in revenge for the killing and when Hanoi violated Paris Accord, the NLF couldn't not joining with the remnant ARVN troops for revolutionary-counterattack Communist Hanoi) and improper domestic surveillance – from indictment by President Ford's justice Department. In the eyes of Attorney General Edward Levi and his aides, George 1's actions verged on obstructing Justice Department investigations. Not least, George 1 had been insistent in protecting former CIA director Richard Helms who might be the Watergate' author for erasing all twenty seven Nixon's letters to President Thieu – aptly named by his biographer "the Man Who Kept the Secrets" – who was ultimately let off with a fine and suspended sentence for lying to Congress. This time Congress do right but William Colby wasn't right because Colby got instruction from Permanent Government which exploited his talent-reputation.

The Eurasia Great Game was aborted when the First emperor of Company Dynasty was out of public 1969 and passed away in 1986. However, the Second emperor [George H.W Bush] was continued his [Harriman] stratagem that I suppose the "New Eurasian Great Game". In the 1980s and 1990s, intensifying U.S military and covert involvement with Iran, Afghanistan, and Iraq set similar cook pots boiling, this rivalry became the so-called Great Game of spies and intelligence organizations. Further heated by the 1991 breakup of the Soviet Union and creation of eight new republics in the Caucasus and Transcaspian

Thank to his father, George-II administration had piles of grand stratagems mounting even before taking office in 2001. George W Bush, like neo-imperialist – so arose the opportunity for a New Great Game resuming from the Old Eurasian Great Game, that time for control of Caucasian and Transcaspian oil fields. In 1993, the resource-war-theorist in Eurasian studies, argued that "this New Eurasian Great Game in the heart of Asia is unfolding not so much among the old colonial powers as among their former minions" – the Caspian and Caucasian states from the Old Soviet Union, as well as Afghanistan, Pakistan, and India from the British sphere.

Central Asia in a New Eurasian Great Game was identified Russia, China, India, Pakistan, and Iran as the players for the game. The interest of the United States, one said, wasn't in being a direct participant but in avoiding conflagration. In the most three years before the attack on the World Trade Center (Retired Marine General Anthony Zinni, who headed the U.S Central Command from 1997 to 2000, lamented that Iraq "reminds me of Vietnam. Here we have some strategic thinkers who have long wanted to invade Iraq. They saw an opportunity, and they used the imminence of the threat and the association with terrorism and the 9/11 emotions as a catalyst and a justification. It another Gulf of Tonkin") the emphasis turned to great-power oil and gas rivalry. The New Eurasian Great Game: Russia and United States competition in the Caspian. In these terms, the United States under President Clinton had clearly started to play. So had a number of Bush allies (Dick Cheney, John Sununu, James

The New Legion

Baker, and Brent Scowcroft) all signed up to counsel the Azerbaijan International Operating Company (AIOC) George-II' members, Secretary States and national security adviser, Condoleezza Rice, as an (Oil-woman) Chevron board member, advised the company on its Tenghiz-Chevroil joint venture in Kazakhstan (considered Kissinger apt to the First Emperor [A Harriman, a Bank-man, and George H W Bush, a Oilman] conformed with Banking, so his favor job was a member of the BNL international advisory board between 1985-1991 and Rice [engaged oilmen]even had a company oil-tanker named after her – a red-hulled, 129,000 ton, Bahama-registered Suezmax behemoth). Typically, Harriman's approach too up residence in the Executive Office Building being similarly Kissinger and Condo-Rice; the blows to their egos because they fully expected to be at President's side as a special assistant to the president for foreign policies; Condoleezza is an intriguing mix of boots, brains, and bravado, rose to become the most powerful woman in the world-top Soviet advisor at age 34 to president George-II, Stanford University's youngest, first female, and first nonwhite provost.

A resource-war theorist also implied a New Eurasian Great Game guided George-II in 2003: "Controlling Iraq is about oil as power, rather than oil as fuel in Harriman's stratagem, and control over the Persian Gulf translates into control over China, Europe, and Japan. It's having our hand on the spigot." Not long after George-II' election in 2000 made his family into theSecond real Dynasty in United States politicians, the crisis of 9/11 – including terrorism, U.S-Saudi-ties, and the question of replacing Saudi Oil and Bases with new facilities in Iraq – took over his presidency. Although this was something none of those involved could have expected, it also spotlighted some hitherto little-debated dynastic disabilities. Clearly, the Bush family's place in Unites States history must rise or fall on its ability to deal with the oil in Middle-East. The concern must be over how those same controversial talents and conflicts of interest will be remembered in histories of the twenty-first-century fortunes of the United States.

At last, the reality is that there is all too much precedent: dynasties, by their very nature, tend toward inheritance and continuity. Despite the new overlay of evangelical Protestantism, the economic record of the George-II essentially extended the practice of the George-I: favoring the small group of rich American while systematically misleading a much large portion of the population.

Bush Crime Syndicate: followed the direction of Godfather [W A. Harriman] and continued keep Harriman's stratagem on track? The Vietnam-War in the mastermind of Harriman's frame-work, but we were insight McNamara in the position executed that war (Kennedy and Johnson administrations). And the Iraq-War, Donald Rumsfeld was activated that war on behalf of Godfather [George-1]. Robert McNamara, Secretary of Defense under Kennedy and Johnson but really under control of the First Skull and Bones Dynasty, William A. Harriman stand-for Permanent Government. And Donald Rumsfeld, Secretary of Defense was directed the Iraq-War, under control of the prince George-II, the "Second-generation" of the Skull and Bones Dynasty.

These were my personal perspectives as a junior commentator: This is a more interesting comparison between two Defense Secretary, Rumsfeld and McNamara. The Vietnam War was a far more damaging and awful conflict than Iraq-War. More Vietnamese died and more Americans died. McNamara has also (sort of) admitted his mistakes, something that Rumsfeld will never do. McNamara also had a complete lack of morality in his judgments – it seems that he saw the Vietnamese as nothing but numbers. Rumsfeld, for as he is, actually might believe in something and maybe that makes him less of a bastard than McNamara who was the architect of the disaster known as the Vietnam-War. He masterminded such terrible ideas as taking South Vietnamese peasants off their land [Phoenix Program] using Agent Orange and other defoliants, and the massive aerial bombing of both North and South Vietnam.

Given all this evidence, why do I argue that Rumsfeld is the worst Secretary of Defense in the nation's history? We must prosecuted Bushes, because McNamara was very much a man of his time while Rumsfeld is an outlaw. Had McNamara not served in his position, history probably would have taken place in a similar way. We still would have gone into Vietnam and hundreds of thousands of people would have died. Did McNamara cause greater damage than another man in the office would have? Probably, But he, like everyone else, believed in the Domino Theory and thought that we had to stop "Red-Menace" everywhere.

Whereas Donald Rumsfeld never represented the majority of opinion in the American public, the military, or even the defense establishment; He and his neo-comrade-buddies decided to engage on a war Iraq, simply because they wanted to. He played a major role in turning the U.S away from the true war on terror and got us involved in an unnecessary war that has killed nearly 4000 Americans and hundreds of thousands of Iraqis. His ideas have plunged the nation into massive debt and severely damaged our credibility abroad. He didn't listen to the nation's military officers (As we have seen even generals who held command in Vietnam War admitted to uncertainty of that war's objectives. Comparable confusion attended the justifications and objectives stated by the George-I, elder Bush in the 1990-91 confrontation with Iraq. A 1974 survey of generals who had commanded in Vietnam found that "almost 70 per cent of the Army generals who managed the war were uncertain of its objectives) preferring to will his ideas into effect rather than listen to reality. No one has done so much to damage the office of the Secretary of Defense as Rumsfeld. No Secretary of Defense has done much to destroy American standing across the world. No previous Secretary of Defense has moved us from a necessary war like Afghanistan into an unnecessary war simply to fulfill the political wishes of a faction of one Oilmen party.

The fantasies of Donald Rumsfeld are different than the fantasies of Robert McNamara in one key aspect – whereas McNamara's fantasies and fears reflected those of both U.S political parties, the defense industry, and the military in 1965; Rumsfeld' fantasies are of his own making and were made active by his own will and the will of a few powerful friends [Oilmen] who happen to control the current administration. For that, and all the unnecessary death, destruction, and decline of American standing in the world that has come from it; I should name Donald Rumsfeld the worst Secretary of Defense in the history of the United States.

"But all above were just unfair, we must account for the Skull and Bones Dynasty Crime Syndicate were must calling American involvement in Vietnam and Iraq-War "a crime against humanity" then rejected a resolution that would have condemned "the appetite of Hanoi and Moslem-Jihad to wage cruel and inhuman war". So called Vietnam and Iraq War were 'two parallel one destruction'. US having new words in its vocabulary as Boat-People, Reeducation-Camp, Killing-Field...

ONCE A DERAILED PERMANENT GOVERNMENT WAS OUT OF TRACK:

The New "Eurasian Great Game" or George H W Bush reigned Second generation of the Skull and Bones Dynasty wasn't "American-First" its strategy was out track to "Oilmen-First" The Bush-family's hunger for power and practices of crony capitalism with a moral arrogance and backstage disregard of the democratic and republican traditions of the U.S government. As we will see, their generations of involvement with clandestine arms deals and European, Middle Eastern rogue banks will do that. This is special true of Bushes' ties to the Wall-Street financial world and the War Industries Complex. After generation by generation of connection to foreign intrigue and the intelligence community, plus three generations of immersion in the future of secrecy, deceit and disinformation have become Bush political hallmarks. The Middle Eastern financial ties of both Bushes presidents exemplify this lack of candor, as do the origins and machinations of both Bushes wars with Iraq.

The first volley in the U.S Attorney's office in Chicago came in 2001, for this reason, the verdict against Libby came down aimed on Vice President Dick Cheney exploded with public anger – George-II chose Cheney because he was coherently affiliated with George-I, his father lead the pack, formed a triumvirate [George H W Bush, Dick Cheney, and Donald Rumsfeld] of like-minded leaders who conceived a gloomy April-1975, Saigon Fall. This eventful incident stunned George-II for the rest of his second term. He implied that "It's run its course. Now we're going to move on...who had promised to discuss the scandal – Valerie Plame leak case when the trial was over." – Imperialist breakdown, rattled; though a Cheney loyalist as Libby cooked up his stories to protect Cheney, he was convicted, but it's the Vice President who is under a cloud. Libby trial spotlighted a Vice President whose overbearing style has become one of the

The New Legion

Administration's biggest problems. But my perception is really not only Cheney that the Bushes are focused on narrow interests as well and as result have too little vision of the vast potential for achievement, to face the common challenges of this generation. The legal justice on display in the Libby verdict, or, to be more precise, the Cheney verdict; under pressure of his father, George-II stumped just about everyone more one half term ago when he tapped the safe and solid Cheney to be his running mate. But George-II didn't want any trouble. He didn't want a Vice President who preened before the journalist spotlight. He didn't want a policy sparing partner.

His cabinet-officials was chosen by his father, and because he reluctantly got exactly the kind of partner he had to chosen; he now faces the very problem he tried to avoid. Cheney has become the administration's enemy within, the man whose single-minded pursuit of ideological goals, creaking political instincts and love of secrecy produced an independent operation inside the White House that has done more harm than good. As a subjectivist, Cheney as nothing less than the locomotive of the Administration, "there's no way in which he isn't driving the long train on this," said one referring to Cheney's role in pushing, pulling George-II and his administration inexorably toward an invasion of Iraq that once John F Kerry said "We bring money for helping Iraqis not for Halliburton Corporation." Analysis, advocacy – it's all done by Cheney or his protégés or his former mentor [Secretary of Defense Donald Rumsfeld] It's about context, It's also reflective not so much of Cheney's direct influence on the President as it is of his influence on – his dominance of – the decision-making process. It's about providing the facts and analysis to the decision maker that the decision maker needs. George-II is making the decision, but the Vice is directing the process toward the decision that he thinks is the right one. This method is repeated when his father [George-I] at Vice position in Reagan's administration. The father's instincts have never been the son's. Replacing the Vice now would create exactly the unpleasant succession scenario George-I had hoped to avoid when he chose Cheney in the first place. He didn't want someone soaking up all the attention and the very energy as he headed into his last almost two years in office. It seemed like a good idea at the time. Or in other words, Cheney had so rigged the process that important decisions were foregone conclusions, ones that had been reached by the Vice President well in advance.

And what a time it was. Back in the months of George-II first term, aides to Cheney, few times Rumsfeld on behalf of Cheney loved to regale journalists with tidbits about the scope of the Vice President's influence and the intensity of his commitment to protecting the US from a terrorist attack. He was so driven and hands-on, the aides would say, that he and Libby would routinely ask to see raw intelligence rather than the processed analysis put together by the CIA and other agencies. "He a voracious consumer of intelligence," and "Sometimes he ask for raw intelligence to make his own judgment. He wants it all."

So everyone knows now that George-II and Vice Cheney took the country into a deadly, costly and open-ended war on flimsy evidence of weapons of mass destruction. Yes, Congress went along. And yes, the public on balance supported it. But no one was more responsible than the vice president for pushing the limits of the prewar intelligence that did all the convincing. Because the Forty Third President and his cabinet didn't keep the strategy on track American First but as merely the Oilmen. The storm will soon blow over, when former ambassador Joseph Wilson questioned the credibility of that intelligence – and the motives that helped polish it – it was Cheney who led the fight to bring him down. Afterward, the Libby trial prompts the question, why did Libby get into legal trouble in the first place? Why did the Vice Cheney's top aide not simply admit to what everyone knew was true – that he discussed the identity of Wilson's wife Valerie Plame, a CIA officer, with at least one reporter? Since most experts agree that Libby was unlikely to be prosecuted on a charge of revealing her identity, it is hard not to conclude that Libby cooked up his stories to protect Vice Cheney; If Libby had gone a different route and admitted in his grand jury testimony that he had told a reporter about the identity of Wilson's wife.

Vindicated: Fitzgerald, who won the perjury verdict, has compared lying to "throwing sand in the umpire's face". The very question that Fitzgerald would have been; "Were you acting on Cheney orders?" And it wouldn't have been long before Cheney was giving testimony

The New Legion

under oath. There was, said Fitzgerald in his summation, "a cloud over what the Vice President did"

Out influence of both Rumsfeld and Cheney, Secretary of States Condoleezza Rice is executing an unmistakable course correction in US foreign policy, quietly stepping away from the strident and unilateral positions of the neoconservatives and cutting deals with – or opening lines to – the remaining members of the axis of evil. Backed by a strong new team of career diplomats, Rice prevailed on Iraq to invite Iran to a regional conference on security and then swiftly agreed to attend – unwinding Washington's vow just a few weeks ago that it would have no direct contact with Teheran until it stopped enriching uranium. And a few weeks earlier, after working for months with the Chinese, President Bush signed off on a deal with North Korea to freeze it primary nuclear reactor in exchange for economic aid and closer diplomatic ties

While Condo Rice rewires foreign policy, White House chief of staff Joshua Bolten is showing signs that he can match Vice President on domestic matters. George-II administration has said it will retreat on the issue of domestic surveillance and abide by laws regulating wiretaps passed years ago by Congress. And the Democrats in Congress are finding administration officials far more forthcoming with facts and figures about the conduct of the war in Iraq, in part because the White House knows that the next step – subpoenas – won't help their dwindling poll ratings.

"We sure know George-II, if the President wants to end eight years and have people say: 'You lost Iraq, you lost Iran, you lost North Korea, and you made the Middle East worse,' it's not a good moment in history. And so the pragmatists are predominant at the moment. This is their window."

What if the president was himself forced to deviate from its American First? Kennedy had pay the price because didn't want to perform The CIP. Robert Kennedy, because he pursuit a conspiracy of silence to demand with some justice that the Skull and Bones dynasty will be subjected to punish by Trading with the Enemy Act, December 1941. Richard Nixon – Watergate, because he stubbornly protected South Vietnam against Axiom-I (there was never a legitimate non-communist government in Saigon) Whereas, Reagan, because he was dared a decider would embargo export wheat-flour to Soviet Union.

WHAT IS A LIE AND PRETENTIOUSNESS?

Calling someone a liar is a serious charge. It's not quite as bad as calling someone a 'traitor'. Telling the truth is something we take seriously, and we try to hold ourselves to an impossibly high standard. Yes. Lying is a serious matter. In the third year of George-II' term, the approaching 2004 national election unleashed an unprecedented array of America political writing: a flow of books, articles, accounts alleging that the head of White House was a serial prevaricator. Commentators hurled the ultimate L-word – "liar" that the prince George-II' behavior, far from being entirely his own product is rooted in concomitant pattern of deception, dissimulation, and disinformation. Particularly, prince George-II' 2003 commitment to ending taxation of dividends was simply an extension of his father, Emperor-II of Skull and Bones dynasty's frequent calls for reducing capital gains tax rates as the solution to any weakness in the national economy.

Expressed in pretentious language that Bush-family had elevated its patriotic profile in February 1942 by becoming chairman of the United Service Organization (USO) annual fund drive, which was raised $33 million that year to entertain soldiers and sailors. Bush-family was in no way a political target of government prosecutors. As a shrewd politician that the Bushes have many qualities to commend them as a private family – community involvement, generosity to those who work for their interest – is not really the point. They are not a private family. They are a public family, and one that is writing a new definition of the presidency. They're bending public policy toward family grudges and interests.

Significantly, as so often, that friendship was passed down to Emperor-II who as vice president and president maintained the quiet friendship and sometime alliance with now Senator Ted Kennedy. In 1990 Ted Kennedy help George-1 pass the Americans with Disabilities-Act and also broad legislation reforming immigration laws. In 2000 the relationship was extended to George-II when the Bushes and Ted Kennedy gathered for the funeral of Senator Paul

The New Legion

Coverdell of Georgia State. After services, George-II sought out the senator Kennedy in the small crowd. "I heard of you," George-II said with a smile, extending his hand. "I understand that what you do, you do very well." Senator laughed, and the relationship was extended to third generation of Bushes. Then the prince George-II explained how he hoped to work with Senator. "I hope we share some mutual goals" he said. Ted concurred that they probably did. The tacit alliance between these two dynasties would prove helpful at times, but also difficult Kennedy would help hypocrite pass some of his educational reforms in 2001, and two years later Ted would receive the hypocrite Award for "Excellence in Public Service." But Ted Kennedy would also denounce the war in Iraq as *"a failed, flawed, bankrupt policy ... This was made up in Texas... This whole thing was a fraud"*

However, I think Jeb-Bush's behavior was un-sincere. Surprisingly, he had told one reporter in 1986, "I think we could probably beat the Kennedy's in touch football, we could beat them in basketball, baseball, any goddamn sport they want to play." Though over decades the Bushes had prided themselves on being the un-Kennedy's they considered the Kennedy's as competitors.

Politically, Skull and Bones dynasty's Emperor-II, Bushes lies about important things: "The assassinations of Kennedy and Diem" by author Edward Lee. Both of them were killed by hired Mafia-smuggle-gangsters [preventing a conflict between CIA and FBI] "The year of the hare American to Vietnam" by author Francois Xavier Winters, professor University Georgia, Vietnam-War is Kennedy war ...? Because right in time JFK' administration. Two English-authors, Michael Charlton and Anthony Monerieff: Kennedy have responsible for Diem died ...? Vietnamization by Nixon doctrine of 1970, and Watergate scandal – go to war to prevent any oil-strangulation by Carter Doctrine of 1979; Deep-Throat by FBI number two disclosed – the trial of Kissinger by Christopher Hitchens of 2001; In 2003, a book about Prescott Bush, under the title "Duty, Honor, County" by Mickey Herskowitz, (I don't think that way be a honorable truth – remembered, "National-Honor" is national property of the highest value why Trading with enemy?") – The economy, their tax cuts, education, the reasons for going to war, drunk driving, abuse of privilege. Draft-dodging Vietnam, a cocaine habit… But we think their lies only when they feel they have to, for instant: interview on Fox News, on 27 September 2004, decoy- O'Reilly questioned: "The South Vietnam didn't fight for their freedom, which is why they don't have it today? George-II answered: "Yes!"But don't forget "Thus, as the nine-year rule of President Diem came to a bloody end by CIA document declassified" this is a logic answer question for you.

All at often, they know that, most of the time, their venality of Fox News, the Wall Street Journals are only too glad to do it for them. And all the notorious lies, small and large, add up. They create a world view in which the mainstream media is a liberal propaganda machine. It's a worldview designed to comfort the comfortable and further afflict the afflicted. They knew how invested money for the mainstream media according to the Act of Academic-Freedom.

Because the second generation of Skull and Bones [George H W Bush] derailed out off main course-track, to the tracking Oilmen, secret arms-deal and become a notorious, if any Vice president in US history could fairly be known as "the secret-arms-deal Vice president" he would be the one. As for Dan Rather, on the side of "American First", head CBS Station pretends confuse between old style typewriter and computer typewrite. A venal commentator Rather who is cheating, accepting money for doing in not good faith dishonest, as the result, Director Andrew Heyward of CBS News pointed out: "We made a mistake in judgment, and for that, I am sorry" (who gave him the absolute that right? In 1950 Harriman's staffs masterminded the special branch elite-Media must be protected by 'academic freedom') Thereby, just sheer it's simple an apology! And they based on "Academic Freedom" dishonestly they said: "It was an error that was made, however, in good faith and in the spirit of trying to carry on a CBS News tradition of investigative reporting without fear or favoritism." Dan Rather followed Connie Cheung were out of sight of American viewer plus Walter Cronkite, they were definitely in the arms of shadow wizard power in the most disinformation account to Vietnam War. You could realize that in the most world TV channel-show which we never heard a good word to say "Don't go away!" instead of "Please stay with us!" It seemed to me that wasn't very polite of you to serve of people in society as a rude word not used in polite publicity.

Another lie and distorted view of the Vietnam-War: In 1983, a new television serial begins at first session to thirteenth. "Vietnam: A television history" which Permanent Government invest for that propaganda cost 4.6 million-dollar showed-up on T.V entertained 9.7 million viewers, all disinformation, distorted, given a false account, distort facts, not interested in convoying the truth, a tried-and-true methodology, concoct an inflammatory story, and all the lies, small and large, add up that serves Permanent Government's political goal. They create a world view in which the mainstream-media is a liberal propaganda systemized machine. There is merely a Vietnamese American, Doctor Nguyen Manh Hung, professor George Mason University showed up an essay with title "Vietnam: A Television history" a case study in perpetual conflict between the American media and the Vietnamese expatriates" – World Affairs - Vol.147, no.2. Fall 1984, pp. 71-84. Professor Hung' essay was studied by prominent U.S. historians in serious consideration.

Ridiculously, Vietnamese Sea Commandos on DMZ rescued U.S pilots were unappreciated but in contrast humiliated them. Why they didn't ask for two rescuers: Colonel Hambleton and Lieutenant Mark Clark for further information? In contrast, in the United States, the film with head-line "BAT-21" and so many films about Vietnam-War demonstrated on TV by venal film productions, cables told so much lies, distorted, to turn from truth or proper purpose, to misinterpret, to pervert the facts. Why?

In my perspective, the mainstream media has a conservative bias? For decades (1950 till now) the media elite is an apparatus device of Permanent Government which's just shamelessly dishonest; however few media, at least try to be fair. Some were biased against South Vietnam. Because Permanent Government would like to use famous-professors at most Universities as the basis for explaining the war instead of in battlefield by three "axioms": (1) there was never a legitimate non-communist government in Saigon- *"any price Harriman protected Ho Chi Minh trail or his name Harriman's highway"* (2) the U.S. had no legitimate reason to be involved in Vietnamese affairs *"so why CIA fabricated a 'Tonkin Gulf Incident'.* (3)

The U.S. couldn't have won the war under any circumstances *"Paris Peace Talk agreement for honorable withdrawn U.S. troop"* When the CIP done!

So why the P.G isn't interested in conveying the truth, that is not what they're for; are their lies pathological, or are they merely malicious? Yes! P.G invest money trying to push it into the mainstream media, for instant Walter-Cronkite by his notorious-prophecy after one decade testified US couldn't won the war and forced honorable withdrawn. All too often, they succeed, they used the malicious tactics to cripple Saigon regime. They used them to discredit South Vietnam leadership. President Diem regime has two wars, one against the North Communist, and one against the tiny venal American press-corps – reporters Homer Bigart, of the New York Times a two-time Pulitzer Prize winner, and Neil Sheenan with "A Bright Shining Lie" a prizewinning journalist, a twenty-five-year old reporter with UPI. So it was that a handful of American reporters soon became the other enemy, only the reporters would confirm would be right.

Francois Sully of Newsweek who had just been expelled by Diem administration for writing unfavorably about how the war effort was going; so the mood at Saigon – a name that was to become part of the everyday American vocabulary – was already bitter; It was soon to get far worse, for there were. In 1971 this closer-cooperated with CIA, Francois Sully was died innocently in helicopter crashed after his bird took off with the famous Vietnamese Patton- General Do Cao Tri who was be killed because his perfect operation destroyed all COSVN' cargo on Harriman's highway. [Ho Chi Minh trail] And now they're badly using them again [the media elite among the American press-corps] how to silence U.S policy's critics.

To near the end of the war like Vietnam and Iraq-War: The War-Industries-Board Bones [Permanent Government] gave heavy pressure on Congress to cut war budget when the project keyed-up time is over (project accomplished, done for inventory) Once again and again and again, WIB shall have to find a same pretext for on the common cause *"Exhausted the patience of the American people"* by urging anti-war protested movement. (U.S troop stuck in mud of plain of reed in Vietnam and Iraq U.S troop stuck in sand of desert,

The New Legion

but good enough due to keeping America always number One of World-Superpower).

After Vietnam War, when leaving the CIA in early 1977, George-1 began laying the groundwork for a 1980 presidential race. However, so do vanity, ambition, and pretentiousness.

For conforming the Kennedy's analogy war also at hand, early 2001, George-II invited the Kennedy family to preview of Thirteen-Days, a movie about the 1961 Cuban missile crisis. It's why J F Kennedy not only faced down the Soviet Union over nuclear missiles in Cuba but also signed the Nuclear Test Ban Treaty and launched the Peace Corps. In November, he dedicated the new U.S Justice Department building named for former attorney general Robert Kennedy; Senator Edward Kennedy, in attendance, expressed his pleasure. The message was unsubtle: Democrats, too, have dynasties. "The wish for kings is an old and familiar wish, as well known in medieval Europe and in ancient Mesopotamia, but its recent and cringing appearance in late twentieth-century America, in a country presumably dedicated to the opposite premise, coincided with the alarms and excursions of the King of Cold War [W A Harriman] with the presidency of John F Kennedy, and with the emergence of the theater of celebrity." Recent presidential families have come to breed multiple, even dynastic celebrity-hood.

Besides, Harriman's masterminded dishonestly from trust to tragedy. Although, the U.S. acted-government and OSS had found Ho Chi Minh the only Vietnamese great leader of a resistance group sufficiently well organized to provide good intelligence on the Japanese to rescue American pilots and conduct sabotage and other behind the lines operations. But unfortunately, Harriman deprived of Vietnamese's independence for his skull and WIB' warlords interests. Similarly as J.F Kennedy family, Harriman redeemed his early traitorous behavior by putting Ho in world celebrity of UNESCO, but fail, and naming Ho Chi Minh trail, as for Hanoi named Route 559 or prior of 1959 Hanoi called East Mountain Chain (Truong Son Dong) This Ho Chi Minh trail named by Western Europe via the God-father from WIB Bones bribed Mafia made propaganda and the prospect real Ho Chi Minh City after the cruel of Saigon fall, so why I dare said Harriman's Highway not Ho trail!.

Republican Emperor-II, himself derailed across from Democrat Harriman's strategy out track, from the **Shipbuilding** since postwar WW-1 to the developed **Airline** in Vietnam War, Jet-Engine Helicopter Age and specially to Energy developed improvement; stead to focusing on synthetic-fuel he focused on narrow interest unique on crude-oil in Middle East; though, so many resources so close at hand, we can all be Texas. Hell, we can be Saudi Arabia. And we can get along. As a result have too little vision of the vast potential for achievement at home and abroad, for the United States under the kind of leadership we deserve. So why Second Skull and Bones Dynasty, the voters take away his [George-1] job and give it Bill Clinton in 1992… The question continues to be an open wound.

But father and son intentioned to jump on two wars by proclaiming, they hereby find that the defense of Saudi Arabia is vital to the defense of the United States with ultimate goal. To stir the war for Weapons of Mass Destruction: We were genuinely torn about war. On the hand, we are not the believers in the Bushes Doctrine of preemption. We think it could be used to justify wars of aggression, not just by us, but by the Oilmen. And on the other hand, it would be silly to deny that, on 9/11, the world changed. On that day, Americans learned that America was vulnerable to attack. There were hard choices to be made. Americans were confronting an enemy that was everywhere and nowhere. The person who had to make choices was the men with all the facts: The Bushes or the second emperor of Skull and Bones dynasty.

Telling the truth is something we take seriously, and we try to hold ourselves to an impossibly high standard. For example, Coulter's book is not really titled "The Treason Diet" It's titled "Treason": Liberal Treachery from *the Cold-War to the War on Terrorism*.

When the Middle-East War was over or we are going to wait until the reconstruction of Iraq was complete, major international oil companies-based at the end of century, would become even closer to Skull and Bones' policymakers and their Intelligence Agencies than they had been in 1920 until now. Not surprisingly, after WW-II and Cold-War stage of the energy industry's deepening connections to national security, aerospace, government services, and overseas construction contracts brought Bushes New-York and Washington influence to the fore.

Two George presidents, following Prescott Bush's lead, likewise seems to have most enjoyed the financial and international side of the energy business – consider Zapata Offshore, for example, with its deep-sea-rigs, international subsidiaries and tax angles, and tropical breezes of foreign intrigue off Cuban and Arabian shores.

"J.F Kennedy standpoint": should this trading with alien property custodian be abolished? If JFK was still alive all these above never took place. And today, Americans reducing petroleum use instead of hydrogen fuel cell technology truly becomes a viable alternative; we found ourselves in the New World Order. J.F Kennedy dream of using our blessings to better the world has always clashed with the opposing isolationist heritage to "avoid foreign entanglements". In my perception of the world around us are constantly changing, this will be the true issue with which we will have to come to grips in this century. The world at our gates demands it of us.

For engaging the myth that to question the validity of the Vietnam and Iraq-War is to betray the troops in the field, equating support for soldiers with military escalation is insidious. True support would be to remove them from harm's way. But I take exception to Iraq for affirmation that the cause – removing a dictator Saddam Hussein – was worthy. That's just as dishonest as saying we need to continue the war to support our troops. Because is the Civil-War likely Vietnam that we unleashed a noble cause? Or was the arrogant pretext of imposing Western values on an ancient civilization just camouflage for establishing military bases and expanding the American empire?

In reality the Second Skull and Bones generation's motives for invading Iraq were "to liberate a country from a dictator, perhaps to find and destroy some dangerous weapons." They made no mention of securing an oil supply, establishing military bases in the Middle East and promoting neoconservative ideology. Those less altruistic motives are the elephant in the small room that everyone refuses to acknowledge. The WIB and Skull and Bones cannot withdraw troops from Iraq because they are protecting oil, military bases and neoconservative' egos.

One of the foundations of US democracy is the acceptance of different ideologies, including religion. It's time for Sunni and Shiites to get over their mutual 1,300-year-old grudge. I Americans can accept a multitude of religious creeds among their compatriots then surely Iraqis can accept differences in the same religion. The sectarian war between Sunnis and Shiites would be comparable to a civil war in the Unite States between Roman Catholics and Southern Baptists. If Iraqis cannot tolerate slight differences in practice of the same religion, how can they embrace democracy? I can't escape the conclusion that the solution-equation to Iraq's problems cannot be military. Sunnis and Shiites have to sort this one out themselves; and the most the US can do is try to be an honest sincerely broker between them

Observer historical perspective on the differences between the Shiites and Sunnis was quite enlightening. Two groups have a great deal of historical baggage to unload it they are to find peace instead of an unending civil war. But one destroyed a perfectly clear historical perspective by claiming that "there could be no more bitter legacy of the Bushes Administration's fateful decision to go to war in Iraq" than an intramural death match between the two groups. This conflict has been going on for centuries – The must to blame it on the Bushes Administrations instead of those responsible.

Meditation on the revenge
by full of lies and prevarications

In the third year of George-W Bush' first term, the approaching 2004 national election unleashed an unprecedented array of US political writing: a flow of books alleging that the president of the United States was a serial prevaricator. Commentators hurled the ultimate L-word – "liar" – with abandon. In connection to foreign intrigue and the intelligence community, plus three generation overlapped with Harriman of immersion in the culture of secrecy, deceit and disinformation had become Bushes, Second Skull and Bones generation political hallmarks.

In 2003, a book about Senator Prescott Bush, prepared with the cooperation of his family, was published under the title "Duty, Honor, Country". Its author, Mickey Herskowitz, a Houston sportswriter

The New Legion

long known to the Bushes, but author could imaged in the deep hell Prescott Bush turned it down because internet online: "A Harriman along with Prescott. Bush financed the German Nazi's rise to power. Their Union Banking Corporation was closed in 1943 by US government for Trading with the Enemy?" (http://www.answers.com/topic/w-averell-harriman, page 5, 1/22/2006)

In same year 2003, their meditations on the causes of retaliated revenge – Old man said: "Eaten bread is soon forgotten." All reports were full of lies and prevarications. LB Johnson's confession in (http://www.anwers.com/topic/w-averell-harriman on page 4) the assassination of Diem could indicate some complicity on Harriman's part; additional LBJ' statement to Hubert Humphrey, Democrat senator. "We had involved the crime to kill Diem… now this happened right in our country!" Consequently, WIB-Bones was intent on revenge: "*The vice president ordered to kill president for taking over?*" For more than four decades emerged a witness named Billie Sol Estes, 78 years olds. He said in the tape having some serious allegations that LBJ ordered to kill JFK: At Paris Estes together with another author journalist William Reymond, published by Flammarion, 400 pages-edition, title "JFK, le dernier témoin" and a video on channel Cannal, plus title "JFK, autopsie d'un complot" author Bernard Nicolas and William Reymond showed on Monday, October, 27, 2003, in short Estes explained JFK and LBJ not closed? (but in reality Johnson and Harriman were not closed; In March 1964 Harriman was given charge of African affairs at the Department of States, and the next year he was appointed ambassador at large for out of LBJ' sight, although he publicly supported the president Johnson. But, as my perspective, privately Harriman [Emperor-I] worked to change policy, especially in the matter of negotiating with the Democratic Republic of Vietnam in carrying out **axiom-1** – Vietnam unification. Because Harriman, U.S. policymaker, and finally Johnson must appoint him as the U.S. representative at the Paris Peace Talks in 1968) His serious allegation indicated a guy Cliff Carter said: "LBJ shouldn't order Mac Wallace to kill the president!" Estes implied Mac Wallace, the sniper hired by LBJ. An anonymity fingerprint – on fifth-store, Lee Harvey Oswald sniped JFK, the special agent found out another anonymous fingerprint – in 1988 (two year after

Harriman passed away) an expert I.D examiner, Nathan Darby gave a determination of that fingerprint of Mac Wallace who maybe was hired by LBJ? [Estes confirmed by himself who trust in him]

All allegations above it seemed to me in President Diem' case – They prosecuted on charge to the bullets but not the right-finger pull the trigger? Those less altruistic motives are the "elephant in the small room". I put the events into my perspective that "the healthy-oil-men" among the Skull and Bones together with the War Industries Board Bones intended to kill a Warrior of Peace such J.F Kennedy and President Diem for executed-performance the "CIP" [Counter Insurgency Project] in Vietnam-War; as A .Harriman said "With the passage of time, our objectives in Vietnam will become more and more difficult to achieve with Diem in control" as same President Kennedy? I think. Whereas the rumor of President Diem was smuggles opium so JFK kill him – Americans maybe easier understandable because that often existed in a poor country but none of Vietnamese at all to believed it right.

GEORGE H W BUSH, A GIFTED INTELLECTUAL?

Skull and Bones Dynasties' single minded focus has been on three major areas: *"Intelligence, National Security, and Energy"* The Harriman and Bushes' dynasties ties to a community notorious for disinformation and disinformation in sphere National Military Intelligence, (NMI) also go back to two World Wars as former Justice Department official John Loftus has contended that Prescott Bush, ostensibly a newly commissioned artillery captain, was brought into military intelligence through British auspices. By the period 1917-1918 as Head of WIB, some of Samuel Prescott Bush's friends from Yale and Skull and Bones were already working closely with the British. As for George-1, the alternatives were that he might have been taken into the OSS before naval flight school, the a CIA connection might have been made at Yale University, or that his company Zapata Offshore could have become at least partially a CIA front sometime in the 1950s or early 1960s.

The Bushes has been acting very strangely lately with the arrival of Bush Junior in the White House, it was immediately plain that secret

The New Legion

intelligence would receive a high status and more money. While the CIA may have been the creation of a Democratic W A Harriman, it now seemed to be strongly by the Bushes, notably conservative Republicans and specially the presidents 41st and 43rd. Alarm bells began to ring for those who remembered past CIA excesses and who for years had campaigned for restrictions, oversight and even abolition. **But these sounds were soon drowned out by the deafening roar of 9/11.**

The CIA's attempt in the 1980s to say that it was a different George-1 who had worked for it in the early 1960s was distinctly unconvincing. Such covert relationships on the part of both George-1 and George-II would have nurtured the practices that are textbooks stuff at the Center Intelligence Agency. Skull and Bones was regarded as the fount of Secrecy, Elitism, and Hubris: In its eighty years heyday, Yale' number one secret society stood for all three attitudes, well documented in several books and studies. In George-1's case, prior to Yale he belonged to another secret society, AUV, at Andover. These societies had a considerable overlap with the OSS and the CIA for which they were good preparation. Bones-men, in particular, were conditioned to level with each other and to keep secrets from (or deceive) outsiders that Evan Thomas and Walter Isaacson, in their book, "The Wise Men" described how seriously A. Harriman took the society.

Until in 1962, a senior OSS officer during World War II, Casey had also been an acquaintance of grandfather of George-II the two had worked together in launching the National Strategy Information Center, which advocated U.S use of political and covert operations. The NSIC' obsession led some to assume that it was a CIA front. In the so called "Carter Doctrine of 1979" when Oil was becoming a critical factor – In Vietnam War, brought US combat invaded South Vietnam was so called "Kennedy involvement" – the CIA a spearhead [tool] of Permanent Government tried promulgated it – In Vietnam War, such as the rubbish war material left on the spot operation in Vietnam which was so called "Vietnamization" (how much costs to send these shits back to America including the cost of antirust-paint, sent back to US will never happened in WIB' policy) Who's known behind these slogans were the Skull and Bones together WIB members' conspiracies. Naturally Oilmen and defense experts in Washington had their own new strategic thinking to do.

By Saigon Fall, 1975, oil was becoming a critical factor to the CIA, where George-1 took over in December. Coincidence with a few months earlier, Henry Kissinger, Secretary of State had made it clear that the United State would go to war to prevent any strangulation of U.S and world oil supplies, a pledge later restated by the White House in the so called "Carter Doctrine." By this point, Second Emperor of Skull and Bones dynasty had come to depend on the Middle-East for about 30 percent of its oil, and his strategist staffs began to look for more diversity in supply, increasing purchases from Nigeria, Venezuela, and Mexico.

American excessive dependence on the wrong energy sources, controlled by the wrong people; though American have known for a very long time that its heavy reliance on petroleum products and other fossil fuels has been terrible for the environment. With the growing evidence of global climate change, the potential price of U.S oil addiction has grown from the exorbitant to the horrifying. And we've known at least since the early 1975s that dependent on oil as a primary energy source has exposed us to the risk of supply interruptions, price shocks, economic chaos, and political blackmail from a well-organized cartel centered in the Central Asia. Perhaps only the Oilmen like George-1and II dynasty advised in influence by another oilman such as Dick Cheney – could have formulated such a policy.

The "New Eurasia Great Game" was forced to deviate from its usual initial course [Harriman's initiative.] Pragmatically "was one of the last occasions on which the Bushes-dynasty publicly acknowledged the link between energy-policy and national security? – Bushes implied "nothing to do with oil, literally nothing to do with oil." Oil had to be a factor in this dynasty calculation, even if the motivation was less about short-term US oil supplies and more about future geopolitical power – Bushes' ambition to control the global oil flows without which potential rivals like the European Union and China could not challenge US hegemony. By next decade, according to the oil resources experts, a New Game guided Bushes-dynasty: "Controlling Iraq is about oil as power, rather than oil as fuel; and estimates, three-quarters if the Gulf's oil will go to Asia, chiefly to China. United States hands would have to be the pumps." Or control over the Persian Gulf translates into control over Europe, China, and Japan. It's having Bushes and Dick Cheney hand on the spigot.

Their focused on narrow interests confirms my worst fears: It's time to issue a United States declaration of independence from oil. American spent twenty billion dollars a year on oil imports from the Persian Gulf. Too often these funds pour into the pockets of some of the planet's most uncooperative and repressive regimes. And they can too easily be diverted to finance the very 'terrorists' who seek to destroy American.

George H W Bush's intelligent superiority which my original ambition was to identify and explain the George-I related Soviet-Union transformation. I found a greater basis for dismay and disillusionment than I had imagines. He, beside his political syndrome, was the spearhead in very defeat to the collapse Soviet Union. In the past, he might have been taken into OSS before naval flight school, that a CIA connection might have been made at Yale, or that his company Zapata Offshore could have become at least partially a CIA front sometime in 1950 nor early 1960s. The CIA's attempt in the 1980s to say that it was a different George Bush who had worked for it in early 1960s was distinctly unconvincing. Such covert relationship on the part of both George-I or II would have nurtured the practices that are textbook stuff at the CIA.

After Vietnam War, the US became a pitiful, helpless giant. There was a secret strategy in the method of "On the Strongman Side" which the Company-dynasty called the "Inventory Event." Now in turn Soviet Union must full support to all communist countries taking place on US in charge from 1950 until the exhausted-occupation Afghanistan. Meantime US incited the world wide revolution let them voted with theirs feet in the craps who won. The people were just coming to understand, were trapped between two Superpowers; they began to realize that the center of gravity was the people... and that winning hearts and minds was not just a slogan; it was the only route to winning the war. [Actually, China used this slogan by economical approach like magic weapon to compete counter U.S.]

So the second epoch 1980 of the strategy 'On the Strongman Side' George-I as Vice president but he was the very policymaker. He proclaimed how 'the roll-back' military forces. He praised US freedom-fighters in Vietnam, we had it right and we did it right, and hard to escape the feeling, "God we let them [Vietnamese] down; we were in the Cold War; we were fighting communism. In 1961 because of Bush's CIA experience – and perhaps also because of influence of the White House chief of staff, James A Baker III, who had manage the Texan's 1980 nomination campaign – President Reagan issued National Security Directive 3 (remembered now George-I was the Leader Skull and Bones to Second generation) naming the Vice President to head a Special Situation Group to identify national security crises and plan for them. His policy in slogan "no more arm race" with Soviet Union if WIB (War Industries Board) invest all property they have for massive armaments buildups, secret diplomacy, and cover actions, a new era of clandestine arms races, perhaps as much George-I' doing as Reagan's, was about to unfold in defeat Soviet Union at Central Asia.

In one view, weather weaponry: Soviet Union got so much trouble almost every years, she needed the assistance from Canada and US for a huge amount of flour-wheat and potatoes for making Vodka. Typically in 1970, she needed a large dozen-million tons imported from North America. Russia's winter arrived at late October, though cold weather the crop still evolution developed until the December harvest. The habitants with hope having wet snow cover the paddy-plain, the grains enveloped with fresh snow but never frozen if not too rigid-cold. Unfortunately the winter 1970 was very cold without snow, the habitants be panic-stricken on the severe weather. The temperature goes down below -10 centigrade frozen all the grains, even the weather recovered better, the warmer but the grains closed cover by icy too long and rotten, soft or having gone bad. Russia emergency proclaimed for rescue in supporting 20 million-tons wheat-flour and 20 million-tons of potatoes. The US and Canada responded immediately. This ugly weather inflicted Soviet Union didn't to dream of one day becoming the Number One superpower by the very-fashioned war game National Liberation Front, a dream World Communism. A weaker Soviet Union could no more help their small communist countries at worldwide because she got economic difficulties too.

Together Cuba and Vietnam were subjected to the weather weaponry. Cuba couldn't raise sugar canned and Vietnam was the same and all fishes in Mekong Delta were disappeared and perished (likely used high-tech beam spot light in constant temperature over permanent spot, no humidity and rigid dry or cold) This weak point urged Soviet to restrain to go war with US. The risk of lost Siberia submerged so many natural resources being to China hand? In the past, six states located at Southern Soviet being smuggled the Chinese immigrated invasion there. Soviet must ponder what or which strategies for defense that risk of confrontation with US were, too bad; immediate China was a real immediate enemy not United States. The Soviet Union leaders should political meditation – about US ambassador to Soviet, A Harriman 1943-1946 about his two books: "Peace with Russia" and "America and Russia in a Changing World". Eventually, they agreed a common goal that China will became an immediate enemy of both Russia and America.

Now the good axis of evil implied by KGB and his partner CIA were a perfect compact to carry out the New World Order without "Yellow peril". As for US, in 1972 at China, President Nixon said: "I do not agree with that position, as shown in the communiqué, and I will not withdraw our forces from Japan, because I believe that our interest in peace in the Pacific is to restrain Japan. All the things that we have talked about require our forces staying"

There must be some evil-tricks of KGB and CIA to play the fool – a laughing-stock or magic trick: A Skull and Bones founder, A Harriman played a special representative to the US President Kennedy, Nuclear Test Ban Treaty, 1963. Almost two decades later there were taken place SALT-2: America side destroyed 60 B-52 in contrast Soviet destroyed 1,500 IRBM (Intermediate-Range-Ballistic Missiles) situated at Ukraine targeted to Western Europe. A Soviet delegation arrived to US for surveyed B-52 at Omaha and Wyoming, slicing by pieces; also the film video saw showing up slicing Soviet missiles apart but regardless about the number of warheads and not reporting how many missiles destroyed. There must be few magic-tricks about it. There are some signs indicated in secrecy of two commitment-partners. In the world U.S number One and Russia number two of world superpower. That Harriman's testament implied in his two books, edited 1959 and 1971, in short Russia and U.S together changing world. So why up to now, in keeping peace world order the cohesion of Russia, U.S, and Japan must be triangular-strengths as a united pact. Russia offered Japanese exploited natural gas resources from Siberia to Japanese instead of China.

Russia understood in the immediate prospect of 'yellow-peril'. When China burst into overpopulation, the mass exodus of Chinese to the Central Asia or Siberia will occurred; underneath of deep layer covered by snow a huge natural resources [coal, crude oil, natural gas] ever exploit yet. Siberia's superficies was 2.900,000 squared miles or 7.511,000 Km2, population less 40 million. Politically, Russia is willing that U.S being the Superpower and together with Russian to confront with the threat from China which was actually a powerful economic growth. But other aspects of China's rise are real and troubling. Remembered China is a one-party state, not a democracy.

When climate-change skeptics mock the fear about a rise of a very few degrees in temperature, a few degrees above normal can mean the difference between life and death, species survival and extinction. About from 120 to 180 millions the Chinese, because the salt at sea level come up devastated all cultivation along the sea-coast farm land, must immigrated to anywhere and nowhere for survive; naturally they must escaped to Southeast Asia. We have only way just wait and see.

On May, 8/ 2004 suddenly, former Defense Secretary McNamara warning Soviet had 82,000 including more than 7,000 missiles intercontinental; McNamara implied destroyed US instantly, but a conspiracy of silence to destroy 1.3 billion peoples. However, the US's National Resource Defense Council confirmed skeptical these missiles may be reached to US mainland in 20 or 30 minutes. These systems were in alert round the clock. In US, the SOP (Standard Operation Procedure) the defense commander has only 3 minutes to make decision, and 10 minutes in contact with the president. Now after 30 seconds, the decider thumb up for 30 minutes thereafter, and plus more 20 to 30 minutes the missiles will hit the targets. But

The New Legion

with Chinese totalitarian regime could shorter the space of time instantly.

All above procedure was slow and inaccurate, as for China reacted too secrecy and instantly by her missiles attacked systems stemmed from totalitarian regime. When she was strong enough, everywhere on earth has China Towns, communities, and neighborhoods over population, and badly needed female for psychological development of an emotionally and mentally mature. She takes opportunities during Chinese warships escorted crude-oil tankers passed Suez Canal and instantly salvo all of their missiles on the Pentagon targets. Thirty minutes later every country stooped for surrender. Somehow Chinese couldn't all be killed. Instantly, China will become number-one world superpower?

How CIA help out KGB overthrown communism. The two incidents offered tantalizing clues: one checking out Soviet air defense capable to detect the enemy aircrafts at both Low and High altitude. In the early 1980s, an Korea Airline on course from Seoul to Alaska at midnight, was shot down by SAM-2 on Soviet territories, Island Sakhalin of Sea of Okhotsk, on board having couple dozen of US citizens died innocently, all passengers and crewmembers were perished (US have high-tech electronic to give the dog the bone – don't tantalize Soviet) In the early morning, the US have the conversation proof-evidence between ground control defense system and pilots MIGS. President Reagan strongly opposed the inhumanity action against innocent civilians, urged all UN boycotted to Soviet athlete to compete incoming event international Olympic physical sports. And second game at low altitude. Soviet knew in silence that the U.S laid a trap but not a least justified proof to test-confirmation.

On May, 30, 1987 a Youngman Western Germany his name Matthias Rust pilot a small aircraft from capitol Helsinki, Finland crossed Soviet border straighten airway heading to Moscow by passing away from sophisticated air defense missile SAM-2, crossing 400 miles and landed on Moscow-plaza. Rust is the laughing stock of everybody around the world. But Moscow residents laughing in Soviet air defense system's face; Vice President Bush has a good laugh at KGB. But Gorbachev laughed a bitter laugh to become the laughing stock of not for all the capital Moscow but world wide (CIA did a damn good job, a conspiracy to overthrow the communism of silence. As an experience pilot, I had 1,600 hours flying time on Cessna L.19 Bird-dog, I knew how drift angle with the light aircraft flown for a distance 400 miles. Definitely Rust having Tacan and ADF by electronic sensor guidance devices, based on heading direction to radio Moscow's station. Rust was 15 months in prison and released afterward to go back home country)

Strangely, to force a laugh, Gorbachev takes this opportunity to discharge Defense secretary, admiral Sergei L Sokoloy, unsavory reputation a hard-line hawkish, once he intents to sent nuclear-submarines to destroy US, now is discharged immediately; admiral Dimitri-T-Yasov takes on charge. Lieutenant General Vladimir Kruichkov actor KGB; and a large commander general must be replaced. Now Gorbachev felt free without opponents. Gorbachev ménage to cooperate with US transforming Russia becoming out of communist dictatorship; He orders his military forces to perform his brass-hat maneuvers in standby out of the Eastern Europe's revolution movements, destroying Berlin's Wall, assassinations communist-cadres and self declaration democracies. Right in Vietnam, "glasnost" and "perestroika" the styles imitated by more recent Gorbachev was acted enthusiastically about reforming a new society in Vietnam; but unfortunately failure because some China influences emerged in the communist political bureau staff and without Soviet aid-supports. Though Gorbachev persuaded Vietnam must pro-United States and trying keep out of China influence. This matter felt into a US's scrutiny plot of post Vietnam in pretext "Agent Orange and MIA" (in 1973, Paris Talk, the problem again came under the close, rigorous scrutiny of the post-Vietnam's road map) So Vietnam was trying the best in moving toward friendship. She believe she should normalize her relation and should be able to continue her discussions in the pretext "MIA and Agent Orange" and released all South Vietnam officers out of her reeducation camps in return, US conditionally accepted training Vietnamese officers as well as military veteran of South Vietnam did in containment.

Leaving Hanoi back to Moscow, Gorbachev signed a decree establishment building 21 manufactures for Pepsi-Cola, McDonald fast food, the new US style-life.

In short, it was both an intellectual change of perspective and emotionally satisfying experience to jettison the false guilt about that Vietnam War that I had been carrying around for a more quarter of a century. Doing so has enabled me to relearn in my perception values. I'm deadly certain that from 1917 till 1969, W.A Harriman was deserved a "great strategist," and from 1960 till 2,008 (1960-1969 George-I, an apprentice diplomat, a surrogate for A. Harriman) George H W Bush was deserved an above the best "Expert Counterespionage-War", but unfortunately he was walking out of track "American-First" aimed to the most his backers called them – 'Oilmen'. Consequently his Bush's dynasty will be rebuke to the hermetic power-sharing arrangement at the top of the "None-American-First". His son became a lone ranger increasingly isolated, faltering in Iraq-War, out of favor with his own Republican party. And Afghanistan, Iraq-wars The Economist emphases "war without end, No exit". But similar Vietnam-war, the US Permanent Government would like use that stage of war for LAB-testing to Future Combat System for New generation of weapons. He will frustrated by the lack of appreciation shown of his Soviet Union collapsed work. It seemed to me, he himself attempted to frustrate his other son, Jeff Bush by denying him access to the media for next presidential campaign.

As was the development of the so called imperial presidency in the debut 1960 of Emperor-II, Second Skull and Bones generation, the emergence of a dynastic presidency is contrary to the American political tradition, and the shorter its duration the better. And how dynastic the United States future will be, and with what consequences, remain to be seen. The tendencies may be nipped in the bud; the first decade of the 21st century may turn out to be anomaly. What can be said today is that the circumstances of the United States in these tumultuous years have taken a turn that would have surprised and presumably appalled the nation's founding fathers.

INSTEAD OF MORE OIL TODAY AND HYDROGEN FUEL CELLS IN AN INDEFINITE TOMOROW

A greedy dynasty derived no benefit [synthetic fuel] from the course of crude oil. Second Skull and Bones Dynasty [emperor-II, George H W Bush] can do it by restrained its self from lucrative and instead of more synthetic fuel yesterday and hydrogen fuel cells definitely today. Consequently, for eventful years from hell, every American knew that Bush-Dynasty took the country into a deadly, costly, and open-ended war on flimsy evidence of weapons of mass destruction. As a result, for long past-decades, U.S made "muscle-car" inflicting in desperation meanwhile Japanese car became practical-fashioned for mankind in today. For instant, in 1933 Germany, Adolf Hitler, who took power had seen the perils of insufficient oil during his own wartime military service; as chancellor, besides ensuring supplies from Romania, he launched a hugely successful program of producing synthetic fuels through the Germany-invented hydrogenation process. According to oil economist Daniel-Yergin, Hitler prided himself in knowing more about economics than his staff-generals did. In U.S there've an old Manhattan Project to begin the process of creating a foundation for energy independence and an oil-free future. Why not we've borrowed this term for our energy independence proposal because it conveys the right sense of urgency and focus and the right combination of public resources and private innovation that we need today; Luckily, President 43rd forced to sign the Energy-bill in the best interest of the country which is the battleground where the fight for energy independence must begin, however too late.

On December, 19/ 2007, US President expressed at Energy Department that was important issue, it's time to issue an American declaration of independence from oil and improves our environment. We will have the technology to manufacture cars that give far better gas mileage. Our auto producers and auto workers rose to the occasion with a new generation of cars that performed better using less energy. We can achieve the same efficiency again while giving Americans the kinds of vehicles they wish to drive. So far so bad, we

The New Legion

already spend billions dollars for year on oil imports from Persian Gulf. Too often these funds pour into the pockets of some of the most uncooperative and repressive regimes. Worse, they can too easily be diverted to finance the very terrorists who seek to destroy our country.

Unfortunately, in the past Bushes-Dynasty maintained their selfish. While waiting for synthetic fuel process, in May 1945, "the need for oil certainly was a prime motive" in the decision to invade Russia; unfortunately, after (1943) U.S tankers fed an almost insatiable demand at peak consumption marked a turning point. By late 1944, after U.S bombers had smashed Hitler's synthetic-fuels production, German aircraft – including potentially decisive jet fighter-bombers just becoming operational – lacked fuel because Luftwaffe aviation gasoline had shrunk to just 10 percent of what was needed. In the Pacific, Japan lacked fuel for its ships and aircrafts, using them only for desperate maneuvers. The Japanese turned to wood-turpentine and pine roots for fuel – and to suicide missions that pilots flew with gas tank only half filled.

For my energy independent imagination because it conveys the right sense of urgency and focus and the right combination of public resources and private innovation that we need today – The goal is simple but revolutionary: for the first time in human history, to harness the natural world around us to light and power the world we live in. The wind, the sun, water, and a rich array of crops can provide us with secure forms of energy at reasonable costs for a modern twenty-first-century economy. The significance of synthetic fuel was so crucial goal if we would assume "a moral equivalent of war!" – Ethanol was a essential production of United States, and the first record of U.S among 9.66 billion gallons, we reached got 44.5 percent, secondly Brazil, and few from European countries (U.S Department of Agricultures Conservation Reserve Program) Until we reach that degree of sustainability and even after we do so, we can use new technologies and innovations to recast existing sources of energy – like oil, coal, and natural gas – so that we consume them more cleanly and efficiently. And by seizing the amazing opportunities presented to us by American agriculture, we can make the renewable fuel content of gasoline grow to billion to billion gallons in the next decade. Because, I'm especially sensitive to concerns about energy supplies and prices, we're the ultimate energy-consuming region, with virtually no production, little diversity inn sources, and a lot of dark days and tough winter weather to force up prices. A new strategy for renewable energy sources is that it may finally begin to break down the regional differences of interest and opinion and create a genuine national consensus on energy: Sun, Wind, and Water are available resources – in varying degrees, of course – all over the country. There are a lot more natural-gas reserves in more parts of the country there than is oil. Beside, in the future, U.S coal shall be a significant crucial for our capacity energy. United States will be a world coal-leader – from West Virginia to Pennsylvania toward New-York… We're exploited only from 3-5 percent, and still having abundant coal instead needed crude-oil:

I believe it's important to be comprehensive in five planks energy policy.

1 – Create alternative fuels, from hydrogen fuel cells to biomass plans that use agriculture byproducts to generate energy.

2 – A new push to make US cars and trucks more energy-efficient by now reducing petroleum use in the long interim period before hydrogen fuel cell technology truly becomes a viable alternative.

3 – Plank in our energy independence plan is to launch our country's first really systematic effort to tap renewable energy sources, reserves that are almost infinite.

4 – to pursuit a comprehensive effort to expand supplies of natural gas, the cleanest and most American of fossil fuels.

5 – To restore the place of U.S number-one-abundant in coal-minerals as a valuable resource and help it shed its longtime image of having a negative impact on the environment.

Do so, this project would break the back of our independence on oil and foreign manipulation of our energy supplies, our economy, and our national security posture in the Persian Gulf and elsewhere. It would put us on the fast track to a future where most of our energy needs are met from clean, domestic, and renewable sources.

The New Legion

It would radically reduce pollution, especially the greenhouse gases that scientists believe contribute so much to potentially catastrophic global climate change. And it would be good, not bad, for our economy.

Concern for the environment is a value that U.S. administration will put America back into mainstream of respect for scientific evidence, technological progress, and bipartisan action on energy and the environment. Those who deny our responsibility for stewardship of the earth and its resources will be dismissed from positions of influence. And while there are legitimate differences of opinion on many issues of environmental and energy policy, we will not tolerate to craft policies, special pleaders seeking government-imposed privileges to despoil the earth or control our energy supplies. And we should be committed to building a national consensus based on the national interest to pursue a smart and effective strategy for a clearer environment and energy independence.

Our main concerns will also have to think globally. America is about to be overtaken by China as the world's largest emitter of CO_2 from energy use. For years Americans had brushed off the rest of the world as other countries had pleaded for the America to get its house in order. Now as China's CO_2 output threatens more intense hurricanes, droughts, blizzards, and heat waves in the America, the tables are turned, and we will certainly want China to control emissions. In fact, since CO_2 mixes freely in the atmosphere, every country's climate depends on the whole world's actions. Many climate shocks have already become more common man-made disasters. When climate-change skeptics mock the fear about a rise of a few degrees in temperature, we should remind them of how it feels to have a 105 fever. A few degrees above normal can mean the difference between life and death, species survival and extinction, as Polar Bear. According to scientist prophesy, the historic area as Jamestown, Virginia and Cape Canaveral, Florida will disappeared under sea-level which levered up one more meter equivalent 39-inches. Chairman institute, Jonathan Overpeck warning 25,000 square-miles included 22,000 square-miles below sea-level such as Louisiana, Florida, North and South Carolina, Texas, Pennsylvania, and the capital Washington D.C. However, a few actions on our part could make the difference between a healthy planet and one that falls into an environmental tailspin. The time has come for action. The earth's future is in our hands. You should persuade the President 43rd do something!

Admittedly, in order to perform the CIP included Jet-Engine of Helicopter and Civilian Airline industry has developed efficiency over 48 years, with technological upgrades more than doubling efficiency. There are tweaks in aircraft operations that could nip carbon emissions even further. Jet-engines are uniquely polluting, and the carbon they emit at high altitudes appears to have a greater warming effect than the same amount of carbon released on the ground by cars or factories. One of the biggest problems, as "the Intergovernmental Panel on Climate Change" (IPCC) put it bluntly recently: "The growth in aviation and the need to address climate change cannot be reconciled," The IPCC point out, is that the carbon emitted by air travel currently has "no-technofix." As messy a source of pollution as electricity generation and ground transportation are, technologies do exist that could drastically cut carbon from power plants and cars. Not so for planes: the same airplane models will almost certainly be flying on the same kerosene fuel for decades. How cut back on emissions of greenhouse airline gases. Traveling by jet transport is a dirty business. As passenger load increases, then so hard the environments look for way to cut back the carbon.

All too often, we don't, in-fact, have to make a choice between jobs and environment. In fact, protecting the environment will only help generate jobs – the high-value-added jobs of the future.

And for that matter, of basis respect for "God's Creation", during last three decades have demonstrated with compelling evidence that cleaning up our environment will strengthen, together with the welfare of "Second Class" in existence, I means their still survive: the greedy with which large WIB wealthy companies swallow up their smaller competitors, not weaken, our economy while Second Class was existed long ago, now its disappear.

Moreover, we have proved beyond any reasonable doubt over the last few decades that a good environment, a sound economy, and a high quality of life not only can but must go hand in hand. But despite such remarkable achievements, old problems like smog and rainwater pollution and deforestation are obviously on the rise again, and new and potentially catastrophic problems like global climate change call for bold and novel actions. Instead of rising to meet this challenge of defending our national heritage of water, air, and land from polluters, however, the Second-Skull and Bones dynasty emperor [George H W Bush] and his clique have all too often unconditionally surrendered to the demands of polluters.

In emergency hurry up, we need smarter, tougher enforcement in part simply to keep up with new dangers to our environment and our health. There are some eighty thousand chemicals registered for use in the Unites States, each day Americans are exposed to hundreds, even thousands of them. They are released into our water, air, and land and into our food chain. But we need to raise our sights much higher to deal with new environment threats, which we must convert into new environment opportunities. The most controversial of these, obviously, is the challenge of global climate change and the greenhouse gas emissions that scientists are increasingly certain contribute to it.

George-II Environmental Record: If any vice president in U.S history could fairly be known as "the secret-arms-deal vice president" George-1 would be the one; and George-II is the worst environmental president in our nation's history. As you read this, his-interested coterie of industry-mills are dismantling the protections that we take for granted. *"Each of us understands that our prosperity as a nation will mean little if our legacy to future generations is a world of polluted air, toxic waste, vanishing-forests. We encourage our people to join together in renewing our commitment to protecting the environment and leaving our children and grandchildren with a legacy of clean water, clean air and national beauty"*

Because our air, water, and wildlife are under attack; how could this have happened under the watch of a man who spoke so passionately and with such quiet eloquence to this very issue in his very first presidential "Earth-Day" speech? What if the Company-Dynasty [Skull and Bones dynasties] don't care about pigs, or pig shit, or family farms, or mountaintops, or this pfiest-a-mahoosey, or environment; Oh God they are walking into a major disaster for mankind, aren't respect for God's creation. In 1995, a spill from one of these lagoons killed a million fish in the Neuse River of North Carolina. Every year since, dead fish have continued to wash up onshore by the tens of millions. These fish are falling prey to a previously unknown life form spawned in the pig shit basins and carried into river waters. As the Federal Environment Protection Agency, the nation's leading energy producer, Texas had been responsible for some of the nation's worst environmental problems, notably air pollution. – Houston overtook Los Angeles as the smoggiest U.S city in 1999 – and hazardous wastes in the chemical districts alongside the Houston Ship Channel.

However, we would distinctly remember "the Rio-Summit" of 1991, which laid the initial groundwork for what later became the Kyoto-Protocol on global climate change. It was a good moment for our country and in our lives. In a continuation of the great bipartisan tradition of environmentalism that George-1 made a commitment at Rio to the United States' assuming a role of leadership in meeting the challenge of global climate change and addressing the broader issue of an international consensus on sustainable development. He understood clearly that if America did not lead by precept and by example on these issues, there was no hope at all for voluntary action by developing countries to avoid catastrophic damage to their environment as they began to industrialize.

Unfortunately, no wonder Texas has a world-class pollution problem, the abrupt abandonment of Unites States leadership on these environmental issues has been one of the most disastrous steps taken by George-II' administration, affecting not only our environment but our global alliances and our international reputation. Bushes and Oilmen ignored the increasingly solid scientific consensus that greenhouse-gas emissions, especially the carbon dioxide released by power plants and automobiles, were contributing significantly to climate changes that could eventually wreak havoc on our weather, our coastlines, our water and food supplies, and on our general quality of life. They would commission a Kyoto process study by the NAS (National Academy of Science) to assess the evidence for global climate change and its link to greenhouse --gas emissions. When the NAS promptly came back with a study that confirmed what most of us already knew along with an expression of urgency about the need for immediate action, George-II and his Oilmen publicly rejected their conclusions as the work of "the bureaucracy." It was clear that these Oilmen had fully abandoned the proud environmentalist tradition of our world-leader. Instead, they cast their lot with the know-nothings and the do-nothings whose agendas coincided with interests of America's and the world's worst polluters.

"Orange Agent", what makes the Kyoto situation especially frustrating is that US already have experience in the effectiveness of multilateral cooperation in addressing environmental problems. It's no secret that my experiences in South Vietnam have led me, along with other US veteran, to feel a special responsibility for healing relations between two nations. The idea was to assist Vietnam's leadership and people in taking a fresh look at how the country was developing, at a time when Saigon was in danger of becoming another Beijing, a city whose air is so dirty that its residents commonly wore surgical mask on the streets long before the advent of SARS. We brought corporate executives, scientists, and engineers from around the world to the table with the Vietnamese to discuss how that country could find cleaner way to develop and keep higher incomes in tandem with higher standards for air, land, and water quality.

Why these Oilmen didn't comprehend that the countries that want to work with Americans on protecting the environment were the same countries that could work with Americans to rid the world of terrorism. And rich country must help underdeveloped countries get on the low-carbon track by, for example, compensating them for ending the deforestation that leads to carbon emission as well as a loss of biodiversity. The right timing for a global agreement is keyed up time. In the coming time, the US and the rest of the world will begin negotiating a set of standards to follow the "Kyoto-Protocol" which expires in 2012. The new rule regulations need to embody certain key realities: all countries must join; the world's power plants, automobiles fleets and buildings will have to shift to low-carbon technologies, no more muscle-cars like US had made; a world price must be charged for emitting carbon into the atmosphere to provide a market incentive for companies and government to make the changeover.

In human history for the first time to harness the natural world around us to light and power the world we live in. The water, the sun, wind and a rich array of crops can provide us with secure forms of energy at reasonable costs for a modern twenty-first-century economy. Until we reach that degree of sustainability and even after we do so, we can use new technologies and innovations to recast existing sources of energy – like oil, natural gas, and coal – so that we consume them more cleanly and presented to us by American agriculture, we can make the renewable fuel content of gasoline grow to billion to billion gallons in the future.

I wish for the first time a guaranteed national commitment to reduce our dependence on foreign oil with a dedicated trust fund to help pay for its cost. Because, why not, we can send a powerful message to diplomats, politicians, policymaker, and leaders around the globe that climate change is a necessary battle for our common future. The World Wildlife Fund (WWF) warning "drought raged, water will not enough for mankind, countries lead were India, Bangladesh, northern China. Hymalaya chain mountain, the water from snow was limited 1/3 world life maybe terminated due to temperature increased 0.6 to 0.7 degree centigrade - The mankind on the brink of annihilation

IS CHINA THE NEW SUPERPOWER?

That is wishful thinking. China is developing fast, but it has a long way to go. It is only the beginning of the 21st century, and many challenge lie ahead. Its economy depends on trade with the United States, even though the U.S has an unmanageable trade deficit with China. Has she got what it takes? As China emerges as an international power, to be a manufacturing giant, she must get the know-how. Lack of oil was the country's worst catastrophe? In the past, petroleum was just as important at the Asian end of the Axis. Japan was even less well endowed consumer, having to import most of the rest from the Unites States which incited Japan went to war, now was for to China turn? Fuel concerns also dominated Pacific Strategy shrinking oil inventories forced the attack on Pearl in December 1941 "to safeguard the Japanese invasion of the Indies and the rest of Southeast Asia by incapacitating the American fleet and, thereafter, to protect the sea lanes, particularly the tanker routes for Sumatra and Borneo to home islands"

The New Legion

Well before Japan and Germany surrendered in 1945, however, US petroleum geologist had brought Washington policy-makers unwelcome news: The Middle East had huge reserves and future production capacity that far surpassed those of the United States, where reserves were being depleted.

Actually, the US and China were both gas guzzlers. Because the US tied down in Middle East, a dawn of a new dynasty has arrived. How to deal with it? Will that lead to a confrontation with the US? The Economist, August 27, 2005, "The Oiloholics" Could in the sky having two suns? On the rise of China's power and its prospects for the 21st century blends two treasured subjects, China and US, and explores not only China's extraordinary rise but also how U.S and China will interacted in the 21st century. Observer says, "Watching China now is like being in one of those science-fiction movies where you can see a whole new planet take shape before your eyes!" It's a story that could have many different outcomes: China could fulfill its sense of destiny and become the next great superpower, or it could succumb to internal strife, as it has many times in its long history. In the past, when somewhere having protests or aggressive to US, in the most South America, for instant: US sent the Marine for pacification like Grenada, Dominican Republic, Panama, Guatemala; President Teddy Roosevelt "speak softly and carry a big stick". If isn't okay, US reacted by tactical "gunboat diplomacy" but now we don't hear that term again and again. That meant up to now the relative power of American is going to decline.

Firstly, China pondered about immediate closer and easier ways, "the White Coal policy" influence to small countries from the river upstream of Yunnan province. Upstream at the controversial Lancang (the Chinese name for the Mekong) river cascade, blasting continues, not within earshot of the MRC (Mekong River Commission) headquarters, but its political reverberations are felt all way to the delta in Vietnam. Two dams have already been completed in China's Yunnan province and six more are scheduled to be built. These are designed to exploit the rapid fall of the level of the Mekong's main tributary as it flows through Yunnan. China performed in "secrecy." She is carrying out the projects to dam the Mekong in almost total secrecy – Bangkok Post: The rap of a River, Jan/2003.

The Vietnamese government complains that China's dams on the Mekong reduce the volume of water and allow seawater into the Mekong Delta which produces half of Vietnam's food supply. Whereas Cambodia side "We would like to avoid confrontation in the region" The Mekong River Commission reported on April, 3, 2003: "The Mekong's low levels at present are related to the dry conditions that have persisted since last year, according to a preliminary technical analysis released today by the MRC." The MRC meeting at Vietnam on March, 26 and 27, 2004 included four members: Thailand, Laos, Cambodia, and Vietnam at ninetieth, discussing about the river level and exploit it in the reason preventing flood and trying persuaded the two countries in the upstream as Myanmar and China. "They discussed how to detail a regulation on supervision of water use; to accelerate preparations for the signing of agreements to finance flood control projects, and cooperation among nations in the Mekong River basin as well as promoting dialogues with the two countries in the upstream, China and Myanmar (in the conspiracy of silence, Skull and Bones scope was had the hate like poison between the countries in Southeast Asia and China and his subordinate Myanmar, a gloomy confrontation)

The Rivers Watch ESE proposed the subject: "A river of controversy" In general, governments (China and Myanmar) upstream of a dam do not inform downstream communities about the quantities and timing of water released. This has caused serious droughts, floods, and overall agricultural losses in many cases. The news AFP, at Bangkok stated on November, 11, 2004, subject "Asia's Mekong River under threat from China: experts". The spokesman Terry, in environment included 200 experts meeting at Bangkok on November, 15, 2004 – "China's aggressive dam building and development plans threaten fish stocks and add to pollution of Southeast Asia's strategically important Mekong River, environmentalists warned

China's plan to build eight dams on the river and to dynamite obstacles to allow boats to travel freely poses the greatest threat, environmental group Terra said at the meeting in Bangkok on managing the waterway. We are already seeing farm lands suffer and a lot of erosion as flood patterns is regulated by energy

The New Legion

demands in China instead of seasons. Said spokesman Witoon Permpongsacharoen:

- Up to 90 percent of the water taken from the Mekong River is used for agriculture providingan economic lifeline for 75 percent of the population of the Lower Mekong Basin, according to countries on the lower section of the river.
- Witoon said existing Chinese dams were already having a major impact on fish stocks. "80 percent of people in the region depended on fish for protein and all species are under threat," he said
- Only the latter four have signed on to the Mekong River Commission which aims to coordinate management between the countries.
- Witoon said China's refusal to cooperate with lower Mekong countries remained an obstacle to long term sustainability.

U.N/UNDP on title: "*Mekong River development may trigger conflict.*" During the monsoon months, from around June until September, the Mekong flows at a rate of 50,000 cubic meters per second. Thus, communities dependent on the Mekong downstream, such as those in Vietnam, stand to be affected the most by any changes in the river. This is the case when the river's natural flow drops during the dry season to allow the intrusion of salt water, which destroys the land set for agricultural use the Vietnamese along the river banks.

Japan invested 1.5 billion-dollar for 13 among 23 projects in this organization Mekong Watch at Tokyo. "There are an additional 23 plans for more dams, and Japanese aid is related to 13 of them. For example, the Japan International Cooperation Agency (JICA) is conducting a development study for the Nam Niep Dam (hydropower) Japan is expected to offer around 1.5 billion USD in financial assistance over the next three years for the development of the region during a two-day Japan ASEAN summit starting on Thursday, Kyodo news service reported. In talks with Vietnamese Prime Minister Khai, Prime Minister Koizumi reiterated Japan's commitment to help develop the Mekong River Basin, saying Japan wants to promote projects that will be beneficial to the people in the region" (reports VNA news and Kyodo December/2003.

On June/24/ 2004, 12 organizations and 30 professors, scientists, experts in the sphere environment, together a signed report to China officials for the matter: "serious and urgent concern about the ecological destruction caused be Chinese logging firms and their associated companies in the N'Mai Hku area of northern Myanmar, Kachin State on the border of Yunnan Province, People's Republic of China.

What should Vietnam do after it has been elected into the U.N Security Council as a non-permanent member? Moving further to form a regional-neutrality which included Vietnam, Cambodia, Laos, Thailand, and Myanmar; As all five nations are afraid of China's expansionism and the exploitation of the upper source of the Mekong River, they may be pleased to join Vietnam in a regional neutrality of these five countries. The China will caught in the U.S trap, a clever trick designed to make a reveal a secret as scandal lobby in 1974, Kissinger implied the Islands Paracel (Hoang-Sa) maybe in the South China Sea in the world map. Do you think before withdrawn from Vietnam, due to congressional Amendments, Cooper-Church' 1970, and 'Case Church' 1973 – the United States set an avoidable trap then China fall into it? The first prospect became a hot spot confrontation between a big Sino-nation with the Small-countries in this region. Thereby, on January, 19/ 1974 China seized Paracel (Hoang-Sa) Islands. (A historical sea battle, between South Vietnam Navy with China – South Vietnam Navy-HQ.4, HQ.5, HQ.10, and HQ.16 engaged against giant China Navy-forces. China was been destroyed two battleships sunk by 127mm gun attacker from by HQ-16 and damaged another two. South Vietnam casualty during 30 minutes fighting, our Navy HQ-10 was destroyed by enemy, the commander and vice trying stay fighting and heroic died together with their sunk-HQ-10, as for HQ-16 was serious damage by enemy torpedo, retreat back to Danang Base)

And again on April 14/ China 1988 seized (Truong-Sa) Spratly Islands by power. Early 1995, great Sino expansionism, again Chinese occupy Mischief Reef of Philippine. March 25/ 1995 Philippine Navy detains four Chinese fishing vessels near Alicia Annie Reef.

February/ March 1995 – Philippine Navy removes Chinese markers on: Pennsylvania Reef, Jackson Atoll, Second Thomas Reef, First Thomas Shoal, and Half Moon Shoal. Manila also tries to halt China's advance into the Spratly Islands, blowing up makers and detaining Chinese fishermen. But its diplomatic and military weakness doesn't bode well for the attempt, waiting for good opportunities together the Southeast allies. This solution was delivered by French President De Gaulle in 1966, but no one paid attention at the time, due to the nationalist-communist conflict being too large and both sides believing in protecting themselves. Now the situation is different under the globalization and democratization. Nations now can live peacefully without paying too much to ideology, as globalization is prevailing.

After the Cold War, the U.S military strategy has been much changed to cop with world process situation. The U.S new military organization headquarters is PACOM located at Honolulu to react if a very complicated situation might exert with the China's expansionism toward Southeast Asia. Where recently the Vietnam officers were sent to study the joint cooperated PACOM' tactical and strategic maneuver if go to the war with China, (very soon, Vietnam will be equipped with sophisticated weapons such as Navy patrol-cruiser, destroyer with up-date launching missiles) then Vietnam having a very good chance of opportunity to restored these islands Paracel and Spratly. But firstly, and ideally Japan should be given equal power of the opportunities for upgrading from Agency of Self Defense to Department of Defense Ministry. (Japanese inaugurated her Self Defense Forces by her constitution in hold-peace 1946 after surrender – remembered that the sea-war between Russia and Japan (1904-1905) Japanese Navy defeated the allies Russian, French, and Germany at North Eastern Pacific, while U.S. and England not involvement, and Vietnam defeat the French colonialist force at Dien Bien Phu)

But this matter's too soon taking place. If it happened, of course we will won, then the U.S has been overcome the trauma U.S/VN syndrome. 58.000 U.S freedom-fighters been praised the great-heroes for free-world. In fact, this organization [PACOM] was established in Philippines 1899-1902 where and when the U.S forces dominated in occupation cover all ocean Pacific toward East of Africa, estimated a half world specific square feet and cover a half potential world economic. The most best competent U.S force was in alert 24/24 for this acting organization. The significant matter China tried increased sophisticated military forces the most aerospace and nuclear carrier. I reminded that in 1972, Mao Zedong once expressed to President Nixon and Kissinger "the prospect WW-III will take place on Pacific ocean." Mao read in his mind: "sacrifice Old China country to create a new alien-Great-Sino nation on America continent" Because after nuclear annihilation Chinese couldn't all died! This 21st century is a chance of new emerged Great China on the world. So a perfect popular remedy for the New World Order is to divide China in many nations prior she became world' superpower.

And already a commercial giant, China is aiming to be the world's next great power. Oil and natural gas were the necessary blood for 184 countries around the world. Today they dispensed 82 million-barrels but 119 million-barrels in 2030. At that time, I estimated Chinese century was being already a commercial giant China is aiming to be the world's next great power. Will that lead to a confrontation with the Unites States? Apparently, If Emperor-II is focus on a New Eurasian Great Game by identified India, Pakistan, Iran, Russia, and China as the players. The interest of the United States, we guessed, was not in being a direct participant but in avoiding conflagration. Before the attack on the World Trade Center, the emphasis turned to great-power oil and gas rivalry. This New Eurasian Great Game was headed U.S.- Russia Competition in the world-Caspian. In these terms, the United States under President Bill-Clinton had clearly stated to play. So had a number of Bushes, with Dick Cheney, James Baker, and former national security adviser Brent Scowcroft all signed up to counsel the Azerbaijan International Operating Company. Prince George-II' future national security adviser becoming State-Secretary similar Henry Kissinger, Condoleezza Rice, as a Chevron board member, advised the company on its Tenghiz-Chevroil joint venture in Kazakhstan – as for Kissinger, a member of the BNL international advisory board (they made a pact not to tell anyone that their motto).

The New Legion

So why even United Nation, Western Europe, and United States against China continued support Somalia genocidal regime, but China was still sent 1500 volunteer-troops to protect the oil pipe-lines and military aid for this country. Iran was closed ally with China by her natural gas and oil resources. She paid nor dollars not Euro but by military materiel equipment equivalent about Seven billion dollar a year and imported 14percent Iran's oil. In reality, Iran has become coherently the engineer of China's economic growth.

A Chinese state-owned company owns 40% of the oil concession in the South of Sudan, and there are reported 4000 Chinese troops there protecting Beijing's oil interests. (By contrast, despite the noise that China made when one of its soldiers was killed by an Israeli air strike on a U.N post in Lebanon recently, there are only 1400 Chinese troops serving in all U.N peacekeeping missions worldwide)

"Is China playing a position role in developing democracy [in Africa]?" was contrast with United States, asks the resource-war theorist of the South African Institute of International Affairs. "Largely not" Human Right Watch goes further: China's policies in Africa, it claimed during the Beijing summit, have "propped up some of the continents' worst human-rights abusers." Most notoriously, China has consistently used its place as a permanent member of the U.N. Security Council to dilute resolution aimed at pressuring the Sudanese government to stop the ethnic slaughter in Darfur. China doesn't support unsavory regimes for the sake of it. Instead China's objective is to insure a steady supply of natural resources, so that it economy can sustain the growth that officials hope will keep a lid on unrest at home. That is why China has reached out to resource-rich democracies like Australia and Brazil as much as it has to such international pariah as Sudan and Burma, both of which have underdeveloped hydrocarbon reserves. There's nothing particularly surprising about any of this; it is how all nations behave when domestic supplies of primary goods are no longer sufficient to sustain their economies. But China has never needed such resources in such quantities before, so its politicians have never had to learn the skills of getting them without looking like a dictator's friend. Now they have to.

From Iran, China and United States: The Energy-War might be exploded? No! It seemed to me It should exploded at Suez Canal while the Chinese escorted crude oil tankers to refill at Venezuela, because as closer as possible for salvo in-effect every of categories of a special-nuclear missiles in the superior performance by Fengshui-powers, secretly controlled by the totalitarian spontaneous quickie-reaction. That's signified the outcome of "21st China-century" – the aftermath of WW-III emerges the New Great-Sino on Western hemisphere speaking English.

Long ago, the battle against communism and atheism is not only for Vietnamese, but more importantly it is a contemporary battle between Pope John Paul II, now Pope Benedict XVI and the Western world and the main force of atheism in the world today which is the Chinese communist Party. Chi Haotian, Ex-minister of Defense and vice-chairman of China's Central Military Commission recently in his speech posted on the internet argued that it is atheism in China, or equivalently, the tradition of loyal to the king which was taught by Confucius (not loyal to the Masters of Religion) which allows the CCP to reign and control the 1.4 billion people of China. Chi Haotian and the CCP are preaching atheism and suppressing all the movements of region, especially Falun Gong and churches such as Catholicism, Islamism…

According Charter 2000 of the Viet Democratic Side's International Forum, it seemed to me the must rejected Chi Haotian's argument, as I pointed out that scientific and technological progress will soon awaken the Chinese intelligentsia and the people of China to reconsider all the values of the Chinese society, including those of Confucius and of the CCP. The mono-party system would simply be unable to survive within a society which reevaluates all the time the values of the society to cope with the rapid progress, on all facets, of the world. Should China think of the 21st century being the Chinese century, its present mono-politics system can't survive the test of the age when all the values are permanently reevaluated. The Chinese intelligentsia and the people of China will ask for more liberties once they attain a high level of scientific and technological progress. We can't think of a Chinese century with a China of mono-politics, as

The New Legion

Chi Haotian argued that the CCP will be successful in its way to maintain a one-party ruling system!

Pope Benedict XVI as well as leaders of the Western world are surely doing everything to awaken the society of China as well as recently Soviet Union to become a free society as the people of China's spiritual and intellectual demands are more and more modern and sophisticated day to day, while China enters a new phase of scientific and technological explosion. As a result, other facets such as citizen rights and politics will also be reviewed by the intelligentsia and the people of China accordingly.

China's prospects now are as bright as ever, the opportunities of its people improving each year. It would take a particularly stupid or evil group of leaders to put that glittering prize at risk in a war. Chi Haotian and General Zhu Chenghu, Chief military political bureau, announced "We are sorry the must bombardments for a hundred big towns with full scale nuclear war could lead to the annihilation of the Americans" based (but too soon) on "fenghui power". So note: Chi Haotian; "The War Is Not Far from us and is the Midwife of the Chinese Century" was published on February 15, 2005 on www peacehall.com and was published on www.boxun.com; on April 23, 2005. This speech and a related speech; "The War Is approaching us" are analyzed in The Epoch Time original article: "The CCP' Last-ditch Gamble: Biological and Nuclear War?" (Forwarded by vnmd2002@yahoo.com: Nuoc-Viet@yahoogroups.com,8/17/05,3.50PM)

MANAGEABLE POWERLESS WITH THE LOSS OF FENGSHUI POWERS

Because early 21st century China defiant challenge a new flag from five stars to six stars; the big one signifies "Great-Sino," a great star emerged as superpower dominated five little stars which means five world's continents, stemmed from the thoughtful of General Zhu, and Chi Haotian chief military political bureau announced on February, 15, 2005 "We are sorry the must bombardments for a hundred big towns with full scale nuclear war could lead to the annihilation of the Americans" Obviously aftermath of a nuclear war, China's not all died! China didn't have any choice (In my political judgment, just guessing about the dangerous of a totalitarian regime, for instant, on the seaway escorts Chinese oil tankers through Suez canal to Venezuela, abruptly everywhere and nowhere the salvo attacked new sophisticated carrier-nuclear warhead bombardment toward the heart of United States and unsurprisingly 30 minutes later all world countries must be unconditional surrender to "Great Sino")

Apparently, we must manipulate to displace Fengshui power veins to another place for out of its effect. In the Yih-King (Oxford 1882) German professor Richard-Wilhlem and English professor James Legge (1815-1897) author of nine philosophies masterpieces (Oxford 1891) about "Tao-the king or Textes of Taoism." English translator James-Legge once said: "as if he was leaping up, but still in the deep." – waiting for next millennium development goal. Coincidently, in fact, the consequence illegal, immoral, demoralization, terrible thing American did: assassinations, not drug abuse but the stereotypical problems of drugs, civil unrest, out of control inflation, racial conflict,fragging, atrocities, gasoline shortage so much greatest tragedies in made up a tired America, a divided and deeply fractured America.

Additionally, because, in fact the America's vulnerable economy equation, for recovering at any price, strongly we must do it again (CIA and KGB once, together overthrown Communism, remembered CIA was a special 'tool' of Skull and Bones: first dynasty was Democratic W.A Harriman, and second by Republican Bushes) because the second dynasty is out of track toward American First. That the Bushes-dynasty may be preparing for war with Iran; and Iran is on the agenda. The most 40 percent of the world's oil needs to pass each day through bottleneck in the Strait of Hormuz. Two unfinished wars – one on Iran's eastern border, the other on its western flank – are daily depleting America's treasure and overworked armed forces. Most of new elected 44th president's allies in those adventures have made it clear they will not join another gamble overseas. Whoever becoming 44th U.S president wouldn't considered this main target is Middle East unrest set similar cook pots boiling but merely deviated to China, must be the original-troublesome China. Moreover, the China's equation of her new-flag with six stars can be dangerous for world stability. On the sky isn't have two suns, the U.S could have potential elimination a China totalitarian? The Tibet and some

The New Legion

nations from far-northwest of China closer [Central Asia] might separated by America help via under the U.S. Freedom Support Act? I recalled a French proverb "Broken eggs must be a fried chow-treat." The so called America's vulnerable economy will overcame not too far in prospect to enter upon a new phase of 21st century? The U.S policymaker will wise enough to carry it on.

There was requested one decade from 1962 to 1972 Mao-Zedong said "Just neglected the birth control for ten years". So when President Nixon came to see Mao 1972. China already increased population about 350 millions which population implied manpower good enough for created one New Chinese country on the America territory in meantime to need erased the Old China by nuclear-annihilated. Absolutely if WW-III will take place Chinese people couldn't all perish? Up to now mankind has car-bombed, airplane-bombed, few flesh bombed, team bombed, and one day, one country bombed. China recently have created everywhere on earth the Chinese communities, China-Towns, neighborhoods, the most in South America, Canada and Africa. For one certain moment, China badly needed war for resolved an equation earth-overpopulation and China badly needed women for mental, physical stabilities. Nowadays, China have 110 million males needed females, every year increased more 11 million male-singles. Why not don't make war? Mao-Zedong, he can use a little bamboo-leaf to cover the blue lens of American eye, covering him seeing the summit of Everest-Mount in front by the pretentious behavior: "we will still not considerer ourselves a super power" Blink for a moment and you can imagine that – but deeply in Mao-Zedong' heart, I think He believe that the 21st century is China's century.

In meeting with Kissinger, Zhou Enlai, Prime minister said "Though we have developed our industrial complex perfectly, we will still not consider ourselves a super-power...we find a way to implement any overall agreements we had reached in a way beneficial to peace between our two countries in Asia and in the world. The Indochina question is indeed a crucial problem, both for Indochina people and for the world. Therefore, we would welcome your excellent coming… because we are moving towards friendship, we believe we should normalize our relations and should be able to continue our discussions in accordance with such relations... and China's legitimate rights in the United Nations must be restores that all strategic-matter which United States would favor to One China.

Something we must mentioned, a Zhou Enlai shrewd enough, he reacted by asking Kissinger to invite President Nixon coming to China before via Soviet. But Kissinger already having the agenda timetable Nixon came to Soviet first prior to China. (How would Zhou Enlai known this Axis of Evil of two demons exploited in the world war by merchant of death in war industries?) Zhou probed into his conversation with Nixon and Kissinger and find out: "... also discourage Japan from supporting a Taiwan independence movement..." Nixon responded: "I know the Prime Minister's position is that we should withdraw our forces from Japan. I do not agree with that position, as shown in the communiqué, and I will not withdraw our forces from Japan, because I believe that our interest in peace in the Pacific is to restrain Japan. All the things that we have talked about require our forces staying"

But up to now, who tell who know "Has China the will to become a Big Power?" Spontaneously, The China's next generation implied: "For New World Order, China, once she achieves Great Power status, is to bring about a world order without resorting to war or violence. A peaceful world is one where there is no coercion but patient persuasion. To rid this world of turmoil, China must be decisive and willing to be a Great Power. Without Great Power status, how can China bring about a peaceful and tranquil world?" That felt something logically? The answer was boasted by the new China generated leaders. However China want to see the island, Taiwan reunited with the mainland one day. The Unites States, although it has a One-China-policy and has no formal diplomatic mission in Taiwan, is committed to defend Taiwan from an unprovoked attack by China. (*The island has been a place evacuated by CIA – First Flight evolved from the Civil Air Transport Service (CATS) the island has been governed independently since the defeated forces of Chiang Kai Shek's followers retreated there in 1949. But in the future Taiwan automatically becoming a state as same time China has divided a dozen republic states. In the second chunk of Eurasian Great Game, started in 1950, when Harriman came back to US with his talent-gifted-staff* *strategists worked right in the Executive Office Building – in 'Asia-Chunk' having Korea and Vietnam Wars, each created two decades hostility – China 1952-1972 and Vietnam 1975-1995. Since 1960, the 34th Squadron's U-2s had flown over China, spying on the Lop Nor nuclear test site and Kansu missile range. First Flight's -123 had proved a tough target for SAM and MIG, penetrating the mainland 200 time (SOG-Colby's secret war) CIA air experts at Takhli, Thailand, were tasked to help Colby plan the North Vietnam aerial penetrations; he couldn't have found a more capable group. Colonel Harry "Heinie" Aderholt, likely the most experienced special operations officer in the USAF, had finished the CIA's Tibet airlift, where unmarked C-130s had penetrated Chinese-occupied Tibet to parachute supplies and guerrillas to the pro-Dalai Lama resistance. Also, on loan to the CIA for secret projects since the Korea War, Aderholt's Thailand based organization had been redirected to support the CIA's expanding guerrilla force in Laos, using Air America planes, when the infiltration analysis job was assigned. You ever thought one day Taiwan and Tibet become the Independent Republic states?)*

The United States can also encourage China's diplomats to recognize that irresponsible policies will diminish China's long-term influence. As China expands its global reach, it will find itself exposed to all sorts of pressures – of the sort it has never had to face before – to behave itself. Already, there are voices in Africa warning China that actually it is acting just like the other purpose than substituting "White colonialism" instead "Yellow colonialism". Whereat did African get so angry? Meantime talk about peace and cooperation and development which sound great to U.S and Western ears – but underneath is a question of brutal competition for energy for markets and for resources. How can that competition be managed? China competes aggressively for natural resources. How can the US and allies convince the China – the key may be to identify more areas in which China's national interests align with the West's and where cooperation brings mutual benefits.

Whereas, half century ago, China's secrecy stratagem has planned a secret highway for one opportunity seizure Australia after destroyed US instantly by special nuclear annihilation when her preparedness to stir the war was done. She trusted herself a totalitarian regime having the reacted advantage than US government led so much time pondering for war- declaration. But other aspects of China's rise are real and troubling. China is a one-party state, not a democracy. China's military buildup is best seen as a corollary of changes in Chinese society. Where Chinese military doctrine was once based on human-wave attacks, it now stresses the killing power of technology. China's prospects now are as bright as ever, the up date sophisticated weapons and the opportunities of its people improving each year. It would take a particularly stupid or evil military-group of leaders to put that glittering prize at risk in a war. There's nothing new, or particularly frightening, about such a transformation; it's what nations do all the time.

A more than four decades ago, there were in the past, about 2.5 millions Myanmar-Chinese and secret Chinese residents living in Myanmar. China and Myanmar were close neighbors, linked by mountains and rivers, with a common border of over 1300 miles enjoying a long-standing friendship. The Myanmar people had called the Chinese "pawpaw" means "full brothers". There had been frequent exchange of visits between their leaders. Overhauling oil wells and building a new dockyard for repairing ships as well as helping build a major highway that would connect the southern Chinese province of Yunnan to the Indian Ocean through county Thaton, Burma, along Triangle Kumon range to the rivers: Nujiang, Sittang, and Salween through the high land Shan-Plateau raising opium smuggling, cultivation, opiate of the tribal: Poppies and poverty are everywhere, and opium has many uses, including as a medicine, even its smoke to treat the children's illnesses.

Coordinated or must synchronize with Ho chi Minh super highway, now called IIH (International Indochina Highway) for her Australian occupied anticipation. (I have some stranger, ridiculous view-points that I couldn't comprehend "why US Strategic Air Command (SAC) dropped 14.5 million-tons bombs on Indochina, but only 6 millions among them just dropped on South-Laos from Mu-Gia Pass to Tchepone, Attopeu, south Laos provinces, straight tracking like as arrow reaching about 900 miles; the real meaning of air-campaign "the rolling thunder" that Colonel NVA Bui Tin said only 0.19 damaged on Route 559 [Ho Chi Minh trail] or less one-percent damage, no one NVA soldier got killed but merely hear real sound 'rolling-thunder'. This is so strangely to me as a spy-pilot witness, all bombardment targets on mountain area that KGB forced Hanoi to derail into Laos' territories instead parallel with Laos/Viet border. NVA named 'West Truong Son' (western-chain-mountain-range, NVA general Dung expressed: this West Truong Son went to South expensed Five month instead East Truong Son only One month) CIA and KGB created this strategic Ho Chi Minh trail for economical or military causes? What the axis of evil's conspiracy of silence? So why China has extended to Myanmar a great deal of assistance in projects of agriculture, industry, transport, electric power, education, health and human resources development. Chinese companies have initiated a large number of projects in Myanmar, setting up factories in the form of whole investment or joint ventures, covering as many sectors as oil and gas exploitation and processing of forest and marine products. The U.S frequently put on eye on these two strategic-highways.

The sentiment, or something like it, can be heard a lot these days in Chiang Saen, a town on the Mekong River in northern Thailand, where locals used to subsist on whatever they could make from farming and smuggling – until Chinese engineers began blasting the rapids and reefs on the upper Mekong so that large boats could take Chinese-manufactured goods to markets in Southeast Asia. In South America, Chinese investment is building roads and railways, opening textile factories and digging oil wells. You hear it on the farms of Brazil, where Chinese appetite for soy and beef has led to a booming export trade. Through its foreign investments and appetite for raw materials, the world's most populous country has already transformed economies from Angola to Australia. Nowadays, China is turning that commercial might into real political muscle, striding onto the global stage and acting like a nation that very much intends to become the world's next great power.

The theory of China doctrine aimed "sound like an oil drop spreading on the paper" that China would applicable, extending from its own neighborhood; while Unites States exports to Southeast Asia have been virtually stagnant for a past decade, Chinese trade with this region is soaring. Yet actually China's relations with its neighbor are nothing but light and sweetness, often at the expense of the United States. There are signs that China's behavior is changing in more constructive ways. China fought a war with Vietnam 1979. For years, it supported Communist movements dedicated to undermining governments in nations such as Singapore, Malaysia, Philippine, and Indonesia.

In the northern reached of Thailand and Laos, you can find whole towns where Mandarin has become the common language and the Yuan the local currency is always keep low trade value so it is not aid from the U.S but trade with China – carried on new highway being built from Kunming in Yunnan province to Hanoi, Mandalay and Bangkok, or along a Mekong River whose channels are full of Chinese goods – that is transforming much of Southeast Asia. And strangely, The Ho Chi Minh trail now have been developed for becoming International Superhighway for China's interests which the most 40 years ago USAF-B.52 , the Strategic Air Command demolished rocky-mountain with 6 million-tons of bombs and C-123 for Air-defoliation in "the Hot-Tip" campaign, tracking for the land cleared reference for the beginning early NVA' pioneers as road-constructors. An eagle nurtures a nest, she would see a little Eagle Chic there; absolutely, she doesn't want an ugly water-bird-chic born there. Thereby, there need be a war between China and the U.S? No but yes! The beginning conflicts between the regional countries firstly against a giant nation and the U.S would engaged later one. That is an eternal basis fundamental procedure that U.S policy's schemer anticipated in U.S stratagem. The Islands Paracel sound like belonging to China in Kissinger's lobby scandal in 1974 was a cunning trick [at a stage to manage the defeat in the first volley ball in U.S Congress in 1970 aimed "Cooper-Church" and "Case-Church"] that U.S led China fell into the trap in stirring war with their neighbors in the future.

Early 1995 Chinese occupy Mischief Reef – Sparring over the Spratly islands. Manila tries to halt China's advance into the Spratlys, blowing up markers and detaining Chinese fishermen. But its diplomatic and military weakness doesn't bode well for the attempt.

But in an interview with the REVIEW, Philippine President Fidel Ramos stood his ground: *"I will not hesitate to take the necessary protective measures for our territory."* Shortly after the discovery of the Chinese presence, the Philippine Congress passed a 50 billion-peso ($2 billion-dollar) armed-forces modernization program.

The Philippine occupies eight of what it calls the Kalayaan (freedom) islands, and maintains a military airstrip on one Pagasa. Taiwan has troops on one island in the area and Vietnam occupies four others. China, Vietnam and Taiwan claim the entire Spratleys area, while the Philippines, Malaysia and Brunei lay claim to parts of it. Perhaps ironically, Vietnam publicly backed Manila's protest, despite occupying islands in the same area, some of which have been reinforced recently. The Vietnamese have been China's most vocal critics over the Spratleys issue, and are still smarting over the sinking of two of their patrol craft by Chinese warship in another part of the island-chain in 1988. Vietnam is expected to join the Philippines as a member of Asian in July/1995, so bilateral relations are naturally close.

A legacy of decades of reliance on the Unites States to protect the archipelago, that era ended when CIA motivated Philippino protest to take back two U.S Bases (Clark field Air Force Base and Navy Subic Basy) which were forced to close in 1992. When President Ramos ordered a beefing-up of military forces in the Spratlys theatre after the Chinese structures were discovered; the same operational maneuver of Vietnam 1974 – the Air force could draw on only elderly F-5 jet fighters, with dubious operational capability. These were to be pitted against China's comparatively modern range of destroyers, frigates, submarines and thousands of jet fighters.

Stemmed from the first volley in Congress came in 1970, "Cooper-Church" authored a bill that cut off funding of all military activity in "Southeast Asia". That measure narrowly failed in its original "Eurasian Great Game" stratagem. So did the U.S' anticipation? Admiral Richard Macke, the commander in-chief of the U.S. Pacific Command, sought to backtrack. Asked by the REVIEW during a visit to Jakarta in early March how the Chinese managed to spend four months building structures on Mischief Reef without the U.S. knowing about it, Macke retorted: *"I didn't say we didn't know anything about it...and I'm not going to talk to all the information we* have available to us," he said. "But we don't get surprised an awful lot." Could he elaborate? "Not in this forum."

Strangely, a week later, the REVIEW posed again the same question about Mischief Reef to another important visitor, Admiral William Owens, vice-chairman of the Joint Chiefs of Staff. *There are a lot of things that go on in the Spratlys on any given day,"* he replied. *"The complete intelligence-sharing of every thing that goes on in the world is not a policy of our military. But we do care a lot about sharing important intelligence with our allies."*

Bushes Head of the China-America Chamber of Commerce

Magically, after transformed the Chinese leadership was like an **Asian version of Skull and Bones,** secretive and select. Three year after Red China took the advantage of take over the Paracel Island. In August 1977, Deng Xiaoping invited Four Big American companies to China to discuss the exploitation and development of offshore oil reserves. The group arrived to watch a ceremony in Tiananmen Square, where thousand of marchers paraded in precise formation carrying Red banners. Then the real work began in the following days when they held a series of closed door meetings with Chinese Officials, Deng Xiaoping who made a point of telling George H W Bush that Deng was welcome in China anytime. Immediately, George-1 invited his old partner Hugh Liedtke, who was now Chairman of Pennzoil. He was interested in drilling for oil in China. Right after meeting, George-1 took Hugh Liedtke to a private meeting with the foreign trade minister. Pennzoil wanted a crack at drilling for oil offshore in the East China and South China Sea. One of the Four was Pennzoil. A year later, Pennzoil became the first oil company to drill in China.

The New Legion

Below you're reading an article that Saigon being oppressed by a ruthless military Red China while the U.S turned her face to another side:

In February 1972, under the authority of the Permanent Government [Skull and Bones] President Richard Nixon along with Kissinger made a historic trip to China. In Beijing on June 22, 1972, Kissinger told Zhou the U.S. acknowledged its North Vietnamese enemy was a "permanent factor" and probably the "strongest entity" in the region. "And we have had no interest in destroying it or even defeating it" he insisted. After more than a year of testing to make sure that the messages were right and "sincere," on January 16, 1974, the Communist China took the advantage of the opportunity and made a move to take over the Paracel Islands in the South China Sea. While Uncle Sam looked the other way and considered that was a local dispute, the Navy of The Republic of Vietnam made a stand and fought back, repeating an epic episode of Vietnam history. A small group of islands named Paracel (Hoang Sa) are located approximately 200 nautical miles due east of Danang. And, although too small to be inhabited by a permanent population, they were never-the-less an important historical and strategic possession of Vietnam. This claim of sovereignty dates back centuries. However, the Peoples Republic of China felt they could displace this claim based upon a proclamation made by them in September 1958, and acknowledged by then North Vietnamese Prime Minister Pham-Van-Dong. Contradicting this disputed proclamation, the South Vietnamese Government continued to maintain a small weather observation garrison on Pattle Island, the largest island in this group. And no action was initiated by the Peoples Liberation Army (PLA) to displace this presence.

On January 16, after delivering six South Vietnamese Army officers and an American observer [that's as maybe a CIA agent] to the Paracels for an inspection tour, the former USS Bering Strait (AVP-34), WAVP-382/WHEC-382 Bering Strait, now Vietnamese Navy Patrol Cruiser Ly-Thuong-Kiet HQ-16, discovered two Chinese "armored fishing trawlers" were laying off Drummond Island supporting troops from the PLA that had occupied the territory. In addition, Chinese soldiers were observed around a bunker on nearby

Duncan Island, with a PLAN landing ship moored directly on the beach. The CO of HQ-16, CDR Le-Van-Thu, reported his findings back to the regional headquarters in Danang, and also sent over 15 people to guard the small island of Money. CDR Thu' report was routed immediately over to Saigon, where a hastily formed meeting by President Thieu and his cabinet decided to attempt eviction of the PRC forces. Overnight on January 18, a small South Vietnamese force comprised of Destroyer Escort Tran-Khanh-Du HQ-4 (ex-USS Forster, DER-334) and the Patrol Cruiser Tran-Binh-Trong HQ-5 (USS Chincoteague (AVP-24), USCGC Chincoteague (WAVP-375) (WHEC-375)) were dispatched from the Danang area under the overall command of Captain Ha-Van-Ngac. Patrol Craft Nhat-Tao HQ-10 (ex-USS Serene AM-300) which was proceeding to Danang for repair of one of her engines, was also diverted to join the small flotilla of VNN ships that was converging on the Paracels.

While waiting for the arrival of the other ships, CDR Thu on HQ-16 landed a team of Vietnamese commandos on Robert Island (Cam Tuyen) to investigate some PRC flags installed on this tiny spit of land. No PLA forces were present on the island, so the naval commandos returned to their ship. However, shortly after their arriving back aboard, two PLAN Kronstad-class guided missile gun boats started churning up the waters in the vicinity of the collection of small islands. The possibility of peaceful restoration of the islands became highly unlikely. Permission to attack the intruding PRC forces was transmitted to Captain Ngac later in the day of January 18, with one stipulation: President Thieu wanted the Navy to try to "parley" with the Chinese first. Accordingly, the commander of the VNN task force arrayed his ships around Duncan Island during the evening in preparation for a confrontation early on the morning of the 19[t.h]. Meanwhile, two additional PLAN T48-class gunboats arrived in the area. This had the effect of further deterioration to an already very tense situation.

As the tide crested on the following morning, HQ-5 lowered a brace of rubber landing craft over the side, heading for Duncan. Twenty Vietnamese Navy commandos, led by a lieutenant junior grade, waded through the surf and onto the high ground waving a white flag, indicating a desire to talk. Instead, the larger than expected Chinese ground force began advancing toward the small party from several directions. Captain Ngac ordered a retreat. As the Vietnamese began nudging their boats back into the water, the PLA troops opened fire. A Lieutenant and two of his men fell dead in the raging surf.

The flotilla commander, in direct radio communications with the VNN Headquarters staff in Saigon, requested instructions. After only a short period of deliberations, the word from Saigon was emphatically relayed:

"Shoot" - Captain Ngac immediately translated the order into action as his four vessels began moving toward and taking on the two armed trawlers, one landing craft and four missile-gunboats with devastating fire. The melee that resulted was fast paced, close in, and deadly. The two groups of ships were some times as close as only 1600 yards as they blasted away at one another. One of the PLAN gunboats (K-274) was sunk outright. And another (T-389) was damaged so badly that it was beached on Duncan and lost. The remaining two PLAN gunboats were also damaged.

But HQ-10 took a direct hit from a surface-to-surface missile and, spewing smoke and fire from her bridge went dead in the water with her guns silent. HQ-16 also received damage from an errant five inch round from HQ-5 but continued to fight on scoring additional hits. A seaman below decks on the Nhat-Tao rushed up to the gun deck to find the gun crew dead and the 40 mm weapon jammed. Although not a gunner's mate, Seaman Tay cleared the gun and resumed firing on the PLAN vessels. The Chinese concentrated their firepower on this renewed source of danger, and Tay quickly went down fighting as the fate of his ship became all too evident. "HQ-10 was going under" After only thirty-five minutes (10:25 to 11:00 AM) the furious battle was over. Both groups of ships began rapidly pulling away from one another. The PLAN toward Hainam, and the South Vietnamese in the opposite direction toward Danang;

As the disengagement took place, word reached Saigon from the Americans that, although the US would not provide assistance in what they deemed to be a local dispute, they did advise that radar reports from US Naval sources indicated that a flight of MIG-21's had taken off from Hainam headed toward the Paracels, with at least one Chinese Guided Missile Cruiser also moving in that direction at high speed.

With this news, and indications of rapidly moving surface radar contacts approaching the area from the north, the only recourse for the Vietnamese was to retire completely. Captain Ngac ordered HQ-4 to escort the crippled HQ-16 back to Danang. HQ-5, with the commander of the flotilla on board, would begin an "expanding square" search for survivors from HQ-10. But even the search effort was abandoned and further emphasis made for all South Vietnamese ships to withdraw as it became increasingly clear that further threats from the PLAN could be expected. Information obtained in later years proved this to be a wise decision, as two PLAN Hainam Class submarines were directed to guard the approaches to the Paracels on October 19. Therefore, it would not be until several days later that a Dutch tanker and a Vietnamese fishing boat pulled only thirty-seven survivors of the sunken Nhat-Tao out of the South China Sea; This from the eighty-two sailors on board HQ-10 when the battle began. Commanding Officer Nguy-Van-Tha was not among those who were rescued having been killed when the missile hit the bridge area. A few days later, the Chinese returned in force to finish the occupation of the entire chain of islands of the Paracels. The Chinese government announced to the world that they had captured forty-eight prisoners, including the one American. These were the garrison forces on Pattle and neighboring Money plus the six ARVN officers that had arrived in the days just before the battle. Up until today, the Government North Vietnam has not lodged a formal protest, and the Paracels remain claimed and in the control of the Red China.

Why did the South Vietnamese Navy challenge China with its more powerful fleet?

That seems like a logical question; perhaps best answered by men who fought there, from a Vietnamese language article published in 1998; Twenty four years ago, US Navy officers stationed in Vietnam thought that the South Vietnamese Navy should have quietly withdrawn from the Paracels. They never did expect that "Little South Vietnam" would pick a fight with the giant China. "Why would you engage a superior force with no hope of succeeding? Even those who did not directly participate in the battle would answer as follows: "To defend my country, even to the death. The South Vietnamese Navy was determined to fight. The Paracel Islands were and are a part of Vietnam's heritage. The Vietnamese vowed to defend it. Our ships exchanged fire with the invaders and fought with all their strength. Many worldwide observers, who at first wondered at our actions, later looked on with admiration at our courage. A nation's destiny is in the hands of its own people"

A tribute to the Navy of the Republic of Vietnam

On January 19, 1974 this proud Navy fought against the huge Chinese Navy in Hoang-Sa (Paracel Islands) archipelagos without any help or support from the U.S. Seventh Fleet. Sailors who abandoned ships scattered to the sea. The U.S. Navy offered no assistance. U.S. Naval Historians have never mentioned a word about this sea battle.

The ill-equipped former DER Foster (VNN HQ 4) with torpedo tubes without torpedoes, long range radar that had been stripped off after changing hand from the US Navy, was all but useless. Former U.S. Coast Guard WHEC craft, with slow 5" guns, could not get the upper-hand on the high speed Chinese gunboats. The aftermath was VNN PCE (HQ 10) was sunk. Two Chinese gunboats were sunk and some were damaged. The Hoang-Sa (Paracel Islands) was lost. After 1973 the U.S. sharply reduced its support. The VNN had to use its ammunition sparingly. A victory at Tuyen Nhon changed the Viet Cong's movements towards Saigon. The Viet Cong commander offered millions of Đong (Piaster) for Lt. Commander Le Anh Tuan's head.

On April 1975 Task Force 99 blocked a Viet Cong attack on Saigon from Tay Ninh and alerted a surveillance post for the VNN fleet to evacuate via the Long Tao waterway to safety. On April 30, 1975, after Duong Van Minh called Republic of Vietnamese Armed forces to surrender, Lt. Commander Le Anh Tuan committed suicide when his river flotilla was ambushed by Russian made T-54 tanks. Many boats were abandoned in Vung Tau and in South Vietnams waterways. Officers and enlisted sailors felt betrayed by their comrades and allies. The only way they could save their miserable lives was to draw close to their families. Sadly, Commander Ha Ngoc

Luong killed his wife, children and then committed suicide at the Nha Trang Naval Academy.

After April 30, 1975 some LST crewmen, with AK-47s held behind their backs, trained Viet Cong sailors to run those types of ships. They did so while watching dirty pigs and chickens feeding on the former proud ships decks. Officers were separated from their families. They had to do duty in forced labor Re-education Camps for years. They tried to escape Vietnam by all possible ways. With their experiences as sea going sailors, many were successful. Some succeeded in reaching free countries and began rebuilding their lives.

The Viet Cong Navy updated the former DER Foster (HQ 4) and began using her as a training ship. They armed WHEC with missiles. Today they are still using some former VNN LST for cargo ships. Their fleet has dozens of gas turbine Petya gun boats with torpedo launchers. The Ukraine is planning on selling them some 2,000 ton Gepard frigates and Molniya missile boats equipped with Moskit supersonic anti-ship missiles under Ukrainian license. Vietnamese shipyards will build these types of ships for Viet Cong Navy.

The China was caught in a U.S trap?

Unsurprisingly, on early January, 2008 Navy-China raised a new flag with six stars, means one more star in hindsight her composed the islands Paracel and Spratly the theatre the South China Sea belong to Yunnan province (Geneva 1954 agreement, Secretary of Russia, English, French, and China – Zhu Enlai signed accepting Vietnam has two states: one North Vietnam and one South Vietnam that two islands Paracel and Spratley belong South Vietnam proper-sovereignty, Vietnam will won if this matter proved by international judge – Skull and Bones lay a good trap for Great-Sino in 1974, be caught in a U.S trap few decades later after they had detected oil well there) In early 2008 Great-Sino raised its flags on all the islands on South China Sea (Paracels and Spratlys) increased 5 million Km2 to her belonging. The area is potentially rich in oil and natural gas, though geologists debate the exact amounts that could be extracted. The challenge wasn't only with Southeast Asian countries alone but more involved with Japan, Australia, US; due to China's ambition on crude-oil and natural gas. "Wait and see what will happen in this century" World War Three explodes on the Ocean-Pacific adverse for that name?

Vietnam was the first class with 1.9 BOE, equivalent 10,000 cubic-feet. Malaysia and Thailand in the second with 1.8 BOE, according the natural resource-war theorist international 1994 – by Professor Charles J. Johnson – energy resource VN, chapter 10 "in the direction of fly-dragon" until at least 2030 Chinese oil exploitation couldn't to carry out the eve drill technique. But surely, the United States was already contracted lease with Vietnam for exploitation – Conoco, Caltex, Mobil, Texas Co… off shore of Vietnam the ceiling sea-floor was hard stony creek, the under wave so turbulence, the must inclined drill with sophistical high-tech. One drill missed cost three million dollar (price estimated 1970) So China dream was never come true. Meanwhile the U.S warships frequently came back and forth anchored at Vietnam visitation. In the 2007, U.S. Commander Admiral Seventh Fleet, Timothy Keating twice visited Vietnam and very soon Vietnam and U.S. have signed a military cooperative treaty. U.S. would like equip to Vietnam missile-launch-destroyer and patrol cruiser just I guess.

"Apparently, China was a big pity giant, ugly fat and slow. When United States celebrated 50 years anniversary of Vietnam-War 1975-2025 this pity giant will already sliced many pieces prior her becoming qualified to oil drilled exploitation. Many challenge shall took place in the prospect, on the course road-map "Eurasian Great Game" stratagem. And the United States once again repeat the approach-procedure as China was even less well endowed consumer, having to import most of the rest from the United States, which was avoidable incited great China went to war; nowadays was for China turn? Or on the earth after WW-III, global population have survived a couple hundred million people and China then been an earth leader in population. So wait and see! What the hell taking place.

However, there is so hard and never happened that you ever feel mesmerized by what China fears – remember this: China is still a poor country (GDP per head in 2005 was $1,700, compared with $42,000 in the US) whose leaders face so many problems that it is reasonable to wonder how they ever sleep. Corruption is endemic and growing

(CIA played the excellent experience lesson-ruled similarly in South Vietnam) U.S Permanent Government lobbied to lift sanctions under the U.S. Freedom Support Act, repeated every procedures against aid to ethnic minorities, tribe montagnards…claimed that the sanctions were largely the result of biased lobbying by human-being-Americans. Protests and riots human right violations, by rural workers are measured in the tens of thousands each year. China is an environmental dystopia, its cities' air foul beyond imagination and its clean water scarce. The most immediate priority for China's leadership is less how to project itself internationally than how to maintain stability in a society that is going through the sort of social and economic change that, in the past, has led to chaos and violence. And yet for all their internal challenges, the Chinese seem to want their nation to be a bigger player in the world, by success in advancing its interests abroad despite turmoil at home. Most Chinese, the survey found, believed China's global influence would match that of the US within a decade – pledged billions dollars in investments in Cuba, Chile, Brazil, Argentina predominance in commercial business. China-leader played host to leaders from 48 African countries in Beijing, went to Vietnam for the annual Asia-Pacific Economic Cooperation summit, slipped over to Laos for a day and then popped off for a six-day tour of India and Pakistan. You could feel China is playing a global game now – "Look at parts of Asia, look at Africa, and look at Central America." China is seeking only way counter with U.S on economic competition in low labor. China doesn't used war but killed U.S by her economic booster in people way of lives.

However, what will be China's priorities? What does it fear and what does it want? The first item on the agenda is straightforward: it is to be left alone. China brooks no interference in its internal affairs, and its definition of what is internal is not in doubt. The status of Tibet, for example, is an internal matter; the Dalai Lama is not a spiritual leader but a 'Splittist' whose real aim is to break up China.

As for Taiwan, China is prepared to tolerate all sorts of temporary uncertainties as to how its status might one day be resolved – but not the central-point that there is only 'One-China.' Cross that line and you will hear about it. China's defense of its right to be free of interference has a corollary. China has traditionally detested the intervention by the great powers in other nations' affairs. To the US invasion of Iraq, saying, "They felt they can't allow that sort of meddling in what they see as a nation's internal affairs." China's commitment to nonintervention means that it doesn't inquire closely into the internal arrangements of others. China's aid and investments are attractive to Africans precisely because they come with no conditionality related to governance, fiscal probity or other concerns of Western donors, but secretly the necessary of dispatched the Chinese people who in formed the so called China-Towns for incoming WWW-III;A New China country out of the Old-China annihilation by Fengshui-Power vein?

Disastrously, China is a one-party state, not a democracy; but other aspects of China's rise are real and troubling. Few U.S policymakers and business leaders like to say there is something inevitable about political change in China – that as China gets richer, its population will press foe more democratic freedoms and its ruling elite, mindful of the need for change, will grant them. Could be! But China is becoming richer now, and if there is any sign of substantial political reform – or any sign that the absence of such reform is hurting China's economic growth – it is, to put it mildly, hard to find. Does China's lack of democracy necessarily threaten U.S interests? One answer to that question involves looking back to the Cold-War. Based on Harriman's great strategist of performed in "Espionage-War" and "Counter-Espionage-War": The Soviet Union wasn't a democracy, and although the US contested its power in all sorts of ways, American policymakers were content to live with the reality of Soviet strength in the hope that communism'

Appeal outside its borders would wither and Soviet's political system would become more open. Is that how the US should treat a non-democratic China?

As an experienced China watcher now at Iraq we saw almost every day taking place 'Car-Bombs" what is different between Muslim and totalitarianism and China leaders count on so much at "Fengshui Power Veins" equation, like theorem in 21st century will be China-Century! So we are warning that living with a more powerful, non-democratic Beijing would not be easy for the American. In crucial ways, the American has less leverage over China than it ever had over the Soviet Union. This lack of leverage over Chinese behavior may make for an uncomfortable future. We will see a time when a powerful China not only remains undemocratic but also sustains unpleasant regimes in power, as it does today in such nations as Zambia, Burma, Iran, Pakistan…Because China is particularly against any attempt to spread democracy but in contrast, China wants to build speed bumps on the road to political globalization and liberalization in her way. We should know, "talk about peace and cooperation and development, which sound great to American ears – but underneath is a question of brutal competition for energy for resources and for markets.

How can that competition be managed? And how can the US and its allies convince the Chinese not to support rogue regimes? The key may be to identify more areas in which China's national interests align with the West's and where cooperation brings mutual benefits. China competes aggressively for natural resources. That equation is shifting due US production has slipped down an estimated in future, this is an event of the first magnitude; Take it a break-times! Because the Skull and Bone had a long stratagem about the Eurasia Great Game: "The Eagle formed his nest in which should be born a small Chic Eagle, surely not a small Chic Waterfowl" Obviously, Harriman's Super-Highway for the US interest not for the China's interest; that Indochina-International-Highway soon becoming the approaches for US allies invades and divided China in dozen Republic China countries likewise Soviet Union which the US consider as a fruit "Durian", that skin-peel is so hard so tough but US can be a peeler for it, and done! now China look like its flesh, thereby whenever the US feel his expenses more than swallow up the earnings, then just go ahead to repeat the Freedom Support Act like for final victory will remedy all past set-backs in Soviet Union. In my view this event is similarity the triumvirate of Skull and Bones counter a triumvirate of LBJ, JFK, and his brother Bobby in the earlier 1960s. But focus on a common similar goal. Both of these two triumvirates were supremely confident that the advantages of the Capitalist system would ultimately prevail eventually though different way.

The New Legion

To set a good example in 1996, the last episode of the "Old" Eurasian Great Game but the beginning of the "New" that George-I activated for his own narrow interests. George-I, second Skull generation, lobbied to lift sanctions under the US Freedom Support Act against aid to Azerbaijan, the oil-reach former Soviet republic in the Caucasus, which had been motivated by concern over Azerbaijani ethnic cleansing of the Abkhazians. He claimed that the sanctions were largely the result of biased lobbying by Armenian Americans, but in 1997 Brown and Root bid on a major Caspian project from the Azerbaijan International Operating Company. On a related front, Halliburton supported overturning the Massachusetts "Burma Law" which discouraged the state government from awarding contracts to companies doing business in repressive Myanmar. The complicity of Halliburton's Burmese operations in major human rights violations had been asserted in a 2000 report by Earth Rights International. Similarly, He lobbied heavy against the U.S Iran-Libya Sanction Act of 1995, trying to secure an exemption so that Halliburton could participate in the development of Iran's offshore oil fields, as well as in the Persian Gulf. Although his deputy, Dick Cheney's stewardship of Halliburton also raised some questions of domestic business ethics overcharging the government, fraudulent accounting practices, and the like – the more important issues concerned two large topics: First, Halliburton's growing role as something of a US "private military adjunct," and Second, the extent to which this emergence drew upon Dick Cheney's positions as Secretary of defense then Vice president of the United States. As noted, Cheney launched the Defense department's with Donald Rumsfeld in privatization effort (1992 till 2007) took advantage of it as CEO of Halliburton from 1995 to 2000, and then helped to extend and entrench the "private army" aspect as vice president.

Why don't gas companies drill more wells? Gas and Oil companies, the most Halliburton, are flush with profits, so they could afford it. And Halliburton one of the world's largest natural-gas producers, in the inter-contiguous 48 states, easily accessible fields are running full tilt, these are unconventional sources – low permeability coal-bed methane, shale gas, and gas sands. So high energy costs will shave up too much a point off Americans fiscal income nowadays; this equation George-I should resolved in early 1960 [synthetic fuel] but now, it was too late. We do know who grows corn, soybeans and wheat has seen the price of fertilizer, which is made in part from gas, rise heave-charges to consumers. It'd why for some companies the run up in fuel prices is one more reason to ship jobs offshore. Domestically, jobs have vanished since then companies are building plants overseas, where natural gas goes for a small fraction of the price it commands in the America. As a result, "we've lost a lot of jobs to China because of the labor-cost difference," and "Now we're starting lo lose jobs in energy-intensive sectors – It's a shame the US hasn't put in place these policies." [George H W Bush, a policymaker of the Emperor-II Skull and Bones focusing on Crude-oil instead of the Synthetic-fuel]

Meantime, Chinese says "But if they decide to do something (energy) they achieve it!" China will defeat US by economical approach not nuclear weapons. There need be no wars between China and the U.S, no catastrophes, no economic competition that gets out of hand. Today nuclear weapons are a blunt instrument, because Chinese were everywhere around the world. Surely U.S. does not want to suicide. Problems cannot be solved through bombs. They are of little use. They hate it. They need economy and safe lives in seeking peace, love, friendship and justice. Once again, China repeated in opposition to nuclear weapons. Mankind thought, it has been developed just to kill human beings. It' isn't in the service of human beings. For that reason, China often address to the U.N General Assembly, China suggested that a committee should be set up in order to disarm all the countries that possess nuclear weapons. Automatically, China becoming a warrior for world peace! Remembering, in 1972 Mao-Zedong said: "The Chinese Government completely disapproves of the proposition of the Soviet [why not US] government to hold a five-power nuclear conference… We propose is that all nations of the world, whether large or small, should come together to discuss this problem and reach agreement and thorough destruction of nuclear weapons, and as a first step, should reach agreement on the non-use of nuclear weapons. It won't do to lasso us. The Soviet Union has such a scheme." The conjunction of an U.S immense military establishment and a large arms industry [WIB] is no longer used in the mankind experience. Even the total influence – economic, political, and even spiritual – is felt in every world wide countries. We should recognize the imperative to stop in used for this merchant of death. Yet we not fail to comprehend its grave implication for our future generation. The potential for the disastrous rise of misplaced power exists and will persist.

Scientific-activists concerns about pollution and potential harm to wildlife from such a large industrial operation. Groups like the "ACEEE" the American Council for-an-Energy Efficient Economy say we could cut natural-gas prices less in the next five years if we would, for instance, mandate efficiency targets for power plants and offer more financial incentives for renewable fuels like wind and solar. Can we do it? The ACEEE would say we could ease out of our gas crunch with realistic conservation efforts. As for China, The CERS (China Energy Research Society) expects: Water power – A geothermal plant in her national wide produced a cozy runoff – and no carbon emissions – going green all steamed up as the world's biggest country is starting to go geothermal. Last year alone, China added 102 gigawatts to its electrical grid – roughly twice the total capacity of California's. There are eventually geothermal resources in almost every province in China. "Geothermal pumps will even be used to heat and cool some of the venues at the 2008 Olympic Games in Beijing.

So why I am with my definite knowledge, just guessing: The Skull and Bones dynasties literally terminated at the end of its second term 2008, but in reality on investigated date 'the leak of CIA operative Valerie Plame's identity 2003; this is a more interesting comparison with Skull and Bones dynasties in which in my perceptions has two disguised emperors: the First was under the reign of Democrat William A. Harriman (1917-1969) and the Second was Republican, George H W Bush (1960-1969 apprentice: till to the Paris peace talks on Vietnam, Harrimanwas chief U.S negotiator, especially in the matter of negotiating with the Hanoi, I dare said donation Saigon regime to Hanoi, that's! and last to 2:19pm, November/ 19/ 2006, Republic Death Rattle) In fact, I'm uncomfortably aware that I still must dilute my enthusiasm with a cold splash of reality; While it's perfectly delightful to have been so thoroughly vindicated for predictive posts like: "Republican Death Rattle," "Bushes Death Rattle," and "Skull and Bones Graveyard Nov/2006."

The prince George-II Crime Syndicate – at the direction of his Godfather George-I – found itself forced to make him an offer he couldn't refuse, the most W Bush's cabinet included Donald Rumsfeld, Vice president Cheney was rendered all the sweeter because President Loser had pompously proclaimed barely too earlier that the most would all remain until the administration's end...then had to admit the lie when he was called on it. The Vietnam-War was a far more damaging and awful conflict than Iraq. More Vietnamese died and more Americans died. The First emperor has also (sort of) admitted his mistakes, something that The Second emperor will never do. The First also had a complete lack of morality in his judgments – it seems that he saw the Vietnamese as nothing but numbers. The Second, for as awful as he is, actually might believe in something and maybe that makes him less of a bastard than the First. Given all this evidence, why do I argue that George H W Bush is the worst emperor of US history? Because W .A Harriman was very much an emperor of his time while George H W Bush is an outlying. Had W .A Harriman not served in his position, history probably would have taken place in a similar way. We still would have gone into Vietnam and hundreds of thousands of people would have died. Did W .A Harriman cause greater damage than another man in the office would have? Probably! By the, like everyone else, believed in the Domino Theory and thought that we had to stop communism everywhere

Back to Vietnam War, every month the National Intelligence Estimates report to Mr. President-eyes [President Nixon] only the Status of the war and explanation to detail if needed in Oval Office. Strangely, it was so different between two disguised emperors, [the acting emperor-II, George H W Bush] In earlier 1972, that emerged of strange event, the NIE reported to President-eyes only, but Henry Kissinger, a superman dared hold it in secret, of course he was a powerful key-creator covered NSC, State Department, Pentagon, White House

What the NIE expressed? (1) North Vietnam prepared to overrun Saigon. (2) China, Mao Zedong okay. (3) Soviet Union, Leonid Brezhnev ultimately rock and roll war materiel supplies as soon as possible to Hanoi's hand 700 tons of sophisticated weapon for gloomy April/1975 – Saigon fall, invasion Cambodia, and counter attack to Red China 1979.

Nowadays in turn George-II, The National Intelligence Estimates mainstream media was published on December, 3/2007 – Why? This is a cold splash on Bushes of reality. Washington Post states "Blow", George-II stunned into silence on 2/12/2007. Why George-II didn't hold it? It's easy understandable because the emperor-II was out of track off on the course "American-First". Bushes are focused on narrow interests for their backers 'Oilmen' and 'Merchant of death,' as a result have too little vision of the vast potential for achievement. His loyalist Carl Rove, lady Karen Hughes… resigned. George-II isolated became The Lone Ranger. He became a liar to Congress and US citizens. "Iran banned the nuclear deployment since 2003 she could at least 2015" repeat the scene Iraq with Weapon Mass destruction" Lying liars who tell them. They want go to war due a merely oil-energy resources. Additionally, the emperor-II was still urged his son go ahead to Iran-war: "Elder Bush [George-I] still jumping in" New & World Report on November 19/2007 (We recalled in Korea-War, President Truman [William A Harriman, policymaker] brought U.S troops under umbrella of United Nations, all allies recognized their duties in keeping world peace and order. But Iraq-War you knew what the stranger hell!

In the Iraq-War, at the direction of his father, George-I never represented the majority of opinion in the American public, nor United Nation, not neighbor Canada and Mexico, his military, or even the defense general establishments. He and his neo-con oilmen buddies decided to engage on a war in Iraq, simply because they wanted to instead of synthetic fuel development in the world safe-way. He played a major role in turning the US away from the true war on terror and got US involved in an unnecessary war that has killed more than 4,000 Americans and hundreds of thousands of Iraqis. Bushes' ideas have plunged the nation into massive debt (2007 only CIA expended 43, 5 billion-dollar- World in Figures ed. 2007, p 238) and severely damaged our credibility abroad. Bushes didn't listen to the nation's military experienced officers, preferring to will their ideas into effect rather than listen to reality on the battlefield.

Faded into darkness by the Laws of Nature: Alas, the reality is that there is all too much precedent: dynasties, by their very nature, tend toward inheritance and continuity. Just reviewed in the past: Roman Empire, the ancient Romans from 27 B.C to A.D 395; Genghis-Khan 1162-1227, founder of the Mongol empire; Napoleon, surname Bonaparte 1769-1821, Emperor of the French 1804-15; Nazism, Adolf Hitler and Militarism-Japanese 1933-1945; Communism last **70** years (based on my perspective) from 1917 till on May, 30/ **1987**, that significant day a Youngman Matthias Rust landed his light aircraft at Moscow Red-Plaza, Gorbachev got a chance to reorganize his governed system. And the United States, the Skull and Bones Dynasties from 1917 till when the verdict against Bushes came down, it was also a rebuke to the hermetic power-sharing arrangement at the top of the White House – special case: 'the leak of CIA operative Valerie Plame' CIA officer identity on July, 7/**2003**. From now on, I thought the CIA's job is on course for America First not for Oil-coterie any more, and the Skull and Bones has been rattled by American First and to self abolishment – "Republican Death Rattle 2006" and "Skull and Bones Graveyard 2008" (the end of prince of Emperor-II' term) I can best sum-up the Skull and Bones Dynasty lasted **86** years. According all above, China believed her turn in the 21st century.

While the CIA may have been the creation of a **Democratic** president (Harry Truman) but an author-creator Democrat W. A. Harriman, it now seemed to be strongly favored by **Republican**, with the arrival of George-II in the White House, it was immediately plain that secret intelligence would receive a high status and more money; notably conservative Republicans and especially the second reigned generation of Skull and Bones' Alarm bells began to ring for those who remembered past CIA excesses and who for years had campaigned for restrictions, oversight and even abolition. But these sounds were soon drowned out by the impact deafening roar of 9/11.

Despite the new overlay of evangelical Protestantism, the economic record of the George-II president essentially extended the practice of the George-I: favoring the small group of rich Americans while systematically misleading a much large portion of the population

The New Legion

including eliminated Second Class in US society's disappearance. George Bush, himself proved unmasked an operation inside the White House that was secretive, unforgiving and overbearing.

And how should United States navigate through a world where its enemies seem everywhere and nowhere? To win the war against terror, the United States must do a better job of communicating and extending its values – but not just with its words or even with its weapons, as important as its military strength is to keeping the peace. Today nuclear weapons are a blunt instrument because the China's presentation, overpopulation were everywhere on earth; so problems cannot be solved through nuclear-bombs? Ultimately, the best way to maintain the fine line between good and evil, right and wrong, civilization and chaos is to do our best to maintain it in each of our own lives. We need logically – actually nuclear bombs are a blunt instrument!

We will never view ourselves as invulnerable in the old way again. The world isn't necessarily any more dangerous today than it was before on September/ 11/ 2001; in fact, it's probably less so because we have killed or captured so many terrorists. But we are still under threat, and we are now much more cognizant of the danger. And somehow, we must learn to live lives of joy and confidence despite the presence of that dark shadow. After 2008 presidential election, the next Dynasty may have found the right approach. As the United States, once again finds itself in an endless war or war without end, no exit – this time against terror, or perhaps against fear itself – the equation of President 44's true legacy seems specially loaded. What is the best approach for the United States to navigate through a world where its enemies seem everywhere and nowhere at the same time? What can American learn from the way the 44th President was trying to redefine the United States acted position in the world and to invite Americans to be part of that change? True, the dynastic trend in the America goes deeper than the Bushes. Pragmatically, the must be Democratic runs and makes for president in 2008. Unfortunately, Democrat divided and deeply fractured party in which J.F Kerry and Edward Kennedy joints together with Republican McCain because the interest of War Industries Complex [American First]. The failings and lingering grudges of his next president family's own would-be dynasty will be fair game. And thus American may learn – for better or worse – more about the transformation and perils of American politics. This chapter, however, is about the dynasty that all Americans already have and what it stands for. This is the direction in which national politics and national discussion must turn first.

But Permanent Government didn't mind about a white cat or black cat which one catch more mouse should be okay! Dare Hillary Clinton swear as Kennedy did … if she was on power seat: *"Nobody is going to force me to do anything I don't think is in the best interest of the country!"* for instant "Health Care System Revolution is her ultimate reformed goal in her new administration; so why P.G intends to use money-tactics crippling Hillary's presidential campaign for the victory of their decoyed unpopular Black-Obama.They used them (mainstream media in venal press-corps) to discredit Hillary Clinton and magically put Obama into the seat of power. And they're using them again now to silence Bush-dynasty critics.

As for Caroline Kennedy! Though while it's perfectly delightful to have been so thoroughly vindicated for predictive posts like "Republican Death Rattle, Skull and Bones Graveyard" In contrast with her support, however she will be frustrated to advocate the Democrat presidential candidates who wouldn't dare to reform (changed) the already fixed-policy strategy with a grave challenge. The possibility that Emperor-II, [George H.W Bush] was an architect, his role would help to involve a serial major political scandal of 1980s: October Surprise (1980-81) – Iran-Contra (1984-86) – Iraq-Gate (1981-90) – His son's restoration (2000) – and now **Election-Surprise** (2007-08) no one believe Obama beat Hillary. In fact, the new presidential candidates' statements in which that are intended as publicity for a particular becoming president cause. Any president wouldn't aimed to hurt the interests of a tiny group [WIB Bones] of rich Americans of military-industrial complex; when they recalled her father, her uncle and L.B Johnson in his historic address of 31 March 1968. President Johnson announced he would not seek reelection. This is the first historical phenomena in the United States. The Watergate scandal, President Nixon stalemated his resignation, meanwhile he can, despite congressional pressure, to declare an amnesty for himself; but why he didn't? Whereas Prince George-II

The New Legion

was below 34 percent American mistrusted but still safely on power seat, tell lie weapon mass destruction in Iraq, still remain until the administration's term-end. American applauded the old fart's departure with ill-concealed glee and then helpfully suggested that Prince George-II ought to step down, too (In the case of Nixon, the public extremely reluctant to remove Nixon, by RJ Ellis, *"Polarization and Presidentialism"* Society, no 3 & 4, 1999, pp.8-11)

As for the world diplomats who considered J.F Kennedy was still a great-man ahead of his time. He was convinced that America true power came from Democratic ideals, not military power-mighty whereas Emperor-I and II [William A Harriman and George H W Bush] used half military/intelligence in the Axis of Evil might for prevail enemy. Kennedy's presidency included some of the tensest moments of the Cold-War, but absolutely he was convinced the true power came from democratic ideals, as similar conception with South Vietnam president Diem. He has proven the bigots wrong and made our nation greater. Personally, I hope the dream we have struggled to realize can be extended to the rest of the planet. Because the most effective way to demonstrate America's strength was not to threaten its enemies; it was to live up to the country's democratic ideals and "practice what it preaches about equal rights and social justice" So why Kennedy's triumvirate tried to bring the Skull and Bones to the American justice by the alien property custodian under the Trading with the Enemy Act of December 1941.

In actual fact, "solution for America," personally I think no one better lead American as Republican McCain to respond this complicate, so fragile world situation, but he failed. Though what a loathsome creature Republican Emperor-II is? The Skull and Bones in Second-Generation is out of track American First, its consequence was illegal, immoral, terrible thing that it did. - A divided and deeply fractured America. However, for overhauling damage control to readjust back on course of roll-back to "**original** Eurasia Great Game", the genuine American First [Company Dynasty] on behalf of Republican party to recovering its power in investing a large dollar to mainstream media propaganda to support strategically the Black un-prominent senator Barrack-Obama in temporary. The Permanent Government is an indispensable invisible component of the American

First machine that has taken over America. They employ a tried-and-true methodology. First, they concoct an inflammatory story that serves its political goals. They try to push it into the mainstream media by their pathological, or are they merely malicious? It seemed to me that the **"presidential campaign surprise"** in 2008, because you do know how many percent White, how many percent Asian, then naturally you can imagine the magnitude of voter surely much less and less count on the skin color overwhelming in the actual America prisons. If Hillary Clinton failed in the election 2008 that will be an excellent stratagem of Permanent Government with its perfect background from under ground experience; of course Hillary, she has to be more than vigilant. She has to fight back. She dared to expose those who bear false witness for the false witness bearers that they are. And has she to do it in a straight-forward, plainspoken way? Though the black un-prominent senator Obama will be on the power seat as President of United States, but the policy in the Hillary Clinton hand with experts Robert Gate and Joe Biden: True, the new dynastic trend in the United States goes deeper than the Skull and Bones dynasties; If Hillary Clinton runs for seizure US' policy, the failings and lingering grudges of her family's own would-be dynasty will be fair game, but she'd never made because George H W Bush been played in the game. And thus we may learn-for better or worse-more about the transformation and perils of American politics. This The New Legion book, however, is about the dynasty we already have and what it stands for. This is the direction in which national politics and national discussion must turn first. Meditate on this presidential election campaign, you find its phenomenon beyond belief, so I named a 2008 'presidential campaign surprise'.

Bush family has never produced a doctor, scholar, teacher, judge, or lawyer of note; that dynasty's single-minded focus has been on three major areas: National security, Energy, and **Intelligence**, for leadership. It not like emperor-I [Harriman] who would focused on becoming a great world strategist so why two times attempt to seize the U.S. power seat but fail in 1952 and 1956 (presidential campaigns) Apparently, the reality is that there is all too much precedent: dynasties, by their very nature, tend toward inheritance and continuity. Despite the new overlay of evangelical Protestantism, the economic record

The New Legion

of two Bushes presidencies essentially extended the practice of the favoring the small group of rich American while systematically misleading a much large portion of the poor population. As for the Civil liberties lawyers complained that 9/11 was becoming an unwarranted cloak for secrecy as Bushes family single-minded focus has been on very area "national intelligence security" If national security was obviously involved; dynastic security had become a hidden new context. The world isn't necessarily any more dangerous today than it before was on September 10, 2001; in fact, it's probably less so because American have killed or captured so many terrorists. But American is still under threat, and American is now much more cognizant of the danger.

The destabilizing environment in which we may commit forces to confront many of these threats may be further degraded by the effects of overpopulation, economic depression, depletion of basic resources, and the urbanization. The world has become reliant on natural resources and raw materials that come from increasingly unstable regions, with the compounding problems of a poor infrastructure and environment. Access to energy resources, timber, water resources, metals, and rare gems, etc…is becoming a growing rationale for intervention and conflict in many parts of the world. To win the war against expansionism, terrorism, America must do a better job of communicating and extending her values – liberty, tolerance and respect for others, dignity for every life – but not just with her words or even with weapons, as important as her military strength is to keeping the peace. No one can predict the future, but we can make judgments on the growing number of threats that now face us. Some of these will not be what we have grown used to preparing for. In recent years, an arc covering a large part of the earth's surface – from North Africa to the Philippines, and from Central Asia to Central Africa – is chaotic and in turmoil. We are going to be dealing with this turmoil for decades. At this moment in Iraq, we are dealing with the Jihadis, who are coming in from outside to raise hell. Shite on Shite, Shite on Sunni, Kurds on Turkomans. Right now, the military in Iraq has been stuck with that bullshit. In Somalia, we were stuck with that bullshit. In Vietnam, we were stuck with that bullshit. It is not a new role but old principle procedure of WIB (War Industries Board) and it is going to continue for their scam.

We are now a Skull and Bones empire. Not an empire of conquest in the traditional sense. We are an empire of influence. Our power, our values, our promise affect the world. We are more than Woodrow Wilson's (1913-1921) beacon. We are an expectation of better things. The world demands of us the delivery of the promise we project. We are seen to have an obligation to share our light. We are, however, reluctant to deliver. We have never comfortably settled on our role in the world or on our obligations to the other citizens of this planet. The Wilsonian dream of using our blessings to better the world has always clashed with the opposing isolationist heritage to "avoid foreign entanglements." As historian Walter A McDougall, in "Promised Land, Crusader State," has described the delusive impression do gooding, Wilsonian uplift, and "welfare imperialism" that accompanied America's 1960s march into the Indochinese quagmire. That the National Security Council [Permanent Government] on September, 21, 1960 declared it a goal of American policy in Vietnam to the so called "create in that country a viable and increasingly democratic society" mean created Vietnam-War 1964-1973 (Gulf Tonkin Incident 1964 to Paris Peace Talk 1973)

Subjectively, I have faulted U.S intervention in Vietnam as evidence of American arrogance of power – attempts by the United States to be the World's Policeman. But there is another dimension to American arrogance, the international version of American domestic Great Society programs where American presumed that American knew what was best for the world in terms of political, social, and economic development and saw it as American's duty to force the world into the American mold – to act not so much the World's Policeman as the World's Baby-Sister. But I'm pretty sure, it is difficult today to recall the depth of U.S arrogance. As for Iraq, if however, Bushes dynasty succeeds in bringing about regime change in Iraq, they will set a historic precedent – for Iraq, which could become the first Arab democracy; for the United States, which will demonstrate to all the compatibility of its interests and ideals; and for the world, which America will have made a safe and more just place.

The New Legion

In my perspective, this will be the true immediate issue with which we will have to come to grips in this century. The world at our gates demands it of us. But at last, nowadays, China the new superpower, that is wishful thinking? Too soon it taking place, how did you think? In this beginning of the 21st century, which is the relative power of the United States is going to decline, many immediate-challenges lie ahead and let that unsavory China is going to rise? Already a commercial giant, Great-Sino is aiming to be the world's next great power. But other aspects of Great-Sino' rise are real and troubling. China is a one-party state, not a democracy. Should American no sweat? Does Great Sino' lack of democracy necessarily threaten U.S. interests? The equation to that solution involves looking back to the Cold War. The Soviet Union wasn't a democracy, and although the U.S. contested its power in all sorts of ways, American policymakers were content to live with the reality of Soviet Union strength in the hope that totalitarian communism's appeal outside its borders would wither and Russia's political system would become more open. Is that how the U.S. has to treat a non democratic China! Why not China acted with characteristic shrewdness and insight that:

- "The Inter-government Panel on Climate Change," The biggest problems which IPCC put it bluntly recently.
- How to fight Bacterial, Contagious, or Viral Diseases.
- Drought raged water will not enough for mankind, countries lead were India, Bangladesh, and particularly included her own northern China.

Pragmatically, If Americans should pardon and forgot to loathe having to accept Republican McCain in a seat in White House. Because in this world unrest situation, no one better than McCain in qualified to meet criteria-requirements to command and control the worse unusual atmosphere. But first of all, the U.S. badly needed something good to come after enduring so much bad fracture, deeply divided: assassinations, civil unrest, out-of-control inflation, demoralization, gasoline shortages, drug abuse, fragging ... The U.S must ready stand and *"roll-back"* to South China Sea in Pacific Ocean to help back-up the Southeast Asian countries to restore in recovering their sovereignties, integrity of all islands that Great China had recently seizure by power in the last century. [Paracels, Spratleys] "Resolved this solution first and gain an advantage over a tiny opponent Iran-issue in Center Asia later and worldwide"

Will that lead to a confrontation with the United States, either Economic-War or Military-War. China shall won by gaining an advantage over the U.S. of a population and cheaper goods? "Doesn't the U.S. wait until 2030, when China became the First superpower capably having had drill oil platform high-tech and 'oil-sand' technique exploitation." Remembered that the sky never have two existed suns. And two Chinese Generals, Zhu Chenghu and Chi Haotian, Chief Military Totalitarian Political Bureau, *"The war is not far from us and is the midwife of the Chinese Century!"* and *"We are sorry the must bombardment for a hundred big towns with full scale nuclear war could lead to the annihilation of the Americans"* They tried to sacrifice one billion and half population on Old China territories (not car-bomb but nation-bomb) and creates a New Chinese state on Western-hemisphere speaking real good English and abundant of freshwater in the Great-Lakes of north America after WW-III over.

Asked China *"If the hard sharp skin* [Soviet-Union] *of Durian fruit was already peel off... what will do next for its flesh?"* And asked American policymaker *"That cake was baked long ago... what would come next?"*

EPILOGUE

FOR NEARLY FIFTY YEARS the US defense policy was defined by conflict with the Soviet Union. From the Berlin airlift in 1948 to the Korea 1950, Vietnam escalation in 1965 and to the Star Wars initiative in 1983, the US has been seen as willing to pay any price to halt the spread of Communism. In the 1980s, the Soviet Union itself ceased to exist, and the US became the only superpower. It seemed to me, geopolitical theory, the Asia met Europe represented the hinge of world politic as W A. Harriman's doctrine: 'Eurasian Great Game.' But George-1 resumed "New Eurasian game," had done as CIA director, so in the 1980 to 1990, intensifying US military and covert involvement with Iran, Afghanistan, and Iraq set familiar cook pots boiling, further heated by the 1991 breakup of the Soviet Union and the creation of eight new republics in the Caucasus and Trancaspia. Splitting into latter-day Khanates, Circassian mountain republics, and bristling encampment of missile-bearing, Tatar, Emperor-II' New Eurasian Great Game was once again in play. This New-Game's time for control of the Caucasian and Transcaspian of fields; so it sound like "this new game in the heart of Central Asian is unfolding not so much among the old colonial powers as among their former minions."

First, however America changed its defense policies. Every country today realizes that a nation cannot live alone but also depends on the other countries. Economic success will give power to a country; therefore a strong economy and global trade are more important to defense than a large military without financial support.

At the Yalta Conference in 1945, US President Franklin Roosevelt and Soviet leader Joseph Stalin agreed that East European nations were entitled to self-determination within a Soviet Union zone of influence, but Stalin breached the agreement. And US specialist diplomat George Kennan, [Averell Harriman's buddy] said that wherever the Soviets could successfully challenge Western institutions, they would do so. He recommended that American policy toward the Soviets be firm and vigilant containment of Russian expansive tendencies and quote;

President Harry S. Truman, in his address to Congress in 1947, saw the Soviet Union as an aggressive ideological foe bent on global domination that could be stopped only by the forceful use of US power, and most American leaders felt they had responsibility to prevent the spread of Communism.

Also, after World War II, a number of countries that had been colonies of European Communist government had been claimed to the American Supreme Court, so the American Justice did not judge this case, but the American government always introduces itself in justice. If someone destroyed to the American country, the American government quickly struck back, did not need to the United Nations Organization, and trampled the public opinion down.

Second, the American Executive always tramples the American people down. It has not respect the sovereignty of the American people. For example, the American government is authorized to freely find out of the own information like mail, telephone, conversation, and email of its sacred people because the American government thinks that its people look like to cast between two fires, or the fish lays between a knife and wooden chopping board. Moreover, when the American government secretly releases important information's spy of state, the American assistance secretly gave this important news to An American reporter. After that, the American government declared against the American reporter who was illegal action to be traitorous nation, the American Court imprisoned this reporter because the American government has joyfully been playing its demagogy policy. In this event, I think that the American government looks like the Vietnamese Communist government because the Vietnamese Communist government always worried to the former soldiers of South Vietnam might throw its reign and should rebuild the Republic of Vietnam. Therefore, the Vietnamese Communist spies had been disguising themselves in South Vietnamese rebellions, trapping the innocent people, and sending them to jail. In the United

States of America has this case, because the American spy disguises in one to Al-Qaeda terror, conquers them to be the terrors, and traps them. According to a skillful spy does good job, has high duty, and is to have a spy's conscience, he has never had using a terror's cap, which is not covered on the innocent people' heads, because the honest people do not become the crime. But the American spy straps them when the honest Americans did not have any spy network, or Al-Qaeda organization supports to the honest Americans. Perhaps, the American discrimination policy has been taking an assumed terrorism to the innocent American heads in order to support its invading war policy. For example, in Liberty City, Miami, Florida, an American spy takes the cap of terrorism to cover to the American heads because the American spy has been learning from the terrorism of communism. I have known them from the American news that seven Americans did not have any weapons, secret strings and terror's organization from Middle East. The only having American spy has built this situation. If the American spy did not trap them, they might not do that. We knew that an excellent, moral, and conscientious spy, who has never used his terror's cap in order to cover to any innocent man because the American Democracy did not allow any spy to do this, but the spy's duty, has been finding out to punish the national betrayer without any trapper network.

Third, the American Legislative betrays its voters because the American voters voted them in order to serve their people, to help poor Americans, and to build their nation. However, when they came in power into the American Legislative, they cannot do right these duties. For example, the American people have been paying a lot of tax to their nation than other people in the world. If an American person did not pay tax to his or her nation, the American Court might judge him or her because he or she was not good citizen. Moreover, their American Legislative did not concern to many homeless Americans because nearby eight millions of homeless Americans did not have any law for helping them, but the American Legislative was available to sign the biggest bill, which has risen up many billions dollars to spend for the invading war without the unreasoned rights. For example, the Vietnam and Iraq Wars have been spending over ten thousands of billion dollars, so the American people are to be the money debt of foreign countries going up ten thousands of billion dollars. If it is good of the American Legislative, it cannot let its people have more debts. In fact, some American Legislator corrupted like Tom Perry, who did not dedicate his duty to his nation, but he was a worm of the American social. With regard to a world power, it symbolizes for the true, the good, and the beautiful, should not be deceived to anyone or country, and but must be won all of the hearts of people. However, the American Legislative seems to forget these methods of a work power. Significantly, when the American Legislative created its law in order to invade to Vietnam, skilled more than three millions of Vietnamese innocent people, and deceived one million soldiers of South Vietnam, but the American Legislative did not compensate any penny to the Vietnamese people and soldiers, did not apologize to them, and not follow any law of war of the United Nations.

In conclusion, we realize that Capitalism and Communism are different. Communism has been applying its military dictator in order to trap, to oppress, and to trample the human being down, but Capitalism applies its individual character in order to develop democracy, intellectual standard of people, and many right freedoms. However, when I was living in Vietnam for the long time, the communist dictator freely investigated my house without court order, I was covered a cap of national reaction by the Vietnamese communist spies, I did not have any right to request for compensating when my property was nationalized by the Vietnamese communist reign. Next, I have come to the United States of America, seen these returned views, and perhaps released that the American Democracy only welcomes to the rich and powerful men, so it is available to trample the weakest and poorest down.

The most people in the world think that the United States of America that a country is the greatest of democracy than other countries in the world. However, emperor-II [George-1] has become a leader, the American democracy seems to be lost its great role in itself and where will the American Democracy go to the future? George-1, especially the pioneering work, he had done in China, afforded George-1 plenty of business opportunities, trying transformed the Chinese Leadership was like an U.S version of Skull and Bones, totalitarian regime, secretive and select. Then he held a series of closed door meetings with Deng Xiaoping for *"Second-Class's elimination"* in both China and U.S societies by cheap-labor. Because the right democracy always protects its people, it does not discriminate behaving any class or race. If the factual of democracy is right, its people are never trampled down by the powerful, or dictatorial or military dictatorship, or totalitarianism, so the people and government look like the fish and water.However, under my eyes look to the true events when I wear with my white glasses without any color, I see the obviously events of the United States of America. Therefore, I do understand some reasons of the American democracy that have been going down because the American Justice, Executive, and Legislative gradually leave their people, so the human-right of the American people was to be cold.

First of all, the American Justice betrays its people because it did not recognize any human rights of the American people. For example, the American people have been working hard in order to earn good money, paying the federal tax, state, and many bills in their lives, and making their right duties. After working day has gone, the American people wish to peacefully rest. No one must not be bothered them. However, their little dream is not right because the American Justice did not recognize this. It allowed to the American police that they have right to conduct a search of the American houses, do not need any court order and think to the American houses, which look like an American casino, but the American guarders protect the American casinos. In fact, the American social is the same as communism. The American people are to be the good tools when the powerful uses them and throws them to the garbage. Otherwise, the American Justice only protects its powerful and rich men. It did not concern to the weakest and poorest of the American people.

Now I realize that US Capitalism meant the worst aspect of the Super-Communism, a totalitarian regime had evolved its own version of hindsight Permanent Government in which a freewheeling representative activist as on 21, November 1970, movie-star from Hollywood, Jane Fonda at University Michigan, audience-2000 students *"If you understood what Communism was, you would hope, you would pray on your knees that we would some day become communist"* she declared. Actually, then the U.S was an eventual to adjust a Super-Finest-Communist country now.

SOURCES and NOTES

- Nguyen Hoang and Beginning of Vietnam's Southward expansion," in A. Redi (ed.) Southeast Asia in the Modern Era (Ithaca: Cornell University Press, 1993) pp, 42-85

- Military History Institute of Vietnam, Victory in Vietnam, p.338 – lbld, p.350

- Australian Minister for Immigration Michael MacKellar vas quoted as saving that 'about half the boat-people perished at sea,' basing this conclusion on 'talks with refugees and intelligence sources. 'Thus, he said in 1979; 'we are looking at a death rate of between 100,000 and 200,000 in the last four years.' The Age Newspaper, The Boat People: An Age Investigation (Middlesex Penguin Books 1979) p.80 According to James Banerian, the International Red Cross estimated that 300,000 boat people perished in their attempts to reach safety. Loser Are Pirates, p.2

- On line http://www.whatarewefightingfor.com and http://www.democracy-project com/archives/003279.html

- From Enemy to Friend NVA Colonel Bui-Tin. Naval Institute Press 2002, p 107-114.

- http://www.ussvorktown.com/yorkown/apology.him

- http://www.gwu.edu/%Ensarchiv/NSAEBB/NSAEBB/NSAEBBfflindex.htm

- Prime minister Zhou Enlai http://www,gwu.edu/~nsarchiv/NSAEBB/NSAB193/HAK%206-20-72.pdf

- http://www.findarticles.com/p/articles/mi m1571/is I I 18/ai 84184983

- Meet the Domestic Enemy, Magazine, author John Perazzo on March, 20, 2007

- American dynasty, author Kevin Phillips.

- In the Company of Heroes, author Michael J Durant with Steven Hartov

- Goodnight Saigon, Charles Henderson

- Ly Tuong VNAF bulletin quarterly.

- A Southern Remembrance of Cao Bien in p.p. Paper & J. Heinen (eds) Liber Amicorum: Melanges effects on Professor Phan Huy Le (Hanoi: EFEO, 1999) pp.241-258.

- General Cao Van Vien et al... The US Adviser (Washington: US Army Center of Military History, 1980) p. 142.

- Lieutenant General Ngo Quang Truong, Territorial Forces (Washington: US Army Center of Military History, 1978) p.134.

- "In Search of Vietnamese Classical Moments," in G. Holst-Warhft & D.R McCann (eds) The Classical Moment: View from Seven Literatures (NY:Rowman & Littlefield, 1999) pp. 117-129.

- Commanders WIEU [Weekly Intelligence Estimate Update] 27 September 1969.

- Remarks Lexington, Kentucky, John Paul Vann Papers, Patterson School of Diplomacy and International Commerce, University of Kentucky, Lexington, Kentucky, Vann suggested that, to put Vietnam in perspective, it was useful to know that during 1971 there were 1,221 US servicemen killed in Vietnam and during the same year 1,647 people were killed in New-York City.

- Major General Nguyen Duy Hinh, Lam Son 719 (Washington: US Army Center of Military History, 1979 p. 5.

- Brigadier General James Lawton Collins. Jr. The development and Training of the South Vietnamese Army, 1950-1972 (Washington: Department of the Army. 1975) p.101.

- China and Vietnam: Looking for a new version of an old relationship," in J. warnder and Lun Doon Huynh (eds) The Vietnam War: Vietnamese and American Perspectives (INY: ME. Sharpe. 1993) pp 271-248.

- "Voice Within and Without: Tales from stone and paper about Do Anh Vu" in K.W. Taylor and J. D. Whitmore (eds) Essay into Vietnamese Pasts (Ithaca: SEAP, 1995), pp 59-80.

- Seth Mydans, "A Fallen Saigon Rises Again in the West," The New York Times (5 April 2002)

- Notes by Vincent Davis of a telecom during which Vann described his December, 15 1969 presentation at Princeton, Paul Vann Papers. Patterson School Lester A. Sobel ed...South Vietnam: US Communist in Southeast Asia, Volume 6: 1971 (New York: Facts on File, 1973) p.211

The New Legion

- Remark, Lexington, Kentucky, 8 January 1972, Paul Vann Papers, Paterson School
- Ellsworth Bunker Interview, Duke University Living History Project
- Durham, North Carolina 2 March 1979.
- "Perception of encounter in Shui Ching Chu 37," Asia Journal (Seoul National University, Korea 2, 1 June 1995): 29-54.
- As quoted in Rene Sanchez, "In Little Saigon," The Washington Post March, 3/ 2000.
- Seth Mydans, The New York Times November, 7/ 2000
- Nguyen Qui Duc- The Boston Globe April, 30/ 2000.
- "Surface Orientation in Vietnam: Beyond Histories of Nation and Region," Journal of Asian Studies 57, 4 (November 1998): 949-978.
- How I began to teach about the Vietnam War, Keith W Taylor Cornell University of Michigan Quarterly Review. Ann Arbor: Fall 2004.
- VNAF Quarterly bulletins and reports.
- Remembering Vietnam, Lewis Sorley, A lecture delivered at the National Archives Washington D.C April, 30/ 2002.
- Lieutenant General Fred C Weyand, Senior Officer Debriefing Report, CG II Field Force, Vietnam, March, 29/ 1966 – 1 August 1968, MHI [US Army Military History Institute] files.
- Message, Abrams to Johnson, MAC 5307, 040950z June 1967, CMH [US Army Center of Military History files
- Lieutenant Dong Van Khuyen, RVNAF Logistics (Washington: US Army Center of Military History, 1980) p. 57.
- Time, April 19/ 1968.
- Douglas Pike, PAVN: People's Army of Vietnam (Novato: Presido Press, 1986) p 225
- Jame Banerian, Losers Are Pirates (Phoemix: Sphinx Publishing, 1985) p 182.
- Message, Abram to Laird, MAC 04039, 020443z May 1972, CMH files.
- Ambassador Ellsworth Bunker, Oral History Interview, Lyndon Baines Johnson Presidential Library p I: II
- Commanders WIEU, April 22/ 1972.

- "Battle Ready", Tom Clansy with General Tony Zinni (ret)
- Historian Tran Trong Kim , "One dusty-Wind" Saigon, Vinh Son 1969 p. 75
- The secret meeting between Sainteny and Ho Chi Minh (translated by Jean Sainteny, Histoire d'une paix manqué, Paris 1953, p. 171.
- King C. Chen, Vietnam and China p.82)
- Diary "Mémores d'un Viet Cong, nxb Flammarion Paris 1985
- US Veteran Dispatch –www.usvetdps.com
- A Bright Shinning Lie, Neil Sheehan – Home Bigart of the New York Times.
- Hope and Vanquished Reality, 2001 New York, Center for A Science of Hope, ICIS (International Center for a Science)
- Stanley Karrow, Vietnam Viking New York 1983
- L'Harmattan, Paris "Prisonier politique au Vietnam.
- Uncertain Greatness, Roger Moris NSC
- Leslie Gelb "The Irony of Vietnam.
- "The Vietnam Wars 1945-1990, Harper Perennial, p 102, Marilyn B Young.
- Vietnam Syndrome "Lodge in Vietnam" Anne Blair, Yale University Press. New Haven 1995 p 190
- Lost Victory, William Colby, Contemporary Book, Chicago, 1989
- "No More Vietnam, Nixon, Arbor House, New York, "Beyond Peace" Random House, NY 1994.
- Ambassador Jacques de Folin "Indochine 1940-1955: La fin d'un rêve, Edition Perrin Paris 1993.
- The Washington Post (28 December 1968)
- Colonel Stuart Herrington, "Fall of Saigon," Discovery Channel May 1, 1995.
- Douglas Pike PAVN p 310.
- In J Edward Lee and Toby Haynsworth, ed White Christmas in April (New York: Peter Lang 1999 p 67
- The Boston Globe (30 April 2000)

- Seth Mydans "A War Story's Missing Pages" The New York Times (24 April 2000)
- Vietnam magazine August 2000.
- Letter General Bruce C Clarke to Brigadier General Hal. C Pattison 29 December 1969, Clark Papers, MHI
- Message, Abrams to General Wheeler and McCain, MAC 13555, 0710007z October 1968 CMH files
- As quotes in Joint Chiefs of Staff, The History of the Joint Chiefs of Staff: The Joint Chiefs of Staff and the War in Vietnam, 1960-1968, Part III (Washington: JCS Historical Division, 1 July 1970) p 51-7.
- King C Chen, Vietnam and China, p 82.
- "The Post Vietnam Formula under siege" and "Political Science Quarterly", Kenneth E. Sharpe.
- "The Kissinger transcripts: A Verbatim Record of US Diplomacy, 1969-1977.
- Colby's secret war, The secret war against Hanoi, Going North, Crossing the fence
- "From trust to tragedy" by Ambassador Frederick Nolting.
- "America's secret power in a democratic society" Oxford University, press, 1989, Lock K.Johnson
- Teaching intelligence in the Mid.1990s – National intelligence study center, University Yale, Georgetown, Bradley, Michigan
- "An ailing body, when Congress checks out" by N J Ornstein and Th. E Mann, Foreign Affairs, vol. 85, no 6, Nov& Dec 2006.
- "The evangelical boom" Walter R Mead "Religion& US Foreign Policy, vol. 85, no 5. Sep& Oct 2006.
- "Red and Yellow colonialism, Switzerland, April 2004.
- "Cuoc Chien Quoc Cong" at North Vietnam 1945-1946, Le Manh Hung (The Ky 21 Magazine, USA, September 1995.
- "From Colonialism to Communism" Hoang Van Chi (Pall Press, 1964)
- Philippe Devillers: Leclerc et l'Indochine1945-1947 (Albin Michel 1992)
- King C. Chen: Vietnam and China 1938-1945. (Princeton University Press, 1969)
- "Ly-Tuong" VNAF quarterly, August/ 2004.

- "Why We Were in Vietnam," Norman Podhoretz, Simon & Schuster, New York, 1982.
- "No More Vietnams" Richard Nixon. (Arbor House, 1985)
- "Why Vietnam?" L.A.Patti, Berkeley University Press, 1980.
- "Vietnam 1945, The Quest For Power (University of California Press, 1995)
- "Capitalism and Socialism, ed by Michael Novak, Washington D.C 1979, p.21.
- "The Collapse of the Second International"- V.I Lenin, Collected words, vol.xx1, pp. 213-217.
- "Ho Chi Minh' Education and Young Organization" (censured some excerpt by Le-Duan) p 33-37, 2002, on May, 10, 1969.
- "Polarization and Presidentialism" Society, no 3&4 1999, pp. 8-11 – In the case of Nixon, the public extremely reluctant to remove Nixon- R.J Ellis.
- A book 394 pages, author Magaret-MacMillan "Nixon and Mao: The week that changed the world." Praised by historian Warren I. Cohen, Maryland University: author was a well researched and analytically sound popular history- Foreign Affairs, May- April 2007.
- Mark Riebling – Was Deep Throat a CIA Officer? 1o/17/2007. Clues suggest that his name was Cord Meyer http://www.markriebling.com/deepthroat.html.
- "U.S and Russia:" 200 years of Diplomatic relations (1807-2007) by A. Isbakov-Moscow
- "Putin's plan: back to the USSR or forward to a strong, democratic Russia?" Russia and U.S edition Dec. 19, 2007.
- "The USSR's nightmare still hovering!" by Russia-historian Professor Vitaly Zakatnova.
- "The future, starting today"- Russia, Dec. 19, 2007, p.h3
- "From Enemy to Friend, NVA Bui Tin- Naval Institute Press 2002, p. 107 to 114
- Yearbook, Chinh Dao VN 1-C 1955-1963 Houston, Texas; Van Hoa 2,000 p.279-280
- SS-VN Relation 1945-1967, book p.3-5 and Air Gram A-20 June/3/1963 and Frus 1961-1963 p. 111-277.

- "Vietnam Buddhist Congregation" (1963) "Vietnam Buddhist Struggle History (1964) Quoc Tue and Thich Tue Giac.
- He dead of the Cold War kings" and "The assassinations of Diem and JF Kennedy" with their stories of both men's death by Mafia might have been related to drug trafficking.
- "Religion and Politic" Chinh Dao p.328-329
- "The storm has many eyes, Henry Cabot Lodge
- "Natural gas and Geopolitics: From 1970 to 2040, edited by David G Victor… Cambridge University Press 2007
- "The Rap of a River" Bangkok Post-Jan/ 2003
- "The Post Vietnam Formula under Siege" Kenneth E.Sharpe and "Political Science Quarterly.
- "Vietnam a History" editions Viking, Stanly Karnow New York 1983, page 225.
- "Briefing emerging economies – Dizzy in Boomtown," the Economist, Nov/17/2007, p.83
- The White House, Memorandum of conversations – Top secret – Sensitive eyes only, pp. 27-29 – Washington D.C 1972, translated by Cao The Dung, Communist Party – history and legend – T.H "Bien Tuong – hu cau p.879.
- The Economist Weekly on 17/Nov/2007, in cover "America's vulnerable economy"
- "The Irony of Vietnam: The system Worked, by Leslie Gelb. The different between Nixon and Ford president without election. United States manage the defeat or roll-back
- "Christ's Mission", US News & World Report, April, 17, 2006 – New debate about the role of Jesus in the world.
- "The Oiloholics"- The Economist, August 27, 2005. "Next Stop Iran?"- photo B-1
- "The Other Enemy," by David Halberstam's books include Best and The Brightest, a chronicle of American involvement in Vietnam.
- "Assassination in Saigon" by Robert Shaplen who, long a correspondent for the New Yorker in Asia and elsewhere has written six books about Vietnam. "Voices of Dissent"

- "Uncertain Greatness, by Roger Morris, National Security Council staff opposed Kissinger with his president Nixon about North Vietnam' bombardment.

- "The Irony of Vietnam": The system Worked, policy different in Vietnam between Ford and Nixon – U.S withdrawn not engaged anymore Kissinger advisers to Ford.

- "The trial of Henry Kissinger," 2001 by Christopher Hitchens, it sure different from the inside

- "Indochina Migration and Refugee Act IRAP, May, 23, 1975: $455 million for Vietnam and Cambodia.

- "The Vietnams as partners in Trade" by Nguyen Tien Hung: North and South Vietnam as partners in trade, the Washington Post turned down for edited! Why?

- "We betrayed you!" General Westmoreland said at Indochinese Refugee Authored Monograph Program.

- Journalist James Reston of New York Time said: "well, there is no doubt these were very categorical Congress commitment": Low house, 466/0 votes and High House 98/2, Senator Gruening and Morse voted against.

- Abramson, Ruby. Spanning the Century: *The life of W A Harriman, 1891-1986 (1992)*.

- McCullough, David. Truman (1992)

- Truman, Harry S. Memoirs. Vol.2, Years of Trial and Hope (1956).

- "Military man, a politician, and a movie star." – Premier Ky: Who Rules Vietnam? Newsweek, no 27/Sept/1965, p-32.

- "The Post Vietnam Formula under Siege" and "Political Science Quarterly" by Kenneth E Sharpe. (A stage from 21/Sept/1960-NSC to 1970: CIP performance)

- The corruption is policy, or disaster? http:perso.orange.fr/chuchinam/ the revolution exerted only on communist regime and Soviet and Eastern Europe collapse.

- "Strategic Policy Consulting" News-Telegraph; United Press International; Reuters.

- Treachery p—How America's friends and foes secretly arming our enemies? Crown Forum (French, Russia, and China arms smuggling to support Saddam Hussein.

- PBS station "Vietnam: A television history" – Washington Post evaluated this chronicle-films "VN a television history is extraordinary, 1983.

- Vietnam' Communist Party – History – Reality and Myth by Lu-Tuan (ARVN Major Nguyen Cong Luan)

- Pope diary "Memory and Identity" edited by Rizzoli, Vatican, Gioan Phaolo-II

- Newspaper May, 7, 2007: "The Charter 2000 movement successfully organized the ceremony to announce results of the Ly-Tong contest on May 18, 2007 in Toronto, Canada.

- "The Vietnamese communist party destroyed the hope of the people of Vietnam by continuing the mono-party election (May 20, 2007) and arresting many dissidents as well as trying them with heavy sentences up to 8 years in jail plus years of "administrative surveillance"

- Wall Street Journal, "Memo to Hanoi" (Chris Smith, Bart Stupak and Frank Wolf.)

- Diary: "The Longest Road: The Communicative Hope" p, 290-392.

- "Hope and Vanquished Reality" 2001, New York, edition Center for A Science of Hope belong JCIS (International Center for Integrative Studies)

- Interim Platform, Vietnam Progression Party (VNPP) announced to be self-established in Vietnam on September 8th 2006.

- "Police Chief to Apologize for Racial Slur" by Stephanie Sandoval, *The Dallas Morning News*, 12-January-2006 and *Vietnam Weekly News*.

- "Polarization and Presidentialism" R.J Ellis- Society, no 3, 4 1999, pp.8-11 "In case of President Nixon, the public extremely reluctant to remove Nixon…"

- "Nixon and Mao: The week that changed the world" by Margaret MacMillan, book composed 394 pages. Professor of history, Warren I Cohen, Maryland, University high asset her valuable master piece: "well researched and analytically sound popular history-Foreign Affairs, May-April 2007

- The White House, memorandum of conversation- Top secret- sensitive- Exclusive eyes only – meeting between Kissinger [power broker] and

Vinh-Van-Truong

Zhu Enlai on 20/6/1972 witnessed by Winston Lord and John D. Negroponte.

- Politics in America-Members of Congress in Washington and at home" by Alan Ehrenhalt, ed. 1758 pp, Congress quarterly inc
- Vietnam Relations of the United States Department Telegram or Telegram 243.
- "The Fate-full of 1963" Robert S McNamara, In Retrospect, Tragedy and Lesson of Vietnam, chapter3
- A small group of anti-Diem activists end run, "swords and Plowshares", diary Maxwell D Taylor.
- CIA Saigon station reports to Center Information Agency at Washington "Buddhist leaders were optimistic that President Diem could be overthrown within six months and were organized for a struggle of several months.
- "Iraq and The Spectre of Vietnam" historian professor, Martin Stuart-Fox, University Queensland, Australia.
- "From Enemy to Friend" NVA Colonel Bui Tin- Paris October 2003.
- The Newsweek "Paris Match" on April 25, 2005 interviewed U.S. POW Senate John McCain, repeated Axiom-I, stance of U.S Permanent Government, was explained the Vietnam-War in universities 1960: "*Les Sud Vietnamiensn'ont jamais cruque le gouvernement en place à Saigon était legitime. Ils savaient que Hồ Chí Minh était un nationaliste qui rechercherait l'unification du pays. En Irak, les elections ont prouvé que les Irakiens croient que leur go4444444444444444444444444*```````` ``````````*vernment est légitime...*"Once McCain came back at Hoa-Lo "Hilton Prison, he said *"The bad guys won the war!"*

ABOUT THE AUTHOR

VINH TRUONG IS A former Project Delta pilot, spent 13 years in the Communist prison, the so called "Reeducation Camp," escaped from fresh water of Mekong Delta to the salt water in Pacific Ocean, drifting to an nearest island Palawan, Philippines during 14 terrible days and night. A boat-people resettled in United States since November 1989. October, 2007 retiree at 70 years old, now living at 8331 NE Brazee ST, Portland OR 97220, amateur writer for enjoy retirement, and merely a pretend gossip columnist

The author can be contacted by e-mail at:
vtruong2602@yahoo.com

www.ingramcontent.com/pod-product-compliance
Lightning Source LLC
Chambersburg PA
CBHW070713160426
43192CB00009B/1175